Luke Rivington, Herbertus Vaughan

The Primitive Church and the See of Peter

Luke Rivington, Herbertus Vaughan

The Primitive Church and the See of Peter

ISBN/EAN: 9783743330214

Manufactured in Europe, USA, Canada, Australia, Japa

Cover: Foto ©Lupo / pixelio.de

Manufactured and distributed by brebook publishing software (www.brebook.com)

Luke Rivington, Herbertus Vaughan

The Primitive Church and the See of Peter

The Primitive Church
and the
See of Peter

Nihil obstat.

SYDNEY F. SMITH, S.J.

Imprimatur.

HERBERTUS CARDINALIS VAUGHAN,

ARCHIEPISCOPUS WESTMONASTERIENSIS

Die 19 *Martii,* 1894.

The Primitive Church

and the

See of Peter

BY THE REV.

LUKE RIVINGTON, M.A.

MAGDALEN COLLEGE, OXFORD

WITH AN INTRODUCTION

BY THE

CARDINAL ARCHBISHOP OF WESTMINSTER

LONDON

LONGMANS, GREEN, AND CO.

AND NEW YORK: 15 EAST 16th STREET

1894

INTRODUCTION
BY THE
CARDINAL ARCHBISHOP OF WESTMINSTER

OF course we desire to convert all men—especially our own countrymen, as loving them best—to the Catholic Religion. Could it be otherwise? We believe the Catholic religion to be the one only true religion, founded by Jesus Christ upon the Rock. We should fail, then, in love for God did we not strive to extend His Kingdom, which is His Church upon earth; and in love for our neighbour, did we not endeavour to persuade him to become one of God's liegemen and a sharer with us in the Divine life of the Faith and of the Sacraments. It is no matter of doubt or of indifference that is at stake, but absolutely the most vital, the most personal, the eternal interest of man.

But any kind of conversion will not do. The conversion must be real, genuine, and based on solid grounds. That is to say, it must rest not only upon conviction, but upon a right conviction, a conviction rooted in the right fundamental principle. To come into the Catholic Church simply on account of the beauty of her ceremonial, the reasonableness of this or that set of doctrines and practices, or her venerable antiquity and her attractive traditions, or as a mere refuge from persons or systems that have bred dissatisfaction and distrust, is to enter the Church without a conviction rooted in the right fundamental principle. What is that principle? Simply this: that the Catholic Church is the Divine Teacher, set up in the world by Jesus Christ, and that our attitude towards her must be that of a Disciple. The Disciple does not pick and choose according to his taste, nor, when the Divine Teacher is once accepted, can he be ruled by private judgment and understanding. Our Lord Himself shows us this by His own method of procedure. When He had announced, 'My Flesh is meat indeed, and My Blood is drink indeed,' many said, 'This saying is hard, and who can hear it? And after this many of His Disciples went back and walked no more with Him. Then Jesus said to the twelve, "Will you also go away?" And Simon Peter answered Him, "Lord, to whom shall we go? Thou hast the words of eternal life. We have believed and have known that Thou art the Christ, the Son of God"' (John vi.). Christ, therefore, gave no countenance to those who would believe only that which was agreeable to their notion of fitness or possibility. He gave them no explanation of *how* His Flesh and Blood were to be eaten and drunk. He demanded this, and this alone, that they should recognise the Divine Teacher, and having found Him, that they should take up their due position as learners or disciples. There was no compromise, no halting; if unwilling to accept this fundamental principle, the position of a Disciple, they might all go away, aye, even the twelve. The vital question, then, is, Where is the Divine Teacher? Some, prompted by private motives, with subtilty and sophistry, evade the question, or answer it in a way to leave themselves an escape from the plain obligation of a disciple. Their aim is to stay as they are. To them the Church is a vast organisation incapable of articulate speech, or it is made up of branches, each of which has an independent voice, but without any one living, visible, audible authority to control the whole.

Now it is best, in this matter, to come to close quarters, and to deal with a definite member of the Church—namely, with the Head. If the Church is visible at all, it must have a visible Head, at least as visible as the body itself. It is the essential business of the head to speak and direct. It controls the body, according to certain divine laws. It secures to the whole unity of thought and of action. Without its presence and influence the members must either fall into dissolution or destroy one another. Where, then, is the visible Head of the Catholic Church? For a thousand years the English people professed, with one accord, the Pope to be their religious Head. They acknowledged one centre of authority, the See of Peter; were led by one Supreme Shepherd, the successor of Peter; and they were consequently united, by the profession of the same Faith and Sacraments, in one religion, with the whole of Christendom.

There is one passage, so aptly setting forth the doctrine of the Catholic Church, in a letter from King Edward II., A.D. 1314, directed to the Sacred College of Cardinals, during the vacancy of the Holy See, that I quote it not only for its own intrinsic merit, but as showing the belief of the English nation.

'When Jesus Christ, the only begotten Son of God, had consummated the mystery of man's redemption, and was about to return to His Father, lest He should leave the flock He had bought with the price of His Blood bereft of the government of a shepherd, He delivered over and entrusted the care of it, by an immutable ordinance, to blessed Peter the Apostle, and in his person to his successors, the Roman Pontiffs, that they may govern it in succession. He willed that the Roman Church, who, for the time, presiding as the Mother and Mistress of all the faithful, holds, as it were, the place of God upon earth, should by salutary teachings direct the peoples of the said flock, scattered over the whole world, in the way of salvation, and show them at all times how they should behave themselves in the house of God' (Wilkins, vol. ii. p. 450).

Three hundred years earlier King Edward the Confessor notifies in a solemn charter the extraordinary devotion which the English people had ever had towards St. Peter and his successors: 'summam devotionem quam habuit semper gens anglorum erga eum [Petrum] et vicarios ejus' (Wilkins, vol. i. p. 319).

And three hundred years before that, again, Bede was teaching and writing that 'Whosoever shall separate himself in any way whatsoever from the unity of Peter's faith, and from his communion, can neither obtain pardon of his sins nor admission into heaven' (*Hom.* xxvii. Giles).

The lesson of history teaches unmistakably that the

unity of the visible Church can be preserved only by its normal union with its visible Head.

The Churches, planted among different and antagonistic races and tongues—for instance, the French, the German, the Italian, the English Churches—are all one in Faith and the Sacraments, through their submission to the See of Peter.

So long as the spiritual authority and headship of the Pope was recognised by the English people, they remained united in creed and religion. It was not Canterbury, but Rome that was the source and the touchstone of unity. Though after the apostacy of the sixteenth century the names of the old sees were retained, with their accumulated wealth, their extensive patronage, their State protection, Canterbury and the rest of them were unable to hold the English people in unity of faith and practice for a single generation. Though backed up by the sovereign and the whole legislative power of England, and by a code of the most drastic penal laws, they were speedily reduced to the pitiable condition of seeing the people fall away from them in all directions. The nation that had been conspicuous for its religious unity during a thousand years became, from the moment it rejected the authority of the Holy See, a by-word throughout Europe for religious rebellion and sporadic dissent. Had there been, as we are assured by some, no essential change in religion, but only a healthy reform and a purification from errors and abuses, how came it to pass that this purified and perfected religion began its career by falling into discredit with the people of England,

and to such an extent that religious dissent has become quite as characteristic of the last 300 years in England, as religious unity and peace had been of all the preceding ages of our history? I will only add that the leaders of the Established Church need not throw the blame of this upon the English people. Had the various countries of the Continent, which are still united in one faith, withdrawn, like England, from the guidance of the Chief Shepherd, they too, like England, would long since have been similarly torn to pieces by religious strife and discord.

The recent revival of Catholic doctrines and practices in the Church of England is very wonderful. It is a hopeful sign. It is a testimony to the patristic dictum that the human mind is 'naturally Christian.' It exhibits a yearning, and a turning of the mind and heart towards the Catholic Church. It is a national clearing the way for something more, and is to be regarded as a grace from above. It may be all this; but it is not yet obedience and submission to the Divine Teacher. A whole cycle of Catholic doctrines might be picked out one by one and strung together, and passionately professed, upon grounds of private judgment; but that is not submission. It is one thing to recognise that the pasture is sweet and wholesome, and another thing to recognise and to obey the voice of the Shepherd. Goats may enter into the pastures of the sheep, and may select at will the herbs, the grasses and clovers they most fancy, and may doubtless deem them sweet and delicious; but this does not constitute them sheep of the fold. The sheep hear the voice of their Shepherd and they follow Him. He chooses the pastures; He leads His sheep into them. The relations of sheep and Shepherd correspond to those of disciple and Teacher. And hence it is clear that no one ought to be received into the Catholic Church unless he come into the fold through the gate, of which Peter, the chief shepherd, is the keeper.

Indeed, I may add, that people who, through negligence or inadvertence, have been admitted into the Church without having mastered the fundamental doctrine that they are to be disciples and learners of a living Divine Teacher, are apt, upon encountering temptation, scandal, contradiction, or disappointment, to leave her. They had indeed been within the fold, but they were not of it, because they had never really recognised the Shepherd.

A word on two classes of difficulties raised against the Catholic Church by her professional opponents.

First, intellectual difficulties: no doctrine is free from them, not even the existence of God and the immortality of the soul. Difficulties arise from the limitation of our faculties, from mists of ignorance, from prejudices, antipathies, and sinful conduct. The sun is shining, but we see it not while dense fogs or clouds and storms interpose between it and ourselves. We see it not when our vision has become gravely affected, or when we close our eyes. It is a common practice with the opponents of the Catholic Church to endeavour to hold souls back by arraigning before them a multitude of difficulties and objections against the doctrines of the Church. To this two things may be said.

First, it would be easy to string together a most formidable array of difficulties quoted and examined by Catholic theologians in their great scientific works on theology. But it is obvious that it would be necessary to be a trained theologian, or to spend a lifetime in research, were it needful to give detailed answers to them all. Then there are works, like those of Dr. Littledale and others, written in order to blind and mislead: made up of calumnies, misquotations, and a calculated admixture of truth and error. These are often intended to shock and alienate the moral sense quite as much as the intellectual. If they do not finally succeed in this, at least they may succeed in creating perplexity, anxiety, and delay.

Now, instead of entering into a maze of objections, into a labyrinth of difficulties, a shorter and more satisfactory course should be taken. Find the Divine Teacher, find the Supreme Shepherd, find the Vicar of Christ. Concentrate all your mental and moral faculties upon finding the Head of God's Church upon earth. This is the key to the situation. The learned work to which these words serve as introduction is intended to aid this inquiry, by setting forth for this doctrine various of its reasonable motives of credibility. If only you find the Divine Teacher, you may leave all objections to the doctrines he teaches to answer themselves. And if you find him not, then answers to the difficulties brought against his teaching will go for little.

Secondly, moral difficulties have to be met—ingrained antipathies, traditional prejudices, fears and anxieties: fear to offend and grieve parents, guides, and loved ones ; fear of temporal consequences, loss of station, of influence, of fortune, possibly poverty and want ; anxieties as to whether the call be of God, whether to trust Him without clear insight into the future ; perplexities as to the difference between the motives of credibility and the divine certainty of faith. All these are very real and sharp trials ; but these, or others, are to be expected, for it is said, 'Son, when thou comest to the service of God, stand in justice and in fear, and prepare thy soul for temptation. Humble thy heart, and endure ; incline thy ear, and receive the words of understanding, and make not haste in the time of clouds. Wait on God with patience ; join thyself to God and endure, that thy life may be increased in the latter end ' (Ecclus. ii.).

Faith is a gift of God. No man can acquire faith by study alone, as by his own skill. 'No man can come to Me, unless it be given him by My Father' (John vi.). Or, to quote the Council of Trent :

'If any man saith that without the prevenient inspiration of the Holy Ghost, and without His help, man can *believe*, hope, love, or be penitent as he ought, so as that the grace of justification may be bestowed upon him, let him be anathema ' (Sess. vi.).

The motives of credibility which may be learnt by reading and study do not produce the absolute and perfect certainty of faith. They lead a man to see that the objects of faith are worthy of belief ; they show him that he is under an obligation to give to them the assent of faith. But it is grace, it is God, who inspires the soul with the pious inclination to believe, the '*pia affectio ad credendum.*' The certainty of faith rests, not indeed upon the motives of credibility, or upon facts or arguments that may or may not be evident in themselves, but upon the veracity of God Who has revealed them.

Or, as the Vatican Council defines it:

'Faith is a supernatural virtue, whereby, inspired and assisted by the grace of God, we believe that the things which He has revealed are true; not because of the intrinsic truth of the things, viewed by the natural light of reason, but because of the authority of God Himself Who reveals them, and Who can neither deceive nor be deceived.'

And again:

'Though the assent of faith is by no means a blind action of the mind, still no man can assent to the Gospel teaching as necessary to obtain salvation, without the illumination and inspiration of the Holy Ghost, Who gives to all men sweetness in assenting to and in believing the truth. Wherefore, faith itself, even when it does not work by charity, is in itself a gift of God, and the act of faith is a work appertaining to salvation, by which man yields voluntary obedience to God Himself, by assenting to and co-operating with His grace, which he is able to resist.'

And further on the same Council declares:

'That we may be able to satisfy the obligation of embracing the true faith and of constantly persevering in it, God has instituted the Church . . . which both invites to itself those who do not yet believe, and assures its children that the faith which they profess rests on the most firm foundation; and its testimony is efficaciously supported by a power from on high. For our merciful Lord gives His grace to stir up and to aid those who are astray, that they may come to a knowledge of the truth; and to those whom He has brought out of the darkness into His own admirable light He gives His grace to strengthen them to persevere in that light, deserting none who desert not Him' (*Cap. de Fide*).

All this shows that the assent of faith is concerned with the will as well as with the intellect, and that a man who is seeking to come to a knowledge of that article of faith which declares that God has left a Divine Teacher to guide men safely in the affairs of salvation, must give himself to prayer and to humble repentance and contrition as much as to study and to reading. 'The prayer of him that humbleth himself shall pierce the clouds, and he will not depart till the Most High behold' (Ecclus. xxxv.).

HERBERT CARDINAL VAUGHAN,
Archbishop of Westminster.

AUTHOR'S PREFACE.

THE particular theory opposed in this book lies at the root of the controversy which we are forced to carry on with our Anglican friends on the subject of Church government at the present moment. It is the theory of the lawful independence of National Churches. Even the Magna Charta has been enlisted in the service of this theory by so able and respected a writer as Lord Selborne. The expression 'Let the Anglican Church be free' is held by his Lordship to express the determination of the Church of England in that century to be independent of Papal jurisdiction.[1] The present jurisdiction of the See of Canterbury is referred to the general question of the independence of National Churches by so eminent a writer as Dr. Stubbs.[2] Mr. Gore goes so far as to deduce from the teaching of St. Cyprian the fundamental independence of each bishop in the whole world.[3] And the present Archbishop of Canterbury writes that the 'individual independence of elected bishops' was the Cyprianic doctrine, but that it is applicable only to 'States which have not that intimate union with the Church which the ideal of a Christian nation requires.'[4] In other words, the ideal condition, according to his Grace, is the independence, not of each bishop, but of

[1] *A Defence of the Church of England,* by Roundell, Earl of Selborne, fourth edition, 1888. He lays emphasis on the expression 'Anglican,' as though it involved independence of Rome, p. 9.
[2] *Eastern Church Association Papers,* No. 1.
[3] *R. C. Claims,* p. 117, third edition.
[4] *Dict. of Chr. Biog.* (Smith and Wace), art. 'Cyprian.'

each national Church. And this was certainly the doctrine of some of the most eminent teachers in the Establishment in previous centuries, as for instance, Bishop Overall, the author of part of the Catechism in the Church of England Prayer-book.[1]

And this ideal of independence is asserted to be the teaching of history, the natural outcome of the principles which are to be discovered especially in the primitive Church. *There*, we are told, there was no dependence on Rome; *there* was no shadow of centralisation to be seen; *there*, if the Pope comes at times to the front, it is as the occupant of a See, great by reason of its relation to the empire, not because of any special relation to the Apostolic College. It was with this ideal of independence that, according to Dean Church, the Oxford movement was in special and profound sympathy.[2]

In the following pages, the doctrine set forth by John Peckham, Archbishop of Canterbury, in his famous letter to King Edward the First, as that of the Church of England, is maintained as the teaching of the primitive Church.[3] It is, of course, perfectly true that Magna Charta spoke of the Anglican Church being free; but the freedom claimed and granted was not from the authority of the Pope, but from the lawlessness of the king—in a word, it involved, amongst other things, freedom to appeal, when necessary, to Rome.[4] 'The Anglican Church' at that time signified a religious body in the closest communion with Rome, and under her obedience in spiritual matters. For in that same Charter, the Archbishop of Canterbury is called a Cardinal *of the Holy Roman*

---

[1] See the thesis of his *Convocation Book.*

[2] *Oxford Movement*, p. 211. He also quotes (p. 47) Hurrell Froude's saying (*Remains*, edited by J. Keble), viz. 'Let us give up a National Church, and have a real one,' *i.e.* if a national Church means lack of discipline. Dean Church thinks that the Oxford movement purged the national Church of its deeper faults.

[3] See quotation from this letter, *infra*, p. 381.

[4] Hume says that by Magna Charta 'all checks on appeals were removed.' He is speaking of appeals to Rome.

Church, and the next words to those quoted by Lord Selborne proclaim the fact that the confirmation of 'the lord Pope Innocent' had been 'obtained' for this very matter.[1] It is maintained in this book that the close communion with Rome which the Church of England thus avowed, and which it cherished during all those centuries from St. Augustine to the sixteenth century, is a principle deeply embedded in the life of the primitive Church.

But when we say that Papal supremacy is found deeply embedded in the life of the primitive Church, what do we exactly mean? No one who appeals to the primitive Church professes to find in her actual life a literal transcript of his own present position. National Churches certainly did not exist in Europe; it would be hard to say what could be included under the national Church of Rome. The appeal must be to something else than a primitive presentation of the form and outward appearance of any system in the nineteenth century. What, then, do we ourselves mean when we say that the Papal *régime* was in existence in the earliest beginnings of Christianity? The question really is as to whether the alleged counterpart in the early Church differs from its successor in the present, in substance, in principle, in essential features. Is the difference, for instance, between the Papal *régime* of to-day and the position of the Papacy in the first four centuries of the Christian era more than between the oak and the acorn? Does the difference between the two argue a dissimilarity of constituent elements, or is it merely the necessary difference between various stages of normal growth?

On meeting some one whom we have not seen since his childhood we are often constrained to exclaim, 'I should never have known it to be you!' Yet it is the same person whom Almighty God brought into the world as an infant, whose powers and appearance have thus developed. This

---

[1] *Viz.* concerning the election of bishops.

simile of the child and the grown man, as well as that of the oak and the acorn, was adopted in regard to the Church by St. Vincent of Lerins, the author of the formula (though not of the truth) of the 'always, everywhere, and by all,' as a test of truth not yet defined.

And yet an idea has taken hold of many minds to the effect that when Dr. Newman wrote his book nearly fifty years ago, now called 'The Development of Christian Doctrine,' he was striking out a new theory,[1] instead of merely illustrating, with that force which belonged to the greatest religious genius of this country, the theory on which the Church has always proceeded in teaching Christian history. His first title may be thought to countenance the idea; but the second corrects it. And St. Vincent of Lerins is a sufficient witness that the theory which Cardinal Newman so expanded and illustrated was not new even in the fifth century.

Dr. Döllinger only reflected the general teaching of the Church when he wrote, sixty years ago, with his usual felicity of expression, the following passage:

'Like all other essential parts of the constitution of the Church, the supremacy was known and acknowledged from the beginning as a divine institution, but it required time to unfold its faculties; it assumed by degrees the determined form in which the Bishop of Rome exercised systematically the authority entrusted to him for the preservation of the internal and external unity of the Church.'[2]

And some years afterwards the same writer says of the Papacy:

'Its birth begins with two mighty, pregnant, and far-reaching words of the Lord. He to whom these words are addressed realises them in his person and in his acts, and transplants the institute to which he has been appointed into

---

[1] Cf. Canon Bright's *Lessons from the Lives of Three Great Fathers* (Preface), where he assumes this.

[2] *Geschichte der christlichen Kirche* (1835), vol. i. p. 365

the centre of the infant Church, to the Roman capital itself. Here it grows up in silence, *occulto velut arbor ævo* ; and in the earliest times it manifests itself only in particular traits, till the outlines of the ecclesiastical power and action of the Bishop of Rome become ever clearer and more definite. Already even in the times of the Roman Empire the Popes are the guardians of the whole Church.'[1]

I venture to call this view of the matter more in accord with history than that proposed by the respected writer to whom I have alluded,[2] which in effect prescinds all real development from the action of the Papacy, if it is to be acknowledged as of divine institution.

It is the repudiation of the necessity of a real development which seems to me the greatest blot in a book which appeared last year under the auspices of the Bishop of Lincoln, who has made himself responsible for its general accuracy as well as its thesis. I have incorporated in this book an answer to the main points of that work. I have not, however, included an account of the Acacian troubles, because I have dealt with these elsewhere ;[3] but, in point of fact, the teaching of the Council of Chalcedon (with which this book closes) is such as to establish the fact that the law of Christian life is communion with Rome, and any seeming exceptions must be treated as such, and must not be quoted as establishing a principle of action in the future. To the history of that council I venture to draw the especial attention of the reader, because I am not aware of any English work that contains as full an account of its various acts. And it is only by seeing certain expressions in their context that their full value can be gauged, as establishing, not what St. Leo claimed (though that has its value),

[1] *The Church and the Churches*, p. 31. Eng. trans.
[2] Bright's *Lessons, &c.*
[3] In the *Dublin Review* for April 1894, where I have shown that communion between Rome and the East was not broken off at that time, but only suspended in some of its effects, and that consequently no argument can be derived from the existence of sanctity in some members of the Eastern Church.

but what the Church at large received without consciousness of novelty or usurpation.

I have sometimes referred the reader to the original of Dr. Döllinger's writings, but more often to the English translation, since the former is much less accessible than the latter.

I have, in conclusion, to thank his Eminence the Cardinal Archbishop of Westminster for so kindly enriching this volume with an introduction, and the Censor Deputatus, Father Sydney Smith, S.J., for going beyond the necessities of his office in the way of many helpful suggestions.

NOTE.—Since the above lines were written, a book has appeared [1] by the Regius Professor of Ecclesiastical History in the University of Oxford, containing a chapter on 'Papalism and Antiquity,' which consists for the most part of a *critique* on a book of mine published in 1889.[2] Lest the following pages (especially the last two hundred) should seem a miracle of anticipation, I may as well say that the chapter in Canon Bright's work, to which I allude, is a reproduction or recension of an anonymous article by that writer in the 'Church Quarterly Review' for October 1889, characterised by much bitterness against the 'Church of Rome,' calling it an atmosphere of untruthfulness.

I do not propose to descend into the arena of vituperation and invective. But I am able to say that the following pages contain a direct answer to most of the arguments advanced in Canon Bright's 'Papalism and Antiquity.' For after reading his article in the 'Church Quarterly,' when it appeared in 1889, I came to the conclusion that there was need of a fuller account of the Councils of Ephesus and Chalcedon than has yet been given in English, with special reference to the points urged in that article, and now repeated in Canon Bright's recension of the same. It rarely falls to the lot of a writer to be able to produce an answer to such representations of history as Canon Bright proposes in his new book, within a few weeks of their appearance. But it is my good fortune

---

[1] *Waymarks in Church History*, by W. Bright, D.D., Canon of Christ Church, Oxford, Regius Professor of Ecclesiastical History. 1894.

[2] *Dependence; or the Insecurity of the Anglican Position.* By Rev. Luke Rivington, M.A. (Kegan Paul, Trench & Co. 1889.)

to have been able to do this through the accident of having selected the original draft for particular refutation. I would draw especial attention to the treatment of the twenty-eighth Canon of Chalcedon, on pages 437–449, as meeting one of Canon Bright's chief points.[1]

But I feel bound to add a few words here on one passage in Canon Bright's chapter on Papalism, referring to this very subject.[2] The Regius Professor says (p. 234), 'When Mr. Rivington tells us that "nothing more transpired concerning the canon, and it was omitted from the authorised collection of canons even in the East," he omits, and it is no small omission—it is a real *suppressio veri*— to say after Hefele that the Greeks did not adhere to the profession made by Anatolius, and that his successors continued to act as patriarchs under the terms of the new canon, with the full approval of their emperors, and in despite of the protests of Rome.'

Will it be believed that Canon Bright has altered my words by a most important, nay, crucial omission? My words are ('Dependence,' p. 60), 'Nothing more transpired concerning the canon. *No further appeal was made to it at that time*, and it was omitted from the authorised collection of canons even in the East.' Now this statement is absolutely true. Hefele, to whom Canon Bright appeals, says the same: 'From that time Leo continued to exchange letters with Anatolius, and his successor Gennadius, but there was nothing more said between them on the subject of the twenty-eighth Canon' ('Hist. of the Councils,' § 207). But Canon Bright has omitted the all-important words, which I have placed in italics, and thus made my statement refer to the future instead of the present only. The strangest part of the matter is that in his anonymous article, of which he calls this chapter a 'recension' (cf. Preface, p. vii), the words I have italicised above appear in their right place, and he there accuses me only of '*going near* to *suppressio veri*' ('Church Quarterly Review,' October, 1889, p. 133); whereas now, having in his 'recension' omitted the crucial words of my statement, he accuses me downright of that form of literary dishonesty.

But, further, I had actually said on the same page, 'What Constantinople did was to continue its encroachments.' And on the next page but one (p. 62) I have given an instance of an attempt to revive the canon, and of the emperor's fruitless endeavour to induce Rome to recognise it. How, then, can Canon Bright say

---

[1] This canon is cherished as suggesting that Rome's primacy was due to her secular position alone.

[2] His accusation of 'carelessness' on p. 227 will be seen by reference to p. 409 *infra* to be based on a misinterpretation of the passage as a whole.

that I even suppressed this? Nor is this writer correct in saying, 'It is all very well to talk of "the canon invalidated," *i.e.* from the Papal stand-point, but it is the canon which has practically prevailed.' The canon was invalidated from the high Anglican standpoint; for as Le Quien ('Oriens Christianus,' p. 51) points out, a canon, to be a canon of the whole Church, must be accepted by the West. This was repudiated by the West. Even the Illyrians did not sign. And when, centuries after, Constantinople was allowed to take precedence of other Eastern sees, it was not on account of this canon; and in the previous centuries it was not the canon that prevailed, but unjustifiable encroachments. Does Canon Bright imagine that a canon passed under such disgraceful circumstances as I have described below (cf. p. 440)—dropped by the archbishop and emperor in whose reign it was proposed—could override the Nicene settlement? The Pope said, No. And when Acacius came on to the scene and acted on the canon, it was to place heretics, who opposed the doctrine of the Incarnation, as defined at Chalcedon, in the Eastern sees—heretics like Peter the Fuller at Alexandria. Canon Bright, in the same paragraph, quotes Liberatus against me; but my account altogether agrees with that of Liberatus, who in the same chapter speaks of the 'usurpations' of Anatolius, and in the passage quoted by Canon Bright is stigmatising the Erastianism and encroachments that went on under the pretext of that canon, and in the following chapter describes the usurpations of the heretic Acacius ('detectus hereticus').[1] In fact this whole passage in Canon Bright's book is, I regret to say, a tissue of misrepresentations, his accusation of *suppressio veri* being actually supported by omitting the very line which confines my statement to the present, whilst the truth supposed to be suppressed is concerned with the future.

[1] *Breviarium*, cap. xviii.

L. R.

THE PRESBYTERY, SPANISH PLACE,
LONDON, W.
March 30, 1894.

CONTENTS

	PAGE
INTRODUCTION BY THE CARDINAL ARCHBISHOP OF WESTMINSTER	v
AUTHOR'S PREFACE	xvii

PERIOD I. A.D. 96–300.

CHAPTER I.

THE EPISTLE OF ST. CLEMENT; OR THE TYPE SET.

§ 1. The Church of Rome intervenes in the Schism at Corinth, p. 1. § 2. Reasons why St. Clement omitted his Name, 2. § 3. The authoritative Tone of the Letter, 7. § 4. Probably a Case of Appeal, 8 . pp. 1–10

CHAPTER II.

THE CLEMENTINE ROMANCE.

§ 1. St. Clement's Personality, p. 11. § 2. The Clementine Literature, 12. § 3. Its Use by the Tübingen School, 13. § 4. Use by anti-Papal Writers to account for the Expression 'See of Peter,' 13. § 5. Impossibility of this Supposition, 15. § 6. The List of Hegesippus anterior to the Romance at Rome, 17. § 7. Irenæus on the See of Peter, 22. § 8. The Clementines at Rome later than Tertullian, 25. § 9. Historical Results, 29 . pp. 11–31

CHAPTER III.

ST. IRENÆUS, OR THE SOVEREIGNTY OF THE CHURCH OF ROME.

§ 1. His Statement of the Rule of Faith, viz. Agreement with Rome, p. 32. § 2. Protestant Endeavours to wrest his Meaning: e.g. (a) Rome's Orthodoxy secured by the Confluence of Strangers, 34; (b) her 'principalitas' only Primitiveness, 35; or (c) due to her secular Position, 36; (d) *undique*, not = everywhere, 36; (e) *in quâ*, not = in communion with, 37 . pp. 32–38

CHAPTER IV.

ST. VICTOR, OR THE GUARDIAN OF THE COMMON UNITY.

§ 1. The Modes of observing Easter, p. 39. § 2. St. Victor's Attempt to produce Uniformity, 40. § 3. St. Irenæus' Intervention, 42. Note on Mr. Puller's Interpretation, 44 . pp. 39–

CHAPTER V.

THE DOCTRINE OF ST. CYPRIAN ON UNITY.

§ 1. St. Cyprian on the Authority of St. Peter, p. 47. § 2. The Occasion of his Treatise on Unity, viz. (α) Danger to the Episcopal Authority, 50; (β) an unlawful Bishop at Rome, 55. § 3. Teaches Papal Supremacy incidentally, 57. § 4. St. Peter in the Treatise on Unity, 60. § 5. Corollaries, 62 . . . . pp. 47–64

CHAPTER VI.

ST. CYPRIAN ON APPEALS TO ROME.

§ 1. *Résumé* of the Saint's Teaching on Unity, p. 65. § 2. Fortunatus denounced for going to Rome, but not the Principle of Appeal, 67. § 3. Case of Marcian referred to Rome, 70. § 4. Spanish Bishops may be, but do not deserve to be, restored by the Pope, 72. Note on Mr. Puller's Interpretation . . . . pp. 65–76

CHAPTER VII.

ST. CYPRIAN'S ERROR ON BAPTISM BY HERETICS.

§ 1. Doctrine of Unity misapplied; his threefold Error, p. 77. § 2. Convokes a Council on the Subject, 81. § 3. Second Council and Letter to Jubaianus, 84. § 4. Refers the Matter to Rome, 86. § 5. Meanwhile holds third Council and decides in favour of Rebaptising, 88 . . . pp. 77–93

CHAPTER VIII.

ROME'S DECISION AND CYPRIAN'S IRRITATION.

§ 1. St. Stephen's Decision, p. 94. § 2. St. Cyprian's Legation to Rome, 97. § 3. Letter to Pompeius and Firmilian, 97. § 4. Firmilian's passionate Reply, 100. § 5. Did St. Stephen actually excommunicate St. Cyprian? 105. § 6. Did St. Cyprian retract? 111. § 7. Corollary as to Papal Infallibility, 114 . . . . pp. 94–116

CHAPTER IX.

ROME, ALEXANDRIA, AND ANTIOCH, SEES OF PETER.

§ 1. Only Peter left a Successor of his Apostolate, p. 117. § 2. Rome the Rallying-point from the first, 118. § 3. The three Sees of Peter, 120. § 4. Relationship of Rome to Alexandria, 121. § 5. Relationship of Rome to Antioch, 122. § 6. Why these three Sees chosen, 125. Appendix on the Popes' witness to their Office, 127 . . . . . pp. 117–136

CONTENTS. xxvii

PERIOD II. A.D. 300–384.

CHAPTER X.

THE DONATISTS AND THE COUNCIL OF ARLES.

§ 1. The Origin of the Donatist Schism, p. 139.   § 2. The Donatists appeal to the Emperor, who refers them to Rome, 140.   § 3. The Papal Sentence, 141.   § 4. Final in the Eyes of Augustine, as that of Peter's See, 142.   § 5. Case reheard to sift additional Facts, 144.   § 6. British Bishops at Arles, 146.   § 7. Donatist Erastianism, 147.   § 8. Archbishop Laud's Mistranslation, 148 . . . . pp. 139–152

CHAPTER XI.

THE COUNCIL OF NICÆA.

Part I.—Reasons of its Meeting.

§ 1. The good Results of Heresies, p. 153.   § 2. Need of a Council compatible with Papal Infallibility, 154.   § 3. The Circumstances, 155.   § 4. Papal Consent, 157.   § 5. Why the Pope desired a Council, 159.

Part II.—The Council itself.

§ 1. The Pope presided, p. 161.   § 2. Papal Jurisdiction not in Question, therefore not directly mentioned, 164.

Part III.—The Sixth Canon.

§ 1. The three Sees of Peter, p. 166.   § 2. Alexandria's Jurisdiction rested on Rome's Example, 167.   § 3. Or on her Arrangement, 169.   § 4. The original Beginning of the Canon, 170 . . . . . pp. 153–172

CHAPTER XII.

THE POPES THE GUARDIANS OF THE NICENE CANONS.

Part I.—St. Julius.

§ 1. The Post-Nicene Struggle, p. 173.   § 2. Pope St. Julius and Alexandria, 175.

Part II.—The Sardican Canons.

§ 1. Canon III. not concerned with Appeals to Rome, p. 179.   § 2. Canon IV. supposes Appeals, 180.   § 3. Canon VII. leaves it to Rome to decide the Mode of Appeal, 180.   § 4. Received in the East, 181.   § 5. Honouring the Memory of St. Peter, 182.   Note on these Canons . . pp. 173–184

CHAPTER XIII.

THE REIGN OF LIBERIUS.

Part I.—His Personal Grandeur.

§ 1. Defends St. Athanasius, and is exiled, p. 185.   § 2. His supposed Fall, 186.
§ 3. His Stand after the Ariminian Catastrophe, 188.

Part II.—The Meletian Scandal at Antioch.

§ 1. The Consequence of Meletius' Election, p. 190.   § 2. The Council of Alexandria on the same, 194.   § 3. The precipitate Action of Bishop Lucifer 198.   § 4. Eusebius of Vercellæ settles nothing, 199 . . pp. 185–202

CHAPTER XIV.

ST. DAMASUS.

§ 1. His Sanctity, p. 203.   § 2. His Election, 207.   § 3. His central Position, 208.   § 4. His Condemnation of Heresies, 211.   § 5. St. Basil looks to the West, 213.   § 6. St. Damasus differs as to the best Remedy, 215.   § 7. Sides with Paulinus at Antioch, 218.   § 8. St. Basil's Irritation, 219.   § 9. His petulant Expression not Disbelief, 222.   § 10. Believed in Rome's Jurisdiction in the East, 224.   § 11. St. Damasus neither approved nor repudiated St. Meletius, 226.   § 12. St. Jerome's Witness, 227.   § 13. St. Meletius and Paulinus come to Terms, 229 . . . . . pp. 203–232

CHAPTER XV.

THE HOMAGE OF KINGS; OR GRATIAN'S RESCRIPT.

§ 1. The ideal Relation between Church and State, p. 233.   § 2. Realised for awhile under Gratian, 234.   § 3. Relationship between Gratian and St. Ambrose, 235.   § 4. Gratian gives civil Facilities for the exercise of Rome's Supremacy, 235.   § 5. Mr. Puller's Theory as to Gratian's Rescript refuted: (i.) by the Absence of any Protest, 238; (ii.) and by the Words of the Rescript compared with the Letter of the Roman Synod, 239   pp. 233–242

CHAPTER XVI.

THE COUNCIL OF CONSTANTINOPLE (A.D. 381).

Part I.—Theodosius and the Imperial City.

§ 1. Theodosius made Emperor, p. 243.   § 2. Issues a Law defining the Term 'Catholic,' 244.   § 3. Gregory and Maximus in Constantinople, 245.   § 4. Theodosius resolves upon a General Eastern Council, 246.

Part II.—The Council.

§ 1. St. Gregory's Election confirmed, p. 248.   § 2. St. Meletius dies, 249.   § 3. Flavian elected to Antioch, 250.   § 4. St. Gregory resigns, 253.   § 5. Nectarius appointed in his Place, 255.   § 6. How the Council came to be œcumenical, 256.

Part III.—*New Rome; or the Third Canon*, p. 258.

Part IV.—*The Western Disapproval of Flavian's Election*, p. 263.

Note on Mr. Puller's Proof that St. Meletius was out of Communion with Rome, p. 267. Conclusion of Second Period. Councils of A.D. 382 at Rome and Constantinople, 269 243–279

PERIOD III. A.D. 400–452.

CHAPTER XVII.

THE CHURCH OF NORTH AFRICA IN THE DAYS OF ST. AUGUSTINE.

Part I.—*The Letters of St. Innocent.*

§ 1. Cœlestius, condemned in Africa, appeals to Rome, p. 284.   § 2. The Synods of Carthage and Milevis write from Africa to Rome, 286.   § 3. St. Innocent's Rescripts—their Doctrine on St. Peter's See, 288.   § 4. Their Reception by the African Fathers—its Witness to African Belief, 289.

Part II.—*St. Zosimus' Support of the Faith.*

§ 1. Did not sanction Pelagian Statements, p. 291.   § 2. Cautiousness of the Pope, 293.   § 3. St. Augustine and Dr. Pusey, 293.   § 4. St. Zosimus' Encyclical 'confirming the Brethren,' 295.

Part III.—*Apiarius and Papal Jurisdiction.*

§ 1. A Canon quoted of which the Africans ignorant, p. 297.   § 2. Legates *a latere* deprecated, 298.   § 3. The whole Matter a Question of Procedure, not of Principle, 300.   § 4. The Genuineness of the chief Letter open to Question, 303 . . . . pp. 283–304

CHAPTER XVIII.

THE COUNCIL OF EPHESUS—ITS PRELIMINARIES.

§ 1. The Matter in Dispute, p. 305.   § 2. St. Cyril's Action, 306.   § 3. The Papal Intervention, 306.   § 4. St. Cyril asks the Pope for Judgment, 307.   § 5. St. Celestine appoints Cyril his Plenipotentiary, 309.   § 6. Conclusions as to the Pope's Position, 311.   § 7. Anglican Writers on the above, 313.   § 8. Cyril's Action as Plenipotentiary, 315.   § 9. Nestorius, having the Emperor's ear, makes for a Council, 316.   § 10. Meets at Ephesus, without the Bishop of Antioch, 319.   § 11. Celestine (Pope) the real, Cyril the acting President, 321 . . . . pp. 305–328

CHAPTER XIX.

THE ACTS OF THE COUNCIL.

§ 1. Nestorius refuses to appear, p. 329. § 2. The Relation of the Bishops' Judgment to that of the Pope, 330. § 3. The Action of the Council, 332. § 4. The Council's Sentence, 333. § 5. Anglican Writers on the Council's Sentence, 336. § 6. The immediate Result of the Sentence, 336. § 7. The Arrival of Legates from Rome, 338. § 8. The schismatic Synod, 341 . . . . pp. 329–343

CHAPTER XX.

THE SEE OF PETER 'CONFIRMING THE BRETHREN.'

§ 1. The Papal Legates' Judgment, p. 344. § 2. The Council's Witness to the Supremacy of the Pope, 345. § 3. John of Antioch condemned by the Synod, but referred to the Pope, 350. § 4. The Pope's fatherly Care, 354. § 5. The Case of the Cyprians, and Canon Bright on the Expression 'worldly Pride,' 356. Conclusions, 361 . . . . . . pp. 344–361

CHAPTER XXI.

THE FOURTH GENERAL COUNCIL—PRELIMINARIES.

§ 1. Introductory Remarks on the Council of Chalcedon, p. 362. § 2. The Origin of the Council—Eutyches' Perversion of St. Cyril's Writings, 364. § 3. Eutyches condemned at Constantinople, 365. § 4. Eutyches appeals to Rome, 365. § 5. St. Leo blames Archbishop of Constantinople for not sending Report, 367. § 6. Eutyches makes for a Council, 368. § 7. Archbishop of Constantinople prefers a Papal Brief to a Council, 369. § 8. The Position of the Pope in the Thoughts of Christendom, 371. § 9. The Tome of St. Leo, 372. § 10. Revises the Acts of the Synod of Constantinople, 373. § 11. Leo consents to a Council to convict Eutyches, 374. § 12. Describes his Tome as an *ex Cathedrâ* Pronouncement, 375. § 13. Describes the Office of the Council, 376 . . . . . . pp. 362–377

CHAPTER XXII.

THE LATROCINIUM, OR ROBBER COUNCIL.

§ 1. Its uncanonical Composition, p. 378. § 2. Eutyches is acquitted, Leo's Tome suppressed, Flavian condemned, 379. § 3. The Inadequacy of a Primacy of Honour to meet the Case, 380. § 4. The Supremacy exercised by Leo, 382. § 5. Flavian's Appeal to Rome, 383. § 6. Leo insists on another Council, 384. § 7. Demands the Enforcement of the Niceno-Sardican Canon, 385. § 8. The Emperor and Empresses write to Theodosius, 388. § 9. Leo describes his Duty to the whole Church, 390. § 10. The new Emperor decides on a Council, 391. § 11. Anatolius, Archbishop of Constantinople—his Antecedents, 392. § 12. Leo requires his Profession of Faith in accordance with his Tome, 393. § 13. Anatolius sends it and receives Directions, 396. § 14. St. Leo's Tome signed by Anatolius and other Bishops, 397 . . . . pp. 378–398

CHAPTER XXIII.

THE DEPOSITION OF DIOSCORUS.

§ 1. The Work before the Council, p. 399. § 2. Dioscorus condemned, 400 § 3. The Sentence pronounced in the Name of the Pope, 403. § 4. On the Matter of Faith nothing new needed after Leo's Tome, 408. § 5. The so-called Review of Leo's Tome, 409 . . . . . . pp. 399–418

CHAPTER XXIV.

THE DEFINITION OF FAITH.

The Bishops in Danger of adopting an insufficient Formula, p. 419 ; are kept right by the Commissioners and Papal Legates, 420. They have to answer the Question of Obedience to Leo's Decision, 421 ; Principles that emerge, 424 . . . . pp. 419–425

CHAPTER XXV.

THEODORET AND MAXIMUS.

1. Theodoret appealed to the See of Peter, p. 427 ; the Sentence against him annulled, 429 ; his Presence objected to at Chalcedon, 430 ; allowed the Position of Bishop, 431 ; acted as such in the Council, 431 ; compelled to anathematise Nestorius, 432 ; not a Review of Leo's Judgment, 432. II. Maximus of Antioch irregularly ordained, 433 ; condoned by Leo, *ib.*; his Position accepted on that ground, 434 . . . . pp. 426–436

CHAPTER XXVI.

THE BYZANTINE PLOT ; OR THE TWENTY-EIGHTH CANON.

The Ambition of Constantinople, p. 437 ; Rebuff at Chalcedon, 440 ; Opening for a Move, 441 ; some Bishops passed a Canon, 442 ; the Papal Legates protest, 443 ; Imperial Commissioners side with the Bishops, 445 ; Value of the Canon, 447 . . . . pp. 437–449

CHAPTER XXVII.

THE EASTERNS' RECOGNITION OF PAPAL SUPREMACY.

The Bishops write to Leo, p. 451 ; express full Doctrine of Papal Supremacy, 452–454 ; Anatolius does the same, 455 ; Leo and the West repudiate the Canon, 458 . . . . pp. 450–460

CONCLUSION . . . . . [pp. 459–460]

APPENDICES

		PAGE
I.	REV. F. W. PULLER'S INTERPRETATION OF ST. CYPRIAN	461
II.	ARE THE SARDICAN CANONS NICENE?	467
III.	REV. F. W. PULLER ON ST. AMBROSE	475
IV.	THE APOSTOLIC SEE; MEANING OF THE PHRASE	479
	INDEX	483

ERRATA

P. 188, lines 10, 9, 8 from bottom: *for* but its numbers after an interval . . . belied its beginning *read* but its numbers fell off as it continued its sessions after an interval, at the emperor's command, and its end belied its beginning.

P. 189, line 2, *for* mission *read* minion.

PERIOD I.

A.D. 96–300.

CHAPTER I.

THE EPISTLE OF ST. CLEMENT
OR
THE TYPE SET.

I. In the very first document belonging to Christian history, outside the pages of Holy Scripture, the Church of Rome steps to the front in a manner that is suggestive of supreme authority, and that tallies with her whole future attitude towards the rest of the Church. The occupant of the See of Rome comes before us, speaking in the name of his Church, within the lifetime of the Apostle St. John, and settles a disturbance in a region naturally more nearly related to that Apostle than to the Church of Rome. And he comes before us both as in possession of a tradition of divine truth, and as its authoritative exponent to a distant Church. He lays down the law of worship and government for the whole Church as of Divine institution.

The circumstances were as follows:—The Church in Corinth had for some time been torn by dissensions, and had caused the utmost scandal on all sides (§ 47).[1] A few fiery spirits, with a considerable following, had succeeded in extruding probably their bishop and some of his presbyters, if not, indeed, one or more bishops in the neighbourhood, from their sacred office ($\dot{\epsilon}\pi\iota\sigma\kappa\sigma\pi\dot{\eta}$, § 44).[2] The Church of Rome came to the rescue. The persecutions under Nero and Domitian had alone prevented her from intervening earlier (§ 1). But as soon as possible St. Clement wrote a letter entitled, 'The

---

[1] The references to St. Clement's letter are from Dr. Lightfoot's edition—the second, posthumously published in 1890.

[2] St. Clement calls it a schism (§ 46).

Church in Rome to the Church in Corinth,' which Dr. Lightfoot characterises as 'almost imperious'[1] in tone, and which St. Irenæus spoke of as 'most powerful,' or 'most adequate.'[2] In this letter St. Clement speaks of the tradition which the Church of Rome had received from the Apostles themselves (§ 44), as to a succession of rulers in the Church, to prevent strife 'about the name [*i.e.* dignity] of the office of bishop (ἐπισκοπῆς).' Speaking of this government of the Church, he finds its type in the Old Covenant, in the High Priest, Priests, and Levites. He says that the Apostles, in order to obviate strife, ordained as successors in the ministry (λειτουργίας) bishops and deacons. He magisterially reproves the ringleaders of the disturbances in Corinth for attempting to extrude such successors of the Apostles,[3] and says that 'it will be a sin in us' to depose them from their 'sacred office (ἐπισκοπῆς).' Further on, in a passage only discovered of late, he claims their 'obedience unto the things written by us through the Holy Spirit' (§ 63), as he had said a little previously: 'If any disobey the things spoken by Him through us, let them know that they will involve themselves in transgression and no small peril' (§ 59). The letter concludes with saying that they hope soon to receive back again the legates whom they have sent, with a report from Corinth that the peace, which they desire, has been restored.

Such was the first recorded act of the Church of Rome. And it is spoken of in terms of enthusiasm by St. Irenæus, from whom we gather that the Corinthians amended their ways, and the desired result was achieved. It is also alluded to with commendation by St. Ignatius on his way to his martyrdom.

II. Dr. Lightfoot lays great stress on the fact that the name of St. Clement does not appear in this letter, but only

---

[1] *St. Clement of Rome*, vol. i. p. 69. 1890.
[2] ἱκανωτάτην, *Adv. Hær.* iii. 3, 3.
[3] τοὺς . . . κατασταθέντας ὑπ' ἐκείνων [*i.e.* the Apostles] ἢ μεταξὺ ὑφ' ἑτέρων . . . οὐ δικαίως νομίζομεν ἀποβάλλεσθαι, κ.τ.λ. (§ 44). Notice the present tense in the latter word. The Church of Rome treats the action of the Corinthians as incomplete.

that of the Church of Rome.[1] He admits, however, that the letter was written by St. Clement, and calls it an 'incident in his administration' of the Church.[2] But he thinks that St. Clement 'studiously suppressed'[3] his name, as not being in such a position of authority as is involved in the monarchical idea of the episcopate. He thinks that, in consequence, 'his personality is absorbed'[4] in the Church of Rome, and that in this we may discern a vital difference between the first century and the fifth. He says that 'the language of this letter is inconsistent with the possession of Papal authority in the person of the writer;' that 'it does not proceed from the Bishop of Rome, but from the Church of Rome.' It is spoken of, he says, in the second century as 'from the community, not from the individual.'

It will be well at once to warn our readers of a general misconception involved in the use of the word 'monarchical' as applied by certain writers (such as Dr. Lightfoot and Dr. Salmon and others) to the episcopate, and above all, to the Bishop of Rome.

When we speak of the Bishop of Rome as the infallible guardian of the faith, we do not mean that he is placed in a position in which he can act in isolation from the rest of the episcopal body. The very doctrine of Papal Infallibility implies that he never can act apart from the general teaching of the Church. We can always be sure that his utterances, when attended with those conditions which are implied in the exercise of his infallibility, are the exposition of the Church's mind as a whole. If we were to suppose the case of the Pope on the one side, and the whole of the episcopate arrayed against him on the other, we should be obliged to hold that the Pope would be in the right and the rest of the episcopate in the wrong. But such a case never has occurred, and never can. It is involved in our Lord's promise of His presence with the Church in her teaching 'all days unto the consummation of the world,'[5] that the body will never be separated from the head. The Holy Father speaks in the name of his children; and

---

[1] *Loc. cit.* p. 69.   [2] P. 84.   [3] P. 352.
[4] P. 69.   [5] St. Matt. xxviii. 20.

his children will never, as a whole, protest against his teaching.

But not only so. The Bishop of Rome, throughout the ages, has adopted the principle on which St. Cyprian, who especially expounded the monarchical idea of the episcopate, says that he ever proposed to govern his diocese—viz. with consultation. So nothing is more characteristic of the government of the Church by those great Popes, like St. Damasus and St. Leo, in the fourth and fifth centuries, than their use of episcopal assessors. As St. Ignatius speaks of the bishop of the diocese having his *corona*—his circlet—of presbyters, so the Bishops of Rome ever had their circlet of bishops, and made use of their advice in all great matters concerning the general welfare of the Church. When, then, the Popes used the plural 'we,' they were not only using the majestic plural, but they had gathered into their utterances with a special closeness a portion of that great whole in whose name they were justified in speaking. They had held their synod. They were not acting in lone majesty, but in concert with others whom they had gathered into a special closeness of contact with themselves.

Again, the supremacy which belongs strictly to the Bishop of Rome, as the successor of St. Peter, is often attributed, not to the Bishop of Rome, but to the Church of Rome. In the later history of the Church we constantly meet with the supremacy of the bishop spoken of as though it belonged to the *Church* of Rome. To this day we constantly speak of 'Rome' doing this or saying that, while of course we believe that the informing power of the whole is the bishop himself, as successor of Peter and Vicar of Christ. Martin V., in the Council of Constance, condemned the proposition of Wicliffe, that 'it is not of necessity to believe that the Roman Church is supreme amongst the other Churches;' and in the Creed of Pope Pius IV. a similar expression is used by converts on their reception into the Church, viz.: 'I acknowledge the holy Catholic and Apostolic Roman Church to be the mother and mistress of all Churches,' just as in the profession of faith prescribed by Clement IV. and Gregory X., and made by the Greeks after the second Council of Lyons, the words are: 'The holy Roman Church has the supreme and full primacy and sovereignty over the whole Catholic Church.' And, lastly, the Vatican decree runs thus (Constit. 'Pastor Æternus,' cap. 3): 'We teach and declare that the Roman Church, by the ordinance of Christ (*disponente Domino*), has the sovereignty of ordinary power over all other [Churches].'

Consequently, if primitive Christian history presents us with the spectacle of the *Church* of Rome calling herself by this name, and stepping to the front to act with authority in guarding the faith of the Church as to the Apostolic succession of her rulers, and restoring unity to a divided Christian community at a distance, this does not constitute anything like a vital difference between this early expression of authority and the most recent instance of Papal rule. It is at most a difference of terminology. It would not follow that, because an act of authority was done in the name of the Church of Rome, it was not done by the authority of the *Bishop* of Rome.[1] Unless, then, Dr. Lightfoot had been able to show that there was no other possible reason for St. Clement suppressing his name in the letter to Corinth, the fact that he did suppress it would not prove that he did not occupy the position in the minds of the early Christians that he occupies now in the Roman Catholic Church. And yet the argument from silence is the main point urged by Dr. Lightfoot in this matter. 'The language of this letter,' to which he appeals as showing a difference between earlier and later Popes, means its silence as to the name of its author.

But there is more than one possible solution of this silence. If the tradition which St. Epiphanius[2] gives is based on facts, to the effect that after the death of the Apostles Peter and Paul St. Clement refused to occupy the position of bishop in the Roman community out of modesty, the same deep humility might well operate in this, perhaps, first great act of discipline exercised by him towards a distant Church. On the Papal teaching concerning Church government it would be enough for St. Clement to mention the *Church* of Rome; she held 'the principality,' as St. Irenæus says, which, says St. Augus-

---

[1] Cf. *Life of St. Thomas of Canterbury* by Rev. J. Morris, S. J., p. 135.
[2] *Hær.* xxvii. 6.

tine, 'was always in force.' St. Clement was successor of St. Peter because he was Bishop of Rome. He owed his relationship to the Divine Head of the Church, viz. that of His Vicar, to his position in the Church of Rome; and it would not be unnatural, in writing a letter of some severity to the Church at Corinth, that he should simply speak of the Church of Rome, and not mention his own unworthy name. This will only seem far-fetched and fanciful to those who do not reflect that our Lord's description of the vital difference between the head of His kingdom and those of the kingdoms of this world was that 'the principal one' in His kingdom would not 'lord it' over others, after the example of this world's rulers, but would be amongst the rest as He Himself was—their Ruler, their Lord and Infallible Teacher, and yet lowly and meek in heart.[1]

But there is yet another possible, and indeed probable, solution of this suppression of his name, on which Dr. Lightfoot has rested his argument as to the difference between St. Clement and the Papacy in subsequent times. The Church had only just emerged from the most fiery persecutions, and might at any moment be exposed to another. All societies, organised without leave from the civil authorities, were illegal, and consequently the last thing that the head of the Christian community would do under such circumstances would be to flaunt their condition as an organised body before the world. A letter, of such authoritative tone as St. Clement's, with his own name at its head, might easily fall into the hands of strangers; and if St. Peter himself thought it advisable to call Rome 'Babylon,'[2] when writing of the Church of Rome, it might very well seem the part of prudence in the bishop to suppress his name when writing from Rome.

And yet neither of these suppositions is necessary to account for the fact of St. Clement's silence as to his name. Writing as the head of the Christian community, he could write officially in its name. A successor of his did

---

[1] St. Luke xxii. 25–27. And so from the time of St. Damasus the Popes have called themselves the 'servant of servants.'

[2] 1 St. Peter v. 13. Dr. Lightfoot so understands the word 'Babylon' in his *St. Clement of Rome*, vol. ii. p. 491, 2.

the same, St. Soter. And Eusebius expressly says that Clement wrote in the name of his Church,[1] and St. Jerome, that he wrote in the person of the Church.[2]

And this is the explanation of a passage in Eusebius in which he speaks of this letter of St. Clement. St. Dionysius of Corinth, writing to the Church of Rome, describes the letter as 'your Epistle written to us by Clement;' whereas Eusebius says that Dionysius made 'some remarks relating to the Epistle of Clement to the Corinthians,' on which Dr. Lightfoot convicts Eusebius of making an assumption not warranted by the words of Dionysius.[3] But the Greek historian, like all the world after him, considered it was all one, to call it, as Dionysius did, the letter of the Romans 'by Clement,' or the letter of Clement: just as St. Clement of Alexandria speaks of it in both ways, as the Epistle of the Romans,[4] and the Epistle of Clement.[5] All is explained by the principle which St. Cyprian laid down when he said, 'You ought to know that the bishop is in the Church, and the Church in the bishop.'

It would not have been necessary to enter at such length into Dr. Lightfoot's interpretation of this omission of the name in St. Clement's letter, were it not that Dr. Lightfoot's name gives weight to everything that he says, and that many who heartily repudiate his views as to the Christian ministry[6] yet follow him in this particular point.

III. The letter, then, of St. Clement was written in the name of the Church of Rome, and was, as Dr. Lightfoot says, 'the only recorded incident in his administration of the Church.' It was, according to the same writer, 'undoubtedly the first step towards Papal domination.' It would seem impossible to mistake its tone of authority, 'almost imperious,' says the same writer.[7] Dr. Salmon, in his book on 'Infallibility,'[8]

---

[1] *H. E.* iii. 37.   [2] *De Viris Illustr.* 15.
[3] *Loc. cit.* p. 358.   [4] *Strom.* v. 12, 81.   [5] *Ib.* iv. 17, 19.
[6] Mr. Gore has an excellent reply to Dr. Lightfoot's erroneous conception of the episcopate in the early Christian Church in his *Church and the Ministry*, 1889, note A, p. 353 *seq.*
[7] Mr. Gore (*ib.* p. 325) speaks of 'the teaching authority which breathes in his [Clement's] Epistle.'
[8] Salmon's (G.) *Infallibility of the Church*, second edit. p. 379.

maintains that the tone 'is only that of the loving remonstrance which any Christian is justified in offering to an erring brother.' But in his article on St. Clement in the 'Dictionary of Christian Biography' (Smith and Wace), he says, 'Very noticeable in the new part of the letter is the tone of authority used by the Roman Church in making an unsolicited interference with the affairs of another Church.'[1] 'Already in St. Clement's letter an assumption, so natural as to be almost unconscious, of the right to advise and interpose underlies his pacificatory argument.'[2]

It is certainly singular that only a few years after the dogma of Papal Infallibility, always the general belief of Christians, had, in view of emerging denials, been made obligatory, a manuscript, in a Greek monastery, containing strong assertions of the divine authority with which the Church of Rome conceived herself to be speaking, should be suddenly unearthed. Dr. Lightfoot had substituted a long fragment from another writer, as possibly the substance of the long-lost portion of this invaluable letter, and most scholars admired his ingenuity. But a comparison with this suggested complement of the letter, and the actual fragment now recovered, will show how the imagination of a brilliant scholar differs from the actual thoughts of the great Bishop of Rome himself.[3]

IV. There is one passage which suggests an answer to the question, whether this letter from Rome was in answer to an appeal or was an unsolicited intervention. The writer says (§ 44) that 'we do not think that such as these' (*i.e.* men left there by Apostles and of good repute) 'are being justly cast out from the sacred ministry; for it will be no small sin in us, if we should extrude [or depose] from the episcopate those who have offered the gifts blamelessly and holily.'

---

[1] Dr. Salmon, in the preface to his book on the *Infallibility of the Church*, says that much of it was written years ago. It certainly contrasts strangely in its tone of abruptness and heat with his admirable *Introduction to the Study of the New Testament*, in which he takes the same view of St. Clement's letter as in Smith and Wace's Dictionary. Possibly the new ending had not been discovered when he wrote that portion of his work on *Infallibility*.

[2] Cruttwell's (C. T.) *Lit. Hist. of Early Christianity*, 1893, vol. ii. p. 404.

[3] Lightfoot's *Clement of Rome*, 1890, vol. i. p. 178.

It certainly seems as though the case of these bishops (I use the exact equivalent, without meaning thereby to settle the question what exactly their office was) had been laid before the Church of Rome. The Corinthians had removed them from the exercise of their office, as is stated in the next sentence; but in this sentence the writer of the Epistle treats their deposition as not concluded; it is the present tense, as though their act awaited its completion at the hands of Rome. Whether this were so or not, the matter must have been brought before them in some way, for Rome passes most definite judgment as to whether these rulers deserved such treatment, instead of asking for further particulars. The passage in which St. Clement speaks of the 'report' having reached Rome,[1] which seems at first sight to suggest that the Romans had not been directly consulted on the matter, refers only to the statement that the disturbance, of which the main facts seem to have been brought very circumstantially before the Church of Rome, was due to only 'one or two ringleaders.' The expression in the beginning of the letter, 'the matters in dispute *among you*,' does not compel us to suppose that the matters of dispute among them had not been also referred to Rome. For if there had been no appeal, why should St. Clement excuse himself for not having attended to the matter sooner? On the whole, then, it seems most likely, though not certain, that the letter was written in answer to an appeal from Corinth.

Such, then, was 'the first step towards Papal domination' (Lightfoot), or, as we should prefer to call it, the first recorded exercise of authority towards a distant Church. There was no protest; on the contrary, St. Irenæus and St. Ignatius praised it, and Corinth treasured the letter and read it at Divine service on the Lord's Day for years to come.

Such is the dawn of uninspired Christian history. In that first century of the Christian era unity was restored at Corinth by the action of Rome writing a most powerful letter and sending legates[2] to the scene of disturbance; and, according to St. Ignatius, Rome was the teacher of others, with special allusion, it is thought, to this letter: 'Ye taught

---

[1] § 47, *ad finem*.   [2] Clem. *Ep. ad Cor.* § 45.

others' (Ign. 'Ep. ad Rom.' § 3) are words which, as Dr. Lightfoot remarks,[1] 'the newly discovered ending of St. Clement's letter enables us to appreciate more fully'—a letter in which the writer claims to speak with the authority of God.

The least that can be said of this first disclosure of Rome's position in the Church is that it fits in with her present position in Roman Catholic Christendom.

---

[1] *Loc. cit.* p. 71.

CHAPTER II.

THE CLEMENTINE ROMANCE.

I. 'It is very remarkable,' says a Protestant historian, 'that a person of such vast influence in truth and fiction, whose words were law, who preached the duty of obedience and submission to an independent and distracted Church, whose vision reached even to unknown lands beyond the Western Sea, should inaugurate, at the threshold of the second century, that long line of pontiffs who have outlasted every dynasty in Europe, and now claim an infallible authority over the consciences of 200,000,000 of Christians.'[1]

Dr. Schaff here speaks of St. Clement, who, as Dr. Salmon says, 'speaks in a tone of authority to a sister Church of Apostolic foundation, and thus reveals the easy and innocent beginning of the Papacy,'[2] in a letter which, as Dr. Lightfoot observes, forms 'undoubtedly' 'the first step towards Papal domination.'[3]

The reasonable explanation is that he spoke as successor of St. Peter, the Prince of the Apostles. The first recorded utterance of a Christian bishop in uninspired literature speaks in the name of his Church with the voice of infallibility, and that Church is the Church of Rome. His letter was bound up with Holy Scripture, and is to be seen this day in the British Museum amongst the contents of the great Alexandrian Codex of the Bible. According to Origen, Eusebius,

---

[1] Schaff's *Hist. of the Church. Ante-Nicene Christianity*, vol. ii. p. 639 (Edinburgh). 'He was regarded,' says Lightfoot, 'as the interpreter of the Apostolic teaching and the codifier of the Apostolic ordinances' (*St. Clem.* vol. i. p. 103).

[2] Salmon's (G.) *Introduction to the Study of N. Test.* p. 646.

[3] *St. Clement of Rome*, second edition, p. 70. In the first edition it is 'Papal aggression.'

and St. Jerome, he was that Clement whose name St. Paul mentions as 'in the book of life.' According to some modern authorities he was a Jewish freedman, or the son of a freedman belonging to the household of Flavius Clemens (Lightfoot). There can be little doubt that his letter, read as it was in public worship in numerous Churches, as, for instance, in Corinth itself, for many years, made the name of Clement sufficiently well known for a large amount of spurious literature to gather round it in the second and third centuries—a literature which has played an extraordinarily prominent part in modern controversy. It furnishes, according to Dr. Lightfoot, Dr. Salmon, the Bishop of Lincoln, and Mr. Puller, the key to the assertions made by the Christian writers of the third century to the effect that the See of Rome is the See of Peter. The same literature had already been seized upon with avidity by the Rationalist school of Tübingen, and still forms the basis of similar theories concerning the origin of Christianity.

II. This literature contains a romantic narrative in which St. Clement in his travels meets with relative after relative whom he had lost—hence called the 'Recognitions'—and a set of Homilies, containing a great deal of Ebionitish doctrine, and a letter of St. Clement to St. James, which forms a sort of preface to the version which obtained currency in Rome. In this letter St. Clement says incidentally that he was ordained by Peter, a fact which by no means forms a prominent feature of the narrative, and is accompanied in the same breath with the statement that he was commissioned by Peter to send certain sermons to St. James, as the head of the Christian Church. The position of St. James as the bishop of bishops is an important feature of the letter. 'Taken as a whole, the Clementine Romance is,' as Mr. Puller admits, 'entirely un-Petrine and un-Roman.'[1] Its whole tendency is also anti-Pauline—depreciatory, that is, of St. Paul as compared with St. James, in accordance with the Ebionitish doctrine which placed St. James before either St. Peter or St. Paul. It is supposed to have appeared in Rome either in the middle or the end of the second, or in the beginning of the

[1] Puller's (F.W.) *The Primitive Saints and the See of Rome*, p. 45.

third century, or later still. It was never quoted as an authority by early Christian writers, but nevertheless obtained after a while an extensive circulation. It is written with skill and popular effect. To this day most of its readers will admit that there is a certain fascination about it, viewed merely as a romance.

III. Its anti-Pauline tendency was seized upon by Baur and the Tübingen school in general, and vastly exaggerated; and having been thus interpreted, was made to do service in connection with a passage in Holy Scripture which has, from the earliest days of Christianity, been pressed into the service of unbelief. The state of things supposed to be described in the Clementine Romance was held to be a survival of the state of matters which obtained in the early Church, as shown, according to this theory, by the conflict between St. Peter and St. Paul at Antioch. The difference between these two Apostles was held to be vital, instead of concerning only a matter of practical expediency; and so, according to this theory, the early Church began with a conflict as to the truth to be taught, of which we have the remnants in the Clementine literature. Every effort was therefore made to throw back the Clementine Romance into the second century, and as far back in that century as possible.

It would be outside the subject of this book to enter upon the complete and decisive answers which have been given by Christian writers to the Rationalist school of Tübingen on this head.

IV. But this spurious Clementine literature is, as I have said, now pressed into the service of anti-Papal writers. Dr. Salmon, Provost of Trinity College, Dublin, one of the most vigorous opponents of the Papal claims, whilst he exposes the weakness of the Rationalists' deductions from the Clementine literature, nevertheless rounds off one of his paragraphs with the assertion that it 'has had a marvellous share in shaping the history of Christendom, by *inventing the story* that Peter was Bishop of Rome, and that he named Clement to succeed him in the see.'[1] He expresses the same theory elsewhere,

---

[1] *Introd. to the N. T.* fourth edition, 1889, p. 15. The italics in this and the following quotations are my own.

saying that as regards the story of Peter's Roman episcopate, 'the real inventor of the story was an editor of the Clementine Romance.... Though the doctrinal teaching of the Clementines was rejected as heretical, the narrative part of the book was readily believed.' He gives no proof of this, but continues, 'and in particular this story of Clement's ordination by Peter was felt to be so honourable to the Church of Rome that it was *at once adopted there*, and has been the traditional Roman account ever since.'[1] Dr. Lightfoot adopted the same theory, stating that 'its *glorification of Rome and the Roman Bishop* obtained for it an early and wide circulation in the West. *Accordingly*, even Tertullian speaks of Clement as the immediate successor of St. Peter.'[2] I would gladly give this author's proof, but I have been unable to find anything but assertion on this whole subject. The present Bishop of Lincoln has recently adopted the same position in his preface[3] to Mr. Puller's book on 'The Primitive Saints and the See of Rome.' Dr. King is speaking, indeed, of a theory which no one, that I have been able to discover, ever held, viz. that St. Peter was the 'sole *founder* of the Roman See.' But it is evident that he alludes to the theory of St. Peter being held to have been the first Bishop of Rome, and he proceeds to say, referring to Mr. Puller's book (pp. 48, 49), that 'the anti-Pauline Clementine Romance may explain the source from which this invention was derived.' Mr. Puller himself has made it the pivot of his argument against Rome. 'If the author of the Clementine Romance had not been an Ebionitish heretic, with an inherited hatred of the memory of St. Paul, *the world would never have heard of the chair of Peter*. It is strange how, from the very first, the Roman claims have been based upon forgeries.'[4] And when he comes to the crucial passage in St. Cyprian's writings, where that saint speaks of the See of Rome as 'the Chair of Peter and the principal Church whence sacerdotal unity took its rise,' he dismisses St. Cyprian from his array

---

[1] Salmon's *Infallibility of the Church*, second edition, 1890, p. 360.
[2] *St. Clement of Rome*, edition 1890, vol. i. p. 64.
[3] P. xxi. Dr. King is here endeavouring to make room for our 'honesty.' But he starts with imputing to us the above theory, which no Catholic theologian ever held.
[4] Puller's *The Primitive Saints*, p. 50.

of witnesses on this point, as under a prevailing delusion. '*I need say nothing* about the expression, "Chair of Peter," as applied to the See of Rome. By the time of St. Cyprian Western Christians had learnt from the Clementine Romance to apply the title to the Roman See.'[1] Mr. Puller goes further (if his words are to be taken seriously) than his predecessors, for he says, ' No one had any suspicion that the Clementine Romance was a lie invented by a heretic,' for which there is no proof given; and, further, 'the story was accepted on all sides.' In other words, the whole Church believed that St. James was its visible head! 'Some,' he continues, 'like St. Cyprian, accepted it, but without allowing it to modify to any appreciable degree the traditional teaching of the Church. Others, more closely connected with the Church of Rome,[2] fastened on the notion of the chair of Peter, and used that notion to provide an apostolic basis for the growing claims of the Roman See.' It is difficult to see how they would secure 'an apostolic basis' by extruding St. Paul. For the twin Apostles include St. Peter. It was not, therefore, a substitution of St. Peter for St. Paul, but of St. Peter for St. Peter and St. Paul.

V. But the Clementine literature is a subject which deserves a somewhat fuller treatment. I shall accordingly endeavour to show that, supposing 'the corporate pride of the Roman Christians' could be reasonably imagined to be so 'flattered' by the 'unique position which it [this romance] assigned to Clement,' which is Dr. Lightfoot's explanation, it has not been conclusively proved that this romance was the first to call St. Clement the successor of Peter in the bishopric of Rome. It may be shown that there was something else before it— namely, the lists of the Bishops of Rome.

But before entering on this proof I feel that it is necessary to enter a protest against the assumption virtually made by some that the local Church of Rome was in that early age filled with the spirit of the devil. How could this be, if, with Dr. Lightfoot and others, we explain the position of superiority accorded to the Church of Rome by her moral majesty? She

---

[1] *Prim. SS.* p. 54.   [2] Tertullian, for instance, St. Cyprian's master.

presided 'in love,' is his interpretation of προκαθημένη τῆς ἀγαπῆς. The possibility of such a translation of St. Ignatius' words is not now the question; but so Dr. Lightfoot explains her position. This 'practical goodness,' as he chooses to translate the supernatural gift of ἀγαπή,[1] enabled her, according to these writers, to take, and justified her in taking the lead, and led others to acquiesce in a kind of primacy, This (they tell us), together with her position as the Imperial city, went to form her unique position. Was, then, the Church of Rome, the leading Church according to all these writers, so filled with the spirit of lying that she could take the suggestion of a romance in place of her own lists, which we know from Hegesippus she then possessed, whether by oral tradition or in writing?[2] Had she the heart to alter her tale, to drop the Apostle in whom she had gloried, and in whom, conjointly with St. Peter, she glories to-day, sending out her bulls in their twin name?—had she, I say, the heart suddenly to change her attitude towards her known and beloved founders? Did Tertullian, when he came to Rome, instead of examining the lists, instead of listening to what older men could tell him, take up with an incidental expression in a romance, which *no single writer of that time ever quoted*, so far as our records go, as an authority, and of which they rejected the heretical teaching, according to Dr. Salmon? Could all classes in the Church of Rome agree suddenly on a new platform, and no whisper of the fundamental change find its way outside, or produce the slightest protest against this change in the Church's idea of her own constitution? Is it reason, is it common sense, to suppose that in twenty years, which is the utmost space of time that is given,[3] a change so vital was effected, as that the episcopal chair was no longer what it is assumed by these writers to have been, that of the two Apostles, but of one only?

But further, why should the 'corporate pride of the Roman Christians' be so flattered by the story of St. Clement being so prominent, and having been ordained by St. Peter, that it

[1] *Loc. cit.* p. 71.
[2] Hegesippus' expression, διαδοχὴν ἐποίησα may imply that there was no written official list. But he found at least a reliable oral tradition.
[3] *Prim. SS.* p. 48.

henceforth adopted the idea of the see being that of Peter and not that of Peter and Paul? Was, then, St. Peter so far above St. Paul that it would flatter their corporate pride to call it the see of Peter instead of the see of both? Was the glorification of St. Clement sufficient to balance the depreciation of St. Peter, in the same narrative, below St. James? And could Rome ever bear any approach to an Ebionitish view of the Apostle of the Gentiles? Again, who are the writers who were thus, on Mr. Puller's theory, deluded? Men like Tertullian, who belonged to the Church of Carthage! But is it conceivable that Tertullian, with his forensic ability, the first Christian writer of the day, who had been at Rome before the year 200, had never heard of *what these writers suppose to have been* the earlier teaching, viz. that the See of Rome was not the See of Peter, but merely founded by the two Apostles, and that neither of these Apostles held to it any relationship different from the other? Or if they knew of this supposed earlier teaching, can we conceive of their deliberately falsifying or ignoring it without a word of explanation? Is this the way in which the phrase, which was henceforth common to all ages, sprang into existence? If so, the expression 'the chair of Peter' must be considered the symbol of the Church's utter inability to extrude a seriously erroneous doctrine.

Such are the insuperable philosophical difficulties in the theory that the Clementine Romance gave birth to the doctrine that the See of Rome is the See of Peter. There are, however, critical obstacles besides.

VI. We know that Rome possessed at least two lists of her bishops before the Clementine Romance appeared on the scene. In the reign of Eleutherius,[1] a converted Jew, named Hegesippus, came from Syria to Rome for the purpose of inquiring particularly into the lists of bishops from the Apostles' time. He desired, above all things, to establish the connection between the series of bishops and the Apostles in each case, in the East and in the West. Eusebius (not a Roman writer) wrote with the list as made out by Hegesippus under his eye.

[1] A.D. 175-189.

What, then, is the evidence supplied in this matter by Eusebius?

But first we must be clear as to what it is that we are engaged in proving. Catholic theology, then, has always spoken of the See of Rome as, in some sense, the See of the *two* Apostles, Peter and Paul. We join these two Apostles together in all our thoughts concerning Rome, when we wish to be precise and explanatory. Rome has inherited from St. Paul the merits of his martyrdom and a peculiar inheritance of watchful care, as her patron conjointly with St. Peter. But from St. Peter she has inherited his character of foundation in a unique sense, as compared with the other Apostles (who are also foundations), and that possession of the keys which was bestowed on Peter. This possession of the keys is something beyond their mere use and exercise, such as the rest of the Apostles received for the purposes of their temporary mission, as founders of Churches throughout the world. Those who do not belong to us are not generally aware that we never commemorate St. Peter in the Holy Mass, or the other sacred offices of the Church, without immediately also commemorating St. Paul, nor St. Paul without at once adding a memorial of St. Peter. The Feast of June 29 is not with us the Feast of St. Peter, as it is in the calendar of the English Church, it is the Feast of St. Peter and St. Paul. And every Pope sends forth his bulls in the name of the two Apostles. As, then, a person could not argue from the latter fact that the See of Rome is not held by us to be in a special sense the See of Peter, so neither could one argue from a mention in any early writer of a relationship of the See of Rome to the two Apostles that such a writer did not *also* believe in a special relationship to the Apostle Peter on the part of the same see. To prove similarity of teaching between primitive and modern Rome, we should look for the use of both expressions. This is exactly what we do find in Tertullian, who speaks of Rome as the see into which the Apostles Peter and Paul 'poured all doctrine (*totam doctrinam*),' and says at the same time that St. Clement was ordained to it by St. Peter.[1] Tertullian, I notice in passing,

---

[1] *De Præscr. Hær.* 32 (A.D. 200).

does not say that St. Clement was the immediate successor of St. Peter, but simply that St. Clement, Bishop of Rome (whom all the world knew, and who was the teacher of others), was ordained by St. Peter himself. This is all that his argument requires, since it is to establish the apostolicity of the Church of Rome. It was necessary for this purpose to show not only that it was founded by two Apostles, but that they both, or (which was at the least the same thing) one of them, had instituted a successor, as in the case of the other Churches which he mentions.

And now to return to Eusebius. Dr. Lightfoot[1] has furnished us with a most exhaustive critical investigation of the relationship between the list made out by Hegesippus and the History and Chronicle of Eusebius, and has gone far to prove that the latter had the very list of Hegesippus in his hand, through the medium of a Syrian writer in the time of Elagabalus, named Julius Africanus. But that he had, somehow, the list of Hegesippus may be deduced from his own words.

What, then, does Eusebius, resting on the list made by Hegesippus in the middle of the second century, say concerning the relationship of St. Clement to St. Peter?

There is now no question as to his making him the next but one to Linus. What, then, was the relationship of Linus to Peter?

There are two sources from which we gather the witness of Eusebius—his History and his Chronicle. In his History he says[2] that Linus was the first appointed to the bishopric of the Church of the Romans after the martyrdom of Paul and Peter. This is an expression which decides nothing; for we should say that Henry III. was the first king of England after John, meaning to include John amongst the kings. The word 'after' may be used of a successor in the same chair, the first *successor* being called the first bishop *after* the original occupant.

---

[1] See the whole of the interesting discussion on the 'early Roman succession' (pp. 201–345) in his *Clement of Rome*, vol. i. Every line will repay perusal.

[2] *H. E.* iii. 2.

But immediately afterwards Eusebius uses an expression which suggests a difference of relationship between St. Peter and St. Paul to the bishopric of Rome. For he says[1] that Linus obtained the bishopric of the Church of the Romans '*first after Peter.*' Here we have Peter alone connected with the bishopric. But further on there is another expression, when he speaks of Clement as ' holding the third place of those who acted as bishop *after both Paul and Peter.*'[2] Here the series of bishops obviously begins with Linus, but the exact relationship to the two Apostles is not defined. In another later passage[3] he speaks of Telesphorus as receiving the bishopric ' seventh from the Apostles,' which may mean after their death, or in succession to them.

So far, then, Eusebius is found to speak ordinarily of Linus, coming after the Apostles, as the first bishop, but on one occasion he speaks of him as the successor of Peter alone. Both are true, according to the teaching of theology.

But besides his History, Eusebius drew up a Chronicle, which appears to have contained the list from which he took that which he gives in his History. This is a matter of general agreement. But that Chronicle is not extant. We have only a few extracts in Syncellus, a Greek writer of the ninth century, and three versions in other languages—viz. Armenian, Latin, and Syriac. The first of these, the Armenian, was, according to Petermann, who has translated it into Latin,[4] from two sources—the original Greek and a Syriac translation. The first part, according to Petermann, with whom Lightfoot agrees so far,[5] is from the original Greek. In this, whilst Clement is counted as third from the Apostles, there is a passage of supreme importance, in which the writer says : ' The Apostle Peter, when he had first founded the Church of Antioch, sets out for the city of Rome, and there preaches the gospel, and stays there *as prelate of the Church* for twenty years.'[6] It also so happens that we have this very passage in the original preserved by Syncellus : ' but he [*i.e.*

---

[1] H. E. iii. 4.   [2] iii. 21.   [3] iv. 5.
[4] It can be seen in the British Museum in A. Schoene's beautiful edition, in which the various versions are placed side by side.
[5] *Loc. cit.* p. 213.   [6] ii. 150.

Peter], besides the Church in Antioch, also first presided over that in Rome until his death.'[1]

And the Latin version by St. Jerome confirms this, for St. Jerome, who made the translation, says of Peter, 'He is sent to Rome, where, preaching the gospel for twenty-five years, he perseveres as bishop of the same city.' And yet St. Jerome calls Linus 'the first bishop after Peter.' Thus the Chronicle of Eusebius coincides with the History. St. Peter was Bishop of Rome, but being an Apostle also, the bishops are sometimes counted from Linus [2] and not from the Apostle, sometimes from one Apostle, sometimes from both.

The Syriac version again confirms the Armenian and Latin on this particular point. It has an excerpt from the Chronicon, which says that 'Peter, after he had established the Church at Antioch, presided over the Church at Rome for twenty years.'

The later Greek and Oriental chronographies establish the same point. Cardinal Mai published one which was drawn up professedly 'from the labours of Eusebius,' in which the lists of bishops open with the statement, 'Peter first acted as bishop (ἐπεσκόπησεν) in Rome,' whilst in the same century Nicephorus, the Patriarch of Constantinople, gives a list of 'those who acted as bishops in Rome from Christ and the Apostles—I. Peter the Apostle.'

Dr. Lightfoot has (it seems to the present writer) proved that both the History and the Chronicon of Eusebius derived their lists from Hegesippus.

But not only so. He seems to have established another point of great importance for our present purpose, and that is the connection between a passage in Epiphanius and the original list of Hegesippus. He thinks that this list really appears in Epiphanius, 'Hær.' xxvii. 6. Now St. Epiphanius speaks of both Peter and Paul as at once Apostles *and Bishops* in Rome, and gives the name of Linus next. He then goes on to explain how it was that although St. Clement was a con-

---

[1] ὁ δὲ αὐτὸς μετὰ τῆς ἐν Ἀντιοχίᾳ ἐκκλησίας καὶ τῆς ἐν Ῥώμῃ πρῶτος προέστη ἕως τελειώσεως αὐτοῦ (*ibid.*).

[2] This must not be understood as though Linus, Bishop of Rome, did not succeed to the pontificate of the Universal Church; but the apostolate was something besides that.

temporary of the two Apostles, yet the others succeeded 'to the episcopate before him,' viz. Linus and Cletus. Here, then, according to some very satisfactory reasons given by Dr. Lightfoot, we are in closest contact with Hegesippus, who wrote, be it remembered, in the middle of the second century. And the writer who is considered to give us most directly and unquestionably the results of Hegesippus' work in Rome is also the writer who enters most largely into the question of St. Clement's relationship to St. Peter. He was, according to St. Epiphanius, ordained by that Apostle, but could not be prevailed upon to take upon himself the responsibility of the sole episcopate on their death, until, Linus and Cletus having both died, he was at last 'forced' into it. It is, of course, only conjecture that the subject of Clement filled a special place in the 'memorials' of Hegesippus, as it did in St. Epiphanius' work; but, supposing this to be the case, we have another side-light thrown on the prominence which the name of St. Clement obtained in the East, whence came the Clementine Romance. Hegesippus was himself a Syrian Christian, who visited Corinth and Rome. Julius Africanus, through whom Eusebius derived his knowledge of Hegesippus' work, was a native of Emmaus. And the Clementine Romance hailed, in its original dress, also from the East.

The result of all that has been said is, that what we can glean from Eusebius and St. Epiphanius concerning Hegesippus' work, which was written in the middle of the second century, points to a belief already established, that St. Clement, at whatever interval, occupied 'the chair of Peter'— a belief, therefore, which was in existence before the Clementine Romance could, on any theory, have made its appearance in Rome or the West.

VII. But there is one more witness, and that of the first importance, viz. St. Irenæus himself.

In his list of the Bishops of Rome we have again, according to Dr. Lightfoot, the same work of Hegesippus, though this is denied by many scholars. However, the witness of St. Irenæus is of importance in itself, because it is often supposed to contradict that of Tertullian.[1] But that is an idea which

---

[1] *St. Clem. of Rome*, Lightfoot, p. 204.

arises simply from a misinterpretation. In his first mention of the succession of the Bishops of Rome ('Hær.' i. 27, 1), St. Irenæus speaks of Hyginus as *the ninth*, which makes St. Peter the first, as Hyginus was the eighth *after* the Apostle. He repeats this on another occasion ('Hær.' iii. 4, 3). Dr. Lightfoot here conjectures that the reading may be wrong; but admits that 'all the authorities are agreed' as to the correctness of the reading. His only reason for supposing that the reading may be wrong seems to be that it does not fit in with his theory that St. Peter ought not to be counted as a Bishop. The reading appears in St. Cyprian, Eusebius, and St. Epiphanius. But St. Irenæus also says in another passage ('Hær.' iii. 4, 3) that the Apostles Peter and Paul entrusted the ministry of the episcopate to Linus, and that Clement came 'third.' This seeming contradiction is explained by the consideration mentioned above, viz. that Linus might be called first after Peter, or second, according as the writer meant to speak of those who were only Bishops as one body by themselves, by reason of the apostolate of St. Peter, or of the bishops as actually commencing with him who was Apostle and Bishop all in one. The episcopate of Linus, although inheriting the peculiar powers of St. Peter's episcopate, *i.e.* of his universal pontificate (though not of his apostolate considered in its fullest sense), would naturally be due to the joint action of the two Apostles.

Thus the see was founded by the two Apostles; the first person who was bishop without being one of the Twelve was appointed by their common action. This bishop inherited those features of St. Peter's apostolate which were special to him, and accordingly he might be spoken of either as the second Bishop of Rome, or the first after Peter, or the first after the martyrdom of the two Apostles, or, in fine, the first after Peter and Paul, Apostles and Bishops: the former because of the relationship of St. Peter to Rome as the originator of its universal pontificate, the latter because of the connection of St. Paul with Rome as fellow-labourer with the Prince of the Apostles, and its joint patron in the courts of Heaven. No one of these terms excludes the other. St. Irenæus does not contradict Tertullian, nor Tertullian St. Irenæus. A see founded by two Apostles is not necessarily the see of both or either. The expression settles nothing. St. Gregory founded the See of London, but was not its bishop. If it seemed good to one Apostle to take the See of Rome under his special care, and form to it a special relationship, there would be nothing in the fact of the foundation of the community having been due to co-operation to prevent his so doing. It cannot be said that St. James founded the See of Jerusalem, and yet he was its first bishop. And, conversely, although St. Paul, coming on to the scene after St. Peter, assisted in the foundation of the organisation of the Christian community at Rome, it was not necessary that he should also be its bishop in the same sense as St. Peter.

Why, then, should Tertullian speak of Clement as ordained by St. Peter if Linus was the first bishop? The two facts I have shown are not mutually exclusive. There is nothing unreasonable in the first part of the explanation given by Rufinus in his preface to his translation of the Clementine Recognitions, viz. 'Linus and Cletus were indeed bishops in the city of Rome before Clement, but during the lifetime of Peter, that is to say, so that they bore the care of the episcopate, whilst he fulfilled the office of the apostolate.'[1] We must, however, add that they also reigned after St. Peter, and when it came to the successor of the Apostle, now in glory, one must come before the other, and whether from humility, as St. Epiphanius thought, or from whatever other cause, St. Clement came third. But it is more likely that it was settled by the two Apostles that Linus should be the first successor of Peter before their death, and hence the account in St. Irenæus. They did not, they could not, hand on precisely their own position, for they were Apostles; but 'they committed the ministry of the episcopate to Linus' ('Hær.' iii. 3, 3). St. Clement, however, especially from his great Epistle, filled a place in men's eyes which the others did not, and so for Tertullian's purpose it would be enough to say that he was ordained by St. Peter, not thereby excluding the other two. Tertullian wished to insist on the succession of doctrine, and mentions the connection between the well-known Clement and

[1] *H. E.* iii. p. 4.

St. Peter as sufficient. He received the bishopric from St. Peter, whether as first or third was not material to the point.

VIII. But this is not all. The question now occurs, When did the Clementine literature appear in Rome? Was it before Tertullian wrote? The Tübingen school did its best to force the composition of these writings as far back in the second century as the middle. The Bishop of Lincoln (Pref. to 'Prim. SS.' p. xxi.) fathers Mr. Puller's theory, which is apparently the same as that of Dr. Lightfoot, and nearly that of Dr. Salmon. The latter writer renders his own theory more difficult to maintain, by making this literature 'not older than the *very end* of the second century,'[1] in at any rate the form in which it appeared at Rome. In this case it would have been contemporaneous with Tertullian's account, and one does not see how Tertullian could possibly have gone counter to the supposed older tradition at once. Mr. Puller speaks of its appearance at Rome as 'an event which probably intervened between the time of St. Irenæus' treatise and the time of St. Cyprian,'[2] which is too vague for his thesis. Accordingly he settles its date further on, purely, however, on the grounds of his own assumption as to the effect of that literature. He says, 'There is much reason for supposing' (but, like Dr. Lightfoot, he does not give the reasons for this, which is the pivot of the whole argument) 'that the notion that St. Peter himself consecrated Clement to the Roman See is wholly due to the Clementine Romance, and *therefore* that romance *must* have established its influence in Rome some time during the last twenty years of the second century, between the year 180, which is the approximate date of the treatise of St. Irenæus, and the year 200, which is the approximate date of the treatise of Tertullian.'[3]

Mr. Puller realises the importance of establishing a date for the Clementine literature anterior to Tertullian's account of Peter having ordained Clement. And it is not too much to say that the argument of his book altogether halts if this

---

[1] *Introd. to N.T.* fourth edition, p. 14. The italics are my own.
[2] *Prim. SS.* p. 44.
[3] *Ibid.* p. 48. The italics are my own.

cannot be established. The 'very end' of the century, which Dr. Salmon gives as its date, will not really serve the purpose; for who could believe that a new novel, making St. James the head of the whole Church, could in a year or two, or in five years, induce the Roman Christians to tell such a lie on behalf of their 'corporate pride' as to ignore their older lists and (supposed) older tradition on the authority of a book written in the interests of Ebionitism?

There is, however, an interesting piece of evidence which goes far to prove that neither the Tübingen Rationalists nor the anti-Papal writers are correct in assigning this Clementine literature to any part of the second century. In the 9th book of the 'Recognitions' of Clement, as preserved in Rufinus' translation, there are nearly ten chapters which are almost identical (in many places absolutely so) with a treatise of which Eusebius gives a copious extract, written by a Syriac theologian named Bardesanes, born at Edessa, and famous for his philosophico-theological speculations. The Syriac original of the treatise, of which Eusebius gives the extracts in Greek, was discovered by the late Canon Cureton in 1843 and published in 1855. Cureton thought that Bardesanes [1] himself wrote the treatise, but it was possibly written by a disciple of his, who incorporated the arguments of a treatise of his master. So that in that case what follows would apply to the substance of the Bardesanes dialogue, not to its form. But I will speak of it as Bardesanes'.[2]

The first question that arises is, which borrowed from the other—Bardesanes from the Greek 'Recognitions,' or the 'Recognitions' from Bardesanes? Dr. Hort points out what

[1] His proper name is Bardaisan. See a valuable article on this Eastern writer in Smith and Wace's *Dict. of Chr. Biogr.* by Dr. Hort.

[2] *I.e.* by way of giving to the maintainers of the earlier date the benefit of the doubt. I have no doubt myself that the writing is that of a disciple. I have not discussed the only supposition that would militate against the following contention as to the date—the supposition, namely, that an earlier form of the Clementine Romance reached Rome, and that the chapters from the treatise of Bardesanes were added in a subsequent edition. Probably no critic would maintain that. And it must be remembered that the crucial passage about Clement occurs in the Epistle to James, which is obviously the covering letter, so to speak, to the *Recognitions*, and *no part of an earlier original*. Rufinus, who had the original in his hands, expressly says that it was of later date.

most people will consider one adequate reason for believing that the 'Recognitions' borrowed from Bardesanes.¹ The Syriac original of Bardesanes 'contains various names and particulars pointing towards a Mesopotamian origin, which are obliterated partially in the Greek dialogue and still more in the "Recognitions."' If, therefore, we considered the 'Recognitions' to be the original, we should have to suppose that Bardesanes took the matter from them and inserted these names and other particulars into his Syriac narrative as he went along. On the other hand, if the treatise or dialogue of Bardesanes (or his disciple) is the original, from which the writer of the 'Recognitions' borrowed these chapters, he did what was only natural, viz. dropped the allusions to Mesopotamia in giving the narrative its Greek dress, a process usual with a compiler such as the author of the 'Recognitions' appears to have been, and even with a mere translator who might wish to recommend the story to Western minds. Probably few scholars will hesitate which theory to adopt. So that the 9th book of the 'Recognitions' may be said with good reason to have been taken from the famous treatise of Bardesanes.²

It only remains to determine the date of the original treatise or dialogue of Bardesanes. Now, there is a lengthy note of great value on this subject appended to an article by M. Priaulx³ on 'Indian Embassies to Rome, from the Reign of Claudius to the Death of Justinian,' contributed to the 'Journal of the British Asiatic Society,' in 1862, p. 289. The article is not written with reference to our present subject, but purely from an antiquarian point of view. M. Priaulx is showing reason why the date assigned to Bardesanes' writings by the early Christian writers is erroneous. His name is connected by these writers with Antoninus Pius, Antoninus Verus, and Marcus Antoninus, to whom Eusebius says Bardesanes presented a copy of his book, adding that he wrote it in consequence of the persecutions of the Christians by Marcus (A.D. 167-177), and about the time that Soter, Bishop of

---

¹ *Loc. cit.*

² The consensus of scholars is in favour of the Eastern origin of the Clementine Romance as against Baur.

³ Referred to by Dr. Hort, *loc. cit.* I have given a fuller account of this.

Rome, died (A.D. 179). Now, Bardesanes was born A.D. 154.[1] He was, therefore, only seven years old when Antoninus Pius died, and twenty-five when Soter died. But when he wrote the dialogue in question, or its substance (if it was that of his disciple Philip in its present form), he was able to allude to a former work of his, which makes it probable that he was in middle age. But there is a note of time, which forces us to place the earliest limit of the treatise considerably later. It says that '*as yesterday* the Romans took Arabia and abrogated all their ancient laws, and more especially that circumcision with which they were circumcised.' This could only refer to the conquest by Trajan (167), or by Severus (196), (cf. Eutropius, iii. 18), when Arabia was reduced to a province. In the one case Bardesanes would be only thirteen; consequently we must suppose that he wrote, not then, but soon after the death of Severus (A.D. 211). If we suppose this treatise to have been written in 214, it would have been written eighteen years after the conquest, and at the age of sixty. Now, at that time the Emessine Elagabalus was on the throne, who specially affected the name of Antoninus. Nothing would be more natural than for Bardesanes to present his book to the emperor, and to address him as Antoninus, the name by which he was known in Syria. Further, it would be most probable that the Christians would know of the honour of the book being thus presented, whilst it would also be most natural that amongst subsequent writers a confusion should arise as to the name Antoninus, as its application to Elagabalus was not known at that time, so far as we can tell, in Greece or Rome. Hence the mistaken transference of date to the time of the Antonines in the second century by Eusebius and others.

By this ingenious conjecture, based on sound principles, new light seems to be thrown on the date of the 'Recognitions,' and Dr. Hort is probably quite correct in his estimate of that date. They could not have appeared at Rome until well into the third century. Consequently the theory of the writers with whom I have been dealing, as to Tertullian having adopted the incidental notice in the Clementine Romance

---

[1] *Edessene Chronicle*, A.D. 154.

about St. Clement having been appointed to the Chair of Peter, must be dismissed, and some other more solid ground for that writer's assertion must be adopted. No other needs to be sought than the list of the Bishops of Rome, which Hegesippus found in existence, whether orally or otherwise, in the middle of the second century, which, according to Eusebius, made Linus, Anencletus, and Clement all successors of St. Peter. There would be no difficulty in supposing that St. Peter ordained Clement, whether we accepted St. Epiphanius' explanation or not.

IX. There is also no difficulty in supposing that the Clementine literature, on being introduced into the West, would contain what I may now assume to be the common tradition of the West as to St. Clement having been ordained by St. Peter, although thinking him to be the first successor, as an Eastern story well might; whereas the idea that, in order to depreciate St. Paul, the Ebionitish writer made Rome the See of Peter only, and so determined the whole future of the Church, first misleading the keen apologist Tertullian into assuming as the common teaching of the Church an heretical trick of less than twenty years' standing, is in the highest degree improbable from the view of merely natural criticism; but when we look at it from the supernatural view of the Church, as the Body of Christ and the home of the Spirit of Truth, and remember that, according to the admission of all, the Church of Rome, the leading Church from any point of view, the Church which, according to Dr. Lightfoot, owed her great position to her moral ascendency, as well as to her secular position: when, I say, we remember that she, the centre of the Christian world, adopted that view of her relationship to St. Peter which is implied in the supposition of this ordination, viz. that she is 'the chair of Peter,' then the theory that 'the corporate pride' of the Roman Christians led them to a guilty participation in a mere falsehood becomes quite untenable.

Novels are often based on facts, or at any rate contain a certain number of historical facts; and it is unreasonable to assume that every statement in the Clementine Romance is untrue because it is a work of fiction. Anyhow, Tertullian in A.D. 199 or 200, could not have derived his ideas from a romance which does not seem to have reached Rome before the time of Elagabalus, *i.e.* well into the third century.

It results, then, from what has gone before, that (i.) St. Irenæus taught that, whilst the See of Rome was founded by the two Apostles, Peter and Paul, it was also in a special sense the See of Peter; that (ii.) so far as we can glean anything positive from Eusebius about the list of the Bishops of Rome, drawn up by Hegesippus in the middle of the second century, it also included a special relationship of St. Peter to that see; that (iii.) Tertullian, after or during his visit to Rome, wrote as an ascertained fact that St. Clement was ordained by St. Peter, although he does not say that he was his immediate successor; that (iv.) the Clementine literature reached Rome after Tertullian had left; and that (v.) in its Western dress it wove into its tale the common tradition of the West to which Tertullian had made allusion.

NOTE.—Since writing the above I have seen a very able essay on the Clementine literature in the 'Studia Biblica' (vol. ii.), edited by Professors Driver, Cheyne, and Sanday. The writer, Dr. Bigg, considers that Uhlhorn has conclusively proved the Eastern origin of this literature, and that 'there can be no reasonable doubt' that the work called the 'Homilies' ' was well known to the author of the "Recognitions" ' (p. 183). He shows, as others before him, that there must have been an earlier form on which both the 'Homilies' and the 'Recognitions' drew, and says that this 'must not be fixed too early.' He suggests about A.D. 200. But his only reason for this seems to be his assumption that 'the Clement legend,' in which he seems to include the ordination by Peter, was contained in the older form. Dr. Salmon, rightly, denies this ('Dict. of Chr. Biog.' art. *Clem. Lit.* p. 511). Dr. Bigg admits that the argument against heathenism is of a late type. As yet, however, not a shadow of proof has been produced that the earlier original of the 'Homilies' and 'Recognitions' appeared at Rome. Much less can it be supposed, in the face of Rufinus' statement to the contrary, that the letter of St. Clement, which mentions his ordination by St. Peter, belonged to the earlier original. The 'Recognitions' is, obviously, the form in which the literature first appeared at Rome, and the said letter of Clement was, as Dr. Salmon says, 'the preface to the "Recognitions"' ('Dict. of Chr. Biog.' art. *Clem. Lit.*).

Dr. Bigg gives a very plausible account of the reason of the circulation of this literature at Rome. He thinks that Alexander of Apamæa brought with him to Rome, 'as a new Gospel, the volume which had been dedicated to Elxai among the Seres of Parthia by an angel ninety-six miles high. The particular article of this revelation, on which he relied for success, was a baptism which washed away all, even the most hideous sins, without any discipline or penance at all' ('Hom.' xi. 26-7). Alexander arrived in the city of Rome during the reign of St. Callixtus (A.D. 219-222), in the midst of the storm about remission of sins after baptism, and 'such an improvement on the terms of Callixtus might be expected to win over many of the looser Christians.'[1]

Whatever may be thought of this ingenious conjecture, it suggests that there are other reasons for the popularity of this literature more probable than that given by Dr. Lightfoot and others.

But even if all these critical difficulties could be solved, one irrefragable proof of the untenableness of the view against which I have been contending would still remain. According to that view, the Romans wished that their see should be the See of Peter rather than the See of the two Apostles. It seemed to them more honourable; it 'flattered their corporate pride,' says Dr. Lightfoot. But why, unless St. Peter was superior to St. Paul? The mere fact that St. Peter was first in order, but not in jurisdiction (*primus inter pares*), could never be a sufficient reason for dropping the name of St. Paul. The Romans were not Ebionites that they should despise St. Paul. They must, on Dr. Lightfoot's theory, have considered Peter, on independent grounds, head and shoulders above his brother Apostle, if, in less than twenty years, they could reverse their (supposed) former history, and claim for their see the name of Peter only. St. Paul tells us that 'he laboured more abundantly than they all;' how could St. Peter tower above St. Paul, except on the supposition that our Lord had appointed him to be the supreme ruler of the Church? Our adversaries in this matter have to suppose the very point which they are concerned to deny, viz. the supremacy of Peter, in order to find a motive for the supposed adoption by the Romans of this Clementine literature as the guiding star of their local history.

[1] *Studia Biblica*, vol. ii. p. 189.

CHAPTER III.

ST. IRENÆUS, OR THE SOVEREIGNTY OF THE CHURCH OF ROME.

THE Epistle of St. Clement is alluded to in a remarkable passage in the work of St. Irenæus against heresies. He has just given the Church's rule of faith, which is, agreement with the Church of Rome, by reason of her 'more powerful sovereignty' as compared with other Churches. He then proceeds to speak of one special instance of her exercise of sovereignty, viz. 'the letter of the Church in Rome to the Corinthians on behalf of (εἰς) peace,' which letter he describes as most adequate or powerful (ἱκανωτάτην). He describes it—according to one reading, the *Church* of Rome, according to another, her letter[1]—as 'forcing them together (συμβιβάζουσα αὐτούς) and renewing their faith,' delivering 'the tradition which it had recently received from the Apostles,' *i.e.* St. Peter and St. Paul.

I. In the passage of which this is the sequel, St. Irenæus, I have said, gives the Catholic rule of faith. Nothing can be more clear and simple. It is, ultimately, agreement with Rome. The deposit of the faith was delivered by our Lord to the Apostolic College; and if we wish to know what that faith is, we have only to consult an Apostolic Church. But the easiest way of all is to consult the Church of Rome, because all must agree with, or (which comes to the same thing) have recourse to, that Church. She was founded by two Apostles, the most glorious of all, so the saint avers, and her Church is the most renowned and the greatest of all. She has a more powerful sovereignty than the rest, and by reason of this, all other

---
[1] *Hær.* lib. iii. 3, 2.

Churches must have recourse to, or agree with her, so that in her, by union with her, the faithful everywhere have preserved the deposit of revealed truth.

Such is the plain teaching of our saint, who united in himself such special qualifications for expressing the Church's rule of faith. St. Irenæus combines the experience of East and West, and unites the second century with apostolic times. He was an Eastern and had been trained by St. Polycarp, who himself had sat at the feet of St. John. And he was a Western bishop.

In the treatise from which the summary of his teaching, just given, is taken, he is engaged in pointing out the way in which the Christian faith may be known. Dr. Lightfoot observes that, in this second century, 'the episcopate is regarded now not so much as the centre of ecclesiastical unity, but rather as the depositary of apostolic tradition.' The two things, however, go hand in hand. St. Irenæus himself mentions them together in specifying the effects of St. Clement's letter as 'compelling them to unity and renewing their faith.'[1] It was as the guardian of the faith that the Church of Rome presided over the Universal Church. St. Ignatius speaks of her as ' presiding in the place of the region of the Romans ' (an expression which indicates not the extent, but the centre of her presiding authority), and says that she presides ' over the [covenant of] love.' Dr. Lightfoot translates this 'in love' instead of ' over *the* love,' and understands the love, not as the supernatural gift of the Holy Ghost, but as ' practical goodness,' in a word, philanthropy, instancing her great generosity in alms. But Dr. Döllinger appears to be right in regarding 'the love ' as the equivalent of ' the Church.'[2] And it was as the guardian of the faith that the Church of Rome presided over the covenant of divine love. This involved her

---

[1] *Hær*. lib. iii. 3.
[2] ' Gleich darauf nennt er sie προκαθημένη τῆς ἀγαπῆς, was nicht wie die alte lateinische Uebersetzung hat, præsidens in caritate heisst, sonst hätte Ignatius ἐν ἀγαπῇ gesagt; ἀγαπή bedeutet wie ἐκκλησία bald . . . auch die grosse auf Liebe gegründete und durch Liebe zusammengehaltene Gemeinschaft aller Gläubigen,' &c. Cf. for the use of the genitive with προκαθημένη Theodoret's letter to St. Leo; he uses προκαθημένη τῆς οἰκουμένης (presiding over the world) of the Holy See.

D

being the centre of unity; for it is of the essence of the guardianship of the faith that those only should be admitted into the one teaching body, or remain in it, who hold the one faith, and this involves a central authority and source of decision.

Now this is what also results from the famous passage of St. Irenæus quoted above. The Church of Rome has a sovereignty, and it is connected with the preservation of the faith.

II. But, as Dr. Döllinger says, 'For three hundred years there have not been wanting writers who have endeavoured to wrest these words from their evident meaning.'[1]

I shall here only deal with such as have been adopted by writers in this country. But first, I will give the translation ordinarily adopted by Catholic writers, amongst whom I am glad to be able to number Tillemont and Bossuet.

'It is necessary that every Church, that is, the faithful who are everywhere, should agree with this Church; in which that tradition which is from the Apostles has been preserved by those who are everywhere.'

To this rendering exception has been taken in the following particulars:—

(a) It is said that St. Irenæus does not say that every Church must *agree with* the Church of Rome, but *must resort* to it, and that by every Church is meant the individuals amongst the faithful who find their way to the city of Rome.[2]

Now, it may be admitted that the words *convenire ad* may mean physical recourse, but it must be remembered that it is to the Church, not to the city of Rome that this centripetal movement is said to be 'of necessity.' And it is every *Church* which must resort to the Church of Rome. The following words—'those who are from all sides'—explain, but must not be allowed to explain away, the word Church. It is as organised communities, not as individual men of business, that every Church must resort to the Church of Rome. The necessity also can hardly be that which arises from the fact that Rome was the centre of secular life. Men who came to

---

[1] *Geschichte der christlichen Kirche.* Landshut, 1833, B. 1, p. 355.
[2] *Prim. SS.* p. 36. Gore's *R. C. Claims*, p. 97.

hawk their wares, or consult the market, or plead their civil causes, are hardly the persons likely to promote the integrity of the faith. Whilst such men as Hegesippus found their way to Rome, men like Alexander of Apamæa did the same. And, as a rule, it is either the wealthy, or the secular-minded, or the ne'er-do-wells of a community who bend their steps to the metropolis, and this would not contribute to the preservation of the faith. The mere fact of a confluence of streams will not keep the waters sweet; there must be some preservative power in the centre.

Nor is there any need to see in the word 'necessary' anything more than a deep-seated attraction which drew men to the Church of Rome on another ground. The word used by St. Irenæus is the regular word in ecclesiastical Latin, as is the corresponding word in Greek, for such necessity. St. Cyril uses it as expressing the obligation under which he lay of writing to the Pope about Nestorius.[1]

It is, therefore, more natural to translate *convenire ad* as 'agree with,'[2] and to understand *necesse est* of that necessity which arose from the commanding position of the Church of Rome and the supernatural operation of the Holy Ghost. But even if we translate *convenire ad* 'resort to,' it must be borne in mind that a *necessary* resort of all *Churches* to the *Church* of Rome implies supremacy in the latter.

(b) To what was the commanding position of the Church of Rome due according to St. Irenæus? Our answer is, to its superior sovereignty, as not only an apostolic but, as in after times it was called, *the* Apostolic Church; to its having, as St. Irenæus puts it, been founded by the two most glorious Apostles, to which we must add the fact that one of those two most glorious Apostles was he to whom our Lord had said, 'Thou art Peter,' which signifies a special association with the Rock of Ages.

---

[1] Cf. *infra*, p. 308. And also see the letter of the Council of Ephesus to St. Celestine: ἔχρην ἅπαντα εἰς γνῶσιν τῆς σῆς ὁσιότητος ἀνενεχθῆναι τὰ παρακολουθήσαντα γράφομεν ἀναγκαίως (Labbe, t. iii. p. 1196).

[2] This is Canon Bright's translation in *The Roman Claims tested by Antiquity*, p. 8.

Dr. Pusey and Mr. Keble understood by the word 'sovereignty,' merely *primitiveness* or *origin*. They saw that the words must apply to the Church, and not to the city. Dr. Döllinger completely shattered to atoms this same translation, as given by Gieseler. ' Die Häretiker würden natürlich einen Beweis für diese absolute Nothwendigkeit einer Uebereinstimmung, die blos auf den Vorzug des Alters beruhen soll, gefordert, sie würden erwiedert haben, dass jüngere Gemeinden allerdings von dem Glauben der altern abweichen könnten.'

He scouts the idea that such an 'illogical conclusion ever entered the mind of St. Irenæus;' and he shows that the word 'principalitas' means in Irenæus' writings 'supreme authority,' and points out that Rome was not the oldest Church.[1] Indeed, it may be added that St. Irenæus expressly calls Jerusalem the mother Church in point of antiquity ('Hær.' iii. 12, 5).

(c) But whilst understanding the 'principality' as meaning sovereignty, others, as Mr. Puller, understand it of the imperial position of the *city*. But this is absolutely excluded by the context. It is the apostolic origin of any Church that gives it, according to St. Irenæus, its commanding position; it is the specially apostolic character of the Church of Rome that gives it its peculiar position amongst the apostolic Churches. Bossuet calls such an interpretation as that given by Mr. Puller 'trifling' with the matter; Hefele calls it 'ridiculous' (*lächerlich*); Perrone, 'most absurd.' For, as Bossuet says, St. Irenæus was speaking, in the previous sentence, of the Church of Rome as founded by the Apostles Peter and Paul, not in her imperial aspect. And the words 'more powerful' imply comparison with the Churches ('every Church') which he has mentioned in the same breath, and with which he contrasts the Church of Rome as 'the most ancient and the most universally known.'

(d) Some writers, as Mr. Gore and Mr. Puller, have laid great stress on the word translated 'everywhere.' It is literally 'from all sides.' And they seem to imagine that this suggests the picture of an assemblage of the faithful from all

---

[1] *Geschichte der christlichen Kirche*, p. 357.

quarters in the city of Rome. But it may equally represent the view of a writer regarding the faithful as living in all quarters of the globe, and connected with the centre not by physical movement, but by the tie of a common faith. It is, however, certain that the word is used by the Latin interpreter, and that the corresponding word in Greek was also used by St. Irenæus (for in this case we have the original in the Bodleian MS.), for 'everywhere' simply. St. Irenæus speaks of the four Gospels as 'breathing, or blowing, incorruptibility *everywhere* and revivifying men.' The word for 'everywhere' used here is the same as in the passage we have been considering;[1] and it is obvious that it means a radiation from a centre, not *vice versâ*.

Further, St. Irenæus does not say that the apostolic tradition was preserved *through* these merchants, and lawyers, and appellants, and heretics, and faithful, that gathered haphazard to the city of Rome, but *by* them—which reduces the supposition that he meant these business travellers at all to an absurdity.

Once more, the interpretation given by Canon Bright (*loc. cit.*), viz. that the *principalitas* was 'a sort of "primacy," involving a moral guarantee of its soundness of belief, which led St. Irenæus to say that every Church that was itself true to apostolic tradition " must needs agree with it "'—implies the very doctrine which he is endeavouring to exclude. For it must be asked: If all orthodox Churches are *necessarily* found to be in agreement with the Church of Rome, what is this but ascribing infallibility to that Church? This, indeed, is what St. Irenæus does ascribe to Rome, an ascendency in matters of faith which makes her teaching the test and norm of the Catholic faith. And so he goes on to show that as a matter of fact other Churches, such as Smyrna and Ephesus, do agree with Rome.[2]

(*e*) Lastly, it has been objected that the words 'in which' (*in quâ*) may refer to 'every Church,' and not to the Church

---

[1] *Hær.* lib. iii. cap. 11, n. 8. Gk. πανταχόθεν. Lat. *undique*. Cf. also *prædicationem vero Ecclesiæ undique constantem* (24, 1), and *prædicatio veritatis ubique lucet.*

[2] Mr. Puller has misunderstood this passage.

of Rome. But this, again, necessitates the absurdity of supposing that every orthodox Church is necessarily in agreement with Rome, and yet that Rome is not infallible, or the equal absurdity of supposing that the chance business men who found their way to Rome for secular purposes kept Rome right in the faith—or the people, for instance, who brought with them the Clementine Romance. The words *in quâ* are well explained by Dr. Döllinger, as stating that the faithful throughout the world were 'in' the Church of Rome—that is, in communion with it as the centre of unity. The corresponding word in Greek would be that which is used by St. Paul of our being 'in Christ,' and the exact phrase of the Latin interpreter, whose translation is all that we have of this passage in St. Irenæus, is used by the African bishop, St. Optatus, whose work St. Augustine recommended, viz. '*in which* one chair [*i.e.* the chair of Peter] unity might be preserved,' *i.e.* that in communion with this one chair, &c.[1]

The plain and simple meaning, therefore, of St. Irenæus remains in possession. All Churches must agree with the Church of Rome, so that if you know the faith of the Church of Rome you know the faith of the whole Christian Church.

---

[1] 'D. h. in ihrem Schoosse, in der Gemeinschaft mit ihr als dem Mittelpunkte der Einheit' (*loc. cit.* p. 358).

CHAPTER IV.

ST. VICTOR, OR ROME THE GUARDIAN OF 'THE COMMON UNITY.'

ONE of the legal methods of preserving the evidence of a claim is to subject it, periodically, to a challenge *pro formâ*. And one method of discovering how far a claim holds good, such as that which Rome makes, is to see what happens under circumstances that press heavily on the obedience of those over whom it is made, leading them in the natural course of things to dispute it. Resistance does not disprove authority; while a resistance which falls short of disputing the authority itself indicates a sense of its lawful existence. Such an occasion occurred in the second century of the Christian era. A portion of the East came into collision with Rome on a matter on which *Rome proved to be right*, although the Pope thought it well not to press the matter beyond a certain point. The circumstances were as follows.

I. In the Asiatic Churches a multitude of Jews had entered the Christian fold, and had kept to various Jewish customs, under the eye and apparently with the sanction of the Apostle St. John. Amongst these customs was that of celebrating the Paschal Feast on the same day as their unconverted brethren. In the West it was observed on the Sunday after the 14th Nisan—always on a Sunday. Amongst those who now observed the feast on the same day as the Jews were some whose belief as to the idea of the feast was the same as that of the rest of the Christian world. But there were also some whose teaching as to the idea of the festival itself was erroneous, and whose observance of it differed altogether from that of the Church.[1] In fact, the observance

---

[1] 'Many of the orthodox Quartodecimans thought that the main feature of the Paschal Feast lay in the commemoration of the death of Christ, of whom

of this Queen of Festivals, on which St. John the Apostle appears to have allowed some external difference, had come to be connected with Ebionitish teaching. It would therefore only be a matter of time for an endeavour to be made to bring the whole Christian world into unison on such an important matter, for though it was not a matter of faith, it was closely connected with the faith.

Rome had her observance handed down from the Apostles Peter and Paul; and her observance was destined to be the rule of action for the entire Church. In the beginning of the century she had made an endeavour to achieve a greater uniformity, but had ended with acquiescing in the continuance of the dissimilarity of practice. Anicetus received Polycarp to communion at Rome, although Polycarp adopted the Asiatic mode of observing the Feast. Soter went a step further and insisted on uniformity, at least in Rome itself.

II. But when Victor ascended the throne matters had become much more serious, and the Asiatic observance of Easter was adopted by certain schismatics, who were also infected with Montanism.[1] It became a matter of moment to stop the dissimilarity of observance in the Church itself, or to dissociate it from false teaching. St. Victor decided upon the first, but succeeded only in effecting the second.

Mosheim, the German Protestant historian, has said that the action of Victor in this matter, and the reception with which it met, prove that in that age the power of the Roman Pontiff was not such as that he could cut off from the whole Church those of whose opinions and practices he disapproved. He has been followed in this by the author of 'The Primitive Saints and the See of Rome,'[2] who contends that the account of the matter in Eusebius shows that the loss of communion with Rome did not involve loss of communion with the rest of the Church. There is a sense in which this is true, but it is not the sense in which this writer uses the expression. There was, in early times, a measure of separation from Rome which was not *intended* to involve separation from the whole body.

---

the Paschal Lamb was the type.' Cf. Jungmann, *Diss.* ii. 65, who gives a short account of worse heresies into which some of the Quartodecimans were falling.

[1] Cf. Jungmann, *Diss.* ii. 79. [2] Pp. 24-31.

This lesser separation was a serious loss, but was meant to fall short, by a great deal, of the excommunication under anathema.¹ For the latter a distinct and formal notification of its terrible infliction was necessary. Moreover, this latter and more extreme measure might be preceded by the former. With these remarks I will proceed to narrate what actually happened, and to show that matters never came to the point which would necessitate our speaking of these Asiatics as being under anathema, and so in actual schism.

St. Victor first collected the evidence of the whole Christian world,² except Asia, and then requested Polycrates, the Bishop of Ephesus, to summon the Asiatic bishops in council, in the hope of inducing them to relinquish their purely local practice. Polycrates obeyed. The Asiatic Churches, however, came to the conclusion that they would adhere to their own custom. Polycrates, their leader, went so far in the way of exaggeration as to speak of their own practice as though it alone were 'in accordance with the Gospel,' and they pleaded the authority of St. John the Evangelist and St. Philip. They may have meant only that their custom had been permitted by the Apostle. Anyhow, if they dreamt of an Apostolic *prescription*, we are not obliged to think that they were historically correct in their assertion.

The result of their answer to St. Victor was that he decided upon strong measures. The warmth with which they defended their custom must have seemed to him suspicious, as though they were erecting it into a matter of belief, or were really in danger of doctrinal error. For it must be carefully remembered, that the question of the Paschal observance involved not merely that of a day, but in many cases (known only too unhappily to the Pope) of the meaning of the feast.

St. Victor, therefore, decided, or at least threatened, to excommunicate the Asiatic Churches 'from the common unity,'³ as Eusebius expresses it. He set to work to do it; *he made the endeavour*; he took the first step.⁴ He issued his notice of

¹ Cf. Döllinger's *Geschichte*, Periode II. *ad finem*; and quotations from De Smedt in Jungmann, *Diss.* ii. 75.
² Euseb. *Hist. Eccl.* v. 23.   ³ τῆς κοινῆς ἑνότητος.
⁴ πειρᾶται. Euseb. *in loco*. The word involves no more than the endeavour which the head-master of a school might make to enforce a salutary rule, but

excommunication, of downright excommunication, to the effect that they were cut off from the common unity (ἀκοινωνήτους). Unfortunately we do not possess St. Victor's letter; consequently it is impossible to say whether or no the excommunication was contingent on their obedience at the next Easter.¹ But it is most reasonable, and most in harmony with what we know of such excommunications in after times, as, for instance, St. Celestine's excommunication of Nestorius—to suppose that these Asiatics were to be excommunicate if they adhered to their custom at the following Easter. But as soon as they received the Papal injunction, or, at any rate, before the time came for compliance with it, *i.e.* before the following Easter, some bishops protested.² Their protest, however, consisted only of exhortation or entreaty: ' they exhorted,' says Eusebius. This they did in no measured terms, but went beyond the limits of the respect due to the office of St. Victor.³ Their complaints were probably a more bitter edition of Polycrates' previous letter, in which that bishop pleads his own virgin life as a reason why he should be heard, and says he cares for no threats— not a very edifying form of correspondence.

III. Peace, however, came from the mediation of the same saint, who wrote that ' it is necessary for every Church to agree with the Church of Rome, because of her more powerful principality or supremacy.' St. Irenæus (the author of the words) wrote from Gaul a letter couched in more deferential terms.⁴ He

from which he might desist owing to the fear of rebellion. Mr. Puller greatly exaggerates its force (*Prim. S. S.* p. 30).

¹ So Döllinger, *Geschichte*, p. 289.

² 'The sentence did not please all the bishops' are the words of Eusebius, which implies that there were some, probably many, who thought St. Victor in the right.

³ πληκτικώτερον. Mr. Puller has translated this 'very severely.' But πληκτικός implies bitterness—' objurgatione acri ' is Dindorf's translation of the positive. ' Severely ' is a word which suggests the tone of a superior rebuking the fault of an inferior, or of a usurper. ' Bitterly ' (the correct translation) is a word which describes the tone of a dissatisfied inferior protesting against his superior's action. And ' *very* severely ' misses the point of the ending of the word. It is not πληκτικώτατον, but is in the comparative degree, implying excess, ' more than the occasion warranted ' in the judgment of Eusebius.

⁴ προσηκόντως. This seems to be in contrast with the πληκτικώτερον or excessive bitterness of the Asiatics. He was amongst the number of those who were displeased with Victor's determination, but differed from them in tone.

agreed with Rome about the observation of Easter, but realised the impossibility of bringing the Asiatics into line under present circumstances. Possibly also he did not realise as keenly as St. Victor did the mischievous tendency, under present circumstances, of the Asiatic [1] custom, which gave it a very different colour from the same custom in the time of his predecessors. He pleaded, as he had a right to do, that it was not in itself a matter of faith, which, of course, St. Victor himself allowed. And he 'warned' St. Victor of the consequences of persisting in his threat, or sentence.[2] The Asiatic blood was up, and a schism was possible. He referred to the precedents set by Pius the First, Hyginus, Telesphorus, and Xystus, as not having 'cast off any merely for the sake of a form,' showing what he thought of the power possessed by the Bishops of Rome. He therefore advised [3] St. Victor with all becoming respect (προσηκόντως) 'not to cut off whole Churches.' The Churches, therefore, were not, to the mind of St. Irenæus, as yet excommunicated; but it was, according to the same saint, within the power of St. Victor to cut them off. Bossuet exactly hits the point when he paraphrases St. Irenæus' advice as being to the effect 'that a rigorous right is not always to be used.' Not a hint is given all round that any one of the Churches disputed St. Victor's authority. Had any other portion of the Church talked of cutting off whole Churches from the common unity, it would only have made itself ridiculous. But when the threat comes from Rome the whole Church is astir; and there is one thing that no one says—neither St. Irenæus nor the rest of the bishops said, 'It is ridiculous, you have no such authority;' but they exhort, and protest, and warn, and entreat him not to do so.

[1] It must be remembered that Eusebius in speaking of Asia means, not the peninsula, but Asia in the restricted sense customary at that time. Cf. De Smedt, *Diss.* ii. cap. 1, note 1.

[2] I have put the alternative, because I do not think it possible to determine for certain which it was. Eusebius' account, not containing St. Victor's letters, is not sufficient to enable us to decide. Catholic writers are to be found on both sides. It seems to me that the evidence, on the whole, is in favour of a threat only.

[3] παραινεῖ = recommend. We have hardly an exact English equivalent for the word in the original—'admonish' has with us more idea of superiority, and 'advise,' perhaps, a shade more of softness than the original.

St. Victor's endeavour failed; for he found the opposition to this exercise of discipline too serious. It was a bold attempt to effect the more perfect unity of the Church, and to prevent the intrusion of heretical tendencies. He had thought to enforce, under pain of excommunication, a more uniform observance of the Festival of the Resurrection throughout the Church. The endeavour unfortunately failed, owing to the passionate tenacity with which he found the Asiatics wrongly adhered to their national custom. He found he could not persist in downright excommunication, even of the lesser kind, with any hopes of gaining the end in view. It was not a matter of faith, and therefore, whilst he showed his care for the unity of the Church and his jealousy for the faith—not directly assaulted, but indirectly endangered by a line of action which easily lent itself to error—he showed his wisdom in ceasing to contend for his point when he saw the spirit of obstinate partisanship which his endeavour evoked. He desisted from the final step, in accordance with the respectful remonstrance of St. Irenæus. Eventually the Universal Church settled down to the Roman mode of observance. The whole incident discovers the actual centre of Church life in that century. St. Victor sets in motion synodical action throughout the Church, gathers up the results which are sent in to him, lays down the conditions of adherence to the common unity, and his ruling ultimately prevailed throughout the Church, as it does to this day, concerning the observance of the Queen of Festivals.

NOTE.—Mr. Puller contends that St. Victor cut off these Churches of Asia from communion with Rome, and *endeavoured* to go further, *i.e.* endeavoured to cut them off from 'the common unity,' but that in this he failed. From which he argues that no degree of loss of communion with Rome involves loss of communion with the rest of the Church.

It is to be noted that he appears to understand ἀκοινωνήτους, 'separated from communion,' as meaning separated from the local Church of Rome, and not 'from the common unity,' as the context in Eusebius suggests. And indeed he goes so far as to state that ' Eusebius tells us that, while Victor, *speaking for his own Church,* announced,' &c.; whereas Eusebius merely says that Victor announced, &c. And to clench the matter, in summing up he inverts the order of Eusebius' words, and so draws his conclusion from them. He puts the proclamation of St. Victor (to the effect that those Churches were excommunicated) first, and the endeavour to cut them off from the common unity last.[1] This is not the order in Eusebius. The endeavour was being made, and the first step was to issue the proclamation. So that unless they repented and altered their rule of observance at the following Easter, they incurred the downright excommunication (ἄρδην). The next step was not what Mr. Puller states it to have been. He says, 'The other bishops objected to Victor's proceeding; they refused to withdraw their communion from Polycrates.' This latter sentence is not contained in Eusebius' account. What the bishops did was not to 'refuse,' but to *exhort*, and to reproach with some bitterness. And since their exhortations, enforced by St. Irenæus' letter of more becoming tone, availed with St. Victor, matters never came to the point of *refusal* on the part of the bishops. The breach no sooner opened than it closed. So that the moral to be drawn from this incident in the early life of the Church is something very different from what Mr. Puller describes it. He says (p. 31—the italics are my own), 'The right way of dealing with such claims,' *i.e.* those of the Vatican Council, 'if we may judge by the example of St. Irenæus and other holy bishops [2] of his time, is to inveigh against the claimant strongly and to upbraid him severely, and to *refuse to give in to his claims*.' On the contrary, if we take the few facts we possess, there would be 'exhortation' to desist, there would *not* be the same upbraiding, for that was too bitter (πληκτικώτερον), there would be 'becoming' (προσηκόντως) admonition as to a too dangerous exercise of rightful authority, but there would not be (if we are to judge by Eusebius' account of the whole matter) any denial of the authority itself. Professor Harnack, the most brilliant German Protestant writer of the day, says that Victor 'ventured by an edict . . . to declare that any Church which did not adopt the Roman method was excluded as heretical from the communion of the one Church. How could Victor have ventured on such an edict . . . if it was not already established and recognised that it belonged to the Roman Church, as its distinctive prerogative, to determine the conditions of

[1] P. 30.
[2] The bishops who agree with Mr. Puller seem always to be holy. He denies the title of saint to Victor, just as he does to St. Stephen, St. Damasus, St. Gelasius, St. Celestine, St. Zosimus. These holy men were all Popes. In the same way Dupin and Tillemont are Roman Catholic divines, the Ballerini and others are only 'Ultramontane.'

the κοινὴ ἕνωσις, when essential doctrines of the faith were in question?' ('Dogmengeschichte,' i. p. 868.)

In the course of his description of this incident Mr. Puller also settles a question of translation without sufficient authority. St. Victor 'requested' Polycrates to summon the bishops in his parts, and Polycrates did so. Mr. Puller finds in this an argument against the supremacy of the Holy See. He considers the Greek word to imply equality. But the word used by Polycrates is equally applicable to the request of a superior, as may be seen by consulting Liddell and Scott's Greek Lexicon, 7th edition. It would, indeed, be hypercriticism to the last degree to lay stress upon such an expression at all, for who does not know that superiors will often, out of courtesy, express their desires, as Popes usually do now, instead of issuing a peremptory demand? But in point of fact ἀξιόω by itself implies neither superiority nor equality on the part of the person who makes the request. That must be determined by other considerations.

Once more. There is no authority for saying, as Mr. Puller does, that 'everything went on as if nothing had happened.' The obstinacy of these Asiatics had received a check, and it seems not improbable that some further measure of conformity to the Roman mode of observing the Paschal Feast followed upon the stand made by St. Victor; if we may trust the letter of Constantine, respecting the Nicene Council, it would certainly seem as if this incident had had an effect for good.

With regard to the question as to whether St. Victor actually excommunicated the Asiatics contingent upon their obedience by the following Easter, or only threatened to do so, it seems to me that Firmilian's evidence is very strong. He says in reference to the day of celebrating the Paschal Feast, that 'there was not at any time a departure from the peace and unity of the Catholic Church on that account.' ('Ep. Cypr.' lxxv.) Tillemont makes a poor attempt to get out of the plain meaning of this sentence. And Firmilian's position in Asia Minor makes him a specially valuable witness in this matter. It is true that I have given reasons for questioning his evidence in the rest of the sentence, but they do not apply to this point. Firmilian's argument is that St. Stephen, in excommunicating (so he asserted) the Bishop of Carthage on such a question as that of baptism by heretics, was acting contrary to St. Victor and others on the question of Easter.

CHAPTER V.

THE DOCTRINE OF ST. CYPRIAN ON UNITY.

THE teaching of St. Cyprian, and certain portions of his life, have been claimed as the special justification of the Anglican position in early history. Dr. Pusey, in his preface to the Epistles of this saint, says, 'The Epistles of St. Cyprian are the more deeply interesting to us in that he, who has been called "the ideal of a Christian bishop," has been almost involuntarily chosen as the model of our Church.' He considers that St. Cyprian 'maintained in act the abstract independence of Churches, which he had in theory maintained.'[1] Mr. Puller, in his book on 'The Primitive Saints and the See of Rome,' maintains that 'both his writings and the story of his life remain as a perpetual witness against the Papal and in favour of the episcopal constitution of the Church of God,'[2] and even goes to the length of saying, in another place,[3] 'The defenders of the English Church may safely stake their case, so far as it relates to the Papal claims, on the witness borne by St. Cyprian.' It is necessary, therefore, to enter more fully into the teaching and life of this saint than would be otherwise natural, premising that to stake the defence of one's ecclesiastical position on a single saint is contrary to all Catholic ideas of divine faith in the Church.

I. It will be admitted on all hands that St. Cyprian's eye is perpetually fixed on one saying of our Lord's when he thinks of the government of the Church. 'Thou art Peter; and on this rock I will build my Church . . . and to thee will I give the keys of the kingdom of Heaven,' are to

---

[1] *Lib. of the Fathers. St. Cyprian*, pref. p. xvii. [N.B. The references to St. Cyprian's writings are to the Oxford edition; but where the number of an Epistle differs from that in the Benedictine edition, I have referred to the latter thus, B.x.]

[2] P. 357.　　　　　　　　　　　[3] P. 363.

St. Cyprian the all-important words in regard to Church authority.[1] At the same time, it is undoubtedly the case that St. Cyprian is full of the necessity of obedience to the *bishop of the diocese*, and that he distinctly speaks of the Church having been 'settled on the bishops.'[2]

The point, therefore, to be considered is the connection between the episcopate of the Church and the Apostle St. Peter—whether, according to St. Cyprian, it excludes the sovereignty of the Bishop of Rome.

Some of the most brilliant German Protestant writers, such as Neander and Harnack, and, amongst Americans, Schaff, maintain that St. Cyprian's teaching necessarily issued in the Papal form of government. Amongst Anglican writers, some agree with these German historians, whilst others, such as Dr. Pusey and his followers, hold that St. Cyprian maintained the necessity of the episcopate, and, at the same time, its entire independence of the See of Peter. The former hold that if the episcopate be considered as a matter of necessity, by reason of its relationship to Peter, its dependence on the successor of Peter (if there be such) necessarily follows; the latter, that if all bishops are the successors of Peter, there is no room for a special relationship to the Apostle on the part of any one see.

The position maintained in the following pages is that the Papal supremacy is already there. St. Cyprian regards the saying of our Lord to Peter as the root of all authority in the Church. Other Apostles were associated with Peter; but St. Cyprian *separates him off from the rest*, as well by the stress which he lays on the commission given to him (compared with the very rare occasions on which he mentions the rest), as by the definite expression so often repeated in his writings, that the Church was founded by Christ *on Peter*. It is to our Lord's saying to Peter that St. Cyprian perpetually recurs, which he regards also as giving the form of unity to His Church subsequently to the death of that Apostle (Ep. lv. 6, lix. 18). St. Peter was, in the teaching of Cyprian, the beginning of a divine institution, which issued in a stream

---

[1] Cf. *Ep.* xxxiii. 1, lxvi. 7, lxxiii. 7, lix. 8, lxx. 5, lxxi. 2, lxxiii. 7. *Tr. on Unity*, § 3.   [2] *Ep.* xxxiii. B. xxvii.

of bishops throughout the world. The Apostles founded various communities of Christians, each with their head to succeed themselves; but the authority of all is traced, in the Cyprianic literature, to the words of Christ to Peter, repeated in part, and in part only, to the rest of the Apostles.

Thus the bishops were the successors of the Apostles, but of the Apostles considered as a college, with Peter at their head. On Peter the Church was founded : *it was founded, too, on the Apostles*, but on these only, I must repeat, as forming a body of which Peter was the head; and the Church is for ever founded on the bishops, because the episcopate has succeeded to the rule of *Peter*,[1] having come into being through the missionary initiative of the several Apostles, scattered throughout the globe, who were all of them associated with Peter.

So that when St. Cyprian says that the origin of heresy and schism lies in the misfortune that 'the head is not sought,'[2] it is not our Lord simply, but our Lord considered as the Creator of an institution, whom he contemplates. In fact when he says 'the head is not sought,' he may be said to mean broadly that the *original institution* is overlooked, the originating words of our Lord, who is our Divine Head, are not borne in mind.[3] By these words an authority was placed on earth; for the saint goes on to speak of Peter having received the keys. And this he insists upon by way of showing that the martyrs and confessors in their prisons were disturbing the unity of the Church, in overlooking the bishop of the diocese, who derived an authority from our Lord's

---

[1] *Ep.* xxxiii. St. Francis of Sales explains the different ways in which St. Peter and the rest of the Apostles were foundations. 'They were foundations of the Church equally with him [Peter] as to the conversion of souls and as to doctrine; but as to the authority of governing they were so unequally, as St. Peter was the ordinary head, not only of the rest of the whole Church, but of the Apostles also' (*The Catholic Controversy*, by St. Francis of Sales. Burns and Oates, 1886, p. 249).

[2] *De Unit. Eccl.* § 3.

[3] Elsewhere he says that the remedy, 'when truth is in jeopardy, is to recur to the evangelical fountain, and the apostolical tradition, that the rule of our action may come thence whence both our order and origin have taken their rise.' And again, 'If we revert to the head or origin of the divine tradition, human error ceases' (*Ep. ad Pompeium*).

words to Peter which did not belong to *them*, as they suffered, or awaited their crown. And, again, the Novatianists, of course to a much greater extent and in connection, not with great truths, as was the case with the confessors, but with great iniquity, were overlooking the head, who in that case was the legitimate Bishop of Rome, who, as legitimately rooted in the past, was himself, and not Novatian, the head and root of the Church.[1]

II. For St. Cyprian wrote his treatise on Unity to meet the necessities of the day, and the form which it took was determined by those present needs. It is, therefore, necessary to enter upon these somewhat at length, if we are to understand why St. Cyprian laid such stress on obedience to bishops.[2]

(*a*) The early part of his episcopate was occupied with the danger which had arisen to the discipline of the Church from an unintentional encroachment on the bishop's office on the part of the confessors and martyrs in the Decian persecution. The occasion of this encroachment was as follows. The Church taught that, owing to the solidarity of the Body of Christ, the suffering of one part availed to diminish the punishment of another. During the persecution many Christians had failed to confess the faith, and had incurred the ban of the Church. The question arose as to how and when they should be restored after their lapse. It was the custom to have recourse to the martyrs and confessors in their prisons, and to obtain from them a certificate to the effect that they desired for the applicants a release from the punishment due

---

[1] 'For this has been the very source whence heresies and schisms have taken their rise, that obedience is not paid to the Priest of God,' *i.e.* (as generally in St. Cyprian's writings) the bishop (*Ep.* lix. 6, B. lv.).

[2] 'For schisms and heresies have arisen, and do arise, from the bishop, who is one and presides over the Church, being despised by the proud presumption of some' (*Ep.* lxvi. 4, B. lxix.).

[3] It is the consideration of these circumstances that gives the true answer to Mr. Puller's objection in his *Prim. SS. and the See of Rome*, p. 351. He says, 'You may read the whole treatise on unity from beginning to end, and you will not find one single word about Rome, or about the Pope, or about any Papal jurisdiction derived from St. Peter.' The treatise was written (so St. Cyprian tells us himself, *Ep.* liv. B. li.) to meet special needs, and, as will be seen, Papal authority did not come into question.

to their sin of apostasy. This, in the proper course of things, was presented to the bishop, who decided upon the extent to which the combined effect of the martyrs' prayers and the penitence of the lapsed should affect the latter. The applicability of the sufferings of the confessors to those who sought their intercession was admitted on all sides; and the right of the bishop to grant an indulgence, or remission of the temporal punishment due to the sin of apostasy, was unquestioned. But it lay with the bishop to decide in each particular case; for the temporal punishment could only properly be remitted to those who gave signs of contrition for the sin they had committed; and it also rested with the bishop to determine the extent to which the martyrs' certificates should be available to shorten or dispense with the natural term of penance. In a word, the present teaching of the Church on the subject of indulgences [1] was in full vogue; only the confessors had been led to give their certificates without due reference to the bishop.

Now St. Cyprian felt that the whole discipline of the Church was at stake, through the imprudence of these imprisoned confessors, in giving certificates irrespective of the applicants' penitence and without proper authorisation from the bishop. He accordingly wrote to certain persons on the subject, and sent all his letters to Rome for the inspection of the clergy there.

Rome was just then without a bishop. It had been part of the plan of the persecution under Decius to weaken the body by depriving it of its head. 'He ... persecutes the rulers of the Church that, its pilot being removed, he may .... make shipwreck of the Church.' Accordingly St. Cyprian had been compelled to flee into retirement, and the Bishop of Rome had been martyred, for there, St. Cyprian says, Decius would rather have seen a rival emperor than a bishop of God. Accordingly the election of a new bishop in the place of Fabian, which St. Cyprian calls 'the place of

---

[1] An indulgence is a discharge of the debt of temporal punishment due to forgiven sin, obtained by the application of the treasury of the Church, as Tertullian called the merits of the martyrs. Of course the merit of our Lord is the source of all other merits.

Peter,' was rendered impossible for nearly two years. But the local Church of Rome was still at the head of the Christian world. Although her clergy could not act with the authority of the Roman Bishop, they were still the object of special deference and respect. The aroma of infallibility lingered in the vacant see. The Roman clergy had already written to Cyprian in regard to his flight from persecution, in consequence of some unfavourable comments that had been made, probably by those who were preparing the way for a schism. St. Cyprian, in no way resenting this intervention of the Roman clergy, first wrote to know if the letter was really theirs, and then, on finding that it was, defended his conduct. 'I have thought it necessary to write this letter to you, wherein an account might be given you of my acts, discipline, and diligence .... What I have done my epistles will tell you, which I sent, as occasion required, to the number of thirteen, and which I have transmitted to you.'[1] No one, surely, will suppose that the Roman clergy ever dreamt of sending an account of *their* 'acts, discipline, and *diligence*' to Carthage.

St. Cyprian then proceeds to detail his proposed method of dealing with those who had lapsed under persecution. In this portion of his letter he shows still more strongly what deference he felt to be due to the chair of Peter in Rome, even when the administration of the Church there was in the hands of the inferior clergy. 'Nor in this' (*i.e.* his attitude towards the lapsed) 'did I lay down a law, or rashly make myself its author. But whereas it seemed right that both honour should be shown to the martyrs, and yet the violence of those who desired to throw everything into confusion be checked— and, moreover, *having read your letter lately sent to my clergy* through Crementius, the archdeacon, to the effect that those should be helped who, having lapsed, were seized with sickness, and who, repenting, desired communion—I thought it right to abide by what was your opinion also, lest our conduct in the ministry, which ought to be united and to agree in all things, should in any respect differ.' He then speaks of referring matters to a council at Carthage after the peace, that

[1] *Ep.* xx. B. xiv.

we 'may with the assistance of your counsel also set in order and restore everything.' He speaks elsewhere (Ep. xxvii.) of the letter of the Roman clergy having helped him much; whilst the Roman clergy, careful not to assume the prerogatives of their bishop, say that Cyprian 'wished us to be found not so much judges as pastors in counsels.' At the same time they speak of the inerrancy of the Church of Rome, its faith having been celebrated throughout the world—a fact which (they say) the Apostle would not have mentioned 'unless this vigorousness had derived its root of faith from that time *and thenceforwards*.' But they are the more compelled to wait before giving any definitive judgment as to the lapsed, 'because since the decease of Fabian, of most honoured memory, on account of the difficulties of circumstances and the times, we have no bishop yet appointed who should settle all these matters, and who might, with authority and counsel, take account of those who have lapsed.' He also mentions later on that this epistle of the Roman clergy 'was sent throughout the world, and made known to all the Churches and all the brethren.'[1]

The Roman clergy then, whilst waiting for a bishop to be appointed, who could settle matters 'with authority' as well as 'counsel,' meanwhile applauded St. Cyprian's intention of refusing to devolve the work of the bishop in the restoration of the lapsed on the confessors and martyrs. Their certificates were to be allowed their due weight; their sufferings were to be admitted in lieu of the temporal punishment which those who obtained the certificate would have been bound to undergo; but the whole matter was to be submitted in each diocese to the 'head' of the Christian people therein.

---

[1] *Ep.* lv. 3. It is difficult to understand how any one could twist this incident, naturally suggestive of the authoritative position of Rome, into an instance of dissimilarity between the 'Cyprianic' and the 'modern Roman' theory of the Church's government. It has, however, been said (*Prim. SS.* p. 60) that on the latter theory 'there would probably be some reference to the fact that a pope would soon be elected who would be able to ratify what the archbishop had done.' This is exactly what the Roman clergy did say to Cyprian in regard to the archdeacon's action during the vacancy of the see. Mr. Puller most unjustifiably substitutes the 'judgment' of the archbishop for 'their conscience' in that note. No 'surprise' is expressed.

The danger that was threatening them was, according to St. Cyprian, that of disregarding the divinely appointed head. And he finds the divine institution of a head in our Lord's words to St. Peter. He writes to the lapsed (Ep. xxxiii.), saying that 'Our Lord, whose precepts and warnings we ought to observe, determining the honour of a bishop and the ordering [1] of his own Church, speaks in the Gospel and says to Peter, " I say unto thee, that thou art Peter, and upon this rock," &c. Thence the ordination of bishops and the ordering of the Church runs down along the course of time *and the line of succession*, so that the Church is settled upon her bishops, and every act of the Church is regulated by the same prelates. Since, then, this is founded on divine law, I marvel that some have had the bold sincerity to write to me as if they were addressing letters in the name of the Church, whereas the Church consisteth of the bishop and clergy and all who stand.'

St. Cyprian, therefore, distinctly understands the 'rock,' in St. Matthew xvi., to be St. Peter; and the bishops enter into their share of the keys through succession from Peter, who is thus, in a very true sense, the 'root' of the Catholic Church and the source of its unity. She is 'built on Peter, for an origin and for the ordering [2] of unity.' The rock which, according to St. Cyprian, is Peter, has expanded itself in ' a line of succession,' and the Church consists of those bishops who flow from Peter, together with the clergy and the faithful. Included amongst those bishops is, of course, according to St. Cyprian (however mistaken he may be in the judgment of Mr. Puller [3]) the occupant of the chair of Peter. The bishop is the head of the Church in each diocese, because he is part of the stream which has flowed from Peter; and this stream is, all along its course, invested with divine right because its source is of divine institution, coming from the creative words of the Heavenly Master, 'Thou art Peter,' &c.

So far St. Cyprian's teaching, though not couched in the terms of modern theology, is yet in substance identical with that of the Roman Catholic Church at this hour. In the

---

[1] *Ratio.* Oxford translation.
[2] *Ratione.* The same word in the letter just quoted.
[3] *Prim. SS.* p. 54.

district of Westminster, for instance, the 'head' must be sought (*caput quæritur*), and the 'head' is the bishop who comes down from Peter, and so is part of that *enduring* living foundation on which Christ built His Church, and on which it will remain until the end of the world. St. Peter is not, according to St. Cyprian, as some would make him, *only* a symbol, but he is the *origin* of the Church's unity, and communion with Peter is an essential feature of the Church's life. Consequently, the lapsed must know that their restoration to the Church is to be regulated by the bishop, not simply by certificates from the martyrs. And the Bishop of Carthage would not lay down a law on the rules to guide the bishop's action without consulting Rome.

(*b*) But another event in the life of St. Cyprian turned his thoughts towards the subject of unity, and led to a further explanation of its origin and nature. An Anti-Pope arose at Rome, and St. Cyprian flew to the aid of Cornelius, the legitimate Pope. In an important passage he insists upon the regularity of Cornelius's appointment, and the consequent sin of opposing him. There cannot be two bishops over the same see, and those who through their own fault are in communion with the wrong one are outside the supernatural sphere of the Church, and their very martyrdom would lose its merit. There was, says St. Cyprian, already a properly appointed bishop when Novatian was ordained, and consequently the Novatianists were in schism. It was not a question of what were the powers or rights of the See of Rome; St. Cyprian had no call to dwell on these. The question was as to the rightful occupant of that see. And St. Cyprian determines this question by insisting on the unity of the Church—its necessarily visible unity. Cornelius was the Bishop of Rome, received as such by the brotherhood of bishops. He was appointed, says St. Cyprian, ' when *the place* of *Peter* and the rank of the sacerdotal chair was vacant '—*i.e.* not merely the bishopric but the ' place of Peter' (Ep. lix. B. lv.); therefore no other could, by any possibility, be the bishop of that same city. The Church cannot be visibly two or three. It began with one, it was founded on one by the voice of the Lord, and it must continue one. It cannot be, like the kingdoms of

Israel and Judah and the garment of Ahijah, visibly disunited. This, he says, 'has been the very source whence heresies and schisms have taken their rise, that obedience is not paid to the Priest of God [*i.e.* the bishop]; nor do they reflect that there is for the time one high priest in the Church and one judge for the time in Christ's stead, whom, if the whole brotherhood would obey according to the divine injunctions, no one would stir in anything against the College of Prelates: no one after the divine sanction had, after the suffrages of the people, after the consent of our fellow-bishop, would make himself a judge, not of his bishop, but of God; no one would by a rent of unity tear asunder the Church of God.'[1]

It is not difficult from a passage like this to see what St. Cyprian would have thought of ordaining an archbishop to a see, whilst the bishops of the province were in prison, in protest against the authority (which they believed to have no 'divine sanction') under which the said archbishop was ordained, whilst the rest of the Church were not consulted or communicated with. In other words, the present Archbishop of Canterbury has no means of tracing himself to Peter, according to Cyprianic tests, and can therefore have no share in the keys of Peter. For St. Cyprian was led to lay stress on the obedience due to the bishop in each diocese, not because he viewed the bishop as standing alone and deriving his commission from our Lord in such a way that he could act independently of the rest of the Church, but as one of a compact brotherhood visibly united.[2] And whilst he had an office to fulfil, which he could devolve on no one else, and for which he was ultimately responsible to our Lord alone, his share in the keys of the kingdom came from his being one of the numerous heads who are visibly connected throughout the world, and who are therefore *in connection with* the blessed

---

[1] *Ep.* lix. B. lv.

[2] *Episcopatus unus, episcoporum concordi numerositate diffusus*—one episcopate diffused by a visibly united (*concordi*) multitude of bishops (*Ep. ad Antonian.* lv.). The Oxford edition translates this '*throughout* an harmonious,' &c., as though the abstract episcopate were one thing and the visible channel another.

Apostle Peter. 'Our Lord built the Church on Peter' is the refrain of the Cyprianic doctrine.

Thus far, then, the circumstances under which St. Cyprian wrote his treatise on Unity would not necessarily, nor even naturally, lead him to the subject of Papal jurisdiction. It was the rights of bishops over the laity, and the test of a lawful occupant of any see, Rome included, which occupied his attention; the relationship of bishops to their mother-Church, whether in Carthage or in Rome, would have been irrelevant to his theme.

III. At the same time he does in this part of his life incidentally touch on the See of Peter and its relation to the other sees of the Church, and in so doing he shows that he held strictly, in theory, to the supremacy of the See of Rome. Peter had, according to our saint, his official representative in the Bishop of Rome. 'The place of Fabian' (the Pope), was, according to St. Cyprian, 'the place of Peter,' an expression which, as a matter of fact, he uses of the See of Rome alone. But further, in writing of Novatus who had gone from Carthage to Rome to join the schism of his all but namesake Novatian, he describes the wickedness of the Novatians in 'setting up for themselves, without the Church and against the Church, a conventicle of their abandoned faction;' and then he proceeds to say, 'After all this, they yet in addition, having had a pseudo-bishop ordained for them by heretics, dare to set sail and to carry letters from schismatic and profane persons *to the chair of Peter*, and to the principal [or ruling] Church, whence episcopal unity has taken its rise.'[1]

Now it is obvious from these words that St. Cyprian did not regard Carthage as being the See of Peter in the same sense that Rome was, for they went, he says, from Carthage *to* 'the chair of Peter.' Rome was, therefore, the chair of Peter in some way differing from Carthage, for it is described simply as 'the chair of Peter.' They were not going to every see—they were not about to make a tour of the globe, but going to Rome.

Again, this 'chair of Peter' is, according to St. Cyprian, the 'principal Church.' Now we have seen that this expression and its Greek equivalent occurring in St. Irenæus can-

[1] *Ep.* lix. 18, B. lv.

not mean the most ancient or the mother-Church. It means the ruling Church. Since Irenæus wrote those words about Rome, Tertullian had defined the word as meaning 'that which is over anything,'[1] as the soul presides over and rules the body. At one time of St. Cyprian's life hardly a day passed without some study of Tertullian; at spare moments he would say, 'Give me the master,' by which they understood that he wished to read Tertullian. We can, therefore, be fairly sure what he meant by the principal Church, viz. the sovereign ruling Church. When, therefore, these heretics went to Rome, they went, according to our saint, to 'the chair of Peter and the ruling Church.'

Again, it is the ruling Church 'whence sacerdotal [*i.e.* episcopal] unity took its rise;' *i.e.* not the College of Bishops, for that took its rise from all the Apostles, but the 'unity' of the College which took its rise from the chair of Peter, *i.e.* from Peter considered as the origin of a succession.[2]

We have, then, here from St. Cyprian a distinct enunciation of the Catholic and Roman teaching concerning the office of the See of St. Peter. It was not directly the mother of the episcopate, regarded as a line of mechanical succession, but of its unity: that is, of the episcopate, regarded as bound together in visible communion and invested with divine authority.[3]

But St. Cyprian adds yet another point. The 'chair' suggests the teaching office, as 'the princedom' implies government. And St. Cyprian adds that the Romans are 'they

---

[1] *De Animâ,* c. 13.

[2] Mr. Puller (*Prim. SS.* p. 55) considers *sacerdotalis unitas* to be the same as *collegium sacerdotale*, which is quite inadmissible, and he thus prepares the way for his strange contention that St. Cyprian is speaking of the chair of Peter as the mother-Church of Africa only. But St. Cyprian gives not the slightest hint that he is speaking of Africa only. And the word he translates mother (*principalis*) had already another signification as applied to Rome. Mr. Puller quotes a passage from Tertullian, which Gieseler quoted *à propos* of the passage in St. Irenæus; but Dr. Döllinger replied to Gieseler that we must adhere to the ordinary meaning of the word as expressly defined by Tertullian (*Geschichte,* &c., *loc. cit.*). And St. Augustine's expression, 'in which the sovereignty was ever in force,' is a kind of echo or commentary of the same.

[3] At present the See of Peter is the mother of all the successions, for all have had to be replenished from her.

to whom faithlessness can have no access.' Such is his ground of security when he contemplates these men sailing from Carthage to deceive the chair of Peter as to the correctness of his teaching. At this period of his life warm words of encomium invariably spring to his lips when he speaks of Rome; but his words, each one of them, contain serious teaching. Here the mention of Rome suggests the absurdity of these people supposing that the original source of episcopal unity will be untrue to its perpetual office on the momentous question which they wished to stir.

But, after all, it may be said that the sovereignty attributed to the chair of Peter did not amount to much, seeing that St. Cyprian goes on to deprecate these people having gone to Rome, instead of being content with having their cause tried at Carthage. But did St. Cyprian mean by his protest against their sailing to Rome to deprecate any appeal under any circumstances? It will be seen presently that this was not his meaning. He considered that, in this particular case, the number of the bishops who had tried these men was sufficient to settle the matter. So that the reference of matters to Rome depended, in his judgment, on the adequacy of the local episcopate in any given case to meet the needs of the occasion.[1]

St. Cyprian, therefore, expresses his confidence that these men will gain nothing by scuffling off to Rome, since it is the very source of unity, and the Romans are they 'to whom perfidy can have no access.' Unity (he says in effect) took its rise from the chair of Peter, and as it arose thence it will remain secure there.

If now we compare the most recent exposition of this great passage in St. Cyprian with its Catholic interpretation, we have these results.

On the one hand, Mr. Puller passes over the expression of our saint, 'the chair of Peter,' as being, in his judgment, the result of a delusion wrought into the Western Church's mind within the second century by the Clementine Romance, a delusion which (he admits) was shared by the primitive saints for ever afterwards! He translates 'principal' as

[1] Cf. p. 69.

'original,' in defiance of Tertullian's definition and St. Augustine's explanation. He subordinates the primary idea in the term 'episcopal unity' to the secondary, by translating it 'the episcopal body considered as a unity,' instead of keeping 'the unity' as the substantive word; and lastly, he narrows the contents of the word 'principal,' as though it related only to Rome and the West, and especially Africa.

On the other hand, in the Catholic interpretation, the words are taken in their plain, naked simplicity. Rome is 'the chair of Peter and the sovereign Church, whence the unity of the episcopate took its rise.' Here St. Peter is seen to be not a mere symbol, but the very source and commencement of a stream of unity (which is St. Cyprian's own simile), and the Apostle is a real foundation, not detached and built, as it were, in the air—not a source separated from its stream—nor a type with no genetic relationship between him and the unity he represents, but the edifice is continuous with the foundation, growing up from it and on it, so that it is true, as St. Cyprian is so fond of saying, that Peter is he 'on whom the Lord built the Church.'

IV. We are now in a position to understand the full meaning of the famous passage in his treatise on Unity, written subsequently to the events described above, but in reference to them. After the opening paragraph, St. Cyprian at once proceeds to state, as he had done before in his letters, the cause of heresy and discord.

It proceeds from this, that men do not go 'to the origin of the truth' (possibly 'unity' is the true reading), nor is the head 'sought, and they do not pay attention to the heavenly Master's teaching.' He our Master, has taught us where to find the head: namely, in the successor of Peter. 'For He said to Peter, "Thou art Peter, and on this rock I will build my Church, and the gates of hell shall not prevail against it; and I will give thee the keys of the Kingdom of Heaven." *Upon one He builds His Church*, and although He gives to all the Apostles after the resurrection equal power, yet'— What is the restriction introduced by the 'yet'? What is the modifying truth? It is that this gift to the rest of the Apostles does not exhaust the arrangement which Christ made for His

Church. This gift does not interfere with the fact that He built His Church on one, for although He gave the rest equal power (*e.g.* to consecrate the Eucharist, to absolve, to teach infallibly, to found Churches), '*nevertheless,* in order to manifest unity, He, by His own authority, instituted the origin of the same unity, so that it should begin from one.'

Mr. Puller does not venture to translate the word 'manifest' by 'symbolise,' but throughout he appears to understand them as equivalent. But it is one thing to symbolise and another to manifest; and our Lord secured the manifestation of unity by 'providing' (*disposuit* [1]) an actual origin 'beginning from one' (ab uno incipientem). And then, that there may be no mistake, and that none may imagine that the difference between the rest of the Apostles and this 'origin of unity' which Peter was made, amounted to a difference in the power of the priesthood, he repeats that undoubtedly 'the other Apostles were what Peter was, invested with an equal share of honour and power, *but* the commencement [of the Church] starts from unity, that the Church of Christ may be shown to be one.' And this unity is a thing to be held, and 'he who holds it not, does he think that he holds the faith?' [2]

Thus St. Cyprian traces all heresies to a neglect in looking for, or to, the head. *Nec caput quæritur.* The head is the bishop viewed as the heir of the promises made to Peter. He is in each place the link for the time being [3] of the chain which reaches down from the original head—namely, the Apostle Peter. For St. Cyprian never speaks of the Church being founded on St. James, or on St. John. He knew that they were foundations, but not in the unique sense in which Peter was. According to St. Cyprian the See of Rome was the See of Peter, and the chair of Peter was the principle of cohesion to the Christian episcopate. He was the Primate of the Christian Church, and showed his humility in not pressing this point at Antioch; [4] and his chair inherits the Primacy

---

[1] 'Unitatis ejusdem originem ab uno incipientem suâ auctoritate disposuit.' Cf. the use of *dispositio* in Roman law for an 'edict.' *Tr. on Unity,* § 3.

[2] *Tr. on Unity,* § 4.   [3] Cf. Appendix I.

[4] *Ep.* lxxi. 2. Cf. p. 83 for the explanation of that passage. Dr. Döllinger remarks: 'Der Sinn ist: Petrus hätte sich dem Rechte nach auf seinen Vorrang berufen können, aber in jenem Momente, als Paulus ihn mit gutem

bestowed on him, for it is the principal or governing Church. They only are lawful bishops who, having been duly elected (a matter which was subject to arrangement on the part of the Church) are built into the one foundation and form part of that visibly compacted body, which resembles, not (so he says) the kingdoms of Israel and Judah, and the garment of Ahijah, but the seamless robe of Christ. Such is the (strictly Papal) teaching of St. Cyprian.

V. This teaching of St. Cyprian has an important bearing on the relation between orders and jurisdiction. 'We have orders,' it is said; 'is not that sufficient?' According to St. Cyprian it is not sufficient. We might be living in the deadly sin of schism in spite of our orders. We might be in possession of sacraments, yet without the sanctifying effects of the sacraments, from lack of jurisdiction. The Church, in St. Cyprian's teaching, is a visible kingdom; it is a compact body, and the ceremony of episcopal ordination will not of necessity introduce a man into that network of holy organisation which alone traces itself up to Peter, 'on whom the Lord built the Church.' We must be in communion with the rest of the Church in this sense, that our episcopate is acknowledged as a part of the succession from Peter by the compact brotherhood of bishops which comes down from the blessed Apostle Peter. Ecclesiastical intercommunion may be temporarily suspended, but we must be an acknowledged portion of the one Church, having inherited the legitimate succession and not forfeited our place in that one stream which, flowing from Peter, is 'diffused throughout the world by a concordant multiplicity of bishops.' And as 'episcopal unity took its rise,' according to St. Cyprian, 'from the chair of Peter,' so from the chair of Peter it will always flow. To take a single instance, Nestorius and his followers forfeited their place in that compact unity, that 'concordant multiplicity.' Their decendants accordingly have no jurisdiction wherever they may be. Their episcopate is not part of the kingdom of Christ. It is not enough that they have orders, if they have; the flaw in their title is that they cannot trace to Peter 'on

Grund tadelte, wäre es Hochmuth und Arroganze gewesen' (*Geschichte*, Periode I. p. 360).

whom the Lord built the Church.' For in the year 431 they were extruded¹ from the unity of the episcopal brotherhood, just as afterwards the followers of Photius departed from the same unity. Wherever the Nestorians are, they are members of what St. Cyprian would call a 'conventicle of their own, beside the Church and against the Church.'

The same would be true, according to Cyprianic principles, of the legalised episcopate in this country if its orders were admitted to be true. It never established itself in the kingdom of Christ, according to those principles. There was no authority recognised by the Church that confirmed the election of Parker. Eleven days after his consecration he confirmed the others, who yet were supposed to have elected him to the see. What could be in more flagrant defiance of all Cyprianic teaching ?

Again, according to Cyprianic principles, where there is already a bishop in communion with the rest of the Catholic Church, exercising his jurisdiction, it would be a most grievous sin to consecrate another and introduce him on to the same field of work. For instance, there was in Quebec a bishop, in communion with the Catholic Church, exercising legitimate jurisdiction. Some two hundred years afterwards one appeared with the title of bishop, with letters patent from England. It was, if this person was in other respects a bishop, the deadly sin of schism on Cyprianic principles. Eventually the whole ground occupied by the Catholic Church was mapped out into districts, to which bishops, at least in title, were ordained by the Archbishop of Canterbury, and sent out to labour in a sphere already assigned to a Catholic bishop. 'The Queen has been pleased by letters patent, under the Great Seal of the United Kingdom, to reconstitute the bishopric of Quebec, and to direct that the same shall comprise,' &c. 'Her Majesty has also been pleased to constitute so much of the ancient diocese of Quebec as comprises the district of Montreal to be a bishop's see and diocese,' &c.² It is clear

---

[1] For the authority with which this was done, cf. pp. 334-336.

[2] I need hardly say that the laws of the Church of England, and not Her Gracious Majesty, are responsible. All Catholics must feel a special regard towards the present occupant of the throne.

from this, which is but one instance of a series of similar acts, that the Church of England at any rate does not proceed upon the lines of St. Cyprian's teaching. That saint must have denounced her line of action with all his fiery vehemence as destructive of his cherished principle, that there can be but one bishop and one altar. The only imaginable defence is that the Church of England is the entire Church of God on earth. The denunciation could then be left to St. Augustine, in his writings against the Donatists.

CHAPTER VI.

ST. CYPRIAN ON APPEALS TO ROME.

I. The essential points, then, in the teaching of St. Cyprian on the Unity of the Church are these. Every Christian finds himself under the rule of one pastor, who has to give an account of his rule to the one Lord of all (Ep. lv. B. lii.). To this one pastor or bishop the faithful in that district owe obedience in matters of faith and discipline.

But this bishop is one of a compact body visibly united by intercommunion with all the rest; and he derives his authority from the words of our Lord to St. Peter in Matthew xvi. 18. He is part of a stream whose united volume flows through the ages from that apostolic source.[1] He must be an accepted member of the great brotherhood of the 'one episcopate.'[2] The episcopate is one body, and when one bishop has been regularly appointed to a district, no one can come in after him and claim the authority of Peter.[3]

These were the two points on which it was necessary to lay unequivocal and almost exclusive stress at the time when St. Cyprian wrote his treatise on Unity. The encroachments of some of the martyrs and confessors on the office of the head of the diocese in which those who applied to them lived, placed that office in jeopardy in the early part of his episcopate; in the second, the legitimate occupancy of the See of Rome was questioned by Novatus and Novatian. The question could not be determined by any reference to the

---

[1] 'De fonte uno rivi plurimi defluunt . . . unitas tamen servatur in origine' (*De Unit. Eccl.* c. v.).

[2] 'Episcopatus unus, episcoporum multorum concordi numerositate diffusus' (*Ep.* lv. B. lii.).

[3] 'Quisquis post unum qui solus esse debeat factus est, non jam secundus ille, sed nullus est' (*Ep.* lv. 6, B. lii. 8).

rights of the Bishop of Rome when once elected; it was the legitimacy of his election which was in dispute. This St. Cyprian decided by asking who was the acknowledged bishop already in possession, legitimately elected, and in communion with the whole brotherhood of the legitimate clergy throughout the world. The Church, he maintained, cannot be likened to the kingdoms of Israel and Judah.[1] He expressly repudiated this state of things as a type of what could happen in the Church of Christ. The Church, he says, in effect, as he sets aside this discord under the Old Covenant, has an external visible unity of her bishops; *not because they themselves are visible, but because they are visibly united.* ('De Unit. Eccles.' § 6). He recurs to this contrast between the Old and New covenants in his letter to Magnus (Ep. lxix. B. lxxvi.), and maintains that, so far from the two kingdoms of Israel and Judah being in any typical and ecclesiastical sense like the Christian Church,[2] our Lord's words about the Samaritans show that the ten tribes were not members of one kingdom in the sense in which people must be one in the Christian Church. 'The Lord ratifieth us in His Gospel, that those same who had then severed themselves from the tribes of Judah and Jerusalem, and, having left Jerusalem, had withdrawn to Samaria, should be reckoned amongst profane and heathen' (*loc. cit.* § 5).

The further question, as to the instrument and guardian of episcopal unity, did not at this period of his life call for any detailed treatment on the part of our saint. This question,

[1] 'When the twelve tribes of Israel were torn asunder the prophet Ahijah rent his garment. But because Christ's people cannot be rent, His coat, woven and conjoined throughout, was not divided by those it fell to. Individual, conjoined, coentwined, it shows the coherent concord of our people who put on Christ. In the sacrament and sign of His garment He has declared the unity of His Church' (*De Unit. Eccles.* § 6).

[2] For the opposite contention cf. *The Primitive Saints and the See of Rome,* p. 227, where the writer maintains a theory of unity expressly condemned by St. Cyprian. The same position was maintained by Dr. Pusey, as where he says (speaking of St. Cyprian's words, 'as the sun has many rays,' &c.): 'The oneness here spoken of is, according to Roman Catholics, fulfilled in the organisation of the *whole* Church; whereas, according to Anglo-Catholics, it is fulfilled in each bishopric, each bishop, viewed by himself, being a full representation and successor of St. Peter' (Cyprian's *Tr. on Unity,* § 4, note 6).

however, is plainly answered in his writings. For the whole authority of the episcopate is traced to Peter, not, indeed, to the exclusion of the other Apostles, but as to their head, their representative, and summary. And allusions to the See of Peter occur precisely on those occasions when it would be natural for the topic of the centre or source of unity to come into incidental notice. When the five schismatics sailed to Rome, to try and hoodwink the Pope as to their number and importance, St. Cyprian expresses his security that they will not succeed, for they are going to the very see which is the source of episcopal unity—'the chair of Peter and the Sovereign Church, whence episcopal unity took its rise.' And when he is persuading a brother-bishop that Cornelius is the legitimate occupant of that see, and he comes to the point where he has to insist on the fact that Cornelius superseded no one else, but that the see was vacant, he calls the see by its Christian name, 'the place of Peter.' It was at once a Christian see and a special see, 'the place of Fabian, that is, the place of Peter, and the rank of the sacerdotal chair was vacant.'[1] The See of Rome was thus in one respect the same as every other see, *i.e.*, in respect to the *Sacerdotium*; it was a 'sacerdotal chair,' but it was also, in its own way, 'the place of Peter.' And his whole attitude towards that see was up to this time one of peculiar respect, deference, and veneration, as the centre of the Church's visible unity.

I shall now examine his teaching on appeals to Rome.

II. A fact that must strike us at once is that St. Cyprian denounced in no measured terms a certain small body of schismatics who repaired to Rome in the hope of persuading St. Cornelius, the Pope, that they were true bishops. But whilst the fact that they repaired thither showed their knowledge of the value set on Rome's favourable judgment, their idea was not in the least that of an appeal in the regular sense of that term. The circumstances were as follows.

An heretical bishop, named Privatus, who had been condemned by ninety bishops, had come to Carthage and made one Fortunatus bishop over the Novatianists there. He had

[1] *Ep.* lv. 6, B. lii.

gathered round him four men whom St. Cyprian called [1] at the outset 'desperate and abandoned.' They were Felix, made bishop outside the Church, and Jovinus and Maximus, who had been condemned first by nine bishops, and then had been excommunicated a year since by a larger council—by 'very many of us.' These were joined by one named Repostus, who had lapsed into idolatry during persecution. These five men (says St. Cyprian), joined by 'a few who have either sacrificed or have evil consciences, chose Fortunatus to be their pseudo-bishop.'

It was thus a little body which had no standing in the Church and no right of appeal. Sailing to Rome was a piece of impudence which our saint justly denounced as such. These 'desperate and abandoned' fellows, as he calls them more than once, informed the Pope that twenty-five bishops were present at the ordination of Fortunatus. They had made the boast in Carthage itself that as many as twenty-five Catholic bishops were about to assist from Numidia. 'In which lie,' says St. Cyprian, 'when they were afterwards detected and put to shame (five only who had made shipwreck of the faith having met together, and these excommunicated by us), they then sailed to Rome with their merchandise of lies, as though the truth could not sail after them and convict their false tongues by proof of the real fact.' [2]

Such were the circumstances under which St. Cyprian very naturally, and with no prejudice to the general principle of appeals to Rome, invoked the decision of the African bishops that causes should be heard in Africa itself. These men were condemned criminals, condemned for moral delinquencies and heresy, and they did not repair to Rome to reopen the case of their own crimes, but to persuade Rome that they had at their back an imposing array of bishops, and that Cyprian was dealing unjustly with the lapsed.[3] They said nothing about their past condemnation, of which St. Cyprian, therefore, had to inform the Pope. Their cause had been heard, and sentence had been passed against them. Fortunatus

---

[1] *Ep.* lix. § 12, B. lv. [2] *Ep.* lix. § 13.
[3] Cf. the latter part of the letter.

himself was only a *pseudo*-bishop; he was, in reality, a presbyter under Cyprian's jurisdiction. As such *he had no right of appeal straight* to Rome, if indeed at all, under the peculiar regulations of the African province.[1] Anyhow, if he wished this sentence reversed, his obvious duty was first to clear himself in Africa, and then at least to observe the proper form of appeal. Instead of this, 'having had a pseudo-bishop ordained for them by heretics, they dare to set sail and to carry letters from schismatic and profane persons to the chair of Peter and the principal Church, whence the unity of the priesthood has taken its rise, remembering not that they are the same Romans whose faith has been commended by the Apostle, to whom faithlessness can have no access.'

On one only plea, according to St. Cyprian, could such a transgression of the Church's laws be even imagined by any one to be justifiable—*i.e.* on the supposition (absurd enough) that the authority of the legitimate African bishops, who had tried and condemned them, was insufficient *in point of numbers* as compared with these 'desperate and abandoned' men. It was this on which they had laid stress. But it was false. They had been twice condemned, on the last occasion by a numerous assembly of legitimate bishops. These men themselves were neither legitimate bishops nor numerous. They were desperate and abandoned men, and few.[2] Those who judged them were sufficient in point of number and of weight. 'For,' as St. Cyprian continues,[3] 'if the number of those who passed sentence on them last year[4] is reckoned together with

[1] Cf. Aug. *Ep.* xliii. (al. clxii.).

[2] 'Nisi si paucis desperatis et perditis minor videtur esse auctoritas episcoporum in Africa constitutorum.' 'Unless the authority of the regular (*constitutorum*) bishops in Africa seems less than [that of] a few desperate and abandoned men.' Such an ellipse is common with Cyprian. If, however, 'paucis' be taken as the dative governed by 'videtur,' the context still forces us to understand 'minor' as expressing comparison in point of number—'less than theirs.' But the immediate context suggests the first translation as the true one.

[3] B. lv. § 15. The Oxford edition is doubtless correct in including this sentence in § 14. It is probably from not reading on, that some writers have been led into the mistake of supposing that the saint is comparing the African bishops with the Pope.

[4] The allusion is probably to the original smaller number, viz. nine.

the presbyters and deacons, *more were then present at the judgment and trial than these same men* who are now seen to be joined with Fortunatus.' St. Cyprian, in his reasoning here, in no way offends against the general principle of appeals to Rome as formulated in the Vatican decrees.[1] He is dealing with a particular case in which the appellants, if such they could be called, had no standing in the Church and no ground of appeal.

III. On the other hand, in dealing with the case of an heretical bishop in Gaul, St. Cyprian distinctly acted on the supposition that the Pope was the proper person to set in motion the excommunication of the leading bishop in that region.

It would seem that St. Stephen, who had succeeded to the throne of Peter after the martyrdom of Lucius, had been slow to use his authority to the extent required, as St. Cyprian thought, in a case that was now brought before him. Marcian, Bishop of Arles, had withdrawn from the communion of the Church and attached himself to Novatian. He boasted that he had not been excommunicated, but had himself withdrawn, and no new bishop had been appointed. Application had been made to the Pope by the bishops of the province, but, for reasons which we cannot tell, he had not as yet acted in the matter. Accordingly, Faustinus, Bishop of Lyons, who belonged to the same province,[2] had on his own account communicated with St. Cyprian, whose fiery nature was calculated to hasten a matter over which St. Stephen was taking his time. We often think the physician can attend to us and heal us more quickly than is perhaps possible. St. Cyprian wrote to the Pope and reminded him that the management of such a matter belonged to the episcopate,[3] and, as he implies, the requisite aid in this case could only come from St.

---

[1] The author of *The Primitive Saints*, &c. says: 'It is for Ultramontanes who profess to venerate St. Cyprian and the early Church to consider whether they are prepared to accept his teaching or not.' Ultramontanes are prepared to accept St. Cyprian's teaching, but not Mr. Puller's translations.

[2] 'In eadem provincia' (*Ep.* lxviii. B. lxvii.) is to be referred to Faustinus. Lyons and Vienne at that time were included in the province of Narbonne (cf. Ammianus Marcell. lib. xv.).

[3] 'Cui rei nostrum est consulere et subvenire.' For Mr. Puller's mistranslation of these words see *infra*, p. 76.

Stephen himself. St. Cyprian urged St. Stephen to effect this. He therefore urged the Pope to write 'letters of plenary authority [lit. most full letters [1]] by means of which, Marcian being excommunicated, another may be substituted in his place.' He presses the Pope to immediate action on the ground that bishops have no 'greater or better office' to perform 'than by diligent solicitude and wholesome remedies to provide for cherishing and preserving the sheep.' He likens the flock at Arles to sailors who need another harbour, owing to the unsafety of their present one—and this new harbour he wishes St. Stephen to provide. They are like travellers whose inn is beset and occupied by robbers, and who seek other safer inns in their journey. These safer inns and this safer harbour ought, St. Cyprian contends, to be provided by St. Stephen by letters of excommunication—'letters by which, Marcian having been excommunicated, another may be substituted in his place.' It was not *advice* that the bishops of Gaul needed; St. Cyprian could give that. That, indeed, was all for which St. Cyprian himself was asked, and his reply was his urgent request to St. Stephen that he would, not advise, but direct letters of excommunication. The excommunication of a bishop was no new matter; but as the martyrs of Vienne and Lyons had called to the Pope to aid them, so now the bishops of Gaul had appealed to the Pope, and to their thinking had been left too long without the requisite aid. St. Cyprian, therefore, reminds St. Stephen that Marcian was trading on the lack of a formal excommunication, as though 'he had not been excommunicated by us.' It only needed, in Cyprian's judgment, formal letters of excommunication to be issued by Stephen, with a mandate to elect a bishop in his place. He therefore asks him to comply with his prayer, and to notify with whom they are henceforth to communicate.

St. Cyprian, indeed, not only by his request to the Pope concerning letters of excommunication and letters of communion, but by an incidental expression also, shows what

---

[1] Or, not merely a 'Papal brief,' but also a full exposition of principles. Cf. the contrast between 'per libellum aditio' and 'plenaria interpellatio' in the law of Honorius and Theodosius 'de Naviculariis per Africam,' adduced by Constant. *Ep. Rom. Pont.*

position St. Stephen occupied in his theory of Church government. Marcian was to be formally excommunicated because of his Novatian teaching. 'Let him not give, but receive sentence' (§ 4). Accordingly, St. Cyprian urges upon St. Stephen that his predecessors in the see ('our' predecessors, he calls them, so full is he of the perfect unity of the Church) had given judgment on Novatian's teaching. They, he says— *i.e.* Popes Cornelius and Lucius, whom he has just mentioned by name—'they, full of the Spirit of God and in the midst of [1] a glorious martyrdom, decided that communion (*pax*) should be granted to the lapsed, and by their own letters they sealed their decision that the fruit of communion and peace was not to be denied them when penance had been done; which we all everywhere altogether judged. For there could not be a difference of thought (diversus sensus) amongst us, seeing that there was one Spirit in us' (in quibus unus esset Spiritus). I do not see how one could better express the mutual relations between the Holy See and the rest of the Church, and the common *charisma* of infallibility possessed by the Pope and the Church, than in these golden words. What do they teach? They say that the Popes decided the question, full of the Holy Ghost; that the whole Church agreed, and that it could not be otherwise, considering they were under the influence of the same Spirit (cf. p. 330).

Accordingly, St. Cyprian says that St. Stephen is bound to honour the judgments of his predecessors by his own 'weight and authority.' [2] Marcian, therefore, will be deposed, and the name of his successor notified by the authority of the Pope. Marcian's name disappeared from the diptychs.[3]

IV. Once more, before the turn in his life, St. Cyprian showed his acceptance of the principle of Papal jurisdiction. I say the principle, for he objected to the particular exercise in this case. Two bishops had been deposed in Spain for

---

[1] 'Constituti.' I have for this word adopted the Oxford translation.

[2] He had given as his reason why Stephen should excommunicate Marcian: 'Servandus est . . . Cornelii et Lucii honor gloriosus; illi enim dandam esse lapsis pacem censuerunt' (*Ep.* lxi.), on which Döllinger remarks: 'The word *honor* frequently occurs in the writings of St. Cyprian with the meaning of *auctoritas* or *potestas*' (*Hist. of Ch.* Period I. cap. 3, § 4).

[3] Cf. Mabillon, *Annal.* tom. iii. p. 452.

having taken out certificates of idolatry[1] during the late persecution. Their names were Basilides and Martial. Moreover two bishops had been appointed in their place, Sabinus and Felix. Basilides, and probably Martial also, appealed to Rome. Obviously it was not the first time that such an appeal had been made. St. Stephen, as St. Clement before him, restored them, or ordered them to be restored to communion, whether by reason of the irregularity with which their case had been conducted, bishops having been appointed in their place without his cognisance (which St. Cyprian's words in Marcian's case [p. 71] show to be an irregular proceeding), or whether St. Stephen was simply taken in by Basilides' statement, we do not know, as the necessary evidence is not forthcoming. But several bishops of the region appear to have accepted the Pope's ruling, and communicated with Basilides and Martial; and accordingly Felix and Sabinus looked round about for help in the shape of counsel and advice as to what they were to do. This is expressly stated by Cyprian. To him they naturally went for such help, considering the prominent part he had taken in the matter of the lapsed during persecution. St. Cyprian held a council and advised their people to cling to them as their real bishops. The probability is, as Baronius thought, that these two were sent to Rome with the conciliar letter to help towards their acceptance by the Pope.

The important point, however, for us is the way in which our saint dealt with the authority of the Pope. He nowhere denies it as a matter of principle, but he sees some restriction in its claim to obedience. He considered that the Pope had been overreached, and says that although there was some fault in this in the way of negligence, the real sin lay at the door of the bishop who had deceived the Pope.[2] He is describing the aim of this bishop—it was 'to be replaced unjustly in his episcopate from which he had been rightly deposed.'

[1] *I.e.* certificates of having sacrificed, which saved them from civil punishment, whether they had actually sacrificed or not.

[2] 'Hoc eo pertinet ut Basilidis non tam abolita sint quam cumulata delicta, ut ad superiora peccata ejus etiam fallaciæ et circumventionis crimen accesserit' (*Ep.* lxviii.).

Not a word has St. Cyprian to say against the possibility of a bishop being replaced in his bishopric by the Pope. Had our saint held the view that the Pope could not restore a bishop who had been deposed by his surrounding colleagues, it must have appeared. But no, the power of St. Stephen is not for a moment questioned. It is the certainty of Basilides' crimes that is put forward as the ground for considering the restoration null and void.[1] The injustice consisted in the certainty of his crimes. St. Cyprian writes with some emotion—indeed, to some extent, without the self-restraint which one would desire; but he does not even remotely hint at any lack of authority on the part of the Pope. He says that he is 'far away and unaware of the true state of the case' (§ 5), not that he is assuming a power which he does not possess. Instead of settling the matter by that obvious rejoinder, he holds a council and decides that St. Stephen has been deceived by false statements, and that Basilides, so far from deserving reinstatement in his bishopric, has only added to his crimes by the falsehoods he has told the Pope. For the position of Basilides is really one, says St. Cyprian, which had been provided for by Pope Cornelius and the rest of the bishops. So that our saint is avowedly acting under the shelter of a Papal decision with which the whole Church had agreed (§ 6).

It is unfortunate that we have no sufficient evidence on which to form a judgment as to the whole case. We have only Cyprian's side. And he does not exhibit a very judicial tone of mind, so far as the scanty record goes. There is no appearance of his having consulted St. Stephen on the matter at all, which, whatever the latter's position, would, to say the least, have been a matter of courtesy. We do not know on what grounds St. Stephen formed his judgment, nor what exactly his judgment was. St. Cyprian's own account is taken only from the aggrieved party. And if St. Stephen could be deceived, so could St. Cyprian. And if, as the latter says, St. Stephen was too far off, St. Cyprian was further off. The

---

[1] Compare the case of Bishop Grosseteste, who, whilst owning himself bound to filial obedience to the Holy Father, felt that His Holiness could not be aware of the candidate proposed by him.

intercourse between Rome and Spain was greater than that between Spain and Carthage; and Spain was more closely connected from a civil as well as ecclesiastical point of view, with Rome than with Carthage. And why did Felix and Sabinus go to Carthage instead of to Rome, where they might have disabused the Pope of his prejudice, if such it was, against their case? St. Stephen's character was, according to St. Vincent of Lerins, that of a 'holy and prudent' man. According to St. Dionysius, he assisted all parts of Arabia and Syria by his letters.[1] We have a right, therefore, to suspend our judgment as to his negligence, on the principle of 'audi alteram partem.' What we gather for certain from the letter of Cyprian is, that in spite of some vehemence, he did not dispute the principle that the Pope could, where just cause existed, restore a deposed bishop of Spain. The editors of Migne's magnificent collection of the whole literature on the subject endorse the supposition of Baronius, that Felix and Sabinus went with the letter of the Carthaginian synod to Rome, and that St. Cyprian's intent was to move St. Stephen to sanction the deposition of Basilides and Martial. But in point of fact our materials are insufficient for understanding the matter fully, and we do not know the sequel. It looks as if it would not be difficult for the Evil One to produce a rupture between these two saints, one of whom was full of holy vehemence, and the other of holy prudence. 'Coming events cast their shadow before.'

NOTE.—It is astonishing how anyone could fail to see in the affair of Marcian of Arles an emphatic testimony to the strictly Papal method of government as existing in the Church at that time, and taken for granted by St. Cyprian. Rigaltius, whose inaccuracy in regard to the text of this letter was pointed out by Baluze,[2] has, however, been greatly followed by anti-Papal writers. He is quoted at length in the Oxford edition of the Fathers,[3] but the editor (Dr. Pusey) felt compelled to add in a note that Rigaltius 'seems anxious to understate the eminence conceded to Rome. A

---

[1] Euseb. lib. vii. c. 2, 4.
[2] *Epistolæ S. Stephani. S. Cypr. ad S. Stephanum* (*Ep.* i. p. 1027, note 10. Migne, 1865).
[3] Vol. iii. pt. 2, p. 217 (1844).

deference does seem to be paid to him, not on account of his nearness only; he exercises an eminent authority, although only [sic] as the executive of the rules of the Universal Church.'

But the most recent anti-Papal writer [1] contends that it was only for the sake of obtaining St. Stephen's *advice* for these bewildered bishops of Gaul that St. Cyprian wrote. Our saint, however, says nothing about advice. He is, indeed, made to speak of advice by this writer's translation, according to whom the words, ' It is ours to advise and come in aid' are the equivalent of the Latin ' cui rei nostrum est consulere et subvenire'![2] It is easy after such a manipulation of the text to make out that ' St. Cyprian presses on Stephen the duty of writing *a letter* of *counsel* and help.' But, even if this writer's incorrect translation of the above words could be passed, the words could not be considered exhaustive of what St. Cyprian wished from the Pope. A letter of counsel and help is not exactly the equivalent of ' letters to the province,' whereby, Marcian being ' excommunicated, another may be substituted in his place.' Yet these are what St. Cyprian asks the Pope to send. And, again, letters to ' signify plainly to us who has been substituted at Arles in the room of Marcianus [*loc. cit.* § 5], that we may know to whom we should direct our brethren and to whom we should write,' are something more than mere counsel and advice. They imply an ' eminent authority.'

[1] Rev. F. W. Puller, *Primitive Saints and the See of Rome*, pp. 62-65.
[2] Cf. Facciolati on the word *consulo*. ' Cum dativo significat habere rationem et curam alicujus rei, tueri, providere, prospicere.' Forcellini's edition, by J. Bailey, F.R.S. (1828).

CHAPTER VII.

ST. CYPRIAN'S ERROR ON BAPTISM BY HERETICS.

WE now come to the events in St. Cyprian's life which have dimmed the splendour of his glory and led some to invoke him as the patron of their isolated position. If from his throne of glory he could shed a burning tear of sorrow, it would, I conceive, be over the false views of history that can select an incident in his otherwise holy life, which his glorious martyrdom threw into the shade, and indeed washed out, and which forms no proper basis of a theory of Church government. The Donatists perpetually quoted Cyprian to St. Augustine; he replied, not by denying his error, but by pointing out his determination not to break with Rome.[1] There are those in our days who are fond of quoting his quarrel with Rome (which St. Augustine calls a brotherly altercation) on a question which he considered one of variable discipline only, and treating of it as though he thought it a matter of faith and essential discipline. We will give a short summary of this unhappy episode in his career.

I. It was apparently his conflict with the Novatians which led St. Cyprian into his error concerning baptism by heretics. His fundamental tenet was the sin of breaking with the society founded on Peter. It was a sacred principle, but he drew a conclusion which conflicted with the Church's teaching. Heretics were separate from this one society, and therefore, he added, they could not baptise, for they could not give the Holy Ghost to others, being themselves bereft of His grace. He did not realise that heretics might nevertheless carry with them some *débris* of Catholic truth, and above all an indelible 'character' with some rights and privileges still remaining.[2] Their baptism was indeed 'vain and profit-

---

[1] Cf. *Ep.* 93, 40.   [2] Cf. Freppel's *Saint Cyprien*, 1890, p. 321.

less, having a semblance but nothing real *as an aid to holiness*,' as St. Athanasius said;[1] but although it was shorn of its sanctifying effects, it was not therefore void of all value in the supernatural sphere. But St. Cyprian had already exhibited symptoms of pressing his thesis, that outside the Church there is no salvation, to an excess of rigour. He had said in his treatise on the Unity of the Church, speaking of schismatics, 'Their waters soil instead of purifying,' and 'their illegitimate birth gives children to the devil, not to God.' His very horror of heresy and schism became a stumbling-block to him. We cannot, moreover, but feel that the influence of his master Tertullian was not without its effect. Tertullian had himself broached the false opinion that it was impossible to receive baptism amongst heretics; and Agrippinus, one of St. Cyprian's predecessors in the see of Carthage, had begun to rebaptise those who had received baptism only at the hands of those in schism. Cyprian followed suit, but he met with opposition from some of the bishops of his own province. The position which St. Cyprian assumed was that those who had received baptism from heretics ought to be rebaptised, *but* that it was one of those matters of discipline about which they might disagree, without forfeiting each other's communion.

It was a question which had already agitated one part of the East. Two synods, one at Iconium and the other at Synnada, had issued decrees in favour of rebaptising, and Firmilian, Bishop of Cæsarea, in Cappadocia, had taken a prominent part in promoting this discipline. He had even gone to the length of rebaptising some who had received baptism from a bishop who had fallen into the sin of idolatry under persecution. But as in Africa so in the East the practice was novel, and if we take the East as a whole, Firmilian had few followers. Still the matter was now assuming serious proportions, as the Novatians at Rome had begun to rebaptise Catholics when they induced them to apostatise, and the influence of Cyprian's name was a serious addition

---

[1] Mr. Puller, in quoting this passage (*Prim. Saints*, p. 73) seems to have misunderstood its meaning. St. Athanasius does not deny the validity of baptism by heretics, but its sanctifying effects.

to the confusion. He was consulted by eighteen bishops of Numidia as to the practice of rebaptising which his predecessor, Agrippinus, had introduced, and he decided in favour of the practice. This was the beginning of the disturbance in Africa. St. Cyprian alleged various reasons of minor consequence, such as the impossibility of the water being blessed by priests out of communion with the Church, or of the oil used in baptism being consecrated by those who being outside the Church had neither altar nor church; but his main reasons were derived from the oneness of the Church, the unworthiness of the minister, and the incapacity of the subject.[1]

The whole of St. Cyprian's reasoning shows the truth of St. Augustine's remark, that the matter had not yet been thoroughly sifted and elucidated.

And St. Cyprian maintained his point with such logical acumen and eloquence that St. Augustine says he should probably have thought the same, seeing that the matter had not then been discussed in all its bearings in a plenary council. We may gather from what St. Augustine also says that, in spite of this, he would have submitted to the ruling of the Holy See, as he evidently considers St. Cyprian should have done, and indeed thinks that he possibly did.[2]

St. Cyprian's three points, on which he insisted, contained each of them a separate misunderstanding.[3] In insisting that because there is but one Church no baptism outside the Church could be valid, he did not realise the doctrine first expounded in all its fulness by St. Augustine concerning the 'soul' of the Church. He limited the supernatural action of our Lord to the confines of the visible Church.[4] Again, in denying that a heretic, being himself without the grace of God, could be the minister of that grace to others, he was

---

[1] Freppel's *Saint Cyprien*, p. 329.
[2] 'Fortasse factum est' (*De Bapt.* lib. ii. cap. 4).
[3] Cf. Freppel, *loc. cit.* p. 329 seq.
[4] As Bishop Freppel says: 'A precise distinction between the visible Church (or assemblage of the faithful under the government of legitimate pastors) and the invisible Church, formed of all whom divine grace has sanctified, would have sufficed to remove all difficulty.' St. Augustine answers: 'Ecclesia quippe omnes per baptismum parit, sive apud se, sive extra se' (*De Bapt. c. Don.* i. 14). And again: 'An extra unitatem Ecclesiæ non habet sua Christus?' (*Ibid.* iv. 9).

really establishing, what he repudiated in word, the dependence of the sacrament on the dispositions of its minister. He drew, indeed, a distinction between those within the Church who were living in sin and those without the Church who had no share at all in divine grace. But he was again seriously trenching upon the full teaching concerning the visible Church, and endangering the very idea of a sacrament.

And in laying stress on the impossibility of men who were in rebellion against God receiving a sacrament which conferred divine grace, he was ignoring the difference between the reception of a sacrament and its sanctifying effects. St. Augustine points out that St. Cyprian ignored the *character* conferred by the sacrament of baptism which did not, indeed, involve the recipient's sins being forgiven, but which made the reiteration of the sacrament impossible. Its effects slumbered till the baptised person made his submission to the Catholic Church. Infants baptised by heretics would, on St. Cyprian's teaching, forfeit heaven; but St. Cyprian could never be induced to enter on that part of the subject. In fact the whole subject was one which had not, in St. Cyprian's day, formed part of the ordinary teaching of the Church, and was new to many. There was, therefore, room for question and discussion. At Rome, whither heretics always found their way only to be extinguished by the Apostolic tradition, which it was the special province of Rome to guard, the matter had been dealt with, as St. Augustine says, in accordance with a traditional discipline received from the Apostles themselves. And this Apostolic tradition was destined to prevail, but not without a struggle.

There was at Rome a pontiff who was, to use the words of St. Vincent of Lerins, 'a man holy and prudent.' He had, perhaps, already shown some prudence in abstaining from precipitate action in the case of Marcian of Arles, and had evinced a repugnance to proceed to extreme measures in the case of the two Spanish bishops who appealed to Rome. But his zeal for the faith committed to his charge would not permit him to act with remissness in this case. St. Stephen felt himself bound to resist this innovation on the immemorial practice of the Church with the most determined energy. It was resisted by the Episcopate of the Church as a whole, but, says St. Vincent of Lerins, 'Pope Stephen, of blessed memory, who at that time was prelate of the Apostolic See, resisted, in conjunction with his colleagues, yet more than they, thinking it fit, I suppose, that he should surpass all others in the devotedness of his faith as much as he excelled them by the authority of his station.'

This 'holy and prudent' Pope saw that the practice of the Church on this matter of rebaptising was closely connected with the faith, and he had already threatened to suspend communion with Firmilian and his sympathising bishops until such time as they brought their practice into accord with what he knew to be Apostolic discipline.[1] St. Cyprian, however, persisted in viewing the matter as one of pure discipline, and not involving a matter of faith, although worth maintaining at great cost. And further, as we have said, he considered all along that the practice pursued at Rome involved the admission that *forgiveness of sins* was conferred by the baptism of heretics in the same way as by baptism in the visible Church.

II. On being appealed to by the eighteen Numidian bishops for advice on the subject, some of their colleagues being opposed to the practice, St. Cyprian convoked a council of about thirty bishops, and they decided in favour of rebaptising. About the same time he was applied to by a Bishop of Mauritania, named Quintus, on the same subject, to whom he wrote an answer which has been preserved. He emphasises

---

[1] Their actual excommunication was averted through the representations and entreaties of St. Dionysius of Alexandria. Stephen had written, says Eusebius, 'as neither about to communicate with *them*.' Mr. Puller's translation, 'saying that he would not communicate with them' (*Prim. Saints*, p. 329), which he thinks represents St. Stephen as having already effected a separation, goes beyond the Greek, which is as I have written it—' he had written . . . as not about to communicate with them either.' The Greek is simply in the future. Not possessing the letters, we could not say whether Eusebius is speaking of a *sententia ferenda* or *lata*—an actual or conditional excommunication—were it not for the context, which shows that the excommunication was not actually carried into effect. St. Dionysius averted it by his prayers and entreaties. He gained his namesake at Rome and Philemon over to his way of thinking. They had previously thought with Stephen that the rebaptisers ought to be excommunicated.

G

two points—viz. that baptism is one, and therefore cannot be repeated, and that ancient customs are not always to be followed. On the first point he adduces a passage from Holy Scripture, which he misquotes, having, we may presume, an incorrect copy. He relies on a passage in Ecclesiasticus (xxxiv. 30), which he gives thus: 'He that is washed by one dead, what availeth his washing?' A heretic is dead, and therefore what is the use of the washing, or baptism, administered by him? But the passage really runs: 'He who washes himself after having touched a dead body, if he touches it again, of what use is his ablution?' In dealing with the question of custom he expressed himself with more conciseness than caution, so that his words have been (wrongly) interpreted as a depreciation of tradition. He says that we 'must not frame a prescription on custom, but prevail by reason'—words which, without proper explanation, may be said to contain the microbe of Rationalism. But elsewhere he says that 'custom without truth is only ancient error'—which is certain; only it is equally certain that such a custom would not prevail in the Church. The Bride of Christ is incapable of the stain of adultery, as he himself teaches elsewhere; yet she would be unchaste if she sanctioned a custom contrary to truth, to the extent that, as a matter of fact, she had taken home to herself this custom. She had, as a whole, upheld the validity of baptism conferred by heretics. One of the bishops at the third council held at Carthage on this subject said that ' Jesus Christ said " I am the truth," not " I am custom," ' which is true enough; but it is also true that He said to the Apostles in sending them out to teach, 'I am with you all days to the end of the world,' and consequently no custom on so important a matter could attain to prevail in the Holy Catholic and Apostolic Church.[1] St. Cyprian did not really disagree with the rest of the Church as to the value of tradition, but as to the fact in this particular case. 'A sound critic,' says Bishop Freppel, 'should pronounce judgment in accordance with the entire trend of the discussion, not abuse a word which has escaped in the heat of argument.' Both

[1] Cf. Freppel's *Cyprien*, p. 337, 1890; and Rohrbacher, *Hist. de l'Eglise*, iii. pp. 306-7. Paris, 1892.

St. Cyprian and Firmilian maintained that the contrary tradition was a human one—one 'that had crept in amongst some.'[1] This was Firmilian's root mistake. He denied, or was unaware of, the antiquity and universality of the tradition against rebaptising; in other words, he failed to see that it had the two great marks of being a divine tradition—viz. antiquity and universality.[2]

Having insisted on the duty of upholding the unity of the Church, of yielding in nothing to the enemies of faith and truth, and of not laying down the law on the growth of custom, but seeking to triumph by reason, St. Cyprian appeals to the conduct of Peter at Antioch. He had begun his letter by mentioning that 'some of their colleagues' were in opposition—those, of course, who had led to the Numidian bishops consulting him on the question. And seeing that a second council was considered necessary, these African bishops who differed from their Primate, and probably thought that he was setting himself up as a sort of bishop of bishops, must have resisted the decree of the first council in the previous year. St. Cyprian, therefore, in a letter to a bishop named Quintus, deprecates the idea that he is forcing his own judgment in pressing concordant action on these African colleagues, and at the same time supplies them with a model of acquiescence in the suggestion of another. He adduces the example of the Primate of the Apostles. Peter himself did not, on the ground of his Primacy,[3] refuse to accept a better mode of carrying out

[1] *Ep. ad Pompeium*, lxxiv.
[2] Freppel, *loc. cit.*
[3] St. Cyprian did not 'point out that, if in consequence of this priority' (as the author of *Primitive Saints, &c.* translates *primatum*), 'St. Peter had expected St. Paul to obey him, he would have been guilty of insolence and arrogance' (*Prim. Saints*, p. 358). He assumed that St. Peter had a primacy which he might have pressed, but did not out of humility. St. Augustine (*De Bapt.* lib. ii. c. 1) quotes this passage of St. Cyprian, and speaks of 'the Apostle Peter, in whom the primacy over the Apostles is pre-eminent, with such surpassing grace,' being 'corrected by the later Apostle Paul.' And then, in comparing St. Cyprian with St. Peter (as having erred, but as not likely to resent St. Augustine's revision of his judgment on baptism by heretics), he expresses a fear lest he should be reviling Peter by the mere comparison. He says: 'For who is ignorant that *principality* over the Apostles is to be placed above any episcopate?' But if 'there is a distance between the grace of the chairs' (*i.e.* if the position of the Prince of the Apostles is beyond that of any bishop) 'their

their common faith, 'giving us thereby a pattern of concord and patience, that we should not pertinaciously love our own opinions, but should rather account as our own any true and rightful suggestions of our brethren and colleagues for the common health and weal.' He then quotes from i. Cor. xiv. 29, 30, as containing St. Paul's teaching 'that many things are revealed to individuals for the better; and that we ought not each to strive pertinaciously for what he has once imbibed and held, but if anything has appeared better and more useful, willingly to embrace it. For to have what is better offered to us is not to be instructed, but to be defeated.' He then reminds them, through Quintus, that he is himself only following the judgment of one of his predecessors, Agrippinus, who had acted after 'common counsel;' 'whose sentence, being both religious, and legitimate, and salutary, in accordance with the Catholic faith and Church, we also have followed.'

Thus, earnestly and in all humility, did our saint endeavour to bring the whole array of bishops in his own province into conformity on this practice, which, although not in his estimation a matter of necessity, yet called for harmonious action. But he treads on dangerous ground when he speaks of his discipline in the matter as a development or improvement on previous practice.

III. But in the following year St. Cyprian found it necessary to call a second council at Carthage, to consider particularly, amongst other matters, this same question. For the African bishops who had dissented from his ruling were not so easily brought into line.

This second and larger synod decided that 'those who have been washed without the Church and have, amongst heretics and schismatics, been *tainted by the defilement of profane water*, when they come to us and to the Church which is one, ought to be baptised;' and, moreover, they decided that all who had once left the Church, or had been ordained amongst the sects, could only be received back into lay communion.

glory as martyrs is one.' Neither St. Augustine's nor St. Cyprian's words can be satisfactorily explained except on the supposition that they understood St. Peter's relation to the Apostles to be one which could demand obedience. St. Augustine thus explains 'primacy' by 'principality.'

They ought not 'to retain those arms of ordination and honour wherewith they rebelled against us. It is enough that to such on their return pardon be granted.'

Closely following upon this council, St. Cyprian wrote a long letter [1] to a bishop named Jubaianus, in which he uses the arguments noticed above in answer to a letter forwarded by this bishop, and remits to him the letter of Quintus and the decree of the synod. In the course of this letter he repudiates the argument drawn from the fact that Novatian the schismatic Bishop at Rome, had taken to rebaptising. It is no concern of ours, says St. Cyprian, what he may do, who, like an ape, claims to himself the authority and truth of the Catholic Church. 'We who hold to the head and root of the one Church know . . . that he hath no hallowed office.' The 'head and root' was the Bishop of Rome, who traced to Peter (cf. p. 49), or perhaps, more strictly speaking, Peter himself, whom they reached *through Stephen and not through Novatian*.[2]

It was in this letter also that St. Cyprian, in defining what the Church is, where it is to be found, says in effect what St. Ambrose said, 'where Peter is, there is the Church.' He deals with the question as to where and by whom remission of sins can be given. And he at once says, that 'to Peter first, on whom He built the Church, and from whom He appointed and showed that unity should spring (§ 7, Oxf. transl.), was this power given.' And then he quotes the words spoken to Peter and the Apostles on Easter-night. So that, according to St. Cyprian, unity was to spring from Peter by our Lord's institution, and the power of remitting sins was

---

[1] *Ep.* lxxiii.

[2] Mr. Puller (*Primitive Saints*, p. 345) has mistaken the meaning of this passage through imagining that St. Cyprian is arguing with the Novatians. He is arguing with Jubaianus, or rather his correspondent, about Novatian. 'We' (*i.e.* you and I and others) 'hold to "the head and root of the one Church"' (*i.e.* the legitimate Bishop of Rome), 'and consequently we know that "nothing is lawful" to Novatian, because he is out of that one Church, separate from the head and root of the one Church.' Mr. Puller also argues that St. Cyprian could not mean Stephen by 'the head and root of the one Church,' because 'St. Cyprian was opposing Stephen' (p. 346). But this is an anachronism. Stephen had not yet appeared on the scene. Moreover, even if he had, St. Cyprian would still have held that he was the head of the Church. He would have added, that although such, he was going beyond his powers in insisting on obedience in this matter. Cf. Appendix I.

possessed in that body which had originated with the Apostolic College, of which St. Peter was the head, and his chair the origin of its unity.

It seems that the letter which Jubaianus had forwarded laid down the proposition that 'All, wheresoever and *howsoever* baptised in the name of Jesus Christ, have obtained the grace of Christ.' Against this proposition St. Cyprian urges his strongest arguments, and with some reason.

He concludes this forcible and eloquent letter with a disclaimer which is the real key to all that followed. He refuses to consider his practice in any other light than as a matter of discipline, which he had no intention of erecting into a general rule. He refuses to judge others in this matter. Each bishop is to do what he thinks right, having the 'free exercise of his judgment.' (§ 22.) This was the burden of his teaching on this subject, that it was a matter in which each bishop was free to administer his own diocese as he thought fit. There seems little doubt but that St. Cyprian knew that a different practice prevailed at Rome. But he did not place this matter on a level with the treatment of the lapsed; there the dogmatic faith seemed to be more nearly concerned, and on that point it seemed to him necessary that the practice of all the Churches should be one (cf. p. 52). Accordingly he submitted his judgment on that question to the Roman clergy.

The weak point in St. Cyprian's attitude was that, whilst he again and again declared that every African bishop should be free to act as he thought best, he yet supported his own practice by considerations of great dogmatic importance. He says, 'We ought to keep firmly the truth and faith of the Catholic Church;' and yet he is for leaving each bishop free to do as he thinks best. If it was part of the Church's faith, how could he leave it open? If it was not part of the Church's faith, was he not too vehement and somewhat overbearing? But as St. Augustine says, in regard to the whole matter, on which he so profoundly disagreed with St. Cyprian, 'We are men.' There are inconsistencies from which saints are not wholly free.

IV. The matter having gone thus far, St. Cyprian turned to

Rome. He had done the same before. Even when the see was vacant he had written to the clergy who administered the affairs of the Church there in the following words;[1] 'I have thought it necessary to write this letter to you wherein an account might be given you of my acts, discipline, and diligence.' Again, 'Nor in this did I lay down a law,[2] or rashly make myself its author. But . . . I thought it right to abide by what was your opinion also, lest our conduct in the ministry, which ought to be united and to agree in all things, should in any respect differ.'

Accordingly he now sends his report of the two synods, together with his letters to Quintus and Jubaianus, to the Pope. The matter, he says, concerned their 'common honour,' *i.e.* the dignity of the priesthood and the privileges of the Christian name,[3] and accordingly it was especially needful that they should 'confer' with St. Stephen's 'weight and wisdom' (vel maxime tibi scribendum et cum tua gravitate et sapientia conferendum). St. Cyprian and the bishops of the synod end with carefully defining their attitude towards their African colleagues, whose contrary practice had led to the question of the Numidian bishops and to the whole discussion. They say that they know that these 'certain bishops are unwilling to lay aside what they have once adopted (or imbibed), nor will they readily change their practice, but will to retain certain ways of their own which have once come into use among them, keeping the bond of peace and concord with their colleagues. *In which matter* we put no force on anyone, nor do we lay down the law[4] (cf. Ep. xx.), since every prelate has the free use of his own will in the administration of his Church,' *i.e.* in this matter. We must emphasise the words 'in which matter,'[5] to save St. Cyprian from the grossest inconsistency as compared with his conduct in other matters.

Such, then, was the state of things when St. Cyprian carried

---

[1] *Ep.* xx. B. xiv.   [2] 'Nec in hoc legem dedi.'
[3] That this is the meaning of the expression 'pro communi honore' (§ 3) seems quite certain, from the use of the word 'honores' in § 2, and from the 'honoramus' in the sentence immediately preceding. It is translated 'by reason of mutual respect' in *Prim. Saints*, p. 74, in disregard of the context.
[4] 'Nec legem damus.'   [5] *Ep.* lxxii. § 3.

the matter to Rome, 'assured' (so he says to St. Stephen) 'that you, in virtue of the truth of your religion and faith [will] approve of things that are equally religious and true.'[1]

The point, then, on which St. Cyprian considered that St. Stephen ought to be consulted (*conferendum*) was one on which the African bishops refused to judge others or to use any force save that of persuasion, to bring them into line. It was not a matter of faith, and therefore it was one on which each bishop could use his own judgment in the administration of his diocese. There were bishops in Africa who did use their own judgment, and who refused to conform to what they considered a novelty. St. Cyprian accordingly used every effort short of force to persuade them that they were going as close to betraying the faith as it was possible to do without actually forfeiting the communion of their colleagues. These refractory bishops, as he deemed them, pleaded ancient custom on their side; and St. Cyprian replied that his custom was not new—it was, in fact, about twenty years old in Africa—and that the discipline which he advocated corresponded to the 'better things revealed,' of which the Apostle Paul had spoken as possible in the Church. As for those who had lived and died in the past having been baptised by heretics, and not rebaptised on their reconciliation to the Church, they must be left to the mercy of God. As for the succession of the episcopate from the Apostles—lost according to this theory—St. Cyprian did not enter upon that question. In fact, as St. Augustine says more than once, the question was one which had not been thoroughly sifted and elucidated.

V. One more council, and that a still larger and more important one, was now held at Carthage. The exact occasion of this council is a question of great difficulty. It is often thought to have been occasioned by the reception of St.

---

[1] I have given these words in full because (quite unaccountably, as it seems to me) they have been adduced as a proof that St. Cyprian could not have believed 'the Pope to be the infallible monarch of the Church' (*Primitive Saints*, pp. 75, 76). Surely to say that if you believe a thing to be true you believe it will be sanctioned by authority is not saying that that authority is fallible. If anything, your words would show the contrary. As a matter of fact, as will be shown later on, the question of infallibility, as defined by the Vatican decrees, does not come under discussion in this whole matter.

Stephen's answer to the African bishops. But there is this (as it seems to me insuperable) difficulty in the way of considering it to be an answer to St. Stephen's letter, viz. that the letter is not once mentioned. No parallel, I suppose, can be adduced to this save the refusal of Dioscorus at the Robber Council of Ephesus to read the Tome of St. Leo. But who would institute a parallel between our saint and that miserable archbishop? Bishop Freppel thinks that it was a supreme act of homage to the Holy See that prevented St. Cyprian from discussing St. Stephen's letter in synod, when he disagreed with it. This seems to me highly improbable. St. Cyprian's holy passion for unity might arrest his vehement opposition to the decision of St. Stephen at any moment; and he might feel that he who had spoken of the See of Rome as 'the chair of Peter, and the principal Church, whence episcopal unity took its rise,' could not be the man to dissect and depreciate a decision of the successor of Peter in open synod, however he might tear it to pieces in writing to an individual like Pompeius.[1] But there are reasons why he could not have yet received that letter.

For the difficulty is that, not only is there *no mention* of the letter of St. Stephen—the letters of Jubaianus to Cyprian, and of Cyprian to Jubaianus alone are said to have been read, and the letter of St. Cyprian to St. Stephen[2]—but the answers of the bishops and the words of St. Cyprian are not in the least what we should have expected had they met under the 'irritation' which St. Augustine attributes to Cyprian on the receipt of St. Stephen's letter. They speak of some 'amongst us' upholding heretics and opposing Christians. And the whole record exactly fits in with the supposition that the opposition of some African bishops had become so serious as to call for a fresh council on their account alone.

Add to this, that St. Augustine nowhere supposes that these bishops in the third council are answering St. Stephen, and in places where many writers have seen an allusion to the Pope, he discerns none. He refutes every remark they make, and shows the fallacies in St. Cyprian's reasoning point

---

[1] Cf. *Ep. ad Pompeium*.
[2] Cf. speech of Bishop Crescens of Cirta, Mansi, t. i. p. 954; also St. Cyprian's speech, *infra*, p. 91, lines 26, 27, 28.

by point, but he nowhere understands that our saint's remarks are aimed at the Pope. What things St. Cyprian did 'pour out in irritation' against St. Stephen in his letter to Pompeius, he does not 'rehandle' (*retractare nolo*), both because they lay on the dangerous border-land of harmful dissension,[1] and because they were the same in substance as the points he had already discussed.[2] The effusions of Cyprian under irritation were evidently confined, according to St. Augustine, to his letter to Pompeius.[3]

Once more, had the council been dealing with St. Stephen's letter, the bishops must have met the salient point of that letter more directly and more frequently. The point of St. Stephen's ruling was, as we shall see, connected with traditional custom; but only two of the bishops in the council deal with this point at all, and they only repeat words which had been uttered by St. Cyprian in his answer to the writer mentioned by Jubaianus, and that answer was avowedly written before St. Stephen's letter reached Africa.

The only supposition on which it can be maintained that this council was held after the reception of the papal decision and by reason of it, would be that St. Cyprian read it and showed it to none of the bishops,[4] and then called a council in which absolute silence was kept as to its existence; or that all these bishops had seen it, but all agreed not to mention it, but to deal instead with the anonymous correspondent whose letter Jubaianus had forwarded to Cyprian. They must have decided to ignore the main contention of St. Stephen's letter, and simply assert their determination to adhere to their own judgments, without saying one word as to the position in which they found themselves, of separation from 'the chair of Peter, the principal Church, whence episcopal unity took its rise,' and from those Romans 'to whom,' according to St. Cyprian, 'faithlessness could have no access.' But what council ever met to discuss a proposal or decision from another part of the Church, without dealing directly with the terms of the decision in question?

---

[1] 'Periculum perniciosae dissensionis habuerunt' (*De Bapt.* v. 25).
[2] 'Eadem quippe ipsa dicuntur, quae jam satis discussa sunt.'
[3] Compare *De Bapt.* v. 25 with v. 23.
[4] Pompeius asked for a copy of it; but he was absent from the council.

All, on the contrary, is perfectly clear on the supposition that the dissentient African bishops had shown their hands sufficiently to make it evident that they meant to adhere to the known custom of Rome, even without having received any definitive sentence in their favour, and that this was the cause of the synod. St. Cyprian, probably, in his enthusiasm, and the conviction that he was right, counted, as indeed he says,[1] on Rome taking the same ground as he and the greater part of his colleagues in Africa had assumed, viz. that all should be left to go on with their old customs; and thus he would be left free to bring the dissentients in Africa into harmony with his own practice. He may have thought that Rome would even adopt the 'better way' which had been revealed, as he deposed, to himself and others. But, anyhow, he must have counted upon the question being left sufficiently open to leave him free to do his best to produce uniformity in his own province. We cannot suppose that he was deliberately breaking the peace of the Church on a matter which he admitted to be amongst those on which a different line of action could be permitted. St. Augustine does, indeed, accuse him of unintentionally producing a rupture; but that is quite a different matter.[2]

The Council, then, opened with reading the correspondence between Jubaianus and Cyprian, and the letter which the latter had written to St. Stephen in the name of his colleagues. St. Cyprian then made the opening speech, saying that they had met to discuss the question raised in the correspondence between himself and Jubaianus, which, we must remember, included a letter written to the latter, arraigning the policy of Cyprian. He says further that each bishop is to say what he thinks, judging no one, nor removing anyone from the right of communion, if he holds a different opinion.[3]

It is difficult not to feel that St. Cyprian might very naturally be accused of unduly pressing the whole matter, and of using his great position for the purpose. His position in the Latin world was second only to that of the Bishop of Rome. But his was not an apostolic, much less *the* Apostolic See. He could appeal to no divine institution in regard to his

---

[1] *Ep.* lxxii. 3.   [2] *De Bapt.* v. 25.   [3] Mansi, t. i. p. 953.

see. His relationship to his bishops was not that of the Bishop of Rome towards the episcopate. To assume such a relationship on the part of any one bishop to any other in those parts would be the assumption of a *self-constituted* relationship. They had no right to such a position. In issuing an edict, therefore, they wished to be careful not to act as Tertullian, St. Cyprian's master, had, in his fallen days, accused Zephyrinus, the Pope, of doing, viz. 'I hear that an edict has been issued, and a *peremptory* one indeed, to wit, the Chief Pontiff, that is the bishop of bishops, proclaims, "I remit to those who have done penance the crimes," &c.; this is read in the Church, and openly announced in the Church.' ('De Pudic.' c. i.)[1]

They were not, says St. Cyprian, in Africa about to issue a general edict which would control the action of every other bishop. Although Cyprian was their Primate, he was not Pontifex Maximus of the Christian religion, and he did not mean to act as if he were. 'For no one of us constitutes himself bishop of bishops, or drives his own colleagues to the accepting of obedience by the terrorising of a tyrant, since it is open to every bishop to form his own judgment, in the free use of his liberty and power, and he can no more be judged by another than he can judge another. But let us one and all look for the judgment of our Lord Jesus Christ, who alone has the power by Himself both of setting us over (others) in the government of his Church, and of judging concerning our act.' St. Cyprian could not mean to say that a Marcian of Arles could not be judged by any bishop, nor a Privatus (cf. p. 67) be deposed from his see. He could not mean to put himself at variance with the whole practice of the Church in his own and after times. What he disavowed was obviously either the exercise of authority on a matter which he considered to be merely one of variable discipline, or the use of his primacy in a tyrannical way. His words contain no judgment as to whether anyone had been divinely constituted bishop of

---

[1] Whilst there is an obvious reference to Tertullian's words, there is no necessary reference to St. Stephen. We often say 'I will not act the Pope' without meaning to deny that there is someone who *is* entitled to act as Pope.

bishops. They merely remind the African bishops that no one of themselves held such a relationship.

'What,' says St. Augustine, 'can be more mild? What more humble?' And he elsewhere insists upon it that St. Cyprian meant what he said, and did not use these words of meekness merely to cajole [1] the bishops into speaking out their minds, with the view of afterwards bearing hardly upon them. No, the purpose of his speech was honestly to encourage them to say what they really thought, in spite of their Primate's presence. St. Augustine compares with these words what St. Cyprian said to Jubaianus and to Magnus, and says that it is apparent from these just quoted that smaller things were dealt with on which there had been no clear 'declaration,' but which 'being still unlocked were being sought for with great effort.' He considers himself to be in a different position from Cyprian, 'holding now the custom of the universal Church which is to be acknowledged on every side, and which has been confirmed by general councils.

The council decided that the custom of rebaptising those who had been baptised by heretics was the better way.[2]

[1] 'Securitate captaret' (*De Bapt.* vi. 7).
[2] The Bollandist Life of St. Cyprian (Fr. Suyskens, S. J.) takes the same view of St. Cyprian's use of the expression 'Bishop of bishops.'

CHAPTER VIII.

ROME'S DECISION AND CYPRIAN'S IRRITATION.

I. There are no means of deciding how long an interval elapsed between the dispatch of the letter to Stephen [1] and the papal decision in reply. Neither have we the reply itself. The actual decision was, it would seem, contained in one short sentence. That single sentence, however, is evidence sufficient, and more than sufficient, to justify the esteem in which St. Stephen was held by all antiquity, and in particular the epithet which St. Vincent of Lerins applies to that Pope in recording this passage of Church history. 'St. Stephen,' he says, was a man 'holy and prudent.'

Let us suppose for a moment that St. Stephen had been carried away by respect for St. Cyprian's great name in the Church. A false principle as to the sacrament of baptism, nay, as to the nature of more than one sacrament, would have spread like wildfire throughout the Church. It was a very natural deduction from the truth of the unity of the Church, and from a high esteem of the privileges and gifts of the Church, to suppose that these could not be conferred even in any germinant way, or dormant character, by those who were outside the visible fold. But it was a false inference, for it involved a wrong answer to the question as to whether the sacrament in its process of bestowal was wholly Christ's, or in fact, the gift of the instrument. So that the matter, although a question of discipline, really bordered upon the vitals of the faith. It had, however, not yet been elucidated in all its bearings. The Church, as she passed along the stream of time, was discovering more and more the meaning of her deposit of truth. But she entered into the full significance of her treasures through the gradual settlement of difficulties as

[1] Cf. *supra*, p. 88.

they emerged, one by one, and called for patient discussion and then final settlement. The full meaning of the 'character' of the initial sacrament of the Christian covenant was now entering upon a further stage. But it could not be weighed under all circumstances; and perchance the present were unfavourable to its calm investigation. There was no possibility of a general gathering of the Church's rulers; at any rate a few months hence, even if the Pope had thought of a wider council, a new fiery persecution set in, during which he was destined to win the martyr's crown.

What, then, did St. Stephen do? He laid down the ancient custom, and he forbade innovation upon it. He took the side of the dissentient African bishops. He indicated the dangerous nature of the new departure, and so far from allowing the practice, which had set in, to be one on which difference could be permitted, he thought that those who persisted in it must forfeit that ecclesiastical intercourse with the rest of the Christian Church which was the sign and seal of their being true to the one faith. 'Abstinendos putat,' said St. Cyprian—'he [Stephen] thinks they ought to be excommunicated.' St. Stephen reminded St. Cyprian that he was the successor of that Peter, of whom he had written so well in his treatise on Unity, on whom our Lord built his Church; that he occupied that chair of Peter of which St. Cyprian had once spoken so warmly, and was the head of that 'ruling Church whence sacerdotal unity took its rise.' He therefore put St. Cyprian on his obedience. He decided that: 'If any shall come to you from any heresy whatsoever, let there be no innovation but (let that be observed) which has been handed down—viz. that hands be laid on such in sign of penitence.'[1]

It will be noticed that in this decision the Pope avoided the language to which St. Cyprian demurs in his letter to Jubaianus. He does not say 'All, *howsoever* baptised'—for that might be taken to include an alteration of the form of baptism—but 'whatsoever heresy.' The point in dispute was as to whether those outside the unity of the Church could baptise. The adjudication of St. Stephen was that they

[1] Cf. Jungmann, *Diss. Hist.* iv. 76.

could, the use of the proper form being understood. So it was, as a matter of fact, always understood.

Thus St. Stephen refused to enter upon the dogmatic portion of the dispute, but simply laid down the line to be followed in practice. He issued no *ex cathedrâ* definition on the matter of faith, but directed the action of the Church. He decided that the new method of dealing with the baptism of heretics was closely allied to heretical notions concerning that sacrament, and therefore authoritatively forbade its continuance. He discountenanced St. Cyprian's programme of letting alone those who adopted a different method of discipline. It was a matter on which the Church ought to be at one. So much so that he was obliged to tell our saint that he should no longer be able to hold communion with him if he persisted in his present course.

As the successor of that Apostle on whom our Lord had built His Church, he felt compelled to insist on conformity in Africa to the custom followed in Rome, which, as St. Augustine more than once asserts, had come down from the Apostles themselves.

There was one point of view from which St. Cyprian's action was less dangerous than if the truth had lain the other way. He was rebaptising those who did not need it. Had he been omitting to baptise some who needed it, the case would have been one for insisting on immediate obedience; but as it was, he only did what involved no loss to others. This action, however, might lead to false views concerning the validity of the sacrament, and, indeed, was based on such false views; and, as a matter of fact, part of St. Augustine's life had to be spent in refuting St. Cyprian's arguments, and wresting his authority from the lips of the Donatists. St. Augustine, however, was able to insist upon St. Cyprian's example as of more account than his unfortunate arguments against the validity of baptism by heretics. He would not break away from the Church. This was, to St. Augustine, the virtue of virtues in St. Cyprian's life. There was a stain in that life which he knew his glorious martyrdom had washed away;[1] but there was one grand

---

[1] *Ep.* xciii.

grace exhibited, the grace of charity which held him within the unity of the Church when he might have headed a schism, and had indeed every temptation to inaugurate an independent national Church.

II. On receiving St. Stephen's decision, St. Cyprian seems to have immediately sent off legates to Rome with the hope of inducing the Pope to change his mind. But in vain. Nothing, indeed, could have been more inopportune than the appearance of these African bishops in the Eternal City just at that moment. The Pope was in the midst of trouble from the Novatians, and the Novatians had begun to rebaptise those whom they allured from the Catholic Church. These African bishops would find themselves at one with those pestilent heretics, and the great name of Cyprian would add to the confusion. St. Stephen determined that the Africans should not stay in Rome a single night. They were bidden to depart home at once. And judging from the number of events which crowd themselves into [1] these few months, they must have left Rome immediately. The matter was not one on which St. Stephen was prepared to receive a mission, and, if we may trust what Firmilian says on the subject, Catholics were forbidden to shelter the legates a single night. If, indeed, as is almost certain, St. Stephen knew of the third Council of Carthage, held, as that was, either with the knowledge of his decision or, as is more probable, in view of what they knew to be the practice at Rome, he was fully justified in taking decisive measures to prevent resistance spreading. Anyhow, he would not admit them to conference ; there was, indeed, no necessity, seeing that they did not come by appointment.

III. These African legates, therefore, returned home, and a messenger was immediately dispatched to the East. St. Cyprian knew that he had sympathisers there, and would fain take counsel with those who had already entered upon a somewhat similar career. He wrote and told Firmilian, the great Bishop of Cæsarea, in Cappadocia, that St. Stephen— to quote the words he used to another bishop (Pompeius)—

---

[1] Cf. Dom. Maran. *De Vita Cypriani*, and Tillemont's admission that everything must have been done with the utmost speed, *infra*, p. 100.

H

'thinks that priests of God, defending the truth of Christ and the unity of the Church, are to be excommunicated.' We may take it for granted that Firmilian had not been actually excommunicated, for it would have been contrary to all St. Cyprian's previous teaching to have sought help from him if he had. Let alone any deference to the See of Rome as the chair of Peter, she was on any view of the matter the mother-Church of Africa, so much so that St. Augustine expressed his conviction that it was impossible to find an instance in which Eastern bishops communicated with African bishops except through Rome. But Firmilian was now, or at any rate had been but recently, engaged in the same discussion, and accordingly St. Cyprian turned to him to see if together they could induce the Pope to reconsider his decision. Mere messages of sympathy would be out of the question with such earnest souls; the question was, what was to be done?

But before we consider Firmilian's answer, it will be well to recollect the only indication of St. Cyprian's mind which we have from his own pen. He wrote about this time to a bishop, who was not present at the Council of Carthage, but who had asked to see St. Stephen's letter. St. Cyprian, judging from the ending of his reply, sent him the decision of the council, at which we know from the Acts this bishop had himself voted by proxy, and at the same time poured out in the bitterness of his soul what he thought of the Pope's letter. St. Augustine, whilst refuting one or two statements of this letter of Cyprian's, refuses to go further, on the ground that he had already dealt with similar statements, and that it would be better to pass by the rest, as it had in it 'the danger of pernicious dissent.' One would gladly do the same,[1] but as the letter has been dragged into the question of St. Cyprian's allegiance to Rome, one is forced to produce its statements in some fulness. It must be premised that we do not possess St. Stephen's letter itself, and that St. Augustine, with all his great love for St. Cyprian, speaks of this letter as bearing the marks of irritation.

[1] St. Vincent of Lerins compares the Donatists' action in bringing forward St. Cyprian so prominently in this matter to that of Ham towards his father.

St. Cyprian then, in this letter to Pompeius,[1] speaks of St. Stephen's error as that of 'upholding the cause of heretics against Christians and against the Church of God'—of things in the Pope's letter as 'arrogant, beside the purpose, or self-contradictory,' 'written without due instruction and caution.' He says that St. Stephen 'communicating with the baptism of all has heaped up the sins of all in one mass into his own bosom,' and that he, 'forgetful of unity, adopts the deceitful defilements of a profane immersion.' After using arguments which St. Augustine has shown to be fallacious, he pursues his declaration against the Pope thus: 'Does he give glory to God who communicates with the baptism of Marcion? Does he give glory to God who judges that remission of sins is given by those who blaspheme God? ... Does he give glory to God who, the friend of heretics and enemy to Christians, thinks that priests of God, defending the truth of Christ and the unity of the Church, are to be excommunicated? ... let us cast aside our arms, let us yield ourselves captives, let us deliver over to the devil the ordering of the Gospel, the appointments of Christ, the majesty of God: be the sacramental oaths of our divine warfare loosed, the ensigns of the heavenly camp abandoned; let the Church bow down and give way to heretics, light to darkness, faith to faithlessness, hope to despair, reason to error, immortality to death, charity to hatred, truth to falsehood, Christ to Antichrist.' All this, and a great deal more, which he proceeds to describe with his own fervid eloquence, was to happen if the baptism by heretics was not disallowed. All this would happen if the practice followed on all sides in this country at this day, by every considerable religious body in existence, is to be countenanced! We are all of us against Cyprian in this matter, and yet, according to Cyprian, 'if the fear of God abides with us, if regard to the faith prevail, if we keep the precepts of Christ, if we maintain the sanctity of His spouse incorrupt and inviolate, if the words of the Lord cleave to our thoughts and hearts,' &c., we shall reverse our practice, and the Roman

---

[1] *Ep.* lxxiv.

Catholic will rebaptise the Anglican,[1] and the Anglican will rebaptise the Roman, and each will rebaptise the Wesleyan, and we shall generally deny to one another the name of Christian.

IV. All this, however, is nothing compared with what Firmilian poured forth in answer to St. Cyprian. Dr. Döllinger thus describes the two letters:—' We are acquainted with the sentence of the Pontiff only through fragments which have been preserved by St. Cyprian and Firmilian: by the first in his severe and harsh letter to Pompeius, and by the second in his bitter and passionate answer to St. Stephen, addressed to St. Cyprian. Both endeavour to place the opinions of the Pope in the most unfavourable light.'[2]

It has been argued, with much force, by the Benedictine editor of St. Cyprian (Migne's edition), that the legates must have been sent to Rome after the *second* council held at Carthage on the subject of baptism, because from this letter of Firmilian's we find that St. Cyprian's messengers were to return to Africa before the winter. If they left Africa after the third council, the legates would have had within a few months to journey to Rome, and thence back to St. Cyprian, and St. Cyprian's messenger (Rogatian) must have left Cappadocia at once and returned to Africa before the winter had set in. Tillemont admits the difficulties of this supposition, but maintains that it was, nevertheless, possible. The Bollandist writer of St. Cyprian's Life agrees with Tillemont, as also does Hefele. We have, indeed, only to suppose that the legates, *as soon as* they set foot in Rome, were told that their errand was a hopeless one, and induced to return *at once*, and that the deacon sent by Cyprian, on their return to Cappadocia, was detained by Firmilian the *shortest possible time* consistent with the bishop being able to put pen to paper and write off a reply. This will probably account for much of the peculiar character of that letter. Twice does Firmilian speak of being pressed for time. Rogatianus, the deacon, was waiting—' Your messenger was in haste to return to you, and the

---

[1] As a matter of fact, where the right matter and form has been certainly used, this is never done.

[2] *Geschichte*, Periode I. § 29, p. 304: ' mit Bitterkeit und Leidenschaft.' Firmilian's letter is found amongst St. Cyprian's, *Ep.* lxxv.

winter season was close at hand.' Firmilian must have read St. Cyprian's letter again and again with a certain feverish haste, and even (he says) 'committed it to memory.' He seems to have at length reached the boiling-point, and as the fire kindled, he poured forth a burning stream of indignant rhetoric against Stephen, which has hardly its equal in ecclesiastical literature for nervous eloquence, passionate indignation, and bitter invective.

He opens with expressing his joy at finding the blessing of concord with his correspondent, and says that for this experience of unity with the African Primate he has to thank Stephen, although, he adds, the Pope has not thereby done a good work any more than did Judas, who was an instrument of the blessings of the Passion. After a beautiful passage on unity, he excuses himself for repeating the same things as Cyprian has said, whilst he adds some things by way of accumulating proof, and he regrets that he has been unable to consult his annual synod.

He then attacks what St. Stephen is supposed to have said; he denies that the Apostles could have admitted those who had been baptised by heretics without rebaptising them, because there were no sufficiently execrable heretics to baptise—a version of history of which St. Cyprian could not have approved. He then says that Stephen, unlike his predecessors in such matters as the observance of Easter, has now made the first 'departure from the peace and unity of the Catholic Church . . . breaking this peace with you . . . defaming the blessed Apostles Peter and Paul, as if they had handed this down'—the tradition is therefore human. He then protests against following heretics (as if St. Stephen meant this, when he quoted their custom to show the ancient tradition of the Church), and deposes that 'a heretic cannot lawfully' (he means validly, or else he misrepresents St. Stephen) 'ordain, or lay on hands, neither can he baptise or do any spiritual act.'

He then attacks St. Stephen for maintaining what he never did—viz. that remission of sins can follow from the baptism of heretics simply,[1] and scouts the idea that any

---

[1] The remission of sin followed upon conversion—the baptism then taking effect, and issuing in sanctification.

reasonable person would either maintain or believe 'that this mere invocation of the names would suffice for the remission of sins and the sanctification of baptism' (showing that he missed the point of the Church's doctrine in the matter), and then gives an instance in which it would be absurd to suppose this. He next emphasises the unity of the Spouse of Christ, and says that 'the synagogue of heretics is not one with us, because neither is the spouse an adulteress and a harlot. Wherefore neither can she bring forth the sons of God, unless, indeed, as Stephen seems to think, heresy brings them forth and exposes them, but the Church takes them up when exposed, and nourishes as her own whom she did not bring forth.' His misunderstanding of the teaching of St. Stephen is here again complete.

He then enters upon the subject of Apostolic Succession. 'Christ said to Peter alone, "Whatsoever thou shalt bind," &c., and again in the Gospels, when Christ breathed on the Apostles only, saying, "Receive ye the Holy Ghost; whosoever sins ye remit," &c. The power then of remitting sins was given to the Apostles and to the Churches which they, sent by Christ, established, and to the bishops who succeeded them by vicarious ordination.' And then follows a passage of supreme importance as regards the Petrine prerogatives of the Bishop of Rome. 'Herein,' says Firmilian, 'I am justly indignant at such open and manifest folly in Stephen, that he who thus [1] boasts of the seat of his episcopate, and contends that he holds the succession from Peter, on whom the foundations of the Church were laid, *introduces many other rocks*, and establishes new edifices of many Churches [*i.e.* admits the reality of many new Churches] whilst he defends, by his authority [the position] that baptism is there'—amongst them. 'For those who are baptised, without doubt, fill up the number of the Church.'

One cannot but pause here to notice two things. First, the piteous misunderstanding of the teaching of St. Stephen into which Firmilian had fallen, which, nevertheless, has its

---

[1] 'Thus' (*sic*), not 'so,' as in *Primitive Saints*, p. 84. 'So' introduces the idea of excessive, unjustifiable boasting, which is not necessarily contained in the adverb 'thus.'

bright side, for if¹ this had been the teaching of Rome, he would have been justified in opposing it. Secondly, the tremendous witness which Firmilian's words bear to the recognised position of the Bishop of Rome. Firmilian is not indignant that St. Stephen put forth with such prominence his position as the successor of Peter. He has no expressions of astonishment at this, as though it were a new claim. And yet it is inconceivable that he should not have exclaimed against the presumption of such a claim had it been unwarranted or new. No, Firmilian is only indignant that he, in the very moment and act in which he realises and places in prominence his relationship to Peter, should be making *other* rocks, by admitting the validity of heretical baptism. He goes on to argue that the successor of Peter himself 'in a manner effaces the truth of the Christian *rock*.' In fact he effaces himself. In this he is worse, says Firmilian, than the Jews. They had a 'zeal for God;' Stephen has none at the very moment when he (truly enough ²) proclaims that he occupies by succession the chair of Peter, 'for he concedes to them the greatest of all graces.' He might just as well go on 'to join their assemblies and mingle his prayers with them and set up a common altar and sacrifice (§ 18).

He then deals with the argument from custom, and says that the Jews clung to their old custom when Christ came, 'disregarding the new way of truth.' Firmilian, like St. Cyprian, at one moment depreciates custom, at another claims it in his own behalf.

And now his passionate indignation altogether gets the better of him. His words, beginning with the mention of Stephen in the third person, suddenly burst into an apostrophe: 'When thou communicatest with the baptism of heretics, what else dost thou but drink of their mire and mud, and, after having been cleansed with the sanctification of the Church, becomest defiled with the contagion of others' filth?

---

¹ See p. 79 for the real state of the matter.

² I have inserted these words mainly as a balance against the unjustifiable assumption made by some that Firmilian is condemning St. Stephen's claim. He does not say this: his words by themselves pass by the question of the justice of the claim, but they presuppose it.

.... Yea, thou art worse than all heretics ... thou abettest their errors ... and increasest the darkness of the night of heresy. And whereas they confess that they are in sin and have no grace, and therefore come to the Church, thou withdrawest from them the remission of sins which is given in baptism, in that thou sayest that they have been already baptised and, outside the Church, have obtained the grace of the Church' (again the same misunderstanding as to the teaching of Rome), 'nor dost thou consider that their souls will be required at your hand when the Day of Judgment shall come, who deniedst to those atheists the drink of the Church; and to such as long to live thou wast the cause of death. And withal thou art indignant! See with what ignorance[1] thou dost dare to blame those who contend for the truth against falsehood; ... it is plain that the ignorant are vehement and given to anger, whilst through poverty of counsel and argument they are easily moved to wrath, so that the Holy Scripture *says of no one more than thee*, "An excited man provokes[2] strifes, and an angry man heaps up sins" (Prov. xxix. 22). For what great strifes and dissensions hast thou provoked through the Churches of the whole world! What a great sin didst thou heap upon thyself when thou didst cut thyself off[3] from so many flocks! For thou hast cut thyself off. Do not deceive thyself, since he is truly schismatic who has made himself an apostate from the communion of ecclesiastical unity: for whilst thou dost think that all may be excommunicated from thee, thou hast excommunicated thyself alone from all. ... What can be more *lowly* and *meek* than to have disagreed with so many bishops throughout the world, breaking peace with them each by varying kinds of discord—now with the Easterns (which we feel confident you [in Africa] are aware of), now with yourselves, who are in the South; from whom he received episcopal legates with patience and meekness enough, so that he did not even admit them to a hearing[4]—nay, further, so that,

---

[1] 'Imperitia.'   [2] 'Parat.' Some editions have 'parit.'

[3] By taking the line of condemning the new practice—'dum enim putas omnes a te abstineri posse, solum te ab omnibus abstinuisti.' It is 'posse.' It obviously refers, not to power in any, but in this, case.

[4] 'Sermonem colloquii communis.'

mindful of love and charity, he instructed the whole brotherhood not any one of them to receive them into his house, so that on their coming there, not only peace and communion, but roof and hospitality should be denied them? This is to have kept the unity of the Spirit in the bond of peace, to cut himself off from the unity of charity, and to make himself in all things strange to the brethren, and to rebel against the sacrament and the faith with the fury of contumacious discord. With such an one, can there be one body and one spirit, with whom, perchance, there is not one soul, so slippery is it, so shifting, so uncertain?'

Here at length Firmilian comes to anchor. He proposes to return to the 'greater question.' But he can only restrain himself for a few sentences. For he winds up with saying, 'And yet Stephen is not ashamed to give support to such against the Church, and for the sake of upholding heretics to divide the brotherhood; nor, further, to call Cyprian a false Christ, a false Apostle, a deceitful worker. He [*i.e.* Stephen], conscious that all these marks are in himself, was beforehand, so as lyingly to object to another what he was himself deserving to be called.'

This unique specimen of correspondence closes with using the plural, as though it were the opinion of several bishops.[1]

V. The question occurs as to how far this extraordinary letter, with its misinterpretations and obvious exaggerations, can be held to prove that St. Stephen issued a formal sentence of excommunication against St. Cyprian.

It is necessary to repeat,[2] that excommunication is a wide term, including that suspension of ecclesiastical intercourse between various portions of the Church which did not mean that either of them considered the other to be in schism. If

---

[1] I have never been able to discover on what grounds the assertion is often made that St. Cyprian published this letter himself. The mere fact of its having been ultimately bound up in the collections of St. Cyprian's letters proves nothing, for those collections were subsequent to his time. Indeed, the supposition that he translated it himself into Latin (we do not possess the original) is mere conjecture. Fr. Suyskens (S. J.), the author of the Bollandist Life, does not believe that he did. The matter has not received its final settlement.

[2] P. 41.

at any time during the strife between Rome and Africa, the question had been asked at Rome, 'Which is the legitimate Bishop of Carthage, Cyprian or Fortunatus?' there can be no doubt that the answer would have been, 'There is only one Bishop of Carthage, and that is Cyprian.' It is necessary to mention this, because the Cyprianic struggle has been pressed into the service of a theory which regards communion with Rome as a matter of perfect indifference in determining the schismatic position of a religious body.[1] But it is one thing to be so separated from the chair of Peter as that another bishop could be placed by Rome in the same city as its true and legitimate bishop; it is another thing to be only so far out of communion as that ecclesiastical intercourse is suspended. In these days of quick intercourse, when we can confer together by the flash of wire, or at any rate by the rapidity of the rail, the same state of things could not arise as in the times of Cyprian. It is the part of the inspector, in determining the alleged identity of a stream with a certain source, to examine into the elements of which the two are composed, and to decide upon the existence or non-existence of the same essential ingredients in each. So with the question of the identity alleged to exist between the Rome of to-day and the recognition of her position on the one hand, and on the other hand the Rome of St. Cyprian's time, and her relationship to the rest of the Church under the very dissimilar circumstances of the third century. Could the Church, as we observe her in action in that century, have developed into a heap of *independent* National Churches with no sort of intercourse without parting with principles then deemed essential? The answer that has been given is, that 'if St. Cyprian and St. Firmilian were really excommunicated, and if they nevertheless refused to alter either the teaching or the practice condemned by Rome, then it is clear that neither of these saints nor their colleagues in Africa and Asia Minor could have considered that communion with the Pope was an essential matter.'[2] In other words there can be independent National Churches.

---

[1] Cf. *The Primitive Saints and the See of Rome*, ch. ii.
[2] *Ibid.* p. 325.

It is natural, in answer to this position, to ask why both St. Cyprian and Firmilian were so disturbed, if their communion with Rome was not essential?

But the full answer is, first, that the evidence for the excommunication of St. Cyprian and Firmilian *in the fullest sense of the term* is not (to say the least) plain. Baronius and Mansi think that the excommunication was carried out, but it is not clear what measure of separation they understand by the term. They have not, however, been followed by Catholic writers in general. Pagius, Natalis Alexander, the Bollandists, Hefele, Döllinger, Freppel and Jungmann, to mention no others, do not consider that the evidence at our disposal is sufficient to justify us in saying that the excommunication was actually carried out. The only direct evidence is Firmilian's letter. But a letter so full of misrepresentations, and of bitter invective, is (to say the least) not above suspicion as evidence on such a point. Firmilian made out that all the world was against St. Stephen: St. Augustine, with greater truth, spoke of Firmilian and his sympathisers as a handful compared with the bishops who held with Stephen. It would be in perfect keeping with the rest of the letter of Firmilian if, on learning from St. Cyprian that the Pope contemplated excommunicating those who *persisted in* maintaining their custom, he proceeded to picture the excommunication as actual, and forthwith declared that this would be tantamount to cutting *himself* off, and leaving himself without any in the Church to symbolise with him; only in his rhetorical and passionate way of speaking he said, 'By doing this, you *have* cut yourself off and stand alone.' Of course it was ridiculously untrue to say that St. Stephen had been disagreeing with so many bishops '*throughout the whole world*, breaking peace with them *severally* in *various* modes of discord;' but the expression need not be pressed, occurring as it does in such a letter, any more than the assertion that the Pope wished to excommunicate 'all' should be pressed.

And St. Dionysius' words referring to St. Stephen's previous communication with Firmilian himself, viz. 'he wrote as not about to communicate with them either,' cannot fairly be pressed as necessarily meaning more than that he was not going to communicate with them if they persisted in their own line. Certainly, Firmilian nowhere drops a hint that he and his colleagues were under actual excommunication. His wrath is reserved for the Pope's condemnation of St. Cyprian. He never says, 'We are in the same case: he has excommunicated us.' And yet it is inconceivable that he should not have said so, if it was the fact. Nor can it be successfully maintained that the case of Firmilian and his colleagues was on all fours with that of St. Cyprian and the African bishops, in the absence of all records on the subject. Although their case was the same in substance, it does not follow that it was the same in detail. The same sentence was passed on what they did; but not necessarily the same on those who did it.

On the other hand, St. Augustine's testimony is definite and emphatic, to the effect that the peace in all essentials was kept between St. Stephen and St. Cyprian.[1] This is the point of his argument against the Donatists, viz. that St. Cyprian was, indeed, wrong in his teaching, but that he kept in communion with the Pope. Again and again he lays stress on this. He enlarges upon it in some of the most beautiful passages of his many writings against the Donatists, who claimed St. Cyprian for their patron saint. Now it is not reasonable to suppose that St. Augustine was mistaken on this point. It was the tradition of the African Church on the subject. No Donatist replied that St. Augustine was mistaken in his facts, as some one must have done, since it is not in one work alone that St. Augustine elaborates his point. So that the whole African Church in the following century was unaware of any such rupture having taken place between St. Stephen and St. Cyprian as is implied in the stricter sense of the term excommunication. It would be in vain to reply that St. Augustine had not seen Firmilian's letter; for had complete excommunication taken place it must, *apart from that letter*, have left a sufficient impression on the African

---

[1] *Lib. De Bapt. c. Donat.* passim. In one passage St. Augustine notices the tremendous effect which a secession on the part of St. Cyprian would have had. 'If he had separated himself, how many would follow! What a name he would have made for himself amongst men! . . . but he was not a "son of perdition"' (lib. i. c. 18).

Church for St. Augustine to be unable to take it as certain that these two saints did not proceed to complete rupture.

It is, however, most probable that St. Augustine had seen Firmilian's letter. He had no call to refer to it directly, for he was engaged in dealing with Cyprian's authority alone; and it is not possible that such a savage production would commend itself to his sweet and gentle disposition. But some words addressed to the Donatist Cresconius seem to imply that he was at least aware of its existence;[1] and it is to the last degree improbable that, knowing its existence, he should not have been aware of its contents. This at least seems certain, viz. that the Donatists knew of its existence; and yet, to judge from a later work of St. Augustine's, in which he repeats his argument from St. Cyprian's remaining in peace with St. Stephen, the Donatists did not feel that anything in Firmilian's letter justified them in objecting to St. Augustine's assertion that the peace remained practically unbroken between the Pope and St. Cyprian. In his third book against Cresconius, he says, 'Whatever you have thought ought to be brought in from the letters of Cyprian and those of certain Easterns, that they decided against the sacrament of baptism given amongst heretics and schismatics, in no way hinders our cause, if we keep to that Church which Cyprian did not desert, although many of his colleagues would not consent to this judgment' (against the baptism of heretics).

St. Augustine shows himself, in the following sections, thoroughly conversant with what the Easterns had written on the subject.[2] It is, therefore, but reasonable to conclude that he was fully aware of the contents of Firmilian's letter, indeed of the whole history of the matter. He speaks, indeed, of

---

[1] Dr. Pusey, in his note to *Lib. of the Fathers, Cyprian's Epistles*, vol. ii., says that Firmilian's letter 'is probably alluded to by St. Augustine, *C. Cresc.* iii. 1 (as the Benedictine Edd. also think), "whatever," &c., and *De Unit. Bapt. c. Petil.* c. 14. St. Augustine probably did not notice it further because the Donatists relied on the authority of St. Cyprian, not of an Eastern bishop' p. 269).

[2] He speaks of 'letters,' not merely one letter, as is implied in *Prim. Saints*, p. 332, n. 6. The plural includes St. Cyprian's, but does not limit the Easterns to one.

some letters not having come into his possession, but that is not in reference to this particular branch of the subject.

St. Augustine's evidence, therefore, to the effect that the rupture between St. Stephen and St. Cyprian was anything but complete (that it certainly did not include any actual excommunication), includes the evidence of the Donatists, and indeed gives the tradition of the African Church generally; and his judgment seems to have been formed with a full knowledge of what took place between Firmilian and his colleagues on the same subject.

It may be asked whether Firmilian's statement about the episcopal legates is not to be taken as true, and whether, if it be true, it does not furnish a proof that St. Cyprian was excommunicated.

To which it must be answered, first, that there would be nothing surprising if there were some exaggeration in Firmilian's description of the legates' reception, considering the character of the letter as a whole. But, secondly, the reception accorded to the legates, supposing that Firmilian's words are to be taken *au pied de la lettre*, would not prove excommunication. On another occasion legates were sent away from Rome (by Hormisdas the Pope), not, as was afterwards thought and stated, because they, or those from whom they came, were considered excommunicate, but because their presence there was certain to lead to trouble. What has happened once may happen twice, and we have seen good reason for supposing that the presence in Rome of legates on so hopeless an errand as that of these African prelates was particularly inopportune at that moment. So that all we can argue from their being sent back is that St. Stephen was not prepared to argue the question, but decided to deal with this Legatine mission most peremptorily. It would show St. Cyprian that he really meant what he said. St. Augustine's testimony to the preservation of peace in essential matters between Stephen and Cyprian, in spite of what he calls the 'brotherly altercation,' in which Cyprian was unduly excited (*commotius*), is of greater weight than the incident described by Firmilian.[1]

[1] The student of history needs to be warned against Tillemont's article on

On the whole, then, there is, to say the least, not sufficient ground for asserting that things ever proceeded beyond a threat of excommunication. It is not necessary to accuse Firmilian of deliberate falsehood. There is a great difference between telling a falsehood and indulging in exaggeration. This latter Firmilian certainly did when he spoke of Stephen standing alone, and of the strife extending to the Churches of the 'whole world;' and the statement of a writer who can call the Pope 'worse than all heretics,' when, as a matter of fact, that Pope was guarding an Apostolical tradition, is not a safe foundation on which to build a theory of Church government.[1]

VI. But, after all, the second clause of the sentence quoted above[2] is the more important, viz. 'if they [*i.e.* St. Cyprian and Firmilian] refused to alter either the teaching or the practice condemned at Rome.'

This writer assumes that they did refuse. The historical record, so far as it goes, is all against him. St. Augustine expressly says that the Easterns altered their teaching. He blames the Donatists for separating themselves from them in consequence.[3] He says of the Easterns that 'they rescinded their judgment, by which they had decided that it was right to agree with Cyprian and that African council.' He then insists upon using the word 'corrected' in opposition to the Donatists: these Easterns (he says) 'corrected' their judgment, although we know from the Council of Arles that some persisted in their erroneous custom. And St. Jerome tells us

---

St. Cyprian. He is by no means trustworthy. He says that St. Augustine would have changed his opinion if he had read Eusebius. Now, we know from St. Augustine himself that he had read Rufinus' paraphrase of Eusebius. And that translation or paraphrase is stronger on this point than Eusebius himself. Eusebius says only that Stephen 'bore it very ill,' or was very much displeased with Cyprian's resistance. Rufinus says that Stephen thought that 'neither were they to be communicated with who rebaptise.' St. Augustine did not consider that Rufinus' heightened translation justified him in concluding an actual 'excommunicatio major.' Therefore Eusebius's milder term would not have led him to such a conclusion (Cf. *Bolland. Series*, Aug. 2, § 4).

[1] Mr. Puller's accusation (*Prim. SS.* p. 327) against the writer of these pages is based on a misrepresentation. Nothing is said about the African legates in *Authority*—the passage quoted refers to Stephen's standing alone.

[2] P. 106. [3] *C. Cresc.* lib. iii. cap. 3.

that the African bishops themselves 'issued a new decree.' They too corrected their judgments. What St. Cyprian himself did, whether he led the way (as is probable) in the direction of submission, the records do not say.[1] And it is in reference to this and not to the former incidents that St. Augustine speaks of some documents having perished. He thinks it 'suitable' (*i.e.* reasonable) to suppose that St. Cyprian himself corrected his error; but supposes that the records of this may have been destroyed by the Donatists. If he did not correct his error, then, says St. Augustine, there was his martyrdom, endured within the unity of the Church, which he had the grace not to leave; and his suffering would have washed away whatever was faulty in his conduct in this matter. St. Augustine, with the most tender humility, says that he deemed it better to pass over those things which Cyprian poured out in irritation against Stephen ('ea præterire melius ').[2]

The whole matter is admirably summed up by a saint who has a special right to speak on such a subject.

St. Vincent of Lerins,[3] the author of the golden rule that when there has been no authoritative decision on a subject of debate the faithful should see what has been held 'by all, everywhere, and always,' writing in the next century, thus describes the part played by the Pope in this whole matter.

---

[1] St. Augustine distinctly says that St. Cyprian not only tolerated others, but 'was himself tolerated' (*et ipse toleratus est*) (*De Bapt.* iv. 9). This must refer to a time subsequent to the third council. He also says that St. Cyprian 'remained in unity with him'—*i.e.* Stephen—which implies that there was reconciliation. St. Augustine thinks that St. Cyprian might easily have yielded even to 'one uttering the truth' (*i.e.* Stephen), 'which perhaps took place' (*De Bapt.* ii. 5).

[2] St. Augustine considers only three solutions possible: (1) that Cyprian did not say all that he is quoted as having said, since the Donatists were fond of forging documents; or (2) St. Cyprian 'afterwards corrected this in unison with the rule of truth;' or (3) his great perseverance (*perseverantissime tenuit*) in clinging to the unity of the Church covered this blot. Besides, he says 'there is this, that, as a most fruitful bough, the Father purged away whatever there was in him to be blotted out by the sickle of his passion'—*i.e.* his 'martyrdom' (*Ep.* xciii. *ad Vincent.*).

[3] There is something very surprising that a book which is entitled *The Primitive Saints and the See of Rome* should not contain one solitary reference to St. Vincent of Lerins, who has yet generally been considered (though wrongly) the patron saint of the Anglican theory of universal consent.

'When therefore they all from every side cried out against the novelty of the thing' (*i.e.* rebaptising those who had received their baptism from heretics) 'and all the bishops all round began to resist it each according to his own zeal, then Pope Stephen, Prelate of the Apostolic See, together with his colleagues, but beyond the rest, withstood [the novelty], thinking, as I presume, that it would be proper if he excelled all the rest in devotion of faith as much as he surpassed them in authority of place.' And 'what then was the upshot of the whole business? What but the usual and customary issue? Antiquity was retained, novelty exploded.'[1]

This happy conclusion seems to have been reached under the successors of St. Stephen.[2] The contest was abruptly terminated by the storm of persecution which soon broke over the Church. In a few months' time St. Stephen won his martyr's crown. He has been reckoned a saint both by the East and West.[3] He is described as a 'holy and prudent man' by St. Vincent of Lerins; and St. Augustine was able to challenge the Donatists to find a flaw in his episcopate.[4] Almighty God set His seal on his sanctity by permitting miraculous effects to follow from his remains, which now lie in the church of San Silvestro in Capite in the Eternal City, a church which has been granted for the special use of our Catholic fellow-countrymen. Of what passed during the first few months of the year in which St. Stephen attained to his reward we have no record.[5] But we know that St. Cyprian

---

[1] Vinc. Ler. *Commonit.* c. 9.

[2] Mansi, however, who is appealed to as a kind of oracle in *Prim. Saints*, p. 328, considers it *possible* that this took place in St. Stephen's lifetime. He considers Natalis Alexander more cogent in this matter than would appear from the passage quoted by Mr. Puller.

[3] In the Greek Church he was invoked as a martyr on the same day as in the West, but also on the following day, or on Aug. 30 or Sept. 7. In a very ancient Constantinopolitan codex he is spoken of as 'the holy, sacred martyr Stephen, Pope of Rome.' His name occurs in the Menology of the Emperor Basil (cf. *Boll. Ser.* Aug. 2). It is to be regretted that the author of *The Primitive Saints and the See of Rome* should have deprived of his crown one who wears it with such good credentials.

[4] 'Episcopatum illibatum.'

[5] Some writers consider that St. Dionysius' efforts for peace were then made and were successful. They must have been made under great difficulties, for the Bishop of Rome seems to have been under persecution for some months.

was in full ecclesiastical intercourse with his successor; and since both Eastern and African bishops dropped their novel custom and their resistance to the decision of Rome, we may assume that St. Cyprian did the same.

VII. But why did not St. Stephen issue an *ex cathedrâ* decision on the matter of faith, and so end the contest? It will be better to discuss this question more at large when we come to consider the Council of Nicæa. Meanwhile it may be enough to reply that possibly St. Stephen did not feel that he had at his disposal those means to which the promise of divine 'assistance' has been made according to the Vatican decree. Infallibility is not the power of stepping forward at any moment and settling a question; it is only the security of divine 'assistance' when the successor of St. Peter is led to define. He does not bear definitions within his head at all times, ready to flash out at a moment's notice; their possibility and their materials lie in the circumstances of the Church. St. Stephen felt that his duty lay in securing the prevalence of the right practice; in upholding the merciful view which he did; in risking for this purpose the attachment of a great bishop, the Primate of Africa, to the unity of the Church. He probably knew that the attachment of a Cyprian to the Catholic Church would stand the strain, as it did; and he could leave it for others to elucidate the difficult questions which had arisen, and which were solved by the general life of the Church. The great Archbishop of Alexandria, St. Dionysius, wrote to St. Stephen's successor for guidance on this very subject, alleging as his reason for writing his wish *not to go wrong*.[1] He thus testified to the confidence which was felt in the guidance of the Holy See, which, indeed, had now piloted the Church through a storm more terrible than that of persecution. It secured a mode of discipline which nearly affected the very idea of a sacrament, and it left the full elucidation of the matter to the thought of the episcopate in general. Papal infallibility has its purposes in God's gracious mercy; but it is not a *deus ex machinâ* under all circumstances. The present Archbishop of Canterbury has noticed, and I fear I must say a little exaggerated, the odds against

---

[1] Eus. *H. E.* vii. 9.

which St. Stephen had to contend, and, whilst considering that Cyprian was not actually excommunicated, attributes the victory of Stephen to the justice of his cause.[1] But we may see more than that. His action must have unconsciously impressed upon the Church the trust that she could place in her God-given pilot. Not that she could have stated the infallibility of the Pope in the terms of the Vatican decree, but that her belief in it was there, amidst the mass of her convictions, mixed up with her general sense of the authority of the successor of Peter. It was not yet separated off and made to live before her consciousness in distinct and clear outline; for the Church does not live by theological definitions, however much she needs them in view of emergent error. St. Cyprian fought against a particular exercise of authority, not the authority in principle; but for aught we know he ended by recognising the security of its shelter even in this matter. His can hardly be a test case, because history deserts us at the critical point. But we may believe that ere he won his crown he may have entered more fully into the meaning of our Lord's words, 'I am with you all days,' as he contemplated the faith of the Romans, and the power of 'the chair of Peter and the sovereign Church, whence episcopal unity took its rise,' to bind together the Church in unity of faith, even though it involved at times the severity of a father's love.

Bishop Freppel thus sums the matter up from a controversial point of view. A discussion arises in Asia Minor and Africa on a point of discipline, in regard to which both of the parties equally appeal to ancient custom. The question is new, and touches, on the one hand, the notion of the Church; on the other, the general theory of the sacraments. Two great bishops resolve it in an erroneous sense; around them people adhere to their opinion; they possess the prestige of knowledge and sanctity. Further, it must be said, their solution of the question has something in it to dazzle men's minds: at first sight it seems to safeguard Catholic unity, because it traces a deeper line of demarcation between heresies and the Church. Well, it needs only a few lines from the pen

[1] *Dict. of Chr. Biogr.* (Smith and Wace), art. 'Cyprian.'

of the Pope to overthrow all that scaffolding of texts and syllogisms. The partisans of innovation may resist as they please, write letter after letter, assemble councils; five lines from the sovereign Pontiff will become the rule of conduct for the universal Church. Eastern and African bishops, all those who at first had rallied round the contrary opinion, will retrace their steps, and the whole Catholic world will follow the decision of the Bishop of Rome. If there is in this an argument against the supremacy of the Pope, we can desire nothing better than that our opponents should discover many similar ones in their historical studies.

CHAPTER IX.

THE THREE SEES OF PETER.

I. THERE is another incident in the life of the third century which gives us an important glimpse into the relationship that existed between Rome and the rest of the Church. It occurred at a time when the Bishop of Rome and the Bishop of Alexandria were of the same name—namely, Dionysius. They were both saints, and we are indebted to a third saint for an account of the correspondence that took place between them—namely, Saint Athanasius.

But to understand the full bearing of the incident to which I allude, it will be necessary to bear in mind what we know of the relationship between Rome and Alexandria from other sources.

Now, no one supposes that the Holy See could have often intervened directly, at such a period as the third century, in the affairs of the various provinces throughout the world. We know, indeed, from St. Jerome that in the next century its action was felt over the whole Christian Church in various ways. But considering the nature of intercommunication in those times this could only be occasional. What actually happened was as follows.

The 'keys' were originally given to St. Peter, but the College of Apostles was presently associated with him—each one of them with immediate universal jurisdiction from our Lord, and each secure of divine assistance in promulgating the faith delivered to the Apostolic College, which consisted of Peter (their head) 'and the rest.'[1] Their infallibility was necessary for the function they had to perform, that of being the first founders of Christian Churches. It was not needed

---

[1] Acts ii. 37.

after this, and never claimed by their successors, with one exception—viz. the successor of St. Peter. They went out into the wide world and founded sees, without occupying them themselves. Being each of them confirmed in grace and infallible, the position of subordination which they occupied in regard to St. Peter was never emphasised as is the case where there is opposition or rebellion. They left to the Churches which they founded the deposit of truth which they bore with them from Jerusalem. They had no successors in their apostolate, in its fulness. The apostolate—which is of the essence of the government of the Church—lapsed at length in each case into the hands of one see, which remained for all time 'the Apostolic See.' The rest of the Apostles were succeeded by bishops, and their sees, although apostolic in origin, were no longer apostolic in the full sense of the term, having no longer that immediate universal jurisdiction, and that infallibility in delivering the deposit, which was the peculiarity of the apostolate. They could thus be called apostolic, but in a subordinate sense, and they very soon ceased to be so called at all. The whole Christian world understood what was meant by ' the Apostolic See.' St. Vincent of Lerins, in a passage quoted above, does not think it necessary to do more, when speaking of Rome, than to call it ' the Apostolic See.'

Whilst the Apostles, as a rule, left no successors of their universal jurisdiction and of their infallibility, there was one exception. It was not St. James,[1] whose see occupied at the Council of Nice a subordinate position. It was St. Peter, whose see was assumed at that council to possess the Primacy.[2]

That primacy was, *in principle*, as has already appeared, and as will appear still more plainly when we come to the Councils of Ephesus and Chalcedon, all that it is now in the hands of Leo XIII.

II. But in point of fact the bishops who immediately succeeded the Apostles, scattered as they were throughout the

---

[1] Hegesippus says of the first Bishops of Jerusalem: προηγοῦνται πάσης ἐκκλησίας ὡς μάρτυρες καὶ ἀπὸ γένους τοῦ κυρίου (Eus. *H.E.* iii. 32). He is speaking of Palestine, not of the Church everywhere.

[2] Cf. ch. xi. p. 168.

world, enjoyed a certain measure of autonomy as a matter of necessity. It was owing to physical circumstances that they were in any measure externally separated, and not from any idea of the value of 'episcopal independence.' When Africa, in the next century, pleaded for a court of first instance of a more satisfactory nature, which would diminish their attendance at Rome, it was not with a view of cutting themselves off from Rome but of dealing with the witnesses themselves in the first instance, at first hand and on the spot. As a matter of fact the letter in which this matter is (if it is genuine) most urgently pleaded, was signed by a bishop who had at that very time lodged an appeal at Rome against his superior bishop ; so that he could not have been supporting episcopal independence of Rome.

Such an idea is, indeed, foreign to the very idea of a kingdom, such as in those days they held the Church to be. And throughout the world, however autonomous, from the stress of circumstances, distant provinces might remain, intercommunication was kept up by *epistolæ formatæ*, or letters of communion, between all parts of the Body of Christ. To be outside the circle of Christian life embraced by these *literæ formatæ* was equivalent to being no longer within the Christian Church. There was no idea of an underlying unity when there was external separation of a formal and final character. St. Cyprian expressly repudiates the idea. They knew of one Church, one only Church, numerically one—not many, separated one from the other, and never communicating at each other's altars.[1]

But when, through the withdrawal of the χάρισμα of infallibility which the Apostles each enjoyed, any doubt arose in the Churches as to whether a bishop was handing on with accurate fidelity the deposit of truth communicated by the apostolic founder of a Church (or cluster of Churches), then St. Irenæus' rule came into force. The natural thing would be to compare the teaching with that of the nearest Apostolic Church, and finally, if need arose (or at once, if opportunity

---

[1] Communion might be temporarily suspended, as it was for thirty-five years during the Acacian schism, but in such cases it is clear that it was suspension, and not a perfected breach.

occurred, or the occasion called for it) with the Church of Rome, with which it was necessary to agree, said St. Irenæus, *ob potentiorem principalitatem*, because of her more powerful principality. And as the lapse of time separated men from the days of the Apostles, they looked more and more to the permanent Apostle of the Christian Church, the one predestined seat of infallibility and universal jurisdiction. It required the fortunes of time to bring out the powers of her 'Apostle.' But such the occupant of the See of Rome was from the first —not as confirmed in grace, nor possessing inspiration, but as secured from error by special divine assistance under certain circumstances of his teaching.

The amount, therefore, of intervention on the part of the Holy See in the affairs of the Church might be expected to increase with the growth of the means of intercommunication. Nothing in the history of the Church up to this hour has gone beyond the principle involved in St. Clement's letter to the Church at Corinth. But the principle has expressed itself more vividly and widely with the expansion of the Church. And the measure of autonomy forced upon the scattered communities of the early Church during the days of persecution would naturally give way to increasing centralisation, as the possibilities of exhibiting her law of unity multiplied.

III. Meanwhile that external unity which is a note of the Church was being matured in the circles of Christian communities which were nearest to the centre of unity. The Bishop of Rome and his council of bishops formed the first and central knot. But from the first there was a wider circle, embracing a large portion of the East, distinctly gathered round this centre. Three great sees appear in the early Church, each of them counting St. Peter as the head of their catalogue of bishops. Each of them was a See of Peter, for at one (Antioch) St. Peter himself resided temporarily, and to the other (Alexandria) he had sent his disciple St. Mark, whilst he lived for a longer period, and died, at Rome. These two sees, therefore, occupied quite a unique position in Christian history. In the language of St. Gregory they were, with the See of Rome, the three measures of meal which the woman took and leavened the whole. They appeared at

Nice with prerogatives which were left untouched, as being
'ancient.' Each of these sees occupied from a secular point
of view a great central position, but each of them traced its
real glory in the Christian covenant to its connection with
the Prince of the Apostles.

The Church, then, was not as many seem to imagine, all
but invertebrate in that third century, but was already highly
organised. There was no such thing as episcopal independence. The two commanding sees of Antioch and Alexandria,
with their immense provinces of subordinate sees, as soon as
they come into the full light of history, appear in a relationship of subordination to Rome. For instance, in the latter
half of the third century Alexandria conducted herself on a
most important occasion as in such a relationship, under the
following circumstances.

IV. The Sabellian heresy had sprung up in the region of
Pentapolis, which, as we know from the 6th Nicene Canon,
belonged to the 'Greater Metropolitanate' (or, as it was afterwards called, 'the Patriarchate') of Alexandria.

The Patriarch St. Dionysius had on a previous occasion
written to Pope Xystus II. on the subject of rebaptism,
giving as his reason for writing, 'that I may not err' (Euseb.
'Hist. Eccl.' vii. 9). He now wrote to Xystus' successor,
named also Dionysius, to inform him of the fact that the
Sabellian heresy had emerged under his rule. And at the
same time he wrote to two of the Egyptian bishops. In his
letters to these bishops he laid great stress on the reality of
our Lord's humanity. This caused certain persons in the
Province—not merely (as Canon Bright expresses it [1]) 'some
Africans,' but 'brethren,' probably bishops [2] of the diocese [3] of
Alexandria—to suspect him of leaning towards the Arian
heresy. And in consequence the Arians afterwards quoted
him as on their side. St. Athanasius, in a graphic account
of the whole matter, indignantly repudiates the accusation

---

[1] 'The appeal or application to a Bishop of Rome on the part of some
Africans,' &c. (Bright's *Roman Claims tested by Antiquity*, p. 9).

[2] It is *possible*, but unlikely, that pure presbyters would thus appeal straight
to Rome; ἀδελφός is the word frequently used of bishops in the Athanasian
literature.

[3] In the early sense of that word.

thus levelled against his saintly predecessor. He tells them in a magnificent letter exactly what happened. The offended 'brethren' (or bishops) in their zeal for orthodoxy reported their archbishop to the Bishop of Rome, who at once wrote a letter on the subject of Sabellianism and Arianism, adjusting the balance of truth which these opposite heresies variously disturbed. He also wrote to the Archbishop of Alexandria for him to explain[1] what exactly it was for which he was accused, on the ground that as the complainants not having explained it, he was in the dark. St. Dionysius, in no way resenting, but rather welcoming, the 'interference' of the Pope, at once sent a letter to His Holiness, saying that another was to follow, that the Pope might not think him dilatory in clearing himself from the accusation, however vague. His reply was sufficient. And St. Athanasius tells the Arians that they have only succeeded in forging a weapon against themselves in quoting St. Dionysius of Alexandria in their favour. 'For they have brought two things into prominence: first, that Dionysius of Alexandria having cleared himself, they have him against them; and secondly, the fact of Dionysius [the Pope] having written as he did against those who say that the Son of God is a creature, shows that not now [*i.e.* in the days of St. Athanasius] for the first time, but long ago (ἔκπαλαι) their heresy had been *anathematised by all.*'[2]

Here, then, is the principle of appeal at work concerning an Archbishop of Alexandria to the Bishop of Rome; here is another instance of the unvarying orthodoxy of the occupants of the Holy See; and here, again, is an instance of how the Church was governed on the subject of the Homoousion long years before the Council of Nice. St. Dionysius the Pope, as supreme guardian of the faith, had ruled Arianism out of court long before that council had met. The Arian doctrine had, says St. Athanasius, been 'anathematised by all.'

V. In the same century the relationship of Rome to the third Petrine See (that of Antioch) was emphasised through

---

[1] δηλῶσαι. Bishop Pearson's suggestion (δηλώσας) does not square with the course of events as narrated in the same paragraph. And there seems no motive for the suggestion except that it gets rid of an awkward fact.

[2] St. Athan. in *Sententia Dionysii*.

the obstinate resistance of its bishop to the ruling of no less than three synods. Paul of Samosata (so called from his birthplace) had denied the Divinity of our Lord and the personality of the Logos. The Logos, according to this bishop's heretical teaching, was only the Divine wisdom infused into the man Jesus of Nazareth, who was therefore called the Son of God. His position as Bishop of Antioch and his great ability were sufficient to alarm and disturb the whole Eastern Church. The Bishops of Syria, Palestine, and Asia Minor assembled in synod in the year 264 and condemned his teaching. Paul promised amendment in some respects, in others he denied the charges. A second synod, however, had to meet in consequence of his continued heterodoxy, and then a third, and he was ultimately deposed and excommunicated. But he refused to give up the episcopal palace to Domnus his successor, and the bishops appealed to the emperor to enforce their decision. Aurelian, who was the emperor, decided that whoever received letters from the Bishops of Italy [1] and the Bishop of Rome must have the episcopal residence. Rome gave its letters to Domnus, and Paul was extruded.

Now it may be said that it was very natural for the Emperor of Rome to exalt the Bishop of Rome, and if it were not for the historical context in which this method of solving a dispute between bishops occurred, one might easily, with Gibbon, set it down to a natural desire on the part of a heathen emperor to draw all matters, Christian as well as civil, to one centre. But not even a heathen emperor would try to appease a quarrel amongst Oriental bishops by a mode of action alien to their ideas of propriety, such as this would have been on any but the Papal theory. But the imperial settlement occurred in that same second century of the Church's life,[2] in which St. Victor had acted as one who had the right to determine the conditions of inherence in the common unity; in which St. Irenæus said that all Churches must resort to, or agree with, the Church of Rome because of her more powerful principalship; in which an emperor had expressed his fear of a bishop at Rome as of a rival to his own position of authority; in which the Bishop of Rome

[1] = the *Papal Consistory*: cf. p. 124.   [2] Counting from Pentecost.

had temporarily settled the question of the rebaptisation of heretics, pending a general council, relying avowedly on his succession to Peter; the century in which another Bishop of Rome had received an appeal against the Bishop of Alexandria, and the latter had proceeded at once to clear himself from the charge of heresy—all these witnessing to a general conviction on the part of bishops and Popes that the 'chair of Peter' was the normal centre of the Christian Church, and making it natural for an emperor who wished to see peace restored, to refer the matter to the Pope and his council as the recognised arbiter of Christian disputes.

The emperor was just then at Antioch, after his victory over Zenobia, and seventy bishops had decided against the Patriarch Paul. It would therefore have been natural for the emperor to settle the matter at once in favour of Domnus, had he not seen that it could be settled by a higher ecclesiastical authority in accordance with the rules of the Christian community. It is reasonable to suppose that either the bishops at Antioch themselves suggested the reference to Rome as the final court, as Ballerini suggests, or, as the Gallican Fleury supposes, that 'it was sufficiently notorious even to the heathen that the true religion of the Christian body lay in communion with the Roman Church.'[1] The judgments of Rome were invariably passed in synod—in a synod not of all the Italian bishops, but of a select number, varying according to circumstance. They were the normal organ of Papal decisions. To this synod the emperor had the matter referred,[2] for, says Bossuet, he had noticed that the Christian body was contained within the communion of the Roman Bishop.[3] Accordingly Eusebius praises the action of the emperor as 'most religious.'[4]

Thus in those primitive days no idea of the independence of national Churches seems to have entered the mind of the Christian community. The whole Church was one vast

---

[1] *Hist.* tom. ii. lib. 8, c. 8.

[2] Throughout the whole history of the Church up to this day the Popes have been accustomed to act in concert with some kind of consistory.

[3] *Discours sur l'Hist. univ.*

[4] Eus. *H. E.* vii. 30: αἰσιώτατα περὶ τοῦ πρακτέου διείληφε.

brotherhood, with its relations of interdependence between the various centres or sees. And all tended upwards to one common centre, which appeared as such, as the need of a central authority made itself felt, and the possibilities of its exerting its influence increased. Rome, Alexandria, and Antioch gradually emerge as three distinct and greater centres; whilst between themselves an order is observed which places each of these Eastern sees in a relation of subordination to the West, that is the See of the one Eternal City, destined to be such by virtue of her relationship to the Prince of the Apostles.

VI. And if we ask why Alexandria took precedence of Antioch, the answer is to be found, not merely in its civil position, but in the law originally laid down by our Lord in sending His Apostles through the world. They were to go first to the Jews. Accordingly they went first to those cities in which the greater number of Jews resided, making them the centre of their operations. Thus the extension of the Church followed the framework of the Jewish organisation, rather than, as some appear to imagine,[1] merely the civil order. As the Jewish Sanhedrim in Palestine received their jurisdiction from the central bureau at Jerusalem, so the Christian communities, composed of Jewish converts, so long as they continued to be so composed, owned Jerusalem as their metropolis; but when, as Dr. Döllinger has pointed out in his admirable summary of the growth of the metropolitical system, these Churches were destroyed under Adrian, and a new Church, composed mainly of converts from paganism, was formed at Ælia, the metropolitical jurisdiction in Palestine was transferred to Cæsarea, whose Church took precedence of Ælia owing to its apostolical foundation. It had been founded by St. Peter in the conversion of Cornelius, the first Pagan who embraced Christianity.[2]

The same principle explains the order of Alexandria in the gradation of sees. St. Peter sent his disciple St. Mark

---

[1] *E.g.* Mr. Puller, in his *Primitive Saints, &c.* p. 18 *seq.*, and the Bishop of Lincoln in his preface, p. xv.

[2] Döllinger's *Hist. of the Church*, Period I. ch. iii. § 3. See the whole section.

thither, and was thus held to have been its real founder. It was the largest centre of Jews outside Judæa; its ethnarch took precedence of all other heads of the Jewish people in their dispersion, and consequently it took precedence even of Antioch, also a Petrine see.[1] And its metropolitical jurisdiction, confirmed by the Nicene fathers as having existed from the beginning, covered, not the political, but the Jewish division. The Bishop of Alexandria held sway over the Pentapolis and Libya, which politically belonged to the African, not to the Egyptian province. The area of his jurisdiction was thus conterminous with that of the Jewish ethnarch, not of the imperial prefect or proconsul.[2] Rome was the centre of Jewish life in the West, and in Rome St. Peter abode, with intervals of absence, for twenty-five years, and thither came also the great Apostle of the Gentiles, whose name was to be for ever linked with that of St. Peter in the prayers and thoughts of the Christian world, in regard to the Eternal City. As a matter of fact the centres of Jewish life were also the centres of political grandeur; and it was, we may say, in the providence of God that on the division of the Roman Empire the constitution of the Church rarely crossed or overlapped the articulation of the civil order. But in principle it might on any occasion, as it actually did in the case of Basilinopolis at the Council of Chalcedon. Ordinarily, however, the political centre would naturally form the ecclesiastical metropolis, as there could be no fresh Apostolical foundation. Eventually no Apostolical see presented a permanent and uninterrupted succession, save only the See of St. Peter. Alexandria and Antioch were destined to be submerged in the troubles of the Church, and to-day Rome alone of all sees in the world can trace her line of descent straight up to an Apostle.

[1] So St. Ambrose, when insisting on the truth that it is the Holy Spirit who cleanses the soul, the Church being His instrument, runs through the sees in order, 'It was not Damasus' (Bishop of Rome) 'that cleansed, it was not Peter' (Bishop of Alexandria), 'it was not Ambrose' (Bishop of Milan), 'it was not Gregory' (Bishop of Constantinople). He omits Antioch because of its trouble about its bishops (*De Spir. Sancto*, lib. i. n. 18).

[2] Mr. Puller (*Prim. SS.* p. 14 *seq.*) does not seem to have realised this: hence the undue stress which he has laid on the civil position of these sees. One does not see on what grounds, according to his theory, Canterbury takes precedence of London.

The Witness of the Popes concerning their Office.

But before going further it will be well to consider an argument which has been much insisted on of late. It has been said on behalf of the Anglican position: 'Our contention is that the idea of a divinely appointed supremacy over the whole Church, as a prerogative of the Roman See, arose very largely out of the exorbitant claims made by the Popes. It follows that exaggerated [1] claims in favour of the Papacy, when they occur in the writings of the Popes or of other persons living, so to speak, in a Papal atmosphere, and when they stand in marked contrast with the general teaching of the Fathers and Doctors of the Church, cannot be quoted, at any rate controversially, on the Papal side. *We* regard them as the proofs of Papal ambition. In connection with this subject it is surely permissible to refer in all reverence to our Lord's own words, "If I bear witness of myself, my witness is not true" (St. John v. 31).' [2] And again, 'No candid person will press statements about St. Peter written by Roman Popes or by Antiochene Fathers.' [3]

It will be well, before proceeding to consider the witness of the fourth century, to examine the value of the above statement. And I shall begin with the passage quoted from Holy Scripture.

Our Blessed Lord had been bearing witness concerning Himself. He had called Himself the Son of God; He had said that He was about to raise the dead, and to judge the whole of the human race. Those who saw in the tone of authority with which He spake an evidence of the truth which He delivered were amongst the very elect of God. But, although what He said was strictly true, He vouchsafed to add another testimony to His own, and so to make His witness to Himself complete and formally true, according to the received notions of legal testimony. He accordingly

---

[1] Mr. Puller explains what he means by exaggerated claims in the opening of his Preface (p. xxvi), viz. 'the claim to a supremacy or primacy of jurisdiction as of divine right.'

[2] *Primitive Saints, &c.* p. 97, note 3.   [3] *Ibid.* p. 123.

referred them to the witness of the Baptist, who, as an acknowledged prophet, was to them an accredited witness, summing up the testimony of the Jewish teaching Church. The Baptist had borne the same witness by the river Jordan as our Lord had now borne concerning Himself.

Our Lord, therefore, rested His claim to their acceptance on two grounds, His own witness and that of the Baptist, the two together satisfying the formal requirements of their Law. To His own it was enough that He 'spake with authority' in a way that none had ever done, touching chords of their hearts which no power had been able thus to sweep with the hand of a master, proclaiming Himself the real author of their inmost being. St. Peter, when our Lord appealed to the twelve as to whether they would leave Him, replied at once, 'Lord, to whom shall we go? Thou hast the words of eternal life.'[1] There was a richness, a fulness, in His teaching that met the imperious needs of their souls as no other teaching ever had. To them it was a felt truth that, as our Lord afterwards said, 'Although I give testimony of myself, my testimony is true.'[2]

Now the Church is the extension of the Incarnation, and as our Lord was in the world, so is she. The same feature that strikes us in the teaching of our Lord meets us in the teaching of His Church. She speaks with the tone of authority; she bears witness of herself. And as there is no logical alternative between considering that either our Lord (may He forgive the words) uttered blasphemy when He bore the witness that He did to Himself, or that He was what He said He was, literally and fully Almighty God, so is it with His Church, and so is it with those who represent His Church from age to age. As the late Dr. Liddon, in one of the most remarkable sermons that this century has produced,[3] drew out the proposition that our Lord could not be a sincere man— could not be considered a good man—if He was not Almighty God, seeing what He said of Himself, so is it true to say that no Pope who gave himself out as supreme ruler of the

---

[1] St. John vi. 69. [2] St. John viii. 14.
[3] *Bampton Lectures on the Divinity of our Lord and Saviour Jesus Christ,* Lect. iv.

Catholic Church, or acted as such, could be a good man unless the claim was just, since he must have taken the name of God in vain with his eyes open, of set purpose, in the supreme acts of his sacerdotal life. On the other hand, if St. Peter was appointed by our Lord to be head of the Apostles, and if each Pope in succession felt himself to be the successor of that Apostle, then it became a mere duty to bear witness to his office, and no sin could be greater than for such a one to make acts of humility at the expense of divine truth. If he should hide the truth, if he failed, when occasion demanded it, to 'magnify his office,'[1] he must hear the condemnation of the Divine Head of the Church, 'O thou wicked and slothful servant.'[2]

Much, therefore, will depend on the circumstances under which the Popes bore witness to their office. The position maintained in this book is that the witness they bore was of such a character, and under such circumstances, as to render it of great value. And it seems to me altogether unphilosophical, and that is the same as saying that it is in violation of the laws of historical investigation, simply to set aside their witness as nothing worth. They are quoted in this work for what they are worth. Their witness is not valueless because borne by themselves, neither is it conclusive unless supported by other testimony.

Now consider the character of the witness borne in this third century. It is unvarying. And it has after it an unvarying testimony of sixteen hundred years. It is not, therefore, the witness of one man, but of many, and of men placed in a post, according to their own judgment, of the highest responsibility. How is it that Pope after Pope no sooner sits on the throne than he is filled with the same consciousness of world-wide responsibilities? What was there in that one See that spread the infection to each successive occupant, so that he articulated with such perfect simplicity the same teaching concerning his relationship to the rest of the Church? Is there any sign of ambition, except in the mere fact that each Pope acted as Ruler of the Universal Church, to plead which against hem in controversy would be to beg the ques-

[1] 2 Cor. x. xi. xii.   [2] St. Matt. xxv. 26.

tion? Why is it, in the judgment of such writers as I have quoted, always ambition on the one side, and not rather rebellion on the other?

Let us look at the circumstances under which the claim comes to view. It was in the ages of persecution. In the second century the violation of the laws proscribing Christian worship and the Christian society was often connived at officially, but the laws existed in all their tremendous severity, ready at any moment to be put in execution. Wherever the Christian society existed, it lived under the vigilant observance of a sleepless foe, and, of all things, the imperial power dreaded its centralisation.[1] St. Peter had suppressed the name of Rome in his Epistle, calling it Babylon; St. Clement suppressed his own in writing to Corinth. Each of them wrote under violent persecution.[2] But they wrote. And the Bishops of Rome not merely wrote, but they acted as the rulers of the Church under circumstances which rendered any exhibition of a centralising power a matter of almost certain death. During this time the Church of Rome acquired a name throughout the Church for practical goodness, and for steadfastness of faith; so that the clergy of Rome in writing to St. Cyprian could assume that the Apostle's commendation of their Church was understood to apply to all time.[3] And St. Cyprian does not hesitate to speak of the Romans as those 'to whom faithlessness could have no access.'[4] Are we to suppose that their bishops, chosen as men whom they could trust to lead them, were in each case tainted with the diabolical sin of ambition? They were mostly martyrs, and they all had of necessity the martyr's end before their eyes. In that stormy third century, which passed in alternations of extreme tolerance and passionate persecution, no Pope sat on the throne with any fair prospect of dying the common death of ordinary men. St. Zephyrinus reigned during the persecution under Severus; St. Callistus was imprisoned, half starved, severely beaten day after day, finally thrown into a well, and

---

[1] See this beautifully developed in Mr. Allies' *Throne of the Fisherman*, c. vi.

[2] St. Clement in a short breathing-time between two persecutions.

[3] Cf. *supra*, p. 53.   [4] *Supra*, p. 59.

so won his crown; St. Urban fell a victim to the sensual monster Heliogabalus; St. Pontian was exiled; St. Anterus died in the persecution of Maximin; St. Fabian suffered under Decius, and the Christians were unable to elect his successor for two years, so fierce was the persecution. At length Cornelius, of a noble Roman family, occupied the see for little more than a year, and died in exile. St. Lucius, who succeeded him, was presently banished, and received the well-known letter from St. Cyprian congratulating him on possessing the twofold honour of the bishopric and of suffering for the faith. After a short reign St. Stephen held the post for four years, and ended with a violent death, whilst his successor St. Sixtus was seized as he offered the Holy Sacrifice in the catacomb, and beheaded in his episcopal chair. Truly in that first half of the third century the See of Peter was baptised in blood. One bishop now died in peace—St. Dionysius, but the roll of confessors recommenced in St. Felix, who died in prison, and in St. Caius; and the white-robed army of martyrs received another recruit in St. Marcellinus, with whom this blood-red century closed. For three years the see was vacant owing to the violence of the persecution.

Now, five times in this century, amongst the scanty records, the Pope comes out to view as ruler of more than the local Church of Rome. In each case his action is drawn from him by dangers threatening the faith of the Church. The Holy Feast of Easter, the Queen of Festivals, was in danger of being associated with false teaching. St. Victor attempted to produce a uniformity of practice in its observance, in which he was thwarted by one portion of the Church, though supported by the greater whole. St. Irenæus prevailed upon him not to use his authority further. During the fierce persecution under Severus many Christians lapsed, and some would have closed the door of repentance to such for ever. St. Zephyrinus came forth and opened the gate of mercy, as the High Priest of the Christian religion. So Tertullian described him. Under St. Stephen the African Primate had started on a dangerous career, and might have carried all before him in a practice which must have ended in depraving the doctrine of the Sacraments. Whole provinces were exposed to the danger of being carried away with the novelty, when the Pope stepped forth and put a stop to the danger, acting avowedly on his position as successor of Peter. The vigilance of St. Dionysius the Pope, so praised by St. Athanasius, was exercised towards the saintly Dionysius of Alexandria, in view of possible dangers to the cardinal point of the faith, whilst St. Felix achieved the peace of the Church by deposing the Bishop of Antioch.

There is no room for the accusation of ambition in all this. In each case it was care for the faith.

The only answer usually given to the various evidences of a supremacy having been accorded to the See of Rome in this century, is that in the most marked instances there was resistance, and that the authority recognised in the Bishop of Rome was only a tribute to the imperial position of the city.

But as regards the latter, it is at any rate not this that comes to the front in the record. The central position of the See of Rome is, according to St. Irenæus, due to her principalship as compared with other Churches, which we have seen cannot mean her secular position. Her priceless prerogative is, according to Tertullian, that she possesses ' all doctrine ; ' her peculiarity, according to St. Cyprian, is that she is in a unique sense ' the chair of Peter ' and the original source of episcopal unity. St. Clement claims to be heard not by reason of the natural position of his city, but on supernatural grounds ; whilst St. Stephen speaks of himself as the successor of Peter, which neither St. Firmilian nor St. Cyprian deny.

And as regards the resistance offered to these early Popes, to what does it amount ? In each case the Pope proved to be in the right; his judgment was always followed in the event by the whole Church. St. Victor's ruling as to the Easter Festival became the ruling of the whole Church ; St. Stephen's likewise ; so with that of St. Zephyrinus or St. Callistus. St. Dionysius' judgment is quoted by St. Athanasius as the condemnation of Arianism, and St. Clement's brief was at once obeyed. Never once, no, not in any one single line in the record we possess, is the one word found, which was needed on the theory of those who defend separation from Rome —' You have no such authority in matters of faith.' St.

Cyprian contended that the matter of rebaptisation did not come under that head; St. Victor did not pretend that the Asiatics were directly opposing the faith.[1] Thus the resistance, such as it was, on the other hand, will not bear the weight of argument placed upon it.

And yet the exhibition of authority is at once wide in its range and consecutive in its action. The truth as to the Christian ministry is defended by St. Clement; Gnosticism is condemned in two of its chief leaders (Cerdon and Valentine) by St. Hyginus; the heresies of Valentine and Marcion by St. Pius. Valentinianism, asserting itself under St. Eleutherus, found in that Pope its active opponent. It was his successor, St. Victor, who was the first, according to Eusebius, to excommunicate the forerunner of Arius, viz. Theodotus, 'the leader and father of this God-denying apostasy, the first one that asserted that Christ was a mere man.'[2] The dangers that beset the faith in regard to the Festival of the Resurrection were, as we have seen, met by the same Pope, and those that assailed the Sacrament of Penance and the mercies of its provisions, by his successor, St. Zephyrinus. The restriction which an unchristian severity placed on the restoration of those who lapsed under persecution were discountenanced by St. Cornelius, and the denial of the validity of the heretics' baptism was condemned by St. Stephen. St. Dionysius, as I have said, anticipated the Council of Nice in the condemnation of what afterwards went by the name of Arianism, and the letter of St. Felix to the Bishop of Alexandria concerning Paul of Samosata, the heretical Bishop of Antioch, is extant to prove him worthy to take his place in this illustrious line of guardians of the Church's faith.

Thus far, then, the See of Rome is prominent, but not in the way of ambition. No see could show such a line of martyrs; no see could produce such a record of active guardianship of the divine deposit which had been committed to the Church's care. At the same time the way in which she assisted others in their distress by her munificent and unfailing

---

[1] ὡς οὐκ ὀρθοδυξοῦντας (Eus. *H. E.* v. 24) does not amount to more than tha they were wrong on the particular point, which was not a matter of faith.

[2] Eus. *H. E.* v. 28.

almsgiving was such as to lead some, like the late Dr. Lightfoot, to assign her great position in the Church universal, what he calls her 'leadership,' to her 'practical goodness.' But in truth, her practical goodness was both the result of a supernatural gift and the witness afforded by the Father to the representative of His Son on the earth. St. Ignatius, of Antioch, speaks of the Church of the Romans as presiding in their region, and also as presiding over the brotherhood of divine love. He does not mention the Bishop of Rome himself; it was the last thing he would do. He was himself being hauled by the imperial decree, in deference to the bitter natural prejudice, to be devoured by the lions at Rome. To point out one as the head of the community in the city of Rome itself would have been like procuring the instant death of the Pope. If St. Peter would not mention Rome, except under the pseudonym of Babylon, neither would St. Ignatius draw attention to the fact that at Rome there was a head to the illegal organisation of the Christian community. He calls it the Church of the Romans, and says that it presides over 'the love,'[1] over a 'communion founded on love and preserved by love.' Its presidency was justified by its practical and supreme exhibition of the spirit of love; but it was derived from a divine appointment.

Therefore in these first two centuries after Pentecost, the Popes had produced an accessory evidence of their divine appointment to be the guardians of the faith. Their 'works' testified. In the fourth century their witness to themselves begins. But it does not stand alone. It does not offend against the canon of Jewish law concerning testimony, which our Lord claimed to satisfy. The most astonishing fact about the witness of the Popes concerning their office is that it never

---

[1] Dr. Döllinger's original rendering is obviously the correct one. 'He [Ignatius] first says: ἥτις προκάθηται ἐν τόπῳ χωρίου Ῥωμαίων, in which words he does not confine the authority, but only describes the situation, of the Church of Rome. He afterwards names this Church προκαθημένη τῆς ἀγάπης. These words do not signify *præsidens in caritate*, as the old Latin translation rendered them, for then St. Ignatius would have said ἐν ἀγάπῃ. Ἀγάπη signifies, in the same manner as Ἐκκλησία, sometimes a smaller assembly of the faithful at the sacred love-feasts, sometimes the entire body of the faithful of all the Church—a communion founded on love and preserved by love.' For the original of this translation, see p. 33.

varied. There is not a solitary exception. Wherever their witness is recorded, it is of the same nature. It is as though the speech of 260 men of different nationality, temperament, and circumstances, stretching over eighteen centuries and a half, were the speech of one person, as indeed it was, for these several witnesses were the vicars of one Lord, Who spoke through them to successive generations. Already in these first two centuries Greece, Athens, and Africa, as well as Rome, had contributed their occupants to the throne of the fisherman. But all alike contributed the same witness, as they exhibited that same feature, of rulers conscious of worldwide responsibilities, and fulfilling them with prison or death before their eyes. When, then, a Pope speaks in these early ages concerning his office, it is reasonable even for a controversialist to listen, considering the subsidiary testimony with which that office comes before us; considering also the responsibility attaching to that office, according to the Pope's own conception of it. The permanent is a shadow of the eternal; and this permanent consciousness of holding a position fraught with such tremendous responsibilities suggests a more than human origin.

Our Lord did not admit, as Mr. Puller appears to imagine, that His witness to Himself was worthless even from a formal point of view, for it was part of the testimony. The Baptist's witness, and His own works of mercy, formed the rest. So with the witness of His vicars concerning (not, indeed, themselves, but) their office, it must be taken into account; and it would be no sign of 'candour' to omit it, but would indicate an inadequate appreciation of the nature of testimony.

In the following pages, therefore, the Popes' witness concerning their office will be emphasised, though not to the exclusion of other witness, but as being in harmony with it, each being the counter-signature of the other. The reception of that witness on the part of the Church at large will be considered as forming its necessary complement, and by this I understand the reception by the Church *on the whole*, not taking an occasional murmur, or the resistance of a single province, for the settled conviction of the whole Church. A boy's grumble is not the same as a permanent rebellion, neither is every resistance to a particular instance of authority, or to a particular method of procedure, tantamount to a repudiation of the authority itself. St. Peter was resisted by the Judaising Christians; but they came round to his judgment. All Apostle that he was, he yet had to explain to those of the circumcision, which in charity he did, the rationale of his action, and they acquiesced ($\dot{\eta}\sigma\upsilon\chi\alpha\sigma\alpha\nu$).[1] In Africa, for a little moment, some bishops resisted the mode of procedure adopted by Rome, but they never questioned her authority as supreme: their successors incorporated the very mode of procedure into their code.[2]

[1] Acts xi. 18.   [2] Cf. Period III. ch. x.

PERIOD II

A.D. 300—384

CHAPTER X.

THE DONATISTS AND THE COUNCIL OF ARLES.

THE fourth century opened with two schisms, one of which led to some of the most important literature which the Church possesses. The first in point of date was the Meletian schism in Egypt, which led to the boundaries of the Alexandrian diocese being specially mentioned in the 6th Canon of the Council of Nicæa. The second occurred in Africa, and was the occasion of some of St. Augustine's most important writings on the subject of the Church, in the end of this century and the beginning of the fifth. He threw his fiery genius into the question of how far scandals affect the note of sanctity which the Nicene Creed attributes to the Catholic Church.

I. The centre of the schism was Carthage. Some discontented presbyters had expressed themselves dissatisfied with their bishop and had accused him of having delivered up the sacred volumes to the heathen during persecution, and of having failed in charity towards those who refused to do the same,[1] and had to suffer in consequence. At his death Cæcilian was elected for his successor, and was consecrated by Felix of Aptunga. Seventy bishops of Numidia were on their way to the consecration, which, however, was performed before their arrival. Finding themselves disappointed of their claim[2] to have a hand in the consecration of a primate of the only city

---

[1] Those who gave up copies of the Holy Scriptures were called *Traditores*.
[2] In the other parts of Africa the presiding bishop might be of almost any see, as the office was attached to seniority, not to the see.

of Africa which was metropolitical,[1] and discovering also a party in Carthage ready for schismatic action, one of these Numidian bishops, named Donatus, consecrated a bishop in opposition to Cæcilian. The latter was accused of having been a *traditor*, and the new schism was supported by the immense wealth of a lady named Lucilla, who had been hurt by the disciplinary action of Mensurius, the predecessor of Cæcilian. The new-elected bishop of the schism was one of her household, named Majorinus.

II. The schism soon assumed formidable proportions in the North of Africa, so that the schismatics made the endeavour to gain the imperial condemnation of their opponents. They appealed to the emperor himself,[2] for which in after times St. Augustine perpetually reproached them.[3] The emperor, however, not yet Arianised and Erastianised by contact with Eusebius of Nicomedia, referred them to Rome.[4] They had asked for a judgment from the Gallic bishops, as being in their estimation specially free from the taint of 'tradition,' or the delivery of the sacred volumes to the heathen.[5] There is no evidence that they had any idea of the case not being submitted to Rome; but as Rome invariably decided matters with the assistance of a council, they had asked, and it was agreed to, that the assessors in this case should be several of them Gallic bishops and the rest Italian. There is nothing in the records we possess to sanction the assumption which Archbishop Laud makes, viz. that these bishops were forced upon the Bishop of Rome. St. Augustine says that Constantine 'sent' the bishops to Rome; but that only applies to his ordering them to go, and supplying them with facilities for the journey. It is in the last degree improbable that there was no concerted action between the emperor and the Bishop of Rome, who was himself an African, named Melchiades. The question to be decided was not one that

---

[1] St. Augustine says that their claim had no foundation, the Bishop of Carthage being properly consecrated by a neighbouring bishop, as the Bishop of Rome by the Bishop of Ostia (*Brevic. Collat. c. Donat.* 3ii diei, c. xvi. 29).

[2] Optat. Milev. *c. Parmen.* lib. i.   [3] Aug. *c. lit. Petil.* lib. ii. cap. 92.

[4] Aug. *Ep.* 166; Euseb. *H. E.* x. 5.

[5] Probably they also thought that the Gallic bishops would be more under the sway of the emperor, whom they hoped to influence.

concerned the faith, but as to a matter of fact; but as it had to do with bishops the emperor relegated the matter to Melchiades and his assessors. This, according to St. Augustine, was in accordance with the rules of the Church. The emperor all through expressly and strongly deprecated the idea of his sitting in judgment on bishops on such a matter.¹

III. Cæcilian was acquitted by the bishops at Rome. St. Augustine almost always calls the decision 'the judgment of Melchiades,' as though its force was due to his position amongst the bishops.² Optatus gives the judgment actually delivered by him. Melchiades said with respect to Cæcilian, 'I decide that he should deservedly be kept in his ecclesiastical communion, his *status* being unimpaired.'³ And so St. Augustine, in his account of the conference with the Donatists in the following century, calls it 'the judgment of the Roman bishop Melchiades, by which Cæcilianus was purged and absolved.'⁴ And yet it is also 'the decision of the bishops who sat at Rome,' on which Constantine declined to pass judgment himself,⁵ whilst the imperial official at the tribunal in Africa asked if 'they had anything to say against the council and the judgment of Melchiades, by which Cæcilian was purged and absolved,' *i.e.* from the charge.⁶ Elsewhere St. Augustine calls the said decision 'the judgment of the Churches beyond the seas founded by apostolical toil,' alluding to St. Peter and St. Paul.⁷ Again and again St. Augustine insists that the judgment of Melchiades ought to have been final, and further, that in repudiating that judgment the Donatists were putting themselves out of communion with the whole world, and putting the whole world into the position of *traditores*, because the whole world 'believed the judges who absolved [Cæcilian] rather than the accusers who incriminated him.' But in his letter on the Donatists in

---

¹ Mansi, t. ii. p. 748.
² *E.g.* throughout the conference with the Donatists in 411.
³ Optat. c. *Parmen.* lib. i.
⁴ *Ad Donatistas post Collationem liber unus*, cap. xiii.
⁵ *Loc. cit.* cap. xliv. 29.
⁶ *Brevic. Collat. c. Donat.* 3ii diei, cap. xviii. 33.
⁷ *C. Crescon.* lib. iii. cap. lxvii.

398, St. Augustine has a passage of the very first importance as throwing light on his ideas of Church government. He is contrasting the sentence of Melchiades with that of the seventy Numidian bishops who favoured the Donatists' candidate. He says, ' And yet of what character was that final sentence issued by the blessed Melchiades?—how innocent, how complete, how prudent and peace-making! By that judgment he both did not venture to remove from their ecclesiastical position [1] colleagues against whom nothing had been proved, and whilst chiefly blaming Donatus alone, whom he had discovered to be at the head of the whole matter, he gave the rest the free option of recovering their position, being prepared as he was to send letters of communion even to those who it was shown had been ordained by Majorinus : so that in whatever places there were two bishops, owing to the dissension, he [*i.e.* Melchiades] would confirm the one who had been first ordained, whilst another flock should be provided for the other to rule. O best of men, O Son of Christian peace, and Father of the Christian people!' ('Ep.' 43, al. 162.)

IV. From the passages just quoted, we gather that the ecclesiastical status of the bishops in Africa rested with Melchiades, whose judgment in the matter was to a Catholic final. 'Because Constantine' (St. Augustine says elsewhere) ' did not dare to judge the case of a bishop, he delegated it to be discussed *and terminated* by bishops, *which also was done in the city of Rome* under the presidency of Melchiades, the Bishop of that Church, with many of his colleagues.' [2] But the sentence was the sentence of Melchiades, according to St. Augustine. It rested with him to 'send letters of communion' to the bishops in Africa, whose case was under consideration, and it was for him to 'confirm' them in their ecclesiastical status. He did in synod confirm Cæcilian in his position at Carthage ; and accordingly St. Augustine says that Cæcilian 'was able not to care for the multitude of enemies that conspired against him when he saw himself in communion with

---

[1] 'De collegio'—*i.e.* from amongst his own colleagues, from his own partnership—but that the above is the meaning is clear from the actual words of the sentence given by Optatus, which I have quoted on p. 141.

[2] *Ep. ad Donat.* 105, 8.

the Roman Church, in which the principalship of the Apostolic chair has ever been in force, and with the other lands, where the Gospel came to Africa itself, *where* [*i.e.* in the West] *he was prepared to plead his cause* if his adversaries attempted to alienate those Churches from him.' ('Ep.' 43, 7.)

Nothing, it seems to me, can be clearer, if one takes into account the whole of St. Augustine's writings concerning the Donatists, and they are considerable and full of details and of summaries that by their repetition and precision enable us to form a fair estimate of his idea of Church government—nothing, I say, seems to me clearer than that St. Augustine considered that the canonical justification of the position assigned to Melchiades in this matter was the fact that the See of Rome was the See of the Apostle Peter, and not that it was the imperial centre. The latter never once appears in the whole of St. Augustine's voluminous writings on the subject of the Donatist schism; the apostolical character and consequent jurisdictional primacy of the See of Rome is written in characters so large that I am unable to understand how anyone could deny it to be the teaching of our saint. If there be any one passage in which this conception of the See of Rome seems to be contradicted, I make bold to say that the evidence on the other side is so overwhelming that such a passage must be interpreted by the great mass of statements *vice versâ*. I do not know of any such passage, after reading through this long correspondence on the schism; but if there be such, it must be capable of the interpretation I have suggested. It is clear from the passages quoted above, that St. Augustine had no idea of causes of bishops being terminated in Africa. If proof positive were needed in addition, we have it in the last sentence of the chapter in that same letter, in which he speaks of the principalship of the Roman Church in connection with the judgment at Rome of African bishops. He there blames the Donatist bishop, Secundus, for having condemned bishops in their absence, forgetting that such bishops could not only appeal to the judgment of other colleagues, but especially to that 'of the Apostolical Churches,' —to that they could 'reserve their whole case.' There was no Apostolical Church in Africa; the only one to which they could appeal was at Rome. There he sat who was not only what the occupants of other Apostolical Sees were, but 'the Father of the Christian people.' (Cf. p. 142, line 19.)

V. 'But the Donatists appealed from the judgment of the Pope, Melchiades.' They did. And this was one of the counts in the heavy indictment which St. Augustine brought against them. He tells us how the emperor himself deprecated such an enormity, on the ground that bishops were the proper judges of bishops.[1]

Why, then, did not the emperor simply enforce their obedience, instead of waiting to issue the decrees which he afterwards did, depriving them of their churches? What the emperor did was to assign them a fresh tribunal, composed for the most part of Gallic bishops. It is here that a number of writers have jumped to a conclusion which is not warranted by the facts. It was not an appeal from Rome to a larger council. Mr. Haddan, in his article on 'Arles' (Smith and Cheetham's 'Dictionary of Christian Antiquities'), falls into a mistake which Mr. Ffoulkes, in Smith and Wace's 'Dictionary of Christian Biography,' stigmatises as 'either as gross a misconception or as wilful a misstatement as ever proceeded from a learned man.'[3] Mr. Haddan says that St. Augustine calls the Council of Arles, to which the case was now remitted, a 'universal council!' It is extraordinary how widespread the error is, that St. Augustine called the Council of Arles 'a plenary council of the universal Church.' As a matter of fact, he only says that if the Donatists were not satisfied with their judges at Rome, 'there remained a plenary Council of the universal Church,' *but that they had not availed themselves of this.*[4] The Donatists, after the sentence of Melchiades, pre-

---

[1] *Ep.* 43, 7.

[2] *Ep.* 162. S. Optatus, *c. Parmen.* lib. i. says that the emperor spoke of them 'just as infidels' for appealing to him.

[3] Mr. Ffoulkes is speaking of Bishop Hefele, who commits the same mistake.

[4] St. Augustine does not suggest this alternative as though the rest of the episcopate could review a Papal decision on a matter of faith, but on such a question as this it was open to the Pope to use as his organ of judgment a fuller council. A plenary council, such as St. Augustine suggested, *would include the Pope*, through his legates or by his confirmation.

tended that some facts had not been brought forward concerning Cæcilianus' consecrator, Felix of Aptunga. Nay, more, they declared that Melchiades had himself been a *traditor*, and consequently was not qualified to act as Bishop of Rome. These were all matters of fact, and Constantine decided upon having them cleared up in order to leave the Donatists, who were disturbing the civil order in Africa, no room for further complaint. Accordingly, the emperor had the matter sifted by his proconsul in Africa, and 'gave these Donatist bishops another council, at Arles.' The question was not a matter of faith; but still Constantine refused to do anything but appoint fresh judges. It was not a higher court. For though the Pope was not there himself, his legates were, and they presided over the inquiry. Mr. Haddan makes an assertion in the 'Dictionary of Christian Antiquities'[1] which is both incorrect and misleading. He says that the emperor 'summoned other bishops from Sicily, Italy (not the Bishop of Rome, he having been one of the former judges), etc.' But the Pope was represented by four legates, Claudius, Vitus, Eugenius, and Cyriacus,[2] which shows that the council was not an appeal to a higher court, but merely the assignment of fresh assessors, 'other bishops,' '*alios episcopos*,' as St. Augustine says, sitting with the representatives of Pope Sylvester, who had now succeeded to Melchiades.[3] It was granted, says St. Augustine, in spite of the great authority of the council at Rome ('tantæ auctoritatis episcopos'), whose numbers were not commensurate with its authority; and it was granted 'not because it was now' (*i.e.* after the council at Rome) 'necessary, but as a concession to their perversities, and out of a desire to restrain such great shamelessness in every way ('omnimodo cupiens tantam impudentiam cohibere').[4] It was, indeed, a concession on the part of Rome also; for it is reasonable to suppose that Constantine was acting in concert with St. Sylvester. The emperor was himself in Gaul; and the impudent Donatists, as St. Augustine calls them, had a special leaning to the

---

[1] Article on 'Arles.' [2] Mansi, t. ii. p. 470.
[3] Cf. Döllinger's *Ch. Hist.* Period II. cap. v. sec. 2. 'Almost immediately after his accession this pontiff [Sylvester] sent his legates to the Synod of Arles.'
[4] *Ep.* 43, 20.

Gallic bishops. He therefore arranged for the council to meet at Arles in 314. It was not, then, a plenary council reviewing the decision of Melchiades, but arose from a determination on the part of the emperor to give these Donatists no excuse for not submitting. He flatly refused to hear them himself, but instead handed their case again to the episcopate, consisting this time of Papal legates and other bishops, whose number is variously estimated—according to a false reading of St. Augustine, two hundred, but according to the list of signatures we possess not more than thirty-two. The emperor was himself present, although only a catechumen, but as the business of the council did not relate to matters of faith, his position was not as abnormal as it would otherwise have been.[1] He had submitted the matter to investigation in Africa by his proconsul; for the Donatists had raised the question of the canonicity of Felix's consecration, which had not been explicitly dealt with at Rome. He had hoped that Ingentius, who had confessed to having forged a letter in the name of Cæcilian, might make his confession before him, but he had eventually preferred that the matter should be dealt with by a synod of bishops. The synod decided against the Donatists. In other words, the synod decided that there was nothing in the supposed fresh matter to induce the new Pope to reverse the judgment of Melchiades.[2]

VI. The Synod of Arles has a special interest for us, as two British bishops—one of them the Bishop of London—attended it. And a matter was decided there which throws light on the contention of the British bishops that their rule for observing Easter was the right one. 'The British bishops' (say Haddan and Stubbs) 'must have consented to the following canons amongst others.' Amongst them they give the

---

[1] It is not certain who presided. Mr. Ffoulkes is certain that Marinus of Arles did not (*Dict. of Chr. Biog.*, art. 'Marinus'). Ballerini thinks it is possible that he did. It is not a matter of controversial importance, considering the purpose and nature of the council. Chrestus, Bishop of Syracuse, signed first. But we cannot argue safely from the list of signatures. Probably the legates were, after all, the presidents

[2] A reversal which, had it taken place, would not have trenched upon the infallibility of Melchiades, since it was not a matter which came within the scope of Papal infallibility.

following:—'In the first place, concerning the celebration of Easter, it shall be kept at one time and on the same day throughout the world by us and *as thou shalt by letters, according to custom*, direct.'[1] This canon occurs in the letter addressed by the synod to the Bishop of Rome 'as thou shalt by letters, according to custom, direct,' referring to him. It is clear from this that St. Victor's efforts to procure uniformity in regard to the Paschal Feast had not been without effect, for in 314 it was a 'custom' for the Bishop of Rome to 'direct' the Churches as to the day of its observance. The British bishops in their controversy with Augustine merely clung to what they had received from Rome, in ignorance that it had been changed.

VII. The council sent a letter to the Pope, expressing their conviction that their sentence against the Donatists was even more lenient than it might have been, if the Pope had been present in person—*te pariter nobiscum judicante*.[2] But as he could not leave those parts 'in which the Apostles daily sit'—*i.e.* St. Peter and St. Paul—they have drawn up the decrees, which they send, hoping that he will communicate them to the rest of the world—of course, supposing that he approved them. The letter speaks of St. Sylvester as not only sitting where the Apostles St. Peter and St. Paul sit—*i.e.* as occupying the see founded and guided by them—but also as holding 'the greater dioceses,' and it decided that persons who had been baptised by heretics with the proper form should not be rebaptised, but should be received by imposition of hands—passages from which we can form some idea of the religious teaching in this land in the fourth century.

The Donatists' next step after this decision at Arles was condemned by the emperor and all Catholics. They again appealed to His Imperial Majesty from the judgment of the episcopate. It is unfortunate that we have no record of the motives which induced the emperor to rehear the case. We

[1] *Ecclesiastical Councils* (Haddan and Stubbs), vol. i. p. 7, note.

[2] Mansi, t. ii. p. 469. Some writers (*e.g.* Dr. Wordsworth, *Theophilus Anglicanus*) consider that the word *pariter* involves an assertion of equality in judgment. But it must be admitted that the word does not necessarily mean anything more than our English 'together with,' which would admit of any amount of inequality between the parties thus acting together.

know that he disapproved of their step, and very reluctantly yielded.[1] He allowed them to come to Milan, but only to reiterate the original sentence against them, and eventually to deprive them of their churches.

VIII. The Council of Arles, however, has another interest for us, besides the fact that our fellow-countrymen were present. In the movement out of the Calvinism which had flooded the land since its change of religion, the party of decency and order, as we may fairly call the followers of Laud, stood between two fires; on the one side from the Puritans, who brought their king and archbishop to the scaffold, and on the other side from the Catholics, who urged the return of the High Church party to the bosom of the Catholic Church. The grounds on which they defended themselves have more than an antiquarian interest for us in England, for indeed many of the arguments used then for the purpose of preventing the chivalrous champions of ecclesiastical order from submitting to Rome are repeated in the controversial books of the present day. Amongst them is to be found an argument supposed to be derived from the Council of Arles. We have already seen that Mr. Haddan, in Smith's 'Dictionary of Christian Antiquities,' made a point of Rome not being summoned to it, ignoring the fact that Papal legates attended, and that he appeared to view it as an appeal to a plenary council of the universal Church from the judgment of the Pope. Mr. Ffoulkes, we have seen, considers it ' as gross a misconception or as wilful a misstatement as ever proceeded from a learned man ' ('Dict. of Chr. Biogr.' art. 'Marinus') to say (as Mr. Haddan does) that St. Augustine called the council universal. It is not surprising that some who lean much on history should say, as nowadays many do, ' Whom *are* we to believe?' History, as the Catholic Church gives it to us, placing its key in our hands, is one thing; history without that key may easily become a labyrinth in which a lifetime may be spent in futile attempts to find the centre. But Archbishop Laud succeeded in impressing on his generation a view of history which contented a great many, and which it is, therefore, a

[1] He asked pardon of the bishops, St. Augustine says (*Brevic. Collat.* pars 3).

matter of interest to examine. I shall take the argument by which he repels the evidence adduced by his adversary, the Jesuit, from St. Augustine's words, quoted above, about the 'principalship,' or sovereignty of the Roman chair.

First, he gives an account of the origin of that principalship, or sovereignty, or primacy, which certainly was not St. Augustine's. He says: 'The Roman patriarch by ecclesiastical constitution might, perhaps [sic], have a primacy of order; but for principality of power the patriarchs were as even, as equal, as the Apostles were before them. . . . The truth is, this "more powerful principality" the Roman bishops got under the emperors when they became Christian.'[1] Now St. Augustine, writing about the first Christian emperor, and he not yet baptised, says that this principality 'has *always* been in force' ('semper viguit,' Ep. 43, 7).

But Laud proceeds: 'And to prove that St. Augustine did not intend by *principatus* here to give the Roman Bishop any power out of his own limits (which God knows were far short of the whole Church), I shall make it most manifest out of the very same epistle. "For afterwards," saith St. Augustine, "when the pertinacity of the Donatists could not be restrained by the African bishops only, they gave them leave to be heard by foreign bishops."' It will be seen by comparison with St. Augustine's words, as quoted above, how thoroughly inaccurate this is to begin with. There was no leave given[2] in Africa. But in the next sentence Laud mistranslates the Latin, and applies the saint's words in his own favour instead of exactly the other way. He quotes, or professes to quote, St. Augustine's own words: 'And yet peradventure Melchiades, the Bishop of the Roman Church, with his colleagues, the transmarine bishops (*non debuit*) ought not to usurp to himself this judgment, which was determined by seventy African bishops, Tigisitanus sitting primate. And what will you say if he did not usurp this power? For the emperor, being desired, sent

[1] *Library of Anglo-Catholic Theology* (Oxford), Laud's Works, vol. i. § xxv. 10, p. 186. All the quotations that follow are taken from this volume.

[2] The Emperor expressly says that the removal of the case to Rome was his own doing, in his letter to Melchiades (Eus. x. 5). But it is obvious from its terms, and from St. Augustine's account (*Ep.* 43, 14), that he was referring them to a tribunal recognised as supreme by the orthodox in Africa.

bishops, judges, which should sit with him and determine what was just upon the whole cause.' It will be noticed that there is rather a lack of logic in these words of St. Augustine as given by Laud. The question, 'And what will you say, &c. ?' suggests that St. Augustine did not think it a usurpation on the part of the Bishop of Rome, whilst the preceding words make the saint stigmatise it as such. But this, as I shall show, is owing to Laud's mistranslation. It will be best, however, to proceed with his deductions.

'In which passage' (says Laud) 'there are very many things observable; as, first, that the Roman prelate came not in till there was leave for them to go to "transmarine bishops."'

There is no evidence whatever that they asked or obtained leave from the African bishops. St. Augustine says that they simply appealed to the emperor, and he remitted the case to Rome.

'Secondly' (says Laud), 'that if the Pope had come in without this leave, it had been a "usurpation."'

Now this point rests on Laud's mistranslation. The words he quotes from St. Augustine are his, all except two little words at the beginning. Instead of the words 'And yet,' St. Augustine asks a question, and uses—no equivalent for the words 'and yet,' but—the particle which marks the beginning of a question.[1] He supposes the Donatists to make the objection; so that the words which Laud professes to transcribe from the pen of St. Augustine as his first view of the case are the words which St. Augustine puts into the mouth of the Donatists and at once proceeds to controvert! His question, 'And what will you say, if he did not usurp this power?' contains his answer, or the beginning of his answer, to the objection which he supposes the Donatists to raise against the judgment of Melchiades. The Donatist is supposed to call it a usurpation; St. Augustine combats the Donatist contention. Laud puts it the other way, and makes it plausible by his mistranslation.

But he proceeds: 'Thirdly, that when he [*i.e.* the Pope] did thus come in, not by his own proper authority,

[1] 'An forte,' &c.

but by leave, there were other bishops made "judges with him."'

Here, again, the 'leave' is harped upon, for which there is no evidence, and assessors are assumed as detracting from the supreme authority of the Pope. But to this hour Popes act with assistance from bishops or cardinals, and in greater matters from a council.

Again: 'Fourthly, that these other bishops were "appointed and sent by the emperor," and his power; that which the Pope will least of all endure.' Laud puts the words 'appointed and sent by the emperor' as though they were quotations from St. Augustine; but he has slipped in the word 'appointed.' St. Augustine only says 'sent'—we do not know with how much concerted action between the emperor and the Pope.

Laud continues with a complete misinterpretation of another passage: 'Lastly, lest the Pope and his adherents should say that this was a usurpation in the emperor, St. Augustine tells us a little before, in the same epistle still, "that this doth chiefly belong *ad curam ejus*, to the emperor's care and charge, and that he is to give an account to God for it."'

Now one would suppose that 'this' relates in St. Augustine to the same as Laud has been speaking of before, as he adduces it to show that the previous affair, as understood by him, was not in St. Augustine's eyes a usurpation on the part of the emperor. Will not any reader, who has not been able to study the passage in the original, be surprised to find that St. Augustine is referring to a wholly different stage of the proceedings, and to a matter which was, according to the teaching of Laud's adversary, well within the power of the emperor? St. Augustine, in this last passage, is dealing with another objection by the Donatists. After the synod at Rome had decided in favour of Cæcilianus' consecration and against the Donatists, the latter brought forward a new point about Felix of Aptunga. This was a matter of fact, which could be determined by a secular tribunal. The emperor ordered his proconsul to investigate it in Africa. The Donatists hypocritically objected in after years that a proconsul was not the proper judge of bishops. St. Augustine reminds them of the way in which the proconsul was commissioned by the emperor, to whom the care of such a matter properly belonged. Besides, St. Augustine urges that they had themselves appealed to the emperor, and if they considered it wrong for a proconsul to investigate the question of Felix's antecedents in Africa, 'how much more blameworthy must they be who wished to make an earthly king the judge of their case!'[1] In a word, St. Augustine is urging the very opposite conclusion to that which Laud deduces from his words.

[1] *Ep.* 43, § 13.

CHAPTER XI.

THE COUNCIL OF NICÆA.

§ I.—*The Reasons for its being convoked.*

I. THE history of the Church consists of the record of her perpetual proposal of divine mysteries to the human intelligence, and of the acceptance or repudiation of her authority by a nature wounded through the fall in Eden. One result of that fall is the reluctance that men feel to submit to a master. There is no man that is not called at some time of his life to sacrifice his natural love of independence in obedience to authority. But it is not every man that will bind his intelligence on the mount of sacrifice and merit to receive it back again from God in a new supernatural life. Hence the conflicts of heresy in the history of the Church. The very word heresy implies deliberate choice ; and the deliberate choice which constitutes heresy is a determined rebellion against the authority that, bringing with it adequate credentials, proposes the subject matter of divine revelation.

The history of the Church is, therefore, the history of a series of conflicts between authority and the rebellious instincts of our fallen nature, which protest against rule, dominion, and lordship, even though submission be the portal of Paradise itself.

But these conflicts with heresy were not all so much loss to the Church. As the original rebellion in Paradise was the *felix culpa* which led to the greater gift of the Incarnation, so the lapse of heretics led to the Church bringing out her stores of wisdom and exhibiting the majesty of her divinely given authority. There is no better cordial for drooping courage than a study of the evolution of her grandeur as she rode through the storms of the fourth and fifth centuries. The majesty of her Divine Head was assaulted and in danger of being undermined under every conceivable aspect. But without these assaults we might have been poorer in our knowledge of what the Church was and what she could do. It has been well said that 'it was not until after some conflict that the Church exercised her full authority as guardian of the ancient faith in all its integrity, whose duty it is to repress all error, and all principles that may lead to error, among Christians. By this conflict the Church was led of necessity to unfold, with ample fulness, the truth of her doctrine, which was at first more implicit, and although perfectly understood, not fully expressed; to define it more particularly and in distinct formulas against every error. This is a service which heresies have at all times conferred upon the Church.'[1]

And there is no spectacle in all history more worthy of our admiration than the serene majesty with which the Holy See articulated the teaching of Jesus Christ through all the storms that raged against the Church in the days of persecution. But with the fourth century came the era of great councils, beginning with that held at Nicæa and ending with that held at Chalcedon. These stand apart, with features of their own, and have obtained a position which St. Gregory the Great likens to that of the four gospels. It will be my object in the following pages to exhibit the share which the Holy See took in the destruction of heresy and the orderly exhibition of the deposit of truth committed to the Church's care during this era of her conciliar action.

II. But why, it has been asked, a council at all, if the Pope is himself infallible? Might not the Church have been spared the trouble of meeting in council at all?[2] Indeed, it has been said that the fact of the Nicene Council having been held is the most perfect refutation of the assertion made in

---

[1] Döllinger's *Ch. Hist.* Period I. cap. ii. § 7.

[2] This was the argument constantly used by Dr. Pusey: *e.g.* 'Had Papal infallibility been then believed, Sylvester, or St. Damasus, or St. Celestine, or St. Leo might by themselves have set at rest the heresies of Arius,' &c. (*Sermon on the Rule of Faith*, 2nd ed. Preface, p. 18).

the Vatican decrees that the *ex cathedrâ* infallibility of the Pope was always known to the Church. It is asked, 'On the principle of the Vatican dogmas, why did not Pope Sylvester close the question by an *ex cathedrâ* judgment?'[1] and it is added that 'the negligence, on the part alike of the Church and the Pope, was simply treasonable '—*i.e.* on the supposition that Papal infallibility was a known truth.

All these objections are based on a misconception of 'the principle of the Vatican dogmas.' It is no part of the doctrine of infallibility that the Pope was able at any moment to 'close the question,' when he had to deal with such people as the Arians; just as it is no part of the Church's teaching that our Divine Lord could close the question about His heavenly origin in addressing the Jews in the synagogue at Capharnaum. And yet He was in a higher sense infallible.[2] It cannot be argued that our Lord was not Almighty God because the people said, 'If Thou be the Christ, tell us plainly,' and because He taught them in a way which did not convince them all. And so with His Vicar. It might need a longer management, or a different mode of expression from an *ex cathedrâ* judgment, to bring the Arians to their bearings and 'close the question.' The writers who have advanced this objection believe the Nicene Creed to be as authoritative an expression of revealed truth as can be had; but the Nicene Creed did not 'close the question.' The Pope is not more infallible than the whole Church, and yet the voice of what the objectors would consider the whole Church has not sufficed to close the question for some of their own teachers.

III. But the objection thus confidently urged against the truth that under certain circumstances the successor of Peter is secure of divine assistance against leading the Church astray (*i.e.* is under certain conditions infallible), ignores the circumstances under which the Council of Nicæa was assem-

---

[1] *The Roman Claims tested by Antiquity*, by W. Bright, D.D., Prof. of Eccles. Hist. in the Univ. of Oxford, 1877, p. 9—one of the books recommended in the list drawn up by the English Church Union. Cf. also Preface to *Lives of Three Fathers*, by the same author.

[2] Canon Liddon, in his last *Bampton Lecture*, was perfectly right in arguing that our Lord alone was infallible in the sense in which he uses the term; he was mistaken in his exaggerated idea of what is involved in Papal infallibility

bled. It was not a new question that it had to discuss. It was not one on which anyone had the slightest doubt as to the judgment of the Pope. It has already been observed that the real forerunner of Arius was excommunicated, in the person of Theodotus, by Pope St. Victor. And the first open conflict on the subject of the term *Homoousios* (or consubstantial) as applied to the Eternal Son, had been set at rest by another Pope, St. Dionysius. His namesake of Alexandria had used similes concerning the relation of the Son to the Father which were liable to misrepresentation, and had withdrawn them, and informed the Pope that he only did not use the word consubstantial because he did not find it in Holy Scripture, but that he believed and taught the doctrine therein contained.[1] St. Dionysius, the Pope, in his synod, had declared the doctrine signified by the term to be of faith, and set his seal to the use of the term itself (*Homoousios*) without, however, making it a matter of absolute obligation on the whole Church. It was henceforth used at Rome and Alexandria as the fittest symbol of the relationship of the Son to the Father. So that Christians were not left in doubt as to the faith up to the hour of the Council of Nicæa. St. Athanasius (*loc. cit.*) says that the gist of the Arian heresy had been condemned on this occasion (c. 262) by the Pope St. Dionysius, 'and so was long ago (ἔκπαλαι) anathematised by all.'[2] For St. Dionysius and his synod had proclaimed that the Son was in no sense a creature, but was of one substance with the Father.

In the beginning of the fourth century the heresy reappeared in the teaching of a priest at Antioch, named

---

[1] Athanas. *De Sententia Dionysii*, n. 14.

[2] It has been said that the word ὁμοούσιος was condemned by the Council of Antioch in 269 (*e.g.* Salmon on *Infallibility*, p. 292). St. Athanasius, St. Basil, and St. Hilary *seem* to allow this. But St. Athanasius says that he had not seen the letter of the Council nor been able to learn its contents. St. Basil appears to be speaking of the Council of Ancyra, a semi-Arian council in 358, for he gives their known motives and assigns them to Antioch. St. Hilary makes the two councils say exactly the same thing. Dr. Döllinger has an exhaustive note on the subject (*Ch. Hist.* Period I. cap. ii. sec. 7), and concludes that its rejection by the Synod of Antioch, in its true meaning, is ' contrary to all historical evidence.' De Smedt argues forcibly that the term, though not the doctrine, *was* repudiated at Antioch (Diss. vi.).

Lucian, among whose pupils was the priest of Alexandria, named Arius, of great parts and most attractive ways. This is not the place in which to give his teaching in detail. Suffice it to say that in his descriptions of the Son, or Logos, or Word, of God, whilst he exalted Him far above all other creatures, placing His origin even before time, he yet denied to Him strict eternity, or a real generation from the Essence of the Father. His teaching spread like wildfire in the East, even Eusebius, Bishop of Cæsarea, the father of Church history, being carried away by it. It is an unutterable loss to history that Eusebius was thus out of sympathy with the real mind of the Nicene Fathers. Whilst, therefore, he indulges in a grand description of the council, he has omitted all that we most wish to know.

The teaching, then, which had been condemned by St. Dionysius was spreading over the East. What was the Pope to do? Hold another Council in the West and issue an *ex cathedrâ* judgment on the whole question? But the question had already been closed by St. Dionysius. Should he, then, excommunicate every bishop who was not teaching in perfect accord with Rome? But it needed the apparatus of a council to discover who were, and who were not, teaching the true faith.[1] The Arians were proverbially slippery.

IV. The step actually taken was due to the fact that in the Providence of God the Emperor Constantine now occupied himself with the Eastern portion of his empire. He had seen the unity of the Church in the West. He found the East torn with dissension. After attempting to introduce the idea that the contention was for nothing real, and discovering his mistake, he resolved that the bishops should meet together, and so be brought to some definite issue. He might, of course, have done as the three emperors did half a century later—

---

[1] 'Almighty God did not will that it should be by the voice of one man that heresies should be slain. He had an office for the Universal Church throughout the world. He had an office for the Church, as a whole, to bear witness to the truth' (Pusey's *Sermon on the Rule of Faith*, Pref. p. xxxiv.). This, which Dr. Pusey thought a conclusive argument against the Vatican Decrees, is, nevertheless, part of the teaching of those decrees. One of the most curious phenomena of contemporary history is the continued misunderstanding of those decrees by Dr. Pusey and others.

issue an edict that all who wished to retain their churches must teach the religion handed down by the Apostle Peter to the Romans—but Constantine was not yet baptised, and it is impossible to suppose that a Pio Nono would have advised such a remedy under the circumstances. The idea of a council on a larger scale than had yet been tried was suggested to the emperor by the episcopate. It was convoked, says Rufinus, a contemporary, 'by the advice of the bishops, *ex sententiâ sacerdotum.*'[1] It was not likely to be the suggestion of Eusebius, nor the rest of the Arianising bishops. They had not yet gained the emperor's ear, and it was the last thing they would desire. Judging from a statement of the sixth Council, composed entirely of Eastern bishops, and held subsequently to the time when the extent of the claims of Rome were, by the confession of all writers, distinctly understood, the idea of the Nicene Council was not due to the emperor, but to the Pope himself. Rome and Alexandria were in close correspondence on the crisis, and it is in the highest degree probable that they had agreed that the best way of assisting the East was by a solemn consultation. This is looking at the matter from a purely historical point of view. Such notices as we have all suggest that the idea came from Rome and Alexandria.

V. And the reasons why St. Sylvester might reasonably and not 'treasonably' (as the above-mentioned writer insists [2]) prefer a conciliar judgment in the East to an *ex cathedrâ* judgment from Rome itself, were possibly such as these:

An *ex cathedrâ* judgment was usually given with a certain solemnity of circumstance, such as a council of the bishops who were in Rome, and those, besides, whom the Pope might be pleased to select. Such an authoritative utterance, making the *term* '*Homoousios*' a condition of Catholic communion (which was all that was needed, the doctrine having been already settled) might have been sent from the West to the

---

[1] Lib. i. cap. 1. Dr. Salmon flatly contradicts Rufinus. He says (*Infall.* p. 289), 'The bringing it together was entirely the emperor's idea.' But he gives no authority for his assertion, and appears to have forgotten the quotation given above.

[2] Bright's *Roman Claims*, &c. loc. cit.

East. This would have been the 'despotic' method of rule. But the 'politic'[1] mode of action was clearly to have the council in the East, and to call upon the bishops there to exercise their judgment upon the matter. For it is part of the episcopal office, according to the Vatican decrees, to use its judgment, and the free use of the same in no way interferes with the truth of Papal infallibility, as defined by those decrees. To judge after the Pope is not to act as his superior, but as a subordinate judge. It is not proclaiming his judgment useless, but following it spontaneously as the norm. Whilst a discordant judgment would subject the bishop to anathema, a concordant judgment is of value. In a council information would be given, personal contact with the orthodox would do its proper work, an Athanasius (although but a deacon) would exert the influence due to his character, and the unity of the Church would be made plain.

Moreover, it cannot be too carefully borne in mind that Papal infallibility does not mean inspiration, but only Divine assistance. Such assistance requires the Pope to use human means to ascertain the truths to be proclaimed : *e.g.* discussion may be necessary to enable the Pope to decide as to whether this or that is in the deposit, whether it is the logical outcome of such and such a revealed doctrine. And among such means of arriving at the truth, one of peculiar efficacy is that of convoking a General Council and taking the witness of the Fathers. Thus, a General Council may be included in the action of infallibility, although the ultimate result in the shape of the final definition is only certain by reason of the *charisma* bestowed on the Holy Father. In the case of the first four councils, the decision of the Pope was already formed, and, therefore, they were not needed for that purpose, but they were conducive to the ends which the Holy Father had in view, and were, therefore, suggested or accepted by him as the case might be.[2]

The way, then, in which St. Sylvester elected to govern the Church was by a council in the East, which the emperor

---

[1] Readers of Aristotle will remember his distinction between the despotic and politic methods of government.

[2] It was in the council that they discovered that nothing short of the use of the term *Homoousios* would avail. Cf. Athan. *De Decr. Nic. Syn.* n. 20.

hailed for the fulfilment of his own desire for the unity of the Church as the safeguard of his empire. St. Sylvester knew well that Papal infallibility does not act like magic. The writers from whom I have quoted appear to imagine that he had only to raise his voice, and if the doctrine of infallibility had been held by the Church, 'the question would have been closed.'

But the visible Church consists of wheat and tares; and the Arians would not have accepted the consubstantiality of the Son, though an angel from heaven proclaimed it. The decree of the head of the Church would have sufficed for some of these Easterns; but the decision of the head in conjunction with the rest, with the 'conjudication' of the associated teaching body, viz. the episcopate, which can never be reduced to a mere vicariate of the Pope, would be a stronger argument to those who were inclined to resist. It was more imposing, and required less faith. Rome and Alexandria had already consecrated the term *Homoousios* to express the faith. It was now to be seen in the face of day by an evident and imposing manifestation that there was no place in the Church for any who taught the contrary. The bishops, directed from Rome,[1] were in the exercise of their prerogative, by the grace of their consecration, to proclaim before the world their adhesion to what, as a matter of fact, had been the teaching of the Holy See, and of such bishops as Alexander of Alexandria. They did not, as I have said, come to decide an open question. The legates (cf. p. 164) came full charged with their master's judgment, and the rest of the bishops with the teaching which had been theirs all along—they came to proclaim that there was but one teaching in the East and West, in the body and the head, and that that teaching attributed proper Divinity to the invisible Head of the Church.

So that the palmary instance of history contradicting the statement of the Vatican decree[2] is derived from the fact that St. Sylvester considered that the circumstances of the case demanded the apparatus of a council rather than an *ex cathe-*

---

[1] See p. 164.

[2] 'The Nicene Council is the best instance one could take—the best on all grounds' (Bright's *Roman Claims, loc. cit.*).

drâ judgment from himself. That is to say that, *given* Papal infallibility, it ought to have been exercised in the particular way laid down by these writers;[1] and since it was not so exercised, it could not have been known to the Church; 'the negligence on the part alike of the Church and of the Pope was simply treasonable.' In point of fact, St. Sylvester seems to have exhibited that genius for government which, it has been remarked by an unfriendly critic, is an inalienable inheritance of the occupants of the See of Rome. To bring the East into line with the West, he used the instrument of a council composed of bishops, mostly Eastern, together with his own legates, instead of issuing a fresh decree straight from Rome. We do not know what the action of his legates was in the council, as the record has perished. We can only judge, if we can judge at all, by that of the Papal legates at the Council of Ephesus, when we first have a full record of conciliar action. And in that council their position was one of undisputed superiority.

§ II.—*The Council itself.*

I. The council, when it met, consisted almost entirely of Eastern bishops. Not more than five Western bishops attended. There was no need of the presence of more, and the assembly would have been indefinitely delayed had the presence of others been required. Arianism, as Mr. Allies remarks, was an Eastern malady. And it was enough for the West that the legates of the Holy See were on the spot, bringing with them, as is expressly stated by Eusebius, the authority of St. Sylvester.

The Pope presided by his legates, consisting of Hosius, the Bishop of Cordova, in Spain (who had been acting at Alexandria[2] in the affair of Arius, and was the trusted friend of the emperor), and two priests named Vito and Vincentius. These three signed first, Hosius obviously not in virtue of his

---

[1] I have quoted only from Dr. Pusey and Dr. Bright; but the instances in which I have noticed the same assumption in Anglican writers are practically innumerable.

[2] The action of Hosius, a Western bishop, at Alexandria, suggests some other than a purely imperial commission. He was probably Papal legate throughout the whole affair.

see, but as legate. The two priests signed next, and then Alexandria, Antioch, and Jerusalem. Some writers have endeavoured to evade the force of this fact, by suggesting that Hosius was made president, as the emperor's favourite, and from general respect for his character. One can hardly suppose that the suggestion could be due to anything but the exigencies of a theory which is opposed to the idea that Rome presided. Could anything be more entirely opposed to all that we know of the relationship between the greater and lesser sees of Christendom than the supposition that the emperor's will placed an inferior Western see over the Sees of Rome, Alexandria and Antioch? It is admitted on all hands, that long before the Council of Nice the See of Rome was considered to be the See of Peter, and we have already seen that there is irrefragable proof that Alexandria acted as at least in some sense subordinate to Rome. It is freely admitted on all sides that Rome had a primacy of honour by those who deny her primacy of jurisdiction. Yet, according to this strange theory, her primacy of honour did not involve even the presidency at the first Œcumenical Council. What *did* that primacy of honour involve? Further, the sees are, even on this theory, placed in their usual order *after* the president's signature, viz. first the papal legates, then Alexandria, and then Antioch. But we are asked on this theory to believe that above these greater sees thus placed in their order, a lesser see of the West signed, not as representing the first see in Christendom, but as president—Cordova, Rome, Alexandria, Antioch, Jerusalem!

I have said that this supposed arrangement could only have been by the emperor's desire, for it is impossible to suppose that Papal legates suggested such an order, or that Alexandria and Antioch would otherwise have suffered a suffragan of the West to take precedence, when a question as to their own jurisdiction over their suffragans was coming on for discussion.

Mr. Puller [1] quotes the case of Marinus, Bishop of Arles, at the Council of Arles, who is supposed by some to have presided.

---

[1] *Prim. SS.* p. 143, note 3.

But it is not certain that he did;[1] and he was the bishop of the place, and the council was in no sense œcumenical, but was convened under peculiar circumstances (cf. p. 145). Hosius was not Bishop of Nice, but of a see in Spain. And is it conceivable that, if Hosius had acted as president, a lesser Western see over all the great Eastern sees, in the East, the precedent would never have been quoted? Could the Council of Chalcedon have blamed Dioscorus for sitting as president in the presence of papal legates, by the express order of the emperor, at the Robber Council of Ephesus, and no one have pressed the point that at Nice even a lesser Western bishop had sat above even Rome, not to speak of Alexandria and Antioch? The idea is so unsupported by any historical evidence, that it would have been natural to pass it by, had not several recent writers made a chivalrous attempt at foisting it into the history of the council.

It is, then, on the list of signatures alone that such writers rely; it is from the same list that we may derive a sound argument for the presidency of the Pope at this council. It is not only from the account of Gelasius of Cyzicus that the proof is derived, but from the inherent improbability (I had almost said impossibility) of the opposite theory, granting the accuracy of the list of signatures, which is not denied. These lists, referred to by Gelasius, supported by the strongest internal probability, and the analogy of the mode of procedure at subsequent councils, constitute an amount of evidence which is opposed merely by the fact that Hosius' name occurs first, and the assumption that he signed in his own right.

And it is necessary also to protest against the idea that in this instance Gelasius of Cyzicus may be discarded as of no value.[2] Photius of Constantinople, before his fall, bracketed Hosius and the two Roman priests as forming the Papal legation, quoting Gelasius. And Photius must have been relying not only on his own judgment, but also on an Eastern tradition to the same effect. But Gelasius of Cyzicus could hardly

---

[1] Cf. *Dict. of Chr. Biog.* art. 'Marinus.'

[2] Mr. Gore (*R. C. Claims*, p. 100, 3rd ed.) altogether fails to appreciate the argument derived from the lists of Gelasius. Nearly every assertion which he makes in the note, in which he speaks of this subject, may be fairly questioned.

have created an Eastern tradition. Besides, Gelasius is not giving his own authority, which would be of comparatively little worth, but professes to be copying from older lists. What is the exact authority of those lists no one can say; but Gelasius evidently had some other lists besides the one from which Eusebius copies, and they agreed on this point. The Eastern tradition in favour of the presidency of Rome at the council must have been strong for it to be adopted as it has been into the Græco-Russian liturgy. In the office of St. Sylvester the following address to him in reference to the council occurs:—' Thou hast shown thyself the supreme one of the Sacred Council, O initiator into the sacred mysteries, and hast illustrated the Throne of the Supreme One of the Disciples.' Here is the presidency of the Council of Nicæa attributed to St. Sylvester, as the successor of St. Peter, ' the supreme one of the Apostles.'

That the legates exercised a real influence is involved in the statement, made in the same century by St. Damasus and a synod of ninety bishops, that the 318 bishops at Nicæa were ' directed from the city of the most holy Bishop of Rome ' in the work of the council, whilst the Council of Rome in A.D. 485 states that the 318 bishops there assembled ' referred the confirmation of things and the authority to the holy Roman Church.'

II. The official records have perished, probably destroyed by the Arians when in possession of the Eastern sees. Hence it is not open to argue anything from the silence of the bishops on this or that subject. It would be arguing, not from the silence of the council, but from the absence of records. When Mr. Puller says that '*undoubtedly*,'[1] if the idea ' (*i.e.* of a primacy of jurisdiction as possessed by the Bishop of Rome) ' had been presented to the synod, and if *any claim* on behalf of the Pope had been urged as of divine right, there *can be no question* that a repudiation of such claim *would* have been made in *unmistakable* terms,' he is arguing not from history but from preconceived ideas. But when he goes on to say, ' But as a matter of fact the claim was not made, and therefore the whole conception that underlies the Vatican decrees was

---

[1] The italics in this sentence are mine.

ignored,'[1] he first manufactures his history and then makes an unsound deduction from his fabrication. How can we say that 'as a matter of fact the claim was not made,' when we do not possess a single record beyond the creed and canons?—when, moreover, the learned are not even agreed as to the number of canons? Who has interrogated the Nicene Fathers to know what was said, seeing that all documentary evidence has perished? But supposing that the claim was not made, how does this prove that 'the whole conception underlying the Vatican decrees' was 'ignored'? It proves nothing either way, unless it can be shown that there was occasion for making the claim. But how can we suppose that such a claim would come in *à propos* of the business of the synod? Surely these strong assertions, 'undoubtedly,' 'there can be no question,' need some other ground on which to rest. The fact that the original documents were at some time or other, in the case of each of the greater Eastern sees, in the hands of the Arians, and the tendency that we know the Arians exhibited to forge and mutilate documents, must make us very careful how we use even those we do possess. Where great institutions rest upon them, where traces of them are found in other writings, and when there is corroborative evidence in the West, we may trust them. But as to arguing from their silence, and calling it 'significant,' one is compelled to say that those who build such tremendous issues on such a sandy foundation are having recourse to a most dangerous expedient. St. Boniface, addressing the bishops of Thessaly, reminds them that the Nicene Fathers did not venture to lay down anything regarding the See of St. Peter, because they knew that 'that was bestowed by the word of the Lord.' As an hypothesis this is equally rational with that of the supreme jurisdiction of the Pope having been ignored; as a matter supported by evidence, it has more in its favour than the latter hypothesis. The history of matters immediately subsequent to the council will show that this must have been the case; for it is not reasonable to suppose that St. Julius, St. Liberius, and St. Damasus could have acted as they did, if the primacy of jurisdiction had been 'ignored' at the Council of Nicæa. We

[1] *Prim. SS.* p. 147.

must not take history piece by piece, but trace the continuous development of an institution, if we would understand its real meaning.

§ III.—*The Sixth Canon.*

I. There is, however, one canon which gives us a glimpse of the nature of the Church's government. It ran thus:— 'The Roman Church has the primacy' (or, 'Let the Roman Church have the primacy,' or, as the true version probably runs, 'It is the ancient custom that the Roman Church should hold the primacy'). 'Let the ancient customs be maintained, which are in Egypt, Libya and Pentapolis, according to which the Bishop of Alexandria has authority over all those places, since this is also customary' (or 'there is a like custom') 'to the Bishop of Rome. In like manner in Antioch and in the other provinces these privileges are to be preserved.'

As it is disputed by some whether the first clause about the Roman Church formed part of the canon, I will leave that for the moment as though it did not exist. And I will also suppose that the canon ends here, although I think there is good reason to suppose that there was at one time more in the canon.

One thing that must strike the most casual observer at once is the fact that the Church comes before us after her three centuries of persecution with her hierarchy of bishops already in order. Three sees come before us with titles to jurisdiction already possessed. The council did not originate their jurisdiction, and settled not to meddle with it. Their words do not even imply that they *could*. The force of ancient custom is too much for them. Whence the ancient custom was derived, on what authority it was based, they do not say; we can settle that from other sources. The Sixth Canon gives no hint as to whether these customs, all or any of them, relied on divine institution or on ecclesiastical agreement. The three sees that come before us in this important canon are the sees of Peter, and their relationships were, according to the Fathers of Nicæa, of ancient origin. Within the jurisdiction of one of these Petrine sees a quarrel had arisen. Meletius, an Egyptian bishop, had risen against his patriarch (so to call him by anticipation) and formed a schism. The council had already dealt with metropolitans; it now proceeded to deal with greater metropolitans,[1] those bishops who had metropolitans under them. They decide that there is nothing to be done but to adhere to the jurisdictional extent of the See of Alexandria as it had been mapped out in the past.

II. But the Fathers in this canon give a reason for not interfering with the jurisdiction of Alexandria. They say that the ancient customary jurisdiction of that see should remain what it is, 'since [or because, ἐπειδή] the same is customary with the Bishop of Rome.' Thus the most marked distinction is drawn between the position of Rome on the one hand and the great sees of Alexandria and Antioch on the other. Rome's cognisance, or Rome's example, whichever be the true interpretation, is quoted by the Nicene Fathers as determining the question of Alexandria's rights of jurisdiction.[2]

If the expression used in this canon—viz. 'since this is customary also with the Bishop of Rome'—means that such exercise over other bishops was the custom also with the Bishop of Rome, then Rome's patriarchal sway is held up as the norm and sufficient justification of a similar authority on the part of the Bishop of Alexandria. The council does not touch upon the origin or ground of Rome's organisation of her jurisdiction. That did not come within its purview. It spoke of her patriarchal sway as settled *and as settling their own decision* (ἐπειδή). It has been said that the absence of any reference in this canon to the unique and sovereign position of the Bishop of Rome 'is a proof, if proof were wanted,

[1] Cf. *Valesii Observ. in Soc. et Soz.* 3. viii. So Jerome, John Scholasticus, Patr. of Constantinople, and Petrus de Marca.

[2] Mr. Puller describes the canon as going on 'to cite the case of the Roman See as parallel to the case of the Alexandrian See' (*Prim. SS.* p. 145). But the canon *goes on to cite* the *parallel* case of the Roman See *as the ground* for continuing her rights to Alexandria. This Mr. Puller omits to notice. Mr. Gore's summary of the canon is equally misleading: 'The Fathers in the Sixth Canon recognised in Rome a quasi-patriarchal power in her own region like that which they acknowledged equally in Alexandria and Antioch. They recognised nothing more' (*R. C. Claims*, 3rd edit. p. 96). Surely they suggested a great deal more when they gave this as *the reason* for their own action.

that the First Œcumenical Council knew nothing of the doctrine of Papal supremacy.' And the Bishop of Lincoln has recently called special attention to this proof, quoting these words and saying, 'We need to bring our minds to the consideration of such words.'[1] The same writer (Dr. Bright) urges in the previous sentence that since they were touching on jurisdiction they were bound to go on and speak of Papal jurisdiction if they believed in it. The best answer would be to ask, Why? If that jurisdiction were under dispute, one could understand why they ought to have gone on to speak of it. If not, there is no conceivable reason why they *must* enter upon such a subject. The proof to the consideration of which we are asked 'to bring our minds' is of the nature of a *petitio principii*. We may with much greater justice ask why the Fathers quoted Rome's relationship to the sees of her patriarchate as an adequate reason ($\dot{\epsilon}\pi\epsilon\iota\delta\dot{\eta}$) for so all-important a decision as that the jurisdiction of Alexandria was not to be interfered with. Mere antiquity would not be sufficient. The Nicene Fathers were not a body of antiquaries concerned to preserve the shape of an edifice from mere love of the antique. The custom must have been based on sufficient authority, and this authority they give—'since' (that is, because) 'this is customary to Rome.' The reason given suggests that Rome is something more than Alexandria and Antioch—nay, than the whole Council of Nice, for Rome's action is assumed as the true norm of ecclesiastical government. The council did not confirm anything in this matter as a superior court, it only followed custom. It *gave* nothing, except its adhesion to the customary jurisdiction already settled. It dealt with Alexandria and Antioch, but only to declare the type which Rome had supplied by her action in her own neighbourhood to be a sufficient authority.[2] On this ground they considered the protesting bishops bound to obey their Metropolitan at Alexandria.

[1] Cf. his Preface to *The Primitive Saints and the See of Rome*, by Rev. F. W. Puller, p. xvi.

[2] This seems to be the view of it taken by the Eighth Gen. Council, actio x. cap. 17, but not quite certainly. It is the interpretation given by Nicolas I. in his letter to the Emperor Michael.

III. I have given this interpretation first because of the great authority it can claim. But I cannot conceal from myself that, as compared with a second, adopted by Baronius and Bellarmine, it labours under certain disadvantages. In the first place it gives, indeed, a reason for the general principle of patriarchal jurisdiction, but not for the particular instance; and it was the particular instance which was the point in hand. That is to say, it is not clear how the reason given on this interpretation would account for the decision that those Egyptian bishops in particular should remain under Alexandria. And, secondly, the canon does not, in some of the oldest versions, speak of a *similar* exercise of jurisdiction as customary with the Bishop of Rome, but it says, ' since *this* is customary to the Bishop of Rome.' What is ' this ' ?

Taking the words simply as they stand, the canon may be said to assert that the subjection of the Egyptian bishops to Alexandria was customary with the Bishop of Rome. That is to say, the jurisdiction of Alexandria over these bishops had been the arrangement with respect to them recognised and acted upon by the Bishop of Rome himself, and that consequently things must remain as they were. They could not interfere with the ancient custom which had been thus recognised by Rome. The arrangement had been made with the cognisance of Rome. We can hardly doubt that the Papal legates had been instructed on this question. And they may have given the information that the bishops of Rome had long ago originated, or arranged, or consented to this jurisdiction of Alexandria. In this case the Nicene Fathers' judgment, when they said ' Let the ancient customs hold good, &c.,' would be equivalent to saying, 'Let these bishops remain under the See of Alexandria, since this arrangement is of long standing, it being customary with the bishops of Rome to act upon it '—as had actually happened in the previous century in the case of the bishops of Upper Nubia and St. Dionysius of Rome and his namesake of Alexandria.

On the supposition that the supremacy of the Church of Rome was a universally recognised truth, this would be a most natural way of speaking. It is here advanced, however, not as a positive proof of that doctrine, but as a reply to the various conjectures on which the writers above quoted rely, arguing from the supposed silence of the fragmentary records which we possess, and particularly of this canon. The argument advanced by Dr. Bright and emphasised by the Bishop of Lincoln, to the effect that if the Church had believed in the supremacy of the Church of Rome, it must have said so in this canon, may thus be met in two ways: first, by insisting on the precarious nature of the argument from silence, in the absence of the Acts of the Council; and secondly, by showing that it cannot be fairly deemed beyond dispute that this canon was not meant to give the authority of Rome as an all-sufficient reason for these Fathers not venturing to innovate on the customary relationship of Alexandria to her suffragan sees. There is, moreover, this indisputable fact, on which Pope Nicolas I. laid stress in his celebrated letter to the Emperor Michael, that whilst the council described the jurisdiction, more or less, of Alexandria and Antioch, it did not do the same in regard to Rome. Rufinus, indeed, supplies us with some information in regard to the patriarchal jurisdiction of Rome, speaking of the suburbicarian churches, but as his interpretation is not generally accepted as part of the canon, we cannot say under what form mention was made of those churches.

IV. This whole contention will be greatly strengthened if we consider the probability that this canon had for its heading, or rather, for its first sentence, the words read by the Roman legates at the Council of Chalcedon, viz. 'The Church of Rome always held [or, Let the Church of Rome always hold] the primacy.'[1] Aetius, the Archdeacon of Constantinople, is supposed to have read out a copy of the canon without this heading. But there is no suggestion in the Acts, as we have them, that this was by way of contrast to the legates' version, which came from Lilybæum. It is hardly

---

[1] The full reading is very likely 'Let the ancient custom remain that the Church of Rome should,' &c. (cf. Vincenzi, *De Sacrâ Monarchiâ Hebr. et Christianorum*). Canon Bright is hardly fair in saying 'the *Prisca Versio* tries to blend the original with the Roman gloss.' The *Prisca Versio* is a real authority, and from an old Greek version.

conceivable that he should have read this canon at all; for each side was asked to read the canons on which they relied. The Papal legates relied on that portion of the Sixth Canon which places Alexandria and Antioch, and not Constantinople, next to Rome; the Easterns relied on the Third Canon of Constantinople. Aetius probably read this alone, and not the Sixth Canon, which carried on the face of it his condemnation —in fact, the bishops' resolution had departed from the canon which Aetius did read, being, as Dr. Bright euphemistically phrases it, 'more astute than candid,'[1] or, as we might put it, somewhat dishonest. The imperial commissioners, in summing up, decided that from all that had gone before it was clear that Rome held the primacy, but as that was not the point in question, they proceeded to the subject of Constantinople's place in the order of sees.

The occurrence of this Sixth Canon in what the Archdeacon of Constantinople is supposed to have read, is probably due to the copyists, one of whom put the Sixth Canon in the margin, and another eventually introduced it into the text, a most frequent mode of corrupting the text, as all textual critics are aware.

So that, so far from the legates' version of the Sixth Canon read at Chalcedon being a forgery,[2] it is probably the insertion of the other version which is, I will not say a forgery, but an error in the transcriber.[3]

Thus the Council of Nicæa, as a whole, suggests the unique position of the Bishop of Rome as something more than that of the Duke of Norfolk to the rest of the English peerage.[4] It does not discuss Papal jurisdiction; for, on the hypothesis of its truth, it would be beyond the province of a council to enter upon such a question, which neither was, nor could be, submitted to its consideration. It did not speak of Papal infallibility; it had met together to show that the teaching of the West was also the teaching of the East, to express the

---

[1] *Canons of the First Four General Councils*, 1892, p. 223.

[2] As the Bishop of Lincoln, Dr. Bright, and Mr. Puller assert (cf. *Prim. SS.* Preface, p. xxi.).

[3] For a further treatment of this subject, cf. *infra*, on the 28th Canon.

[4] The simile selected in *Prim. SS.*

unity of the teaching Church, and to settle a question of the first importance in regard to jurisdiction in the East, in the settlement of which it alleged the practice, or the cognisance, of the Bishop of Rome as its sufficient warrant for adhering to the long-established relationship between Alexandria and its suffragan bishops. It cannot be too often repeated, in view of the argument from silence, that the Acts of the Council are not forthcoming, having been, it may be, destroyed by the Arians when in possession of the Eastern sees. And besides the work of destruction, these heretics were busy in the work of forgery. Consequently, we have to be careful about arguing from what we do possess, and still more careful about arguing from what we do not possess. It is not until we come to the Council of Ephesus that we are able to see the Church in conciliar action in the comparative daylight of anything like adequate records.[1]

[1] I do not forget St. Athanasius' work on the Decrees of the Nicene Synod; but that does not validate the argument from silence.

CHAPTER XII.

THE POPES THE GUARDIANS OF THE NICENE CANONS.

AFTER the Council of Nicæa it seemed as if the Church had entered upon an era of triumph. But one catastrophe changed the whole face of things. A bishop with Arian sympathies gained the ear of Constantine, and henceforth the whole weight of imperial influence was brought to bear upon the establishment of heresy. St. Athanasius seizing, as he once did, the bridle of the emperor's horse, and insisting upon his abating his opposition to the Catholic Faith, but in vain, was a symbol of what was going on. Constantine was persuaded that he was enforcing the Nicene Faith; and Eusebius was victorious all along the line, in both mounting himself, from throne to throne, in the teeth of Nicene regulations, and in deposing the orthodox bishops. And the weapon that he victoriously opposed to the Council of Nice was a synod convoked by the emperor.[1] It was a line of action to be repeated in the history of the Church—viz. a synod of bishops, under the influence of the Crown, deciding as to the government of the Christian Church. And it entered upon the platform of Church history under the patronage of the deadliest foe that the Church has ever known. It was the darling project of an Arianising emperor under the influence of an Arian bishop. In this case, however, the bishop was the foe, the emperor the instrument. It was not yet the theory of the independence of National Churches, but it was akin to it, and its natural parent. The supremacy of the Crown was ousting the supremacy of the Holy See. Imprisoned or exiled bishops in communion with the See of St. Peter (reminding us of

[1] For an interesting expansion of this, see *The Throne of the Fisherman*, by T. W. Allies, ch. vi.

events in the sixteenth century) were the immediate result of the alliance between Church and State which sprang up through the wily machinations of Eusebius, Bishop first of Berytus, then of Nicomedia (when the Court was there), and lastly (on the Court's removal), Bishop of Constantinople. In concert with the emperor, the whole constitution of the Church was soon further assailed by the attempt of Eusebius' successors to base the jurisdiction of patriarchs, not on their connection with Apostolic origin, but on the secular position of their city. It was the world against the Apostle; the crown against the crozier; Cæsar usurping the prerogatives of Peter. Constantinople, but a few years ago, was a spot all but unknown, whose bishop was suffragan to the Bishop of Heraclea. Now it was New Rome, and its bishop aspired to be a second Pope. The Pope was the successor of St. Peter, and therein his strength lay; but that Apostle had selected the centre of the world for the base of his operations, and as the centre had shifted, why might not the new imperial city be also the centre of a new patriarchal jurisdiction? The answer was, that Peter, not Cæsar, is the governor of the Christian Church.

And under the difficulties which now emerged, in some sense the greatest that the Church had as yet had to meet, the government of Peter became the salvation of the Faith of Nicæa. As the Church entered upon her new course of alliance with the State, the Eastern bishops more and more discovered a fatal weakness incident upon their proximity to the new centre of secular power on the shores of the Bosphorus. On the other hand, the genius for government and the inherent strength and majesty of the Holy See became more and more pronounced, under circumstances of unparalleled difficulties. It is evident that the full meaning of the Nicene canons *could* only gradually make itself felt; and the same is true of the guardian of those canons, viz. the Apostolic See. The history of this eventful period is orientated by a remark made by St. Gregory the Great in reference to a later Bishop of Constantinople: 'As to what he says, that he is subject to the Apostolic See, I know not what bishop is not subject to it, if any fault be found in bishops.' When 'fault is found in bishops' then the primacy develops its stores of wisdom and authority to correct the fault. This is precisely what happened in the post-Nicene period. Until then, as Mr. Allies points out in his 'Throne of the Fisherman,'[1] bishops had not learnt to struggle with one another for place and power, and the need of a head was not so keenly felt. But when ambition came to curse the East, then came out to view the controlling power of the Sovereign Pontiff.

This, then, is the salient feature of the next fifty years after Nicæa, viz. the Holy See 'confirming the brethren'[2] in the East. The Court bishop in the East was the new factor in the Church's life and the source of unceasing trouble. Court and bishop together did their best to deprave the Church's faith. They must have succeeded but for the unbending firmness of the Holy See, for a council could not guard its own canons. So far the Apostolic tradition had been guarded by the See of Rome; and now the position at once occupied by that see, when the Fathers of Nicæa had dispersed to their various homes, was precisely that of guardian of the Nicene interpretation of the Apostolic tradition against refractory and Erastian bishops. The government of the Church was, in fact, not merely episcopal but apostolical; episcopacy was unequal to the strain that ensued, but the Holy Apostolic See gave strength to the episcopal brotherhood.

It was in the course of the struggle that now ensued between Catholic and Erastian bishops that St. Julius, the reigning Pope (who, after the short reign of St. Mark, had succeeded St. Sylvester, the president of the Council of Nicæa), wrote a letter of even exceptional importance, which has been fortunately preserved to us by the care of St. Athanasius. This letter has an important bearing on the Nicene canons; it is quoted at length by St. Athanasius, and it affords irrefragable witness to the existence, in the Nicene period, of the entire claim on the part of Rome to a divinely instituted authority over East and West alike. It has, moreover, in view of modern discussions, the advantage of having been protested against by those who were opposed to the Nicene Faith. And yet its

---

[1] Ch. vi.   [2] St. Luke xxii. 32.

author, St. Julius, was canonised by the Church, and his name figures in St. Athanasius' life and writings as the great defender of the faith.[1]

His letter, which St. Athanasius gives with obvious approval, deals with a canon drawn up by a synod of Eastern bishops, which was meant to silence St. Athanasius himself. The Emperor Constantius, listening to the falsehoods by means of which the Eusebian heretics succeeded in deposing Athanasius, Eustathius, and Paul, the orthodox bishops respectively of Alexandria, Antioch, and Constantinople, had assembled a council of bishops at Antioch, who passed the following canon:—'A bishop who has been deposed by a council may not resume his office, nor be restored by any subsequent council, if, after his deposition, he has dared to execute ecclesiastical functions.' The canon was specially aimed at St. Athanasius, who had been 'deposed' by the Council of Tyre, and after his return from banishment had zealously resumed his work as bishop. This Council of Tyre was an assemblage of bishops presided over by the Arian emperor, determined to oust St. Athanasius from the See of Alexandria, and the Council of Antioch had thus stamped this synod with the character of finality. 'But,' says Socrates, 'Julius, Bishop of Old Rome, was not there, nor did he send a representative, although the ecclesiastical canon expressly commands that the Churches shall not make ordinances contrary to the judgment of the Bishop of Rome' (ii. 8). And Sozomen says (iii. 10): 'Julius wrote that they had acted against the canons because they had not called him to the council, the ecclesiastical canon commanding that the Churches ought not to make canons beside the will of the Bishop of the Romans.'

They had chosen to have their own council under the emperor in isolation, although, as Theodoret says, 'Pope Julius, adhering to the law of the Church, both commanded them to repair to Rome and summoned Athanasius to trial' ('H. E.' ii. 4). 'Both they and we were summoned,' says St. Athanasius himself.[2]

---

[1] Mr. Puller, in his *Primitive Saints, &c.* p. 138, has nothing to say against St. Julius. He even calls him saint, a title which he denies to every other Pope in that century. [2] *Apol. c. Arian.* n. 1.

These bishops, then, averred that the decision of the Council of Tyre should not be subject to appeal, on the ground that it was a council of bishops under imperial leave. It was on this point that the Roman Pontiff at once joined issue in his celebrated letter preserved by St. Athanasius. In the course of that letter he accuses these bishops of violating the discipline of the Church. They had condemned the Bishop of Alexandria, St. Athanasius. But 'why,' asks St. Julius, ' was nothing said to us about the Church of Alexandria in particular? Are you ignorant that this is customary, for word to be written to us first, and then for a just sentence to be passed from this place? If, then, any suspicion rested upon the bishop there, notice thereof ought to have been sent to the Church of this place [*i.e.*, Rome]; whereas, after neglecting to inform us, and proceeding on their own authority as they pleased, now they desire to obtain our concurrence in their decisions. . . . Not so have the directions of the Fathers prescribed. This is another form of procedure, a novel practice. . . . What we have received from the blessed Apostle Peter, that I signify to you.'[1]

It was, then, according to St. Julius, a novel practice in the middle of the fourth century for a council of bishops to proceed to censure the second Petrine See, that of Alexandria, on their own authority, *instead of obtaining a just sentence from Rome*. The latter, he says, was the usual course, sanctioned by antiquity. And the authority thus to decide was, he adds, derived to Rome from ' that which we have received from the blessed Apostle Peter.' And this was under the very shadow of the Nicene Council. To this the reply of the Eusebian heretics was that ' it was not his [Julius'] province to interfere.' The Eusebians, in their endeavours to overthrow the Nicene faith as to our Lord's Divinity, adopted the programme, as we learn from St. Hilary, that things settled by a council in the East should be simply accepted by the West, and *vice versâ*. It was all important for their cause that they should not be interfered with by the unyielding orthodoxy of the Apostolic See. They did not dream of a province settling

---

[1] Athan. *Hist. Tract., Lib. of Fathers*, p. 56.

such things all by itself, without *any* communication with the rest, not even if the whole East were to be called one province —that would have been to rend the Church in twain—but they did hope to withdraw themselves from any active intervention on the part of Rome, such as had hitherto obtained as a matter of course. But, as we have just seen, both Socrates and Sozomen—Eastern historians—and Theodoret and St. Athanasius (by implication) speak of the idea of canons being made without the concurrence of the Bishop of Rome as unheard of up to that time. But what is still more important is that the Council of Sardica (if the Sardican canons were really passed by that Council) or the Nicene canon itself (if the Sardican canons are really Nicene) condemned the Eusebians in this their endeavour to settle matters of high importance without reference to Rome. It will be necessary, therefore, to devote our attention to the canons which go by the name of Sardican.

§ II.—*The Sardican Canons.*

I have elsewhere[1] shown that it is quite possible that these canons represent actual decisions of the Nicene Fathers; but whether this be so or not, they certainly embody the mind of the Church in the fourth century. Only seventeen years after Nicæa St. Julius could speak of the 'custom' of referring judgment on the Bishop of Alexandria to Rome as one of the directions of the Nicene Fathers, with the approval of St. Athanasius, himself Bishop of that Eastern city.

Let us, then, waiving the question as to whether they are actually, or only virtually, Nicene—passed, that is, at Nicæa, or an accredited appendix to that council, passed at Sardica—examine their witness on the subject of appeals to Rome.

Three are of special importance in relation to this subject.

I. *Canon Three* decides against bishops passing from province to province, 'lest we should seem to close the door of charity.' If this were Sardican, it may have had special regard to Eusebius, who had passed from Berytus to Constantinople; if Nicene, it may have been concerned with his passage from Berytus to Nicomedia, where he was bishop

[1] Cf. Appendix II.

when the Council of Nicæa sat. The canon further provided that in the event of a bishop having a 'case' against another bishop the metropolitan should convene a provincial synod. If the accused lost his case he was not to be allowed simply of himself to appeal to some neighbouring bishops, as was the tendency, but if he wished it, an appeal was to be arranged for him, and in the same region. There is no question here of appeal to Rome in the full technical sense. But 'Julius, the Bishop of Rome' (if that be the true reading—for some copies have 'Sylvester,' which would be the true reading if the canon was Nicene in its origin), was to be asked to settle the judges that should form the new synod, if it was thought well for the case to be reheard. In deciding this, which consisted in asking Rome to select the judges, the unusual formula adds as a reason, 'Let us honour the memory of the Apostle Peter.' Supposing this to be Sardican, it would contain a judgment upon the Council of Tyre. The irregularity of that council consisted in the fact that not only did the emperor call a council without consulting the Holy See, but he actually selected the judges. The Greek historian Socrates says of the Council of Antioch: 'Julius, Bishop of Old Rome, was not there, nor did he, indeed, send a representative, although *the ecclesiastical rule* expressly commands that the Church shall not make canons without the consent of the Bishop of Rome' (ii. 8). It is difficult to suppose that Socrates refers to anything here but a canon of Nicæa. But be that as it may, the device of the Eusebians was a radical innovation on the constitution of the Church. Had such a course been permitted, Arianism, which was so successful in attracting to itself first Constantine, and then, still more decisively, his son Constantius, would have gained the day. Had it been allowed to the emperor to convoke councils for cases of appeal, without reference to the Holy See, as Constantine had done in the case of Tyre, and Constantius in the case of Antioch; had it, moreover, been permitted to the Crown to appoint the judges, the most fundamental feature of the polity of the Church would have been destroyed. It would have ceased to be Apostolical in its government; and, when the empire was separated into various nations, each tribe would have had its own independent national Church. The theory of independent national Churches would have become a fact, the unity of the Church would have disappeared, and the guardianship of the holy faith been rendered impossible. No wonder, then, that the Sardican Fathers, if the canon was theirs, determined still to honour the memory of the Apostle Peter; or that the Nicene Fathers (whose canon we may suppose it to represent) in view of fundamental principles necessary in the immediate future, rather than of such bitter experience as the Sardican Fathers would have had, said amongst themselves, 'Let us honour the memory of the Apostle Peter,' in the future as in the past; and that the African Fathers, in this their commentary recorded these utterances of Nicene Fathers used in the discussion about the canon.

II. *Canon Four* deals with appeals to Rome. What was to happen in the case of bishops who, having lost their cause in the second court, had thence appealed to Rome? Their see must not be occupied by another. This was a matter which the Nicene Fathers could easily foresee would be likely to happen in the future, or if the canon be Sardican, this had already arisen; and here it is no longer the informal utterances of members of the council, and the particular occupant of the Holy See is no longer mentioned. It is now simply 'the Bishop of Rome.'

III. *Canon Seven*, again, deals with the case of a bishop who, having been condemned in the court of first instance—viz. the synod of his province—appeals, without recourse had to a second synod, straight to Rome. It will then, according to the canon, belong to 'the Bishop of Rome' to say whether he thinks it is a case for revision; and if he decides in the affirmative, it will rest with him either to remit the case to the bishops of the province adjoining that in which the condemned bishop lives, or to send a legate *a latere*, who can undertake the case, either by himself or in conjunction with the bishops of the neighbouring province.[1]

---

[1] I have here adopted Jungmann's interpretation of these canons in preference to Hefele's. The Ballerini have an invaluable dissertation on the

IV. Now these canons obtained reception *eventually* in the East as well as (at once) in the West. They were, strangely, unknown in Africa during the first part of the fifth century; but the African bishops were in a small minority, and the canons were eventually incorporated even in their African code. They must, therefore, be admitted to represent the mature judgment of the Church, or, to be more accurate, the matured expression of her mind. Men cannot put themselves back into the beginning of the fourth century, and into the position of some African bishops (for the evidence is against St. Augustine having refused to receive them when fully made known); they cannot adopt as the basis of their permanent position an episode in the life of one portion of the Church which did not represent its maturer thought—they cannot, I say, do this—which is what some have claimed to do, and then call themselves by the name of Catholic.

Constantinople and Alexandria, although their (probably corrupted) copies of the sixth Nicene canon did not contain these said provisions, had not a word, so far as history tells us, to say against the justice of the regulations contained in these canons; whilst they certainly incorporated them eventually, as did Africa herself, into their code.

And yet these canons suppose a mode of unity which is irreconcilable with any but the Papal form of government. They barred the possibility of independent national Churches. They nipped that natural tendency in the bud. They do, indeed, condition appeals to Rome, but they assume their necessity. They do not inaugurate them. In neither of these canons is the question entertained as to whether there ought to be appeals at all. They suppose that there will. The third canon does not deal with appeals to Rome at all— in the strict sense of the word, it only provides for requests to Rome for the selection of judges in a fresh local court of appeal. Hence all that has been said about the words ' Let us honour the memory of the Apostle Peter' *inaugurating* appeals to Rome falls to the ground.

subject in their unrivalled edition of St. Leo's letters, but Jungmann's treatment leaves nothing to be desired (*Diss. Hist. Eccles.* vol. ii. pp. 15-27. Ratisbon, 1881).

V. But even if this canon could be proved to deal with direct appeals to Rome, it would be fair to argue that the memory of the Apostle Peter may be just as much honoured by adhering to an old custom as by a new arrangement. That is to say, the words do not indicate a novelty. And the defence which has been set up, that the canon specially mentions Julius by name, and that therefore the arrangement applied to him personally, and to him alone, in his lifetime, fails to account for the previous words, 'Let us honour the memory of the Apostle Peter.' It is as successor of Peter that Sylvester or Julius is to be asked to appoint judges; and Julius' successors were, equally with himself, the successors of the Apostle Peter.

But the fourth and seventh canons do deal with the subject of appeals to Rome, and in them, at any rate, the name of the Pope is dropped, and the general term for the office is used.

Whether, then, Nicene or Sardican—whether already in existence or soon to be passed, these canons bear out the statement of Julius to the Eusebians that they had offended against the established order of the Church in not recognising that, in the case of ordinary bishops, the appeal lay eventually from East to West, and that in the case of the Bishop of Alexandria the appeal lay straight to Rome.[1]

Before passing on, it may be well to notice a fallacy concerning the relationship of the Popes to the canons. It is often said that, for instance, St. Leo denounced the third canon of Constantinople on the ground of the Nicene canon, and it is suggested that this is a sign that he could not fall back on his own authority simply.[2] But the obedience to the Nicene canons, and indeed to other canons of the Church, which the Popes professed, was an act of natural justice, not

---

[1] Dr. Bright lays stress on the fact that St. Julius uses the word 'all,' saying that the Eusebians should have written to 'all of us.' But the word 'all' obviously means all those bishops who were then in Rome, of whom there were several from all parts. And the sequence of the letter, which contends that, in accordance with the rule of the Church, they should specially have written to Rome about Alexandria, establishes the principle of Rome's relationship to her, viz. that of judge.

[2] Bright's *Hist. of the Church*, p. 417, 3rd edition.

submission to a superior power. The canons that they guarded, and by which in many matters they considered themselves strictly bound, were passed by themselves or by their predecessors, through their assent and confirmation. They were not, therefore, a hyper-Papal power, ruling the Popes themselves, for they acquired their force from the Popes. They were, therefore, bound by them in the same way that a king is bound to respect the laws where they affect his conduct, not because they are superior to him, but because he is bound by the natural and divine law to set the example. As St. Ambrose said to the Emperor Valentinian, 'What you have prescribed to others you have prescribed to yourself, for the emperor passes laws which he should be himself the first to keep.'[1] And Theodosius and Valentinian themselves say, 'It is worthy of the majesty of him who reigns to profess himself bound by the laws.'[2] The Popes could dispense from the observance of the canons, as St. Leo dispensed Maximus of Antioch from the results of an irregular ordination, and the council received him as bishop avowedly on the ground of the Papal dispensation;[3] but they were bound, in natural justice, or in supernatural charity, not to dispense without legitimate reason. When, then, a Pope quotes a Nicene canon as the ground of obedience on the part of others, he does not place the canon above himself, but avows his natural obligation to follow in the footsteps of his predecessors, unless cause can be shown why he should in a particular case allow others to withdraw themselves from the operation of the general rule.

Note.—That the third Sardican canon does not relate to appeals to Rome is proved by the facts that the original judges, not the guilty party, are to write to Rome, and that this canon was not mentioned in the discussion between St. Zosimus and the African bishops as to the best mode of procedure in regard to appeals.

In the fourth canon it is to be noted that the effect of the appeal to Rome is suspensive. The bishop is spoken of as *seeming*

---

[1] *Ep.* 32. *ad Valent.*
[2] *De Leg. et Const.* (l. i. Cod. tit. 14): 'Digna vox est majestate regnantis, legibus obligatum se profiteri.'
[3] Cf. p. 435, *infra.*

to be deposed, not actually deposed, until Rome has spoken. There is nothing *here* about the case being heard in the region in which it arose. It was obviously to be heard at Rome.

The seventh canon contemplates another quite different case, and one in which the case *was* to be heard in the province. Mr. Puller appears to have blended them into one; hence his idea that no cases were to be carried to Rome ('Prim. SS.' p. 158). But the seventh canon deals with the case of a bishop passing by the regular stages of appeal, and hence the provision that the case should go back to the province, and not to Rome, as Canon Four implied.[1]

For the witness of Photius to the reception of these canons in the East see Appendix II. *ad finem*.

---

[1] Cf. Jungmann, *loc. cit.*

CHAPTER XIII.

THE REIGN OF LIBERIUS.

§ I.—*His Personal Grandeur.*

I. MORE than half a century elapsed before the second œcumenical council met, and even this was not convoked as such, for the ordinary government of the Church does not lie with general councils, but with the bishops in union with the Holy See. It was to Rome that men looked in the anguish of those days, and not to general councils. In one sense, indeed, the eyes of all were for a while turned to the great Bishop of Alexandria; but St. Athanasius himself looked to Rome. Had the government of the Church rested with independent National Churches, or with an East independent of the West, the Church must have sunk under the Erastianism of imperial Christianity, and the restless activity of Eastern speculation would have wrecked the faith.

Constantius, one of the most dangerous foes that the Church has had, could deal with the fickle, quarrelsome, over-subtle Eastern mind; but with the West and its determined adherence to the Nicene settlement, and its consciousness of strength in the possession of the Apostolic tradition, he could do nothing. His success against Athanasius was at one time terrible; it was only checked by one obstacle—he could not gain the occupant of the Holy See. That see was occupied by one whom the Greek menology in its calendar of saints calls 'the blessed Liberius, defender of the truth,' and he threw the shelter of his impregnable position round the Bishop of Alexandria. The heathen historian Ammianus Marcellinus tells us how this one exception meant everything, and how the emperor could not rest satisfied whilst he had left one stone unturned to win the Roman Pontiff.

Liberius had succeeded Julius. The latter had consolidated the work of the Nicene Council by his brilliant and persistent justification of Athanasius. Liberius received the mantle of Julius, and like Julius stood on the rock of Apostolic tradition. He could say, ' Never was it my own statutes, but those of the Apostles which I guarded and carried out.' [1]

Constantius, accordingly, set to work to win Liberius, which St. Athanasius says would have been equivalent to winning the whole Church to his side. But neither threats nor bribes availed to move the aged pontiff. Firm as a rock he went into exile, 'the admiration of all,' in the words of Athanasius. St. Jerome's account, if genuine, is plainly inaccurate, and in direct contradiction to that of St. Athanasius; for according to St. Jerome—if (I repeat) that passage is genuine—Liberius, before he set out, signed an heretical formula. We may dismiss this as certainly untrue. He went forth, says St. Athanasius, ' the admiration of all.'

II. What he did towards the end of his two years' exile and ill-treatment we shall never know. We know from Sozomen that the atmosphere was thick with Arian calumnies, and that these calumnies did not spare the Pontiffs. In this case it would seem that calumny, which loves to shoot its arrows in the dark, availed itself of a period in the life of Liberius of which we have no authentic information, to suggest that his return from exile was due to his having signed against Athanasius. The formula he signed has never been produced, nor can anyone say what it was. Forgery has been busy about it; for all accurate writers now admit, as Canon Bright does in the second edition of his 'Church History,' that the ' Fragments of Hilary,' on which the accusations have mainly rested (as for instance in Dr. Pusey's 'History of the Councils '), are, at least in great part, spurious. The passage in St. Athanasius' ' Apology,' on which Mr. Gore relies, does not speak of a fall, but merely of Liberius not having completed his term of exile. The passage in the ' History of the Arians ' was written before the supposed fall took place. And Father Bottalla, S.J., has completely demolished the idea that

---

[1] *Ep. ad Constant.* n. 3.

St. Athanasius added it afterwards.[1] *Even if it were genuine, it denies that the incident in Berœa counted for anything.* And there are, besides, these facts, that neither Socrates nor Theodoret alludes to the passage, although they had St. Athanasius' work before them as they wrote; that Nicephorus Callistus, whilst following Sozomen in his account of matters up to this, drops him here; and that Rufinus, though 'with his bark full of malice,' as St. Jerome describes him, was unable to find a reason in St. Athanasius' works for the return of Liberius, which confirms the idea that the passage was not at that time to be found in those works.

As for St. Jerome's witness, those who take their stand on this cannot take it as it is, but are obliged to correct it on one point, which opens the door for a further correction, viz. the excision of the rest, which has no contemporary evidence in its favour. The fact is, that St. Jerome is to be revered for his knowledge of Holy Scripture and his eminent sanctity, and as a witness to the Church's teaching; but in matters of history he is sometimes at fault.[2] Sulpicius Severus, Socrates, and Theodoret are more to be relied on, when they agree; and they agree in knowing nothing of any fall of Liberius. And, further, the passage about Liberius does not occur at all in the famous manuscript of St. Jerome which the Queen of Sweden gave to the Vatican, and which belongs to the sixth or seventh century.

There is, however, another form of evidence which needs to be emphasised. There was in the time of Liberius an active correspondence carried on by the bishops all round. They speak of the councils held, the professions of faith adopted, the zeal of some bishops, the defection of others. There is mutual encouragement and sympathy in the distresses of the times; but there is no mention, no distant allusion, to any idea of Liberius, the Pope, having subscribed a suspicious formula or condemned Athanasius. And yet the principal events of the time were known to these numerous bishops. There is also correspondence between Liberius and

---

[1] *Autorité du Pape*, vol. i. pp. 239-41 (1877).

[2] It is quite another matter to set aside his teaching as to the faith, as Mr. Gore and Mr. Puller do.

Athanasius, but no consciousness of injury in the past nor demand for renewed affection in the future.

No. What Liberius did sign for certain was all in support of Athanasius. What he did sign, as matter of history, was the condemnation of the heretical Councils of Tyre, Arles, Milan, Ariminum; he did sign the confirmation of the Catholic Synods of Rome and Alexandria. The authentic acts of his pontificate include a definition of the Divinity of the Third Person of the Holy Trinity; the reconciliation of the Macedonians; the mission of Eusebius of Vercellæ, and of Lucifer of Cagliari *to the East*; the nomination of Elfidius as legate to Sclavonia; a letter of congratulation and encouragement to the bishops exiled for the faith, as well as general decrees touching the attitude to be maintained towards the penitent signatories of Ariminum.[1]

III. But one of these episodes in the life of this great Confessor for the faith deserves further mention, for it stands on a level with that described by St. Athanasius, and it entitles him to be considered the special instrument of the great head of the Church for 'confirming the brethren' at this eventful period of her history—I mean his action in regard to the Council of Ariminum.[1]

More than 400 bishops assembled there. The legate of the Holy See presided at the opening. It had all the conditions of an œcumenical council so far; it would only need the final confirmation of the Roman Pontiff. It began well with excommunicating the heretics that were troubling the Church; but its numbers after an interval, at the emperor's command, fell off as it continued its sessions, and its end belied its beginning. The legate of the Holy See withdrew, and the bishops, whose number was still very considerable, were induced to send deputies to the emperor who were completely overawed by the imperial presence. So great was the heretical emperor's anxiety to force them into accepting a semi-Arian programme, that although engaged for the onerous ceremonies of initiating new consuls on the following day, he sat up through the greater part of the night occupied with pushing on the signatures to the heretical

---

[1] *Revue des Questions Historiques*, vol. i., art. 'St. Liberius.'

creed. The bishops of the East in the simultaneous Council of Seleucia were equally pliant to the emperor's mission. Eventually, scarcely more than eighteen or nineteen bishops in Christendom remained uncompromised. It was then that, in the language of St. Jerome, 'the world found itself Arian, and groaned.' The faith had suffered an eclipse in the episcopal body. Who was to save the position? It fell to the lot of one man to stand in the breach—and that man was Liberius. The aged pontiff had once said to the emperor, in his memorable interview with his Majesty at Milan (when told that on that occasion, too, he would stand alone), 'If I am alone, the faith will not fail.' He knew himself to be the Atlas whom our Divine Lord had appointed to bear the world of Divine Revelation on his shoulders, on which the government of the Church had been laid. Another occasion for proving the truth of his courageous utterance had now come. Liberius found himself alone face to face with the triumphant Arians, who had overreached the Catholic episcopate at Ariminum and Seleucia. He saved the situation. In the tremendous troubles that beset the East, which led St. Basil to appeal so earnestly to the West for help, St. Damasus was able to point out to the Eastern bishops that 'he whose judgment was to be looked for before all others' had deliberately refused his assent to the Ariminian formula.[1] The three illustrious exiles, Athanasius, Eusebius, and Hilary, had not signed, and the bishops who had been entrapped, as St. Damasus explained, in the East and West, by the wary formula, were with them in heart. But the express repudiation of the formula rested, for the moment, with Liberius, and Liberius did not fail. He authoritatively rejected the proposed formula, and, in so doing, unchained afresh the emperor's wrath. He had once more to leave his beloved Rome—whether for the Catacombs or at a greater distance is not certain—but only to return and erect, through the devotion of his orthodox flock, the Basilica of Santa Maria Maggiore, and to receive the retractation of the penitent signatories of Ariminum, as one who had himself never failed.

[1] Cf. *infra*, p. 209.

Such was the second Pope after the Nicene Council—'the most blessed bishop Liberius,' according to St. Basil; 'the Pontiff of blessed memory,' according to St. Epiphanius; 'the great Liberius, the most holy Liberius,' according to Cassiodorus, and 'in all things most renowned;' 'the thrice holy bishop,' according to St. Ambrose; and, in the words of Theodoret, 'the illustrious athlete for the faith.' In the Menology of the Greeks, he is a saint distinguished as 'the blessed Liberius, the defender of the truth,' 'whose zeal for the orthodox faith caused him to undertake the defence of the great Athanasius.' His exile is there related, and his return, but not a whisper of any defection, the account ending with saying that 'he died at Rome, after having governed his flock well.'

§ II.—*The Meletian Scandal at Antioch.*

But I am anticipating. Liberius had the conduct of another affair, which ended less happily.

I. After the disaster at Ariminum—when the whole body of bishops, saving a few great saints such as Athanasius and Basil in the East, and the Sovereign Pontiff in the West, had yielded to imperial pressure and signed a semi-Arian confession—the Church seemed likely to receive still heavier blows at the hand of the new emperor, an apostate from the faith. But it was Julian's policy to let the bishops slaughter themselves by intestine divisions; and, accordingly, they were allowed to return from their various places of exile and resume their episcopal duties.

Liberius, ever foremost in the faith, at once entered upon the work of pacification and ecclesiastical discipline. He proceeded to lay down the rules by which the Church should be guided in reconciling those who had in any way compromised themselves by complicity with the manifold forms of Arianism.[1] Antioch was naturally one of his chief cares; and he influenced and authorised the great Bishop of Alexandria to convene a council to consider the position of affairs in that central see of the East. The council at Alexandria adopted the rules laid

---

[1] Cf. *Acta Sanctorum* (Bollandist), Sept. 23, § 195, 6, 7.

down by the Sovereign Pontiff,[1] and did its best to conciliate the differences that divided the Catholics at Antioch.

The origin of these differences was as follows. St. Eustathius had been exiled from Antioch through the influence of the Arians. Amongst other things they had suborned a woman to asperse his moral character, who afterwards confessed her perjury. After his death, Meletius had been elected bishop under circumstances which rendered his appointment open to serious objection. He had been to some extent 'led astray by the stranger's hand,' to use St. Gregory of Nazianzus' expression—*i.e.* he had coquetted with Arianism. According to the Arian historian Philostorgius, he had 'feignedly professed the *heterousion.*'[2] According to Socrates, he had signed the semi-Arian profession of faith put forth at the Council of Seleucia.[3] According to St. Epiphanius, he belonged to the party of Acacius, which, if true, was a most serious blot on his life.[4] According to Nicephorus Callistus, he had been originally elected to the bishopric of Sebaste through the suffrages of the Arians.[5] Sozomen said that he was returned by the Eudoxians, the most thorough-going Arians.[6] The See of Antioch being vacant, through St. Eustathius' death, he was promoted to that important post. According to St. Jerome, he was 'transferred to Antioch by the Arian bishops Acacius and George.' But it seems that St. Eusebius of Samosata was assured of his having embraced the orthodox faith. St. Eusebius was perhaps, as Bollandus thinks, the instrument of his conversion. His change was kept a secret from the Arians, but known to a certain number of Catholics in Antioch, who in consequence voted along with the Arians for his appointment to the see. In view of what might happen, when his conversion became known, the Catholics had a written document drawn up concerning his appointment by the Emperor Constantius, which

---

[1] Cf. *Letter of St. Athan.* read at the second Council of Nicæa (Mansi, tom. vii. col. 75, 6), in which he says of the provisions for the restoration of the lapsed: ταῦτα καὶ ἐν 'Ρώμῃ ἐγράφη καὶ ἀπεδέξατο ἡ 'Ρωμαίων ἐκκλησία (cf. *Acta Sanctorum, loc. cit.* 201). They seem to have been drawn up in Rome, and sent by Eusebius to the Synod of Alexandria.

[2] *Eccl. Hist.* v. 1, 5. [3] *Hist. Eccl.* ii. 44.
[4] *Hær.* lxxiii. 25, 6. [5] *Hist. Eccl.* ix. 48. [6] *Hist. Eccl.* iv. 25.

St. Eusebius afterwards refused to resign into the hands of the Arians.

This appointment of St. Meletius was a clear misfortune to the Church. Saintly as he proved to be, full of zeal and of most gentle, winning ways, his election was, nevertheless, the occasion of a separation between the Catholics of Antioch which lasted more than eighty years. 'The sound body of the Church,' says Theodoret, 'was divided into two.'[1] The Catholic bishops who, for the occasion, combined with Arians, could not free the election from the stain of complicity with these great foes of the orthodox faith. To understand, then, the Antiochene troubles of that century aright, it is necessary to bear in mind that St. Meletius entered upon his episcopate at Antioch under false pretences, and that the irregularity of his election could only be set right by some higher ecclesiastical authority.[2]

Meanwhile a numerous party of Catholics in Antioch, in horror at the idea of having a bishop who, however recommended by personal holiness, had yet ascended the throne under such sinister influences, refused their allegiance to Meletius. They chose for their leader a priest, named Paulinus, of irreproachable life and unimpeachable orthodoxy, and nothing would induce them to accept the ministrations of Meletius. Meletius, on gaining the see, had, indeed, at once openly avowed his belief in the *Homoousion*, and engaged the Arians, who procured his election. He was forthwith driven into exile, and so became a confessor for the Catholic faith. But even this did not satisfy this fervent body of Catholics under Paulinus, who had kept themselves during all those years that intervened between the exile of Eustathius and the election of Meletius from all complicity with Arian worship. It had become the fashion to mix with Arians in divine worship to an extent which their more zealous orthodoxy could not brook. It was with these, and these alone, that St. Athanasius, when he went to Antioch,

---

[1] *Hist.* iii. 4.

[2] The account of the Meletian troubles in *Primitive Saints and the See of Rome* (pp. 163-176 and p. 238 *seq.*) fails in accuracy from losing sight of this point. The narrative on p. 163 is altogether misleading. The writer also neglects to give proper stress to the ruling of the Council of Alexandria.

communicated; and this great doctor of the Church interested himself in gaining for them a church of their own. Tillemont suggests that it was a penance which St. Meletius had to bear for his unfortunate antecedents, that he never enjoyed full communion with Rome, nor with the great saint of Alexandria. Even in the great sermon which St. Meletius preached as soon as he had succeeded to the throne of Antioch—holding up first three fingers, and then one, to signify his belief in the Eternal Trinity—there were expressions which St. Athanasius would not have sanctioned, and which St. Epiphanius considered to be open to objection. His actual orthodoxy had by no means established itself in men's minds, as is shown by the various reports which St. Jerome mentions and (according to St. Epiphanius) wrongly credited.

The people of Antioch were now divided into three. St. Meletius' followers, of course, separated themselves from the disciples of Euzoius, the Arian bishop, whom Constantius had intruded after the exile of Meletius, and for this they were praised by St. Gregory Nyssen as keeping themselves free from spiritual wandering.[1] They went and worshipped apart from the Arians in a suburb, in a church called the Palæa. As long as those set over them were professedly orthodox, they had worshipped with them; but now that a declared Arian, like Euzoius, was set over them by the emperor, they separated and preserved their spiritual chastity. Those who acted with Paulinus were often called Eustathians, from the last unquestioned bishop, St. Eustathius. They had a real grievance in the unfortunate election of St. Meletius, and, moreover, are thought by some to have had questionings as to the validity of the baptisms amongst the Meletians.[2] But their fundamental difficulty was the election of Meletius;[3] they were otherwise at one in doctrinal teaching. As Theodoret says, 'The *sound* body of the Church was divided into two parts.'[4] And so high did Paulinus stand in the esteem of all,

---

[1] *Orat. Fun. in Melet.* It was not for keeping aloof from the Paulinists, as Mr. Puller (*Primitive Saints, &c.* p. 166) applies his words. The phrase ἐπεχείρετο would not apply to Paulinus, and the whole sentence implies a long interval before Meletius' second exile. This could only apply to a time before Paulinus had been consecrated.

[2] Socr. ii. 44.   [3] Niceph. Call. ix. 48.   [4] *Hist.* iii. 4.

that he was never interfered with by the emperor, nor spoken of disrespectfully by his adversaries; he and his flock also worshipped by themselves. The parties of Meletius and Paulinus held together in some sort of ecclesiastical intercourse. St. Meletius deposed before Sapor that 'their flocks held intercourse in religion,' and St. Meletius held that those who worshipped with Paulinus, after the latter had been made bishop, were under legitimate authority. 'You have received the care of the rest,' are his words to Paulinus.[1]

II. Such was the state of affairs with which the Council of Alexandria had to deal. Liberius had sent his legates, Eusebius of Vercellæ and Lucifer of Cagliari, now freed from exile, to assist in the composition of the Oriental differences. Their conduct throughout suggests that they were not simply acting on their former legatine faculties, as De Marca and Thomassin thought; they seem to have been entrusted afresh by the Apostolic See with powers of extraordinary jurisdiction and authority in the East.[2] Western bishops could not have acted as they did, on their own authority, without protest both from the East and from Rome. But Liberius had previously joined Eusebius on to his legates to Constantius, and two letters are extant from the same Pope to Eusebius, in one of which he speaks of his legate having 'in no way deviated from the fellowship of the Apostolic See.'[3] It is, therefore, reasonable to suppose, seeing that he acted with authority, that he was in possession of fresh legatine faculties.[4]

The council, then, 'few in number, but of sound faith, and many in merits,' as Rufinus says (lib. i. c. 28), with the

[1] Theodor. *Hist.* iii. 4. Mr. Puller's account of the position, in *Primitive Saints, &c.* ch. iv., is irreconcilable with St. Meletius' statements in Theodoret. Theodoret's statements are not always to be trusted, but in this matter his leanings would prejudice him against the position which he here assigns to the flock of Meletius.

[2] Cf. *Vita S. Liberii* (Stilting, S.J.), *Acta Sanctorum*, Sept. 24, § 202.

[3] Coust. *Ep. Liberii*, iii. v. vii.

[4] Rufinus' statement that the legation was enjoined on Eusebius and Lucifer by the Alexandrian Synod could only mean, if it is not a slip, that the synod determined the special form which their general authority should assume. For Alexandria had not the jurisdiction over Antioch that would be implied; and, indeed, Lucifer did not go to Alexandria at all (cf. Stilting's *S. Liberius*, § 202, *Acta Sanct.* Sept. 24).

Papal legate presiding together with St. Athanasius,[1] followed exactly the rules for reconciling those who had tampered with the orthodox faith which had been drawn up and received at Rome,[2] and it applied the principles thus settled to Meletius and his friends. The ordination of Meletius was dealt with, and not rejected. This we learn from the Seventh General Council (A.D. 787), in which the history of the matter is thus succinctly given :—(1) The holy Meletius was ordained by the Arians; (2) he ascended the ambo and proclaimed the *Homoousion*; (3) the ordination was not rejected.[3]

So far, then, the scruples of the party of Paulinus were in the way to be removed. They could look on the irregularity of St. Meletius' ordination as having been purged by proper authority. The way was cleared for his acceptance as sole bishop, if the two parties agreed. But an event occurred which altered the whole position of things, and henceforth constituted the difficulty of the situation.

After the council, some bishops who remained in Alexandria drew up a letter in the name of the council, written, it would seem, by St. Athanasius, and obviously with the council's consent. This letter was addressed to Eusebius, Lucifer, Asterius, Cymatius, and Anatolius, and was also written in the name of Eusebius himself, amongst others, as having previously given his consent, and being now about to execute its decrees. But—and this is a point of the last importance—it was also signed by the two deacons of Paulinus. Now this involved a decision on the part of the council that the see of Antioch was vacant, until Meletius' ordination was in a manner validated, and he, or some one else, was chosen as bishop of the whole body of the orthodox.[4] The alterna-

---

[1] 'Interfuit et præfuit Concilio Alexandrino cum Athanasio,' *Life of Eusebius from the Archives of Vercelli*, published under the authority of his successor, St. Honoratus. Cf. *Acta Sanctorum*, May 20; *S. Lucifer.* c. v. 45.

[2] *Speech of Sabas* (Mansi, tom. vii. col. 75).

[3] From St. Athanasius' letter to the Emperor Jovian it is evident that Liberius had dealt with the matter of the lapsed bishops before the Council of Alexandria met. Letters had come from Gaul and Britain. Cf. also the Council of Paris, which proves that the Council of Alexandria was not waited for in the West as the initiator.

[4] He was acknowledged as a bishop, but *the* bishop had yet to be chosen.

tive would be, that Paulinus was himself bishop. For these deacons could only appear as legates, either as commissioned by a bishop or on the ground that they represented the presbyterate in the vacancy of the see. Baronius thinks that Paulinus was already known to be a bishop, and that his election was thus acknowledged. But it seems certain that this was not the case. The see, therefore, was considered vacant until, as a first step, Meletius' irregular consecration was formally condoned by a council, in which the Papal legate sat.

But the most important point follows. The letter signed by the legates and sent from Alexandria gave directions to the commission (of which the legates formed a part) as to what should be done at Antioch. 'Call to yourselves all who wish to be at peace with us, and specially those who meet in the Palæa:' *i.e.* the Meletians. They were amongst those who presumably wished to be 'at peace with us,' and the deacons of Paulinus were amongst those who thus spoke. The followers of Paulinus were therefore the nucleus of the Catholic Church.[1] But, further, these commissioners were, 'as teachers and guardians,' to 'embrace all such,' and they were to '*join them*' (*i.e.* the Meletians and others) 'to the party of Paulinus, well beloved of us.' Again, then, the party of Paulinus was treated as the nucleus. And further, 'Demand of them nothing more than to anathematise the Arian heresy, and to confess the faith professed by the Fathers at Nicæa, but also to anathematise those who say that the Holy Ghost is a creature, and separate from the substance of the Christ.'

Twenty years were to elapse before the Council of Constantinople was to meet and testify to the Eastern reception of this latter dogma; but, in spite of this, it was already a matter of faith that the consubstantiality of the Holy Ghost was contained in the Nicene Creed. That is to say, all that

---

[1] Cf. Mr. Puller's contention that the Meletians were the nucleus of the Church. An expression of St. Basil's (mistranslated, as it seems to me) cannot be placed over against the definition of this council sitting avowedly as judge in the matter; yet the position assumed in *The Primitive Saints and the See of Rome* involves the preference of the former to the council's judgment.

the Council of Constantinople was about to declare was already taught under anathema. Liberius had already issued an authoritative decree on the subject.[1] This, however, by the way.

The Acts of the Council of Alexandria were eventually taken by Eusebius and Lucifer to Rome and submitted to the Pope, who confirmed and approved them.[2]

The point, however, that particularly concerns our present purpose is that the Synod of Alexandria emphatically endorsed the action of Paulinus and his party. It also relieved them of the difficulty of accepting the ministrations of Meletius, whilst it recognised the Eustathians under Paulinus as the really orthodox party. It is hardly possible to exaggerate the importance of this synodical decision. Had Mr. Puller, in his 'Primitive Saints and the See of Rome,' given to it its due weight, the whole of his contention about Meletius must have been seriously affected.[3] He would hardly have given us to understand that the Church of England is prepared to sink or swim with the orthodoxy and Catholic position of the Meletian party at Antioch from the beginning. He would hardly have drawn a parallel between the followers of Paulinus and the present Church of Rome in England on the one side, and the followers of Meletius and the Church of England on the other. What conciliar judgment with Papal legates has validated the election of Archbishop Parker? And what comfort is to be drawn from the fact that the followers of St. Meletius were told by St. Athanasius and the Alexandrian synod to join themselves to Paulinus and his disciples?

But, further, the Council of Alexandria entreated the episcopal commission at Antioch not to insist on any other conditions, in the case of those who assembled at the Palæa, and also bade the party of Paulinus to put forth nothing but

[1] Socrates, *Hist. Eccl.*
[2] Cf. Papebroch, *Vita S. Luciferi*, c. v. 45, *Acta Sanctorum.*
[3] Pp. 165-7. He seems to have been misled by the Benedictine editor of St. Chrysostom, whose words he quotes as his authority; but the Benedictine editor is more cautious than Mr. Puller: he only speaks of the endeavour of St. Athanasius, and in terms more capable of being reconciled with the facts than are Mr. Puller's, taken with their context.

what was put forth at Nicæa. Moreover, it decided that the question of the Three Hypostases, as between the East and West, was one of terms only; and it recommended that they should all meet together at the customary place (not at the Palæa) and settle the future place of divine worship according to the wish of all.

III. Thus the peace between the two parties seemed in a fair way to be concluded by legitimate authority. A council of Alexandria had, of course, no sort of right by itself either to purge the election of a bishop in Antioch of its irregularity or to settle matters in general for the great Oriental see by an episcopal commission, much less to elect a new bishop. And yet it seems as though the commission were to superintend this also, in case the Catholics in general should not select Meletius.[1] But the council was acting with the Papal legate;[2] and the legate Eusebius proceeded to execute his commission in conjunction with his brother-legate, Lucifer of Cagliari, who was already on the scene. It was, however, owing to the precipitate action of this latter bishop that the proposals of the council fell to the ground.

On arriving at Antioch, after leaving Eusebius to proceed to Alexandria, according, it would seem, to their mutual arrangement, Lucifer, having sent some one to represent him at Alexandria, found both parties without a bishop. Meletius had not returned from exile, and the Eustathians had only the priest Paulinus to lead them. From all we know of St. Lucifer,[3] his whole soul would go forth towards the Eustathians, or party of Paulinus. They had never compromised, and he was uncompromising to a fault. They had never worshipped along with Arians, and his horror for the Arian heresy was unbounded. They had stood the brunt of the battle; their fiery zeal for the proper Godhead of their crucified Lord had stood the test of thirty years. All the exquisite beauty of Meletius' character could not now tempt them to

---

[1] Cf. *Acta Sanctorum*: *S. Lucifer*, May 20, c. 5.

[2] *Ibid. Vita S. Liberii*, § 195, 6, 7.

[3] Tillemont is mistaken in supposing that the Luciferians were so called because they followed Lucifer into schism; they were disciples of his who went beyond him after his retirement. His retirement was not a schism.

condone the irregularity of his election, and his still (as they deemed it) too tender dealing with the Arian heresy. St. Lucifer accordingly decided to use his papal faculties, as he deemed it certain that anyone who was on the scene would feel justified in doing. He determined to act before the return of Meletius, and, assisted by two bishops,[1] he consecrated Paulinus, against whose character for orthodoxy and personal holiness no whisper had ever been heard, and who had been selected as leader, rather than thrust himself forward. But St. Lucifer had not counted on the devotion of the people of Antioch to the person of Meletius. St. Gregory of Nazianzus, the panegyrist of St. Meletius, thus describes the state of matters in his eloquent discourse on peace:—
'Since, being men, we are liable to sin, our fault was that of loving our pastors to excess, and that we could not discover which of two good men was the more to be preferred, until we agreed to admire them both alike.'[2] He emphatically denies that there was any difference as to doctrine, in spite of St. Basil's assertion to the contrary. He says to the heretics: 'However much you may desire it—*i.e.* to find a quarrel between us as to doctrine—it is in vain ; " besides this there is nothing "—*i.e.* nothing but undue attachment to our several pastors.'

IV. The commission of bishops, with Eusebius at its head, now arrived in Antioch with their peace-making programme, only to find that the proposals of the Synod of Alexandria had been rendered futile by Lucifer's hasty action. The Eustathians were devoted to their new bishop, and delighted to find that their principles in the past had received the sanction of Rome and Alexandria. The Meletians, on the other hand, were not unnaturally sore at the new consecration, devoted as they were to the gracious and winning personality of the bishop, whom they had with such questionable diplomacy helped to the throne of Antioch. Eusebius was naturally disappointed with his brother-legate. If

---

[1] Cf. Jerome, *Chronicon*, and Tillemont, *Luc. de Cagl.* iv.

[2] An endeavour has been made to connect this with another passage in St. Gregory's life. With what success cf. Merenda, *De Vita et Gestis Damasi*, c. 18, § 2.

Rufinus' account be taken literally, he refused to communicate with either party. But considering that he is found shortly afterwards in close co-operation with Lucifer, before the latter shut himself up in Sardinia, we must understand Rufinus to mean that he did not decide as to the legitimate occupant of the see. Of course, if St. Lucifer had held no legatine faculties, and if the jurisdiction of Rome over Antioch had not been acknowledged on all sides, the case would have been simple enough. His consecration of a bishop in Antioch would have been a flagrant act of schism. Neither St. Athanasius nor St. Gregory, nor even St. Basil, could have spoken and acted as they did, unless they recognised the right of the Apostolic See to consecrate a Bishop of Antioch. They must have called it what it would have been, the most monstrous act of interference with the rights of Antioch. But they betray no distant consciousness of any lack of validity in the appointment on the score of the consecration. All that St. Basil, the most determined opponent of Paulinus, resented was that his friend should be ousted. All he pleaded for was that he should not be ignored. All he determined was to communicate personally with Meletius, of whose orthodoxy he was sure, and not with Paulinus, about whom he thought Rome had been misled. He had against him in this St. Athanasius and the Council of Alexandria, who had thoroughly investigated the question, besides St. Epiphanius (no mean authority), some eighty Egyptian bishops, and the entire West. But he declares that if anyone should come from heaven itself, and yet should be demonstrably not walking according to the sound word of faith, he would not communicate with him—an innocent resolve, which is that of every Catholic at this hour.

Eusebius, on arriving at Antioch, expressed his disapproval of Lucifer's action, and yet felt himself unable, with his present powers, to make any amicable settlement of the difficulty. It was the orthodoxy of the Eustathians, and the sanction given to their position by the Council of Alexandria, that constituted the difficulty. For, although the council purged the election of Meletius of its original stain, it had made Paulinus and his party the nucleus of Catholic life round which the Meletians were to gather, and over which it was hoped St. Meletius would be chosen to preside by the spontaneous action of the whole Catholic body. But now that Paulinus had been (however unwisely) ordained by one who had authority to act in the name of the Apostolic See, and had been enthusiastically accepted by the orthodox Eustathians, there was, on the one hand, a difficulty in ignoring him, and, on the other hand, the impossibility of making him the only bishop. There is no parallel in the history of the Church to the state of things which thus arose in Antioch. And, accordingly, Eusebius, declaring it 'wellnigh incurable,' seems to have left Antioch without coming to any definite conclusion. He probably felt that the thing must work itself out, and that meanwhile he could only have recourse to Rome. Thither, with Lucifer of Cagliari, after transacting other business elsewhere, he appears to have taken the decrees of the Alexandrian Synod for the confirmation of Liberius and his account of what had happened in Antioch.[1]

The further development of the matter belongs to the reign of Damasus.

NOTE.—It will be seen from the facts adduced above that Mr. Puller in his book 'The Primitive Saints and the See of Rome,' has given a version of the history of St. Meletius which is inconsistent with the facts of the case as a whole. He has ignored the real character of St. Meletius' election. He has misrepresented the judgment of the Council of Alexandria. He says, 'it recommended that the whole body of Catholics should unite together,'[2] whereas it said that the Meletians should unite themselves to Paulinus and his party. He is wrong about Lucifer having 'immediately afterwards' broken away from the Church. It is, to say the least, a moot point whether he ever broke away; it is certain that he did not immediately afterwards. Paulinus was not ordained by Lucifer without assistant bishops, as Mr. Puller states. There is no discussion (which was at least needed, if not an admission) of the legatine position of Eusebius and Lucifer. Consequently his readers would

---

[1] 'Tulerunt secum Acta Concilii ambo Legati et in Latinum transtulerunt et Romam portaverunt ad Liberium, qui omnia confirmavit et approbavit' (*Vita Eusebii ex Archivio Vercellensi*).   [2] P. 165.

gain quite a false idea, if they trusted to the version he gives, of the whole affair. There are other points in his account which will come under notice later on.

It will be seen also that Dr. Pusey's assertion, quoted by the Bishop of Lincoln (Preface to 'Prim. SS.' p. xxiii), viz. 'St. Meletius, even while president of this second General Council, was still out of communion with the West,' is not borne out by the facts of the case.

CHAPTER XIV.

ST. DAMASUS—THE CHAMPION OF THE 'CONSUBSTANTIALITY' OF THE HOLY GHOST.

I. LIBERIUS having attained to his reward, the great Damasus sat on the Fisherman's throne. Ozanam, in his graphic description of the Church in the following century, says that until the accession of Leo the See of St. Peter had been occupied by saints and martyrs rather than by what we should call men of genius, and that in St. Leo the Church salutes the first genius in a Pope. There is some truth in this. The foundations of the Church's order were certainly laid by the hands of saints in the first three centuries, and, as we have seen, their normal end was the martyr's death. Indeed, the Popes being the infallible guardians of Divine tradition, there was, if we may so say, a certain fitness in their being conscientious even to sanctity, rather than learned in the world's judgment; zeal for the faith—that divine love of truth which will not brook or comprehend in the Church's net the teacher of false doctrine—is what we should most expect in the early occupants of that see which was set for the preservation of the deposit of revealed truth. And such, as a matter of fact, was the characteristic feature of the early Popes.

But in St. Damasus we have something more than this. He was a man of learning as well as of piety; a patron of art as well as a master of the spiritual life. 'Rarely, if ever, in the history of the Church' (says Dr. Lightfoot), 'has a great leader been fired with such zeal for recording the Christian heroism of the past.'[1] He was, moreover, a man of prodigious activity, and at the same time of singular

---

[1] *Apostolic Fathers*, Part I. 'St. Clement of Rome,' vol. ii. p. 444.

caution. He was too, says St. Jerome, 'the virgin Doctor of the virgin Church.' But although St. Jerome implies that there was an ascetic side to his life, he seems to have endeared himself to every class of men. He was called by his schismatic opponents 'the friend of diggers,' in allusion doubtless to his familiarity with the workers in the catacombs and their affection for him; he was called the friend of matrons, doubtless in allusion to the fact that the Roman matrons saw in him an embodiment of true religion, and lavished their wealth on his schemes for the improvement of the city (of which the traces remain to-day), or for the betterment of the poor, or the improvement of the condition of the clergy. To Saint Athanasius, who must have known him well during his stay in Rome, he was the 'beloved Damasus;' in Theodoret's eyes, looking at him from a distance, he was the reproduction of the great Bishop of Carthage, and 'conspicuous for the sanctity of his life.'[1] The emperor soundly scolded St. Damasus' schismatic opponents for disturbing the calmness of his 'most holy mind.' St. Ambrose, who knew him personally, speaks of him as 'the holy Damasus elected by the judgment of God.' Few characters come before us with more manifold recommendations than that of Damasus. His poems are at once scholarly and touching. What can be more exquisite than his poem on Projecta, what more touching than that on his sister Irene, whom he hopes to meet in a better world, and by whose side he asked to be buried? Half his life, he says, has gone from him on losing his sister in her twentieth year:

> Non timui mortem cœlos quod libera adiret,
> Sed dolui fateor consortia perdere vitæ.

But Damasus was above all a ruler. He ascended the throne at a time when firmness and prudence were, above all things, necessary; and the Sixth General Council is witness to the one, when (with a play on his name) it calls him 'the adamant of the faith,'[2] whilst Theodoret says that 'there was nothing that he was not prepared to say and do in behalf of the Apostolic teaching;'[3] and St. Basil is a reluctant wit-

---

[1] *H. E.* v. 2.
[2] Δάμασος ὁ ἀδάμας τῆς πίστεως (Mansi, t. xi. p. 661).   [3] *H. E.* v. 2.

ness to his caution in dealing with the East. Ambrosiaster, bearing witness to his official position (in spite of his own Semi-Pelagianism), really describes the main feature of his life when he speaks of the Church as 'the house of God, of which Damasus is now the ruler.' But though a ruler, he was, to those who knew him, meek and gentle; St. Jerome, his intimate at one time, was particularly impressed with his mildness; and the title, 'Servant of servants,' which he adopted, which has been used by the Popes ever since, points to his humility. His position was one that needed this pivot of the Christian life, for on the one hand no man was ever more maligned by his enemies, idolised by the Christian world, or placed on a higher pinnacle by the policy of a Christian emperor.[1] It is not without special interest that to him also we owe the recitation of the Gloria after each Psalm in the divine office; whilst, above all, it is to his desire and encouragement that one of the greatest gifts of God to Holy Church is to be traced—the translation of the Holy Scriptures into what we may call the vulgar (or common) tongue of Christendom by St. Jerome.

It is to be regretted that some recent writers have taken the side of schismatic and heathen authors, rather than that of the contemporary Christian world, in regard to this great Pope. Dr. Littledale has a passage on Damasus which reproduces the venom of the 'Libellus Precum,' written by two bitter schismatics, whose statements have been proved, where they could be checked, to have been shamefully false;[2] and more recently Mr. Puller has argued from the surroundings of the saint, and from a passage from Ammianus Marcellinus, the heathen historian, to the effect that St. Damasus must himself have been guilty of a luxurious mode of life.[3] Does Mr. Puller think that at a time when the throne of Peter was

---

[1] What is the real value of the saying of Prætextatus (quoted by Mr. Puller as evidence of Papal luxury), 'Make me Bishop of Rome, and I will become a Christian to-morrow'? A Hindu might say the same to the Archbishop of Canterbury—would it be any reflection on his Grace? Tertullian says that the heathen said the same of Christians in his day: which destroys Mr. Puller's application (*Apol.* p. 134).

[2] He quotes them alone as his authority.

[3] *Primitive SS.* pp. 140, 141.

taking the place of the altar of Victory, a pagan historian would be a stranger to the seductive whispers of envy? Is a pagan historian to be trusted altogether in regard to the very Pope who, at the risk of his life, gave the death-blow to paganism in the city of Rome, and conspired to destroy its last altar? No doubt it would be something in favour of Mr. Puller's thesis if it could be shown that pure worldliness led to the position which the throne of Peter occupied in the days of Damasus;[1] but we need something more than the suggestions of a heathen historian, and a petulant expression that fell from the pen of St. Basil, writing to an intimate friend, to counterbalance the unanimous witness of the contemporary Christian world in favour of the 'virgin Doctor of the virgin Church.'[2]

St. Damasus had a good preparation for his life's work. He must have seen St. Julius and conversed with St. Athanasius, and he was the secretary of St. Liberius. He followed the latter, part of the way at least, out of the city when he went forth an exile for the faith 'to the admiration of all,' as St. Athanasius describes him; some think, but without sufficient ground, that he followed him to Berœa. He at one time managed the ecclesiastical affairs of the city in the absence of Liberius; and he had a great deal to do (under the latter and in concert with Hilary, of Poictiers) with the restoration of the bishops who had lapsed at Ariminum. He was therefore a special object of aversion to the Luciferians, in whose eyes a moment's dallying with heresy was an unpardonable sin. These same men were probably the authors of the calumnies

---

[1] Cf. *Primitive SS.* pp. 140, 1. On p. 136 Mr. Puller says that Valentinian's edict 'had to be publicly read in the churches of Rome.' Damasus himself adopted this unusual course in his zeal for the reformation of his clergy. Mr. Puller's account of the bishops of the fourth century (p. 134, *seq.*) needs to be checked by the facts given by Thomassinus, *Disc. Eccl.* t. ii. part. ii. lib. iii. cap. 101, and a grand passage in Döllinger's *Hist. of the Church*, Period II. cap. v. § 1: 'The word bishop was synonymous with just and upright administration of the law.'

[2] St. Jerome, *Ep. ad Pammachium*. Ammianus Marcellinus laid stress upon the gorgeous attire in which St. Damasus appeared in public, and contrasted it with the robes of bishops in the country. Leo XIII. also wears the most gorgeous official robes, and yet he almost lives on air

both against Liberius and Damasus.[1] But no accusation could be successfully manipulated against the faith of Damasus; for there was no occasion (as in the case of Liberius) when he was removed from public ken, and when their calumnies could escape unchecked. But, in concert with the Jew Isaac, they attacked his moral character; only, however, to draw from all sides fresh witnesses to his sanctity.

II. When Liberius died, Damasus was his natural and fittest successor. He was immediately elected by the vast majority, and duly consecrated—'elected,' says St. Ambrose, 'by the judgment of God;'[2] only four out of the forty presbyters of Rome went with his foe. There was no competitor for the throne at the moment when Damasus was elected. Ammianus Marcellinus, looking at matters from the outside, sees in Damasus and Ursinus merely two rivals for a great position. But Damasus was seated on the throne when the opposition began; he was the bishop, and the only bishop, on Cyprianic principles, 'since there cannot be a second after the first; and whoever is made such after one who ought to be the only one, is not a second, but no bishop at all.' St. Jerome expressly says that it was after an interval, however short, that a rival bishop was started ('post non multum temporis spatium,' 'Chronicon').[3] Rufinus says that before the troubles began, Damasus 'had received the episcopate in the city by succession after Liberius.' He did not, therefore, mount an episcopal throne through streams of human blood.[4]

But Damasus having been elected and consecrated, not long—it may be immediately—afterwards, Ursinus, a deacon, stirred up a party against him, and succeeded in getting himself elected and consecrated on a single day,[5] contrary to the

[1] Cf. Stilting's Life of St. Liberius in the *Acta Sanctorum*.
[2] We could hardly have a better judge of the matter than St. Ambrose.
[3] 'A few days after' (Döllinger).
[4] *Primitive Saints, &c.* p. 140. It is strange that Mr. Puller should content himself with saying that 'Ammianus Marcellinus divides the blame equally between the two competitors.' Just what a heathen would do. Mr. Barmby (*Dict. of Chr. Biog.* iv. 1069) thinks it a merit that Ammianus 'shows no bias on the one side or the other of the contest.'
[5] Damasus waited the usual time.

canons, by the Bishop of Tivoli, an old and rough bishop, who usurped for the occasion the office of the Bishop of Ostia. His party seized on the basilica which Liberius had erected on the Esquiline in honour of our Lady, and in the endeavour to prevent the people, who sided with Damasus, flocking into it for their usual worship, a *mêlée* ensued. A savage Prefect of Corn, a considerable official, who took side with Damasus, mismanaged the matter, and a scene of bloodshed ensued. The whole matter (which included two frays) was, as Rufinus, a contemporary writer, says, 'turned to the prejudice of the good and innocent bishop'—*i.e.* Damasus. The judgment of the Prefect of Italy, a heathen, was against Ursinus as ' the author of the dissension '—so at least we may gather from an expression of Valentinian's. And in the second fray, whilst the Prefect of Italy, who was then, it would seem, under the influence of Isaac the Jew, sided against Damasus, the vicar of the city corrected the judgment of his co-official, and Ursinus was banished the city. St. Damasus built a basilica at Nola in thanksgiving for his release from the trouble.

III. No sooner had the reins of government been placed 'by the judgment of God' in the hands of Damasus, than he entered upon a course of procedure which characterised his whole reign. Like others before him, but with still greater frequency, he conducted the affairs of the Church in concert with other bishops. The council was his instrument of rule. So much was this the case that presently 'The Westerns' and Damasus presented themselves to the East as one man. St. Basil sets it down to their own sins that things were so different in the East. He and the bishops that agreed with him saw in the West a unity of faith and action which they fairly envied. But this unity was not obtained without a struggle. Milan, the imperial residence, was the scene of discord at the beginning of Damasus' reign. Ursinus seems to have succeeded in stirring up the embers of Arian misbelief outside Rome, and it found a champion in Milan in the bishop Auxentius. The bishops Ursacius and Valens, the old opponents of St. Athanasius, together with Auxentius, were busy in the same mischievous work. St. Athanasius looked to Rome for the settlement of these difficulties. Already Rome had acted with vigour sufficient to induce St. Athanasius to say, writing to the African bishops, 'We thank him' (*i.e.* 'our beloved Damasus' as he had just called him) 'and those who met in the great city, that by casting out Ursacius and Valens, and others who thought with them, they had preserved the peace of the Catholic Church.' But St. Athanasius imagined that not enough had been done with regard to Auxentius. Various synods had met and condemned them, but Rome, he thought, had not yet spoken plainly. Accordingly he expressed his surprise that Auxentius had not been 'cast out of the Church.'[1] But in reality, Damasus had done more than St. Athanasius knew of. He had not only convened a council and reaffirmed the Nicene faith against Ursacius and Valens, but he had condemned Auxentius in an encyclical, in spite of the support given to him by the emperor. And he had written in the name of the synod to the Illyrian bishops, and through them to the East, a letter which was to set men's minds at rest as to the value of the Council of Ariminum, in which so many bishops had failed.

This letter is of great importance as evidence of the position held by the Holy See in the mind of the Church generally. It appears from St. Athanasius that nothing less than a Roman synod could authoritatively allay the disquiet abroad. But the value of a Roman synod could obviously only be rated thus by reason of its being an expression of the mind of the Bishop of Rome; for the rest of the bishops had no more influence than an ordinary Eastern prelate. Damasus then tells the Illyrian bishops, and through them the whole East, that they must not allow their minds to be swayed by the great number of the bishops who went astray at Ariminum. In this matter numbers do not count, 'for,' he says, 'it is evident that neither the Roman bishop'—*i.e.* Liberius— 'whose judgment was the one to be looked for before all, nor Vincentius, nor others, gave any consent to such decrees.' Now it cannot be supposed that Vincentius and a few others

---

[1] θαυμάζοντες, πῶς μέχρι νῦν οὐ καθῃρέθη καὶ ἐκβέβληται τῆς 'Εκκλησίας. In what follows I have, for the most part, followed Merenda, whose monograph on St. Damasus is to be found in Migne's edition of that Pope's letters, and seems to me a masterpiece of accurate reasoning.

could outweigh the immense number of lapsed bishops in the disastrous Council of Ariminum. Nor could Vincentius, and a few others, *plus* the Roman bishop, counterbalance such numbers, unless there were something special in the position of the latter bishop. Damasus, however, and his synod could assume in those to whom he wrote a recognition of the singular position of the Roman bishop, whose refusal to sign the Ariminian confession nullified the effect of the vast defection on the part of the bishops. The synodal letter also speaks of the bulwark against heresy raised by the Nicene Creed. The Western bishops were, be it remembered, writing to the East, and they thus described the Nicene Council: 'Our ancestors, three hundred and eighteen bishops, *directed from the city of the most holy Bishop of the city of Rome*, a council having been arranged at Nicæa, erected this bulwark against the devil's weapons.'

Later on [1] the Illyrians assented to the Roman programme, condemned certain heretics, and announced their adherence to the 'Consubstantial Trinity.'

But equally important from another point of view is the letter of the emperor accompanying his confirmation of the decrees of the Illyrian bishops. He warns bishops against pleading in the East the faith of their emperor, for that, he says, would be disobedience to the scriptural command, 'Render unto Cæsar the things that are Cæsar's, and unto God the things that are God's.' There was, therefore, no confusion in theory at this time between the temporal and spiritual order—a fact to be remembered when we come to the Rescript of Gratian. The Western emperor only gave civil privilege to that which the spiritual authorities themselves decided.

So far, then, the Bishop of Rome comes before us as the centre of Christendom at a time when the imperial residence was at Milan, and when some of the greatest bishops that the Church ever possessed were engaged in the conflict for the

---

[1] The chronology here is exceedingly difficult. Mansi and Merenda bring in Valentinian's action here. Hefele gives reasons for supposing it to be somewhat later, in the same year as his death (cf. Hefele, ii. 289; Merenda, *Gesta Damasi*, sub anno 370).

orthodox faith. This central position of the Bishop of Rome will appear still more clearly as we proceed. Milan, Treves, Sirmium, Thessalonica, Constantinople, possess in their turn the imperial court; but the headship of the Church remains at Rome. There, hemmed in by an idolatrous prefect, a mixed senate (of which pagans formed the larger portion), a disunited clergy, cosmopolitan heresy represented by the sectaries of Africa, Syria, the depths of Spain, organised calumny incited by the Jew Isaac, and above all, at one time, an anti-Pope at the Esquiline, Damasus proceeded with his work of ruling the Church from Great Britain to Africa, and from Gaul to Constantinople.[1] No mere headship, such as the Duke of Norfolk possesses amongst the English nobility, will explain the attitude of the Church in general towards the Bishop of Rome[2] in this fourth century.

IV. It was the special glory of Damasus that it fell to his lot to guard the Church's faith on two essential points, and to condemn the leaders of the two heresies that took the place of Arianism, during his long and fruitful reign. On both these questions the great St. Basil proved unequal to the task of discerning the germs of evil, and dealing with them with decision. His fight—and no words can describe the grandeur of his stand—was at the first against Arianism; and he ended with writing one of the most magnificent treatises that the Church possesses on the Divine glory of the Third Person. But when Apollinarius started his heretical teaching the Easterns could not believe that one who had deserved so well of the Church had fallen into a new heresy, and Basil least of all. Basil, indeed, thought Apollinarius 'ready to say anything,' but would not openly condemn his doctrine and break with him. Whilst wellnigh the whole East was resounding with his heterodox position, St. Basil would not allow himself to think of him as the victim accused of a fundamental heresy; and he managed to furnish his enemies with weapons of which it needed all the dexterity of an Athanasius to turn the point. There can be no question that Basil was absolutely orthodox on the point himself; but he did not see

[1] *Damase*, par l'Abbé Callen (Paris, 1871).
[2] This is the illustration selected by Mr. Puller, *Primitive SS.* p. 229.

the danger that threatened the Church from Apollinarius. Yet this heretic had begun to organise; he was gaining a following among the bishops, and the East was in danger of being overrun with Apollinarianism as before with Arianism. But, as the Eastern historian notes, 'Damasus, Bishop of Rome, and Peter of Alexandria, having discovered the beginning of the new heresy, condemned it in a council held at Rome as contrary to the Catholic Faith.' [1]

The same was the case with the Macedonian heresy which in part occasioned the Council of Constantinople. It was for a while dealt with too tenderly by the Greeks. St. Basil even incurred blame for his charitable tolerance of it. No blame, indeed, properly attaches to an individual saint for not perceiving the germs of heresy as they first appear; but at this critical moment in the Church's life, when Arianism was being put to death, it is to be noticed that, as a matter of fact, the Holy See was the source of strength to the episcopate in meeting the new forms of heresy that arose upon its grave. That see might be expected to be occasionally deceived by persons who dissimulated to gain its support, as in the case of Vitalis; but in regard to the doctrine at issue it was as a matter of fact the unerring judge.[2]

And the strength of its occupant lay as well in the divine assistance which was pledged to his office as in his own perpetual consciousness of his relationship to the Prince of the Apostles. Thus he says of his promotion:

> Hinc mihi provecto Christus cui summa potestas
> Sedis Apostolicæ voluit concedere honorem.[3]

To the Easterns he wrote: 'It redounds principally to your own honour, most honoured sons, that your love pays the reverence which is due to the Apostolic See.' [4] At the same time he is careful to remind them of his own unworthiness to hold the position.

---

[1] Sozomen, vi. 25.

[2] When St. Basil speaks of the ignorance of the West concerning affairs in the East, on which Mr. Puller lays some stress, he is alluding to cases in which the orthodoxy of particular persons was temporarily in question, not of matters of faith. He exaggerates somewhat into the bargain.

[3] *Damasi Carm.* xxxv.   [4] *Ep.* iii.

We have to this day the distich which St. Damasus wrote in the baptistery, where he seems to have placed the chair of the Apostle. It runs thus:

'One chair of Peter, one only true bath.'[1]

He sat, then, according to his own belief, in the chair of Peter. And nothing, as we shall see, but a recognition of this on the part of Eastern and Western Christendom can explain the action of the episcopate during his troubled reign.

V. The Church in the East had been plunged into the utmost distress. St. Basil's descriptions are heartrending, and he assured St. Athanasius that, in his belief, there was no way of help but for the Western episcopate to assist.

Now, what did St. Basil mean by the Western bishops? Not certainly individual bishops acting on their own account. Neither could they all act together, except by representation. But the West throughout these times was ordinarily represented by the Roman synod. And in what could the Roman synod surpass the rest of the Church, except in the position of its president, the Bishop of Rome? St. Basil in his sixty-sixth letter is thought to allude to the action taken recently by Rome in regard to Auxentius of Milan. He seems to long for something of the same kind, so that the scholiast heads this letter of St. Basil's to that effect. St. Basil tells St. Athanasius that his first idea was to induce the West to send an imposing array of legates, commissioned by a vast synod, which would impress these perverse Easterns by its numbers. He thought that there was nothing like appearance of numbers to counteract the impression produced by the immense array of bishops who had failed in their duty at Ariminum. But this he saw to be impracticable; consequently he fell back [2] on the regular mode of action in the Church. 'It appeared suitable to write to the Bishop of Rome and ask him to *oversee* [the verb of which *bishop* is the substantive form] matters here in the East and to give judgment, so that since it would be difficult for any of the Westerns to be sent by a common and synodical

---

[1] See an excellent summary of Rossi's argument concerning the chair of Peter in the Abbé Fouard's *St. Peter and the First Years of Christianity*, Appendix iv.

[2] Compare *Ep.* lxx. with *Ep.* lxvi.

decree, he [the Bishop of Rome] might act *on his own authority* in the matter, and choose out men equal to the task.' The work which these legates would have to do was that of persuading the Eastern bishops to accept the ruling of the West concerning the disaster of Ariminum, which consisted essentially in the signature of the bishops having been obtained from them by force.¹

Now St. Basil would never have recommended a plan against which these refractory bishops could lawfully exclaim on technical grounds—against which, that is, they could urge that the Bishop of Rome had no right on his own authority to send legates to persuade them to accept the decisions arrived at in the Roman synod. The relation of Rome to the East must have been recognised by St. Basil as that of a superior authority, and he must have been well assured that his Eastern co-prelates held the same view.

St. Basil, however, included in his requests a verdict in favour of St. Meletius and a condemnation of Marcellus, whose followers, as a matter of fact, were at that time siding with Paulinus. St. Basil's attitude towards Marcellus was, as we shall presently see, somewhat impetuous, and it is not certain that he was justified in his expressions referring to the past. The letters were sent to Rome by Dorotheus, a cleric from Antioch belonging to Meletius, and they were graciously received. St. Damasus sent a deacon of Milan named Sabinus, and afterwards the Bishop of Placentia, with the letters previously written to the Illyrians and the acts of the synod held two years before. In these letters St. Damasus had said that the Nicene synod defined 'that we ought to believe that the Father, Son, and Holy Spirit are of one Deity and one substance,' and then that those to whom they were addressed 'ought to approve this by reciprocal letters.' Valentinian's rescript obliged all, so far as imperial authority could go, to believe in accordance with the synod of Rome and the synods of Gaul, that 'there is one and the same substance of Father, Son, and Holy Spirit in Three Persons.'

¹ ἐφάνη δὲ ἡμῖν ἀκόλουθον ἐπιστεῖλαι τῷ ἐ π ι σ κ ό π ῳ Ῥώμης ἐ π ι σ κ έ ψ α σ θ α ι τὰ ἐνταῦθα καὶ δ ο ῦ ν α ι γ ν ώ μ η ν, ἵν' ἐπειδὴ ἀπὸ κοινοῦ καὶ συνοδικοῦ δόγματος ἀποσταλῆναί τινας δύσκολον τῶν ἐκεῖθεν, αὐτὸν αὐθεντῆσαι περὶ τὸ πρᾶγμα (*Ep.* lxvi.).

The Illyrian bishops anathematised all 'who do not hold and preach that the Trinity is consubstantial.'

I have laid stress on all this activity on the part of the Pope, because a recent writer has, as it seems to me, so thoroughly misrepresented the reign of Damasus. Speaking of this period, he says that St. Basil 'over and over again had written to Damasus to ask him, living as he was in comparative peace and quiet [sic], to help the Eastern Churches which were suffering persecution; but nothing was done, although much might have been done.'[1] It will be seen, however, that we can hardly talk of peace and quiet in regard to the life of Damasus, nor is it true to say that 'nothing was done.' As a matter of fact, the letters from Rome led to action on St. Basil's part, for he writes to say in a letter, wrongly headed 'To the Westerns,' that they in the East agreed to 'all that had been done by your Honour in accordance with the canons,' and that they had 'welcomed your Apostolic zeal concerning the true Faith.'[2]

VI. But it is true that affairs were not conducted at Rome exactly as Basil would have wished. St. Damasus and his synod did not agree with St. Basil as to the best method of putting an end to the differences at Antioch. It was considered at Rome that the uncanonical character of Meletius' election needed to be taken into account, and also Rome did not feel such perfect confidence in the orthodoxy of Meletius as St. Basil did. Rome required the matter to be accurately investigated before coming to a decision. St. Basil proposed a legation from Rome to the East; Rome preferred a legation from the East to herself. Considering all that we know of Eastern intrigue, and the terrible state of things in the Eastern Church, it was surely not unnatural that St. Damasus should wish for some more personal and searching

---

[1] *Prim. SS. &c.* p. 171. St. Damasus, as a matter of fact, was in perpetual and pressing trouble in the West—not, it is true, from the emperor, but from other causes.

[2] *Ep.* xc. In the same letter he calls Sabinus his 'fellow-deacon:' the epithet expresses the brotherhood in which one was a bishop and the other a deacon. Attention to such phrases as these would have saved Mr. Puller from pressing the argument on p. 8. In the most Papal of Papal documents, viz. Hormisdas' Formulary, the Pope was addressed as 'brother.'

investigation of the matter. St. Basil was not infallible. As a matter of fact, he had to be defended by St. Athanasius in more than one matter, and he eventually owned himself wrong in the matter of Marcellus. There would be, so Damasus naturally thought, a better chance of an accurate decision if the case were heard at Rome, with some thoroughly trustworthy legates to give information, than if Western legates were thrown into the sea of intrigue and false-dealing which, according to St. Basil himself, characterised the East. This, then, was the state of things as described by him in a letter to Eusebius of Samosata. At Rome they were in favour of a more thorough investigation of matters, on account of which St. Basil speaks of some there being greater sticklers for accuracy than others,[1] and says that these were not pleased with his letters. Accordingly they were sent back by Evagrius, and St. Basil was asked (it was almost a demand, ἀπαιτῶν) to send another letter and to authoritatively arrange for an embassy through men of position and trustworthiness, in order to give Rome a colourable pretext [2] for undertaking that quasi-episcopal [3] visitation of the East for which St. Basil had so earnestly pleaded. One cannot help seeing that St. Damasus wished the embassy from the East to repair to Rome that the whole matter of the Antiochene dispute might be gone into with care. At present he seems to have been acting on the line adopted by Eusebius of Vercellæ, his legate, when he left Antioch—that of withholding express and final sanction to either party.

Evagrius left Basil to consult St. Meletius at Antioch, and received a letter from the former, saying that he did not suppose that anything would come of the whole correspond-

[1] Mr. Puller has paraphrased Basil's words, 'the more accurate amongst those there,' as 'Pope Damasus and the Roman clergy' (*Prim. SS.* p. 285), and he translates ἀκρίβεια 'preciseness.' It should be 'precision.' He adds that St. Gregory Naz. speaks of the Pope and the Westerns as 'the self-styled defenders of the canons.' St. Gregory does not use the word 'self-styled.' He speaks of the Westerns as being, in the matter of Meletius, 'the defenders, *as they allege* (ὡς λέγουσιν), of the canons,' *i.e.* their ground of action is that the canons were violated. He does not treat the matter with irony, but gives in fairness their plea.

[2] εὐπρόσωπον ἀφορμήν (*Ep.* cxxxviii.).

[3] τῆς ἐπισκέψεως ἡμῶν (*ib.*).

ence, considering 'the accuracy of the man and the [unsatisfactory] nature of writing.'[1] Judging from St. Basil's next letter (Ep. cxxix.) it would seem as if Eusebius of Samosata partly agreed with the advice of Evagrius, that St. Basil should at least write again to the Westerns.[2] Letters were accordingly addressed to the West, and in some of them[3] they pleaded that the West cannot afford to do without the East any more than the head can say to the feet, I have no need of you.[4] After describing in detail the fearful calamities that were oppressing the East, they say that 'doubtless many of us ought to run to your dignity and each be interpreters of his own matter [there]'—an emphatic incidental recognition of the central position of Rome in the Christian Church. They could not go to all the Western bishops and lay their matters before them; nor could the West have any claim to such a reference, except by reason of the possession of some right of hearing appeals. This recourse, however (they say), is out of the question by reason of the circumstances of the times.

The letters are exceedingly vague as to what was to be done, and they evade the request for an embassy to be sent to the West. True as it was that bishops could not, without great difficulty, leave their posts, still later on they did, for

[1] τῆς τε τοῦ ἀνδρὸς ἀκριβείας στοχαζόμενος καὶ αὐτῆς τῆς φύσεως τῶν γραμμάτων. I have adopted Merenda's interpretation, although at first sight the ἀκρίβεια would seem to refer to Damasus and not Meletius. But I have no doubt that Merenda is right.

[2] With regard to a note in Mr. Puller's book (p. 173) concerning the headings of some letters that passed between St. Basil and the West, it must be remembered that there is no more depreciation of Papal authority in calling the Pope and the rest 'the Westerns' than there would be of the Queen's in a French statesman saying that he was going to write to 'the English,' including their sovereign. We do not expect modern styles of writing in the fourth century; added to which there is some uncertainty about these titles. It seems quite certain that as they stand they are incorrect, and the scribe who transposed them may have simply headed them of his own accord. As for the title 'Bishops of Italy and Gaul,' the very idea of St. Basil was to get numbers into the proposed demonstration, and the letter was sent straight to Rome. There are occasions when the congregations, which include the Pope, are addressed.

[3] *Ep.* ccxliii.

[4] They also say that they do not write 'to inform your diligence,' ἀκρίβεια. Clearly, therefore, the word has a good sense as applied to the Westerns—implying diligent investigation—not (as Mr. Puller, p. 285) irony.

such a purpose as that of a council, and one cannot help perceiving in them a certain unwillingness to submit to the searching investigation of the matter which was desired at Rome, and which it was doubtless felt would be more impartial there than in the excited atmosphere of the East.

St. Damasus seems, however, to have held a synod,[1] and sent them encouraging letters, and Basil's hopes forthwith rose high; but troubles soon came which materially altered the complexion of matters in his eyes. Vitalis seceded from Meletius at Antioch, and joined Apollinarius, and, it would seem, was presently summoned to Rome.[2] Thither at any rate he went, and there he presented Damasus with a profession of faith which St. Gregory describes as in actual words orthodox, and which, he says, accordingly deceived himself for a while. St. Damasus naturally thought him orthodox; but was cautious enough to hand him over to Paulinus on his return to Antioch, to be dealt with as that bishop might think best.

VII. This action of St. Damasus in regard to Vitalis was, to say the least, a sign of which side he took in the strife at Antioch. It was not, however, of necessity so emphatic a repudiation of Meletius as some have imagined. For Vitalis had quarrelled with Flavian, Meletius' agent at Antioch, and St. Meletius was himself in exile. It was, therefore, natural to send him to Paulinus. Still, it was an open acknowledgment of Paulinus as a proper person to deal with one under accusation for heresy, for St. Damasus seems almost immediately after Vitalis' departure from Rome to have come to the conclusion that he was not quite sure of his orthodoxy, and accordingly he sent to Paulinus a profession of faith which those were to sign who wished to be in communion with Rome.[3] Just at this time Peter also, St. Athanasius' saintly successor at Alexandria, was in Rome, and he, too, emphatically sided with Paulinus. St. Athanasius had himself written

---

[1] Cf. Merenda (*Gesta Damasi*, sub anno 374) for the evidence.

[2] Tillemont thinks he came spontaneously; but St. Gregory speaks of his being required to make a profession of faith (ἀπαιτηθείς), which implies something less than spontaneity (cf. Greg. Naz. *Ep.* ii. *ad Cled.*).

[3] 'Qui . . . tibi, id est, nobis per te, voluerint sociari.'

letters of communion to Paulinus after being at Antioch. Before going there he was inclined towards association with Meletius, but after being on the spot he sent letters to Paulinus. Tillemont has slipped into a mistake in supposing the reverse to have been the case, and Mr. Puller has followed him. But a careful comparison of St. Basil's letters shows that it was really after being at Antioch himself that St. Athanasius came to his final conclusion that communion should be maintained with Paulinus, although this by no means hindered him from intercourse with St. Meletius.[1] St. Athanasius had now won his crown in 373, and his mantle had descended on St. Peter, who now followed him in siding with Paulinus. This was in the year 375 A.D.[2]

VIII. St. Basil was naturally aggrieved at Rome's recognition of Paulinus, and his tone suddenly changes. He wrote to Count Terence at Antioch to say that he 'hears' that the Paulinists 'are now carrying about letters from the Westerns, handing over the bishopric of Antioch to them, and ignoring the most wonderful bishop of the true Church of God, viz. Meletius.'

What right, we may ask, had the Westerns to hand over the bishopric of the central city of the East to anyone? By the Westerns St. Basil meant, according to the phraseology of the time, Rome, which he presently substitutes for 'the Westerns.' What right, then, had Rome to hand over any bishopric in the East whatsoever to anyone? What greater act of jurisdiction could Rome perform than to decide upon the person who was to be in charge of Antioch? Obviously Rome had the right, according to St. Basil. He never once disputes that right in itself. He had shortly before written[3] to Eusebius of Samosata, asking his opinion as to whether he (Basil) could, under special circumstances of persecution, ordain a bishop outside his province, as he had been asked to

---

[1] Cf. the Benedictine note to Basil (*Ep.* ccxiv.; Migne, *Basil. Opp.* t. iv.).

[2] Merenda seems quite conclusively to have proved this: because (1) time must be left for St. Basil's phase of pleasure with Rome before these letters to Paulinus; and (2) Vitalis was not yet bishop (he was made bishop in 376); and (3) Count Terence, to whom St. Basil at once wrote, as being in Antioch, was there only from 373 to 375.

[3] *Ep.* cxxxviii. 2.

do, it being against the canons. But he never once questions this right in the case of Rome. Paulinus had been ordained by a Western bishop, and he was now being established in his position by the Bishop of Rome. St. Basil distinctly refuses to take the ground that the Pope had no jurisdiction over Antioch. In his indignant letter about Meletius being passed over, when expressing the extent to which he was prepared to go in the way of disagreement with Rome, he never disputes Rome's right in itself. On the contrary, he congratulates[1] the Paulinists as having received the letters of communion from Rome. He numbers them amongst the household of the faith.[2] But he is not prepared on that account 'to ignore Meletius, or to forget, for his part ($\dot{\epsilon}\pi\iota\lambda\alpha\theta\dot{\epsilon}\sigma\theta\alpha\iota$), the Church under him.'[3] For this also, he says, 'is the true Church of God.' He then defines his position still more definitely, and says that 'in the case of one who is not walking according to the rule [or word] of faith, he would not receive him, not even if he came from Heaven itself, much less if he was one of the sons of men with a letter of commendation.'[4]

There is nothing in this to contravene the decrees of the Vatican Council itself, as has been recently supposed.[5] Those decrees do not force anyone to receive a person who is demonstrably contravening the rule of faith, whatever letters he may produce. It may be a matter of piety so to do, a question of humility whether we should take our own judgment as our rule, a counsel and a supernatural virtue, but it is not a matter of necessity under pain of sin, for such a decision as that of St. Damasus does not fall under the shelter

---

[1] συγκαίρομεν τοῖς κομισαμένοις τὰ ἀπὸ 'Ρώμης.   [2] οἰκείους τῆς πίστεως.
[3] Μελέτιον ἀγνοῆσαι ἢ τῆς ὑπ' αὐτὸν 'Εκκλησίας ἐπιλαθέσθαι.
[4] St. Basil is probably alluding not merely to Paulinus but to Vitalis, who seems to have kept letters from Damasus to which he was not really entitled, as he was certainly not walking according to the rule of faith. I have transposed the limbs of the above sentence from St. Basil in order to show what seems to me to be the certain meaning. Mr. Puller has slipped in the word 'letter,' and translated στοιχῇ 'agree with '—a meaning which it never bears in Greek. The reference is obviously to Gal. v. 25, vi. 16, where the word is used of persons, not of things. St. Gregory Naz. has the same idea in reference to some Easterns' jealousy of Rome. He says that if angels were to come and occupy the East with their vain rivalries, he would protest (*Carm. de Vita*, 1605).   [5] *Prim. SS.* pp. 238–240.

of Papal infallibity. It was not an *ex cathedrâ* pronunciation, not something concerning the faith itself, not a decision obligatory on the whole Church. It was not even, so far as we know, an injunction on anyone. He passed no direct sentence on Meletius; he certainly did not excommunicate him: St. Basil nowhere implies that. I do not say that what St. Basil said was commendable or exemplary. His fault was that which St. Gregory notices, that of too great affection towards Meletius. What he would have done had Rome refused her communion to Meletius, we are unable to say for certain, but we can make a fair conjecture from what followed.

In the beginning of the following year Dorotheus went to Rome again with letters from St. Basil and the Easterns, and, although a cleric under Meletius, was received as a matter of course.[1] It was in reference to this journey and the proposal that St. Basil's brother, St. Gregory of Nyssa, should accompany Dorotheus to Rome, that St. Basil wrote one of his most petulant letters. It was a private letter to Eusebius of Samosata. He speaks 'of disdainful tempers' and 'Western superciliousness.' If the allusion is to St. Damasus, he was certainly indulging his imagination—he did not know him personally — and there is nothing in Damasus' letters to justify such an imputation, nor was it the impression which those who knew him appear to have gained. It is quite possible[2] that he does not in any way allude to Damasus, for he speaks of being 'minded' to write to their 'head' informally (ἄνευ τοῦ κοινοῦ σχήματος), nothing about ecclesiastical matters except to hint that they (*i.e.* the Westerns, not 'their head,') 'neither know the truth of what is going on amongst us, nor go the right way to learn it.'[3] St. Basil knew that there were some who differed from him, like St. Peter of Alexandria and probably St. Ambrose, who had now been consecrated at Milan, and he seems to have been 'minded'

---

[1] Similarly, later on, Acacius of Berœa seems to have been sent from Meletius to Rome, and to have been at a synod with Damasus. This must have been before 381, when he helped to consecrate Flavian, and after 378, when he was made bishop. The date is significant.

[2] Vincenzi (*De Heb. et Christ. Sacr. Monarchiâ*) thinks it certain that he did not. Cf. *De Liberio et Damaso*, second edit.

[3] *Ep.* ccxxxix.

to write straight to Damasus and tell him that 'these and such as these were misinformed.' He was 'minded,' but did not do it. In that case 'Western superciliousness' did not include Damasus. But considering how generally 'the Westerns' was at that time an expression used for 'Rome and the rest,' as 'Peter and the rest' in Holy Scripture, I am inclined to think that he did simply, though unjustifiably, attribute St. Damasus' action to superciliousness. Baronius, however, has a beautiful remark on this subject to the effect that although a saint may be caught humanly excited and disturbed in mind, he will not be detained in such a frame. Accordingly our saint did not actually write as he felt tempted to do, but in a very different tone. He asked the 'Westerns' to use their 'diligent accuracy,'[1] to 'denounce publicly to all the Churches in the East' certain persons whom he names, 'in order that either correcting their ways they may be in sincere harmony with us, or, persisting in their perversity, they may keep their harm to themselves, being no longer able to infect those near them through unguarded communion with them.' If this was not calling upon Rome to exercise jurisdiction in the East, it would be difficult to imagine what evidence could be produced that would satisfy those who see in the history of these times no indication of lordship over the universal Church. And, be it remembered, the lordship in this case did not simply come from Rome, but was attributed to her. She did not claim it here, but was asked to use it.

IX. So that St. Basil had come to a better mind concerning 'Western superciliousness,' and the same is true of his persistent accusation of carelessness in the matter of Marcellus. The truth about Marcellus of Ancyra is one of the most difficult points in the history of this century, and I shall not pretend to have solved it.[2] What is of importance to note here is that, whether rightly or wrongly, St. Basil modified his judgment as to the treatment of Marcellus, whose case he considered had been so inadequately dealt with at

---

[1] So I have ventured to translate ἀκρίβεια, which occurs again here, and is unquestionably not ironical but laudatory (cf. p. 217, note 4).

[2] For a most careful summary of the case for and against Marcellus, see Hefele's *Councils*, vol. ii. p. 29 *seq.*, Eng. tr.

Rome. At this time and for some while he had considered that Marcellus had rejected 'all the dogmas of our hope;' but in the letter to Eusebius, in which he speaks of Western superciliousness, he refers to what had been *previously* done in the case of Marcellus.[1] One only hopes he does not allude, as Merenda thinks, to the action of the prelates of Sardica, whose judgment in the matter ought to have been sufficient for that period, but, anyhow, he ultimately admitted that there was another side to the matter. And as for his supposing that the Westerns, by whom he probably meant the Pope (though this is not certain,[3] seeing that on this occasion he mentions him separately), could be guilty of 'supporting heresy,' this in no wise shows, as Mr. Puller thinks,[4] that 'St. Basil had no conception of the Bishop of Rome being the divinely appointed monarch of the Church.' A bishop of the present day, believing *ex animo* in the teaching of the Vatican decrees, might say the same as St. Basil did to the Holy Father, for there are many ways (direct and indirect) of giving support to heresy. In this case St. Basil considered that the Westerns had done it through ignorance of the real state of things, and not by any actual decision, but by not acting in a more decisive way. He was at liberty to consider it to be so, and yet might believe in the Pope as the divinely appointed monarch of the Church. We can say this because we have the Church's teaching, especially that of the Vatican decrees, to help us to understand that the Pope's divinely appointed position, though that of a monarch, is not that of a monarch who cannot err. There *are* matters and circumstances in which the Pope cannot err, and in which absolute submission, under pain of mortal sin, is due from every child of the Church; but there are also circumstances in which, however we might shrink from acting upon the supposition, such submission is not a matter of necessity. It is necessary to say thus much because many of the arguments contained in Mr. Puller's book derive their force from this simple truth

---

[1] 'What they' (*i.e.* the Westerns) 'did before.' [2] *Ep.* cclxxi.
[3] Mr. Puller takes it for granted that Damasus is meant. But he does not seem in his whole account to take the context into consideration.
[4] The sentence quoted from Bossuet is inaccuracy itself.

being kept out of sight. They are directed against something that those whom he is pleased to call Ultramontanes do not believe.[1] In this instance Marcellus had at one time at least succeeded in inducing the Westerns in general to consider him orthodox, although St. Athanasius seems afterwards to have written against him without mentioning his name. At the time when he was received by St. Julius, St. Athanasius, and the rest of the Westerns, it is not certain that he was not orthodox at heart, as he certainly was in word; but St. Basil probably knew Marcellus better than most men did, and he was at this time certain that at least in heart he was heterodox. The Pope, however, had only to do with his words and those of his followers, which was the point at issue at this present moment. Marcellus had not been condemned by any synod at the time that Basil wrote; his case had not been formally brought before Rome.

X. St. Basil, however, had calmed down before he joined in writing to the Westerns, and having appealed to their carefulness in such matters, he says that if they will only make it clear with whom they hold communion (and, according to Mr. Puller, 'they' must mean especially Damasus), they will be listened to, both from their being further removed from the scene of trouble, and 'by reason of the grace of God conferred on you for the oversight of those in trouble.' It is difficult to see how this latter sentence can imply anything less than a belief that Rome was in possession of a *charisma*—that is to say, something beyond a mere primacy of honour—in dealing with *Eastern prelates*. The West, of itself, could have no special 'grace' in this matter.[2] We can only explain the sentiment of St. Basil by that consciousness of a *charisma* attaching to the Apostolic See which made it the proper caretaker of the troubled East. He proceeds to say that if the multitude of them agree, as they did, so much the better. Their decrees would be beyond question even by these refractory Easterns.

[1] I know of nothing better calculated to help a diligent inquirer on this subject than Mr. Wilfrid Ward's second volume of the Life of his father. I think it right to mention that some expressions in this book, almost identical with those used by that excellent writer, were in MS. before I had read that Life.

[2] We could hardly apply such expressions to the Duke of Norfolk, who is the chosen type of Papal primacy in *Prim. SS. &c.* p. 229.

He then mentions first the case of Eustathius of Sebaste. He had, St. Basil says, been deprived of his bishopric,[1] but had found a way of recovering it. He went to Rome, and was restored by Liberius; and St. Basil says they neither know in the East what confession of faith he had put before the Pope, nor what conditions Liberius had laid down. All they know is, that 'he brought with him a letter' from Rome, 'reinstating him, and upon showing it he was restored to his position at the synod of Tyana.' No words can add to the force of this last sentence. If the restoration of a bishop by St. Damasus, on his own authority, is not an act of jurisdiction, what is? And the bishops at Tyana took it for granted that a Papal letter directing his restitution was to be obeyed, and St. Basil has not a word to say against their attitude in the matter. At the same time St. Basil is quite right in demanding, as he went on to demand, that they should now know on what conditions Eustathius was restored, not that they might criticise the conditions, but that they might know if he had fulfilled them. The right settlement[2] of the matter must come from Rome, said St. Basil, and letters needed to be written thence 'to the Churches.' He regrets that they could not hold council with the Westerns; but in spite of that he accepts their authoritative action as adequate. Only (he says) Eustathius has changed,[3] and consequently his restoration does not appear to remain valid.

St. Basil then deals somewhat tenderly with the case of Apollinarius, and passes on to Paulinus. He has an important sentence about his ordination. He says, 'If there is anything to blame concerning his ordination, they [*i.e.* the Westerns] would say.' Now, except on the theory of Papal jurisdiction over the East, there must have been everything to blame in Paulinus' ordination; but St. Basil does not seem

---

[1] Viz. by the Council of Melitene.   [2] τὴν διόρθωσιν. *Ep.* cclxiii. 3.

[3] μεταβληθείς. As a rule, the supremacy of the Holy See over the East was in those times exercised immediately only over the Patriarchal Sees, so to call them by anticipation. But this case of Eustathius of Sebaste is one of several instances in which the authority of Rome was exercised immediately over an Eastern bishop of lesser account, and it was on appeal from an Eastern synod, and the right of Rome thus to act was admitted both by the synod and by St. Basil.

to consider that he has any right to object to it. He considers that lies with the Westerns, *i.e.* with St. Damasus. 'What grieves us,' says Basil, 'is his [Paulinus'] sympathy with the dogmas of Marcellus, and admitting his followers indiscriminately to his communion.'[1] 'We ask for your careful oversight (ἐπιμέλειαν) of these things, which will be effectual if you will vouchsafe to write to all the Churches in the East, to the effect that those who deprave . . . . are, if they amend, in communion (εἶναι κοινωνούς), but if they determine to persist in their novelties, you withdraw from them.' It would be difficult to put into plainer language the teaching that if people wish to be in communion with the Church, they must be in communion with Rome.

XI. St. Damasus at once, on receiving these letters from Basil, held a synod (at which Peter of Alexandria was present) and Apollinarius was condemned. Merenda gives most cogent reasons for believing that this was not later than A.D. 377. St. Basil's tone towards Apollinarius at once changed. Before this synod he had said[2] that Apollinarius was 'not exactly an enemy'—now in his letter to Bishop Eulogius and two other Egyptian bishops he speaks of him as outside the Church. The Roman synod had made the difference.

About this time St. Basil seems to have written to St. Peter of Alexandria to express his sorrow that the latter had spoken of Meletius and Eusebius of Samosata, in presence of Damasus, as though they were tinged with Arianism. Peter was probably alluding to the document which the two had signed, addressed to the Emperor Jovian, which led St. Jerome to speak of St. Meletius as having repudiated the *Homoousion*, and which probably influenced St. Athanasius in his cautious attitude towards St. Meletius. St. Damasus appears to have adopted the same cautious attitude, admitting Dorotheus, Meletius' agent, to full communion and calling him 'brother,' but not entering into close intercourse with Meletius. It must be remembered, as has been already remarked, that there was often a separation between a presbyter and his bishop, be-

---

[1] It will be noticed that Mr. Puller's version of this matter does not at all square with what St. Basil here says.

[2] *Ep.* cciv.

tween a bishop and his province, and again between a province and Rome, very far short of depriving them of the sacraments, but still reckoned as a serious calamity in those times. The separation would consist sometimes in the withdrawal of letters of communion, or of mutual access, or of conciliar intercourse, or other marks of that close association between bishops which was the normal state of things.[1] So Sozomen, speaking of the separation between East and West on the occasion of Flavian's ordination, says the Westerns sent 'the accustomed letters' to Paulinus, but 'to Flavian none.' It did not amount to constituting either side schismatics, although strong terms would be often used. But there was a chasm between putting a bishop outside the Church and interrupting the closer intercourse which was the ordinary result of being in communion with one another.

XII. Still, anyone in the East who wished to be completely on the right side would be anxious to know who was in close ecclesiastical intercourse with 'the Westerns,' by which was meant the Pope and the bishops in communion with him, and no one unless already in the meshes of heresy would wish to be thought out of communion with the West in the sense of lacking recognition by them as the lawful bishop of a see. Accordingly, we know from St. Jerome that at Antioch Paulinus, Vitalis, and Meletius all claimed to possess the seal of Rome's recognition.[2] Paulinus could say that he was on terms of closest intercourse, since, amongst other things, Rome had handed over Vitalis to be dealt with by him. Vitalis, having broken away from the faith, on returning to Antioch, still traded on the letters he had received from Damasus, when he had deceived the Pope by a profession of faith which was orthodox in terms, but which he understood in an heretical sense. Meletius was able to say that Rome, although not in closest intercourse with him, had never repudiated his communion.

There is no fair reason for distrusting St. Jerome's statement here. This assertion on the part of each of the three, repeated by their adherents (which shows the general value set on communion with Rome), caused him perplexity, and he wrote to Damasus to ask him with which of the three he was

[1] Cf. Merenda, sub anno 376, and De Smedt, *Diss.* 2, p. 70. [2] *Ep.* xvi.

to communicate. He conceived that he was uttering the usual sentiments of a Catholic Christian, as indeed he was, when he said (in a previous letter) of the 'chair of Peter,' 'Upon that rock I know that the Church is built.' In this second letter he says, 'I meanwhile exclaim if anyone be joined to the chair of Peter, he is mine. Meletius, Vitalis, and Paulinus say that they adhere to you; if only one of them asserted this, I could believe him.' It is natural to suppose from this that all three claimed in express terms to be in communion 'with the chair of Peter.' The expression could not be an idiosyncrasy of St. Jerome's. He knew well the teaching of Rome; he had been eleven years in the Christian Church. All parties were eager to secure his adherence, as he himself says; his praise was already in all the Churches; he was more than the fit age to be a bishop.[1] No one seems to have told him that he should not speak of Damasus as occupying the chair of Peter; all they did was to claim each one to be in communion with that chair. That Damasus himself had all along claimed to sit in the chair of Peter, in more than one sense, is certain. The inscription which he wrote about the material chair of the Apostle, preserved at Rome, showed his teaching concerning the chair of Peter in the metaphorical sense.[2]

St. Jerome, it may be noticed, in his first letter speaks of the use of the term Hypostasis, by some in the singular, by others in the plural, in regard to the Holy Trinity—a controversy which had been laid to rest at the Council of Alexandria, either form of speech being allowed. But now, when Damasus had shown his special favour to Paulinus, the Eustathians, as the party of Paulinus was called, began to

---

[1] St. Jerome, it has been urged, a little before had spoken of himself as 'pene puer.' But it must be remembered that St. Jerome spoke of a person as 'adolescens' up to forty, and he was older than St. Athanasius was when, in the words of Canon Bright, 'he made himself felt as a power in the First General Council,' and older than the same saint when he was made Archbishop of Alexandria.

[2] Mr. Puller, speaking of the Popes pleading their succession from St. Peter as a religious basis for their jurisdiction, says: 'Whether Damasus did so plead it I cannot say' (p. 159). He may rest assured that Damasus was 'guilty' of pleading his succession to Peter throughout his reign.

draw the Meletians, in the absence of Meletius, towards themselves. Consequently St. Basil thought it right to revive the controversy, and to insist upon the importance of the difference between the two expressions. St. Gregory of Nazianzus on the other hand (at any rate later on) deprecated making this different way of speaking of the Godhead a 'dividing' question, since both parties meant the same.

It is clear from what St. Jerome says about some combining him as a heretic 'with the Westerns and the Egyptians'—*i.e.* with St. Damasus and St. Peter—that he was allowed by the former to use the Western expression of *one* Hypostasis in the Triune God (meaning substance) and that St. Damasus' answer led him to communicate with Paulinus, by whom he was shortly afterwards ordained priest.

XIII. And now a new chapter in the affairs of Antioch begins. The law of Gratian in favour of tolerance for almost all to practise their own religion had enabled Meletius to return to his flock at Antioch. He seems at once to have set to work to bring about some kind of peace between Paulinus and himself. All, however, that they could effect was to agree that when either of them died the survivor should succeed to the one throne. The churches remained as they were, the great majority in the hands of Arians, one in the possession of Paulinus, and one in the suburbs in the hands of Meletius. The flocks of the two bishops held communion with one another. Thus much seems to follow from the scene before Sapor later on. In that interview the question was, not as to whether the church owned by either Paulinus or Meletius should pass into the hands of the other, but who should have the use of the churches of the Arians, who by the law of Theodosius were now to be ejected. But we may trust Theodoret's account[1] so far, that the flocks were by that time already in the enjoyment of intercommunion. If it is to be trusted any further, it would establish that Paulinus refused to go further than the compact, which was certainly

---

[1] Theodoret's narrative is coloured by his partisanship for Flavian. It is not altogether reliable, certainly not as to Paulinus rejecting any overtures, which is contrary to the evidence of St. Gregory. But his witness on the other points is disinterested.

not made at that interview. Meletius, according to Theodoret, proposed joint action during their lifetime, but this Paulinus thought unadvisable or impossible. The reasonable supposition, then, is that the compact, which we know to have been made, was entered upon on St. Meletius' return from exile, and hence came the peace, to which St. Gregory alludes as having been established for at least some little while, and the disturbance of which the Council of Aquileia so strongly denounced, upon the ordination of Flavian.[1]

Meletius at once set about the assembly of a council of his friends, one main object of which seems to have been to proclaim their adherence to the orthodox faith, that the Church might be seen to be thoroughly one in the doctrines which had been recently depraved, and on which they were themselves supposed by some to be in a state of hesitation. This great council (A.D. 379), at which the letters of Damasus were read—those from the first Roman synod (sent first to Illyrium and then to the Easterns) and those sent through Dorotheus from his second and third synods—accepted what was afterwards called in the Fifth Canon of Constantinople the 'Tome of the Westerns'—the dogmatic letter drawn up by the Roman synod under the presidency of Damasus, which proclaimed the 'one Deity and one substance' of the Holy Trinity.

Thus the entire West, the whole of Egypt, and the whole Eastern Church had embraced the decision of Damasus and the Roman Church concerning the Divinity of the Holy Ghost.

Meletius sent this important document to Rome, signed first by himself and next by Eusebius of Samosata, and it was duly registered in the archives. The entry in the 'Synodicus Libellus' seems an accurate summary of this eventful inauguration of the long-desired peace. 'Meletius, in his throne of Antioch, convened a divine and sacred synod, which confirmed the divine symbol, and anathematised Marcellus, Photinus, and Apollinarius, and he sent the exposition (of faith) to Damasus and the Western bishops.'[2]

---

[1] Cf. p. 253.

[2] *Syn.* cap. lxxiv. Tillemont labours hard to prove that the compact between Meletius and Paulinus had not been made at this time. Blondel, the

The theory that this all-important document was not sent formally and officially to Rome, but found its way thither accidentally and privately, is so contrary to the ways of that time, so utterly unreasonable in itself, that I should not mention it here, were it not that the author of 'The Primitive Saints and the See of Rome' has so emphatically adopted it.[1] The synod of Constantinople in 382, which is often confounded with that of 381, in its letter to Damasus, assumes that he had received official notice of the adoption at Antioch of this 'Tome of the Westerns.' The formal acceptance of Meletius' subscription as 'Bishop of Antioch' would not prove, as Mr. Puller thinks, that Rome accepted him as the only bishop. The letter of the Council of Aquileia proves the contrary.[2] Neither, if we are to trust Theodoret's account of the interview with Sapor at Antioch, did Meletius himself look upon himself as the only Bishop of Antioch, although he did consider that his flock had been entrusted to him by Almighty God. It was not an unknown thing for two bishops to rule in one city under anomalous circumstances by special arrangement. The Pope, St. Melchiades, gave permission to some of the Donatist bishops to retain their sees when they renounced their schism, so that there were temporarily, and by Papal dispensation, two bishops in one

---

Protestant, and Baronius and Valesius agree that it was. Tillemont's arguments have been met and, as it seems to me, fully answered by Merenda, who points out (in answer to Tillemont's assertion, that a compact so public could not have been broken by the Council of Constantinople) that the very point of St. Gregory's complaint was that a public compact had been broken, and in this he was followed by the older and more reverend bishops. For the disgraceful conduct of the bishops at that synod, which led to St. Gregory's resignation of the see, see pp. 252-3. The compact was disregarded *at* the council rather than *by* the council. The saints were opposed to its breach. Mr. Puller's argument about St. Meletius hinges so much on Tillemont's indefensible line on this point, and on a misunderstanding of the interview with Sapor (cf. *Prim. SS.* pp. 245-7) that it may be well to remind some readers that, in spite of Mr. Puller's attempt to rehabilitate Tillemont whole and entire, and his entitling him a 'Roman Catholic divine' more than once, the authority of Tillemont as a divine counts for nothing with us, and that his history has been submitted to 'corrections' on, so to speak, a thousand points. He was, as Merenda (who frequently exposes his mistakes) called him, 'doctissimus et piissimus,' but neither his learning nor his piety have saved him from serious errors.

[1] P. 242. [2] Mansi, t. iii. p. 631.

city.[1] Dr. Döllinger's summary of the matter is perfectly accurate, viz.: 'The *two Catholic* parties at Antioch had mutually agreed, in 378, that the survivor of the two rival prelates should be acknowledged by all as sole bishop.'[2]

Thus far, then, the Church in the East could breathe again. The peace, of which St. Gregory spoke with real eloquence, was established. It only remained for those in Antioch to wait until one of the two bishops was taken to his reward for the perfect order of the Church to be restored. It would seem that in the same year the Church asked of the new emperor a civil confirmation of this peaceable, if abnormal, solution of the Antiochene trouble.[3]

---

[1] Until a fresh see was found.
[2] *Lehrbuch* (1843), vol. i. p. 91.
[3] Mansi, t. iii. p. 623. 'Partium pactum poposcimus ut . . . permanerent' (cf. *infra*, p. 265, and the note on p. 267).

CHAPTER XV.

THE HOMAGE OF KINGS; OR GRATIAN'S RESCRIPT.

I. During the reign of St. Damasus the relation of the civil power to the Church entered upon a new phase. During the first three centuries the Church had developed her internal relations in doctrine and discipline wholly irrespective of the State; but so soon as Constantine adopted the Christian religion as professedly his own the Church had to adjust her administrative forms to the exigencies of her new position. She had, from time to time, to decide upon what was essentially under her own direction, and her own alone, and what could fall under the joint action of Church and State. But the complete adjustment of her relations to the civil power could only be accomplished when the occupant of the imperial throne was (what Constantine was not) a faithful subject of the Church. Until then, she acted on the principle enunciated by St. Gregory the Great, of obtaining what was practicable and accepting the unavoidable with the best grace possible. But from the first she laid down the principle that the typical relation of the two powers was not that of separation, leaving each to its own sphere of action, but of co-operation, in which the civil power should aid the spiritual in certain external matters, whilst the spiritual announces the laws which must govern every man's exercise of whatever power he has received from God. The Church and the State have each of them received their powers from the One God; those powers, therefore, cannot properly come into conflict. But not only so; they must in the nature of things be meant to act in harmony and co-operate towards the one end of man, his final beatitude. Moreover, when their spheres seem to conflict, the Church is, necessarily, the judge of the limits which each is bound to observe. She has the custody of the laws which govern man in the attainment of his supernatural beatitude, and consequently wherever she may decide that a mode of action is necessary for that end, any exercise of civil authority that contravenes or hinders such action is not the use of a power given by God, but a transgression of the limits within which the civil order was meant to act. The classical metaphor which expresses the relation between the civil power and the Church is that of the body and the soul. The Church's action stands in relation to the civil order as the soul to the body. It was at this very time that this metaphor, which is commonly used in the theology of the Church to express this relationship, was first used by St. Gregory of Nazianzus, and it was at this time that the actual relationship between Church and State approached more nearly than at any previous period to its typical expression.

II. Constantine used the power which the gratitude of Christians awarded him, on the whole, with moderation,[1] but on coming under the influence of Eusebius he began to encroach on the prerogatives of the Church. Constantius altogether exceeded his powers in ecclesiastical matters, and Valens became a scourge to the Catholic Church. Valentinian I. had espoused the orthodox faith, and gave the celebrated reply to a request that he would call a council, saying that it was not for him as a layman to decide upon ecclesiastical matters. But his attitude towards the Church was nevertheless one of reserve; and it was in his son, Gratian, that the Church greeted her first thoroughly filial subject amongst the line of Roman emperors. The first to refuse to wear the robe of the Pontifex Maximus,[2] he was the first to throw himself into the arms of the Church and seek from her, in submission to her laws, the power which he believed could alone make up for his desertion of the ordinary methods of obtain-

---

[1] Cf. Döllinger's *Hist. of the Church*, Period II. ch. v. § 1.

[2] Tillemont and Fleury think this improbable, but cf. Broglie, *L'Eglise et l'Empire Romain au IVme Siècle* (3me partie, pp. 294-299, 1866) for a juster estimate of the incident.

ing his subjects' support. 'It was not the emperor, but the empire which on that day, by his lips, proclaimed itself Christian.'

III. Gratian was, indeed, over-persuaded by his first surroundings to a horrible deed of vengeance on the Count Theodosius; but he presently came under a new influence, which determined his line of action in future, and may be said to have been the instrument in Divine Providence for sparing the Church from the expiring efforts of Arianism. St. Ambrose had mounted the throne of Milan: a man specially qualified to deal with the new state of things, from his acquaintance, during his secular life, with the principles of the civil order, and from his unswerving devotion to the orthodox faith after his consecration to the episcopate. Had Milan been the see of Peter, St. Ambrose would have been the central figure of the age; but not even an Ambrose could make Milan the centre of the Church's unity. It was, however, his to direct the mind and action of the young emperor. The relationship between them was, according to Gratian himself, that of father and son; and the extant letter of Gratian to St. Ambrose is a beautiful example of filial respect in the spiritual order.

IV. Soon after Gratian's accession, his uncle Valens, lying wounded in a hut, was left by his attendants to burn to death, and Gratian succeeded to the entire empire. He took with him a copy of St. Ambrose's treatise on the true faith, as he repaired to Sirmium to enter upon his new honours; and at once proclaimed liberty of worship for all sects except those which were disturbers of the public peace, such as the Manicheans, or were coming into prominence, such as the Photinians and Eunomians. And in this he appears to have afterwards thought himself remiss, as though it became a Christian emperor to forbid any heretics to worship according to their ill-advised conscience. It must be carefully borne in mind, in this connection, that heresy had invariably itself used the civil power when possible, and with an amount and kind of persecution to which neither Gratian nor Theodosius ever stooped, and that for most of the heretics of that time the only persuasive force was that of legal compulsion; but some time in the early part of his reign [1] Gratian appears to have adopted the measure which was of all others the best calculated to bring about the destruction of Arianism in the West. He decided upon making the exercise of spiritual jurisdiction in the West easier and more decisive by ordering that all bishops within the Western Patriarchate who rebelled against being tried by their brethren should be compelled, if cited, to appear at Rome; and it should be the duty of the Prefect of Italy to expedite their appearance there. In the case of 'the more distant parts' (such as Africa) the duty of trying the bishop lay with the metropolitan. We cannot say for certain that the earlier rescript contained more than this. It is not open to us to argue, for instance, with any certainty that the exact provision of the later rescript about the metropolitans was contained in the earlier. Our only data for deciding the contents of the earlier rescript (which is not extant) are the instances of its violation given by the synod of 378. These, it may be noticed, include Parma, which shows that the whole of Italy came under its purview, and also Africa. For both a bishop of Parma and a bishop in Africa are mentioned as having rebelled against the provisions of the earlier rescript. But the complaint against the African bishop appears to suppose a provision of the same kind as is contained for the regulation of matters 'in more distant parts' in the later rescript.[2]

Thus Gratian made the execution of episcopal judgments easier than it had hitherto been. He did not create a patriarchate, but found one in existence. The jurisdiction of Rome, in its actual exercise, differed in the East and in the West. In the East it was for the most part exercised only directly over the patriarchs; in the West it was exerted over individual bishops more directly. The Pope stood to the West in a double relation, that of ruler of the universal Church, and that of patriarch. And Gratian supplied facilities for the

[1] Possibly quite at the beginning—certainly so if this famous rescript is dated 378—for Florentius had been banished six years previously, in accordance, it would seem, with the earlier law. After six years 'repsit in civitatem' (cf. the letter of the Roman Council to Gratian).

[2] Consequently all that Mr. Puller says (*Prim. SS.* p. 157) about Gratian having enlarged the sphere of his earlier rescript in the later one falls to the ground.

exercise of the patriarchal jurisdiction in the West, which were in perfect conformity with the subordinate character of the State in ecclesiastical matters. His great object, according to the synod of 378 and his own rescript, was to keep the trials of bishops to the episcopate. And in doing this he simply supplied legal facilities for executing the judgments of the episcopate, which were arranged in accordance with rules already established by its own action, as, for instance, at Sardica or Nice.

Gratian's action was, we cannot doubt, inspired by St. Ambrose. The Bishop of Milan was himself interested in the new aid given to the administration of the Church. His own church came under the sway of the rescript, and, indeed, profited by it. The result was that after a few years the West was able, in the words (probably) of St. Ambrose, to report that there were not more than two Arian bishops left.[1]

V. Now, this civil aid granted to the judgments of the Holy See was considered by Newton, when he dipped into theology (*sutor ultra crepidam*), to be the starting-point of Papal jurisdiction. Merenda thinks it worth while to notice Newton's theory, but does not think it worth while doing more than notice it. Mr. Puller, however, has made it part of the backbone of his argument against the divine origin of the jurisdiction of the Holy See, 'Was I not right in saying that the pontificate of Damasus forms a new point of departure in regard to *all matters connected with the growth of Papal jurisdiction?*'[2] He compares the effect of Gratian's rescript in 378 with the mode of procedure sanctioned by the Council of Sardica, and considers that it was an enlargement upon the latter without any canonical basis. He thinks that 'by one stroke of his pen the Emperor Gratian created, so far as the civil power could create, a patriarchal jurisdiction over the whole Western empire, and vested it in the Bishop of Rome,'[3] and that this was the only source of the Pope's patriarchal jurisdiction over Gaul, Britain, Spain, and Africa.

---

[1] During the winters of 378-381 Gratian was at Milan in closest intercourse with St. Ambrose, his spiritual guide. The rescript of Gratian must, as has been shown, be assigned to 380.

[2] *Primitive Saints, &c.* p. 159.   [3] P. 157.

Again and again he insists upon the paradox that the only patriarchal jurisdiction possessed by the Pope over the West came to him from the State, *i.e.* from this rescript—'as State-made Patriarch of the West he had a jurisdiction derived from the emperor'[1]—'it was in the time of Damasus that the State made the Pope Patriarch of the West.'[2]

Now (i.), if this was the case, where was the protest against such a violation of canon law? What had become of all that enormous tenacity of the saints to the spiritual and independent character of the kingdom of God? For saints there were most certainly; indeed, it is impossible to suppose that St. Ambrose himself was not a party to this legislation; whilst the bishops of the Roman synod call the earlier rescript of Gratian that 'sentence unquestionably most excellent and worthy of religious princes.'[3] Is it to be supposed that the bishops of that synod, who were themselves concerned, would thus go out of their way to dignify with the title of 'excellent' a detestable act of Erastianism which deprived them of their own liberty? For the synodical letter speaks of the Bishop of Parma as one who had evaded the earlier rescript; and Parma was outside what Mr. Puller considers the area of the suburbicarian churches, in which alone he thinks the Bishop of Rome had a 'full and commanding metropolitan jurisdiction' (p. 182). This bishop had been properly deposed at Rome by the spiritual power ('dejectus judicio nostro'), and ought therefore (they say) to have come under the ruling of the rescript to which they allude. In other words, their spiritual sentence ought to have had its civil effect. He ought no longer to hold his church, as they say he does, and the Bishop of Pozzuoli, although deposed, had crept back into the city; whereas there again the spiritual sentence ought to have had its civil effect. The imperial official, the prefect, ought to have carried it out. Such instances show that according to that synod all that Gratian's rescript was meant to effect was the civil enforcement of spiritual judgments over an area in which those judgments 'ran' by ecclesiastical custom.

But (ii.), further, Mr. Puller relies on a passage in the

[1] P. 182.
[2] *Ibid.*
[3] 'Præclara ista plane et religiosis principibus digna sententia.'

synodical letter which he misinterprets. He thinks that 'during the pontificate of Damasus the Emperor Gratian conferred on the Pope a very large measure of jurisdiction over the bishops of the whole Western Empire,' and that 'this jurisdiction received from the emperor had no canonical basis,' and this theory he bases on a comparison of the rescript of the emperor with the letter of the Roman synod. The emperor, he says, was asked by the Roman synod 'that contumacious bishops should be compelled by the prefect of the prætorium of Italy, or else by the vicarius of the city of Rome, to come to Rome to be tried. *This mention of the officials who were to coerce the refractory prelates limits the scope of the application of the enactment for which the synod petitioned to Italy and Illyricum.* The emperor in his rescript brings in the prefect of the prætorium of Gaul and the proconsuls of Africa and Spain, and thus *extends the system of appeals which he is establishing to the whole of the Western Empire, to Gaul, Britain, Spain and Africa.*'[1]

Now a careful attention to the words of the Roman synod's letter will show that it is not the case that the mention of the officials limits the scope of the synod's petition to Italy and Illyricum.

The letter is addressed to Gratian and Valentinian alone, as being so entirely concerned with Western affairs.[2] It begins with saying that it redounds to their honour and piety that when the bishops 'almost innumerable from the various (*diffusis*) parts of Italy had gathered together to the sublime sanctuary of the Apostolic See,[3] and were considering what should be asked of the emperors on behalf of the state of the Churches, they could find nothing better to ask than what the imperial care and foresight had [already] spontaneously conferred upon them.'

They then say that the emperors, full of the Divine Spirit

---

[1] P. 156. The italics are mine.

[2] It is a mistake to suppose that the omission of Theodosius' name shows that this letter was written before his accession to the throne. There are several instances in the Theodosian Code in which the name of this or that living emperor is omitted. And here there is a reason for the omission, although it would not have been strange if it had been added.

[3] Mr. Puller omits these words.

and having the patronage of the Apostles [Peter and Paul] in their high estate, decided—for the restoration of the body of the Church, which the fury of Ursinus, in his endeavour to snatch a dignity which was not his due [*i.e.* the chair of Peter] had divided in twain—that, the author of the mischief having been condemned and the rest whom he had associated with himself having been separated from him, 'the Bishop of Rome should have the trial of the rest of the bishops of the Churches, so that the Pontiff of religion should judge concerning religion together with his partners and [thus] no injury would be done to the episcopate, if a bishop were not easily subjected to the decision of a secular judge, as might often happen [before].'

After enlarging on the superiority of the episcopal judgments, they say that they would end here were it not that Ursinus and his followers are evading the imperial sentence and wrongly remaining in their Churches, and conspiring in a rash and profane contempt, so as not to 'acquiesce in the judgment of the Bishop of Rome.' They were managing by bribes and threats of death [to the civil officials] to hold their bishoprics. 'Therefore we ask not for a new imperial decree, but the confirmation of the old.' They then instance the case of the Bishop of Parma, who, although deposed by an episcopal sentence, 'shamelessly holds his Church.' And they mention also Florentius of Pozzuoli, likewise condemned, who 'would have deserved a similar rescript.' They then mention the case of an African bishop who had evaded the rescript, refusing to have his cause tried before bishops ('apud episcopos'). And further, the African Donatists were creating disturbance through one Claudianus, destined for bishop in the city of Rome. In spite of the imperial rescript, he too remains in Rome. They then say that the Jew Isaac went so far (alluding, it would seem, to what took place some years before, as an example) as to 'attack the head of our holy brother Damasus with this deceitful aim, viz. that whilst he is on trial, who had been constituted judge over all, there might be no one to pass judgment on the lapsed, or at any rate on those who had seized on the episcopate.' But Damasus' innocence has been proved, so there is an end of that matter. 'Now, therefore, we ask that your goodness would deign to order that whoever shall have been condemned and shall have determined unjustly to retain his Church, or when summoned by an episcopal judgment shall have decided not to present himself, may be summoned to Rome by the illustrious prefects of the prætorium of your Italy, or by the vicar.'

Thus far, it is true, the petition of the synod seems to limit the contemplated action of the rescript to Italy and Illyricum. But the petition does not end here. For the synod proceeds to say: 'Or if a question of this kind shall have arisen *in the more distant parts*' (clearly such as are not contained within the above limits), 'the trial may be held before the metropolitan for local decision (*per locorum judicia*), or if it is the metropolitan himself, he should be ordered to repair, of necessity, without further process, to Rome, or to judges appointed by the Bishop of Rome. And if the metropolitan or any other bishop shall be suspected, it should be allowed him to appeal either to Rome, or at any rate a council of neighbouring bishops.' It is clear that they are acting on the provisions of the Sardican (or Nicene) canons. Now, who was to deal in a civil capacity with these bishops in 'more distant parts'? They were obviously beyond the reach of the prefect of the Prætorium of Italy or the Vicar of Rome. The synod did not enter into that question, possibly because it was obvious who were the officials that would manage the matter in these distant parts, or still more probably because it was not their business to say. The emperor in his rescript does, naturally, mention the officials who would enforce the episcopal sentence or the transference of *venue* in these more distant parts, and *thus he covers the ground occupied by the petition of the synod*. Otherwise the rescript would have fallen short of the synodical request. They mention the officials who would necessarily superintend the cases which they specify as actually pressing; it was unnecessary or beyond their competency to mention the others, but their request goes beyond the jurisdiction of these officials into 'more distant parts.' It is therefore not the case that Gratian was 'extending the system of appeals,' as Mr. Puller puts it; he was merely facilitating the mode of procedure which had already commended itself to the Church. 'The more distant parts' are but covered by his rescript, as they had pleaded in their letter.

Nor is it correct to say or suggest that there is nothing in the correspondence to show that the bishops were resting their case on higher and strictly Papal grounds. The opening of the synod's letter, which speaks of the bishops having gathered together from various parts of Italy [1] 'to the sublime sanctuary of the Apostolic See,' is suggestive; and they speak of Damasus, compared with other bishops, as being 'equal in *office*,[2] but he excels in the prerogative of the Apostolic See.'

And if we go outside the actual letter, as we have a right to do in search of the context, we know that St. Ambrose, probably the virtual author of the rescript,[3] considered that Damasus sat in the chair of Peter,[4] and he held Peter to be the rock in Matt. xvi.,[5] and taught that from the Church of Rome 'the rights of venerable communion flow to all.' [6]

Mr. Puller says, 'It sometimes seems to me that ecclesiastical historians have hardly done justice to the immense importance of this act of imperial legislation.' But two or three words slipped into an imperial rescript were at the best a slender basis whereon to rest so enormous a superstructure as the patriarchal jurisdiction of Rome over the West. And at least it should be absolutely certain that even this basis is sound; whereas it seems quite certain that it is itself without foundation, for the words in Gratian's rescript, appealed to by Mr. Puller, cover no more ground than did the actual petition of the Roman synod.

---

[1] 'Ex diffusis Italiæ partibus.' Mr. Puller (p. 156, note 1) has no right to limit this to the suburbicarian churches. I do not know why he puts asterisks in place of the words 'sublime sanctuary of the Apostolic See.'

[2] *I.e.* what we should call order, as distinguished from jurisdiction, his 'prerogative' embracing the latter.

[3] It was written during the period when the emperor spent the winter with St. Ambrose at Milan.

[4] 'Peter the Apostle, who was Bishop of the Roman Church' (*De Sacram.* lib. i. § 5).

[5] Cf. his hymn *Ipsa Petra canente.*   [6] Mansi, t. iii. p. 622.

CHAPTER XVI.

THE COUNCIL OF CONSTANTINOPLE (A.D. 381).

§ I.—*Theodosius and the Imperial City.*

I. In January 379 Gratian decided upon a step which both reflected the greatest credit upon himself and was fraught with far-reaching consequences to the fortunes of the Church. After the death of his father by Gratian's order, Theodosius the son had retired into private life. Gratian drew him forth by the magnanimous offer of half his empire, which, as De Broglie says,[1] Theodosius first refused with modesty and then accepted with simplicity. History presents few more touching pictures than that of these two young men, of rare virtue, the one forgiven, and the other forgiving, entering upon the government of the empire with devout attachment to the Christian faith. For during his winter's stay at Thessalonica Theodosius, who was by parentage, so to speak, an orthodox Christian,[2] but not yet actually enrolled in the Christian army, fell ill of fever, and in fear of death called upon St. Ascholius, Bishop of Thessalonica, to baptise him, having previously ascertained that the bishop had never given in to the Arian heresy. He arose from his sick bed to exercise the virtue of divine faith which he had received through the waters of regeneration. As he surveyed his imperial charge a huge scene of religious conflict presented itself to his sight For nearly half a century Constantinople had been under the influence of heretical bishops, and the scene of the most dis-

---

[1] Cf. the whole account in Broglie, *L'Eglise et l'Empire Romain au IVme Siècle*, 3me partie, p. 357 *seq.* 1866.
[2] ' ἄνωθεν μὲν ἐκ προγόνων Χριστιανὸς ὑπάρχων, καὶ τῇ τοῦ ὁμοουσίου πίστει προσκείμενος (Soc. v. 6).

graceful turmoils. Each heresy, as it emerged, found its home there, and the Catholic faith had wellnigh disappeared when Gregory left Nazianzus to do his best to revive it in this New Rome, as they delighted to call it.

II. Theodosius determined at once to strike a blow for the true faith. But how was he to define that faith? The Nicene Creed was the very subject of contention, and each formula that was promulgated by way of explanation had been twisted into a new heresy. He decided to begin by insisting on the observance of the rule of faith itself. He would not—as a devout layman he could not—issue any dogmatic definition, but he could insist on the norm of religious truth being observed, such a rule as no Christian could dispute, and as no Christian did dispute *quâ* the rule. In regard to the heresy that was creating fresh confusion at Constantinople, Damasus and the Roman synod had issued a clear decision, and it was accepted at Alexandria by the successor of St. Athanasius. What could be better calculated to reduce to unity the scattered forces of religion than to recall the Easterns to the true centre of teaching? He therefore ordered that the *religion delivered to the Church of Rome by the Apostle Peter*, as expounded by the Pontiff Damasus and by the present Bishop of Alexandria, should be preached by all Catholics. 'We will that all people who are governed by our clemency should practise the same religion as the divine Apostle Peter delivered to the Romans, as the religion proclaimed by him up to this time declares it; and which it is clear the Pontiff Damasus follows, and Peter, the Bishop of Alexandria, a man of apostolic sanctity—that is, &c. Those who follow this law we order to take the name of Catholic Christians.'[1]

Now, nowhere do we discover a single note of surprise at the East being thus called upon to practise ' the religion of the Romans.' In fact the evidence afforded by the incidental notice of the Apostle Peter is of the most irrefragable nature, to the effect that the Christian world, East and West, had

---

[1] 'Cunctos populos quos clementiæ nostræ regit temperamentum in tali volumus religione versari quam divinum Petrum Apostolum tradidisse religio usque nunc ab ipso insinuata declarat.'

learnt to look to the *See of Peter* as the central authority on matters of faith. The religion practised by the Vicar of Jesus Christ, and now held by the chosen successor of St. Athanasius, such was the form of faith delivered from the throne of the imperial neophyte to the Eastern world. It is clear that Theodosius draws a distinction between Damasus and Peter of Alexandria of a vital character. Damasus is the pontiff, Peter the bishop; Damasus is mentioned simply as the pontiff, Peter as a man of apostolic sanctity, as though some reason needed to be given for tacking on his name to that of the pontiff. His adherence to the religion delivered to the Romans by the Apostle Peter was worth mentioning; it suggested what Theodosius required of his own East, viz. a similar adherence. Rome, then, is indicated as the centre; Rome in its connection with the Apostle Peter, and Rome as the seat of the Pontiff of the Christian religion.[1]

Did Constantinople resent such a description of the Christian religion? Was it an idiosyncrasy of the young emperor's?

It is clear that it was, at any rate, the teaching of St. Ascholius of Thessalonica, whose religious pupil the emperor had become, and Constantinople was unable to say that the faith of Old Rome was not the norm for the faith of New Rome. She received her new emperor with open arms, so St. Gregory tells us.[2] There were soon to be plenty in that city prepared to disagree in fact with Rome, and some, as we shall see, in theory; but not the saints or the theologians of the East. Prosper of Aquitaine expressed the conviction of the day as he sang:

> Sedes Roma Petri quæ pastoralis honoris
> Facta caput mundo.[3]

III. The state of things in Constantinople, whither the new emperor now prepared to go, was as follows. St. Gregory, whom the Church specially dignified with the name of 'the

---

[1] Of course the word 'pontiff' could be used of any bishop, but it is here the distinction of terms that is to be noted occurring in a legal document.

[2] 'Cupidus accessit ad sibi cupidissimos' (*Carmen de Vitâ suâ*, 1305).

[3] *l.c.* 'Rome the See of Peter, which has been made to the whole world the head of the pastoral office.'

theologian,' had stirred the city by his eloquent preaching of the true faith, seconded by his great holiness. You might see St. Jerome sitting an eager listener at his expositions of the faith, whilst St. Gregory made use of his unrivalled knowledge of the text of Holy Scripture. But also you might see a figure wrapped in the mantle of the philosopher, and leaving the oratory with the classical staff and his hair in philosophical disorder, full, to all appearance, of enthusiasm for the eloquent bishop as he refuted the Arian, the Eunomian, or the Macedonian. Warned against this man, whose name was Maximus, Gregory nevertheless took him into his confidence, and even alluded to him in the way of defence in one of his public orations. But presently Maximus threw off the mask, and after having intrigued with the enemies of Gregory, induced some Egyptian bishops with (unhappily) the consent of Peter of Alexandria, to consecrate him to the see of Constantinople. Gregory had thus rendered himself ridiculous in his support of Maximus, and in the bitterness of his disappointment retired. On his reappearance to bid a final farewell, the people of Constantinople, enraged at the appointment of Maximus, suddenly settled that the only remedy was to make Gregory himself their bishop. The scene that ensued seems to have baffled description—Gregory resisting, men throwing themselves on his person and forcing him into the episcopal chair, and women crying out, 'If you leave us, you take away with you the Holy Trinity'[1]—*i.e.* the true faith. Gregory consented on condition that his election obtained conciliar sanction, and at once retired a little way into the country. Maximus repaired to Thessalonica to gain the ear of the emperor,[2] from whom he met with an unfavourable reception, and forthwith he turned to Alexandria, where he was also coldly received by Peter.

IV. Such was the state of things when Theodosius approached Constantinople. He seems already to have formed the idea of an Eastern council, and to have consulted St. Damasus in regard to it, through Ascholius, who appears, from an incidental expression in Damasus' reply, to have

---

[1] συνεκβαλεῖς γὰρ, εἶπε, σαυτῷ Τριάδα (*Carmen de Vitâ suâ*, 1100).
[2] Cf. Broglie, *loc. cit.* p. 404.

been for some time past in the position of Papal vicar at Thessalonica.¹ The Pope replied to Ascholius in favour of a council, and condemned the election of Maximus. The letter reads like a private one, so much so that it has been doubted whether it is genuine ; but the verdict of scholars is in favour of its genuineness, and that being so, it seems perfectly clear that the council had the approval of the Pope. It was, however, so far merely an Eastern assembly—in no sense an œcumenical gathering.

Theodosius approved of the nomination of Gregory, and the settlement of the whole matter of the bishopric was handed over to the council ; but meanwhile the emperor went a step further in the direction of maintaining the true faith. In January, 381, appeared a short edict forbidding all heretics to assemble for divine worship. He also went a step further in defining a heretic. He had bidden all Catholics to follow the religion taught by the Pontiff Damasus, and, as a matter of fact, by Peter of Alexandria, and had spoken of the consubstantiality of the Holy Trinity as part of that faith; he now specified the teaching which obtained at Rome concerning the consubstantiality of the Holy Spirit.² Theodoret, in describing the effect of this decree, says that the churches were now to be given to those who held 'the faith of Damasus.³

Thus the consubstantiality of the Holy Spirit with the Father and the Son was at once a matter of faith, and now also a matter of civil obligation for Catholics, before the council met. The French bishops, in their letter to Innocent X. in the seventeenth century, admitted that the anathemas of Damasus were irrevocable before the Council of Constantinople ; and the law of January 381 shows that Theodosius did not conceive of these bishops meeting to discuss an open question.

---

¹ 'Hoc est quod *sæpe* dilectionem vestram commonui, ne fieret aliquid inconsiderate' (*Ep.* v.). For the opposite view maintained by Mr. Puller, relying on the words of Innocent I. to Anysius and Rufus, cf. *Prim. SS.* p. 162. The Pope's words only show when the emperor gave civil sanction to the arrangement, not when Damasus made it.

² Cf. Theod. *De Religione Decreta*, lib. xvi. tit. v. 6 ; Migne, *Patr. Lat.* vol. xlii.

³ *Hist. Eccles.* v. 3.

And St. Gregory treated the question as closed in his preaching to the people, to the chagrin of some, friends of Macedonius, but with the consciousness that they were standing alone in the Catholic Church.

§ II.—*The Council.*

I. Meletius was already on the scene to institute St. Gregory into the bishopric.[1] We may picture to ourselves the meeting of St. Jerome and St. Meletius, the uniform magnanimity of the latter and the enthusiasm of the former for his newly acquired master, St. Gregory, binding the two together. There were many saints at this Eastern council, which began so well and ended so unhappily. St. Basil's brother, St. Gregory of Nyssa, joined the little throng gathered round the eloquent and mortified bishop of the same name, the choice friend of St. Basil, who had passed from his labours on earth to his work of intercession in heaven. Meletius was the hero of the hour; he had already synodically expressed his agreement with the 'Tome of the Westerns;'[2] his people were in the enjoyment of intercommunion with the disciples of Paulinus;[3] he had arranged with the latter that whoever survived the other should be the sole Bishop of Antioch.[4] There were, for the present, two Bishops of Antioch, but that had been recognised by 'the West,'[5] and consequently he came as the symbol of what the young emperor hoped, and the saintlier souls in the East sighed after—continued peace with the West[6] and the inauguration of peace amongst themselves in the East.

The first business of the council was concerned with the bishopric of Constantinople itself. Maximus had been condemned by Damasus in a private letter to Ascholius meant for the emperor's ear. He condemned his appointment to Constantinople on the grounds that it was done by externs, the ceremony performed at an unusual hour, without consul-

---

[1] Socr. *H. E.* v. 8.
[2] Antiochene Synod, 379.
[3] Theodoret. *H. E.* v. 3.
[4] Greg. Naz. *Carm. de Vitâ suâ.*
[5] *Ep. Concil. Aquil.* 5. Cf. Dam. *Ep.* v.
[6] Letter of the Italian bishops to the Easterns (381), 'dudum.' Mansi, t. iii. 623.

tation of the clergy and people, and that the very appearance of Maximus was, according to accounts, that of a philosopher rather than of a Christian.[1] At the same time there were some difficulties about the election of St. Gregory, which probably account for the matter being reopened later on, and for the election of Maximus finding favour for a while, in spite of his character, with the law-abiding West [2] before they had full information on the subject.

The council was presided over, in the natural course of events, by St. Meletius. There were no Papal legates, for the council had not been convoked as an œcumenical assembly. Alexandria was not yet represented; it was in mourning round the death-bed of its patriarch, the saintly Peter. The Bishop of Antioch was, therefore, the natural president, according to ecclesiastical custom, Antioch being the third of the greater sees of Christendom, the third see of Peter. The ordination of Maximus was investigated and repudiated, and so far the East was placing itself in harmony with the West—so far as the judgment of the latter was known. St. Damasus had urged St. Ascholius to use his influence with Theodosius previous to his leaving Thessalonica for the appointment of some bishop against whose election there could be no objection from a canonical point of view.[3] Whether this could be said as to St. Gregory's election opinions may differ. He had been consecrated by St. Basil Bishop of Sasima, and had acted as Bishop of Nazianzus out of affection to his father's memory. However this might be thought to affect the canonicity of his election (translation from see to see being the great flaw in Eastern elections and the source of some of its greatest troubles), his election was confirmed, and it seems as though his first act was to intercede for the Egyptian consecrators of Maximus. They were spared the usual censure.

II. Difficult as it is to settle the order of transactions in

[1] Damasi, *Ep.* v.
[2] If this be the true account of the matter there would be nothing unnatural in a council in the West treating of the subject, on which Damasus would not naturally consider the opinion given by him in his letter to Ascholius as irreformable.
[3] Dam. *Ep.* v.

this council, of which we do not possess the Acts, it seems almost certain that they must have at once proceeded to consider the dogmatic question,[1] and were probably interrupted in their work of proposed pacification by an event which altered the whole course of events for some years to come. Meletius died—not, as Canon Bright expresses it, 'a saint outside the communion of Rome,'[2] but a saint of chequered career, who, originally recognised amongst the bishops of the East by the Pope Liberius, of mild rather than uncompromising nature, yet a magnificent confessor of the faith as against the Arian Euzoius, having thrice suffered exile, was for a while distrusted at Rome, but after publicly signing the 'Tome of the Westerns,' was welcomed by Rome as Bishop of Antioch in her archives. Some while ago he had made the advances to Paulinus which led to a formal compact as to their successor, and he had now endeared all hearts to himself at Constantinople. He ended his life with inducting into the see of Constantinople her first orthodox bishop for more than forty years. He had perhaps also agreed to the principle embodied in the so-called fifth canon of the council, that all at Antioch should be acknowledged as orthodox who, whether they spoke of one or three Hypostaseis, acknowledged the oneness of the Godhead of the Father, the Son, and the Holy Ghost.[3]

III. The death of Meletius was an event which not only plunged the city of Constantinople into a profound gloom, and was felt throughout the East, but it introduced a complication into the subject of the Antiochene disputes. After a funeral, in which the procession of bishops and clergy and others, with their lighted tapers in hand, is described as illuminating the city, and after the body of the saint had left to enter, on its way to Antioch, cities into which, in accordance with the sentiment of the time, no corpse had been allowed to be borne,

---

[1] De Broglie seems to think that the dogmatic question was not dealt with at all till later on, which is, of course, possible. But I hope to show that it is more probable that the course of events was as I have described it.

[2] *Hist. of the Church*, p. 172.

[3] Cf. Canon v. This was a reversal of the judgment of St. Basil on the subject. The actual canon was probably drawn up at a later council in 382.

the bishops met to consider the question of St. Meletius' successor. It was a question which ought never to have been submitted at all.¹ Its proposal can only be accounted for by the state of the Eastern episcopate at that moment. The Emperor Valens had scattered bishops over the East to support the cause of Arianism, who were quite unfit for the sacred office, and many of these had 'conformed' upon the edict of Theodosius, without a religious conviction of any kind.² Their main sentiment was a deep-seated hatred of the West, which had supported the orthodox faith. They were violently Eastern, because they were but faintly orthodox. These men, St. Gregory tells us, had come all sunburnt from the plough, or from the smith's anvil, or the office of the petty scribe, or the baker's shop, or from handling the oar, or from the rank and file of the army.

A great deal is sometimes said about the authority of the Second Council and the galaxy of saints that are supposed to have promulgated the third canon, and to have proposed a successor to St. Meletius. St. Leo, with his provoking accuracy, describes the men who did this part of the business as 'certain bishops.' St. Gregory considered them the offscouring of the episcopal body, and the very dregs of the Christian community. He distinctly states, as Tillemont points out, referring to St. Gregory's account of the council, that there were men loaded with gold who set to work to corrupt the bishops.³ As long as Meletius lived, the question of the compact which he had made did not press, and they would probably have considered it too dishonourable to provide for the perpetuation of the state of strife which St. Meletius plumed himself on having brought to a peaceful issue with the consent of the West. But now came the difficulty; that some of these bishops would have to be under Paulinus, whilst with others there was the still greater difficulty that they would be giving in to the West. Behind Paulinus they saw the Pope, and the Pope was to these abandoned men the symbol

¹ Tillemont says of this that 'some enemies of peace proposed in the council a thing of which they ought never to have dreamt' (*St. Greg. de Naz.* art. lxxi. p. 475).

Cf. Tillemont, *St. Greg. de Naz.* art. lviii. p. 441. Paris, 1703.

² *Loc. cit.*

of the *Homoousion*. They could not deny the truth of the latter nor the rights of the former. They never in the whole strife objected that Lucifer had offended against the canonical rights of the East in consecrating a Bishop of Antioch. Neither St. Basil, nor St. Gregory, nor even these quarrelsome men, seem ever to have suggested that obvious flaw, as it must have been considered, *unless* the Papal regime was, in principle, acknowledged throughout the East. St. Basil distinctly refused, *totidem verbis*, to decide against the validity of the consecration. St. Gregory assumed its validity throughout. A fact such as this is of vital import in determining the general current of Eastern thought as to the canonical relationship of the West to the East. But these half-Christian bishops (as St. Gregory calls them), at Constantinople, whilst they could not plead a lack of canonical validity in Paulinus' consecration, did demur to the shadow of Western patronage which lay on the rights of Paulinus. They had learnt to cherish a certain unchristian bitterness against the West, whilst others were influenced (to a less extent) in the same direction because the West had refused them the particular mode of support which under the leadership of St. Basil they had claimed in their struggle against Valens. Tillemont attributes their malignant spirit to this, and also to the spirit of 'pride, pique, and jealousy.'[1]

St. Gregory indignantly repudiated the dishonourable course on which they were embarking. He rose above their 'low reasons,' as Tillemont calls them—' reasons,' he adds, ' unworthy of a bishop. He sought only the will of God, the honour of the Church, and the good of souls.'[2] He deprecated their miserable attempt to turn the question of religion into a question of astronomy. He urged them, instead of advancing the miserable plea that things should go from the East, where Christ was born, to the West, and not *vice versâ*, to think more of our Lord as the first-fruits of the whole human race, and to allow themselves ' to be a little conquered.'[3]

'This,' as Canon Bright remarks, ' was clearly the right course.'[4] St. Gregory said that it was pardonable in them

---

[1] *Loc. cit.* p. 476.
[2] *Ibid.*
[3] *Carm. de Vitâ suâ*, 1690 and 1653.
[4] *Hist. of the Church*, p. 173.

'in some measure to vex'[1] the West during Meletius' lifetime, and when they were uncertain how he would be received (as was the case before the peace was made), being annoyed— defenders, as they say, of the laws[2]—but now he considered it wanton and inexcusable. Paulinus (he urged) could not live long, and so he entreated this 'mob of youngsters,'[3] to rise above this false patriotism and act for the peace of the Church. He told them plainly that he might resign 'his throne, but not his opinion.'

But 'party feelings proved too strong for this good counsel.'[4]

Flavian, who, it is to be feared, had promised not to accept the bishopric, was elected. He had been St. Meletius' right-hand man, and even if he had not definitely agreed to the compact, it was a sad sight to see one who had been so intimate with Meletius entering upon his new charge by a violation of that saint's most cherished hope. It was a sure renewal of the breach with the West which St. Meletius had so carefully closed, and it was a deliberate prolongation of strife at the very heart of the East.

IV. St. Gregory's disappointment may be imagined rather than described. His high soul, eager for the peace of the Church, revolted from the rude and contemptuous attitude of the uneducated and undisciplined band of young bishops who secured a sufficient majority to carry the dishonourable proposal. He no longer attended the sessions regularly, and since they were held in the episcopal palace, he soon removed

---

[1] *Carm. de Vitâ suâ*, 1614.

[2] Mr. Puller's translation (*Prim. SS.* p. 251), 'these self-styled defenders of the canons,' is not a correct rendering of the original. There is no irony in his words.

[3] *Carm. de Vitâ suâ*, 1636.

[4] *Canons of the First Four Councils*, by Canon Bright, 1892, p. 110. Mr. Puller's account of this deplorable incident is distressingly apologetic and, it must be added, inaccurate. He calls it the action of the Œcumenical Council, and he says: 'It is, I *think, allowable* to express regret that the bishops at Constantinople did not ratify the compact in the interests of peace. What they actually did was canonically legitimate, but *it may be doubted* whether it was wise or charitable' (p. 248). St. Gregory thought it morally wrong. De Broglie thinks that the influence of this saint had waned since the Maximus affair. This is possible; but the reasons St. Gregory gives are sufficient. Tillemont's piety here fortunately gets the better of his Gallicanism.

to another dwelling. The council was thus without a regular head, and the friends of St. Gregory were withdrawing from participation; it was, in fact, nothing in itself but a small Eastern synod.

What was the young emperor doing all this while? In the spirit of a Christian ruler he held himself aloof from the strife, but he sent for his spiritual father, St. Ascholius, from Thessalonica, who, as belonging to the Western Patriarchate, had not attended the council.[1]

At the same time a new element of disturbance entered upon the scene. The Egyptians arrived with their new metropolitan (or patriarch) Timothy. Tillemont remarks that they had been delayed[2] by the necessity of arranging matters on the accession of Timothy.

The Egyptians felt themselves compromised by the affair of Maximus, and that they had been pardoned rather than justified—a humiliation which they owed to Gregory.[3] To add to the complication, the bishops who came at Theodosius' wish from Illyricum brought with them what St. Gregory calls a sharp 'Western breeze.'[4] They must have felt a somewhat disdainful compassion for the intricate quarrels of the East, compared with their own steady simplicity of faith. They were specially scandalised at the constant translation from see to see in the East, and neither they nor Timothy of Alexandria approved of Gregory's elevation to the see of Constantinople. They looked upon the argument that he had never gone to his original see, and had only administered his father's see provisionally, as insufficient; and the whole council became a fresh scene of confusion. Gregory forthwith announced his resignation, which was received with a respectful silence. The fact was that he had proved too uncompromising in his preaching to please those who originally hailed his promotion, and too mortified in his life for the fashionable capital of the East; consequently there was no

---

[1] This is the simplest solution of the difficulties raised in one direction by Papebroch, May 9, *Acta Sanctorum*, and in another by Tillemont, *St. Greg. de Naz.*, note 43, p. 717.

[2] *Loc. cit.* St. Gregory says: ἐξαπίνης κεκλημένοι, but probably means that they came suddenly, having been originally invited.

[3] De Broglie, *loc. cit.* p. 435. [4] *Carm. de Vitâ suâ*, 1802.

section sufficiently enthusiastic in his favour to counterbalance the displeasure of Alexandria and the Egyptians. The Egyptians were in accord with St. Gregory in deprecating the selection of Flavian for Antioch, but this was not sufficient to counteract their dislike to his intrusion into the see of Constantinople in place of Maximus, for whom they had no respect from a moral point of view, but whose election they considered canonically valid.

St. Gregory, therefore, resigned in the interests of peace, and delivered a farewell address, which for theological exactness combined with pathetic eloquence has hardly its equal in Christian literature. He was a man not born to rule such elements of discord as then met in the Byzantine capital; but for holiness, and orthodoxy, and polished eloquence he had hardly a peer in that century. He made his will in the presence of several bishops, leaving what he had to the poor of Nazianzus, whither he now retraced his steps. On his way he passed by Cæsarea, the scene of his beloved Basil's labours, and after delivering a panegyric there on his brother saint, retired to his father's city of Nazianzus.[1]

V. The council had now lost its two greatest saints— Meletius and Gregory, and with St. Gregory several of his friends appear to have more or less withdrawn themselves. We may safely reckon amongst these St. Gregory of Nyssa and Helladius, and the little throng that had gathered round their master, the 'Theologian,' as he was called.

It was necessary to elect another bishop. Amongst the names presented to the emperor was that of a civil dignitary, whose life had been somewhat free, though irreproachable of late, and who in consequence had delayed his baptism. We may guess, though we cannot say for certain, under what influences his name was entered on the list proposed by the bishops. The emperor selected him, and he received all the sacraments at once. His appointment was a scandal and

---

[1] Rufinus says that men had never seen a holier and more blameless life, more brilliant eloquence, a purer and more orthodox faith, more perfect and consummate knowledge. Tillemont has a beautiful description of his preaching. He used to say to the Third Person, 'Thou art my God, and I shall not cease repeating--yes, Thou art my God.'

promised ill for the Church. Constantinople and Antioch were thus, both of them, filled with bishops on whose election a cloud rested. But both of these bishops happily belied their bad beginnings. Flavian, indeed, ended as a saint, and Nectarius set to work to do his duty in good earnest. It must have been now that the council addressed itself to the work of bringing the Macedonian heretics to the acceptance of the full faith concerning the consubstantiality of the Eternal Trinity; but it had lost its one guiding spirit in theology in the retirement of St. Gregory, and its main power of peace-making through the death of Meletius. The Macedonians could not have been impressed with what they had seen of the bishops so far, and they simply refused to accept the teaching that was proposed to them. The imperial influence was brought to bear upon them, but in vain. The emperor pressed upon them the submission they had made to Pope Liberius, but they simply left the council, leaving a letter of warning to their followers as to anything that might be done in favour of the Nicene Creed. They had found that the Nicene Creed involved not merely the *Homoousion* of the Son, but of the Holy Spirit, and one can well imagine that the bishops of the synod had lost their moral influence after the incidents that had marred their sessions hitherto.

VI. But this council has nevertheless taken a high place in the consciousness of Christendom, having attained to the rank of one of those Four Œcumenical Councils which St. Gregory spoke of as next to the Four Holy Gospels. How was this? It was for one act, which brought the East into harmony with the West, and which was confirmed by the Popes. The departure of the Macedonians may have had the effect of hastening[1] the agreement of the bishops in a formula which had already been in use for years, and which expressed the synodical teaching of St. Damasus on the subject of the Third Person of the Holy Trinity. We do not know how or when, after what discussion, if any, the said formula was adopted; we only know that it was not new, and that it *was* adopted. It had already been called by St. Epiphanius the Creed of the

---

[1] So De Broglie.

Church, and the faithful had been required to learn it, almost as it now stood, by heart. If formally adopted after St. Gregory and his friends had withdrawn, we may fairly assume that there had been some discussion before the death of St. Meletius, and that St. Gregory and others had left their proxies or their signatures for the said doctrinal decree. And the list of signatures, as we have it, suggests this. It is clear that the signatures are not those of the bishops given at any one session, they must have been placed together more or less at random; but it is reasonable to suppose that the signatures were each of them attached to some document, though not all to the same. The signature of Timothy of Alexandria, or again of St. Meletius, were neither of them, as the said list would imply, attached to the third canon; for Alexandria never accepted it, and St. Meletius died before it was drawn up. But it is reasonable to suppose that St. Meletius might be claimed as having accepted the form in which the Nicene Creed had been frequently recited by way of explication (with the approval of individual bishops in their several dioceses) before the council met, and that Timothy signed at the council itself. Consequently, the scribe finding both signatures, entered them as though they were attached at the same session and to the whole of the council's doings.

Although we have no Acts, no record of the discussions, nor even of the order or number of the sessions, we have nevertheless the clear testimony of history to these three points—viz. that the enlarged form of the Nicene Creed, such as was already in use in some parts of the East, and was in harmony with the teaching of St. Damasus' *ex cathedrâ* pronunciation in the Roman synod, was agreed to by a sufficient number of bishops to make it the act of the council; next, that the ordination of Flavian to Antioch did not meet with the approval of the council as a whole; and, lastly, that the third canon was, if it was mooted in this council at all, not the judgment of the 150 Fathers, but of a portion only. These are the broad facts for which there is historical evidence; beyond this we seem to be in the region of mere conjecture. When Mr. Puller speaks of 'so many

s

great saints'[1] having approved of Flavian's ordination, he is met with St. Gregory's statement that it was only a 'crowd of youths,' and those of a very unsaintly character, who succeeded in drawing after them some of the 'older stars.' When certain writers speak of the third canon as though it possessed the authority of the Church, they need to be confronted with St. Leo's determined accuracy in calling it only the decree of 'certain' bishops; but when the Council of Chalcedon, eighty years afterwards, admitted the Council of Constantinople into a rank which was denied to it by the Council of Ephesus, it recognised a patent of orthodoxy as having been conferred upon its one unanimous act—viz. the enlargement of the Nicene Creed—a development by way of explication, embracing the truth which Rome had already pronounced to be of faith, and which the Emperor Theodosius had already decided to enforce on those who wished to be called Catholic Christians. The synod thus rose at length from a mere Eastern assembly of great saints, mixed up with a crowd of unedifying bishops, summoned to bring the East into line with the West on the subject of the Third Person of the Eternal Trinity, to the rank of one of those four œcumenical councils which exhibited the faith of the Church on the co-equality of the Son and the Holy Spirit with the Eternal Father, and the Divine Personality and perfect human nature of the one Mediator between God and man.

§ III.—*New Rome, or the Third Canon.*

Before proceeding further, it will be well to consider briefly the so-called canons of this Second General Council. One of them plays such a conspicuous part in the controversy between our Anglican friends and ourselves that it calls for special attention.[2] It has been contended by the former for the last three centuries, that the Council of Chalcedon set its seal to the principle that the primacy of the See of Rome (whatever that primacy may involve, whether actual jurisdiction or merely a position of honour) was due to the secular position

---

[1] *Prim. SS.* p. 148, note 1.

[2] 'That the Bishop of Constantinople should have the prerogatives of honour after the Bishop of Rome, *because it is New Rome.*' Canon III.

of the imperial capital. This will be considered at length when we come to that council. But the action of that council, whatever it be considered to involve, was based on this third canon of the Council of Constantinople. Hence the necessity of considering this canon with care.

Its history is involved in great obscurity. When was it passed? Not, we may safely assert, after Timothy of Alexandria had arrived at the council, unless it were after his departure; neither could it have been passed whilst St. Gregory was president. No one who has read ever so little of his writings at this time will suppose that he would have given his consent to a measure so certain to frustrate his cherished hopes of peace, and prompted by the spirit of overreaching which he so emphatically denounced. One hardly sees, therefore, how it could have been passed at all. Canons were always drawn up at the close of a synod; but this could not have been the case here, by reason of the presence of the Bishop of Alexandria and the Egyptians, who never accepted the regulation contained in this third canon. Neither is there room for it in the previous sessions, considering, not merely St. Gregory's presence, adverse to such a proposal, but his account of the synod, which makes no allusion to it.

Was it, then, a canon of the council in the strict sense of that term?

In considering this question, we must bear in mind that it was never sent to the West, and that, consequently, whenever passed, it was considered not to be a canon which concerned any but the Easterns themselves. It was not, it would seem, sent even to Alexandria, possibly on the ground that it was not considered to affect the question of jurisdiction. On the next vacancy in the See of Constantinople, Alexandria acted as its superior, and placed St. Chrysostom in the vacant see.

It may be said, however, that this was done in defiance of the canon, just as at the next General Council (as it was intended to be) Alexandria occupied the seat of president, above Constantinople, at the order of the emperor himself. But had it been a canon in the ordinary sense of the term, it could hardly have been so completely passed over in both cases.

But, further, on the first occasion on which it was publicly quoted at a General Synod, the Western bishops present denied that it was amongst the canons of the Church at all.

And the evidence is strong to the effect that it was not contained as a canon even in the oldest Greek versions of the canons of the Church. In the Latin version of the canons called the Prisca, which drew its list from very ancient Greek manuscripts, it is placed after the Council of Chalcedon, as though it had made its first appearance, as an œcumenical rule of action, on the occasion of that council, and there is fair ground for supposing that it was missing in the earliest version of the Isidorian collection of canons. Now these two versions, the Prisca and the Isidorian, supply us with our earliest information as to the most ancient Greek manuscripts.

Much doubt, therefore, hangs over this supposed canon on these grounds.

Add to this the fact that the first canon is generally admitted to be not so much a canon as a part of the Tome which was drawn up by the council, and that the fifth and sixth canons are now admitted by all scholars to belong to a second council held in the following year; whilst the seventh is not a canon at all. On all these grounds we have reason for hesitating to call this, which comes in their midst, a canon even of the Eastern Church.

And yet the subject must have been mooted and settled by some authority. Now, Socrates puts the regulation contained in this canon before the confirmation of the Nicene Creed. His account cannot be depended on as giving the order of time; but his placing this decree, as he calls it, by itself, before the time came, according to him, for the canons about bishops keeping to their provinces and looking to provincial synods for the transaction of provincial concerns, seems to suggest that it stood on a different footing from these. It is certainly remarkable that the council of the following year, in giving a detailed description of what was done at the council of 381, mentions the subject-matter of the so-called first canon and of the second, as well as the ordination of Nectarius and Flavian, but makes no allusion to this third canon. Of course, this might be due to a conviction on their part that Rome would never accept the new arrangement. But if it really was one of the first three canons properly enacted, and they mention the subject-matter of the first two, but keep silence as to this, we have to suppose them guilty of a dishonourable reticence.

We are therefore driven to the conclusion that the decree of which Socrates speaks, and to which they allude in their letter to Theodosius, stood on a different footing to the second and fourth canons. It was an arrangement on which they agreed amongst themselves after Timothy had left, and which would therefore concern *any future* ecclesiastical intercourse between Alexandria and Constantinople. It had nothing to do with jurisdiction, but related to the mere question of honorary precedence ($\pi\rho\epsilon\sigma\beta\epsilon\hat{\iota}a\ \tau\hat{\eta}s\ \tau\iota\mu\hat{\eta}s$). It did not concern Rome, as it would have done had it related to jurisdiction; for in that case they knew well Rome would be obliged to have her say. It was, after a time, slipped in amongst the canons.

Theodosius, in his law of July in that same year, adopted the new order of precedence in naming the prelates who in each region were considered orthodox. But this might be due to the petition of the bishops concerning their new decree, not to its figuring amongst canons of the council; though, indeed, it would be unsafe to argue much from the order in the law of July 30, because the persons named therein are so named, not because of the dignity of their sees, but their personal merit.

It is, however, certain that Theodosius approved of the move, and one cannot but see the hand of the *quondam* civil functionary,[1] now bishop of the Byzantine capital, in the whole matter, and consequently Socrates may be so far right in placing this decree immediately after the ordination of Nectarius, that it was due to his particular influence. Theodosius naturally sanctioned, if he did not also promote the arrangement, for although a good Christian, he was an emperor. His successor set it at nought when precedence would have involved jurisdiction, as at Ephesus.

[1] Nectarius.

The reason given in the canon for thus exalting Constantinople over Alexandria contains a curious mixture of fact and fiction. 'Because it is New Rome' was the ground assigned. Now it was true that the precedence of Old Rome over the West, viewing the West as its patriarchate, was in one sense due to her being the capital of the empire; but it was an arrangement which was made by Rome herself in virtue of her higher relationship to the Church. She chose to rule a portion of her world-wide spiritual dominion in the character of Patriarch as well as Pope [1]—that portion which came at this time under the civil rule of the West, of which Rome was the capital, though not now the imperial residence. It is therefore true, as Canon Bright has said, that 'the representation' contained in the canon was 'unfaithful to the facts,'[2] *i.e.* untrue, for 'it is certain' (as the same writer has elsewhere said) 'that the Bishop of Rome enjoyed this pre-eminence not simply because his city was Rome, but also because he held the chair of Peter.'[3] At the same time, whilst wrong in supposing that patriarchal honours could be assigned to a capital because it was a capital by themselves and the emperor, they were right in implying that the patriarchate of the West came about (in one sense) through Rome being the capital; only it was through the choice of the blessed Apostle Peter and his successors selecting the Papal for a Patriarchal centre. We have no reason to suppose that this was meant to be denied.[4] Their mistake may have consisted in imagining that such a matter as even

---

[1] 'In the decrees of the bishops of Rome the distinction between their supreme and patriarchal jurisdiction is not always fully observed; the latter is often supported and exalted by the former; the one influences the other, and not unfrequently both flow on together: that is, the bishops of Rome perform many things both as Popes and Patriarchs. The Popes themselves do not always draw the precise line of distinction; they possessed, indeed, both powers as successors of St. Peter, and often appeal even in acts which were connected immediately with their patriarchal authority to their supreme pontifical power' (Döllinger, *Hist. of the Church*, Period II. cap. v. § 4).

[2] *Canons of the First Four General Councils*, by W. Bright, D.D., Canon of Christ Church, Regius Professor of Eccles. Hist., 1892, p. 107.

[3] *History of the Church*, by W. Bright, D.D., 1882, 1892, p. 178.

[4] It seems inconsistent with the submissive tone of the letter sent in 382 to Rome to suppose that they in any way questioned the supremacy of the See of Peter.

honorary precedence, when it concerned two of the three Petrine Sees (Alexandria and Antioch), could be settled by these Eastern bishops, or that honorary precedence could be for any length of time divorced from actual jurisdiction. May be they thought to bar in the future such action as that of Peter of Alexandria in allowing his bishops to ordain Maximus to Constantinople; and it might not unnaturally seem that Antioch, considering her long-standing divisions, would be better protected by Constantinople if the latter held the place of honour. And they could count on Flavian, in his present position, owing (as he did) his election to the bishops of the council, acquiescing in an arrangement which commended itself to the political and military instincts of Theodosius.

But there mingled with this a certain lust of earthly honour which culminated in the great schism which was consummated through the unrestrained ambition of the ablest and most unscrupulous prelate that ever managed to intrude himself into that ill-fated Byzantine see. The decree which goes by the name of the Third Canon of Constantinople was the germ of the successful mendacity of the arch-rebel Photius.

§ IV.—*The Western Disapproval of the Election of Flavian to Antioch.*

Thus far, then, the synod was thoroughly and exclusively Eastern, in its composition, its range of action, and its internal discord. There was no idea of its aspiring to the rank of an œcumenical synod. But whilst it ended in some confusion and disagreement in regard to the Antiochene troubles, it nevertheless placed itself in line with the West in the matter of dogma. But they sent no official report to Rome, conscious, doubtless, of the impossibility of expecting Rome to accept their choice of Flavian. The account, however, of what had taken place necessarily reached the West, and was animadverted upon by a council that met that year in September to consider the case of two bishops who, although teaching Arian doctrine, refused to be numbered amongst the Arians. These bishops desired to be tried before an œcumenical synod; but St. Ambrose and (we may presume) St. Damasus considered that a small but influential council of thirty-two neighbouring bishops was sufficient to adjudge their case. It was not a representative synod of the West, neither Rome (where Damasus was pressed by fresh opposition from his old enemy Ursinus) nor Spain being represented, although their letter to the East implies that they were acting in unison with Damasus.

Its president was a great and holy bishop named Valerian, and its ruling spirit was St. Ambrose himself. This council, which met at Aquileia, addressed a letter to the Emperor Theodosius, which is of importance as showing that the West had long ago accepted the compact between St. Meletius and Paulinus as to the survivor being sole successor at Antioch. They say that, owing to the dissensions there, they had intended sending legates from the West to compose the strife,[1] but that 'since our desires could not take effect at that time owing to public disturbances, we presume that our petitions were presented to your Piety, in which we asked, in accordance with a compact between the parties, that on the decease of one the churches might remain in the hands of the survivor, and there should be no attempt to ordain anyone over his head.'

Such had been their previous petition, after they had heard of the compact made before the Antiochene Synod of A.D. 379, in which St. Meletius and his friends signed the 'Tome of the Westerns' and sent it to Rome. This, however, had now been rendered useless, owing to what had taken place at Constantinople.[2] Accordingly they proceed to say: 'And

---

[1] 'Qui sequestres et arbitri refundendæ, si fieri posset, pacis existerent' (Mansi, t. iii. p. 623).

[2] Mr. Puller rests much of his argument (*Prim. SS.* p. 249) concerning the continued existence of the breach with Rome and St. Meletius on this letter and the succeeding one from Milan. He argues that the Council of Aquileia did not know of what had taken place at Constantinople, and hence made a proposal about the survivor of either bishop at Antioch. But this is impossible for two reasons, viz.: (1) it is impossible to suppose that they would ask for a 'fuller council' at Alexandria (as they did in this letter) before they knew the issue of the council at Constantinople, and (2) they knew of Theodosius' law of July, for they thank him for passing it, and this law was passed subsequently to the Council of Constantinople, and brings in the name of Nectarius, who was ordained at that council.

therefore we ask and beseech you, most clement and Christian emperors, to convoke the whole body of Catholic bishops to a council to be held at Alexandria, who may fully discuss and settle the question as to who are to be admitted to communion and who are to have their communion with us maintained.'

They had said in the same letter that they were bound to have a care for the Paulinists at Antioch, because they had *long ago* received the letters of both sides.¹ What they intimate is, that they cannot throw over Paulinus and his followers, which the acceptance of Flavian would involve. They had once hoped to send legates, but that being impossible under the circumstances, they had sent letters which they think the emperor must have received,² in which they had asked for the imperial sanction of the compact entered into by the two sides. That compact having been set aside, *i.e.* at the Council of Constantinople, they now ask for a General Council to meet at Alexandria, and consider 'to whom communion should be given and with whom it should be maintained'³—*i.e.* whether they should extend their communion to the followers of Meletius now placed under Flavian. For themselves they wish the compact to stand ('quod stare volumus'). We learn from Sozomen that several at Antioch at once decided to join the party of Paulinus, as they presumed St. Meletius would have wished them to do, and so these Western bishops say that they do not wish any of these to seem neglected, 'who also in accordance with the compact, which we desire should stand, have asked for our communion.'⁴ They therefore ask for a fuller council ('cœtu pleniore') than that of Constantinople, which will have a better chance of restoring peace.

Very shortly after this, another council seems to have met at Milan,⁵ in which the bishops came to the conclusion that it would be better to have the council at Rome itself, to decide the affair of Nectarius, whose ordination they considered

---

¹ 'Utriusque partis dudum accepimus literas' (*loc. cit.*).
² 'Oblatas pietati vestræ opinamur preces nostras.'
³ Mansi, t. iii. p. 634.
⁴ 'Qui et pacto, quod stare volumus, communionem nostram rogarunt' (*loc. cit.*).
⁵ So Hefele and others think. Mansi makes the letter only a second from Aquileia.

illegitimate. From what follows we may assume that St. Damasus himself, whilst he would have supported Gregory as against Maximus, felt that Maximus' ordination had elements of canonicity which were lacking in the case of Nectarius.[1] The letter of this Council of Milan further censures the election of Flavian in place of Meletius. They say that the confusion which had recently ('nuper,' *i.e.* at Constantinople) taken place is indescribable. Things now stand thus, 'We had written long ago' ('dudum,' *i.e.* long before the Council of Constantinople, alluding to the letters spoken of above as having been sent instead of legates, after they knew of the compact between Meletius and Paulinus) 'that, since the city of Antioch had two bishops, Paulinus and Meletius, whom we considered to agree in faith, either peace and concord should be established between them without detriment to ecclesiastical order, or that, at any rate, whichever of them died before the other, there should be no election in the place of the deceased whilst the other lived. But now that Meletius has died . . . it is said that one has been not so much substituted as intruded into his place.' 'And this is said to have been done with the consent and by the advice of Nectarius, the regularity of whose ordination does not seem clear to us. For in the council lately (*nuper*),' &c.

Now from this letter we gather that there had been no formal notification of the enactments at Constantinople, but that information had reached them, as it must have done even before September (the date of the Council of Aquileia) as to the course of events at Constantinople—and information of a sufficiently precise nature to justify them in writing about it to the emperor, and calling it a state of inexplicable confusion. Further, they allude to letters which had been sent to the emperor concerning the compact long ago ('dudum')—that is, as compared with the Council of Constantinople, of which they speak as comparatively recent ('nuper'). These could only have been the letters to which the bishops at Aquileia alluded as having been sent previous to the Council of Constantinople.

[1] This explains the apparent change of front on the part of Damasus. It is, however, quite possible that it was a real change of mind in consequence of information as to what happened at Constantinople.

Now that the compact had been set aside, they ask for a larger council. It is therefore quite certain from these letters that when St. Meletius went to Constantinople he was a bishop accepted by Rome,[1] and absolutely certain that he died in communion with Rome.[2] Indeed, considering what has been advanced above,[3] it may be safely said that he had been in communion with Rome during the interval between the Synod of Antioch (379) and his death. And further, no case has been made out for the assertion that he was ever excommunicated by Rome. It must be remembered that the refusal to acknowledge a person as bishop is by no means equivalent to excommunication, and again, that the refusal of letters of intercourse may mean something much less than a decision that the person to whom they are refused is under the *excommunicatio major*.

NOTE.—It will be seen that I have drawn a perfectly opposite conclusion from the above letters to that deduced by Mr. Puller, 'Prim. SS.' pp. 247-251. He regards them as containing a demonstration that St. Meletius was out of communion with Rome at the time of the Council of Constantinople. It may well be asked, Whence this difference? It originates in the simple fact that Mr. Puller has disregarded the ordinary rules of grammar in his translation of the first letter. He translates the past tense in the Latin by the present in English. 'Oblatas pietati vestræ opinamur preces nostras, quibus partium pactum poposcimus, ut . . . permanerent . . . attentaretur,' is all in the past. But Mr. Puller actually translates *poposcimus* 'we pray,' and *oblatas* as 'should be offered,' and *permanerent* as 'may remain' (p. 250), which alters the whole sense. He then, to make it more complete, understands *nunc Meletio defuncto* as meaning that the bishops at Milan had *now*, i.e. *since the Council of Aquileia*, heard of Meletius' death. One could wish that Mr. Puller had restrained himself a little in making such sweeping accusations about others rendering history an impossibility as he has indulged in on p. 327. Nothing surely can equal the hardihood of turning the past tense into the present, and then making the passage thus translated the pivot of his argument as to the relation of St. Meletius to the See of Peter. As has been

---

[1] They speak of 'two bishops.'
[2] They had 'long ago' sent letters to both. [3] P. 229.

seen in the text above (cf. also note to p. 264), what the bishops are speaking of when they wish the subject of whom they should admit to communion to be dealt with, is *the state of things that had arisen in consequence of Flavian's election,* not the matter of communion with St. Meletius, 'Prim. SS., p. 250 (last line).' So that instead of its being 'perfectly clear from this letter that St. Meletius up to the time of his death was still cut off from the communion of the Western Church, which was so fully represented at Aquileia' (p. 251), it seems perfectly clear that the exact opposite is the truth. As for the West being 'so fully represented at Aquileia,' that is a minor matter, but it is difficult to see how the West could be fully represented, without Rome or Spain, by thirty-two bishops. So that on p. 251 (last line) of Mr. Puller's book the word 'Flavian' should be substituted for the words 'St. Meletius'—in other words, the whole superstructure of argument so laboriously built up by Mr. Puller falls to the ground.

CONCLUSION OF SECOND PERIOD.

§ I.—*Councils of Constantinople and Rome* (382).

BEFORE closing the second period it will be well to take a rapid survey of the action taken by the East and West in regard to the council which met at Constantinople in 381, in order to see how the whole matter ended in peace for the distracted East. Two great synods were held, one at Constantinople and the other at Rome, in 382, instead of a larger one of East and West in one place.

I. The West having (p. 266) expressed its dissatisfaction with the doings of the council at Constantinople in regard to the appointment of Nectarius to Constantinople and of Flavian to Antioch, now demanded a General Council, and suggested Alexandria as the best place wherein to meet. What Theodosius actually did was to summon a fresh synod to Constantinople. Meanwhile St. Damasus (for by the West we must understand St. Damasus and the Western bishops) proceeded a step further and proposed a General Council to meet at Rome.[1] This invitation, however, came too late. Numerous bishops had already met at Constantinople and left their dioceses for the time that would be required for a synod there, and had not made arrangements which would permit of their extending their journey, neither (it would seem from what they say) had they met at Constantinople in such numbers as would be

---

[1] Theodoret speaks of 'the West' calling for a council of Easterns and Westerns. But, as Merenda observes, everybody knows ('nemo qui nescit') that by this expression the Pope is frequently meant (*Gesta S. Damasi*, cap. xx. § 2). Merenda also thinks that the letter written by the Emperor Gratian to Damasus about assembling a synod, mentioned in the *Lib. Synodic.* cap. lxxiv. refers to the Council of Aquileia.

required for an œcumenical council of East and West. This they stated in their letter, which they at once wrote to St. Damasus and the Western bishops. In that letter, after cordially [1] responding to the desire of the West to bring matters to a peaceful issue, and speaking of themselves as 'members' of the West (as containing, it might perhaps be fairly argued, their head [2]), they say that 'it was indeed our wish, if possible, to leave our Churches in a body and gratify the need or desire,' *i.e.* of repairing to Rome. 'For' (they continue) 'who will give us wings like doves to flee away and be at rest *with you*?' In the West was their true home—so the expression used implies; [3] there was their mother, who could gather them under her wings and give them shelter and peace. But this, they plead, was simply an impossibility at present. It was impossible to leave their Churches for so long, or to send notice to the other bishops. They had already 'flocked in eager haste' to Constantinople [4] 'in consequence of (ἐκ) the letters sent by your Worthiness last year after the synod at Aquileia,[5] to the most God-loving Emperor Theodosius.' It would therefore now be impossible to let the other bishops know. This last reason throws some light on this Synod of 382 at Constantinople. It was not the 150 Fathers who met, except by representation. Of course, we know that St. Gregory of Nazianzus refused to attend; and we do not know how many others did the same. They themselves call the synod of the *last* year ('πέρυσι' [381])

---

[1] Several writers on the subject imagine that these Eastern bishops were not sincere in what they said. There is absolutely nothing in the words they use to convey the notion of hypocrisy.

[2] Of course they might mean only to speak of being members one of another, but the context suggests the above meaning.

[3] Mansi, t. iii. p. 583: πρὸς ὑμᾶς. Cf. the well-known expression in St. John i. 1, πρὸς τὸν Θεόν, indicating the infinite communion of the Son with the Father, the πηγὴ θεότητος. The Greek preposition in such contexts is equivalent to the French 'chez vous.' Jerusalem was the mother-Church as the older; Rome was their mother as the present centre of the Church.

[4] συνδεδραμήκαμεν, lit. 'We had run together.'

[5] It is therefore evident that the order of things was this. St. Damasus, in concert with the bishops at Aquileia, had proposed a council at Alexandria. The Easterns were at once summoned by Theodosius to Constantinople, where they received the subsequent invitation to Rome which is recorded in the letter from the council held (as is supposed) at Milan.

œcumenical, not their own—a term which they could hardly have meant to use even of that in its full significance, unless in the sense that the dogmatic decisions, being but an echo of the pronouncements already promulgated in the West, witnessed to the universal acceptance of the teaching of the Roman Synod of 372. Probably, however, they used the word in the same way that the Africans used the word universal, *i.e.* of a Synod of All Africa.

This whole letter is a witness to the fact that the East had no idea of such a thing as the independence of national Churches. Neither provinces, nor even the whole of the East, felt themselves at liberty to plead that they could manage their own affairs without reference to the West.[1]

They then proceed to say that they had adopted the next best course (ὃ δεύτερον ἦν) by way of righting matters and showing their love[2] for the Western bishops. 'We asked Cyriacus, Eusebius, and Priscianus to undertake the work willingly of going to you, and through these we show our own peaceful determination, and how we aim at unity.' They then describe their faith in exact accord with the teaching sent originally by the Roman Synod (372) on the subject of the Third Person of the Holy Trinity, and they refer to St. Damasus and the Westerns for a further explanation of their faith to a certain doctrinal formulary, which they speak of as 'the Tome which was adopted[3] at Antioch by the synod assembled there, and to the Tome put forth last year at Constantinople by the Œcumenical Synod.' This passage proves two things: first, that the Council of 382 did not regard itself simply as a session of the Council of 381, but as a separate synod; and secondly, that the so-called Fifth Canon of the

---

[1] The letter of Theodosius quoted by Mr. Puller (*Prim. SS.* p. 274) does not exist; and though it did once exist, it probably had nothing to do with this matter; and, if it had, it was denounced by St. Ambrose as erroneous in its teaching (cf. Appendix III. p. 479).

[2] I feel myself quite unable to take the line that these bishops were mere hypocrites. Without rating them too high, they must have had the courage of their opinions sufficiently to say so, if they were, as some suppose, all the while offended with the West. At any rate, they thought it best to say the exact opposite. They were not the same as those of the previous year.

[3] I have thus translated γεγενημένῳ, as being a word which does not necessarily imply that the bishops at Antioch drew it up themselves.

Œcumenical Council belongs to the assembly of the Second Synod of 382.[1] The Council of 381 put forth a Tome, and the Council of 382 embodied it in a canon.

What, then, was the 'Tome of the Westerns,' the doctrinal formulary adopted at Antioch and identical at least in substance with that put forth at the Œcumenical Council of Constantinople? Hefele has furnished most convincing proofs[2] that it was the doctrinal formulary addressed by St. Damasus and his synod of 369 to the East, sent formally and officially in 372 in response to St. Basil's entreaties for help. It was all that St. Damasus had seen it in his power to do at that time. He settled the faith, as contained implicitly in the Nicene Creed, concerning the Third Person of the Holy Trinity, and sent back the Eastern legate, Dorotheus, with this formulary. For the rest, he could but wait on Divine Providence to come to the aid of the East. It came in the form of an orthodox Eastern emperor, who entered upon his career of pacification by insisting on his subjects, who wished to be called Catholic, practising 'the religion delivered *to the Romans* by the Divine Apostle Peter,' as taught now by the Pontiff Damasus, with whom at that time the saintly successor of St. Athanasius agreed.

So that the object which Theodosius originally had most at heart when, on leaving Thessalonica shortly after his baptism, he summoned a general council of the East at Constantinople, had now been achieved. The 'faith of Damasus' had already, according to Theodoret, been made the touchstone of orthodoxy at Antioch when the prefect Sapor decided to whom the churches held by the Arians should be handed over. The emperor had further been able to point in the previous year to Nectarius, Timothy, Helladius, Gregory of Nyssa, and others in his law of July, 381, as the orthodox centres in the East, for each of these could now be said to hold, on the vexed questions of the day, that which 'the religion taught up to this time declares to have been delivered to the Romans by

---

[1] The canon runs thus: 'As to the Tome of the Westerns, we also recognised those in Antioch who confess one Godhead of the Father and Son and Holy Ghost.'

[2] They seem to me to amount to demonstration.

the divine Apostle Peter.' And now the council assembled at Constantinople (382) to establish peace could report that their 'Œcumenical' Council of the previous year (381) had professed the same faith, and they were able to tell the West that they unanimously accepted in the East the doctrinal formulary which had issued from Rome in the midst of their troubles under Valens, and had been accepted by St. Meletius and his synod at Antioch, two or three years previously, and by the more General Council of 381.[1] So far, then, as the faith was concerned, the East had now been brought into line with the West.

But peace was not yet restored ; for the new Bishops of Constantinople and Antioch had not yet received the assent of the Bishop of Rome to their appointment. Meanwhile the council, which had been originally intended as œcumenical, met at Rome, shorn of the Eastern contingent that met at Constantinople, but one of the most remarkable synods as concerned its composition that had assembled during the reign of Damasus.

There was St. Ambrose himself, the foremost prelate of his time, the spiritual guide of the Western emperor, and the spiritual father of the great Augustine; the metropolitan of the city (Milan) selected by the emperor for his frequent residence; a bishop who has more vividly impressed his memory upon the West than perhaps any other Western saint of that critical time.

The great Bishop of Thessalonica, St. Ascholius, who had baptised the Eastern emperor, had also come with the special desire of meeting St. Ambrose in the flesh. He came in his anchorite's garment, and found his brother saint ill in bed. St. Ambrose himself describes their meeting,[2] their long embrace, the tears they shed.

There was the great St. Jerome, the student of Holy Scripture, who had drunk in the theology of St. Gregory of Nazianzus from his own lips, to whose inspection St. Gregory of Nyssa had submitted his writings, and who was one day to be the instructor of St. Augustine himself.

There was, above all, the great Saint Epiphanius, one of

---

[1] It had not yet the right to the title Œcumenical.   [2] *Ep.* xv. n. 10.

T

the greatest men of the day; born in Palestine, brought up a Jew, converted by the sight of a monk giving away his garment to clothe a beggar; the friend of St. Athanasius; inhabitant of the Thebaid as an anchorite, where the monasteries rang with the fame of his many miracles; drawn out of his cell against his will and made Bishop of Salamis—a man consulted by East and West, profoundly versed in Hebrew and Syriac and Greek, one who had investigated to its depths every heresy, and who was called 'the Apostle, the new John, the herald of the Lord.'

These great saints were now in the city of St. Peter and St. Paul. And there was one object, which must have had a special interest for them at that time—the chair of Peter. St. Damasus had built a new baptistery, and placed the chair of Peter in it, to which the description he put up in this baptistery alludes—

Una Petri sedes, unum verumque lavacrum.'

St. Optatus, the African bishop, had lately written his work against the Donatists, and in answer to their boast that they had a successor of Peter in Rome, having consecrated a bishop for Rome, named Macrobius, for their own sect, he had written thus, 'In fact, if Macrobius be asked where he sits in Rome, can he say, In the Chair of Peter?—which I am not aware that he has ever seen with his eyes, and whose shrine he, as a heretic, has never approached.'

St. Ambrose, St. Ascholius, St. Epiphanius, and St. Jerome may be thought of in devout reverence at the shrine of Peter, one in their faith, as expressed by St. Ambrose in the Council of Aquileia, that from Rome 'the rights of venerable communion flow abroad to all.'[1]

Unfortunately, the Acts of this important synod have perished, and we can only guess at its decisions by the action of the West towards the East subsequent to the assembly.

Hitherto St. Damasus had expressed his disapproval of Maximus' appointment to Constantinople privately, before the appointment had been made;[2] but the Council of Aquileia,

---

[1] Mansi, t. iii. p. 622.   [2] Damas. *Ep. ad Aschol*

which met by his authority,[1] and was presided over by Valerian and attended by St. Ambrose, who was its ruling spirit, had asked for a general council at Alexandria, in consequence of its being obliged to say in the name of the West that the arrangements of the Council of Constantinople (381), concerning either Maximus, who had apparently appealed to it, or concerning the see of Antioch, would never meet with their approval.

But the Council of Milan had gone further, being doubtless in possession of further details. It had protested against the appointment of Nectarius, and asked the emperor to send his bishops to Rome. That most extraordinary man, Maximus, had appeared in the West, having probably dropped his yellow wig and philosopher's mantle and staff, and had claimed the privilege of appeal. He had not handed in an appeal whilst in the East, and hence his case did not technically come under the operation of the Niceno-Sardican canon. But the principle of that canon might fairly be invoked,[2] and the council did claim that the East should act in accordance with its provision.[3] The East ought to have waited for the sentence of the West, the council says. It disclaims the idea of making itself the court of first instance, but claims to be consulted in the matter.[4] It was one which could not be concluded in the East; there must be a common judgment.[5]

All this must have been reviewed, at the great synod at Rome in 382, by the Pope, by St. Ambrose, St. Epiphanius, St. Ascholius, St. Jerome, and the bishops in synod. What they decided can only be conjectured from the sequence of events, which was as follows:—Maximus was disowned by the West, the two consecrators of Flavian were excommunicated, but towards Flavian himself Rome maintained silence,[6]

---

[1] Cf. *Valesii Nota* apud Sozom. lib. vii. c. 9; and Merenda, *Gesta Damasi* (Migne, p. 328).

[2] Viz. that no bishop should be appointed during an appeal to Rome.

[3] Mansi, t. iii. 632. Not mentioning the canon, but obviously arguing upon its lines. [4] Prærogativam examinis (Ambr. *Ep.* xiii.).

[5] A common judgment is not necessarily one in which all parties are on a par, and all contribute the same amount of authority, but in which all, head and members as well, join. [6] σιωπὴν εἶχεν (Soz.).

neither passing actual sentence upon him nor admitting his claim—placing him, in fact, in much the same position as that held by St. Meletius before 379, *i.e.* neither excommunicated nor adopted by Rome[1]—whilst the East applied to Rome for its approbation of Nectarius, thus acting in accordance with the request of the Council of Milan, that the matter should not be concluded in the East. Theodosius did not consider Nectarius' position safe without Rome's approval; accordingly, a solemn embassy of bishops and imperial officials[2] was dispatched to Rome for her approbation, the emperor asking for a letter of communion to 'confirm the episcopal position' of Nectarius.[3] The Council of 382 had used an expression in the end of their synodical letter to Damasus to the same effect; they express a hope that Damasus and the West will 'congratulate' them on what they had done—a courteous ecclesiastical formula to request confirmation.[4]

It seems also that the Apollinarian heresy was dealt with at the Roman Synod (382). St. Damasus would be particularly anxious for consultation with such as St. Epiphanius and St. Ambrose on this subject. The condemnation of that heresy had been one of the great works of his reign. It had sprung, as so many heresies, from a zealous opposition to one form of error leading to an error on the opposite side. In opposing the Arians, Apollinarius came to imagine that our Lord's freedom from sin was incompatible with the possession of a human soul, and that the possession of two natures, each entire and distinct, was inconsistent with the Unity of His Person. He, therefore, denied that our Lord had a human soul in its higher element or operation (a rational soul), and asserted that this was supplied by His Divinity. As you entered the house of a disciple of Apollinarius you would see written up on the door or portico, a sentence to the effect

---

[1] Mansi, t. iii. p. 640: 'Ab excommunicatione Flaviani cessatum est, et schisma Antiochenæ ecclesiæ ad tempus certum toleratum fuit.'

[2] 'Missis a latere suo aulicis cum episcopis' (Bonifacii I. *Ep.* xv. *ad Rufum*, &c.).

[3] 'Quæ ejus sacerdotium roboraret' (*loc. cit.*).

[4] Nectarius' ordination needed to be purged of its irregularity as contravening the Second Canon of Nicæa.

that Christians should not adore a man who bore God within himself, but a God who bore human flesh. Both St. Basil and St. Athanasius exhibited a certain natural reluctance to condemn Apollinarius himself, though, it is needless to say, themselves absolutely free from any taint of his error. St. Damasus condemned him synodically in a synod (377) and deposed both him and his disciple Timothy, Bishop (perhaps[1]) of Berytus, and the example of the Pope was followed at Alexandria and Constantinople. St. Damasus had been asked to depose these bishops after he had done it. Accordingly he replied, 'Why, then, do you ask me again to depose Timothy seeing that he was deposed by the judgment of the Apostolic See, in presence of Peter, Bishop of Alexandria, together with his master, Apollinarius?'[2]

At this synod of 382 at Rome St. Jerome was deputed to draw up a formulary to be accepted by all suspected or convicted of the heresy of Apollinarius.

After this, various bishops met in the following year at Constantinople, and Damasus in a synod of the same year[3] confirmed all that had been done at Constantinople in 381, 382, and 383 in regard to dogma. The canons were not sent to Rome, and therefore had no œcumenical authority.

After the synod of 382 St. Damasus took St. Jerome for his secretary, and we know from the latter that the Pope was occupied, during the time that remained to him, in settling matters referred to him by synods from the East and West. He had been the centre of the Church's life now for nearly eighteen years, and during all that time he had been constantly employed in either meeting the attacks on his own person or those, more serious still, on the faith of the Church. He had been, as the Sixth General Council called him, the 'adamant of the faith.' As an instance of the way in which he was able to 'confirm the brethren' at times, we may remember his action in regard to the saintly and orthodox successor of St. Athanasius at Alexandria. This bishop's name was Peter. He was driven out of his see by the Emperor Valens, and one named Lucius was intruded. Peter

---

[1] The difficulties of settling who this Timothy was are considerable
[2] Damas. *Ep.* 14.   [3] Mansi, t. iii. p. 642.

betook himself to Rome, and in 377 he returned to Alexandria with letters from Damasus which, says the historian, 'confirmed the faith of the *Homoousion* and the ordination of Peter. Whereupon the people of Alexandria took courage and drove out Lucius and brought back Peter in his place.'[1] Eutherius, Bishop of Tyana, and Helladius, Bishop of Tarsus, two unimpeachable witnesses, probably referred to this amongst other instances when they said, in their remarkable letter to Pope Xystus, 'And often in former times when the tares of heresy were growing up out of Alexandria your Apostolic See sufficed during the whole of that time to convince of falsehood, repress impiety, and correct what needed correction, and to guard the world for the glory of Christ, as well under the thrice blessed Damasus as under several others.'

It was, however, the chief glory of this Pope that he was the chosen instrument of the Holy Ghost to declare His Divine Majesty coequal with the Father and the Son, as part of that Catholic faith which had been enshrined in the Nicene Creed, but which needed explicit statement. This St. Damasus did in his *ex cathedrâ* pronouncement in the synods of 369 and 372, and his utterance gradually gathered into itself the entire Church, issuing in the assent of the great Eastern Synod in 381, which, by its acceptance at Rome, became one of the first four œcumenical councils,[2] so far as its dogmatic decision was concerned. No wonder that the heathen prefect at Rome, as he saw the central position of the see of Peter, the reverence paid to it in the midst of the troubles it met with through an Ursinus or an Isaac (the Jew), should say that he would become a Christian to-morrow if he could be made Bishop of Rome. He would probably have said the same of the bishopric of Milan, as he saw the heads of departments flock to the entertainments which St. Ambrose, himself the most mortified of men, occasionally gave in that city, and as he considered the influence of the great bishop on the Emperor Gratian. No wonder the heathen historian, Ammianus Marcellinus, felt the sting of jealousy as

---

[1] Socr. iv. 37. Sozomen accounts for the fact that Valens did not avenge himself for this insult by his being just then distracted with troubles elsewhere (Soz. vi. 39).   [2] *i.e.* eventually.

he saw the state with which previous emperors had surrounded the heathen religion now transferred to the Christian. He would not understand how a mortified man like Damasus viewed such matters, accepting the ritual of imperial homage whilst he knew that his real strength lay in the divine promise to the blessed Apostle Peter, in whose name, together with that of the holy Apostle Paul, he ruled the Church, and in whose chair he sat.

PERIOD III.
(THE FIFTH CENTURY.)

400–452.

CHAPTER XVII.

THE CHURCH OF NORTH AFRICA IN THE DAYS OF ST. AUGUSTINE.

§ I.—*The Letters of St. Innocent.*

A RECENT writer, whose statements have been often traversed in this book, has said of us, in regard to the subject of this chapter, 'As honourable men, let them refrain from pretending that the Church of North Africa, in the time of St. Augustine, believed in the principles laid down by the Vatican Council. Such a pretence is an impertinence and an act of folly, which must alienate every person of good sense and Christian simplicity who is cognisant of it.'[1] The particular teaching of the said Council against which this writer's remarks are directed is given in the immediate context. It is 'the principle that, *jure divino*, every member of the Church, whether clerical or lay, has an inherent right to have "recourse to the Pope's judgment in all causes which appertain to the jurisdiction of the Church." The African Fathers absolutely deny that right.'[2]

It must be observed in passing, that it is not *jure divino*, according to the Vatican decrees, that everyone has the right of direct and immediate recourse to the Holy See. It belongs to ecclesiastical authority to regulate the channels of access to the supreme authority, which may differ at different times and in different countries. In a word, whilst the principle of appeal is open to all the world, the mode of procedure by which the appeal is set in motion is matter of ecclesiastical arrangement.

Ever since the sixteenth century, or at any rate the seventeenth, the Church of North Africa in the days of St. Augustine has been quoted as an authority for separation from

[1] *Primitive Saints, &c.* p. 203; cf. also the Preface to the work by the Bishop of Lincoln, p. xxxi.   [2] p. 202.

Rome in this country. At the time of the final separation, when Elizabeth had an archbishop made without leave from Rome, and without connection with Rome of any kind, no theory had been struck out to justify the state of things in which men found themselves; but as soon as they sought for the shelter of Church history the Church of North Africa was invoked in justification of the step taken. And when Archbishop Laud endeavoured to defend his position from history he laid great stress on the misunderstanding that arose between Rome and Africa in the beginning of the fifth century over the affair of Apiarius. Dr. Pusey followed in the same line and insisted that 'England is not at this moment more independent of any authority of the Bishop of Rome than Africa was in the days of St. Augustine.'[1]

It is no exaggeration to say that if it can be shown that the Church of North Africa in the days of Augustine held that the Bishop of Rome was the supreme Governor of the Church under Christ, by His divine appointment, one of the great obstacles to reunion between ourselves and many of our fellow-countrymen will have been removed. It is this that I now proceed to show.

I. The fifth century, in its first few years, saw the beginning of a heresy which struck at the roots of all Christian piety. It originated with a fellow-countryman of our own, a British monk named Pelagius, who denied that death was the penalty of sin—that sin had in any substantial way affected our nature, so as to weaken it and make it incapable of fulfilling the commands of God. Pelagius confused grace with the grant of free-will, and held that it was possible by the mere virtue of our free-will to keep the law. He denied that any interior strengthening of our nature was needed, admitting only the necessity of instruction, as by the doctrine and example of our Lord. He held that the assistance which helps us more easily to fulfil the divine commands is merited by the proper use of our free-will.[2]

---

[1] *Eirenicon*, p. 66.
[2] See in Migne's *Patrol. Cursus* a most exhaustive account of Pelagius' teaching in Garnier's *Seventh Dissertation on the Works of Marius Mercator*, in which the above points are dealt with one by one.

The great difficulty of dealing with this false doctrine lay not so much in the nature of the heresy as in the character of the heretics. Pelagius had no scruple about denying and asserting at random, professing perfect harmony with the teaching of the Church when pressed by authority, and proceeding to teach its contradictory when absolved.

His disciple, Cœlestius, was the first to come to the front; and his action in Africa led to an expression of opinion on the value of a decision from Rome which ought to settle the question as to what the Church of North Africa held concerning the authority of the See of Peter.

Cœlestius had found his way to Africa, and disseminated his opinions there. He was condemned by a synod at Carthage under Aurelius, A.D. 412. The synod wrote to Pope Innocent and described Cœlestius as 'struck with anathema and deprived of communion until he should openly anathematise the things objected against him.' Cœlestius appealed to Rome. The African Fathers took no exception to his appeal, which is mentioned quite naturally by Marius Mercator, a contemporary, and later on by Facundus the African writer. He left Carthage and went, not, as it was supposed he would, to Rome to prosecute his appeal, but to Asia. His object seems to have been to get into the priesthood whilst he was yet finally uncondemned. He was ordained priest at Ephesus, and was therefore outside the patriarchal jurisdiction of Rome.

Meanwhile Pelagius had gone to Jerusalem to disseminate his errors in Palestine; there he found a sympathiser in the Bishop of Jerusalem, named John. But at a synod consisting mainly, if not altogether, of priests, a Spanish priest, named Orosius, whom St. Augustine had sent, as he says, to sit at the feet of Jerome at Bethlehem 'to learn the fear of the Lord,' explained what had happened at Carthage, how this Cœlestius had been condemned for false doctrine. Such a difficulty of language, however, arose, and Pelagius seemed so to evade all that Orosius accused him of teaching, that it was agreed to refer the matter to Rome, and John, the Bishop of Jerusalem,[1] concurred, 'confirming,' says Orosius, 'our demand and con-

---

[1] This bishop seems to have believed in Pelagius, without, however, having any sympathy with Pelagianism. Cf. Natalis Alexander, *H. E.* vol. ix. pt. 2.

tention that the parties and the letters should be sent to the blessed Innocent, the Roman Pope, all agreeing to follow what he should decide,[1] but on the understanding that the heretic Pelagius should impose silence on himself meanwhile.'

The Bishop of Jerusalem, however, fearing that Pelagius would be condemned at Rome, seems to have instigated the Bishop of Palestinian Cæsarea, Eulogius, to summon a synod of the bishops of the province at Diospolis, in which Pelagius imposed upon his judges and was declared orthodox. Some of St. Jerome's monasteries were now burnt to the ground, owing to his opposition to this new heresy which Pelagius was now spreading about on the pretence that it had been sanctioned at the synod.[2] There were, however, two wandering bishops from Gaul, named Eros and Lazarus, who at once wrote to Africa and acquainted the bishops there of what had happened in Palestine.

II. A large council of bishops was now held at Carthage to consider what step should be taken. It was contrary to the canons to condemn a man in his absence, and accordingly their plan was to give the sanction of the entire province to the Carthaginian decision of five years ago, and obtain for it the authoritative confirmation of the Apostolic See. I say of the Apostolic See, for this was the point of all their endeavour, not to obtain a condemnation from the see of the great city of Rome, but to obtain the authoritative sanction of 'the Apostolic' See. 'We have considered,' so they write to Pope St. Innocent,[3] ' that we ought to acquaint your Holiness with this which was thus enacted, lord and brother, that the authority of the Apostolic See may be applied to the statutes of our lowliness, for the sake of guarding the salvation of many, and also of correcting the perversity of some.' And after describing the teaching of Pelagius, they say (n. 3), 'And we fear lest we should seem to act unbecomingly in bringing forward before you those very things which you proclaim

---

[1] 'Universis, quid ipse decerneret, secuturis.' *Orosii Apol.* num. 4.
[2] Jer. *Ep.* 24, apud Aug.
[3] Innoc. *Ep.* xxvi. The letters which follow are to be found in most collections of the Councils and in every complete edition of St. Augustine's works. The following quotations are from the Benedictine edition, Paris, 1694.

with higher grace from the Apostolic See.'[1] And, again, ' If, therefore, in what is said to have been enacted by the bishops in the East, Pelagius shall seem to your Reverence to have been justly absolved, still the error itself and the impiety, which now has many champions scattered through divers regions, deserves the anathema of the Apostolic See' (n. 4).

Almost immediately afterwards a synod of African bishops was also held at Milevis, at which St. Augustine was present, having come, it is supposed, from Carthage (where the letter just quoted was probably written by him) to assist in similar proceedings under Silvanus, the presiding bishop of the Numidian province. In the letter of this provincial council to Pope Innocent, the bishops say that they write, in imitation of their brethren at Carthage, ' to the Apostolic See.' They speak of Cœlestius, as well as Pelagius, being still 'in the Church' (n. 3), although the former had been anathematised and excommunicated in Africa. Only his appeal to Rome could justify them in thus speaking. The three saintly bishops, Augustine, Alypius, and Possidius, were present at this council, and the synodical letter to the Pope strikes the same key-note as that of the Carthaginian council. ' Because the Lord, by the special bounty of His grace, has placed you in the Apostolic See,' is their opening salutation. They excuse themselves, after setting forth the heresy, for saying so much to one who is doubtless moved to act of his own accord, and then speak of Cœlestius being still within the Church (n. 3). And they give their reason for wishing for the exercise of authority in this matter in words which ought to be written over every page of those treatises which endeavour to enlist the witness of 'the Church of North Africa in the days of St. Augustine' against the supremacy of the Holy See. They say, 'We think . . . that those who hold such perverse and pernicious opinions will yield more readily to the authority of your Holiness,[2] derived from the authority of the Holy Scriptures.' But whether they will or not, there are 'others who, as your Reverence perceives, have to be cared for quickly and at once.'

---

[1] ' Quæ majore gratia de sede Apostolica prædicas.'

[2] So they speak of it as (i.) something beyond their own, and (ii.) as of divine institution.

At the same time Aurelius, Augustine, Alypius, Evodius, and Possidius wrote besides a joint letter to the Pope to the same effect, asking for his rescripts.

III. We have now to consider the two celebrated letters of St. Innocent in reply, and I shall quote them, not as showing what he claimed, but what the African bishops are found to have accepted without a murmur. These bishops, it will be seen, were either the tamest and most hypocritical of men, or they believed in Papal supremacy.

To the synod at Carthage he writes:[1] 'Preserving the ancient tradition, and mindful of the ecclesiastical discipline, you have in true method added strength to your religion,[2] not less by your present consultation [of us] than by your sentence having approved the principle of referring to our judgment, knowing what is due to the Apostolic See, since all of us who have been placed in this position desire to follow the Apostle himself, from whom the episcopate itself and all the authority of this office has proceeded.[3] Following him, we know how to condemn what is wrong and approve what deserves approval.[4] The same is the case as to your judgment that the arrangements of the Fathers are not to be trodden under foot, in that they decreed, not by a human but by a divine sentence, that whatever is done from the separated and remote provinces they would not consider should be final unless it should come to the cognisance of the Apostolic See, so that whatever sentence shall have been justly delivered should be confirmed by the entire authority of this see, and that just as all waters should flow from their natal fount and the pure streams of the uncorrupt head flow through the diverse regions of the whole world, so other Churches should take from this see (*inde sumerent*) what to teach, whom to cleanse, who should be avoided, as stained with ineradicable filth, by the wave that is worthy of pure bodies.' He then gave his decision.

This one rescript contains the teaching of the Vatican

---

[1] Aug. *Ep.* 181. [2] 'Vestræ religionis vigorem firmastis.'
[3] 'A quo ipse episcopatus et tota auctoritas nominis hujus emersit.'
[4] It is obvious that St. Innocent speaks of the infallibility of the Holy See. It is 'sequentes,' not 'cum sequamur.'

Council entire. Before, however, considering its reception, listen to the sister letter to the Council of Milevis:[1]

'Diligently, therefore, and fittingly do you consult the arcana of the Apostolic office (a dignity, into which flows the care of all the Churches, besides those things which are without) on matters of anxiety, as to what opinion should be held, following the ancient rule, which you know as well as I do has been kept always by the whole world. . . . Why have you confirmed this, unless as knowing that replies are ever emanating from the Apostolic fountain through all provinces to those who petition it? Especially as often as a matter of faith is being ventilated, I consider that all our brethren and fellow-bishops are in duty bound to refer only to Peter, that is, to the author of their own dignity and office, as your love has now referred, what may be for the common good of all Churches through the whole world. For the inventors of wrong must necessarily become more cautious, when they shall see that at the report of a double synod they are separated from ecclesiastical communion by the decrees of our sentence.'

The Pope then proceeds to cut off Pelagius and Cœlestius from the communion of the Church by Apostolic authority ('apostolici vigoris auctoritate') until they repent; and in his reply to the five bishops he says that his sentence will have its effect in whatever part of the world Pelagius may be, and that he has no reason to suppose that he has been absolved by any synod, because, if he had, letters would have at once been sent to Rome. If he has repented, it is not for us, says St. Innocent, to summon him to Rome, but for him to hasten here that he may be absolved.

IV. Now, the important point for the argument of this book is, How did the African bishops, and, in particular, St. Augustine himself, receive this letter? The whole of the Vatican teaching is contained in it. This simple fact is not without its bearing on much that has been written of late. The mere fact that that teaching was fully before the public consciousness of the Church in the year 416 has left St. Leo little or nothing to add in regard to the authority of the

[1] Aug. *Ep.* 182.

Apostolic See. But the important point is, Did the African bishops, did any African bishop, take exception to St. Innocent's definitions of the place occupied by Rome towards the rest of the Church *as the See of Peter*? Did they throw out the remotest hint that, in accepting the net result of St. Innocent's letters, they excepted the passages about the authority with which it was done? Not one. Yet the letter was much before the world. Later on, three African councils quoted one of the very passages in which St. Innocent so clearly defines the office of the See of Peter. This, it will be said, was too late to be a witness of the Early Church. But a very important writer, St. Prosper, a Gallic bishop, writing as a contemporary in defence of St. Augustine against Cassian, speaks of St. Innocent as 'most worthy of the See of Peter.' The expression is significant, for Prosper knew well what St. Innocent had said of that See. Also, 214 African bishops said: 'We determined that the judgment should stand which was issued by the venerable Bishop Innocent from the See of the most blessed Peter.' They are referring to these very letters of Innocent, and again, I say, the reference to the 'See of Peter,' considering what those letters contain about it, is significant. I have been unable to find any single hint in any contemporary writer to the effect that St. Innocent was exaggerating the privileges of his see. Indeed, he hardly went beyond the declaration of the African bishops as to the Scriptural source of his authority.[1]

But what of St. Augustine himself? St. Augustine says that Innocent, 'in reference to all things, wrote back to us in the same way in which it was lawful and the duty of the Apostolic See to write.'[2]

I do not know how it would be possible for St. Augustine to set his signature to the Vatican decrees by anticipation in plainer terms. Of these two great letters of Pope Innocent he says, in another place, challenging the Pelagian bishop, Julian, 'Reply to him [*i.e.* Innocent], yea, rather to the Lord Himself, whose testimony that prelate used.'[3] Again, he

---

[1] The *Liber Pontificalis* speaks of St. Innocent having drawn up a 'constitutum' for the whole Church.

[2] *Ep.* 186, n. 2.   [3] Lib. i. c. *Julian.* c. 4.

says that if anyone should come across Pelagians, he is no longer to exercise towards them a mistaken mercy; he is not to conceal them, but to bring them before their bishop. 'For already two councils have been sent (or have sent) to the Apostolic See about that matter. Thence rescripts have come. The case is ended; would that the error may be sometime ended too!'[1] St. Augustine knew that there were plenty who had already, when he wrote these words, resisted the decision of the Holy See, but nevertheless that decision was authoritative—' The case is ended.'

It has been customary to express the latter sentence in the short maxim, ' Rome has spoken; the case is at an end '—words which, it will be seen, are the exact equivalent of what St. Augustine here says.

Hardly any decree exists in which the position of the Apostolic See has been more clearly defined than in that of St. Innocent; and no decree was received in terms of more unqualified admiration by the Church of North Africa in the time of St. Augustine.

§ II.—*St. Zosimus' Support of the Faith.*

Dr. Pusey[2] has made the relationship of Zosimus towards Pelagianism one of his test cases against the infallibility of the Holy See; but in his handling of that Pope's history he has, in express terms, whether he knew it or not, contradicted St. Augustine, and in his own imaginary history of St. Zosimus he has founded his opposition on an incorrect description of Papal infallibility. It is the old story of the conflict between science and religion. The opposition is always found to be between imaginary facts (or gratuitous deductions) and Christian teaching, or between ascertained facts and a caricature of that teaching. In this case neither the facts exist nor is the representation of our teaching correct.

I. In A.D. 417 Zosimus succeeded St. Innocent, and Cœlestius at once hastened to Rome and resumed the appeal against

---

[1] *Serm.* cxxi. n. 10.
[2] *Sermon on the Rule of Faith,* Pref. p. xiv, and *Eirenicon* pt. iii. pp. 219–226.

the African sentence, of which he had given notice at the time, but which he had failed to prosecute.¹

Zosimus admitted him to an audience. Cœlestius had brought with him a letter of approbation from the Bishop of Jerusalem, and had avowed his desire to submit to the decrees of Innocent.² It is this that alters the whole case, and wrests the memory of this Pope from the accusation which Dr. Pusey so persistently brought against him. It is this that never appears in that writer's arraignment of the Pope. St. Innocent had expressly said³ that if Cœlestius and Pelagius should condemn their depraved teaching, they were to receive 'the usual medicine'—*i.e.* be received back into the Church. They did present documents in which they promised amendment.⁴ Dr. Pusey says that the document which they presented was heretical, and that Zosimus failed in his guardianship of the faith, because he approved a Pelagian confession.⁵ St. Augustine says he did no such thing. He insists upon the fact that, all through, St. Zosimus was entirely on the orthodox side. These are his words:—' Zosimus never said, never wrote, that what they think about children is to be held—moreover, also, he bound over Cœlestius again and again (*crebra interlocutione*), when he was endeavouring to purge himself, to the necessity of consenting (*consentiendum*) to the above-mentioned letters of the Apostolic See' (*i.e.* the letters of Innocent); and he argues that whilst Zosimus eventually condemned Cœlestius and Pelagius, repeatedly and authoritatively ('repetita auctoritate'), what took place meanwhile 'was the most kindly persuasion [for the purpose] of correction, not the most hateful approval of depravity.'⁶ And elsewhere he insists that Zosimus dealt with Cœlestius on the understanding 'that he should condemn what had been objected against him by the deacon Paulinus [*i.e.* at Carthage], and give his assent to the letters which had emanated from his own predecessor,'⁷ *i.e.* St. Innocent. St. Augustine is meeting the cavils of the Pelagians, who wished to make out that the Pope, St. Zosimus,

---

¹ Paulini *Libell. ad Zosim.* apud Baron. ad ann. 418.
² Zosim. *Ep.* i. *ad Africanos.*   ³ *Innocentii Ep.* xxx.
⁴ Marius Mercator, i. 4.   ⁵ *Sermon on the Rule of Faith*, Pref. p. xiv.
⁶ Aug. lib. ii. *ad Bonif.* cap. 3.   ⁷ Cf. *Lib. de Pecc. Orig.*, cap. 6 and 7.

had favoured their cause; and by an appeal to the actual history of the case, he overthrows their contention, and in doing this he answers Dr. Pusey by anticipation.

II. Moreover, St. Zosimus did not absolve these heretics there and then, but wrote to Africa for any 'instruments' of information, and said that if no one offered within two months to present a further case against Cœlestius and Pelagius, he should consider all doubt removed.[1] He had received their letter of entreaty, he says, before he gave judgment.[2] The African Fathers had met and represented to the Pope that his absolving these heretics would cause great confusion. They said that they decided that the decision of St. Innocent should hold good *until* Pelagius should confess that the doctrine he had taught was false.[3]

Zosimus was really acting with the caution of a judge: and as a judge he was in the right. It is the office of a judge to give sentence according to the evidence produced, and Zosimus was, from a formal point of view, right in his decision to hear Cœlestius and Pelagius. They professed amendment, and until evidence of their insincerity was forthcoming, Zosimus was in duty bound to admit them to a hearing. Dr. Pusey is mistaken in nearly every assertion that he makes on this subject. He says that Zosimus 'formally acquitted' Cœlestius. He only promised to do so if nothing from Africa turned up to the contrary, but meanwhile he discovered his insincerity. Dr. Pusey also says that Cœlestius 'presented to Zosimus an heretical confession of faith.' Now St. Augustine expressly says that this document was not heretical. He calls it 'Catholic.' Whence this tremendous difference between St. Augustine and Dr. Pusey?

III. St. Augustine shall explain. He says that Cœlestius and Pelagius promised submission and correction, if in anything they were judged to be wrong. This, according to our saint, stamped the document as Catholic. There were errors contained in it, it is true; but St. Zosimus himself says to the Africans that they have misunderstood the text of his letters, as a whole, 'as though we had given credence to Cœlestius *in all things*, and without discussing his words, had

---

[1] *Ep.* i.   [2] *Ep.* iii.   [3] Prosper, *Lib. c. Coll.* cap. v. n. 3.

assented, so to speak, to every syllable.'[1] It was the submission promised to the Apostolic See, which made Zosimus accept them as worthy of a hearing, and it was this that, St. Augustine expressly says, made the document 'Catholic in its meaning.'[2]

Pelagius said of his confession of faith: 'In which, if anything has been laid down unskilfully or incautiously, we desire to be corrected by you, who hold both the faith and the See of Peter; but if this our confession is approved by the judgment of your apostolate, then, whoever shall affix a stain on my character will prove himself to be unlearned, or ill-willed, or even not a Catholic, and not me to be a heretic.'

This was the addition which in St. Augustine's judgment made the document strictly Catholic in tone.

Cœlestius likewise said, 'We offer them' (*i.e.* their teachings) 'to be approved by your apostolic judgment [lit. the judgment of your apostolate], so that if perchance any error of ignorance has crept in upon us, as being men, it may be corrected by your sentence.'

Consequently, Marius Mercator, whose authority is of great moment, says that Cœlestius 'by frequent answers' gave hopes that he condemned the heads of teaching for which he had been condemned at Carthage, and that this was the reason why 'he was thought worthy of some kindness by that holy bishop' (Zosimus), for he 'was commanded with special urgency' to renounce what had there been objected against him.[3]

I have said that Zosimus was acting in the spirit of a real judge, and this his letter to the Africans shows. They had really acted without the proper procedure. Although (as it proved) substantially right, they were formally wrong. They had acted on the accusation of two deposed bishops, Eros and Lazarus, whose motives were not beyond question, and who,

---

[1] Zos. *Ep.* iii.

[2] He says (*Ep.* clvii. *ad Opt.*) that 'the Catholic faith' is so clear in Zosimus' letter 'that it is not lawful for Christians to doubt concerning it.' And that it was Catholic 'because it is the part of a Catholic mind' to do as Cœlestius then pretended to do, viz. consent to the letters of Pope Innocent (*c. du. Ep. Pelag.* lib. ii. c. 5).

[3] *Common. sup. nomine Cœlestii*, cap. i. § 4.

as degraded from their office, had no longer the right of accusation.[1] Zosimus, who had the care of all the Churches, pointed out the evils that would ensue if such wandering stormy petrels as Eros and Lazarus were allowed to enter upon the *rôle* of accusers of others. And in their previous trial the Africans had failed in duty towards Cœlestius, who had given notice of appeal to Rome; for, although they appear to have respected the appeal, they took no care to have it properly conducted. It must be remembered also that Zosimus did not rehandle the dogmatic question. It was merely with the sincerity of Cœlestius and Pelagius that he dealt, and in this he was deceived. But this has nothing to do with his infallibility. Rome has never taught, Rome does not teach to-day, that the occupant of the Holy See cannot be deceived, but only that when he is led to determine a matter of faith or of the moral law as of obligation on the whole Church, he is secure of divine assistance.

The whole case, therefore, of Zosimus is outside the region of infallibility, as that infallibility is defined in the Vatican decree. As Facundus, the African writer, says, in reference to the whole matter, 'Simplicity, through not penetrating the wiliness of the wicked, ought not to be reckoned a crime;' and, as St. Augustine says, Pelagius could not deceive the Church of Rome beyond a certain point. Zosimus discovered that Cœlestius was not in earnest, summoned him to appear, and on his non-appearance excommunicated and anathematised him.

IV. But he did more than that. He drew up an encyclical on the matter of faith, which consisted of an enlarged form of the decree of Innocent, accepted by the African Church; and by the advice of St. Augustine, the subscription to this was made obligatory on all bishops, and on the laity whenever suspected of heretical leanings.[2] The emperor gave the aid of his civil authority, and St. Augustine of his

---

[1] This, at any rate, was the view of Zosimus. Tillemont has done his best to defend them. But see Garnier's notes to Marius Mercator for an answer (Migne's edition).

[2] In writing to the Africans the emperor spoke of his rescript as agreeing with their decision, which was true. But it was also true that in a higher sense he followed the judgment of Zosimus. Cf. Possidius, *Vita S. Aug.* cap. xviii.

pen, which for some years he devoted to this subject, for the settlement of which he claimed the decree of St. Innocent and the encyclical of St. Zosimus embodying and enforcing that decree.

St. Zosimus, in writing to the Africans concerning his decision to allow Cœlestius a hearing, said: 'Although the tradition of the Fathers has attributed so great authority to the Apostolic See, that no one would venture to dispute concerning its judgment, and has always guarded the same by canons and regulations, and the current discipline of the Church up to this time, by its laws, pays due reverence to the name of Peter, from whom she traces her descent (for canonical antiquity by the judgments of all willed that such power should accrue to this Apostle, derived also from the very promise of Christ our God, that he could loose what was bound and bind what was loosed, an equal condition of power was given to those who obtained the inheritance of the see with his approval, for he has the care as well of all the Churches as in a special manner of this his own see. . . . Since, then, Peter is the head of such authority, and he has confirmed the subsequent desires of all our ancestors, that the Roman Church should be sustained by human *as well as* divine laws . . .), nevertheless, though such is our authority, that no one can withdraw himself from our judgment, we have done nothing which we have not of our own accord brought to your knowledge by our letters,' &c.

I produce this passage by way of showing the kind of teaching which Africa received from Rome, and which nowhere in St. Augustine's voluminous writings finds any contradiction: with which, on the contrary, his teaching, as seen above, fully harmonises.

We look in vain in the history of the Church of North Africa at this time for any disclaimer, any suggestion, that Rome was not the See of the Apostle Peter, and, as such, the inheritor of peculiar powers of jurisdiction. She assumed this position as in duty bound; she instinctively quoted the divine authority by which she acted, and Africa on the whole listened, applauded, co-operated, and obeyed. Such is the only conclusion that can be drawn from the facts quoted above. So dependent was Africa on Rome, that when the Donatists boasted that some Easterns had written letters of sympathy, St. Augustine argued that these Easterns must have been Arians, because ' never would an Eastern Catholic [Church] write to the Bishop of Carthage, passing over the Bishop of Rome ' [1]—in other words, all ecclesiastical communication would come from the East through Rome.[2] And in this great contest with Pelagianism, Prosper, in his historical defence of St. Augustine against Cassian, writes, with the knowledge of a contemporary, that 'the Pope Zosimus of blessed memory added the strength of his own judgment to the decrees of the African Councils, and armed the right hands of all the prelates *with the sword of Peter* to the destruction of the impious.'

§ III.—*Apiarius, or the Dispute as to a particular Exercise of Papal Jurisdiction and the best Mode of Procedure in regard to the inferior Clergy.*

I. But a question arose as to the best method of exercising this jurisdiction of the See of Peter over the Church of North Africa. The course of appeal was in the case of bishops, first, to the province, next to a general synod, and then to Rome. But in regard to priests and deacons, the Africans drew up a canon in A.D. 418 to the effect that these 'inferior' clergy could appeal first to bishops in the neighbourhood then to the primate of a province, or to a national synod, but no further.[3] Pope Zosimus had thought fit to disregard the mode of procedure afterwards laid down in this their canon, by admitting a priest named Apiarius to communion. He afterwards commissioned his legate, Faustinus, to impress upon the Africans that his procedure was not novel, but that its principle had been included in the Nicene canons. The

---

[1] *Con. Cresconium*, lib. iii. cap. 34, § 38.

[2] The communication about the Nicene canons was by agreement with Rome.

[3] Just as in England there is no legal appeal in a criminal case from the verdict of a British jury; which is an instance of the truth that the right of access to the supreme authority is not an essential consequence of its supremacy. The authority, still supreme, may be exercised by an inferior court. It is, in a word, all a matter of arrangement.

Africans had not this canon in their own copies; they therefore asked leave to communicate with the East, and see if their copies tallied with those at Rome, and, indeed, they insisted that they ought to be allowed thus to assure themselves as to the gap in their own copies. Meanwhile, St. Augustine proposed that they should act in obedience to the regulations which Zosimus had included amongst the canons of Nicæa. They did not say that they would not obey, even if their own copies of the canons were found to be correct. They said they would consider the question further.

Now, without entering here into the question whether the canons of general councils were above the Pope or not, it is certain that the Popes regarded themselves as the custodians of these councils, and as bound in conscience to govern according to their requirements. It was, therefore, quite consistent with respect for the Pope's supremacy to plead that he was in this instance departing from the canonical regulations. A Catholic bishop now might do the same, if a case arose; and it may be added, that since the Church has a human side, a little warmth is wont to arise over such contentions when they are of great interest to the parties engaged.

It was, therefore, no failure in obedience, or respect, on the part of the African Fathers, to say what they did on this occasion. The failure would have been in resisting the Papal decision if, after common consultation, it did not harmonise with their own judgment. To this pass, however, matters never came. History deserts us just when we should have wished her to speak; we only know that the Church in North Africa eventually settled down to the arrangement which Zosimus called that of a Nicene canon.

II. But this is to anticipate. The copies of the Nicene canons from the East arrived in 419,[1] and we hear nothing more of

---

[1] There was no sort of infallibility about the version of the canon that Atticus sent from Constantinople; nor is it at all certain that the Alexandrians possessed the canons intact. Neither of them ever acted as though the African contention were vital. And, indeed, the Africans put in a saving clause as to clinging to their own custom, viz. 'if they should be strictly observed by you in Italy.' They imply that they would be guided by Italian custom. Antioch did not send her canons. Cf. note at the end of Appendix II., p. 474.

the matter until four years afterwards, when the same scandalous priest came on to the scene, again appealed to Rome, and was again unhappily absolved. This was under Celestine. Meanwhile the Papal legate had succeeded in making himself obnoxious to the Africans, and they seem to have made an effort to do away with legates *a latere* for ever. They accordingly wrote a letter in which they entreated St. Celestine to send no more legates. They also 'earnestly entreat'[1] him to allow matters to be terminated (they are alluding to the case of the priest Apiarius, not to the case of bishops) where they arose. They cannot suppose that Almighty God would give wisdom to one man (in allusion to Faustinus, who had ' opposed the whole assembly of bishops ') over against innumerable bishops ; and to drag cases all the way to Rome involved the impossibility of having the proper array of witnesses, and as for legates *a latere*, no canon provides for such.

The letter in which these statements occur differs in tone from any other communication from the African Church : it is evidently written with a tinge of bitterness ; but one or two points are worthy of special notice. First, they do not ask St. Celestine not in any case to admit persons excommunicated at a distance (*e.g.* in Africa) to communion, nor do they ask him under no circumstances to reverse the judgments of the Africans ; they only ask him not to do this ' too readily, hastily, and unduly.' They do not oppose the principle of Papal jurisdiction, but urge, as they had every right to do, great care in its exercise. Secondly, they give a reason why the presence of a legate *a latere* is to be deprecated. It is not that he represents a false principle of jurisdiction, but that it leads to pride. Faustinus had evidently been lording it over Africa. They had borne with him so far, for it was not contrary to their faith to be ruled from Rome, but they trust St. Celestine—nay, they are sure they can rely on him—not to send any more, 'lest we should seem to introduce the smoky pride of the world.' These ' executors ' of the Papal mandates were apt, as we learn from St. Augustine, to be accompanied

---

[1] ' Impendio deprecamur.'

with great military escorts, and this did not, so they considered, tend to peace. It did not impress the heathen. It was to be deprecated, 'lest we' (*i.e.* we Christians here in Africa) 'should seem to introduce the pride of the world.' Faustinus was not the inheritor of the Papal *charisma*, and did not understand matters as well as the African bishops themselves. So that they say one could only defend his position on the supposition that God could inspire one man with wisdom to the depreciation of innumerable bishops.

Much capital has been made out of this letter by one or two slight perversions of its terms. It has been assumed, for instance, that the 'one man' to whom the Africans here objected meant the Pope himself. But this is impossible. Not only is it the fact that Faustinus, *as the bishops said*, 'opposed the whole assembly,' and so, obviously, supplied the subject of their remark, but the Africans knew well that in all such cases the Pope never did act alone, he received appeals in Synod; so that the remark about the 'one man' being unequal to a number of bishops cannot apply to his Holiness. Again, a great many writers in defence of their theory have translated the words 'lest we should seem to introduce the pride of the world,' as though, again, the bishops were speaking of the Pope instead of themselves as a body in Africa. Archbishop Laud deliberately turns the 'we' into 'he.' Canon Bright understands it of the Pope, and likewise Mr. Puller—a most unreasonable supposition.

III. Once more, it is constantly argued that the Africans, instead of merely doing their best by earnest entreaty ('impendio deprecamur') to secure a particular mode of procedure, or to limit it to the case of bishops, were resisting the doctrine of Papal jurisdiction in itself. But the whole of the contemporary history forbids such a supposition. The ideal of Church government was, to the African mind, that priests should never be allowed to appeal beyond Africa, and that the cases of bishops should be managed by Papal commissions consisting of African bishops. Rome did not consent to bind herself to the former arrangement, but she had employed the latter. St. Augustine's visit to Mauritania—in the very year of the first council, in which the bishops promised to act in obedience to Zosimus' interpretation of the Nicene canons—is a case in point. The Pope sent St. Augustine, as his commissioner, with some others, to settle the affairs of these Mauritanian Bishops on the spot. St. Augustine was strictly the Pope's legate for the occasion. He tells us himself that he was 'enjoined by the venerable Pope Zosimus, Bishop of the Apostolic See;' and his friend St. Possidius, himself an African bishop, says in his Life of St. Augustine that he (Augustine) went to Mauritania, 'compelled by the letters of the Apostolic See, for the termination of other necessities of the Church,' *i.e.* not merely for a conference with the Donatist bishop Emeritus. St. Augustine gives a glimpse of the cases he had to settle in another passage. They were questions of precedency between bishops. Thus the ideal of Church government in the eyes of the North African Church was not that there should be no appeal to Rome in the case of bishops—not that they should act independently of Rome, but that the authority of the Apostolic See should be exercised through the medium of an episcopal commission, consisting of African bishops, and not by a legate sent from Rome itself. It was a question of procedure, not of the right of jurisdiction itself.

If this letter on which so much has been built is genuine, there is another argument to be derived from it to show that they could not have meant to withdraw their dependence on the Apostolic See. One of the signatories was the celebrated Anthony, who himself just about the same time prosecuted an appeal to Rome against St. Augustine. The Primate of Numidia favoured the appeal, and St. Augustine acted on the supposition of an appeal being a legitimate course of action. The only answer that has ever been given to this is that which was suggested in the 'Defensio Cleri Gallicani,' and which, corrected of its tremendous blunder, appears in Mr. Puller's 'Primitive Saints and the See of Rome.' The 'Defensio' (I forbear to call it Bossuet's, as it is uncertain how far it is his handiwork [1]), in a passage of much bitterness against

[1] Mr. Puller here, as always, calls it Bossuet's, and indulges in some sarcasm against Lupus, who, however, turns out to be accurate, whilst 'Bossuet' commits a huge blunder. I suspect that Bossuet's handiwork is mainly visible in such passages as that on Hormisdas' Formulary.

Christianus Lupus, the eminent canonist, says that if Lupus had read the letter attentively he would have discovered 'that it was written in the beginning of Celestine's reign [which is true], before the replies had arrived from the East about the Nicene canons, at which time we have seen that appeals were permitted by the Africans,' &c.

Now we know for certain that the answer about the Nicene canons arrived in the end of the year 419. Mr. Puller himself admits this. We know also that St. Celestine did not begin his reign until 422. Thus we are told by Bossuet (if it be his writing) that a letter written in 422 or 423 was prior in point of time to some replies given in 419!

Mr. Puller adopts another argument, or rather, the same argument with the omission of this blunder. He says that the interval during which the African Fathers promised to accept appeals to Rome lasted for five years. There is not a word in the records to justify this assertion. It is a pure assumption, and not only does it rely on no foundation of fact, but it apparently contradicts the record. The African Fathers promised to obey St. Zosimus' interpretation of the Nicene arrangements 'for a short time . . . until we had investigated the statutes of the Nicene Council.' The statutes of the council had arrived in 419. Does Mr. Puller suppose that the African Fathers were still poring over those statutes some four years afterwards? Yet he says that during that interval, which he describes as 'five or, as some say, seven years,' 'appeals to Rome from Africa in the case of bishops in accordance with the agreement' were permitted, the agreement being that they should be permitted until they had investigated the Nicene statutes, which had arrived four years since, during which interval they had held council after council, and yet had never, so far as any records go, mentioned the subject! All is plain enough if we suppose that they had learnt something further from Rome, *i.e.* either that the genuine copy of the Nicene Council was that which was preserved at Rome, or that the Sardican canons were a due appendix to the Nicene.

But, on the theory against which I am contending, we have to suppose that Bishop Anthony, strongly disapproving of appeals, yet himself prosecuted an appeal to Rome and induced the Primate of Numidia to back his appeal, and that St. Augustine followed the matter to Rome (all of which is admitted history); and all this was done on the ground that they were living in an interval in which appeals were permitted, but which was shortly to be closed as contrary to the admitted and vital principles of Church government! We have also to suppose that a month or so after the first council had decided upon this interval St. Augustine went off to Mauritania to act as Papal legate, although (on the same theory) the Pope had no jurisdiction in that country. The African bishops behaved, on this theory, much as schoolboys who have a little leave to do a number of things they wanted to do, and take full advantage of the leave; whereas all is plain and natural on the supposition that the African bishops believed, as St. Augustine did, that when Rome had spoken the case was at an end, and not till then, in the case of bishops. On the further matter, as to priests, they wished for an arrangement which would have modified the exercise of the Pope's jurisdiction, without attacking the root principle of that jurisdiction.

IV. But, in point of fact, the gravest suspicion rests on this letter, which has been made to do such service against the principle of appeals. Had such a document been handed to St. Augustine for inspection he must have disclaimed it as no Catholic document. In his conference with the Donatists he objected to the production of documents without dates.[1] The Donatists replied that many councils had no date. St. Augustine to this replied that such might be the case with schismatical councils, but not with Catholic documents. He quoted the prophets in his behalf, who say in whose reign they prophesied. He more than once enunciated this vital principle, that you have no right to bring a document into court, purporting to be that of a Catholic council, unless it has the name of the consul and the day.

This letter, on which Dr. Pusey so much relied, has no date.

[1] Cf. *Breviculus Collationis cum Donatistis*, 3ii diei, cap. xv. 27 : 'Catholicorum concilia consules et dies semper habuisse.'

Further, it comes before us as emanating from a universal synod of Africa—the peer of the great meeting of 419.[1] Yet we have no record of this synod. This would not be fatal if we had the date, but there is no date.

Further, when we examine the list of signatories we discover that their number is fifteen. It adds that there were others—viz. those whom they represented, as would be natural, but it only gives fifteen names. Now fifteen was the exact number of legates fixed upon shortly before to represent a universal synod. But the president was never counted in, so that though fifteen is the right number, there ought to be at least one other name mentioned to make the account correct.

But when we examine the list of signatories we find that it differs altogether from that of the fifteen who were appointed. Why is this? The 'Defensio Cl. Gall.' (Bossuet) says that other legates had been appointed. It is curious that we have no record of this, whilst the names were so carefully recorded, with the provinces, in the unquestioned list issued by the unquestioned universal synod.

But whose names are wanting? Why, instead of St. Augustine, St. Alypius, and Restitutus, the three bishops who had hitherto represented Numidia, we find one bishop of that province, and that is Anthony, the name of the scandalous bishop who had appealed to Rome against St. Augustine. This was the man who is supposed to have represented Numidia instead of those three saints, and to have signed the heated letter against appeals!

I submit that this is an insufficient foundation on which to rest the position that the Church of North Africa repudiated the supreme jurisdiction of that see which it called in every letter, I had almost said in every other sentence of some letters, 'the Apostolic See.' She accepted St. Innocent's letters with all their Vatican teaching, whilst her subsequent writers never allude to this discussion as involving any such repudiation.[2]

---

[1] In my letter to the Bishop of Lincoln (1893) there is a misprint on this subject. The 'not' should be erased on p. 38 as the argument requires.

[2] There is a forged letter which does, but the forgery has been exposed with ample evidence. See also note at the end of Appendix II.

CHAPTER XVIII.

THE COUNCIL OF EPHESUS.

I. A PECULIAR importance attaches to the Council of Ephesus, from an historical point of view, from the fact that it is the first of the Œcumenical Councils of which we have anything like a full and unquestioned narrative. Accordingly, I shall proceed to test the theory of independent national Churches by the history of this council.

It must be remembered that that theory regards the most complete severance from the Apostolic See as compatible with membership in the One, Holy, Catholic and Apostolic Church; and that it appeals especially to the Church of those four General Councils which St. Gregory compared to the four Holy Gospels. I propose, therefore, to show, from a review of the council, that nothing but the most complete misinterpretation of the Acts of this council could enable anyone to consider the above theory as in harmony with the teaching of the early Christian Church.

The council was concerned with the question of the union of the two natures in the One Divine Person of our Redeemer. Was it a substantial or an accidental union? The whole question of the world's salvation hung upon the answer. Both St. Celestine, the Pope, and St. Cyril of Alexandria emphasise this fact. St. Celestine, in his letter to Nestorius, says, that 'we complain that those words have been removed [*i.e.* by Nestorius] which promise us the hope of all life and salvation.' St. Cyril again and again strikes the same note. Dr. Salmon would have done well to have remembered this in his criticisms[1] on this great champion of the faith.

---
[1] *Infallibility of the Church,* p. 312.

Up to the time of the Council of Ephesus expressions[1] had been used concerning the union of the two natures in Christ which were meant in an orthodox sense, but which were liable to misinterpretation. St. Ignatius had spoken of Christ as 'bearing flesh;' Tertullian had described Him as 'clothed with flesh;' and the early Fathers had often used the word 'mixture' ($\kappa\rho\hat{a}\sigma\iota\varsigma$) of the union of the two natures.

But a term had been in use which, if rightly understood, safeguarded the truth of the ἕνωσις of the two natures. I mean, of course, the term $\Theta\epsilon o\tau\acute{o}\kappa o\varsigma$, or Mother of God, as applied to our Blessed Lady. The term had not been as thoroughly sifted, and authoritatively explained by the Church, as it was destined to be, owing to the heresy of Nestorius; but, as the Patriarch of Antioch bade Nestorius reflect, it had been in frequent use.

II. Nestorius had entered upon his career as archbishop with the boast that if the emperor would give him the earth cleared of heretics, he would give him heaven in exchange, and that if His Imperial Majesty would assist him in putting heretics to rout, he would assist him to do the same with his Persian foes. He was inexcusably cruel to his heterodox subjects, but he soon himself plunged into a heresy which cut at the root of the Christian faith—attributing to our Divine Lord a human personality, and thereby denying the substantial union between the two natures. His writings found their way into Egypt, which was in the patriarchate of Alexandria, presided over at that time by the great St. Cyril. St. Cyril was consequently bound to take notice of the danger, and a correspondence ensued between him and Nestorius. St. Cyril at length appealed to the Pope. He held off from this final step as long as he could, from the same feeling as St. Celestine himself expressed when he said that he could have wished never to have seen the letters of Nestorius, 'lest I should be compelled to pass judgment on so serious a matter.'

III. St. Celestine was a man full of zeal for the faith and of great piety, judging from his letters. Dr. Wordsworth appeals to him as the best judge of Cyril's character and

---

[1] Cf. *Cath. Dict.* 'Council of Ephesus.'

conduct, although he mistakes his share in the affair of Nestorius. He says: 'Perhaps there could not have been a more impartial judge of the parties in the struggle than the Bishop of Rome. Celestine was a calm spectator of the controversy, and in a review of it it may be well to enumerate his letters as indicative of his bearing with regard to it, and also as a summary of its history.'[1]

We shall presently see that St. Celestine was by no means a mere 'spectator of the controversy,' and that his letters by no means bear out Dr. Wordsworth's general review of the Council. But that writer shows a true instinct in taking the Pope's estimate of St. Cyril, in preference to that of the latter's enemies, whom Dr. Salmon follows,[2] for St. Celestine's estimate is that of all after time. 'The bishop of Rome,' says Dr. Wordsworth, 'did not suppose Cyril to have been actuated by any unworthy motives in this controversy.' In this matter Dr. Pusey is at one with Dr. Wordsworth.[3]

St. Celestine, on being appealed to by St. Cyril, at once convoked a synod, as was customary with the bishops of Rome, and gave St. Cyril a full and emphatic answer. He authorised him to act for him judicially. So far St. Cyril's action towards Nestorius had been an office of charity, not an act of jurisdiction. He did not think that he would do well even to excommunicate him from his own Church without consulting Celestine, although he says he might legitimately have done that much. When he wrote to the Egyptian monks he was writing to people within his own jurisdiction, but he had now laid the matter before one who could deal with cases that concerned the whole Church, and with the question of deposition as well as excommunication.[4] The correspondence that passed between Alexandria and Rome on this occasion is, however, so important that, at the cost of repetition, I will give a summary of the two letters.[5]

IV. St. Cyril begins with giving his reason for breaking the silence which he had kept as long as he dared. The ancient

---

[1] Wordsworth's *Church History*, vol. iv. pp. 232-3.
[2] *Loc. cit.*   [3] Pref. to St. Cyril's Works. *Lib. of the Fathers.*
[4] Cf. *Antifebronius vindicatus*, pt. i. p. 506.   [5] Mansi, t. iv. p. 1011, *seq.*

customs of the Churches (he says) persuade us to communicate such matters to your Holiness; I, therefore, write of necessity. Nestorius (he says) from the commencement of his episcopate has been disseminating amongst his own people, and the strangers who flock to Constantinople from all quarters, absurd ideas, contrary to the faith. He has sent Nestorius' homilies to Celestine. It was in his mind to tell Nestorius at once that he could no longer hold communion with him; but he thought it better to hold out to him a helping hand first and exhort him by letters. Nestorius, however, only tried in every way to circumvent him. At last a bishop, named Dorotheus, exclaimed in Nestorius' presence, ' If any one shall call Mary the mother of God, let him be anathema.' A crisis was reached by this expression; a great disturbance arose amongst the people of Constantinople. With few exceptions they refrained from communion—nearly all the monasteries and great part of the senate—for fear of receiving harm to their faith. He had found, moreover, that Nestorius' writings had been introduced into Egypt, and in consequence had written an encyclical to the Egyptian monasteries to confirm them in the faith. Copies of this finding their way to Constantinople, Nestorius had resented Cyril's action. He accused Cyril of having read the Fathers wrongly. Cyril says he wrote direct to Nestorius, with a compendious exposition of the faith, exhorting him to conform to this. All the bishops, adds Cyril, are with me, especially those of Macedonia. Nestorius, however, considered that he alone understood the Scriptures. While all orthodox bishops and saints confess Christ to be God, and the Virgin to be the mother of God, Θεοτόκος, he alone who denies this is supposed, forsooth, to be in the right. The people of Constantinople now began, says St. Cyril, to look for aid outside their province. St. Cyril felt that a 'dispensation was entrusted to him,' and that he should have to answer on the day of judgment for silence in this matter. He does not, however, feel that he can confidently withdraw himself from communion with Nestorius before communicating these things to His Holiness.

'Deign, therefore, to decide what seems right (τυπῶσαι τὸ δοκοῦν), whether we ought to communicate at all with him, or to tell him plainly that no one communicates with a person who holds and teaches what he does. Further, the purpose of your Holiness ought to be made known by letter to the most religious and God-loving bishops of Macedonia, *and to all the bishops of the East,* for we shall then give them, according to their desire, the opportunity of standing together in unity of soul and mind, and lead them to contend earnestly (ἐπαγωνίσασθαι) for the orthodox Faith which is being attacked. As regards Nestorius, our fathers, who have said that the Holy Virgin is the mother of God, are, together with us who are here to-day, involved in anathema; for although he did not like to do this with his own lips, still, by sitting and listening to another, viz. Dorotheus, he has helped him to do it, for immediately on coming from the throne he communicated him at the holy mysteries.' He (St. Cyril) has therefore sent his Holiness the materials for forming a judgment.

V. St. Celestine in a beautiful letter, in answer, expresses his joy in the midst of sadness at Cyril's purity of faith. He endorses his teaching, and embraces him in the Lord, as present in his letters. Still (says the Pope) we are of one mind concerning Christ our Lord! He compares Cyril to a good shepherd, and Nestorius not even to a hireling, but to a wolf, who is destroying his own sheep. Our Lord Jesus Christ, whose own ' generation ' is questioned, shows us that we should toil for one sheep; how much more for one shepherd! We ought, therefore, ' to shut him out from the sheep, unless there is hope of his conversion. This we earnestly desire. But *if he persists,* an open sentence must be passed on him, for a wound, when it affects the whole body, must be at once cut away. For what has he to do with those who are of one mind amongst themselves—he who considers that he alone knows what is best, and dissents from our faith ? Let then all those whom he has removed remain in communion [with the Church], and give him to understand that he cannot be in communion with us if he persists in this path of perversity in opposition to the Apostolic teaching. *Wherefore assuming the authority of our See, and acting in our stead and place with delegated authority* (ἐξουσία), *you shall* execute a sentence of this kind (ἐκβιβάσεις ἀπόφασιν), not without strict severity, viz. that unless within ten days after this admonition of ours he anathematises, in written confession, his evil teaching, and promises for the future to confess the faith concerning the birth of Christ our God, which both the Church of Rome and that of your Holiness, *and the whole Christian religion* preaches, forthwith your Holiness will provide for that Church. And let him know that he is to be altogether removed from our body. . . . We have written the same to our brothers and fellow-bishops John, Rufus, Juvenal, and Flavian, whereby *our judgment* concerning him, *yea rather, the judgment of Christ our Lord*, may be manifest.'

It would be impossible to express with greater clearness the claim involved in the Papal supremacy, as understood at this hour, than is done by these two letters. 'Confirm thy brethren' was the divine injunction to the Prince of the Apostles; 'I have prayed for thee, that thy faith fail not; thou, in thy turn, confirm thy brethren.'[1] Celestine was now exemplifying this law of the Church's life, and in doing so he did but add one more to the number of saintly Popes who had already been conspicuous for the support they rendered to the rest of the orthodox bishops in the defence of the great mystery of our Faith: *e.g.* St. Dionysius supporting one bishop of Alexandria previous to the Arian struggle, St. Julius another, the great Confessor Bishop of Alexandrias in the midst of that struggle; St. Damasus supporting the bishops in general in the struggle with the Macedonian heresy; and now, St. Celestine 'confirming' St. Cyril. And in each

---

[1] Dr. Döllinger parodies the Church's application of this text to the successor of St. Peter when he calls it 'far from being a guarantee of infallibility for every single dictum on an article of ecclesiastical doctrine.' No theologian ever laid down such a childish principle, nor did the Church ever call on Dr. Döllinger to believe it. He insinuates the same absurdity when he says, 'the exhortation that Peter should strengthen his brethren by no means involves a promise that he would really do so *in every single instance*.'[*] Our Lord promises the security arising from his own prayer; and that security need not be, and never was, stretched to include 'every single instance,' of whatsoever kind.

It will be admitted, however, that in the subject-matter of Celestine's letter, the very foundations of our holy Faith were concerned.

[*] *Declarations and Letters on the Vatican Decrees*, Eng. trans. p. 12.

case the support was rendered by the See of St. Peter less in the way of argument than by a simple faithfulness to the tradition of the Church: more, that is, in a divine than a human way, more by authority than by dialectic skill. The Church lives on authority, not on argument, even as our Lord 'spake as one having authority,' and not as the Scribes and Pharisees with their subtle dialectic. St. Agatho, when he sent his legates to the Sixth Council, said that they were not versed in subtle interpretations of the Scriptures—such as had so frequently led the East astray—nor were they illustrious in eloquence, but they had something better, viz. a full knowledge of the 'tradition of the Apostolic See, as it has been maintained by my predecessors, the Apostolic Pontiffs.' This was real history, and this they possessed. Nestorius expressed his contempt for the Holy See when condemned by it, and affected to despise St. Celestine. He called him 'one too simple to fathom the force of the doctrines.' But, as Dr. Pusey well remarks,[1] 'It did not occur to Nestorius that divine truth is seen by simple piety, not by proud intellect.' The letters of Celestine are by no means devoid of argumentative power at times; they are, however, more the letters of a man of strong character in high authority than of the dialectician or the orator. He writes as one steeped in the writings of prophets, evangelists, and apostles, but his piety is of a masculine character, and his Scriptural quotations are full of point. This particular letter to St. Cyril played a most important part in the history of Christian doctrine, for it was referred to as authoritative by the council itself, and as determining their synodical act.

VI. The two letters together, St. Cyril's and St. Celestine's, contain the following important points.

(i.) It was an 'ancient custom,' according to St. Cyril, for such important matters as the deposition of an heretical archbishop to be referred to Rome. St. Cyril says that he writes to Rome 'as a matter of necessity.' He does not even separate Nestorius from communion with his own patriarchate until he has written to Rome.

(ii.) He asks St. Celestine to prescribe what he judges best

[1] *Introd. to some Works of Cyril*, p. 64. *Lib. of the Fathers.*

in the matter; to give the *formal decision* on this important case, and to notify his decision to all the bishops of the East. Canon Bright merely calls this writing in 'very deferential terms'[1] to the Bishop of Rome. Would it not surprise some of his readers to know *how* deferential the terms of St. Cyril's letter were? He uses a word which occurs again and again in the Acts of the councils in reference to the relation of the Pope to the condemnation of Nestorius, asking him $\tau υπῶσαι\ τὸ\ δοκοῦν$—words which are a sort of refrain for a year to come; they form the key-note to the proceedings at Ephesus. Bossuet remarks upon this expression, that 'it signifies, in Greek, to declare juridically; $τύπος$ is a rule, a sentence, and $τυπῶσαι\ τὸ\ δοκοῦν$ is to declare one's opinion judicially. The Pope alone could do it. Neither Cyril, nor any other patriarch, had the power to depose Nestorius, who was not their subject: the Pope alone did it, and no one was found to exclaim against it, because his authority extended over all.'

(iii.) St. Celestine adopts throughout his letter to Nestorius, sent with the above letter to Cyril, the same tone of authority as he uses in writing to Cyril. He writes with affectionate anxiety for Nestorius, but with the authority of office. He has no doubt about his prerogative of infallibility in such a matter, and does not hesitate to express his conviction.

Dean Church, in defending[2] his position, and that of others who appeal to the early Church, says that he finds only a mitigated measure of authority 'in the early and undivided Church, and there was no such thing known as infallibility.' And this he calls 'a certain fact,' including in the early and undivided Church the time of the great councils.

But St. Celestine, on being appealed to by St. Cyril to formulate the decision as to Nestorius' excommunication and deposition, at once assumes his infallibility[3] in such a grave matter. The Vatican decree does not go beyond his words, when he says of his own sentence on Nestorius, that it is not so much his, but rather it is 'the divine judgment of Christ our Lord;' and again to the Patriarch of Antioch he says,

---

[1] *Dict. of Chr. Biog.* art. 'Cyril,' p. 766.
[2] *The Oxford Movement*, by Dean Church, p. 185.
[3] As to the matter of faith.

' and let your Holiness know this sentence is passed by us, yea, rather by Christ [our] God.' Just as afterwards the synod, writing to the clergy of Constantinople, calls the executed sentence, being that of Pope and council together, 'the just sentence of the Holy Trinity and their [*i.e.* the bishops' and legates'] divinely inspired judgment.'

(iv.) And again, Celestine is here pronouncing judgment as to what is preached by the 'whole Christian religion,' and decides to cut off Nestorius *from the common unity*.

VII. Dr. Wordsworth speaks of this all-important letter as being simply a statement of 'the orthodox doctrine of the Western Fathers' upon the controversy![1] Celestine, however, states that he is giving the doctrine of the Church of Rome and Alexandria and 'the whole Christian religion,' or, as he expresses it in his letter to Nestorius (going over the same ground), ' the universal Church.' Canon Bright[2] describes it thus:

' Celestine gave Cyril a commission of stringent character (Mansi, iv. 1017). He was " to join the authority of the Roman See *to his own*,' and on the part of Celestine, *as well as for himself*, to warn Nestorius that unless a written retractation were executed within ten days, giving assurance of his acceptance of the faith as to " Christ our God," which was held by the Churches of *Rome and Alexandria*, he would be excluded from the communion of *those Churches*, and provision would be made by them for the Church of Constantinople, *i.e.* by the appointment of an orthodox bishop.'[3]

Now, St. Celestine does not say exactly 'join the authority of the Roman See to *his own*,' which Canon Bright gives as a quotation. There is nothing in the Latin or Greek exactly corresponding to 'his own;' words which would suggest something more than the Papal decision as the source of authority.[4] Neither does Celestine bid St. Cyril warn Nestorius ' on the part of Celestine *as well as for himself*.' He simply constitutes St. Cyril his 'plenipotentiary,' as Dr. Döllinger

[1] *Church History*, vol. iv. p. 210.
[2] *Dictionary of Christian Biography*, art. ' Cyril,' p. 766.
[3] The italics are mine.
[4] Greek σοί, Latin 'adscitâ'—simply terms with which a legate might be commissioned to act.

accurately expressed it.[1] Neither, again, does Celestine speak of the faith held by the Churches of Rome and Alexandria simply, but he adds that it is that of the entire Christian world or religion. And further, which is of much greater importance, he tells Nestorius in the same batch of letters which Cyril was to read and forward, that he will exclude him, not from the communion of ' those Churches ' only, but from the communion also of the entire Christian Church. This latter point is of supreme importance, and it is strange that Dr. Bright should omit it.[2] In this very letter Celestine speaks of Nestorius being separated from ' our body,' by which from the contextual use of ' our,' he could not mean simply his own, nor only his own and Cyril's, but the whole body of the Church. Anyhow, in his letter to Nestorius, which St. Cyril was to read and forward, and which covers the same ground, the Pope says expressly that by this sentence, unless he retracts, he is cut off from the communion of ' the whole Catholic Church (' ab universalis te Ecclesiæ Catholicæ communione dejectum).' This is a vital point, and it is surely not fair to tell the reader that Celestine bade Cyril warn Nestorius that he was to be cut off from the communion of ' those Churches ' (viz. Rome and Alexandria) when, as a matter of fact, he was telling him that he was to be cut off from the communion of the whole Catholic Church. They are words, too, which recur, for in writing to the clergy and people of Constantinople the Pope repeats the sentence in full, which Cyril is to pass on Nestorius. And while he speaks again of the faiths held, not only by the Churches of Rome and Alexandria, but by ' the whole Catholic Church,' he says that Nestorius is to be ' excommunicated from the entire Catholic Church.' The same occurs once more in the Pope's letter to John of Antioch. The Pope there again speaks as clothed with supreme authority, calling his sentence ' the sentence passed by Christ our God,' and it cuts Nestorius off from ' the roll of bishops ' (' episcoporum cœtu ').

St. Celestine thus comes before us at the Council of Ephesus as the foundation of the Church in a crisis of her life

---

[1] ' Bevollmächtiger,' *Lehrbuch* (1843), p. 121.

[2] The same misleading expression (Rome and Alexandria) occurs in this writer's latest work, *Waymarks, &c.* p. 221.

when the reality of our Lord's redemption was at stake, for this was the real point at issue, as he himself and St. Cyril distinctly stated. He is the 'confirmer' of the brethren. He feeds, or governs, the sheep of Christ, supplying them with the τύπος, or authoritative judicial sentence, the form which was to govern their action. He resumes in himself the apostolic government of the Christian Church, and uses the Archbishop of Alexandria, occupant of the second throne in Christendom, to execute his sentence.

VIII. The execution, then, of the Pope's sentence having been entrusted to Cyril, the latter at once wrote to John, Bishop of Antioch, on the state of things. He entreats him to consider what he will do. St. Cyril must have been well aware that he was treading on delicate ground, for Nestorius had been recommended for the See of Constantinople by the Patriarch of Antioch, and the event proved how little John was to be depended upon. Cyril says (M. iv. 1051):

'We shall follow the decisions given by him [Celestine], fearing to lose the communion of such [*i.e.* the whole West], who have not been and are not angry with us on any other account; considering, too, that the judgment and movement is not about matters of little moment, but on behalf of the very faith, and of the Churches which are everywhere disturbed, and of the edification of the people.' In other words, it was an *ex cathedrâ* judgment; it was on a matter of faith.

John of Antioch began well, and wrote to Nestorius, on receiving the Papal decision, urging him to submit, on the ground that, although the time given by the Pope, viz. ten days, was indeed short, still it was a matter in which obedience need not be a matter of days even, but of a single hour; and that the term 'Mother of God,' although capable of abuse, was one which the Fathers had used, and which, therefore, Nestorius could consent to use, attaching to it his own doubtless orthodox meaning. The letter, although urging obedience, differs in its tone from Cyril's, and gives us already a glimpse of a spirit that subsequently led John of Antioch into schismatic action at Ephesus.

St. Cyril wrote also to Juvenal of Jerusalem exhorting

him to assist in writing both to Nestorius and to the people in accordance with the prescribed decree (ὁρισθέντα τύπον), *i.e.* the Papal decision, and suggested that pressure should be brought to bear upon the emperors.

Meanwhile Cyril had summoned a synod at Alexandria, and in conjunction with the bishops, he drew up twelve anathematisms, which he forwarded to Nestorius with the Papal sentence.

IX. Nestorius tried to turn the subject. He artfully appealed to the Pope to know what ought to be done about certain supposed disseminators of Apollinarian errors, with which he ceaselessly charged St. Cyril, and drew up in reply twelve counter-anathematisms, full of erroneous doctrine. But he had devised yet another plan for staying the execution of the sentence—like all heretics, he appealed to the civil power. In this he was probably prompted and joined by others, for there were at that time in Constantinople some disaffected spirits connected with Antioch.

This city—that first heard the name of Christian applied to the followers of Jesus Christ—honoured by the Church as one of the three Sees of Peter—the third 'throne' in Christendom—had long proved a nursery of heretical teaching and religious dissension. Nestorius himself came from Antioch. Whilst there he had come across Theodore of Mopsuestia, the pupil of Diodorus, Bishop of Tarsus, who was the fountain, so far as we can trace things upwards, of all the mischief which occasioned the Council of Ephesus. In opposing Apollinarianism Diodorus had lost the balance of faith, and taught that the union of Godhead and Manhood in the Redeemer was not of substance with substance, but of two personalities; a union of name, authority, and honour. Theodore imbibed his error, and so great and lasting was the magic of Theodore's name that his memory had to be condemned in the Sixth Council. Nestorius had come under Theodore's influence. John of Antioch, in urging Nestorius to obey the Papal decision, alluded to Theodore's withdrawal of certain erroneous expressions as an encouragement; being both of Antioch, they understood the value of such an appeal.

But there was another of Theodore's pupils, the Bishop Julian, a fellow-countryman of Nestorius, who entered into the lists with St. Augustine in favour of Pelagianism, and, with the usual modesty of heretics, compared himself to David, and Augustine to Goliath. This Julian had been deposed by the Holy See for his Pelagian teaching, and previous to the emergence of Nestorianism had found his way to Constantinople with some others in the hope of moving the emperor to call a council to reverse the sentence of the Pope. Two successive Bishops of Constantinople had refused to present him at Court. But it seems, from Celestine's letter to Nestorius, that the latter was on too friendly terms with Julian to please the Pope, and that but for his fear of Celestine he would have presented Julian to the emperor. When the See of Constantinople was vacant, Celestine had been anxious about its future occupant for this very reason, lest he should be one that would use his privilege of introduction in favour of such ecclesiastical 'lepers' as Julian, and lead his Imperial Majesty to call a council for no adequate reason, and so simply disturb the peace of the Church. St. Augustine and the African Church had expressed themselves satisfied with the ruling of the Holy See in regard to Pelagianism. The expression '*Roma locuta est; causa finita est*,' though not the actual words of St. Augustine, are the exact equivalent of what he did say. 'The rescripts have come,' *i.e.* from Rome (which are St. Augustine's words) is the same as 'Rome has spoken,' and the 'case is finished' are his actual words. Capreolus, Bishop of Carthage, writing in the name of the African Church to the synod, goes out of his way to press this point, that the bishops of Africa had accepted the decision of the Holy See, and that the Synod of Ephesus had no right to re-open matters already settled by such authority. He speaks of novel doctrines which 'the authority of the Apostolic See and the judgment of the bishops agreeing together has defeated,' and submits that to treat these as open questions would be to discover a lack of faith. As a matter of fact, the Synod of Ephesus did allude to their case, not to re-open it, but to signify in express terms their adhesion *en bloc* to the decisions of the Holy See.

Julian, however, hoped much from a council, and seeing his opportunity in the appointment of Nestorius to the See of Constantinople, appears to have drawn him into a favourable inclination towards himself, which led him to sound Celestine as to what could be done in regard to such as Julian.¹ There was, indeed, a natural affinity between their heresies. 'Where Pelagius ends, Nestorius begins,' said St. Prosper; and 'Nestorius erred concerning the head, Pelagius concerning the body,' said a council of Western bishops.²

Nestorius then, probably assisted by Julian, turned to the emperor, and made for a general council. St. Cyril had sent four Egyptian bishops to Constantinople to deliver the above-mentioned letters of Celestine and himself to Nestorius with all due circumstance, and Nestorius seems to have been aware of their contents. But before they could reach Constantinople he had represented to the emperor that the Church was in a state of disturbance, and needed the remedy of a general council. Dr. Littledale says that '*the Pope joined* in a petition to the emperor to convoke a general council as the only means of settling the dispute'³—a flight of absurdity which we may leave to Canon Bright to correct, who says that 'Celestine and Cyril were obliged to acquiesce in the decision of the emperor to convoke an œcumenical synod to meet at Ephesus on the following Whitsunday (June 4th, 431) at the request of Nestorius.' It is going a little beyond the facts to say that the Pope and St. Cyril were 'obliged' to acquiesce. The state of things in Constantinople, owing to the presence of Julian and other deposed bishops, may have made Celestine reluctant; but the letter to the synod is full of rejoicing at its gathering. However that may be, St. Celestine gave his consent, and St. Leo's summary of the Council is that it was 'convoked by the precept of Christian princes and the consent of the Apostolical See'—a more adequate summary than Canon Bright's,⁴ who does not mention 'the consent of the Apostolical See.' ⁵

¹ *Ep. Celest. ad Nest.*
² Cf. Chr. Lupus, Append. to *Scholia on the Canons of Ephesus.*
³ *Petrine Claims*, p. 98.
⁴ Bright's *Notes on the Canons of the First Four Councils*, p. 110.
⁵ Preface to *Notes, &c.* p. 6.

Nestorius appears to have worked his plan well. He accused St. Cyril of Apollinarianism, and of generally disturbing the peace of the Church. And it is important to remember that it was to settle the question between Cyril and Nestorius that the emperor, Theodosius II., summoned the metropolitans of the East and a certain number of attendant bishops to Ephesus. It was with no idea of settling matters between Rome and Nestorius, for the emperor had received no intimation of the sentence passed by Celestine. The idea in the mind of the emperor was that Cyril should be on his trial as a disturber of the peace and a restorer of Apollinarianism, and he probably expected Nestorius to take the prominent position. He disliked Cyril, and specially resented his attempt to secure the sympathy of the Empresses on the side of orthodoxy. He was just then growing jealous of Pulcheria's increasing influence, and Cyril had written her a long and magnificent letter on the doctrine of the Incarnation. We know also from a letter of Cyril's that Nestorius hoped to be president. The Council was thus, as Dr. Pusey has well remarked, a 'device of Nestorius,' [1] although it had been seconded by the monks who had been ill treated by him, and had urged the emperor in their despair to convoke a general synod. They did not know what had been done at Rome.

X. But on arriving at Ephesus some time before Pentecost, in the hope, doubtless, of influencing the inauguration of the council, Nestorius was rudely undeceived by the attitude which Memnon, the bishop of the diocese, assumed at once towards himself and his episcopal sympathisers. The doors of St. Mary's Church were closed against them. They complained to the emperor that they could not celebrate the

---

[1] Dr. Pusey's account of the council, written quite at the end of his life as a preface, or a continuation of his son's preface, to some works of St. Cyril, is, probably, the best account of the council that any Anglican has written. He very successfully clears St. Cyril from the aspersions on his character which Dr. Salmon repeats. In that particular point Dr. Wordsworth and Dr. Bright are honourable exceptions to the usual Anglican view of the great saint. Even Dr. Newman, in his Anglican days, falls far below these three writers in the matter (*Histor. Sketches*), and Dr. Salmon ought not to quote his estimate of Cyril as that of 'Cardinal' Newman without noticing the preface which he prefixed as Cardinal (Salmon's *Infallibility of the Church*, p. 307, 2nd edition).

liturgy of Pentecost in the churches of Ephesus. Bishop after bishop, on arriving, must have strengthened Nestorius' conviction that the Papal sentence was accepted, and that the bishops had come, as Count Candidian, the imperial commissioner, afterwards complained,[1] not so much to investigate, as to execute a sentence already passed. Accordingly, as we shall presently see, Nestorius absented himself from the synod.

The day of Pentecost had come, and John, Patriarch of Antioch, had not arrived. Day after day passed, and no Bishop of Antioch. At length bishops came with a message from him that they were not to wait.[2] Some bishops had already fallen ill, many felt the fearful pressure of the want of accommodation, and at last some of them died. As they said the Requiem Mass of one bishop after another, the survivors must have felt keenly the cruelty of the Patriarch of Antioch's procrastination. They knew it to be of set purpose. The synod, in its report to the emperor, assured His Majesty of their conviction that John had delayed from a desire not to be present at Nestorius' condemnation. He allowed friendship to gain the day over zeal for the truth. Accordingly, the bishops began to 'cry out'[3] against Cyril for not beginning; and Cyril yielded to their wishes, himself convinced that John of Antioch did not wish to be present.

On the sixteenth day after Pentecost the synod began its sessions. Dr. Salmon's caustic remarks on the disorderliness of the councils of the Church certainly do not apply to the sessions of this council. He ignores the judicial, orderly, and even majestic tone of the synod itself, and takes his description from circumstances that took place outside the walls of the church, and he relies too unreservedly on the accounts of the schismatics, and further includes in the 'councils of the Church' the Robber Council of Ephesus which succeeded the Œcumenical Council.[4] No wonder he can speak so slightingly of councils, when he confuses 'concilia' and 'conciliabula,' and prefers the accounts of heretics to the narratives of the synod itself. The letter of the synod to the Pope would have

---

[1] Cf. *Acta Conciliabuli adv. Cyrillum.*   [2] 'if I delay.' Cf. p. 341.
[3] Cf. *Ep. Cyr. ad Cler. Const.*
[4] *Infallibility of the Church*, p. 313 et seq.

quite spoilt his thesis, if he had taken that for his authority instead of the letter of the schismatics to the emperor.

XI. Who, then, presided over the council that now met in the Church of St. Mary? According to Dr. Salmon, 'the theory had not yet been heard of in the East which would ascribe the headship of all councils to the Bishop of Rome, present or absent,'[1] and, accordingly, he denies that Celestine was in any sense president at Ephesus. The Bishops of Chalcedon, who asked for delay that they might understand, and thus give an intelligent adhesion to the Tome of St. Leo, thought otherwise, for they speak of the Council of Ephesus as that 'of which the most blessed Celestine, the president of the Apostolic chair, and the most blessed Cyril of great Alexandria, were the governors or presidents,'[2] whilst the Council of Chalcedon, in its definition of faith, expressly says that the Council of Ephesus was presided over by 'Celestine and Cyril.' And the emperors, in their letter after the Council of Chalcedon, confirming the sentence against Eutyches and the monks who sympathised with him, speak of the Ephesine synod as the occasion 'when the error of Nestorius was excluded, under the presidency of Celestine, of the city of Rome, and Cyril, of the city of Alexandria.' The Empress Pulcheria uses the same expression. We have, too, a large number of letters from various bishops to the Emperor Leo, written after the Council of Chalcedon, in reference to the troubles at Alexandria under Bishop Timothy, most of which allude to the Council of Ephesus, and attribute the presidency to Celestine as well as to Cyril.[3] For instance, certain European bishops (and we presume that Dr. Salmon will not rule their witness out of court, coinciding as it does with the 600 bishops of Chalcedon, almost all of them Eastern) depose that the Council of Ephesus was gathered together 'under Celestine, of blessed memory, the successor of the holy and venerable Peter, the guardian of the keys of the Kingdom of Heaven, and under Cyril, Pontiff of Alexandria, of holy memory.' And the bishops of the province of Isauria speak of Cyril, 'who formerly governed the Church of Alexandria, and openly fought against the folly of Nestorius, and was partaker with blessed

[1] *Loc. cit.*   [2] Κυβερνῆται.   [3] Mansi, t. vii. 539-623.

Celestine, the Shepherd of the *Safe* Church of the Romans.' This latter, however, does not necessarily involve presidency. But Julian, Bishop of Cos, in his letter to the emperor, calls the Council of Ephesus that over which presided the thrice blessed 'and most holy Fathers, Celestine, Pontiff of the Roman city, and Cyril, Bishop of Alexandria.' And again, the bishops of Upper Armenia call the council that ' of which the presidents were Celestine and Cyril . . . who chiefly shone for them against the wicked blasphemy of Nestorius.' These are but specimens of the letters of the bishops to the same effect.

St. Celestine, then, was the real president of the council, but he presided through St. Cyril, who sat in his name. Canon Bright says that Cyril presided ' not in virtue of the commission from Celestine to act in his stead, which had already been acted upon in the Alexandrian Council of November—but as the prelate of highest dignity then present, and as holding the proxy and representing the mind of the Roman bishop, until the Roman legates should arrive.'[1] But the Acts expressly state, again and again, that Cyril held, not ' the proxy,' but ' the place ' of Celestine.[2] And it does not follow, because the original commission had been ' acted upon ' in November, that it had been exhausted in June. Its very terms imply its continuance until the sentence was executed or remitted.[3]

St. Cyril's position was probably due to two causes : first, as the Bishop of Alexandria, the second ' See of Peter,' he was the natural representative of the Bishop of Rome; and, secondly, he had been originally commissioned by Celestine to act ' in our stead and place,' in ' the affairs ' of Nestorius. Those ' affairs ' were not yet finished, and there had been no limitation in point of time, nor subsequent withdrawal, in respect of his commission. That Cyril considered himself to be acting as the representative of Celestine, by his commission, appears from his question to Celestine, asking him what he should do in case of Nestorius' retractation. The commission did not express his duty in that event; and Cyril accordingly wrote, as we know from Celestine's letter,[4] to know what his

---

[1] *Dict. of Chr. Biogr.* p. 706. [2] *E.g.* Mansi, t. iv. p. 1123.
[3] Cf. p. 309. [4] *Ep. Cel. ad Cyr.* in fine, Act ii.

duty would be under such a happy circumstance. He wanted to know whether he should treat Nestorius as no longer a bishop, now that the ten days' grace had elapsed. It is certain from this that St. Cyril considered Celestine's sentence as final, and that he only consented to deal with Nestorius as a bishop by reason of Celestine's permission, which accorded to the heretic a fresh opportunity of retractation. St. Celestine says that he leaves that matter to Cyril, in conjunction with the synod. 'It belongs to your Holiness,' are the Pope's words, 'with the venerable counsel of the brethren, to put down the disturbances that have arisen in the Church, and that we should learn that the matter has been completed (God helping) by the desired correction.' St. Celestine also says that if Nestorius continues in his sin, he will reap the fruit of what will be his own act, *manentibus statutis prioribus*, the previous decisions remaining in force.

It is therefore clear that the Pope's sentence was not so much suspended as devolved upon the council. Had the emperor been orthodox, and not caught by the wiles of Nestorius, he would not have been as keen about the council as he was. The Pope, however, acted in accordance with the rule which St. Gregory the Great also afterwards laid down in such matters, viz. that of submitting to the imperial wishes when they did not run counter to the canons. He expresses the fullest confidence in Cyril and the council, that they will execute the sentence he had passed, with the more solemn apparatus of a conciliar adhesion to the τύπος which he had sent to Cyril, Nestorius, and John of Antioch.[1] He looked upon Cyril as the teacher of the council, and virtually owns the commission originally given as still running. The council, therefore, acted with the full permission of the Pope in utilising the imperial convention for giving Nestorius every chance of repentance before executing the original sentence; and St. Cyril acted under commission from the Pope.

There is a letter extant, written by two Alexandrian clerics towards the end of this century, and used by the episcopal legates from Pope Anastasius to the emperor of the same name, which confirms the account here given of St. Cyril's

[1] τὰ παρ' ἡμῶν πάλαι ὁρισθέντα. *Ep. ad Syn.* M. iv. 1287.

position. In this letter they say that, 'whenever in doubtful matters any councils of bishops are held, His Holiness, who presides over the Church of Rome, used to select the Most Reverend Archbishop of Alexandria to undertake the charge of his own place.' In the case of the Ephesine Council, it was doubly natural that the Patriarch of Alexandria should be 'selected' by Celestine as being the foremost champion of the truth assailed, and as having already had to deal with it in Celestine's name.

There were also peculiar circumstances in this case which would have rendered it difficult for St. Cyril to have assumed that presidency with any chance of success, unless he had had such a special intimation of the Pope's wish in the matter, or felt that he was but continuing on the ground of the original commission from Celestine to execute his sentence. For that it was for this purpose that the council, despite the ideas of the emperor, considered itself convoked, will presently appear.

The circumstances that rendered the position peculiarly difficult for St. Cyril were these. At the first session, the imperial letter, which called the bishops together, appears to have been read, at the suggestion of Juvenal, Bishop of Jerusalem, by Peter, the Alexandrian notary, and the question was then asked how long an interval had elapsed since the day fixed by the emperor for the meeting of the synod. Memnon, Bishop of Ephesus, gave the number of days, and immediately upon this St. Cyril proposed that without further delay they should proceed to business, speaking of a 'second decree' which, he says, had been read to them by Count Candidian, the imperial representative. But there is no account (cf. Act I.) of this decree having been read. There is, therefore, a hiatus in the record, which has been either mutilated or abbreviated. But the account of the schismatic synod held by John of Antioch on his arrival, supplies a key to the missing portion of the record. That synod laid the greatest stress on the infringement, by Cyril and Memnon, of the imperial decree. Count Candidian told them he had been induced to read that decree under great pressure. He wished to wait for John before reading it, probably a device for putting off the synod; but Cyril compelled him to read it, on the ground that otherwise they could not know the emperor's desires. Now they knew, apart from this, that the emperor desired them to meet at Pentecost, and that all the metropolitans available were to attend. *The decree, therefore, could not have related solely or principally to that point.* The copy, as we have it, is without the same formal ending as that which was read by Peter, and so we cannot be sure that we have the whole of it. Indeed, its recovery at all is of later date, and the two copies are not in perfect agreement. And Nestorius' letter to the emperor adds one point which is not in the decree as we have it.

It would seem, then, as if this decree (θέμισμα) were something to be distinguished from the letter (γράμμα) read by Peter, and contained some fuller provision for the ordering of the council, which was set aside by the council itself. The letters of the schismatics to the synod, to the emperors, to the empress, to the clergy of Constantinople, and to its senate, all speak of the violation of this imperial decree. In the letter of the schismatics to the emperor they speak of John's absence from the synod under Cyril as contrary to his order, and add that the council had also infringed the imperial decree, as though in some further way.

In point of fact, we learn from St. Cyril that Nestorius had hoped to preside at the council. The emperor, we know, considered Cyril the guilty party. And it seems probable that Nestorius, by accusing Cyril of Apollinarianism, and by his dexterous management of the emperor, hoped to turn the council into an occasion of examining Cyril. Count Irenæus, in writing to the Orientals, says that if the right order, *i.e.* that which the emperor prescribed, had been observed, the constitution of the council would have been different, and the 'Egyptian' (as he called St. Cyril) 'would not have had it in his power' to condemn Nestorius. We may presume that only two bishops would have attended each metropolitan,[1] and those only such as, according to Nestorius' conceit, understood such matters,[2] and we know that Count Irenæus also meant that Cyril *would not have sat as judge, being himself one of those under trial* (οὐδὲ κρίνειν ὡς εἷς ὢν τῶν κρινομένων ἠδύνατο),

[1] Cf. the imperial letter read by Peter.   [2] Cf. *Ep. Nest. ad Imper.*

nor, continues the count, 'would he have been able to touch the matter at all, acting as he did contrary to the judgment of the most noble Count Candidian'—from which it is evident that Candidian's contention was that Cyril could not sit as judge of Nestorius. In fact, the imperial decree must have resembled that of Constantine in regard to the Council of Tyre, and the order of Theodosius later on, by which he assigned the presidency of the Robber Council to Dioscorus.

All this was contrary to the canons. And accordingly, at the Council of Ephesus, St. Cyril, either ignoring that part of the decree which related to the mode of procedure, and in obedience only to the rest, or by the expressed desire of the council, or producing the commission he had received from Celestine, continued to occupy the president's seat; and the council preferred the canons, and the Papal appointment, to the imperial decree. Candidian left the council on the ground, as he said afterwards,[1] that he considered the imperial decree was not going to be obeyed. He had been compelled by Cyril to read the decree against his wish. And he must have seen very plainly that the condemnation of Nestorius was a foregone conclusion. There is no reason, on this interpretation, to suppose that Count Candidian told a barefaced lie, as the scholiast notes in the margin; but merely that he was an Erastian, and sympathised with Nestorius. He would have liked Cyril to have been placed, as it were, in the witness-box; he would have liked a discussion as to what the Church believed on the doctrinal question; whereas there was to be no real discussion, but all would be settled by acclamation, and bishops would simply testify to the faith in which they had been baptised, and for the guardianship of which they had been consecrated to their high office. So he complained that there was no real investigation. In fact, the synod, as we shall see, did not exhibit the features of a debating club, nor enter upon Biblical criticism, but simply gave its judgment, bishop after bishop, as to the heterodoxy of Nestorius and the orthodoxy of Cyril, and (which was as important a point as any) as to whether Nestorius had continued teaching his heresy since the Papal judgment, so that its provisions remained in force.

[1] *Acta Conciliab. adv. Cyrillum.* Mansi, iv. 1262.

In concluding this part of the subject, I must express my astonishment at the utterly unhistorical position which Dr. Salmon has taken up in regard to another point; and that too, whilst he is so vigorously opposing the infallibility of the Holy See on the grounds of history. He gives what he considers a convincing proof against the existence of any belief in that doctrine, drawn from the history of these early councils. He says :

'*The only one* of the great controversies in which the Pope really did his part in teaching Christians what to believe, was the Eutychian controversy. Leo the Great, instead of waiting, as Popes usually do, *till the question was settled,* published his sentiments at the beginning, and his letter to Flavian was adopted by the Council of Chalcedon. This is what would have always happened if God had really made the Pope the guide to the Church. But this case is *quite exceptional,* resulting from the accident that Leo was a good theologian, besides being a man of great vigour of character. *No similar influence was exercised either by his predecessors or successors.*' [1]

It would be impossible to pen a sentence in more flagrant contradiction to the evidence afforded by the history of the Council of Ephesus.

In the letters of the bishops from all parts of Christendom, which Dr. Salmon will find collected by Labbe, after the Council of Chalcedon, the name of Celestine is of constant occurrence, and always as having been the κυβερνήτης, or pilot, in the matter of Nestorius, whilst the bishops themselves speak of him as 'the guardian of the faith' (cf. Act II.), and the council, as we shall see presently, relies on his letter as the τύπος on which it framed its judgment.

Here, then we leave the various parties concerned: Cyril in the performance of his duty, presiding over the council in St. Mary's Church at Ephesus, with some 200 bishops round him ; Nestorius remaining in his own house, prepared to ignore the council—he, as St. Celestine said, who appealed to it, not appearing; John of Antioch remaining at an easy distance from Ephesus out of friendship to Nestorius, in whose con-

---

[1] Salmon on the *Infallibility of the Church,* p. 426, 2nd edition. Cf. *supra,* p. 278. [2] Mansi, iv. 1287.

demnation he was loth to join; Candidian, the Imperial commissioner, having left St. Mary's in disgust at the turn that things were taking; and the people of Ephesus, who had inherited an affectionate devotion to the Mother of God (who had lived nearly four hundred years ago in their midst, and under whose patronage their great church was placed), in a state of the greatest excitement, waiting for her great foe to be condemned; and far away the good Pope lifting up his hands on the mountain, and preparing to send fresh legates to assist the maligned bishop, to whom the Papal sentence had been entrusted.

CHAPTER XIX.

THE ACTS OF THE COUNCIL.

I. So far, then, we have seen that Pope St. Celestine had, at the request of St. Cyril, decreed the sentence of deposition against Nestorius, and then left its execution (if Nestorius should remain obdurate) to St. Cyril and the council; and that the Council (which was, as Dr. Pusey truly observes,[1] in its origin 'the device of Nestorius to ward off his condemnation,' but was agreed to by the Pope) at length met at Ephesus in the Church of 'St. Mary, Mother of God '—' an ill-omened scene ' (remarks Dean Milman [2]) 'for the cause of Nestorius.'

It proceeded to summon Nestorius to answer to the charges against him. Dr. Littledale, in the first edition of his ' Plain Reasons against joining the Church of Rome,' [3] gravely informed his readers that ' the Third General Council of Ephesus disregarded the synodical deposition of Nestorius by Pope Celestine, and allowed him to take his seat as Patriarch of Constantinople.' We have already seen that the Pope had not deposed Nestorius at all, but devolved the execution of his sentence on the council. As to the second assertion, as Father Ryder pointed out,[4] it is ' quite curiously untrue, even for Dr. Littledale.' Nestorius was summoned, but in vain. Three times summoned, he refused to appear. He eventually grounded his refusal on the absence of John of Antioch. The council considered the question of summoning him a fourth time,[5] but the

---

[1] S. Cyr. Alex. *Tomes against Nestorius. Lib. of the Fathers*, Preface by Dr. Pusey.
[2] *Hist. of Latin Christianity*, vol. i. p. 208.
[3] P. 191.
[4] *Catholic Controversy*. Burns & Oates, 1881.
[5] Mansi, t. iv. p. 1138.

threefold summons satisfied the requirements of the canons. They accordingly, after reciting the Nicene Creed, proceeded, in obedience to canonical requirements, to place his teaching before them side by side with the teachings of St. Cyril.

II. The mere fact that the bishops did so seems to some writers to indicate that they did not regard the Holy See as infallible in its judgments. But this is to forget that it was St. Celestine's expressed desire that they should satisfy themselves as to the heterodoxy of Nestorius. And his desire that they should thus give to his judgment a rational adhesion in no way indicates any doubt on his part as to his judgment being, as he himself called it,[1] that of our Lord Himself. It is in strict accordance with Catholic teaching that the bishops should be called upon to act thus. Those who oppose the Catholic Church in these days seem strangely unwilling to take her doctrine as to her claims from her own lips. She does not claim for the Holy See, as Dr. Bright[2] seems to make her claim, an apostolical authority which concentrates, *in the sense of excluding*, all other authority; she does not claim infallibility for the Vicar of Christ as isolated from the body, but as its head, one with the body. This is so important that we will give the Catholic doctrine on the subject, as it is luminously expounded by one who, for his writings on this subject, received the special blessing of Pius IX. Father Bottalla says:[3]

'We maintain, with St. Cyprian and all the Fathers, that the bishops are as the circumference of a circle, so that in order to have perfect unity in the Church they must cleave to each other so far as to keep the pale of Christ's Church entirely closed against schismatics and heretics. Moreover, we maintain that *the bishops must cleave to the centre of the circle, so that they may be gathered into a perfect unity*;[4] and finally, that the chair of St. Peter and consequently the Pope, is the centre and the source of episcopal unity. In this view it is impossible to say that the circle is the centre alone, or that a centre of a circle could exist without any circumference. We cannot say that a human body is the head alone detached

---

[1] Mansi, t. iv. p. 1050.
[2] *Church History*, p. 336.
[3] *Infall. of the Pope*, p. 141.
[4] Which implies an act of judgment.

from the rest, or that there could be a human head separated from a body acting in its normal manner. In like manner we cannot say that the Church without bishops is the whole, or that the Pope might act as Pope in a state of isolation from the episcopal body. . . . If the Church be indefectible, it must be indefectible in unity of government as well as in unity of faith. In no case, then, can we conceive the Pope as in formal isolation from the episcopal body. . . . What is the province of the episcopal element in the monarchy of the Church? It is certain, not only that the episcopal body can never be superseded in the Church by the Pope, but also that it can never be deprived of its inherent jurisdiction in the general government of the Church, although there is no difficulty as to restrictions and limitations being placed by the Pope upon the exercise of their jurisdiction, should necessity require such a course. Moreover, the bishops, either in their own dioceses or in the œcumenical councils, are the natural judges of questions concerning faith, although under the guidance, and subject to the judgment, of the Roman Pontiff. . . . The power given to the aristocratic episcopal body was not intended by Christ to control or to reform the government and the teaching of the supreme ruler of the Church, but to give efficacy to his action on the whole body, to diffuse to every part the streams of divine life, and to draw tighter the bonds of unity which link together the whole structure.'

The bishops, then, according to what some writers will persist in calling the Ultramontane theory, have a real function to perform in a general council. As Benedict XIV. says:[1] 'Bishops in a general council assist (*assident*) the Supreme Pontiff, not as mere counsellors, but also as judges.' But as Fénelon said:[2] 'To judge after the judgment of the Pontiff is to join one's own judgment with that of the Pontiff. On this understanding the bishops in olden times subscribed the decrees of the general councils. Their submission was a judgment and their judgment was submission.'

The bishops, then, at the Council of Ephesus were called upon to pass judgment on the teaching of Nestorius, not with

---

[1] *De Syn. Diœc.* lib. xiii. c. 2, n. 2, 469. Romæ, 1755.
[2] *Instr. Pastor.* April 20, 1715.

the idea that the τύπος, or judicial sentence formulated by St. Celestine, could be revised, but to execute it, and to add the weight of their collective judgment to that of the Holy See. Their united judgment would give to the sentence an extension of weight, without adding to its intrinsic authority.[1]

Dean Milman's sarcasm is the simple truth : ' The Bishop of Constantinople was already a condemned heretic ; the business of the council was only the confirmation of their [Cyril and Celestine's] anathema,' &c.[2]

Or, as Dr. Pusey correctly says : ' The mind of the Church had been expressed in the previous year.'

And St. Celestine had told St. Cyril that, in spite of his having fixed so short a time for Nestorius to consider the question of retracting, he did not regret a certain delay which resulted from the apparatus of a council being called into action.

III. Accordingly the members of the council, after reciting the Nicene Creed, and listening to Cyril's second letter to Nestorius, drawn up in synod in obedience to the commission entrusted to him by the Pope, for the most part one by one, stamped its contents with their episcopal approval.[3] Nestorius' letter was then read and solemnly condemned as containing heretical matter, by most bishops in turn individually, and by the rest collectively. Dr. Salmon's sweeping accusations against the councils of the Church do not hold in regard to at least this session of the Council of Ephesus. ' There was,' he says, ' no idea then but that what one council had done another council might improve on '—an assertion which he makes by way of proving that ' there was no suspicion of its infallibility,' *i.e.* of that of the Nicene settlement.[4] It is difficult to understand how anyone could make the assertion in the face of all that is said to the contrary in the Acts of the Councils, or after reading the answers of the individual bishops in the first session at Ephesus.[5]

It was next proposed by the Bishop of Jerusalem that the

---

[1] ' Extensivè non intensivè '—Bellarmine.
[2] *Hist. of Latin Christianity*, vol. i. p. 206.
[3] Mansi, t. iv. pp. 1138-70.   [4] *Infall. of the Church*, p. 312.
[5] Mansi, t. iv. pp. 1170-78.

letter of St. Celestine should be read, which sentenced Nestorius to excommunication from the universal Church. It was accordingly read, and received without discussion.¹ The place which this letter held in their estimation is seen in the report which the synod wrote to the emperors, in which they speak of it as having 'preceded their own judgment in the condemnation of the heretical dogmas of Nestorius,' and as having been indited by way of 'providing for the safety of the Churches and of the holy and life-giving faith as handed down to us by the holy Apostles, Evangelists, and holy Fathers,'² and the supreme part which it played in the final condemnation of Nestorius is further stated, as we shall presently see, in the very terms of their own sentence. Further letters of St. Cyril's were then read, which, according to the declaration of Peter, the Alexandrian notary, were 'in conformity with' the Pope's letter just read.

The actual delivery of the Pope's letter and of those of St. Cyril, which executed the Papal sentence, was then sworn to by proper witnesses, viz. the bishops who delivered them.

One important point yet remained to be established. The Papal sentence was conditional on Nestorius' continued obstinacy. If he retracted, the council was authorised by the Pope³ to deal with the matter as it might think best. Had Nestorius, then, continued to teach the same heresy ? He had. He had uttered his blasphemies in Ephesus itself. It was enough. It only remained to read some of the writings of the holy Fathers, whose teachings the Pope had delivered,⁴ and, further, the opposed 'blasphemies' (as they called them) to be found in Nestorius' commentaries—together with a letter from Capreolus, Bishop of Carthage, in the name of the African Church, begging that 'the authority of the Apostolic See'⁵ might be respected, and all novelties repudiated—and they could now proceed to deliver the sentence. The terms of the sentence are of supreme importance for determining the place which the Holy See occupied in the judgment of the

---

¹ Mansi, t. iv. p. 1179. ² *Ibid.* t. iv. p. 1239 c.
³ *Ep. Cel. ad Cyr.*, Mansi, t. iv. p. 1292.
⁴ Cf. *Relatio Syn. ad Imperat.*, Harduin. p. 1099.
⁵ Mansi, t. iv. p. 1207.

Catholic bishops at Ephesus. Did they or did they not act in obedience to the Pope? The terms of the sentence leave us in no doubt on this point. There are words in that sentence which are decisive, and which define the Eastern idea of Papal authority. The Fathers of the council speak of themselves as acting in obedience to the Holy See. They say they acted under necessity. They speak of Nestorius' disobedience to their summons having compelled them to enter on the investigation of his impious teachings in his absence; of their having convicted him from his letters and commentaries, and his utterances even in the city of Ephesus itself; and they proceed to say that 'necessarily compelled by the canons and by the letter of our most Holy Father and fellow-minister Celestine,'[1] they had concurred after many tears in the sorrowful sentence to the effect that our Lord Jesus Christ, whom he had blasphemed, pronounces by this holy synod that he is deprived of his episcopal dignity and excluded from the assemblies of the Church.

'Necessarily compelled by the canons and by the letter of our most Holy Father and fellow-minister Celestine!' Such was their position.

First, the canons. The reference is to their having acted in the absence of Nestorius. In several places they speak of their having satisfied the requirements of the canons through their threefold summons of the heretic. They had given him the opportunity of answering the charge brought against him, four bishops having repaired to his house to acquaint him of the position of things; and John of Antioch had expressly commissioned two bishops to tell the synod not to wait for *him*. 'Do your work,' were his words, 'if I delay.' There had therefore been no violation of canon law. By the canons they were free to act, and indeed compelled, although the guilty party was not present.

Secondly, the womb out of which their entire action and their final judgment sprang was the letter of the Pope.[2] They

[1] Mansi, t. iv. pp. 1211-12.

[2] The preposition by which they express their obedience to the canons is ἀπό; that by which they express their obedience to the letter of the Holy Father is ἐκ. That the words 'necessarily compelled' apply to the letter, as well as to the canons, is clear from the conjunctions used.

were compelled to act by reason of the letter of him who was at once their 'Holy Father' and their 'fellow-minister,' in other words, their equal in sacerdotal dignity,[1] but their superior in authority. He had been asked by St. Cyril τυπῶσαι τὸ δοκοῦν, to formulate the dogmatic decree. He had given the τύπος in the letters written to Cyril, Nestorius, the clergy of Constantinople, and John of Antioch, but especially in the letter to Nestorius which was read in synod. The council *could* do nothing else than yield obedience to this letter. This the bishops declare they have done. Their action in condemning the Archbishop of Constantinople *in his absence* from the synod was covered by the canons; their action in condemning him at all was, they averred, a simple necessity after the letter of the Pope. Although exercising a real judgment on the subject, as the record shows they did, they were yet under a moral impossibility of differing from the Papal sentence; they were, they say, 'necessarily compelled [ἀπό] by the canons and by [ἐκ] the letter of the Holy Father;' and in delivering this sentence, which they thus declare to be in its origin and power that of the Pope, they profess to be acting with the authority of our Lord Jesus Christ. It is, they say, His sentence. What Celestine said of the sentence as it passed from his lips, that it was 'the judgment of Christ, who is God,' the Ephesine Council also said of its execution and promulgation by themselves. Pope and council together claim the prerogative of infallibility: the Pope in defining the relationship of Nestorius' teaching to the Christian faith, the council, in judging after the Pope, 'necessarily compelled' by His Holiness' decision.

Bossuet, who frequently soars above the mists of Gallican prejudices, rightly says[2] that the council was not necessary, but it was expedient, on account of the trouble that Nestorius was able to create through his influence at court. The council, therefore, was careful to note that its decision did not derogate from the compulsory nature of the Papal decision, but presumed it; it was, though the act of free men, not, in every sense, a free action; it was a matter of duty to join themselves as members to their head,[3] it was their own assertion

---

[1] συλλειτουργοῦ. [2] *Def. Decl. Cleri Gallicani.* [3] Mansi, t. iv. p. 1200 c.

of their membership in the teaching body. The obligation which was thus laid upon them by the canons could only refer to Nestorius' disobedience to the synod, which compelled it to enter upon the question *without his own defence*. No canon had dealt with his dogmatic error; but the canons provided for the judicial treatment of a heretic. But the letter of Celestine, which laid them under this obligation to obedience, had respect not only to the deposition of Nestorius, but to his heresy,[1] for it provided that his deposition should follow on his refusal to retract his error in regard to the matter of faith within ten days. And although the Pontiff had left the execution of his sentence, including its delay (if deemed advisable) to the synod, he had not left it open to them to acquit Nestorius in the event of his obstinate adherence to his error. This obstinacy had now been established by competent witnesses, and the council, having complied with the provisions of the canons in summoning him three times, was 'necessarily compelled,' in obedience to the Papal sentence, to depose and excommunicate the archbishop. But how, as Ballerini asks, could the Ephesine Fathers be 'necessarily compelled' by the letter of Celestine, unless they were 'necessarily compelled' to preserve a unity of faith with the Roman Pontiff?

Now, how do those writers deal with this momentous utterance of the council who maintain the independence of national Churches?

It is not put in evidence at all by Canon Bright in his article in Smith's 'Dictionary of Christian Biography' on St. Cyril, nor in that by Mr. Ffoulkes on the Council of Ephesus; neither does it appear in Canon Bright's 'History of the Church,' where the sentence on Nestorius is thus described: 'And the prelates proceeded to depose and excommunicate Nestorius in the name of our Lord Jesus Christ, whom he has "blasphemed"' (p. 333).

There is no allusion to the letter of Celestine here.

It does not appear in Canon Robertson's 'History of the Church'—a work which has figured much on the list of books recommended to candidates for ordination in the Established

---

[1] Cf. Ballerini, *De Vi et Ratione Primatus Rom. Pontif.* c. xiii. § 11.

Church. Dean Milman[1] quotes a part of the sentence, but omits the crucial words 'by the letter of our Most Holy Father and fellow-minister Celestine.' He even gives the Greek in a foot-note, with the same omission, marking that there is an omission. Dr. Wordsworth seems to go a step beyond these writers. He omits the crucial word 'compelled.' His version of the synod's sentence is:[2] 'They then declared that in accordance with the canons of the Church, and with the letter of their Most Holy Father and brother-minister, Celestine, bishop of the Roman Church,' &c.

'In accordance with' is certainly not an accurate translation of 'necessarily compelled by,' nor is it even a fair paraphrase of the same. A very strong and exhaustive term is here used in the Greek.[3] And not content with a word which contains the idea of tremendous force, they add to it the adverb 'necessarily.'[4] And it must be remembered that the Greek is the original here; that it was drawn up by Easterns, and that it was the Greek which the Eastern Fathers actually signed.

The sentence thus expressed and signed, the Fathers issued forth from their œcumenical synod. The citizens of Ephesus were in an ecstasy of joy. They had waited for the sentence in eager expectation, not as doubting the truth, but as looking forward to its confirmation. And upon the council's leaving St. Mary's at the close of the day, they burst into the wildest applause, and attended the orthodox bishops home with every token of honour, Cyril coming in, as well he might, for the lion's share of their attention. Torchlight processions and incense accompanied the members of the synod to their residences, and the very ladies of Ephesus turned out to manifest their joy at the vindication of the glory of their sex, the 'great Mother of God, Mary most holy.'

Candidian, the emperor's legate, on the contrary, soon had the notices from the city walls torn down. The synod had defeated his hopes; but he was bent on causing trouble, as the event proved. Dr. Littledale thinks that he makes a

---

[1] *Hist. of Lat. Christianity*, vol. i. p. 211 (4th and revised edition).
[2] *Church History*, vol. iv. p. 216.
[3] κατεπειχθέντες, which is a strong form of ἐπειχθέντες.
[4] ἀναγκαίως. Cf. St. Irenæus on the necessity of agreeing with Rome, p. 86.

point against the ' Petrine claims' of Rome when he adduces the fact that ' no practical impression was made on Nestorius or the bishops of his party'[1] by the Papal sentence; and Dr. Salmon holds[2] that the mere fact that the decision of a council was not received at once on all sides is fatal to the infallibility of œcumenical councils—an argument which would summarily dispose of our Lord's Divinity. One of the most recent theories about our Lord's miracles is that since everybody did not at once yield assent to His claims, no miracles could have been worked; and Dr. Salmon's is only the same argument applied to the Church. Certainly Nestorianism did not cease to be; indeed, it seemed for a moment as though after the council's judgment it might gain the upper hand. But what of that? These writers have failed to appreciate one of the leading facts of human history, viz. the fall of man. Men who could repudiate the truth concerning the Incarnation could and did rebel against the Holy See and against any number of councils. Nestorius, then, and his followers, instead of submitting to Pope or councils, had their weapons ready; and John of Antioch was to be led into serious sin before the ultimate triumph of the great Patriarch of Alexandria.

St. Celestine, foreseeing or being fully acquainted with the difficulties of the position, had sent three legates to reinforce the council. There is no evidence that St. Cyril knew of their near approach. By the time of their arrival the emperor's party had sufficiently exerted themselves to prevent the further use of St. Mary's by the orthodox bishops, who accordingly met in the house of Memnon, the Bishop of Ephesus. The Papal legates had instructions from St. Celestine not to mix themselves up with any discussions, but simply to act as judges and to carry out his sentence. Accordingly, in this new session the bishops submitted their action in the previous session to the judgment of the legates, and asked them to confirm it. Philip, legate of ' the Apostolic throne,' as the Acts describe him, said, in his opening speech, that Celestine had ' long ago decided' the present matters by his letters,[3] but that he now sends fresh letters for ' the

---

[1] *Petrine Claims*, p. 98.   [2] *Infallibility of the Church*, p. 426, c.
[3] Mansi, t. iv. col. 1282, b.

confirmation of the Catholic Faith.' Cyril proposed that the letters of the Pope should be read 'with the honour that befits them.' They were accordingly read in Latin and Greek, Philip having first said that it was in accordance with custom that the letters of the Apostolic See should be read first in Latin. The Papal letter speaks of the synod as being a witness to the presence of the Holy Spirit, and expresses the conviction that the same Lord who presided over the Council at Jerusalem will be present at Ephesus and teach them. All bishops have received the Holy Ghost; all have received a common command to preach the name of the Lord in place of the Apostles whom they succeed. He then refers to Timothy having been left by St. Paul at Ephesus, and compares them to Timothy. The Pope's expression suggests a similar relationship between himself and the bishops in synod to that which existed between St. Paul the Apostle and St. Timothy, Bishop of Ephesus. He ends with the assurance that they will see that what *he has decided* concerning Nestorius is 'in behalf of the security and freedom from trouble of all the Churches,' and that they will therefore not hesitate to give in their adhesion to 'what was long ago decided by us,' which he has sent his legates to execute.[1]

This letter, on being read, elicited applause from the bishops, who, taking up the injunction in the last sentence, cried out, 'This is a just *decision*,' and the synod exclaimed that it thanked 'Celestine, a new Paul' (in allusion to the Pope's reference to St. Paul's admonition to Timothy), 'Cyril, a new Paul' (Cyril who had represented the Pope), 'Celestine, the guardian of the faith (τῷ φύλακι τῆς πίστεως), Celestine of one mind with the synod,' 'one Celestine, one Cyril, one faith of the synod, one faith of the whole world.'

These utterances as to the unity of the Church contain a volume of theology, and taken together with what had preceded them they exactly illustrate the idea of the Church's action in a general council as described above (p. 330.)

The Pope appears in them as the source of infallibility; the council's action is stated to be the sequence of his; it is an actual exercise of judgment in the shape of an intelligent

[1] Mansi, t. iv. col. 1287, b.

adhesion to the Papal sentence; and the result of all is the exhibition of the Church's unity as a whole.

This, too, is the description of the situation given almost in so many words by Projectus, one of the episcopal legates of the Pope. He speaks of the τύπος afforded by Celestine's letters, and says that the Pope has exhorted their Holiness, not as though teaching the ignorant, but as reminding those who know. He applies to Celestine's action the very word, when translated into Greek (as it appears in the Acts), which Celestine had used of St. Paul when he 'admonished' Timothy as Bishop of Ephesus; and speaks of their office as being that of 'bringing the matter to a perfect end,' so that their action was to be the consummation of the apostolic sentence of the Pope.

Firmus, Bishop of Cæsarea in Cappadocia, now answered for the council, and his answer is most important. He speaks of the 'Apostolic and holy throne' having given the 'decision and sentence'[1] in the affair of Nestorius, to Alexandria, Jerusalem, Thessalonica, Constantinople, and Antioch, which (he says) we, the bishops of the synod, have followed.[2] He says that the limit of time allowed to Nestorius by Celestine for reformation had long passed when they reached Ephesus; that the emperor had fixed the time for their meeting; that they had summoned Nestorius and he had not obeyed their summons, and that accordingly they had executed the sentence (τὸν τύπον ἐξεβιβάσαμεν) by passing a *canonical* and *apostolical* judgment against him. Canonical, he doubtless meant in allusion to the terms of the sentence ' necessarily compelled by the canons;' 'apostolical' in allusion to the letter of their Holy Father Celestine, by which also they were 'compelled.'

After this clear description of the situation, Arcadius, the third legate, thanking God for their arrival on the scene, asks that the proceedings of the council be read. Philip the legate asks the same, in accordance with Celestine's injunctions, congratulating the holy and venerable synod that they have 'joined themselves as holy members to the holy head by their holy exclamations'—again a perfect description of the office of

[1] ψῆφον καὶ τύπον. Mansi, t. iv. col. 1290.   [2] ᾧ ἀκολουθήσαντες κ. τ. λ.

a general council as given above by Fénelon, 'Their submission was a judgment and their judgment was submission.' Philip asks for the proceedings of the synod previous to the arrival of the legates to be shown that they may confirm them. Theodotus, Bishop of Ancyra, remarks that:

'The God of all has shown that the sentence of the synod is just by the auspicious arrival [1] of the letters of the Godfearing bishop Celestine, and by the presence of your Piety.'

And the legates retired that night to their residence with the Acts of the first session, to peruse them in quiet.

IV. Meanwhile,[2] John of Antioch had arrived with a following of several disreputable and disqualified bishops, together with a few others who would naturally have formed part of the synod. The former were men who lay under accusation of various kinds, some of them not having dioceses in consequence of misconduct. This description of them is given by the whole orthodox synod, again and again, even to the emperor himself. Strange to say, some writers prefer the statement of these men to the account given by the orthodox bishops of the council. Yet the latter were, according to St. Vincent of Lerins,[3] men of peculiar ability and holiness; and they were on the side of divine truth, engaged in a struggle for the truth of the Incarnation. It is infinitely to the credit of Dr. Pusey that he should have set himself against the stream of Anglican writers on this point. He stands, we believe, alone in defending St. Cyril against the accusation of impatience and in giving the same account of John of Antioch's delay as the synod itself gives. In opposition to Canon Bright's argument [4] that John of Antioch would have wished to be there at Ephesus *before* the arrival of the legates (which supposes that he wished to be there at all, and that he knew of the approach of the legates—both of them gratuitous assumptions), Dr. Pusey

---

[1] ἐπιφοιτήσει—a word which is generally used of the arrival of a messenger from God, especially of the Holy Spirit. Cf. Dindorf, *Steph. Thesaur.* vol. iii. p. 1881.

[2] The second session of the council was on July 10. John of Antioch reached Ephesus on June 27, and held the Conciliabulum the same day.

[3] *Commonit.* i. 42.

[4] *Hist. of the Church*, p. 331, adopted also by Neale, *Hist. of E. Church*, bk. i. § 2, originally suggested by Tillemont.

maintains[1] that John of Antioch might easily have arrived in time, and that there is no conceivable motive for his delay, except what the synod gives on information which it had received from adequate sources. 'Why should he delay,' asks Dr. Pusey, 'except that he did not wish to be there?'

The passage in Evagrius on which Dr. Bright relies, both in his 'History' and in his more recent article in the 'Dictionary of Christian Biography,' is not sufficient to settle the question. Evagrius was an Antiochene, if not by birth at least by residence, and he merely gives the fact that many, doubtless Antiochenes also, thought there was excuse for John: and the reading of the passage is not certain. And Evagrius is certainly inaccurate in the same passage in saying that Cyril asked Theodosius to convene the council, as also in another statement, that Nestorius promised to attend the synod on the first summons.

Hefele's account, according to which John of Antioch's message that they should proceed without him, refers to the time of the reception of his message, and not to a time subsequent to that, is in strict accordance with the only evidence we have; and accordingly, the Protestant editor of Clarke's translation of Hefele's work says in his Preface[2] with regard to Cyril, that 'there seems no reason to doubt that his antagonists purposely delayed their arrival, and gave him to understand that the proceedings might begin. At any rate, the author [viz. Bishop Hefele] appears to have stated the case with all possible accuracy.'

On his arrival at Ephesus, John of Antioch, refusing to listen to the deputation of orthodox bishops, which endeavoured to provide him with proper information, proceeded in the utmost haste to hold a synod of these otherwise unsatisfactory bishops, and after listening to an *ex parte* and most untruthful statement from Count Candidian, deposed and excommunicated Cyril and Memnon.

The turmoil in Ephesus can be better imagined than described. John did not, indeed, express sympathy with the teaching of Nestorius, but he professed to discern a fatal flaw

---

[1] Cf. Cyril of Alex. *Tomes against Nestorius*, Preface, p. lxxx.
[2] Preface to Hefele's *Hist. of the Council*, English translation, p. viii.

in the mode of his deposition by the council, as being contrary both to the imperial rescript and to the canons. It is needless to say that he paid no manner of attention to either of these authorities in his own proceedings. He was completely led away by the disquiet spirits who had gathered round him, some of whom had been deposed by Rome, and others were under accusation for various charges; although he would probably have said that he was not setting himself up against the Pope, but had only taken the part of a man who, although teaching falsely, was being persecuted by Cyril and his associates. Fortunately he was prevented from consecrating another bishop in place of Memnon at Ephesus, as he was minded to do.

CHAPTER XX.

THE SEE OF PETER 'CONFIRMING THE BRETHREN.'

I. Such was the state of things when the true council re-assembled to hear the judgment of the Papal legates as to the execution of the Papal sentence at their first session, whose minutes the legates had now perused at home.

Philip takes the foremost place, and at once declares that the judgment of the synod in its first session had been passed on thoroughly canonical and ecclesiastical lines; and he asks that the minutes be read over again publicly, in order that, 'following the sentence of the most holy Pope Celestine, who undertook this care [*i.e.* the care of this matter], we may be able to confirm the decisions of your Holiness.'

Arcadius seconds Philip's proposal, and the sentence of the synod was read again, containing the crucial words 'compelled of necessity by the canons and by the letter of our Holy Father and brother-minister Celestine,' &c. Then it was that Philip rose and pronounced the definite judgment on the proceedings of the council as it sat, with Cyril at its head, and listened to the most elaborate and careful statement of the relation of the Holy See to the rest of the Catholic Church.

His words are too important to be given in paraphrase only. He says:[1] 'It is doubtful to no one, but rather has been known to all ages, that the holy and most blessed Peter, the prince and head of the Apostles, and pillar of the faith, the foundation of the Catholic Church, received of our Lord Jesus Christ, the Saviour and Redeemer of the human race, the keys of the kingdom, and power was given to him to bind

[1] Mansi, t. iv. col. 1295.

and loose sins; who, up to this time and always lives and exercises judgment in his successors. In accordance, therefore, with this order, his successor holding his place, our holy and most blessed Father Celestine has sent us to this synod to supply his presence.'

He proceeds to say that all having been done regularly, and Nestorius having refused to attend the synod, what has been pronounced against him is 'firm,' holds good, according to the decision of all the Churches, for East and West are present together at this 'sacerdotal assembly.' So let Nestorius know that he is outside the communion of the Catholic Church.

Arcadius followed in the same strain. His points were that Nestorius had been admonished 'by the letters of the Apostolic See,' and then also by the synod; that he had not made use of the time accorded to him for coming round to a better mind; that he had not accepted the sentence of the Apostolic See (τύπον τῆς ἀποστολικῆς καθέδρας) nor the admonition of all the holy bishops; consequently, in obedience[1] to the decisions delivered by Celestine, the most holy Pope of the Apostolic See, and to the decrees of the holy synod (we say), let Nestorius know that he has been deprived[2] of the episcopal dignity, and is excluded from the whole Catholic Church and the communion of all the bishops.

Projectus says that on the same grounds he decides with the authority of a 'commission from the holy Apostolic See, as executor, in fellowship with his brethren, of the sentence,' that Nestorius is forthwith bereft of the honour of the episcopate and of communion with the orthodox bishops.

II. Such is the position which was occupied by the Papal legates. There can be no mistake about the significance of their utterances. It is not possible to express the position of Rome in the Catholic Church in plainer terms. Her position, according to these statements, is that of judge in matters of faith, and of ruler in matters of discipline. That position is traced to a divine institution. She is asserted to be the See of

---

[1] ἀκολουθήσαντες, which is opposed to the non-acceptance or disobedience of Nestorius.

[2] It is the Greek perfect, indicating the still enduring result of a past act.

St. Peter, and as such, by reason of the position of princedom bestowed on him by our Divine Lord, she is proclaimed the head of the Catholic Church. As such she has responded to St. Cyril's request, τυπῶσαι τὸ δοκοῦν, that she would formulate the dogmatic sentence. The synod has followed that sentence, and therefore the legates, in the name of Celestine, the occupant of the Apostolic See, are prepared to confirm the act of the synod. This is the pith of the legates' speeches.

Now if this position was quietly accepted, we have at an œcumenical council an emphatic condemnation of the Anglican position as contradicting and rebelling against that form of unity which Christ established in His Church. If the Anglican position is to be defended on the ground of conformity with the principles of Church life that have the sanction of the œcumenical councils, history must record some protest against the position taken up by the legates at the Council of Ephesus. Anglicans proudly turn to history. No words can be more scathing than those in which Canon Carter [1] and Mr. Gore, for instance, denounce what they are pleased to call Roman Catholic disregard for history, and assert their own superior attention to its verdict. Bishop King, of Lincoln, follows suit.[2] And yet the Anglican Church takes its stand, as did the Lambeth Conference,[3] on the first four œcumenical councils. Well, we open the Acts of the Councils, and what do we find? Here at Ephesus is the teaching of the Catholic Roman Church described in full, and we look in vain for any protest, any one dissentient voice, any sign whatever of disagreement.[4] On the contrary, Cyril forthwith appeals to the synod, saying that the bishops have heard what the legates have said, that the legates have spoken as ' occupying the place of the Apostolic See, and of all the holy synod of God-beloved and most

---

[1] Cf. *Roman Question*, chapter on ' Ideas of Truth ; ' and Gore's *R. C. Claims*, p. 109, 2nd edition.

[2] Preface to *Primitive Saints, &c.*, passim.

[3] Dr. Salmon repudiates the authority of the councils to such an extent that, although his book is used by High Churchmen, its theory is not the same as that of the Lambeth Conference of the Anglican Episcopate.

[4] Mr. Puller (*Primitive Saints*, p. 184) calls the doctrine of Philip at Ephesus ' new and therefore false ; ' the council accepts it as old and therefore true. What Philip said was ' suitable.'

holy bishops in the West;' that they have executed what has been prescribed to them by Celestine ; that they have given their approval to the sentence of the holy synod against Nestorius, and that consequently they should be asked to set their signature to the same, and that the records of what was done yesterday and to-day should be added to the previous Acts.

The whole council responds to Cyril's proposal, and says, ' Since Arcadius and Projectus, the reverend and pious bishops and legates, *and Philip*, presbyter and legate of the Apostolic See, *have spoken what is suitable*, they ought to confirm the Acts by their signature.' [1]

It is enough. We ought to hear nothing about 'history' from those who refuse to obey the See of St. Peter on the ground that it is not the divinely appointed centre of unity to the Catholic Church. We ought, at least, to hear no such accusations as to Rome's disregard for history as are indulged in by some writers, whose position is absolutely excluded by the history of the Council of Ephesus. We ought to hear no more of the theory that the teaching of the Church of Rome is only a continuation of ' a school of thought,' as Mr. Gore holds, or of an ' innovation of the Church's laws,' as Dr. Littledale held, due to the powerful character of St. Leo the Great. The Council of Ephesus was held twenty years before the Council of Chalcedon ; and at the Council of Ephesus the theory of the Church's government which these writers persist in calling an innovation was in full working order, and was declared to be based on a truth acknowledged 'by all ages.' The teaching of the Vatican decree on this subject was the teaching of the Fathers of Ephesus, and it was the rule of their conduct. Consider the whole drama of the council's decision. Commencing with some hesitation, considering the difficult circumstances in which they were placed, the Fathers of the council rise to the occasion, and, amid many tears, as they say, pass their sentence in accordance with, and in obedience to that of the See of St. Peter. They have the emperor against them ; they presently have the patriarch of one of the three Petrine Sees against them ; they have troops of soldiers

[1] Mansi, t. iv. col. 1299.

brought from Lydia against them, and peasants from the worst parts of Constantinople, creating a scene of confusion, and stirring up the indignation of the inhabitants of the city, who were all, nevertheless, on the side of Cyril and the orthodox bishops; but in the face of all this turmoil, the synod calmly and judiciously enters upon the work for which it had been convoked by the emperor, and which had been entrusted to its care (as itself says) by the 'Holy Apostolic See.' And now, reinforced by legates from the Apostolic throne, the whole tone of the synod rises, and with mutual congratulations, the entire body—' the holy members joining themselves to their holy head, not being ignorant [as Philip says] that the blessed Apostle Peter is the head of *the whole affair,* and even of the Apostles '—exhibits its perfect unity in the condemnation and extrusion of the heretic from communion with itself. The bishops had written to the emperor immediately after the first session, but now they write again in bolder terms, informing him that Celestine had indicated the line of judgment which they too had adopted, that he had sent Cyril to hold his place —a direct reversal of the imperial wish—and that he now afresh signified the same mind, having sent letters by his legates, Arcadius, Projectus and Philip. These men (they say) expressed the mind of the entire West, and have declared their oneness with the synod, so that ' the whole world is of one mind.' The synod thereupon ventures a step further, and requests the emperor not to disturb them any more with 'sacræ jussiones' in Nestorius' behalf, and they ask to be released, that they may return to their various homes.

Now it will naturally be asked, How do Anglican writers deal with the crucial words which fell from Philip's lips?

We have failed to find them in full in any Anglican writer.[1] No one of those from whose writings we have quoted has

---

[1] Since the above was written a book has appeared called *Leadership, not Lordship,* in which these words are given; but they are accompanied by a misstatement of the facts. The writer speaks of the words of Philip having been only 'accepted in the sense of not being contradicted in words,' which is not true; and he speaks, in the same sentence, of the 'absolutely independent [*sic*] judgment and action of the council.' This is in simple defiance of the council's own words—' necessarily compelled,' &c.

given his readers the benefit of Philip's speech in full. Neither does any one of them connect it rightly with its context. Dr. Littledale alludes to it only to pass it by as the private opinion of the Papal legate. But this, as we have seen, is not true. It does not occur in Dr. Wordsworth's rather full account of the council, nor in Dean Milman's. Dr. Neale says simply, 'the legate Philip, after dwelling on the primacy [*sic*] of St. Peter's chair,' &c.[1] Dr. Bright is the only Anglican writer of prominence that has dealt with Philip's words, of which his account is as follows:[2] 'Next day, in the third session, the legate Philip, having magnified the successor of Peter as inheriting his authority, joined with his two companions in affirming the sentence against Nestorius.'

This is a somewhat meagre summary of this all-important session; but in a note Dr. Bright gives a short quotation from the said speech with comments: 'Peter (said Philip) was the head of the Apostles, and "even now and always[3] lives and judges in his successors." On the whole, what Rome said in 431 amounts to this: "All bishops succeed the Apostles, but Celestine, as heir of him who was the foremost Apostle, has a right to be foremost among bishops." Rome did *not* say, as she now practically says, "The apostolic authority is concentrated in St. Peter's successor." There is nothing strange in Celestine's charge to the legates to maintain the authority of Rome.'

What Dr. Bright's explanation does not meet is the assertion that the primacy of the successor of Peter is, according to Philip *and the council*, of divine institution; *and* that, taking into account the context of the words, they indicate a belief that the apostolic authority of the Church cannot be exercised in antagonism to the judgment of the 'Apostolic throne.' We must repeat, and it cannot be too often repeated, that the Vatican decree does not teach that the action or judgment of the 'Holy Apostolic See' *exhausts* the exercise

---

[1] *History of the Eastern Church*, bk. ii. § ii. The word ' primacy,' amongst Anglicans, generally means something less than supremacy. In Catholic terminology the two are identical.

[2] *History of the Church*, p. 336.

[3] Fleury and Ceillier omit the word ' always,' although there is no difference in the original.

of apostolic authority in the Church, but that it informs it, to use a scholastic term; it does not exclude the apostolic authority of the episcopate, but is necessary to it; it is not the act of the whole Church, but of the Head of the Church. Only it is involved in the promises of her Divine Head, that the earthly Head, His vicar, shall not lead the members astray, and that there shall never be separation between the Head and members: that is to say, the Church shall never die. The members, by their separation, cease to be living members. The Holy Apostolic See will live on till the day of doom with such members as He alone knows will be joined to their Head, for the gates of hell shall not prevail against her.[1]

III. In the next session of the synod, Cyril, still presiding, brought forward his own case and that of Memnon, the Bishop of Ephesus. John of Antioch had allowed himself to be so far led away by the bad company in which he found himself, that he had synodically condemned, excommunicated, and deposed both Cyril and Memnon. Cyril could afford to treat such madness with contempt. But he had to deal with an emperor who was opposed to him, and with future generations. He might have fallen back simply and solely on his union with the successor of St. Peter; but the matter was one which had arisen since his communication with Celestine. Accounts were already being sent to the emperor by Candidian; and Nestorius and the Patriarch of Antioch both leant on the imperial arm. At any moment he might find himself in prison, as, indeed, soon actually happened. Every moment, therefore, was of importance.

Accordingly the synod met again, and Cyril asked the bishops for their vote on John of Antioch's conduct towards himself and Memnon. In stating their cases he gives a short summary of what had happened, in which precisely the same

---

[1] Mr. Puller (*Prim. Saints*, p. 184), quoting part of Philip's words, adds, 'We must certainly say that all this is new doctrine: new and therefore false; an attempt to give a religious sanction to the great position which the Roman Pontiffs had acquired mainly through the legislative action of the State.' It has been shown above that Mr. Puller's proofs of the 'legislative' origin of the position of the Holy See are derived from misinterpretations of the documents. Here he is face to face with all these Eastern bishops, and what he says was new teaching, they say was the original and universal teaching of the Church.

view of matters as I have emphasised recurs. They had met, he says, in consequence of the imperial edict—but for what purpose? 'For the purpose of confirming by a common sentence the right definition of the Apostolic Faith'—this, and not the settlement of an open question, was the primary object of the council. The ὅρος, or definition, was, of course, the ὁρισθέντα τύπον of the Apostolic See. Their confirmation of this was not the act of a superior authority, for they also confirmed the Nicene Creed, and their very confirmation was submitted to the judgment of the Papal legates, but it was the added strength, as we have already seen, of the exhibition of unity on the part of the assembled bishops. It was the various points of the circumference (to use Father Bottalla's simile) cleaving to their centre; 'following' (as Bishop Firmus, publicly, interpreted the council's action) 'the sentence of the Apostolic throne,' 'urged of necessity,' as the council at large expressed themselves, 'by the canons and by the letter of Celestine,' and in performing their duty the members of the council had proved the heresy recently introduced by Nestorius. So that the purpose of the council was 'to confirm by a common sentence the orthodox decision of the Apostolic Faith, and to attest the heresy recently introduced by Nestorius.' After explaining how the proceedings had been conducted in an orderly and judicial manner, and how John of Antioch had delayed when he might have come, and had brought with him, and been joined by, certain disorderly people, some without sees, some under accusations, he points out that the so-called sentence of deposition which John and some thirty bishops had pretended to pass on himself and Memnon was absurd, considering the number and character of the real synod. Further, the Patriarch of Antioch had violated a rule of the Church in attempting such a thing as the deposition of one occupying 'a greater throne.' That is to say, Antioch had no jurisdiction over Alexandria. Even if it had, the canons of the Church should have been observed, by their citing the accused to appear before them. Such was St. Cyril's view of the position.

Accordingly, on Cyril's proposition, three bishops were now sent to John of Antioch to summon him to appear before the synod. But they found John surrounded with soldiers, and were insulted with the blasphemous talk of his retinue. On the return of the episcopal messengers, Cyril proposed that the synod should at once proceed to declare the sentence of the Conciliabulum null and void. But Juvenal, Bishop of Jerusalem, interposed, suggesting that John should be cited again. In the course of his speech Juvenal roundly condemned the Patriarch of Antioch for not hastening to appear before the holy synod to defend himself before it, 'and to obey and respect the Apostolic throne of great Rome, sitting with us.' The rest of the sentence is untranslatable as it stands.[1] It appears to bring in also 'the Apostolic throne of Jerusalem.' But Juvenal could hardly have spoken of that as 'sitting *with us*,' for it was himself. He proceeds, according to the text, to speak of the throne of Rome as being that see 'by which, or at which, above all it is the custom by apostolic order and tradition for the throne of Antioch itself to be directed and judged.' It has been thought that Juvenal may have alluded to his own see, because he was, as a matter of fact, at that time endeavouring to wrest some of her fairest provinces from Antioch; and at the Latrocinium shortly afterwards he did take his seat as above Antioch, and sided with Eutyches. But it is impossible that he should have claimed in the council at this time what was so manifestly false, and what was actually true of the Apostolic throne of Rome, in several previous cases, such as that of Paulinus of Antioch. He obviously insisted on the same point as St. Cyril did, viz. that only Rome possessed jurisdiction over the throne of Alexandria, and in some way at the same time magnified the greatness of his own see. John was twice more cited, but with similar and even worse results, the bishops being ignominiously treated, John saying that 'since the causes of the court are transferred to the Church, he was transferring the cause of the Church to the court.'

The synod thereupon proceeded on the following day to pronounce all that John of Antioch had done null and void, and to pass sentence of excommunication against him and his associates, until they should acknowledge their fault, adding

[1] Labbe, t. iii. p. 1172.

that 'unless they do that quickly, they will undergo the complete sentence of the canon.' In this session there is no mention of Cyril having presided as in the previous one, possibly because in the condemnation of John of Antioch Cyril was going beyond his original commission, and therefore the Papal legates act alone, their commission by Celestine's express words having a further reach, and including such a step as the deposition of the Bishop of Antioch, although by the same commission they were empowered to act as they did in conjunction with Cyril and with his advice. The synod, thus composed of the Papal legates with so wide a commission as Celestine gave them, might have proceeded to depose John of Antioch as he had pretended to depose Cyril and Memnon. In their letter to St. Celestine they expressly say they might have done so, but they stopped short of this and 'reserved it for the judgment of your Holiness.'[1] Being a matter concerning one of the 'greater thrones,' they left the severer sentence for the Apostolic throne itself, the See of St. Peter, whose care for the Faith they had pronounced in the beginning of their letter to be worthy of all admiration, and to which they said they had written a report *as a matter of duty and necessity* (ἐχρῆν ἅπαντα εἰς γνῶσιν τῆς σῆς ὁσιότητος ἀνενεχθῆναι τὰ παρακολουθήσαντα γράφομεν ἀναγκαίως).

This letter of the synod is of the utmost importance as a defence of Cyril in beginning the synod without John, and as giving the view of the œcumenical council itself as to its own claim to be such, in contrast with the miserable meetings over which the Patriarch of Antioch presided. It says that the council was one gathered from the whole world, since 'it contained your Holiness' representatives, Arcadius, Projectus and Philip, who secured to us the grace of your presence by their own, and supplied the place of the Apostolic See,'[2] which is exactly the teaching of the Catholic Roman Church at this hour. They also speak of the harm that would come to the Church 'if the *greater sees* were to be insulted with impunity, and sentence were to be pronounced upon them by those who have no jurisdiction over them.' As we have seen, they hold that *they*, including as they did the representatives

---

[1] Mansi, t. iv. p. 1330.   [2] *Ibid.* p. 1338.

of the Holy See, had jurisdiction over one of the 'greater thrones,' although, as a matter of fact, they reserved the actual exercise for Celestine himself. They further speak of Cyril as having been the mainstay of the Faith, and conclude with saying that 'they have judged that all that has been decided by His Holiness concerning the Pelagians and Celestians, concerning Pelagius and Celestius and Julian, &c.,' should stand firm, and that they accept the depositions by the Holy See, after reading the letters which His Holiness had sent concerning them.

The story, interesting as it is, of the final acceptance of the deposition of Nestorius by John of Antioch, does not belong to my subject. Passing over this, therefore, I shall conclude with one or two points that are of importance.

IV. Celestine before his death wrote one of his most touching letters to the bishops of the synod,[1] after their dispersion to their homes, full, as all his letters are, of beautiful applications of Holy Scripture, and displaying the firmness of a ruler and tenderness of a father. He strikes the note of joy in the opening sentence; he then congratulates them on having faithfully carried this affair into execution 'with us;' he applies to himself the words of the Psalmist (Psal. xxiv.), 'The innocent and the upright have adhered to me,' showing that he conceived of the synod as the synod conceived of itself, as the executors of his own sentence. He praises their choice of a successor to Nestorius, and congratulates them on the emperor's assent. He then tells them that they must not stop here, they must induce the emperor to rescind his decree about Nestorius being allowed to go to Antioch. He must be removed further. 'Solitude alone becomes such men.'

'We,' says the Pope, 'are further off than you are, but by solicitude we see the whole matter closer. The care of the blessed Apostle Peter has the effect of making all present; we canot excuse ourselves before God concerning what we know. . . . We ought to have care for all in general, but it behoves us specially to assist the Antiochenes, who are besieged by pestiferous disease.'

Such is the care which he evinces for them, in accordance

[1] *Ep. Cel. ad Syn.* March 15, A.D. 432.

with the title accorded to him by the synod, viz. 'our most holy Father,' and with his own conception of his relationship to the Prince of the Apostles. He then decides what shall be done with respect to those who seemed to think with Nestorius. Although the synod had passed sentence on them, 'still we also decide what seems best. Many things have to be looked into in such cases, which the Apostolic See has always regarded.' He accordingly orders that they shall be dealt with in the same way as the 'Celestians,' and desires that the same method of treatment shall also be observed in regard to those who have imagined that ecclesiastical cases could be removed to Christian princes. He then instructs them how John of Antioch should be dealt with in case of his correcting himself.

The letter is that of no usurper; no spark of ambition appears in it. It is that of a God-fearing man providing as father for the wants of his children. There is not a trace of any consciousness that he is doing anything but fulfilling the duties of an office recognised by all; and that office is the government of the universal Church entrusted to him as the successor of Peter. On the same day he writes to the emperor a letter congratulating him on his better mind, and giving him some exquisite exhortations as to the performance of his high functions. And he writes also to the clergy and people of Constantinople, praising Cyril and drawing attention to Nestorius' sleepless energy. But Rome (he adds) is not behindhand in watchfulness. 'The blessed Apostle Peter did not desert them when they were toiling so heavily, for, when the separation of such an ulcer [as Nestorius] from the ecclesiastical body seemed advisable by reason of the putrid decay which became sensible to all, we offered soothing fomentation together with the steel. It was not by the swiftness of our sentence that he became to us as a publican and heathen man. We could not delay longer lest we should seem to run with the thief, and to take our portion with the adulterer against faith.' He treats his own sentence and its execution by the council as all one.

It is difficult to understand how Bishop Wordsworth could call St. Celestine a 'calm spectator of the controversy.' It is not less difficult, after all we have seen, to understand how

Dr. Salmon could say that 'the only one of the great controversies in which the Pope really did his part in teaching Christians what to believe was the Eutychian controversy.'[1]

Sixtus succeeded Celestine, and took up the work in the same spirit. In the following year he wrote to Cyril, praising him for his magnificent conduct and directing what was to be done about the followers of John of Antioch, and eventually wrote a most beautiful letter to John himself after the reconciliation between him and Cyril, in which he did not spare the patriarch for his past conduct, although he acquitted him of any heretical teaching. He summed up the whole matter, saying, 'You have learned by experience what it is to *think with us.*'

V. We are now in a position to estimate the force of a remark in Dr. Bright's history which, since he has repeated it in his latest productions, he appears to consider of some importance.

A case had arisen in the Patriarchate of Antioch which was brought before the bishops of the council, and which they dealt with not very satisfactorily. It was not one of the matters for which they were assembled, and their ' canon ' did not rank with their decision as to the affair of Nestorius.[2] The case was this.

The Cyprians had long endeavoured to establish for themselves an autocephalous position, not, indeed, with no dependence on anyone, for they would anyhow be subject in some matters to the See of St. Peter, but autocephalous in the sense of not depending on any neighbouring province for the ordination of their metropolitans. In point of fact, numerous provinces of the East had from the earliest times[3] been subjected to the Patriarch of Antioch, of which Cyprus was one. It had remained so until the Council of Nice, and its subordination to Antioch was included in the sixth canon of the council. During the Eustathian schism at Antioch this order had been disturbed by the Arians, and on the termination of the schism, Innocent I. had written[4] to the Patriarch of Antioch,

---

[1] *Infall. of the Church*, p. 426, 2nd edition.
[2] It is not included in the collection of Dionysius Exiguus.
[3] *Nic. Can.* vi.   [4] *Innoc. Ep.* xviii. c. 2.

saying that the Cyprians ought to return to their obedience in accordance with the Nicene canons. The Cyprians, however, managed to evade the decision of the Holy See, and they now succeeded in stealing a march on the Bishop of Antioch under cover of his disgrace. The bishops at Ephesus, guarding their decision with an 'if,' waiving, that is, the question of the truth of the Cyprians' representations, not being able to hear the other side from John of Antioch, decreed that supposing the Cyprians to be correct in their facts, they were not to be subjected to the throne of Antioch. They had not, if their statement was correct, belonged to Antioch in the old times; it was not right, therefore, for Antioch to claim jurisdiction over them now. The decision was subsequently reversed, and the Cyprians eventually agreed to submit to their metropolitans being ordained by the Bishop of Antioch.[1] The fact was, as Dr. Neale says, 'that the claims of Antioch in this instance were well founded.'[2]

In this unfortunate decision the bishops appealed to the canons as forbidding any bishop to seize upon, or occupy by force, another province which was not previously under his own or his predecessor's jurisdiction. This Canon of Ephesus, if it can be called such (for it was rather a provision for the Cyprian dispute which was afterwards recalled), is one of the armouries from which Anglican writers derive one of their most curious weapons against Rome. They apply it to the action of Gregory the Great in sending St. Augustine to be over the British bishops. These bishops were not, so they argue, originally under Augustine. They could not therefore by right be subjected to him by the Holy See. But apart from the universal supremacy of the Apostolic See, there is the question whether they were not already under the Bishop of

---

[1] For a complete misrepresentation of this whole matter see Puller's *Prim. Saints*, p. 181. One would imagine, from this writer's statement ('the Church of Cyprus remains autocephalous to this day') that Cyprus had never returned to its position of dependence on Antioch. Mr. Puller seems also to forget that the 'Council of Ephesus' included the Papal legates. But this decision was probably arrived at after their withdrawal, and so was merely a provisional arrangement (pending further inquiry) by which they succeeded in removing Cyprus from the influence of John.

[2] *Hist. of the E. Church*, p. 267.

Rome as Patriarch of the West, in which case the Ephesine decision as to the 'jus Cyprium' would not apply. Certain it is that this decision was never applied to the case of the British bishops until the sixteenth century. No one ever supposed that Gregory the Great had not the right to define the relationship of the bishops in England to the See of Canterbury. Again and again the Church of England has referred to that Pontiff's action in this matter as natural and proper, and even in the hottest dispute between Canterbury and York, when Lanfranc at the Council of Windsor pleaded the action of Gregory the Great, it did not occur to the Archbishop of York to call in question that Pontiff's right, or to use such an expression as Dr. Bright does in reference to it, viz. that of 'pretension.'

But the Council of Ephesus, in decreeing, at a time of irritation with Antioch, that it would not be well to disturb the imaginary ancient arrangement with regard to Cyprus, used an expression which Dr. Bright thinks was aimed at Rome. He makes a great deal of this supposed allusion, which is contained in the mere fact that they used the words 'worldly pride.' This expression, he thinks, must contain a covert allusion to Rome; and a mere allusion of such a kind occurring in an utterance of an œcumenical council is evidently held to be of the greatest importance in indicating the mind of the Church as to the Holy See. It is alluded to in his 'History of the Church' (1860),[1] and it reappears, after twenty-two years, at great length in his 'Notes on the Canons of the first four General Councils.'[2] In deciding that the Cyprians should, if their statement of the case was correct, have the advantage of the Nicene Canon which forbade the bishop of one province to seize by force upon the spiritual jurisdiction of another, the bishops at Ephesus used the words 'secular pride.' Now it happens that the words 'pride of the world,' with another epithet, occur in the letter addressed a few years before to Celestine, purporting to be from a council of all Africa, in which the applicants 'earnestly entreat' ('impendio deprecamur') the Pope not to send any more legates to execute his orders. They do not, as has been pointed out

[1] P. 339, note m.   [2] Pp. 119-20-21 (1882).

above (p. 301), dream of asking him not to issue his orders; but they would rather not have them executed by a legate, after their bitter experience of Faustinus. They complain that the presence of 'executores'—*i.e.* legates to execute the Papal orders—leads them to pomp and worldly pride; so they entreat the Pope to send them no more legates ' lest *we should seem* to introduce the smoky pride of the world into the Church of Christ'—*i.e.* lest we Christians in Africa should belie our calling to be not of this world.

Seeing, then, that this same word 'pride' occurs in the Ephesine decree about Cyprus, by which the bishops favoured the Cyprians' wish to withdraw themselves from John of Antioch, Dr. Bright's imagination carries him at once back to this letter of the African Synod. He thinks that the Roman legates at Ephesus *may have been* absent from that particular session which dealt with the Cyprian case; and that, they being absent, the deacon, named Besulas, who, though present, was not a constituent member of the Ephesine Synod, the bearer of the letter from the Bishop of Carthage (which Dr. Bright seems to forget spoke of the 'authority' of the Apostolic See) managed to introduce into this so-called Canon of Ephesus the words 'worldly pride,' *in allusion to that said letter of the African Council.*[1]

Dr. Bright has to suppose, first, that the bishops at Ephesus had heard of the said letter of the African Council, a most unlikely supposition; next, that Besulas, a deacon, to use Dr. Bright's own words, 'represented Africa at Ephesus;'[2] next, that the wording of the canon was due to Besulas, for which there is not an iota of proof, and then, that he introduced this clever and far-fetched allusion to the African letter, the legates happening to be absent, for if they were present ' Besulas would hardly, perhaps ' (he is not quite certain even of this) ' have quoted his Church's stringent admonition to their principal '—the ' stringent admonition ' consisting, as we have seen, of an ' earnest entreaty.' And if he did not— that is to say, if the decree of the bishops of Ephesus only

---

[1] For the difficulties about this letter cf. p. 303.

[2] Africa was represented through Capreolus' letter, accepting, by anticipation the joint action of the Holy See and the Council; not by Besulas.

referred to the struggle for precedence actually going on between Antioch and Cyprus, and between Juvenal of Jerusalem and the Bishop of Antioch (the natural and sufficient explanation of the term 'pride'), instead of to a matter with which they had nothing to do—' if he did not, the coincidence is among the most remarkable on record'!

The coincidence consists in the use of the words 'smoky pride of the world' in Africa some few years before, and of the words 'power of worldly pride' now, in reference to a fierce struggle for precedence going on before their eyes, with which Rome had nothing to do. And their remote allusion to a letter from Africa, which expresses a fear of secular pomp, not in the Bishop of Rome (as Dr. Bright seems to imagine), but in the circumstances of legations in foreign countries, is, forsooth, introduced by bishops who, as we have seen, were at the moment on the most friendly, affectionate, and submissive terms with the reigning Pope, having just before spoken of their admiration for his care for the Church and for the Faith.

And not only had they expressed their gratitude to the Pope for his guardianship of the faith, but, after concluding the affair of Nestorius, the council gave its hearty adhesion to all that had been settled by the Holy See in regard to the Pelagian heretics. It will be remembered that St. Augustine had claimed this settlement as sufficient without the apparatus of a general council. 'The rescripts have come from Rome; the case is at an end,' was his dictum; and the rescripts contained the fullest possible assertion of the necessity of referring matters of such importance to the Holy See. St. Augustine died just before the Council of Ephesus met. Capreolus, Bishop of Carthage, in response to an invitation to St. Augustine to attend the council, sent the letter alluded to above by the hands of a deacon, named Besulas, in which he deprecated, in the name of the African Church, any fresh investigation of the grievances of Pelagian or semi-Pelagian heretics, on the ground that their matters had been settled by 'the authority of the Apostolic See and the consentient decision of the hierarchy' (of Africa), which had demolished ($\sigma\nu\nu\acute{\epsilon}\chi\omega\sigma\epsilon\nu$) those disturbers of the Church. Accordingly, as we gather from the synod's report of its proceedings sent to Celestine, they entered upon no investigation of these matters. His Holiness did not wish it, and the African bishops, speaking through Capreolus, were anxious that they should not reopen the question. The bishops at Ephesus, therefore, simply accepted the decisions of the Holy See *en bloc*. And it was under these circumstances that Professor Bright imagines the bishops may have introduced a sly hit at Rome by using the words 'worldly pride'!

Conclusions.

To sum up. The following conclusions emerge from the history of the Council of Ephesus.

1. A certain hierarchical order obtained at that time amongst the greater sees of the Church. This order, though an ecclesiastical arrangement as regards the second and third see, ran up to apostolic times.

2. There was a universal conviction on the part of the Easterns that the Bishop of Rome held a unique position as occupant of 'the Apostolic See.'[1]

3. He held this position as successor of St. Peter.

4. This position involved the guardianship of the faith in a special sense, and a superiority of jurisdiction over the 'greater thrones.'

5. The theory of independent national Churches is excluded by anticipation. The nationality of Constantinople, on the one hand, and of Antioch on the other, did not free them from being subject to intervention on the part of the Bishop of Rome when circumstances demanded it; and Alexandria, in spite of its differing nationality, held itself bound in duty to report 'greater cases' to Rome.

6. An œcumenical council, which included the Pope, was infallible; as also was the Pope in determining the question of faith.

These are some of the rigorous conclusions to be drawn from the history of the Church in A.D. 431. Each one of them has its 'text' in the Council of Ephesus.

[1] Cf. Appendix IV. p. 479.

CHAPTER XXI.

THE FOURTH GENERAL COUNCIL.[1]

I. WE have seen that the principles which were formulated in the Vatican decree of 1870 were at work in the early Church from the first. They appear in the first recorded exercise of her teaching power outside the inspired pages of Holy Scripture. St. Clement's letter to the Corinthians was, according to the late Dr. Lightfoot, 'the first step towards Papal domination;' to a Catholic it was the first recorded exercise of Papal supremacy after the death of St. Peter. St. Clement pronounced judgment, uniting with himself the Church of Rome; exercising his prerogative in unison, it would seem, with a council of whose authority he was the informing principle; for it was for ever known in the Church as his letter. He claimed for his judgment the submission of those to whom he wrote, as to the voice of the Holy Ghost, and he denounced the sin of schism as the worst of evils. His letter was successful in its immediate results, and was read for some time in Christian churches as akin to Holy Scripture itself.

We have seen, further, that at the Council of Nice, whose dogmatic decision was clothed with the robe of divine authority in the eyes of orthodox Christendom, the three Sees of Peter appear in command, with Rome at their head. The canons commonly called Sardican, and regarded as of equal authority with those of Nicæa itself (if not, as there is good reason for supposing, the very canons of the Nicene Council itself) recognised in the See of St. Peter the proper court of appeal for such bishops as felt that justice had not been done them in other courts. They applied and regulated an existing

[1] Where the person's name is given to whom letters of St. Leo are addressed I have not always given the number of the letter, which differs in different editions. I have myself used the Ballerini's edition.

principle. When we come to the second œcumenical council, originally an Eastern synod, which became œcumenical through the acceptance of its dogmatic decision by the See of St. Peter, a new state of things was making itself felt. 'New Rome' had come on to the scene; and a struggle for precedence had commenced, which was destined to end only when 'the scourge of God' arose and brought the Byzantine empire to a close. The sword of Islam was the appointed avenger of the pride of that Queen of cities on the fair shores of the Bosphorus.

Rome remained the Eternal City. Whilst again and again the Christian faith was all but wrecked in the East, each heresy that threatened the mystery of the Incarnation finding its home there, the See of St. Peter stood firm throughout.

At Ephesus the judgment of Pope Celestine imposed itself upon the synod. St. Cyril, the Pope's delegate, was the Joshua that fought the battle on the plain below, whilst the Moses of the Christian Law, having delivered his charge to the warrior-bishop, sat on the throne of Peter with his hands upheld by his assisting synod.

But if this is true of Ephesus, it is still more manifestly true of Chalcedon. The throne of Peter was occupied by one of those majestic figures which occasionally dominate the history of a whole period. Well did he merit his name of Leo; and truly has posterity called him 'great.' St. Leo saved Christianity. For again the sum and substance of Christianity was at stake; the Person of its Founder was again in question under another form, and St. Leo the Great was the instrument chosen by the Divine Founder of the Christian Church to vindicate the truth of His Incarnation.

The Council of Chalcedon was the climax of the Church's conciliar utterances in the Person of our Redeemer—the last of the four Gospels, as St. Gregory called the first four councils by way of similitude. It closed a complete series of denials, each one of which was absolutely fatal to a true hold on the economy of redemption.

But (i.) it also led to a fuller knowledge of the treasure of Divine Revelation. The question all through the struggle turned on what was contained in the original deposit; and the Church at large learnt more of the contents of that deposit, she was richer for the struggle, she learnt more of the glory of His Divine Majesty and of His infinite condescension, in whom her hopes are centred.

(ii.) But the Church also learnt more of the meaning of that provision for unity, and of that guardianship of the faith, which her divine Head had instituted. She found that Peter, the foundation laid by Him, 'lives and exercises judgment in his successors,' with a store of unfailing wisdom, the fulfilment of the divine promise, 'I have prayed for thee, that thy faith fail not.' His infallible guidance was equal to combining an unerring hold upon the apostolic deposit, with fresh definition to meet a fresh denial. The memory of Leo never left the Church. He said no more than others had said before him; he uttered no new truth about the See of St. Peter; not a note of surprise, as at any novel claim, was heard, for it was (as had been said at Ephesus) a truth 'known to all ages, and doubtful to none, that the blessed Apostle Peter, the Head and Prince of Apostles, received from the Saviour of the human race the keys of the kingdom; and that he lives and exercises judgment in his successors.' But the circumstances under which Leo had to act ministered to a fuller apprehension of that truth. It was in the counsels of Divine Providence that the whole force of the 'Petrine Privilege' should be felt on a large scale, and under the pressure of unparalleled needs; so that the Church might for ever know where her strength lay and never suffer her locks to be shorn.

II. But to proceed to the actual history. 'A foolish old man,' as St. Leo called him, erring more from stupidity than the subtlety that misled Nestorius, was the cause of the storm that now burst upon the Church—a foolish old man, who boasted that he had kept his vow of continency in the monastic life, and who had all that natural influence which is invariably exercised, for good or evil, by men of recognised austerity.

Eutyches (such was his name) adopted much the same method of argument as Nestorius. As Nestorius accused St. Cyril of Apollinarianism, so Eutyches accused his opponents of Nestorianism. And as Nestorius endeavoured to gain the ear of Pope St. Celestine by accusing others of Apollinarian teaching, so Eutyches endeavoured to win Pope St. Leo to his side by accusing others of Nestorianism. Eutyches took his stand in certain expressions of St. Cyril, so that in the ultimate issue St. Cyril's teaching became the field of battle. St. Cyril was the accepted exponent of the faith against Nestorius; St. Celestine decided in his favour, and the third œcumenical synod adopted St. Celestine's ruling. St. Cyril's exposition was now quoted by Eutyches in favour of a new heresy. St. Leo, in the name of the blessed Apostle Peter, promulgated an *ex cathedrâ* decision called his 'Tome,' condemning this new heresy, and the fourth œcumenical synod accepted his ruling. In this case, too, the 'members joined themselves to the holy head,' as the action of the bishops in condemning Nestorius was described at the Council of Ephesus—after what struggles and calamities we shall now proceed to see.

III. Eutyches was condemned in a synod at Constantinople, upon impeachment by Eusebius of Dorylæum. Flavian, his archbishop, says that, after much fencing, Eutyches threw off all disguise, and said that 'we ought not to confess that our Lord subsisted in two natures after becoming man,' and that 'the Body of our Lord, although born of the Virgin, who is consubstantial with us, is not itself consubstantial with us.' In this, says St. Flavian, 'Eutyches ran counter to all the expositions of the holy Fathers.' The synod proceeded to degrade him from his ecclesiastical rank, and deprived him of the superintendence of his monastery, but they did not go on to expressly anathematise his teaching.

IV. But the matter did not rest there. It was not enough that Eutyches had been condemned by his archbishop. There was no idea in the Church at large of the archbishop's judgment, even though pronounced in synod, being final. There were no such things in the early Church as independent provinces. There was a further court of appeal, recognised, as we shall see, on all sides as part of the Nicene settlement for the government of the Church, and recognised as such at Nicæa, or Sardica, or both, on the ground of the connection of one see with the prince and head of the Apostles, as St.

Peter was acknowledged to be in the Council of Ephesus. There was, in the minds of the whole Church, an 'Apostolic See'—apostolic, not in the sense in which every bishop is a successor of the Apostles, but in a pre-eminent degree—and to that Apostolic See the case was now carried.

We should not expect to find Eutyches exhibiting the methods of a sincere inquirer. He had all the wiliness of a heretic. He looked round about at once for help, and, probably, wrote letters to every quarter whence help might come. He knew that there was friction between his own saintly archbishop and the Archbishop of Alexandria, who proved the most bitter foe to the truth that even the distracted East produced. He may well have known the weakness of the Bishop of Jerusalem, which led him to such unfortunate conduct in the immediate future, and it is therefore exceedingly probable that he proceeded to enlist these bishops in his cause. At any rate, the patrician Florentius afterwards deposed that Eutyches had appealed to an Egyptian and Jerusalemite, as well as to a Roman council, at the end of the above-mentioned synod at Constantinople—but in an undertone. The account given by the monk Constantine may be passed over, as he was convicted of untrustworthiness at a second synod, or session. If, however, Eutyches did write to these other bishops, his letters are not extant; and we can surmise nothing as to their contents. But what is certain is that Eutyches wrote to Rome, and sent the Pope, together with Eusebius' accusation and some testimonies (mostly supposititious) to himself, two documents, one a profession of faith, and the other a notice of appeal which he pretended to have handed in at the Synod of Constantinople. In his letter he asked the Pope to arrange that he might suffer no prejudice pending the appeal, on account of his condemnation by his archbishop, and he asked for a decision on the matter of faith.[1]

At the same time he wrote to St. Peter Chrysologus, Bishop of Ravenna, soliciting his interest. This saintly archbishop replied that he could not intervene in such a matter without the leave of his superior, the Bishop of Rome. He

[1] Mansi, t. v. p. 1015.

appears not to have learnt from Eutyches anything about the synod at Constantinople, and he knew nothing of the dogmatic epistle of St. Leo.[1] He accordingly advises Eutyches what to do. We are indebted to an important discovery of an old copy of St. Peter's letter in Greek, dated between A.D. 453 and A.D. 455, and therefore strictly contemporary, for the whole text of the saint's words. He advises Eutyches 'to attend obediently to whatever is written from the most blessed Pope of the city of Rome, because blessed Peter, who both lives and presides in his own see, gives to those who seek it the truth of the faith.'

Eutyches, in his letter to the Pope, had told a falsehood. He had not really lodged an appeal to Rome *at the synod*. But although he had not done this, his statement that he had is irrefragable evidence that the bishops of the East held that such an appeal, if given in at the right time, must have the effect of suspending their sentence. This was the point of Eutyches' statement, viz. to stay the proceedings. He knew that the Pope had only to suppose that an appeal had been lodged, and he would be able to enforce a suspension of proceedings.

V. Flavian also had written to St. Leo immediately after the synod, sending him the Acts. He notified, indeed, the condemnation of Eutyches to other bishops, but he sent the Acts of the synod to St. Leo alone, as to a superior court. His letter, however, did not arrive in due time, whether owing, as is supposed, to the management of Eutyches and his friends, it is impossible to say.

Accordingly, St. Leo, on receiving Eutyches' letter, wrote at once to the emperor and to Flavian. The letters are both of the highest importance as showing what the Pope could assume as admitted by the Emperor of the East and the Archbishop of Constantinople.

The emperor had taken Eutyches under his patronage, and written in his favour to St. Leo. The latter, having heard only from the emperor and Eutyches, tells the emperor that he cannot give judgment on the case until he has heard from Archbishop Flavian. He blames Flavian to the

[1] Mansi, t. v. p. 1346, 6, *Admonitio*.

emperor for not having sent the Acts of the synod to Rome at once, 'as he was in duty bound to do.' The Pope was not aware that Flavian had dispatched the Acts, but that from some mishap they had been delayed. If the emperor and Eutyches were in concert—or rather Chrysaphius, the eunuch, who had poisoned the emperor's ear in favour of the heretic —to get judgment from Rome before the cause was properly heard, they were much deceived in their estimate of Leo. For the latter simply told the emperor that he was displeased that Flavian had not written, and that he had written to say so, and felt sure that after this 'admonition,' Flavian would send a report of all the proceedings,[1] 'so that judgment may be passed in accordance with evangelical and apostolical teaching.'

To Flavian the Pope writes in terms of censure, for not having done his duty ('quod ante facere debuit') in reporting everything 'as fully as possible.'

It is impossible not to see in these letters plain evidence of the recognised position of the See of Rome as the supreme court of appeal. It was not Valentinian, but Theodosius, to whom St. Leo wrote, and it was of no less a personage than the Archbishop of Constantinople that he complained; and his complaint to the Emperor of the East was, that the archbishop had contravened a rule of the Church in not sending his report to Rome. No mere patriarch could thus write to an emperor concerning a bishop beyond the limits of his own patriarchate; and no one in his senses could have ventured to write thus in a matter which he felt concerned the salvation of the human race, except on the understanding that the rule was clear and undisputed.

VI. This was in February, A.D. 449. St. Leo, though he wrote to the emperor and to Flavian, deferred his answer to Eutyches; but Eutyches, without waiting for the Pope's reply, imitated Nestorius in inducing the emperor to summon a council. He persuaded Dioscorus, Archbishop of Alexandria, who was prepared to act as his patron, to petition the emperor for a general synod, and his Imperial Majesty fixed

---

[1] 'Quem credimus post admonitionem omnia ad nostram notitiam relaturum' (*Leonis Ep.* xxiv.).

the ensuing August for its meeting. Probably the emperor had not yet received the Pope's reply. Certainly, Flavian had not heard of the definite decision of the emperor to plunge the East into all the difficulties of a council when he wrote his answer to Leo. That answer is another most important item in the evidence supplied by the history of the Council of Chalcedon to the recognised position of the See of St. Peter.

VII. Flavian in no way resented St. Leo's censure of his silence. As a matter of fact, he had written and sent the Acts of his synod, but they had miscarried, or been delayed on the way. The archbishop recognised the duty which lay upon him to report proceedings to Rome. He describes the whole situation, narrates the deposition of Eutyches, and says that the latter has appealed to the emperor, thereby trampling under foot the canons of the Church. Further, Flavian tells Leo that what Eutyches had asserted, unknown to him, in his letter to the Pope, viz. that at the synod he gave notice of appeal to Rome, is untrue. He implies that, had it been true, he would have suspended proceedings. Flavian does not afford in this important letter the slightest indication that in his judgment St. Leo was stretching his prerogative in writing to him as he had done. On the contrary, he ends by invoking that prerogative as the only means of securing the peace of the Church. He asks the Pope to be bold with the boldness that becomes the priesthood, to 'make the common cause his own,' and to deign to give his decision by means of briefs in accordance with the canonical deposition of Eutyches at the Constantinopolitan Synod. He asks the Pope thereby to 'confirm' (using not the usual word, but that which occurs in our Lord's command to St. Peter in St. Luke xxii.[1]) the faith of the emperor; and he says that 'the matter only needs your impulse and the help that is due from you through your own consent, to bring everything into peace and calm; and so the heresy which has arisen, and the trouble that has ensued, will be brought to a happy conclusion, with the help of God, through your holy

---

[1] Mansi, t. v. p. 1354. *Leonis Ep.* xxvi.

briefs; and moreover the synod, about which there are rumours, will be prevented from taking place, and so the Churches in every quarter will not be troubled.'[1]

Flavian, therefore, profoundly distrusted the value of the rumoured synod, and looked to the timely exercise of the Papal prerogative as sufficient to secure the peace of the Church.

And in expressing this conviction he bears witness to the fact that an equal reverence was attributed to the authority of the Apostolical See by the rest of the bishops in the East.[2] Otherwise there would be no point in his remark, and no ground for his hope.

The principle, therefore, of Church government which the Archbishop of Constantinople assumed as Catholic was this— he did not consider that matters should necessarily be concluded where they began. There was, as yet, no thought of the independence of national Churches, nor of each province finally settling its own matters. His connection with Rome was intimate and obligatory; and it is clear that it did not depend on the civil position of that city. He wrote to Leo, as to him to whom it belonged to 'vindicate the common affairs of the Churches;' he prayed him to issue briefs which might settle the disturbances of the Eastern Churches, and he alluded to the passage in St. Luke xxii., 'Confirm the brethren.' St. Leo had requested him not merely to notify the deposition of Eutyches, as he would do to other Churches, but to send him the Acts—precisely what is done for the revision of a sentence by a superior court. And Flavian accepts the position to enable St. Leo to do his duty, which St. Leo had said was impossible without a full report of the proceedings.[3] He states distinctly that not only was there no need of the judgment of any other Eastern patriarch, but that not even a general council was needed; and Flavian knew well what the other Eastern bishops thought.[4]

This was in March, A.D. 449. In April Eutyches occupied himself with getting an assembly of thirty-four bishops con-

---

[1] Mansi, t. v. p. 1358.
[2] Cf. 'Obs. Baller. de Diss. Quesn. de Eutych. Appell.,' *Leonis Opera*, t. ii.
[3] *Ep.* xxiii.
[4] Mansi, t. v. p. 1356. *Adnot. Baller.*

vened in Constantinople to discuss an accusation which he had brought against the synod that condemned him of having falsified the documents—an accusation which miserably broke down.

VIII. But in May Leo had received Flavian's report, and he at once took in the whole position. The lion was roused, and from that day onwards his activity, his decision, his wisdom, his piety, his tender charity and his indomitable courage were such as to mark him out as one of the most extraordinary characters that have filled the pages of history, even were we to forget the effect of his noble presence on Attila, leader of the Huns outside the walls of Rome, or his influence over Genseric within the city. He had already given the death-blow to the remnants of Priscillianism; he had baffled the clandestine movements of the Manicheans, and he had sent Pelagianism to its grave. But here was an enemy that threatened to shake the foundations of the Christian religion by a direct assault on the person of its Founder. All that activity, and ingenuity, and worldly prestige, all that the favour of princes and the friendship of the great could do, was enlisted in its favour. But St. Leo was more than a match for these. He was so in virtue of the divine promises to Peter, for we shall see that it was as the successor of St. Peter, *and through the Church's recognition* of the authority of the Apostolic See, that Leo triumphed. Had he been compelled to vindicate the authority of St. Peter's See—that is to say, if men had been able to resist him on the ground that our Lord did not include the successors of St. Peter in His commission to that Apostle—the position would have been an impossible one. But the faith of the Church had been declared in the most explicit terms at the Council of Ephesus. East and West had there agreed on the position that ' it had been known *to all ages, and was doubted by none*, that the blessed Apostle Peter, Prince and Head of the Apostles, received the keys of the kingdom from the Saviour of the world,' and that Peter ' lives and exercises judgment in his successors.' Such were the undisputed terms in which the Papal legates at Ephesus had expressed the general teaching of the Church, which by common consent had been placed in the archives of that œcumenical council, as containing nothing strange to the ears of the assembled bishops of the East.

It was, then, as the successor of the Prince of the Apostles that St. Leo now acted, and that he claimed to act; and no voice in the East was raised to deny this truth, save, indirectly, one, and that was the voice of the man who became the patron of Eutyches, and who was extruded from the Church at her œcumenical council at Chalcedon.

IX. The ides of June had come, and Leo having been already engaged on his longer epistle to Flavian, saw the necessity of taking more stringent measures to meet the difficulties in which Flavian was placed. He decided upon sending legates to Constantinople to inquire into the whole matter, and instead of sending his letter by Flavian's messenger, he sent it by these legates, together with others, addressed to Theodosius, to Pulcheria, to the Archimandrites of Constantinople, to the synod, of which he had now received notice, and in which he acquiesced,[1] and to Julian, Bishop of Cos, of whom more hereafter.

The 'Tome of St. Leo,' as the epistle now sent to Flavian is called, stands almost alone, after Holy Scripture, in the reverence with which it was regarded for ages by the entire Church. Its reception was equalled only by the position assigned in the primitive Church to the letter of St. Clement, the third successor of St. Peter, written to the Corinthians in the first century. It was frequently read in the East after a general council in professions of faith. St. Gregory the Great says (Lib. vi. Ep. 2): 'If anyone ever presumes to say anything against the faith of these four synods, and against the Tome and definition of Pope Leo, of holy memory, let him be anathema.'

It opens with judging Eutyches at once, and then proceeds to that magnificent exposition of the 'sacrament of our faith,' which on its first perusal in youth has impressed so many much as the first sight of the sea.

X. It is, however, with the ending of St. Leo's Tome that

---

[1] This was clearly the case, in spite of the apparent contradiction given at the Robber Synod, which will be explained hereafter.

the purpose of this book is concerned. The Archbishop Flavian (be it remembered), to whom the Tome is addressed, had come before Leo as the judge of first instance, having synodically condemned a monk of his own archdiocese. He brought him before Leo in his letter as already condemned in the Constantinopolitan Synod, to be condemned more solemnly and by a final peremptory judgment passed by the Apostolic See. For he did not merely notify the deposition of Eutyches, but asked for help, and asserted that peace could only be obtained by Leo's approval of the Synod of Constantinople (whose Acts he sent) and by his issuing a brief to that effect. Accordingly at the end of his Tome St. Leo gave his judgment.

Without referring the matter to a council of the whole West, he reviews the synodical acts, and in part confirms, in part disapproves, of the judgment of the Constantinopolitan Synod. He confirms the condemnation of Eutyches; but he reprehends the acts of the synod as irregularly conducted. He blames the bishops for not having proscribed under anathema the heretical saying of Eutyches, 'I confess that our Lord consisted *of two natures* before the union, but I confess only one nature *after* the union.' And then he directs that Eutyches should be received back again if he repents, and gives the exact method of such reception. The matter, therefore, needed to be done more exactly and canonically than in the Synod of Constantinople. Eutyches might have thought that he had spoken some of these words 'rightly,' or that they were such as could be tolerated ('tolerabiliter'), so far as any expression of the synod to the contrary was concerned. 'In order, however,' the Pope concludes, 'to bring this whole matter to the desired end, we have sent, in our stead, our brethren the Bishop Julius and the priest Renatus, with my son, the deacon Hilarus, with whom we have associated the notary Dulcitius, whose faith has been approved by us, trusting that the help of God will be with us, that he who had erred may abjure his false opinion and be saved. God keep thee safe, dearest brother.'

Such was the exercise of Papal jurisdiction contained in this letter, one of the most celebrated documents of Christian antiquity.

It may be noted in passing that St. Leo here calls the priest Renatus his brother; but this letter is sufficient to show what the whole Catholic Church thought of the relation of the Apostolic See to the rest of the episcopate. Here is a palpable exercise of authority, such as only belongs to the judge of a supreme court. None of the other patriarchs are taken into account; St. Leo speaks in full authority, and that he was not usurping an authority which was disallowed by others is certain from the fact that the Council of Chalcedon and the whole Catholic Church accepted the Tome as a solemn judgment within the competency of the Pope's authority. Thus, not only did Eutyches pretend that he had appealed to the Pope, when it suited his purpose, on the understanding that his appeal would be sure to suspend the sentence of the Eastern bishops against him; not only did Flavian send the synodical Acts to be reviewed by the Pope as judge in the matter; not only did Leo act as judge and decide the case so far as could be done at a distance, and send legates to do the rest in his stead—but an œcumenical synod, and the universal Church for ever after, accepted as on a par with the definitions of Nicæa and Ephesus the Tome which contained this exercise of authority, against which not a protest, not a murmur, not a whisper was ever raised.[1]

It is as idle to call the teaching involved in this exercise of authority that of a 'school of thought,' as it would be to call the Catholic doctrine concerning the single personality of our Lord a 'school of thought' simply because a certain number of bishops held aloof from St. Cyril in his contest with Nestorius. It was the school of thought that held its own at Ephesus, as being the only teaching of antiquity 'known to all ages;' and it prevailed in the future of the Church—in other words, it was the teaching, not of a school, but of the Church. St. Leo's Tome never could have been accepted by the Church unless the position of judge which he assumed therein was in accordance with apostolic doctrine.

XI. Together with his 'Tome' or Epistle to Flavian, Leo sent a letter to the Emperor Theodosius, which is of importance as showing the grounds on which he acquiesced in the

[1] Cf. 'Observ. Baller. de Eutych. Appell.,' *Leonis Opera*, t. ii.

convocation of a general council. He says that Eutyches has been proved to have erred—there is no question, according to St. Leo, about that; but since the emperor has settled upon a council at Ephesus 'that the truth may be made known to the unskilful old man,' he, the Pope, sends legates to supply his place. 'The legates,' says St. Leo, 'are commissioned to carry with them a disposition to justice and benignity, so that, since *there can be no question as to what is the integrity of the Christian faith*, the depravity of error may be condemned.' If Eutyches repents—which the kind heart of the Pope always contemplates—the benevolence of the priesthood (bishops in the Greek version) is to come to his aid. Eutyches, says St. Leo, had promised him, in his original petition, that he would correct whatever the Pope condemned.

The idea of the council, then, was that it was a fitting machinery to impress on Eutyches the importance of obeying the Papal decision, and to deal with him properly if he asked pardon. It was in this that the Constantinopolitan synod had come short of perfect justice and charity.

XII. But St. Leo continues with the following descriptions of the position occupied by the decisions contained in his Tome or letter to Flavian. He says to the emperor, 'But what things the Catholic Church universally believes and teaches concerning the sacrament of the Lord's Incarnation are more fully contained in the writings which I have sent to my brother and fellow-bishop Flavian.'[1]

At the same time the Pope wrote to the saintly sister of the emperor, who had brought him up in his tender years under all the best influences of the Christian faith. It was not her fault, if her imperial brother now sided with heretics; and it was to be her lot to assist the saintly Pope in the Church's struggle with the new heresy. To her—the Empress Pulcheria—St. Leo described the error of Eutyches as 'contrary to our only hope and that of our fathers,' and told her that, if he persists in his error, he cannot be absolved. 'For,' he adds, the 'Apostolic See[2] both acts with severity in

[1] Mansi, t. v. p. 1394.

[2] Literally, 'The moderation of the Apostolic See observes this discipline that it both,' &c. Mansi, t. v. p. 1399.

the case of the obdurate, and wishes to pardon those who suffer themselves to be corrected.' It is obvious to remark that he considers the absolution of Eutyches to rest with the Apostolic See. He hopes that Pulcheria will do her best to help on the Catholic faith, and says that he has delegated his authority to those whom he has sent, that pardon may be bestowed if the error is done away.

It is here, as elsewhere, the Apostolic See that is assumed to be the agent in the matter, and the council is to be concerned not with any question as to the true faith, but with moving Eutyches to repentance by the display of unanimity amongst the bishops.

Still more important, if possible, are the terms of the letter which he sent to the Archimandrites of Constantinople.[1] They are his 'beloved children.' He is sending to them persons 'a latere' to assist them in 'the defence of the truth,' not for the investigation of the faith. He sets his seal to their condemnation of Eutyches. If he repents and makes full satisfaction—which is the constantly recurring thought in Leo's mind—then 'we wish him to obtain mercy.' But 'as to the sacrament of the great love of God (*pietatis magnæ*) in which we have justification and redemption by the Incarnation of the Word of God, our teaching from the tradition of the Fathers[2] is sufficiently explained in letters to Flavian, so that you may know from your chief (*per insinuationem Præsulis vestri*) what in accordance with the Gospel of our Lord Jesus Christ *we wish to be established in the hearts of all the faithful*.'[3]

XIII. Still more definite are the words of the Pope to the synod itself, which was to meet in August. He gives as the ground of its being convoked the emperor's wish to add the authority of the Apostolic See to his edict,[4] as though His Majesty desired 'that the meaning of the answer given by the *Prince of the Apostles* to our Lord's question should be declared by the most blessed Peter himself,' *i.e.* through his own see. The object of the council is further defined to be

---

[1] Mansi, t. v. p. 1406.
[2] 'Nostra ex Patrum traditione sententia.'   [3] Mansi, t. v. p. 1407.
[4] 'Ad sanctæ dispositionis effectum'—'dispositio' being a term in use for imperial edicts.

that 'all error may be done away with by a fuller judgment' ('pleniore judicio')—exactly the idea of a council which has been given above.[1] The council was as it were the fuller and more emphatic utterance of the Papal judgment. Its action was to consist in adhering to the judgment of the Apostolic See—in, as it were, prolonging its utterance, and applying it materially and visibly to the person in hand. It was not a higher judgment, not the confirmation of a superior authority, but the sentence of the Pope swelling out and completed by its synodical proclamation, as the sufferings of Christ are completed by those of His followers. His legates were to provide over its actual utterance; they were to determine[2] with the holy assembly of the episcopal brotherhood 'what things will be pleasing to the Lord.' The Pope then goes on to give a sketch of what Eutyches should do, and repeats what he had already said to Flavian, viz. that Eutyches had promised to obey the Holy See in the document ('libellus') which he had originally transmitted.[3]

One other letter he writes on the same day to Julian, Bishop of Cos, in the course of which he says he has sent letters to Flavian 'from which both your beloved self *and the whole Church* may know about the ancient and only faith, what we hold and preach as of divine tradition.'

No sooner had the legates set out with this batch of letters than Flavian's original letter (written immediately after the Constantinopolitan Synod) arrived, containing another copy of the Acts of the synod which he had spontaneously sent to Rome, and which had been mysteriously delayed. Leo at once wrote to him briefly, saying that the synod was not really needed. And he took the opportunity of writing once more to the emperor, excusing himself from attendance at the synod on three grounds: first, because there was no precedent for a Pope attending such a council (except, of course, by his legate); secondly, if there were, temporal necessities at home were in the way (the barbarians were wellnigh at the door); and thirdly, because the case was so clear that there was no real need ('rationabilius abstinendum'). Still he says he sends legates.

[1] P. 330.   [2] Mansi, t. v. p. 1411.   [3] *Ibid.*

CHAPTER XXII.

THE COUNCIL AT EPHESUS, CALLED THE LATROCINIUM, OR ROBBER SYNOD—LEADING TO THE COUNCIL OF CHALCEDON.

I. On August 8, A.D. 449, the ill-fated council met. It had been convened at the express desire of Dioscorus, Patriarch of Alexandria, a man of immoral life and violent temper, animated with furious hatred against Flavian and a determination to protect Eutyches. The Emperor Theodosius seems to have been completely in the hands of his eunuch Chrysaphius, the friend of Eutyches, and to have been perfectly indifferent to canons and laws of the Church. He repeated the experiment which he had made in the affair of Nestorius, of appointing the president of the synod, but this time with success. He appointed Dioscorus president in defiance of the laws of the Church, and he forbade Theodoret, Bishop of Cyrus, to attend the synod, on the ground that he had written against Cyril, but really because he was opposed to Dioscorus and Eutyches. Further, he commanded the attendance of Elpidius with a band of soldiers, with the view of forcing on the condemnation of Flavian, whom he called an innovator in religion. These were terrible auspices under which to commence a synod.

But the emperor did not even stop there. He commanded the attendance of an Archimandrite of Syria, named Barsumas, who was afterwards credited by the bishops at Chalcedon with the murder of Flavian; and not only his attendance was ordered as an anti-Nestorian, which was the attitude that the adherents of Eutychianism assumed, but the synod was ordered to give him a seat and vote, although not a bishop. The position seems at first sight that of a madman. But Theodosius was under the influence of others, and these others were reckless in their endeavours to vent their spite against the orthodox party.

Dioscorus seems to have been consumed with the spirit of jealousy, and he at once accepted the position of president. He sat above the legates, who stood out against this innovation upon the Church's order, and took no regular seat in the council, but stood outside the bishops. Juvenal of Jerusalem, who was infected with Eutychian leanings, and had been joined on to Dioscorus by the emperor as one of the presidents, sat above the Bishop of Antioch, against whom he had long had a grudge; and in spite of the famous canon passed at Constantinople, Flavian, its archbishop, sat below each of these.

II. When the proposal was made to read St. Leo's Tome, Dioscorus simply occupied the time with other matters, and the Tome was never read. Eutyches had a confession of faith read on his behalf, which was accepted. His great point was that he accepted the Nicene Creed and the Ephesine decree—so little did the recitation of the Nicene Creed exclude heresy as to the central dogma of the Christian religion, and so utterly at variance with the facts of the early Church is the contention, now often made, that since 'Romans, Greeks, Anglicans' recite the Nicene Creed, there is sufficient unity of faith amongst them to constitute a visible Church.

Dioscorus accepted Eutyches' confession of faith, and his condemnation was reversed. In vain did the legates plead that the Tome of St. Leo should be read. The letters of St. Cyril were read and interpreted in favour of 'one nature after the Incarnation.' Eustathius of Berytus said that it was not St. Cyril's or St. Athanasius' teaching that there were two natures in Christ, using, however, an expression which refers in Cyril's writings to the One Nature and Divine Personality which existed before the Incarnation. The bishops held their tongues in terror, with Dioscorus before them, surrounded by soldiers and by the monks of Barsumas. They were dumb as the bishops in England in the Convocation of 1531, when in terror of Henry VIII. they gave a silent vote in favour of his supremacy.

Flavian was forthwith condemned. The Bishop of Iconium threw himself at the feet of Dioscorus, and pleaded for Flavian. Dioscorus called for the soldiers, and the place was immediately filled with the rough military, with chains in their hands to lead off refractory bishops. They were locked in for the rest of the night. A blank paper was given them to sign; the sick were not allowed to go out for refreshment until they had subscribed the paper. Flavian now appealed to Rome, and this was the signal for blows and kicks from the monks, headed by Barsumas, and from Dioscorus himself. The old man eventually died of the injuries; but he had lodged his appeal to Rome before he went before another throne to receive the martyr's crown. Well might many of the bishops at Chalcedon, as they thought of this murdered Abel, call Dioscorus a second Cain.

Domnus, the Bishop of Antioch, was deposed, as also Theodoret. Maximus was chosen in the place of Domnus, but the See of Cyrus was left unfilled. Eusebius of Dorylæum, and Ibas, were likewise deposed, the see of the former being left vacant, while that of the latter was filled by Nonnus.

No one knows what became of Bishop Julius, the legate, in this scene of disorder, but Hilarus, the deacon, fled for his life,[1] and escaped to tell the tale to his master at Rome.

Such were the circumstances under which the authority of the Apostolic See was set at nought by a Christian bishop, with the protest only of the Papal legates, the Bishop of Iconium and the martyred Archbishop of Constantinople.

Dioscorus departed in haste and the assembly dispersed. And so, as Bishop Eusebius of Dorylæum afterwards informed the Emperors Valentinian and Marcian, Dioscorus, 'by money and by the brute force of his troops, overwhelmed the orthodox faith, and confirmed the heresy of Eutyches.' The synod was stigmatised by Leo as a 'Robber Council' rather than a true synod, and for ever after it was known by that expressive title.

III. Now let us suppose that the Church at this moment possessed nothing more for the purposes of her government than a 'first patriarch,' *primus inter pares*, with 'a prece-

[1] So Prosper, in his *Chronicon*.

dency, a pre-eminence,' and (in a sense not formal or technical) 'a leadership,' but without 'definite powers'—which is the highest Anglican description of the official position of the Holy See. Suppose, too, that this precedency was owing, not to a divine institution, but to the secular position of the city of Rome, to its having been 'organised by apostolic hands,' and having been connected with 'the majesty of the names of Peter and Paul,' and become 'famous for its bountiful generosity' and for 'its traditional immunity from heretical speculations.' This is the account given by a representative Anglican writer, of the 'place both lofty and distinctive,' 'undoubtedly assigned by ancient Christianity' to the See of Rome.[1]

Would such a leadership have proved equal to the crisis that had arisen in the East under the Emperor Theodosius? Could such a leadership (which does not include the *right* of being appealed to as a higher court) have been able to reverse the catastrophe of the Robber Synod? Could such a position, with no 'definite powers,' no inheritance of rule and judgment from any 'Prince of Apostles' (for this is excluded by that theory), have been a sufficient lever for even Leo the Great to counteract the tremendous success over the orthodox faith which had now been achieved at Ephesus? Peckham, Archbishop of Canterbury, complaining to Edward I. of the conflicts that had arisen in England between the Church and State, says that nothing would avail to set things right except that state of things in which Catholic emperors bent before (1) the decrees of the Sovereign Pontiffs, (2) the statutes of councils, (3) and the sanctions of the orthodox Fathers. And in regard to the first he says, 'the sovereign Lord of all gave authority to the decrees of the Sovereign Pontiffs, when He said to Peter in the Gospel of St. Matthew, "Whatsoever thou shalt bind on earth shall be bound in heaven."'[2] Could anything short of this inherited privilege of Peter, which was the teaching of every Archbishop of Canterbury, and which is the distinctive feature of Catholic and Roman teaching at this

---

[1] Cf. *The Roman Claims tested by Antiquity*, p. 8, by W. Bright, D.D., Canon of Christ Church, Regius Professor of Ecclesiastical History. 1877.

[2] *Ep.* 199: *Registrum Epistolarum*, ed. C. T. Martin (1882), vol. i. p. 240.

hour, be adequate to deal with the state of things that had now arisen in the East?

IV. On what did St. Leo actually rely? He had already expounded the faith which he 'desired to be implanted in the hearts of all the faithful,' as he told the clergy of Constantinople. He had already given an 'interpretatio benigna' to the emperor's desire for a council as necessarily involving the wish to have Peter's answer at Cæsarea Philippi explained by Peter himself (*i.e.* through his see), as he told the synod itself; he had reviewed and revised the Acts of a previous Synod of Constantinople, and laid down the conditions of Eutyches' restoration, and, in his letter to the empress he had assumed, on the ground of his occupying 'the Apostolic See,' the office of absolver of the heretic in case he repented. But he had now to lift up the fallen East. He had the emperor against him; the Patriarch of Alexandria was involved in heresy, a new patriarch had been elected to Antioch, the Bishop of Jerusalem had sided with the enemies of the faith, and but one bishop, besides his own legate, had dared to lift up his voice in favour of the murdered archbishop.

On what, then, did Leo rely in dealing with bishops, patriarchs, and an Eastern emperor? His position as Bishop of Old Rome could avail him nothing, for Theodosius was Emperor of New Rome. His position as occupant of *an* Apostolic See would not suffice; the Bishop of Jerusalem was his equal there. The traditional orthodoxy of Rome would be of no use to him here; the East had gone in for its own opinion. He had with him the hearts of many, but the voices of none, whilst the emperor professed to believe in an Eastern council of bishops under his own royal supremacy. What right had Leo to intervene at all?

The ground that he did assume was his position of Sovereign Pontiff. He knew well that though they might rebel against it, they could not deny it. He knew that the East to a man believed St. Peter to be 'the Prince and head of the Apostles,' and that Peter 'lives and exercises judgment in his successors.'[1] And on this belief he acted throughout. And

[1] Cf. p. 344.

in the whole course of the Council of Chalcedon not a single protest was raised against the assumption made to emperor, empress, to the synod, and to individual bishops—made publicly and given as the ground of his action; there was, I say, not a solitary protest against the perpetual assumption on the part of the Pontiff that he was the successor of St. Peter, and that as such he had the power of the keys, not exclusively, but pre-eminently; with a precedence, not of honour merely, but of spiritual jurisdiction over the entire Church of God. 'It is idle to bid us acknowledge her bishop' (*i.e.* the Bishop of Rome) 'as first patriarch, when he will not be acknowledged as anything short of a Supreme Pontiff.'[1] This is the ground alleged for refusing at this moment to the Bishop of Rome the position which the writer of these words considers was his in the first four councils. It has, however, already been made clear that the Pope's position was something very different from this from the beginning; but the history of Eutychianism and the Council of Chalcedon are distinct in their evidence to the truth that the Pope was held to be the successor of the Prince of the Apostles, and as such was, as St. Cyril called Celestine, 'the archbishop of the universal Church.'

V. Flavian upon his condemnation at Ephesus had handed in an appeal to the Papal legates. He appealed to 'the Apostolic See;' so Liberatus, the African author of the 'Breviarium,' states[2] after inspecting the documents. And Valentinian, the Emperor of the West, distinctly states the same in his letter to Theodosius. 'The Bishop of Constantinople appealed to him' (viz. the Bishop of Rome) 'by formal notice,' *per libellos.*[3] De Marca, whose general line of argument would naturally indispose him to admit this, says, 'It is clearly proved by Valentinian's letter that Flavian appealed to Pope Leo;' and again, 'so as that he appealed to the Roman Pontiff alone.' The Empress Placidia,[4] writing from Rome, says that appeal had been made to the Apostolic See, 'and to all the bishops of these parts.' 'These parts' are not to be understood of the entire West, but of those bishops round

---

[1] *Roman Claims,* &c. by Canon Bright.
[2] *Breviarium,* c. xii.   [3] *Leon. Ep.* lv.   [4] *Ibid. Ep.* lvi.

about Rome, and all others happening to be in Rome, with whom the Popes almost invariably acted in matters of unusual importance. The authority of such a synod was wholly due to that of the Holy See. For no mere Roman synod could have the right to deal with the affairs of an Eastern patriarchate; the authority of such a synod could only come from its president, the successor of St. Peter, in whose name its decisions most frequently ran. When a Pope felt that the unanimity of his council would add any extrinsic weight to the Papal judgment he would naturally mention it, as in point of fact St. Leo did in this case. But its intrinsic value was recognised as being due to the authority of 'the Apostolic See.' Flavian knew well that the Pope usually acted with a synod, and he may have mentioned the synod, as the Empress Galla Placidia seems to imply; or the empress may (quite as probably) have thrown the words in, as being true in fact, although not expressly mentioned by Flavian.[1] St. Leo's letter to Theodosius, speaking of the tears of 'all the churches in our parts,' is headed 'Leo, Bishop, and the Holy Synod, which met in the city of Rome.' But, as De Marca admits, Valentinian's letter is conclusive.

VI. On September 29 (449) St. Leo was holding one of these synods of the suburbicarian sees and of the bishops who happened to be in Rome, assembled to celebrate the anniversary of his own birthday, and conduct the affairs of the Church, when Hilary, the deacon, arrived from Ephesus with the sad news of the Robber Council. The synod was accordingly prolonged to consider what steps should be taken to retrieve the disaster which had befallen the true faith. They had now before them the appeal of Flavian and that of Theodoret. They knew nothing as yet, it would seem,[2] of the death of Flavian, and the election of his successor. They only knew of the triumph of heresy in a council of bishops which had received St. Leo's acquiescence on the understanding that it met to promulgate the condemnation of Eutyches, if he did not withdraw his heretical propositions, and to absolve him by the authority of the Holy See if he did.

---

[1] Cf. the Ballerini's *Observations on Quesnel's Eighth Dissertation*.
[2] This is very clearly shown by the Ballerini.

St. Leo, in concert with his bishops, at once repudiated the council at Ephesus; so that Hilary, the deacon, who was present, could write to the Empress Pulcheria saying [1] 'that everything done in Ephesus by Dioscorus uncanonically and tumultuously and through worldly hate, is condemned by the aforesaid Pope with the whole Western Council,' *i.e.* the bishops at and around Rome. At Chalcedon (Act X.) the legates objected to the reading of the Acts of the Robber Synod on the ground that they had all been rendered null and void 'by the most blessed and apostolical Bishop of the city of Rome,' and the validity of the objection was admitted.

And so, too, all who took an active part in that synod were now separated by St. Leo from the communion of the Apostolic See.

VII. So that Leo did not ask for any fresh council in order to nullify the proceedings at Ephesus, but he treated them at once as null and void. No general synod was needed for that; and Flavian had not appealed to a general synod. Besides the reasons just given, his principles on that point were clearly expressed in his letter to St. Leo ('Ep.' xxvi.), when he said that the exercise of Leo's authority would supersede the necessity of a council; and his experience of the Ephesine Synod would not incline him to repeat the experiment of another council. He appealed to Leo's apostolical authority, in accordance with the canon of Sardica or Nice, and it rested with Leo to exercise that authority as he thought best, by synod or otherwise. St. Leo considered that a council was rendered necessary by the circumstances under which Flavian appealed, not by Flavian's appeal itself. The Pontiff acted in exact accordance with the fourth canon of Sardica, or (as I have said there is good reason for believing it to be) the unmutilated canon of Nicæa, which came to be called a Sardican canon. That canon enacted that 'When any bishop shall have been deposed by the judgment of those bishops who live in the neighbouring parts, and shall have proclaimed that his case is to be dealt with in Rome, no other bishop should be ordained to his see after the appeal of him who seems to be

---

[1] *Leonis Ep.* xl.

deposed until the case has been decided by the judgment of the Roman bishop.'

What, therefore, was necessary according to this Nicene, or Sardican, canon was the judgment of the Bishop of Rome; and the Bishop of Rome had the right, according to this canon, to demand that things should remain as they were, and no bishop be ordained until he had passed his sentence.[1]

Accordingly, in the following January (450),[2] the Pope wrote to the Emperor Theodosius, who, he well knew, recognised in him the successor of St. Peter, in spite of his having yielded to Chrysaphius his eunuch, and thrown his imperial ægis over the reprobate Patriarch of Alexandria. Now it was not a time in which a man like St. Leo, whose whole soul was on fire with zeal for the truth of the Incarnation, would venture on an unsubstantiated claim, or claim an unrecognised position. He must have known that there was no one who would deny his connection with St. Peter, or he would never have run the risk, under the circumstances, of being asked on what ground he ventured to intervene with such a claim. The idea that he acted as 'First Patriarch' is out of the question. There is not a sign of such a thought in the whole history; and the idea that he risked all on a doubtful position, or asserted what was not fully recognised, is preposterous. But the only alternative to this is the supposition that what was accepted without a murmur at the Œcumenical Council of Ephesus was the literal truth, viz. 'That it has been known to all ages and doubtful to none' that Peter was the head of the Apostles, and that 'he up to this time and always lives and exercises judgment in his successors.'

Accordingly, Leo wrote to the emperor and demanded the fulfilment of 'the decrees of the canons drawn up (*habitorum*) at Nicæa.' And in virtue of these he asked that ' you would order that all things should be as they were before any judgment was passed [*i.e.* at the Robber Council] until a larger number of bishops can be gathered together from the whole world;' and that this synod be assembled in Italy, '*so that I*

---

[1] Cf. *supra*, p. 180.

[2] This date has been fixed by the Ballerini through a codex which they recovered (cf. *Leonis Opera, Ep.* liv., and *Diss. de Ep. deperd.* n. 38).

may be present and pass judgment on the whole matter.' [1] The object of the council was that those bishops 'who have erred from the right way may be recalled to a sound mind by wholesome remedies, and that those whose case is graver may acquiesce in counsels (given), or be cut off from the One Church.'

He speaks of the emperor having sent letters, previously to the Robber Council, ' to the see of the blessed Apostle Peter,' and having made him feel sure that truth would be defended, especially considering the trustworthy character of those whom he (the Pope) had sent to the council; then he expresses his certainty that all would have been well with the bishops if they had been allowed to hear his letter to Flavian (the Tome); ' for the tumult would have been so quieted by the manifestation of the most pure faith which, inspired divinely, we have received and hold, that neither unskilfulness would have pursued its folly' (in allusion to Eutyches), ' nor rivalry ' (in allusion to Dioscorus against Constantinople) ' have had the opportunity of doing further harm.'

These words of St. Leo to an Eastern emperor, written after consultation with the Synod of Rome, contain as full an expression of infallibility as is anywhere to be found. One expression, if taken too strictly, goes beyond the Vatican decree. That decree, in formulating the dogma which is here assumed by St. Leo, decides that the Pope does not, in his *ex cathedrâ* pronouncements, claim inspiration but divine assistance. It is clear, however, that St. Leo held the same. Inspiration, in its earlier, wider sense, includes the assistance vouchsafed to the writers of Holy Scripture. But the saint here limits the word by the rest of the sentence, and shows that he means exactly that divine assistance in declaring what ' has been received by us ' (*i.e.* the Holy See), which constitutes Papal infallibility according to the Vatican decree.

The position, then, as St. Leo placed it before the emperor, was this. The synod has gone wrong. That is certain. Had the bishops had St. Leo's Tome read to them they would have gone right. Violence and intrigue prevailed; but Flavian protested and appealed, and so did the Papal legates.

[1] Cf. *Ep.* xliii. and xliv.

It is necessary, therefore, according to the canons, that the Pope should intervene. This, under the circumstance, will be best done by the medium of a general council, whereby alone (St. Leo says) 'all conflict would be brought to an end, and all deviation from or doubts as to the faith cease.'[1]

At the same time he wrote to the Empress Pulcheria, and said that his legates protested, at the synod, that force was being used, and 'that they were not going to be separated by any injuries from that faith which had been most fully expounded and set in order by the See of the blessed Apostle Peter, and which they had brought with them to the holy synod.'

He asked the empress to assist him in getting another synod convoked, and to consider herself 'specially entrusted with a commission (for that purpose) by the most blessed Apostle Peter.'

VIII. Theodosius kept perfect silence. A few weeks after the despatch of these letters the Emperor Valentinian came to Rome with the Empresses Galla Placidia, his mother, and Eudoxia, his wife, and daughter to Theodosius. On the Feast of the Chair of St. Peter they came into St. Peter's for their devotions, and met the sorrowing Pontiff. They were at the tomb of the Apostles in the Basilica, and his Holiness approached their Imperial Majesties, hardly able to speak for the tears and sobs that choked his utterance.[2] He described to them the state of things, and told them of his request for another synod, and induced them to use their influence with their imperial relative to induce him to answer the Pope's request.

Accordingly each one of them wrote to Theodosius. The Western emperor's letter to his imperial relative in the East is of supreme importance. It is, I repeat, impossible to suppose that Valentinian would venture on any disputed ground as to jurisdiction. Valentinian's letter was inspired by Leo. And no one can read St. Leo's letters at this period without feeling that his supreme motive was the honour due to our Divine Lord and his devouring zeal for the revealed

---

[1] *Ep.* xliii.   [2] *Ep.* lvi. 'Galla Plac. ad Theodosium.'

truth concerning the mystery of the Incarnation. No one can read his letters without feeling that a certain piety, humility, and holy charity breathes through every one of them; and therefore no one can reasonably suppose that he was engaged in pushing a usurped prerogative at this momentous crisis. What, then, does Valentinian, thus inspired, say to his imperial cousin? He says, 'The most blessed Bishop of the city of the Romans, to whom antiquity gave the sovereignty over all' (as being the See of St. Peter, as we know Valentinian held), 'has to judge concerning matters of faith and the affairs of bishops,' and that on this account the Bishop of Constantinople appealed to him by a formal notice[1] 'on account of the strife that had arisen concerning the faith.' And so he is induced to write to Theodosius that 'he would acquiesce in the petition of Flavian that *the aforesaid bishop* [of Rome] having gathered all the bishops of the whole world within Italy, may without prejudice, and going into the whole matter, *give the judgment* which faith and the word of divine truth require.' The empress wrote at the same time, describing the scene in St. Peter's, speaking of Flavian's appeal to Rome, and that of the Papal legates. At the same time she wrote to the Empress Pulcheria,[2] and, after describing the tears of Leo, expressed her hope that all that had been decided at the 'tumultuous and most miserable' Council at Ephesus will be treated as null and void, and that 'all things remaining uninjured [*i.e. in statu quo*, as provided by the fourth canon, so called, of Sardica] the judgment will be remitted to the council of the Apostolic throne, in which Peter, the most blessed Peter, first of the Apostles, having received the keys of the heavens, adorned the headship of the hierarchy. For we ought to give the primacy in all things to the Eternal City.'

At the same time Leo wrote to the clergy and people of Constantinople, promising them all possible support from his fatherly care for them, and bidding them use their influence to obtain a plenary synod; and explained to the Empress Pulcheria that human affairs can go smoothly only when the royal and sacerdotal authorities defend those matters which belong to a 'divine confession,' as a reason for Theodosius

---

[1] *Ep.* lv. *Leonis Opera,* ed. Baller. [2] *Ep.* lvi.

and himself working together—a reason, that is, why the emperor should consent to a council. This was in February, 450.

IX. Meanwhile letters were on their way from the clergy and people of Constantinople and from the archimandrites Martin and Faustus, written in the preceding October, and St. Leo wrote one of his most magnificent letters in reply. He speaks of his writings having been directed to the East, 'not only by the authority of the Apostolic See, but also with the unanimity of the holy synod, which had frequently met, that the care which we have for the whole Church may be apparent, by our exhortations addressed to all the faithful and our demand for help in the defence of the faith from the most clement princess.'

Meanwhile, he directs Martin and Faustus to make known to the children of the Church 'what we preach contrary to the impious sense [of Eutyches] and in accordance with the evangelical and apostolical doctrine; for although we have written fully what is and always has been the *sententia* of Catholics, still we add now no little exhortation to confirm the minds of all. For I am mindful that I preside over the Church in his name whose confession was praised by the Lord Jesus Christ, and whose faith destroys all heresies, but above all the impiety of the present error; and I understand that nothing else is permitted to me than that I should spend all my efforts on that cause in which the safety of the Universal Church is attacked.' Accordingly, that there may be no mistake about his teaching, in case they should not have received a copy of his writings, he sends fresh copies.[1]

Such was the tremendous energy of this single-minded hero of the great conflict for 'the only hope of the human race.'

So far as the Emperor Theodosius was concerned, it was all in vain.

X. In the midst, however, of Leo's difficulties, the Providence of God removed Theodosius, after many signs (if Nicephorus is to be relied on) of true repentance. He had

---

[1] *Ep.* lxi.

selected for his heiress a saintly woman, under a vow of perpetual chastity, of whom St. Cyril says that in her 'every kind of virtue and every adornment pleasing in the eyes of the Divine Majesty shone with wonderful splendour.'[1] No woman, however, had as yet held the reins of empire; and accordingly she offered her hand and throne to the most distinguished general of the day, on condition that he should respect her vow. Marcian was a worthy husband to St. Pulcheria, renowned as well for his piety as for his military skill. Everything was now changed, for the emperor and empress regarded their position simply as an opportunity for protecting the true faith.

X. Pulcheria's entreaties to Theodosius that he would accede to the Pope's request for a council to be called in Italy had failed. But in her new position her first care, as also that of her husband, was to carry out the wishes of Leo. The imperial zeal, however, was 'without knowledge,' for their very advent to the throne had made a council unnecessary. But this they did not know; and accordingly they wrote to Leo, acquainting him with the fact that they had acted at his instigation in memory of the scene at St. Peter's, and had issued an edict for the convention of a council.[2] Not in Italy, since the reason for that no longer existed, as it would be best held under their own protecting presence, in the East, where all the disturbance had taken place.

The Pope told their Imperial Majesties that he no longer desired a council. The bishops had signed his epistle to Flavian in such numbers, and so many were daily returning in penitence, that his legates at Constantinople, in concert with Anatolius (who had also signed the Tome of Leo), could manage the rest. But Leo was not the man to quench the zeal of emperors; and since, out of pure love of the truth and devotion to himself, they had issued the edict, imagining it to be his desire, he praised in them what he sincerely admired, viz. their zeal, and consented to send legates.[3]

---

[1] Cyr. Alex. *de Fide ad Pulch. et Sorores Reginas.*

[2] σοῦ αὐθεντοῦντος: at which everything was to be decided by Leo's authority, σοῦ αὐθεντοῦντος ὁρίσωσιν, *Ep.* lxxvii.

[3] 'Doubt has arisen respecting the true faith, as is shown by the letters of

The emperor and empress, in expressing the purport of the council, did not imply that the doctrine contained in the Tome of Leo was an open question. We know they believed the doctrine themselves. But there were some amongst those who had been led away who needed to have it publicly set before them, and the reinstatement of the lapsed but penitent bishops needed some arrangement which would, says Pulcheria, be made 'on the authority of Leo.'[1] Some shorter confession of faith, in accordance with the Tome, was also needed, and desired by the Pope, and all this could be effected in the council. Pulcheria in the same letter informs the Pope with evident joy that the Bishop of Constantinople has subscribed the Tome; whilst the emperor had already told Leo that he looked to him in the cause of the orthodox faith, because he was 'the bishop and ruler of the divine faith.'[2] This, be it remembered, was one of the holiest emperors, if not quite the holiest, that ever ruled at Constantinople.

XI. Before, however, proceeding to the acts of the council, it will be well to consider the circumstances under which Anatolius took his seat as Bishop of Constantinople.

Upon the death of the murdered Flavian the clergy and people of Constantinople had elected to the vacant see the very person who had acted as secretary to the heretical Archbishop of Alexandria (Dioscorus), and was in favour with his sympathiser, the Emperor Theodosius. The latter had relied on him in his ecclesiastical administration, and had probably procured his election as archbishop of his capital. Anatolius, for that was his name, wrote to Leo announcing his consecration. What else he said we do not know. It is not correct to say, as Mr. Gore does,[3] that he 'simply announced his consecration, without asking for any consent to it on Leo's part;' for his letter, as we have it, is confessedly a fragment, and St. Leo's letter to the emperor implies that Ana-

---

the most holy Bishop of Rome,' are the emperor's words. There was no doubt in his own mind as to which was the true faith; and the letters of Leo were all written with the view, not of settling, but of enforcing the true faith.

[1] σοῦ αὐθεντοῦντος (*Ep.* lxxvii.).
[2] ἐπισκοπεύουσαν καὶ ἄρχουσαν τῆς θείας πίστεως.
[3] *Dict. of Chr. Biogr.* art. 'Leo.'

tolius did ask for Leo's confirmation. What, however, we do
know that he omitted was a statement as to his teaching;
he gave no account of his faith.[1] Leo accordingly waited
some months before answering, and then he wrote, not to
Anatolius himself, but to the Emperor Theodosius. Now it
would hardly be possible to give clearer indications of the relation of sovereignty on the part of the See of St. Peter
towards the See of Constantinople than are afforded by this
and some succeeding letters. It must be remembered that
Leo was writing to the Eastern emperor, who was opposed to
his condemnation of Eutyches; he was writing, too, about
the bishop of that city, which was the very apple of the
imperial eye. We know that the emperor had avowed the
sovereignty of the See of St. Peter over all the sees of Christendom by his signature to the 'Constitution' of Valentinian;
but this sovereignty of the Apostolic See was now to be expressed in a form most calculated to excite that emperor's
indignation, and to jeopardise the whole position, unless that
sovereignty were beyond dispute. But in truth the Huns,
tumultuously crowding into Italy and advancing towards
Rome, were not more dreadful in the eyes of Leo than the
incursion of heretics into that vineyard of the Lord, with
which the Eastern bishops declared him to have been entrusted by the Saviour of the world.[2] The time had come
when that energetic nature, which had hardly its peer in that
half-century, must exercise the authority of his position to
the full. The Divine Majesty of his Lord was at stake. It
was enough for Leo.

XII. Now there was just occasion for suspicion as to Anatolius' teaching. Indeed, his conduct after the synod showed
that there was a taint of heresy about him, such as Leo
feared. Accordingly Leo wrote to the emperor, in July 450,
and praised him for deciding to adhere to the Nicene Creed.
It was on this point that Theodosius had been misled by the
Eutychian party. They were for ever proclaiming their adherence to the Nicene Creed, and made believe that they were
contending for that creed and for the Ephesine decree. So
the Pope gives the emperor credit for sincerely believing that

[1] *Ep.* lxix. lxxi. [2] Letter of the Eastern bishops to Leo after Chalcedon.

he was acting in defence of the Nicene settlement; and on this ground he expresses his surprise that Anatolius has not sent him an account of his faith. Consequently he has deferred acknowledging him—'not that he refused his affection, but because he awaited some manifestation of Catholic truth.' He says that he is not exacting from him anything but what every Catholic would do. He then alludes to their predecessors' writings as sufficient tests for those who preceded them. But they are not enough for themselves under present circumstances. Anatolius is to 'read carefully' 'what the holy Fathers have given as guard to the faith in the Incarnation,' 'and he must understand that what Cyril wrote against Nestorius is consonant with this.' Cyril's letter, says the Pope, is a clear exposition of the Nicene definition, and has been placed in the archives of the Apostolic See.[1] Anatolius is to read carefully the Acts of the Ephesine Synod[2] against Nestorius; and he is 'not to disdain to read also my letter, which he will find agrees in all things with the Fathers.'

But this is not all. St. Leo tells the emperor that Anatolius, having recognised that all this is demanded and expected of him,[3] he is to sign the confession of the Common Faith, and make a declaration before all the clergy and the whole people—a profession of faith which is to be 'publicly notified (1) to the Apostolic See, and (2) to all the Lord's priests [*i.e.* bishops] and Churches.' Further, he is to send a written statement as soon as possible, plainly ('dilucidè') declaring that if anyone believes or asserts anything else concerning the Incarnation of the Word of God than what 'the profession of all Catholics and my own' declares, he will separate such a one from his communion. And to expedite this important matter, he says he is sending four legates, whose business it will be 'to declare the exact faith which we hold, *the form of our faith*, so that if the Bishop of Constantinople consents to the same confession of faith, with his whole heart, we may feel secure and rejoice in the peace of the

---

[1] 'Apostolicæ Sedis scrinia susceperunt.'
[2] 'Ephesinæ synodi gesta recenseat.'
[3] 'Expeti desiderarique'—'desiderari' expressing Leo's feeling that something of the kind ought to have been done sooner.

Church. If, however, there is any dissent from the purity of our faith and the authority of the Fathers,' a council must be held in Italy, so that it may not be open to anyone to talk about the Nicene Creed and yet be in opposition to it.

Now, had there been an idea that there was the slightest dogmatic ground for denying the prerogative thus claimed by Leo of dealing with the Archbishop of Constantinople as a subject, and of imposing on him the Roman 'form of faith,' it is not possible to suppose that either Theodosius or Anatolius would not have resented this exercise of jurisdiction. It would be impossible to imagine a more extreme case. There is every circumstance that could emphasise the impossibility of such a tremendous assumption (if it were an assumption [1]) passing muster without a challenge. The archbishop in question was not naturally disposed either to submit quietly to a usurpation for the sake of uniting against a common foe, for he had a tender spot in his heart for the party of Eutyches; he was not the occupant of a see which had no ambition or no political friends, for it was the Imperial see, and was soon about to attempt a rise in the scale of patriarchal honour over Alexandria and Antioch. Here, too, was an emperor not favourable to Leo and the orthodox party, but under the influence of Dioscorus and his friends. Such were the circumstances, and they simply preclude the idea that there was not ample recognition of the headship of the See of St. Peter on which St. Leo could work; for Leo was neither a dullard nor void of care for the faith. He lived for the faith, and he knew something of men.

To Pulcheria St. Leo wrote to exactly the same effect, insisting that Anatolius must without delay acknowledge the 'unskilful folly' displayed by the definition of the Robber Synod. And the reason he gives is the same as Leo XIII. would give under similar circumstances, viz. 'because both my confession of faith and that of the holy Fathers [2] concerning the Incarnation of the Lord is in all respects a concordant and one confession.'

[1] Canon Bright's explanation, 'Leo ... *quietly assumes*,' is simply out of the question.

[2] In each of these letters there is probably a special allusion to the Nicene Fathers, with whom Theodosius misled by Eutyches, claimed to be in harmony.

At the same time he writes to the archimandrites of Constantinople (a still stronger step in some respects), and complains of Anatolius having given no sign, as if there had been no scandals connected with Constantinople, or 'as if [1] the merit of a bishop were not to be demonstrated principally from here.'

Leo seems to have had no fear that he was placing the cause nearest to his heart, the maintenance of the 'peerless sacrament of the faith,' in any jeopardy. If ever there was a case in which the authority of the Apostolic See needed to come forward, it was here, and if ever there was one case more than another in which that authority was used with holy boldness and singleness of aim, it was this. The result was everything that could be wished. Leo wrote in July, and at the end of the month Theodosius suddenly died. The legates appear to have acted promptly, and in November the Empress Pulcheria was able to announce to Leo that 'Anatolius embraces the apostolical confession of your letters,' and has without delay signed the dogmatic epistle to Flavian, which she calls 'the letter of the Catholic faith.'

XIII. Anatolius' letters to Leo are unfortunately lost. Leo answered him [2] and congratulated him, and, after giving directions about the reception of such bishops as had given way at the Latrocinium, he says, 'the favour of communion with us is to be neither harshly denied nor rashly bestowed.' He says that he had received Eusebius into communion, and therefore requests Anatolius to have Eusebius' Church taken care of, and desires that all should know that Anatolius has been received into communion with Rome, 'that those who serve our God may rejoice that your peace has been concluded *with the Apostolic See*.' He further tells the emperor [3] that he has directed the legates to co-operate with Anatolius, and in another letter [4] he tells Anatolius that he joins him with them in the execution of his decree,[5] and gives his directions about the lapsed bishops in general and the leaders in particular.

---

[1] 'Aut non hinc præcipue fuerit meritum demonstrandum.'
[2] *Ep.* lxxx.   [3] *Ep.* lxxxiii.   [4] *Ep.* lxxxv.
[5] 'Executionem nostræ dispositionis.' (Cf. the use of *dispositio* for an imperial edict.)

As regards the latter, if they repent he 'reserves' their case 'for the maturer counsels of the Apostolic See,'[1] and bids Anatolius 'to strive to execute such things as befit the Church of God' in union with his own legates.

At the same time, as if, in God's providence, history was to settle for those who search it the lines of Papal jurisdiction, St. Leo exercised the same authority over the members of the Archdiocese of Constantinople that Zozimus did over Africa. Two Constantinopolitan priests had repaired to Rome to clear themselves of suspicion as to heresy, and Leo sent them back, saying that 'at great cost they had opened their hearts to [literally *in*] the Apostolic See, and shown that they receive nothing save what we, *by the teaching of the Holy Spirit*, have both learned and teach;' and he exhorts Anatolius to assist them, as 'being adorned with the favour of Apostolical communion,' *i.e.* communion with the Apostolic See.

It is difficult to imagine a more perfect anticipation of Catholic ecclesiastical life in the nineteenth century. And so far there is not a solitary protest recorded, not a distant idea that St. Leo was doing more than exercising his proper prerogative in a natural way, and fulfilling the responsibilities of his sacred and divinely instituted office.

XIV. A very important step was now taken by the new archbishop. For the second time he called together his 'home-synod,'[2] and the bishops not merely themselves signed the Tome or letter to Flavian, but sent it to the absent metropolitans.

Abundius, the Papal legate, thereupon returned from Constantinople, and obtained, in accordance with the request of Leo, the subscription of the Metropolitan of Milan and his synod to the Pope's dogmatic epistle. The same had already been obtained from the provinces of Gaul.

So that this letter to Flavian, which had been suppressed at the Robber Council, had now received the signatures of well-nigh the whole Christian world. It was issued as an *ex cathedrâ* pronouncement on the part of the Pope; it had now been received as the dogmatic expression of Christian belief at Con-

[1] *Ibid.* c. ii.
[2] Consisting of the bishops at and around Constantinople.

stantinople, at Antioch,[1] and in the entire West. No bishop who had signed it could henceforth treat its teaching as an open question; it only remained to issue a definition in accordance with it, and to induce the Egyptians to withdraw their complicity with Dioscorus and his teaching, and to arrange the return of the lapsed but penitent bishops. St. Leo had already laid down the conditions of their return, but had made an exception in the case of the ringleaders at Ephesus. This, however, he also eventually left to the discretion of the council on application from Pulcheria.[2]

Such were the circumstances under which Anatolius, the Bishop of Constantinople, took his seat at the Council of Chalcedon.

[1] *Leonis Ep.* civ.   [2] *Ep.* lxxxv.

CHAPTER XXIII.

THE DEPOSITION OF DIOSCORUS.

I. The great council met, not, as was originally intended, at Nicæa, but at Chalcedon, in order that the emperor might attend to his imperial affairs and yet be near at hand in case of need. And it must be borne in mind that it was summoned for the reversal of the Ephesine catastrophe. The Robber Synod of Ephesus had acquitted Eutyches, and grounded its acquittal on his agreement with St. Cyril; it had condemned Flavian, his archbishop, on the false supposition that he differed from Cyril, and so from the Nicene Fathers. But, on the other hand, St. Leo had confirmed the condemnation of Eutyches by the previous Synod of Constantinople, and there was an end of that matter. His position as a heretic was assumed throughout. But the condemnation of Flavian and the pretended agreement of Eutyches with St. Cyril had to be dealt with; and the Patriarch of Alexandria had to be condemned, if he continued obdurate to the last. St. Leo had cherished hopes of his repentance, and accordingly had devolved upon the council the duty of deposing him in case only of his continued obduracy; in case of his repentance the matter would have to be referred again to the Apostolic See.[1]

It was not enough, then, for the council to signify its adhesion to the Tome of St. Leo. It must also make it plain that its adhesion included the clear perception that the two great letters of St. Cyril, confirmed by the General Council of Ephesus (which included the Pope by representation and by

---

[1] 'Reserved for the maturer counsels of the Apostolic See' (*Ep.* lxxxv.)

his subsequent confirmation of the Acts) were not in contradiction with the Tome which they subscribed, nor the Tome in contradiction with them.[1]

Further, it was left to the council to draw up some short definition which would serve as a test of orthodoxy on the point in question. St. Leo's Tome was not intended for that; it supplied the $τύπος$,[2] the mould and the material, the necessary norm and measuring-line, but not a definition adapted for practical purposes; this would be best effected in a council, after an investigation and exposition of the needs of the case.

Again, St. Leo had left it to the council to deal with the cases of those bishops who had been illegitimately extruded from their sees, and whose cases could now be heard in person—such as Eusebius and Theodoret; and the cases of those bishops who had subscribed the condemnation of Flavian by putting their signatures to a blank paper.

Such was the work before the council. It met in the Church of St. Euphemia, on whose intercessions the bishops avowed their reliance, and on whose altar they placed their definition, that it might be presented before saints and angels, and to Almighty God, by her intercessory mediation.

There were at least 600 bishops present, the largest number that had yet met together. They were, almost to a man, Eastern prelates. The scene of their meeting is described in glowing terms by Evagrius, and is to this day one of the most exquisite spots in that beautiful region.

II. Dioscorus at once took his seat as Archbishop of Alexandria. He had just before gathered together ten bishops and executed the farce of excommunicating St. Leo—an act of madness, which eventually afforded the bishops their chief ground for deciding upon his impenitence, and in consequence for carry-

---

[1] It is important to remember this, because some writers, in dealing with the exclamations of the bishops during the council concerning Cyril, seem to imagine that they were quoting Cyril simply, as the authority before which they bowed; indeed, they even suppose that the bishops put the authority of Cyril on a par with that of Leo. But it was because Cyril's orthodoxy had been established by Pope and council, particularly by Celestine and Sixtus (who are expressly mentioned—cf. fifth session), that his authority is quoted.

[2] *Ep. ci. Anatolii ad Leonem.*

ing out the sentence of Leo, committed to their charge. Whether by this means he thought to make it technically impossible for the legates to sit and condemn him, or whether he acted out of mere *bravado*, and by way of insult to the Apostolic See, it is impossible to say. He now sat down in the place of honour, as the occupant of the second see in Christendom.

But the Papal legates intervened, and refused to proceed until Dioscorus was removed from the seat he had occupied. They wished him to go out. They held a commission (said Paschasinus) 'from the most holy and most apostolic Bishop of Rome, who is the head of all Churches, to see that Dioscorus should have no seat in the council.' When questioned further, the legates said that Dioscorus 'had dared to arrange[1] a synod without leave from the Apostolic throne.'

The imperial commissioners wished to resist this decision of the legates, but in vain. They had to obey 'the head of all Churches,' and cause Dioscorus to leave his place. His presence, however, was required, and he was therefore allowed to sit in the middle, without, that is to say, a seat as a constituent member of the synod, which was the gist of the legates' demand. There he maintained that Flavian was rightly condemned by the council which the Emperor Theodosius had convoked at Ephesus. His position really was that the imperial supremacy was sufficient for the case, and that Flavian was involved in heresy.

Accordingly the Acts of the Robber Synod were read. In these the name of Theodoret occurred, who had been deposed by Dioscorus. Theodoret was called for, and he presently entered. A scene of tumultuous confusion ensued. The Egyptian bishops saw in Theodoret only the enemy of St. Cyril. They shouted and protested, and maintained that to admit Theodoret into the assembly was to cast out Cyril, whom Theodoret had once anathematised. The statement, which the commissioners and senate made, that Leo had rein-

---

[1] ποιῆσαι. I have translated the word 'arrange,' as being a term which is both covered by the Greek word, and which fits in with the facts of the case. St. Leo had sent legates, but Dioscorus took precedence of them by order of the emperor, or with his consent. This was his sin in the matter.

stated him in his bishopric, and that the emperor had ordered his presence, availed nothing for awhile with these Egyptian partisans. They were furious at the idea of one who had anathematised their former holy patriarch, appearing in the council in the character of bishop. They cared for neither Pope or emperor, nor for the Patriarch of Antioch, who had likewise testified to the orthodoxy of Theodoret; they believed them all to be unaware of the true character of the man. They were calmed, however, by the compromise of admitting his presence on the understanding that his sitting as accuser should not prejudice the question of his proper place in the synod, which could be settled afterwards, as was in fact done in Theodoret's favour.

The pith of the accusation now brought against Dioscorus lay in the fact that he had suppressed the Tome of Leo; and he persisted throughout that Flavian was rightly condemned, because he had said that 'after the union' (*i.e.* the Incarnation) 'there were two natures in Christ.' Dioscorus and his party were willing to acknowledge that Christ was 'of two natures,' but not that there 'are two natures' in Him.[1]

The obduracy, therefore, of Dioscorus being duly established, it only remained to pronounce sentence, in accordance with St. Leo's direction, in canonical form—which, however, was deferred for another session. The Oriental bishops, *i.e.* those in the patriarchate of Antioch, were in favour of all the leaders of the Robber Synod being included in the condemnation of Dioscorus, but on the Illyrian bishops exclaiming, 'We have all erred: we all ask for pardon,' it was decided, for the present, that Dioscorus alone should suffer deposition.

When the bishops reassembled, neither Dioscorus nor the imperial commissioners made their appearance; the latter, because the deposition of a bishop was so completely the affair of the spiritualty, and the former, doubtless, because he had clearly seen how things were going. Eusebius of Dorylæum, who had been 'deposed' by the Robber Synod, now preferred

---

[1] Mansi, t. vi. p. 690.

his complaint against Dioscorus, and the latter was accordingly summoned in the usual way to attend the synod. Meanwhile, three clerics of Alexandria and a layman were admitted to the synod, to prefer their several complaints against their patriarch. These petitions were each one of them addressed 'to the Œcumenical Archbishop and Patriarch of great Rome, Leo, and to the holy and Œcumenical Synod.' They revealed the fact that Dioscorus was a man of notoriously loose morality and intolerably overbearing temper. The priest from Alexandria concluded by saying to the bishops, 'I, miserable Athanasius, presbyter of the most renowned city of Alexandria, have presented these petitions to the most holy *Œcumenical Archbishop and Patriarch* Leo, and to the most holy Œcumenical Council of holy Fathers and Bishops.' The layman Sophronius concluded in the same way.[1] These petitions, *thus addressed*, were ordered to be inserted in the Acts, and read to Dioscorus in case he came to the synod. But Dioscorus, like Nestorius, refused to obey the summons, saying that he 'adhered to what he had previously said,' thus confessing his obstinate perseverance, and bringing himself under the condemnation of Leo.

III. The sentence was forthwith pronounced by Paschasinus, at the desire of the bishops. Julian, Bishop of Hypepæ, not merely concurred with the rest in calling on Paschasinus to give the sentence, but made the following short speech :—
'Holy fathers, listen. Since in the metropolis of Ephesus Dioscorus held the authority' (from the emperor) 'for judging between holy Flavian and the most religious Bishop Eusebius' (on the one hand) 'and Eutyches' (on the other), 'and issued a thoroughly iniquitous judgment, himself first pronouncing an unjust sentence, and then forcing the rest to follow him— now your holiness holds the authority of the most holy Leo; and all the holy synod, gathered together according to the will of God and the decree of our most pious emperor knows,

---

[1] Mr. Gore (*Dict. of Chr. Biog.* p. 663) alludes to these addresses as the 'expressions of individuals,' as though they were nothing further. It must be remembered that these petitioners were endeavouring to ingratiate themselves, not with St. Leo, but with the council, and that the council was prepared to use their petitions as evidence. The context makes their use emphatic.

as does your holiness, all that was done in Ephesus; and Dioscorus has been thrice summoned and would in no wise obey. We ask your holiness, therefore, who holds, or rather your holinesses' (*i.e.* the other legates), 'who hold the place of the most holy Pope Leo, to promulgate and issue against him' (viz. Dioscorus) 'the sentence contained in the canons. For we all, and the whole œcumenical synod, are of one mind with your holiness.'

The whole assembly reiterated its perfect oneness of mind with Paschasinus.

Let us pause for a moment. The whole enormous assembly of Eastern bishops can hear St. Leo addressed by the Alexandrian clerics as the 'œcumenical' archbishop *par excellence*, and not a word of protest, but the letters are placed in the archives for use in the tremendous scene that is being now enacted—nothing less than the deposition of the occupant of the second see in Christendom.

Again, the deposition of the Patriarch of Alexandria is yielded by the synod to the legates on the ground that they hold the authority of Leo. The authority of the synod in Chalcedon is said to differ from that of the synod of Ephesus under Dioscorus, in deriving from the Bishop of Rome, who, through his legates, is present at the synod, and forms a constituent necessary and sovereign element of that assembly.

Nothing in the life of the Church could require a more sovereign act of jurisdiction than the deposition of the Archbishop of Alexandria. St. Athanasius tells us how St. Julius in the last century said that the canons required that all matters concerning the deposition of an Alexandrian archbishop should be referred to Rome, that 'a just judgment may be issued thence.' St. Athanasius, Bishop of Alexandria, had been deposed by a synod with the authority of the emperor. But the Pope treated the deposition as null and void, reopened the question, and acquitted Athanasius. In the case of Dioscorus, a Bishop of Alexandria was now being deposed, and the whole Church accepted his deposition. But he was deposed by the authority of the See of St. Peter, whose agent was the synod of bishops, including the representative of the Apostolic See. If anyone doubts this, let him ponder the following sentence, adopted by the council.[1]

Paschasinus, Lucentius (bishops), and Boniface (priest), 'holding' (as the Acts say) 'the place of the most holy and blessed Leo, Archbishop of the Apostolic See of great and older Rome,' stood up and pronounced the sentence of deposition on the following grounds:

1. 'Because Dioscorus on his own authority received Eutyches, of one mind with him, into communion when he had been canonically condemned by his own archbishop'—'this he did before he sat in council with the bishops at Ephesus.'

2. 'The Apostolic See has pardoned the other bishops.' They acted under compulsion, and they have repented and have 'continued to adhere[2] to the most holy Archbishop Leo and the holy and Œcumenical Council.' (How could the 'Apostolic See' be said by an œcumenical synod to have 'pardoned' bishops, unless that synod held that the said see represented 'the prince and head of the Apostles'? And what obedience could Eastern bishops owe to Leo, except on the supposition that he was the 'œcumenical archbishop'?)

But Dioscorus 'has continued to boast over those things on account of which he ought to groan and throw himself on to the ground.' (So that his obstinacy, which Leo mentioned as necessary to be established before he was finally condemned, was substantiated.)

3. He did not allow the Tome of Leo to be read—'which not being read, the Holy Churches of God throughout the world have suffered scandal and injury.' (Notice the relation of the Papal utterance to the whole Church of God.)

All this, however (they say), might have been pardoned. But this was not all. The climax was reached when—

4. 'He presumed to issue an excommunication against the most holy and blessed Archbishop of Greater Rome.'

5. Lastly, he had rendered himself technically liable to deposition, for he refused to appear when thrice summoned to a synod. (St. Athanasius also refused to appear when summoned to a synod; but it had been convoked by the

[1] Mansi, t. vi. p. 1046.   [2] ἑπόμενοι.

emperor without the consent of the Pope, as the Eastern historians notice in condemning it.)

'*Wherefore Leo*, the most holy and blessed Archbishop of great and older Rome, by us and by the present holy synod, together with the thrice blessed and worthy of all praise, the blessed Apostle Peter, who is the rock and foundation of the Catholic Church, and the foundation of the orthodox faith, *has stripped him of his episcopate* and deprived him of all sacerdotal dignity. Wherefore this great synod will decree what is according to the canons.'

Anatolius signed first, saying that 'he agreed in all things with the Apostolic throne.' Dioscorus had disobeyed the canons of the holy Fathers and had refused to obey the threefold summons.

Maximus of Antioch recorded his agreement with Leo and Anatolius.

Diogenes, Bishop of Cyzicum, 'consented to those things which had been decreed by the most holy and blessed Roman Archbishop Leo,' and by Anatolius and the present holy and œcumenical synod.

One bishop calls the meeting 'your angelical meeting.'

In the version of this sentence which Leo himself sent to the Gallic bishops the indictment against Dioscorus that he had 'excommunicated' the Pope is omitted, as was natural; otherwise the differences are purely verbal.[1]

The sentence, however, as communicated to Dioscorus, did not give the bishops' reasons in full, but merely mentioned the technical point of his disobedience to the summons of the synod, besides 'his other offences.'

But in their official report to the emperor,[2] which is of the highest importance, they give the grounds of their condemnation in full.

First, Dioscorus had prevented the Pope's letter to Flavian being read at Ephesus.

Next, he had restored Eutyches, 'sick with the impiety of the Manichæans,' to his priesthood and position in his

---

[1] Mr. Gore calls this version 'widely different.' But a comparison of the two line by line will convince the reader that this is not correct.

[2] Mansi, t. vi. p 1093.

monastery '*after the Bishop of Rome had decreed what was fitting*, and had condemned the *perfidy* of Eutyches in saying, "I confess, indeed, that our Lord Jesus Christ was of (ἐκ) two natures before the union, but that there was one nature after the union."'

The quotation is from the Tome of Leo, and shows that they understood the latter part of the Tome as a juridical sentence. Dioscorus had seen this sentence which the Pope passed on Eutyches, and had suppressed the Tome in which it occurs.

Thirdly, his misconduct to Eusebius of Dorylæum was scandalous.

Fourthly, he had received into communion those who had been put out of communion, thereby offending against the canon which 'teaches that those who are excommunicated by one should not be received into communion with others.'

But all this (the synod says) might have been forgiven; in fact, the Pope had expressly said that a door of repentance was to be left to the last. But Dioscorus (probably just before the council actually met) gathered together ten bishops and induced them to execute the farce of excommunicating St. Leo himself. This was the climax of his madness. And so the synod continues to report to his Imperial Majesty by saying that—

Fifthly, 'beyond all this, he has also opened his mouth like a mad dog against the Apostolic See itself, and has endeavoured to effect letters of excommunication against the most holy and blessed Pope Leo, and—

Lastly, 'has persisted in his iniquities and been obstinate against the holy and œcumenical synod, refusing to answer to various accusations brought against him.'

He remains, therefore (so they wrote to the Empress Pulcheria), 'a pillar of salt, and the rulers of the various Churches have regained their sees, Christ our Lord having prosperously directed their course, Who shows the truth in the wonderful Leo—for as He used the sapient Peter, so He uses also this champion of the truth' ('ita et isto utitur assertore'), viz. Leo.

Such is the verdict of the great Eastern Synod, viz. that St. Peter is the rock in Matt. xvi.,[1] and that Leo takes the place, in the Church's government of souls, of the blessed Apostle Peter, being the Vicar of Christ in his direction of the Church—a statement which is correctly summed up in the more modern phrase 'Papal supremacy,' or 'infallibility.'

IV. In the session which followed, the imperial commissioners, who, although not presidents in the ecclesiastical sense of the term, arranged the external order of the assembly, brought forward the question of the faith in which the body of bishops were now to proclaim their unity. Dioscorus, if this is the third session, had now been deposed, and the case of his assistants in the Robber Council—viz. Juvenal of Jerusalem and four other bishops—had yet to be dealt with. None of these were present at this session. The business before the bishops was, according to the commissioners, that of 'expounding the faith purely;' and the object in view was that 'those who seem not to have held the same ideas as all the rest *should be brought back to unity of mind by the full knowledge* (ἐπίγνωσις) *of the truth*, for the lord of the earth holds, as we do, the faith handed down by the 318 Fathers at Nicæa, and the 150, and by the rest of the most holy and glorious Fathers.'

This description of the business before the meeting is of great importance for understanding what follows. It was the 'pure faith' which was to bind the bishops together; and the commissioners themselves had no doubt as to what that pure faith was. It was no open question. Those who were to be 'brought back' were the bishops who had acquitted Eutyches and condemned Flavian, asserting that Flavian had contravened and Eutyches had accepted the Nicene Creed. By voting for the condemnation of Flavian they had seemed to hold ideas which were at variance with the meaning of the Nicene Creed, as interpreted by the Council of Ephesus and by Leo. But the emperor (said the commissioners) held to the Nicene and Constantinopolitan Creed as interpreted by the present Pope.

---

[1] Cf. the 'Sentence' above, p. 406.

On the mention of the emperor's faith in the Nicene Creed, all agreed by acclamation that they held no other faith than that of Nicæa, Constantinople, and Ephesus.

So far all was well; but a Eutychian could say that. Accordingly, Cecropius of Sebastopol rose and introduced the real subject before them. He said that besides these declarations of faith, the matter concerning Eutyches had arisen, and that a dogmatic decision had been given by the most holy archbishop in Rome, 'And we follow him, and have all subscribed his letter.'

The bishops exclaimed, 'We all say this: the expositions given are sufficient; it is not in our power to make another.'

This is a crucial point in estimating the position which St. Leo's letter occupied in their minds. It stood on a level with those writings which had been accepted by the previous councils. It had not been synodically discussed; it never was. The bishops from the first refused to discuss its contents in open synod. *They followed Leo.* They had signed his letter, and that was enough. They maintained that it was not open to them to make another exposition. It had not yet been synodically accepted, but they still had no cause to frame another exposition.[1]

But as Rusticus in the next century annotates the bishops' acclamation, it was not the case that quite all the bishops were satisfied with this. The great majority were of one mind, but it could not be taken for granted that every one of them was agreed with the rest. Accordingly the commissioners proposed that the patriarchs of each of the provinces should, with one or two from each province, pass into the middle and deliberate in common concerning the faith, so that if there should be any difference of opinion, *which they thought there could not be,* that difference might be clearly expressed.

The bishops, however, refused to do this. They were satisfied with things as they were. They flatly refused to make out any written formulary, for those already in existence were sufficient. They had already agreed to Cecropius'

---

[1] It was (they said) Leo's sentence (τύπος) which made it unnecessary. Mansi, vi. 953.

statement that the Pope's dogmatic interpretation sufficed for the Eutychian matter.

V. But Florentius of Sardes pleaded that 'a certain time should be given so that we may approach the truth of the matter with becoming consideration, although most certainly as concerns ourselves, who have subscribed the letter of the most holy Leo, we do not need setting right.'

He considered, and very properly, after the circumstances of the Robber Council, that some did need setting right, but not those who had subscribed to the letter of Leo.

Cecropius, accordingly, proposed that the decisions of the 318 Fathers and of the most holy Leo be read. He prefaced his proposal by saying that 'the faith has been well discussed by the 318 holy Fathers, and has been confirmed by the holy Fathers Athanasius, Cyril, Celestine, Hilary, Basil, Gregory, and now again by the most holy Leo.'

It may be noticed that Leo is here said to have 'confirmed' the faith confessed by the Nicene Fathers, which shows that nothing can be argued from the council being said to confirm the letter of Leo as to its thinking itself a superior court. St. Leo was not superior to the Nicene faith, nor the synod to Leo. In each case the meaning of the word 'confirmation' must be determined by the context. It will be seen that the final confirmation by Leo was certainly that of a superior authority.

The Nicene Creed was read, and amongst the exclamations that burst from the bishops were such as 'Pope[1] Leo so believes!' 'Cyril so believes!' The great point in their minds was that the condemnation of Eutyches did not involve the condemnation of Cyril, and that, therefore, in signing the Tome of Leo they were not disagreeing with what the Church had already taught through St. Cyril.

Two letters of Cyril were then read; the first on the ground that it had been confirmed by the Council of Ephesus, and the second, to John of Antioch, had as a matter of fact been sanctioned by Pope and emperor and the whole Church.

---

[1] ὁ Πάπας, the Pope (Mansi, t. vi. p. 955). I do not lay stress on the definite article, but the occurrence of the word by way of contrast. Cyril was also a pope, but they do not call him so here.

After this the bishops again cried out that 'This is the faith of Leo, the archbishop—Leo thus believes—Leo and Anatolius thus believe!' No one who considers the circumstances under which Anatolius signed the Tome of Leo will for a moment suppose that Anatolius is placed on a level with Leo by saying that they believed alike.

They further cried out, 'As did Cyril, so do we all believe!' and 'Leo the archbishop thus thinks, thus believes, thus wrote!' The whole contention of the Eutychians had been that they were following Cyril, whose letters had been adopted by the whole Church. The orthodox bishops were, therefore, anxious to emphasise the fact that in subscribing to Leo's teaching they, too, were not divorcing themselves from the doctrine of Cyril. They believed both. If they had been asked, Is it likely, is it possible that Leo under the circumstances *could* have led them astray, and differed from those writings of Cyril which had received œcumenical sanction? they would doubtless have replied that it was impossible. But this was not the question before them. They were only dealing with the truth, that as a matter of fact St. Leo did not contradict Cyril. And they no more sat in judgment on the Pope and St. Cyril as superiors than a man acts as superior to St. James and St. Paul when he declares that they do not contradict one another in their doctrine of justification; neither do they put St. Leo on the same official level as St. Cyril by mentioning them together, any more than a man would equalise St. Paul the Apostle and a Greek poet, if he showed that the Apostle agreed with the poet. It must be remembered, too, that St. Cyril's writings had Papal sanction.

The Tome of Leo was now read. At two points, such was the stupidity of some of the bishops of Illyricum and Palestine (who had been exposed to adverse influences) that they could not see how the words of the Tome could be reconciled with St. Cyril's teaching. They did not say that the Tome was wrong, but they did not see their way to reconcile the two.[1]

---

[1] Their difficulty was, doubtless, to distinguish the two concepts of 'nature' and 'person,' especially as their relationship had been expressed in Latin, and had to be translated into Greek. Members of the Church of England may

Aetius the archdeacon ventured to show the bishops that they had forgotten two passages in St. Cyril, and Theodoret quoted to them some words of the saint. They were satisfied that they were mistaken. At the end of the reading the bishops exclaimed, 'This is the faith of the Fathers! This is the faith of the Apostles! . . . *Peter has thus spoken by Leo!* The Apostles thus taught! Cyril thus taught! . . . As Catholics we hold this! . . . Why were not these things read at Ephesus? Dioscorus concealed these things.'

The commissioners and senate asked, 'After all this, who doubts?'

The bishops replied, 'No one doubts.' They saw, then, in Leo's dogmatic epistle the teaching of the Apostles, but specially of the Apostle Peter. They refused to examine the contents of the letter in synod which they had already subscribed out of synod, but persisted that they heard in it the voice of Peter speaking through Leo, and explaining his own confession of faith at Cæsarea Philippi. It is not to be supposed that they used the expression 'Peter hath spoken by Leo' without reference to the teaching then in vogue, and actually emphasised in this very council, that Leo was the successor of Peter. The question before them was not, indeed, whether the successor of Peter *could* be untrue to the teaching of Peter; they were simply asserting that as a matter of fact he was true to the Apostle's teaching. *But* their exclamation suggests their belief that it followed from his official position.

But although no single voice was raised to break the force of the unanimous cry which rose from the bishops, 'We all believe!' and 'No one doubts!' and 'Peter hath spoken by Leo!' still there was something more needed; for they had not merely to believe, but to understand, since they had to meet their former friends, the bishops who had led them at the Robber Synod. They were absent now; but their case had to be dealt with—and amongst these was the patriarch of the Palestinian bishops. If this was the second session, and

remember the difficulties felt by Dean Stanley even in this century on the same subject, when he was endeavouring to suppress the Athanasian Creed.

Dioscorus was not yet condemned, as the order given by Mansi indicates, then they must have been in the utmost need of being well prepared to face Dioscorus, as well as the other ringleaders of the Latrocinium. But if (as so many old copies give the order, and as the Ballerini hold) this was the session immediately after the deposition of Dioscorus, they had still to reckon with the other bishops, to say nothing of their own flocks. And some shorter formulary, some condensed form of the Tome, would have to be provided for practical use; and they would need to have the teaching of Leo thoroughly in hand to know how to comport themselves in the coming trial.

Accordingly Atticus of Nicopolis asked for a concession of five days, so that they might decide upon this. They especially asked to be supplied with the letter of Cyril, containing the twelve anathematisms which had not been read to them, but on which their opponents outside had laid the greatest stress. They say, 'The letter of our lord[1] and holy Father and Archbishop, Leo, who adorns the Apostolic See, has been read to us,' and the expression implies that they receive that without question. But they wish for the other letter of Cyril's. Why? That they may settle their own judgment as to the orthodoxy of Leo? By no means. But 'that we may be properly provided in the time of closer examination.'

Many of the bishops then proposed that they should all look into this together. The commissioners agreed to an interval of five days, during which those bishops who wished might meet at the house of Anatolius and treat in common, out of synod, concerning the faith, 'that those who doubt may be taught.' Those who doubt were not allowed to meet for mere discussion, but for instruction.

The word 'doubt' seems to have roused the bishops, and they disclaimed against there being such a thing as doubt in the matter. 'We all believe as Leo;' 'No one of us doubts;' 'We have already subscribed.'

The commissioners then explained that it was not meant

---

[1] One article governs them all. Hence the translation I have given in the text. Mansi, vii. 974.

for them all to meet together. 'But since it is fitting to persuade all who doubt, let Anatolius choose from amongst those who have subscribed such as he thinks fitted to instruct such as doubt.'

It was not, then, the council that discussed the contents of the Tome in synod, but some of the bishops, who, from difficulties of language, and as the event proved, lack of acquaintance with Cyril's teaching, were willing to be 'instructed' in the house of Anatolius between the sessions. They had signed a blank paper at the Robber Council in fear of their lives. They would be asked by others in Chalcedon and by their flocks at home, whether they understood what they signed now. If they replied that they did not understand, but simply accepted everything on the word of Leo, they would, indeed, have done homage to a truth in owning allegiance to St. Peter in his successor; but what was then needed was not an act of faith in the infallibility of the Vicar of Christ, but an intelligent adhesion to his dogmatic decree, such as was necessary for those who had to teach. The Fathers of the synod did, indeed, in writing to the emperor on this very subject, bestow unlimited praise on the faith which in some did not need any discussion. 'To those who believe, a perception not submitted to discussion'[1] suffices 'for the useful purposes of faith, drawing the devout soul to confess the holy dogma.' But these bishops could not really say they believed with an intelligent faith, when they did not thoroughly *understand* the agreement between Cyril and Leo, although *they assumed its existence*; having a difficulty in grasping the coincidence of teaching by reason of the different languages in which the several letters were written. That this was the principle on which the hesitating bishops acted is rendered quite certain by what they said in the following session. After the legates had described the attitude of the synod towards the Tome of Leo as being precisely the same as their attitude towards the Council of Nice and the Council of Ephesus, and after the bishops as a body had accepted this as their position,[2] the bishops of Illyricum made a declaration in the person of one of their number named Sozon. They said

---

[1] 'Indiscussa.'   [2] Mansi, t. vii. p. 10.

that their hesitation had not proceeded from any doubt as to the orthodoxy of Leo.[1] The only question was whether one or two expressions conveyed the sense which they were quite persuaded was intended by the 'Holy Father.' The legates had elucidated ('nobis dilucidaverunt') the matter. It is therefore beyond dispute that the examination of the Tome was not in their minds connected with the idea of revision but of elucidation.

St. Leo expressly alludes to this scene in the synod with satisfaction. He speaks of the danger of their consent being a mere mechanical and pretended assent,[2] and consequently welcomes the news that some doubted about his 'judgments.' He reckons it a misfortune on their part, and, in the case of some doubts on the part of the ringleaders at the Latrocinium, calls it an evil thing, and due to the instigation of 'the author of dissension,' but rejoices that evil was overruled for good, for it removed all suspicion of an unreasoning, unintelligent adhesion having been given by the other sees 'to that one which the Lord of All has appointed to preside over the rest.' He says that the net result was that what Almighty 'God had previously defined by our ministry,' He confirmed 'by the irreversible assent of the whole brotherhood,' *i.e.* of bishops. It was already, as it came from his own pen, irreversible; for he says it was that which 'God had defined,' but it was further strengthened by the irreversible sentence of the episcopate. That sentence, it must be remembered, contained within it the Pope by representation, his legates being a constituent part of it, and it needed his further confirmation. Further on he says that 'truth shines more brightly, and is more strongly held, when what faith had first taught examination has afterwards confirmed.' It was already of faith; but it received an accession of strength within the soul, when the 'fides quærens intellectum' had enabled that understanding to sit in its light.

The examination, then, of the Tome of St. Leo accorded

---

[1] Mansi, t. vii. p. 30. They say the language is obscure. ἃ ἡ φράσις διϊστᾶν ἠνίττετο. It was a translation.

[2] *Leonis Ep.* cxx. *ad Theod.*

to these less enlightened bishops was an investigation for the purposes of elucidation, not of revision. No orthodox Christian could seriously maintain that any of the bishops were free to revise that dogmatic letter. They were free to examine, but not to reject. Freedom of dissent would indeed be fatal to the infallibility of the Holy See; the liberty of examining, and turning a blind obedience into an intelligent adhesion, in no way derogates from her position of authority. It does but secure that 'the members should agree with the head,' to use the words of St. Leo, by an enlightened and not merely a blind faith.

A palmary instance of such examination occurs in history soon after this—after the council had passed its sentence and promulgated its definition under anathema. Its decision was then, in the eyes of bishops and of Pope, irreversible. And yet, at the request of the emperor Leo, the Eutychians were allowed to re-examine the synodical sentence. In the case of those who after such examination gave in their adhesion, the council was considered to be confirmed anew, not by a superior authority, but by the additional judgment of concurring bishops. Those who refused adhesion were counted as heretics. They were free to examine, but not to refuse obedience. And we have only to ask ourselves what would have happened if these bishops at Chalcedon had refused to listen to the teaching of Anatolius, and withheld their subscription to the Tome of Leo, to see that they, too, were free to examine, but not to dissent, and that their approval was not that of superiors, but the submission of subordinates. There is not the slightest trace in the actual evolution of the synod's action at Chalcedon of any approval as of superiors. The contrary appears quite clearly in the fifth session. The Tome of Leo would have remained the charter of the Christian faith precisely as much if they had disagreed. As a matter of fact, it was involved in the promise of Christ to His Church, that the episcopate should sooner or later adhere as members to their head. One Dioscorus was as much as the Church could bear at that time, and one victory over the truth, such as the Robber Synod, all that Christ willed to allow to the prince of darkness in a single period. And consequently the bishops in the next session subscribed their assent to the letter of Leo as a symbol agreeing, in point of fact (as, indeed, it was bound to do by reason of the Petrine privilege of the Apostolic See) with the faith of Nicæa. They did not say the Vicar of Christ has exercised his prerogative of infallibility (these are modern terms); but the thing was there.

Anatolius, who signed first, said that the 150 Fathers at Constantinople had 'confirmed' the faith of Nicæa. In that same sense he might have said that the 600 Fathers of Chalcedon confirmed the Tome of Leo. In neither case was it the confirmation of a superior authority, but an exhibition of the oneness of the Church's faith.

The Illyrian bishops said that they found the explanation of the legates about the passage they could not understand, nor reconcile with what Cyril taught, helpful and sufficient.[1] And as when some asked of the Apostle Peter how he could reconcile his action with the teaching of the Apostle James and others, he—all apostle as he was—condescended to explain his conduct, and forthwith they acquiesced ($\dot{\eta}\sigma\acute{u}\chi\alpha\sigma\alpha\nu$), so here these bishops, after due explanation, signed the letter of the Apostolic See, saying they were fully assured of its agreement with all previous standards of the Christian faith. They did not by this means judge Anatolius, who had signed long ago, nor the whole of the council, nor its head, St. Leo; they simply recorded their intelligent submission. Any instructed Christian might say 'this or that *ex cathedrâ* pronouncement of the Holy See agrees of necessity with all previous *ex cathedrâ* utterances; but for my part I do not see that it does, though I am bound to believe it. I should like to see as well as believe—I should like to 'believe *and* know.'

There was nothing more than this in what took place at this session in the case of orthodox bishops in regard to St. Leo's dogmatic epistle to Flavian.

In 1845 some remarkable words fell from the lips of Dr. Döllinger, in addressing a company of *savants* as an historian at Munich: 'Gentlemen, the question is this: It is true that the infallibility of the Pope is not a dogma defined

[1] Mansi, t. vii. p. 31.

by the Church; yet anyone who should maintain the contrary would put himself in opposition to the conscience of the whole Church, in the present as in the past.'[1]

It is this that results from our study of the Council of Chalcedon. The conscience of the whole Church was penetrated through and through with that conception of the Pope's relation to the rest of the episcopate which has been defined only twenty years, but believed in for eighteen centuries and a half.

And yet the 'Dictionary of Christian Biography' can admit to its columns the following sentence by Mr. Gore:— 'It will be seen, then, that Leo's letter was treated by the council like the letter of any highly respected Churchman'! (Art. *Leo*, p. 663.)

[1] Cf. *Christianity and Infallibility*. Longmans, 1891. P. 245.

CHAPTER XXIV.

THE DEFINITION OF FAITH.

BISHOP HEFELE has remarked concerning the fifth session of the Council of Chalcedon, that it is 'one of the most important in Christian antiquity.'

In his Tome or letter to Flavian, Leo had censured the Synod of Constantinople for passing by the expression which Eutyches used in its presence, saying, 'I confess that our Lord was *of two natures* before the union, but I confess one nature after the union.'

In the discussions of this fifth session everything turned on this expression. As Neander said, 'The "IN two natures," or "OF two natures," was the turning-point of the whole controversy between monophysitism and dyophysitism.' Anatolius and others were prepared to accept the expression '*of* two natures,' giving to it their own meaning, but not denying the coexistence of the two natures after the union at Nazareth. With Eutyches the expression was meant to exclude their coexistence.

On October 22 the bishops met, without the senators, who were not needed on the matter of faith. The imperial commissioners were present as usual to manage the business part of the meeting.

It was known that the bishops who had met in Anatolius' house had drawn up a formula, and it seems that the Papal legates were more or less acquainted with its contents. The commissioners accordingly ordered the formulary in question to be read, which was done by Asclepiades, Deacon of Constantinople. It had been drawn up at least in concert with Juvenal of Jerusalem and Thalassius of Cæsarea, who had been the offenders at the Robber Synod, and probably by Anatolius himself, Archbishop of Constantinople now, but with antecedents of sympathy with Dioscorus, whose secretary he had been during the persecution of Flavian.

The formula contained the expression 'of two natures.' It was at once objected to by the Bishop of Germanicia, but defended by Anatolius, and the clamorous approval of a mass of bishops filled the church. It was one of those crises in the history of the Church at which, as in a critical passage in the *dénouement* of a well-drawn plot, one involuntarily stops to take breath. Who could stem the tide of secret sympathy with Eutychian teaching which was again setting in? The bishops clamoured for the insertion of the expression 'Mother of God' in the Creed. They were still possessed of the idea that somehow orthodox teaching concerning the 'two natures' in Christ involved the heresy of Nestorius—which spoke of 'two *persons*' in the Incarnate Word. The Papal legates now stepped forward and condemned the proposed definition (τύπος); they announced their determination to quit the scene unless the letter of Leo was strictly adhered to. The bishops, however, still clamoured in favour of their own formula. The commissioners endeavoured to calm the meeting by drawing their attention to the fact that the term which they had inserted in their definition, viz. 'OF two natures,' might be understood in an heretical sense, since Dioscorus had condemned Flavian for using the opposite expression 'IN two natures' of our Incarnate Lord. Anatolius replied that Dioscorus was not condemned on account of his faith, but for the attitude he had assumed towards the Pope, and for not appearing when twice summoned by the synod. The archbishop's sympathy with his old master, Dioscorus, had evidently not been quite exorcised. He was followed in his defence of the questionable formula by the great majority of the bishops.

It is evident that the commissioners perfectly understood the crisis that had now arisen. The bishops had signed the Tome of Leo, but some did not perfectly understand what they had signed; some were still in sympathy with error, and others were still terrified by the ghost of Nestorius and Nestorian proclivities, which seemed to them to haunt all orthodox statements of the two natures in our Lord.

It fell to the lot of the imperial commissioners, placing themselves on the side of the legates (by whom they were guided) to bring the Eastern bishops to a better mind. They brought the matter to its true issue by asking practically whether they were prepared to withdraw themselves from the Supreme Pontiff?

They said, 'Do you accept the letter of Leo?'—a question which, put as it was, shows that the commissioners did not consider the synod a superior authority. In fact the whole tone of the session shows that the bishops had to accept the Tome of Leo in the fulness of its meaning, or submit to be superseded by a council in the West. For this was what the legates had threatened. The bishops, however, exclaimed that they had both received and put their signatures to the letter.

Thereupon the commissioners pressed home the rigorous conclusion that what was in that letter must be inserted in their definition. 'No!' cried the bishops, 'it is not another definition that is being made; nothing is lacking to the definition.' And Eusebius of Dorylæum repeated their statement, 'It is not another definition that is being made.' He held that it was in perfect agreement with the Tome. 'The definition has confirmed the letter,' *i.e.* by its *agreement* with it, just as the bishops at Constantinople are said to have 'confirmed' the Nicene Creed, not as in a superior court, but by a loyal acceptance of it. 'Archbishop Leo,' they continued, 'believes as we believe.' 'The definition contains everything.' 'The definition contains the faith.' 'Leo said the same as Cyril said; Celestine the Pope confirmed what Cyril said; Xystus the Pope confirmed what Cyril said.' 'There is one Baptism, one Lord, one Faith.'

It is to be noticed how they bring in Celestine's and Xystus' confirmation of Cyril's writings, and assert that Celestine and Leo are at one. They would not dispute the orthodoxy of Leo; but they feared, or pretended to fear, lest their submission to his letter should be taken to imply a denial of Cyril's orthodoxy, which had, they say, been guaranteed by two Popes.

The commissioners now appealed to the emperor, who

was near at hand, to know what should be done; and his Imperial Majesty sent word that a commission of bishops (which had already been proposed) must meet, or else a council in the West, as the legates had threatened, would be inevitable.

The Illyrian bishops, whose signature to the Tome after their instruction in Anatolius' house, had evidently been to a certain extent a matter of mechanical obedience, still pressed for the disputed definition, when at length the commissioners put before them straight and nakedly the choice which they must make, viz. Dioscorus or Leo. 'Which will you follow, the most holy Leo or Dioscorus?' 'We believe with Leo' was their immediate reply. 'Then you must admit into your definition the teaching of Leo, which has been stated,' was the commissioner's logical conclusion—alluding to the expression '*in* two natures,' and not '*of* two natures.'

The commission met for discussion, but as there is no record of the nature of the discussion, we only know that they gave up their point and elected to follow Leo, and to insert in their definition the truth that our Divine Lord subsisted 'in two natures:' that is to say, that in His One Person there are two natures, the Human and Divine, unmingled after the union effected at Nazareth in the womb of the Mother of God.

When they returned to the church the altered definition was read, and agreed upon without dissent.

Thus the legates, by their firmness, had saved the position. And they had saved it as legates. Nothing short of the supreme position of Leo could have given to his legates the authority which they exercised so well at this session. After all that had been effected at this wonderful council, it would have ended in a catastrophe, but for the firm stand which they made on behalf of a single preposition, which had become the watchword of the orthodox party. No one else in that assembly could have opposed himself as an impassable barrier to the acceptance of an expression so minute, but so all-important. And the simple issue had at length been presented to these Eutychian sympathisers from Illyricum and Palestine, viz. would they follow Leo or not? They had once obeyed Dioscorus; they were now induced to obey 'the most holy Leo.'

It was a momentous hour in the history of Christendom. And we, whose religion centres in our adoration of our Divine Lord, have to attribute its successful issue to the firmness of the legates of the successor of that Apostle ' who lives and exercises judgment in his successor;' and that firmness was due to the prayer of his Divine Master, through whom he 'confirmed the brethren.' But for the legates, the end would have been professed submission of the bishops to the teaching of Leo, and yet at the same time the adoption of a definition which let in the false teaching which Leo opposed. As it was they 'followed Leo' in their definition, as they professed to have followed him in their subscription to his Tome.

It was probably at this session that the synod drew up the allocution which was afterwards presented or read to the emperor. The synod suddenly glows with warm sympathy towards him whom it had so often called 'the Holy Father,' and it says, 'God has given the synod a champion against every error in the person of the Roman bishop, who, like the ardent Peter, desires to lead everyone to God.' They then go on to deny that Leo's Tome was a different confession of faith from the Nicene. The object of such explanations is (they assert) to stop the mouths of 'innovators'—doubtless in allusion to the late emperor's condemnation of St. Flavian as one who had 'innovated in religion.' They quote amongst other instances the synods of Sardica and Ephesus as having added useful explanations, saying that those who met at Sardica 'against the remains of Arius,' 'sent their judgment to those in the East'—the West had done the same in the person of Leo—and they end with asking the emperor to be gracious in 'setting his seal to their godly decrees, and confirming the preaching of *the See of Peter.*'

So far, then, there were two principles on which the action of the Church had been based.

I. The contention throughout the Councils of Ephesus and Chalcedon was that it was not enough for anyone accused of heresy to say that he was willing to recite the Nicene

Creed. The Nicene Creed needed explanation in view of fresh perversions; that explanation was given by the Church, and these explanations must be received by those who would remain in the Church. The orthodox were those who 'heard the Church,' the present living Church. That which was decided under anathema by an œcumenical council (including, of course, its head), was just as necessary to be believed as the original scheme of doctrine. It was contained in that scheme, and to reject the voice of the living Church was tantamount to rejecting the original deposit of the faith. Men could not go behind the living voice and appeal to antiquity when that voice had decided that Mary was the Mother of God, or that there are two natures in our Divine Lord after the Incarnation. It belonged to the Church to expound her own deposit, and her children must receive as history that, and that alone, which she delivered to them as such. If a member of the Christian Church maintained that his researches into the early Fathers led him to decline the judgment of Celestine upon Nestorius, or Leo on Dioscorus, and to maintain the orthodoxy of the opinions championed by these heretics, he was subject to excommunication.

II. Again, they more and more spoke of the See of Peter; and as their needs multiplied, they had recourse more and more to its judgment as a court of appeal. Nothing, indeed, could exceed in fulness of statement the description of the relation of the Bishop of Rome to the Apostle Peter, given and accepted at the Council of Ephesus; but at Chalcedon the references were more frequent and from all quarters. Rome is the See of Peter to the Emperor Marcian, to the Empress Pulcheria, to the synod at Chalcedon; she is welcomed as such by Flavian, and described as such by St. Peter Chrysologus; her own assertion is *never once questioned* even in the East, though made again and again, and made in such momentous acts of the Church's life as the excommunication of the Patriarch of Alexandria and the dogmatic exposition of the Catholic faith on points on which masses of Eastern bishops were going miserably astray. If Anglicanism consists mainly in a protest against the supremacy of the Pope, not a whisper of Anglicanism was heard during the fourth

General Council, unless it be from the coarse-minded, ferocious heretic Dioscorus, who was deposed and excommunicated by St. Leo through ('per') the instrumentality of the Holy Synod. The exposition of faith given by the Holy See—the Tome, that is, of Leo, or dogmatic epistle to Flavian—was signed by the greater number of bishops before it was brought before the synod; it was not revised, nor reviewed, nor examined, but only publicly read, *in the council itself*. It was virtually enforced in the house of Anatolius upon the Illyrian bishops who were tainted with Eutychianism, and upon the Palestinian bishops, who had been more or less influenced by Juvenal, soon to be their patriarch. They wished to see *how* Cyril and Leo agreed, rather than *whether* they did. For Cyril (as the bishops afterwards said) was confirmed by Celestine, and therefore his teaching was the teaching of the Church. They came to see that Leo's teaching had not contradicted that of Celestine and (said the bishops) Leo resembled Peter in his championship of the faith. The Illyrian bishops were instructed by the Bishop of Constantinople on the points on which their ignorance led them astray, and they subscribed it as what it was bound to be, in harmony with the writings of St. Cyril; their judgment was a submission and their submission was a judgment. And when all strife for the present was over they called it not only the voice of Peter, but 'the doctrine of the chair of Peter' ($\tau\hat{\eta}s\ \kappa\alpha\theta\acute{\epsilon}\delta\rho\alpha s$ $\Pi\acute{\epsilon}\tau\rho\sigma\upsilon\ \kappa\acute{\eta}\rho\upsilon\gamma\mu\alpha$), and this in the presence of the emperor himself.

For at the following session (the sixth) Marcian and Pulcheria, with their imperial suite, were present. The emperor told them why he had convened the synod. He does not say it was to decide open questions. On the contrary, it was convened in order 'that no one in future should venture to maintain concerning the birth of our Lord and Saviour anything else than that which the apostolic preaching and the decree, in accordance therewith, of the 318 holy Fathers had handed down to posterity, and which was also testified by the letter of the holy Pope Leo of Rome to Flavian.' And they asked him to give the force of civil law to the 'teaching of the chair of Peter.'

CHAPTER XXV.

THEODORET AND MAXIMUS.

AFTER the sixth session the bishops continued their meetings, but no longer on the same footing. The council, in its strictly œcumenical character, was closed. The business transacted in the following meetings was of a comparatively local character, and consisted in the settlement of disputes between certain Eastern bishops. Thalassius of Cæsarea, although present at the later sessions, took back with him the record of the council's action up to this sixth session, and no further. Pelagius II. distinctly says in his letter to the Istrian bishops that the authoritative nature of the council ceased after the sixth action, and what followed was concerned with 'private matters.' And St. Leo describes the work submitted to the council as having consisted only of the definition of the faith and the restoration of the bishops who had lapsed at the Robber Synod. The rest of its proceedings, he says, were of a different nature; and accordingly the official report of the synod included in its unquestionable programme only the two matters just mentioned; they placed the rest on a different footing.[1] The emperor had desired the bishops to remain a few days for the consideration of other matters, for the settlement of which it was natural to take advantage of such a gathering. Whilst, therefore, considerable importance attached to the arrangements which were made, they could not claim the same high level of authority as belonged to the series of sessions which culminated and closed with the address to their Imperial Majesties.

I shall select three of their actions, the restoration of

[1] They excuse themselves for entering on the subject of Constantinople's position.

Theodoret, the acceptance of Maximus, and the twenty-eighth canon, as bearing specially on the subject of this book.

I. A great deal has been made of the case of Theodoret, as a supposed proof of the repudiation of Papal supremacy. It will be, therefore, well to state it somewhat fully.[1]

He had been condemned by Dioscorus at the Robber Synod for his sympathy with Nestorius. Thereupon he appealed to Rome. He wrote to Leo and said that 'if Paul, the herald of the truth, the trumpet of the Spirit, ran to the great Peter . . . much more do we, in our littleness, run to your Apostolic throne that from you we may receive healing for the wounds of the Church: for it is fitting that you should have the primacy in all things.' He then enumerates the advantages with which the Apostolic throne is adorned, viz. 'abundance of spiritual gifts as compared with others; superabundant splendour; the presidency over the whole world;[2] abundance of subjects,[3] present rule, and the communication of her name to her subjects; supereminent faith, as in the days of the Apostles; the tombs of the common Fathers and teachers of the truth, Peter and Paul, . . . who arose in the East but died in the West, and from that West now illuminate the whole world—these have made your throne most illustrious.' Then, after setting forth his condemnation at the Latrocinium (Robber Synod) in his absence by Dioscorus, he adds, 'But I await the sentence of your apostolic throne.' He desires to know whether he is to acquiesce in this unjust deposition or not. 'For I await' (he repeats) 'your sentence, and if you should command me to acquiesce in the adverse decision, I acquiesce.'[4]

Again he says to Leo: 'I beseech and entreat your Holiness that your upright and just tribunal would assist me,

---

[1] Canon Bright writes (*Ch. Hist.* p. 417, third edition) about St. Leo: 'His judgments, whether as to an individual or as to a doctrine, were first reviewed and then confirmed,' as a proof of the supposed difference between his position and that of the Holy See amongst ourselves now. The 'individual' is Theodoret. We have seen that his doctrine was not 'reviewed and confirmed' as by a superior court.

[2] τῆς οἰκουμένης προκαθημένη. Cf. St. Ignatius' προκάθηται τῆς ἀγάπης, president of the [covenant of] love—said of Rome.

[3] οἰκητόρων, lit. inhabitants.   [4] ἐμμένω (Theod. *Ep.* cxiii.).

who am appealing to it, and would bid me come to you and show that my teaching treads in the footsteps of the Apostles.'[1] To Renatus, a priest of the Church of Rome, employed as legate to Ephesus,[2] he writes: 'Concerning this case, I beseech your Holiness that you would persuade the most holy and blessed archbishop to use his apostolic authority and bid me fly to your council'[3]—that is, the council which the Pope invariably used in the determination of greater causes. Theodoret adds words which are omitted by Quesnel, who, in defiance of the context, endeavoured to show that it was not to the authority of the Pope himself that Theodoret appealed—words which even if the preceding quotations were to be forgotten would be sufficient to show that it was the exercise of the authority of the Holy See that he was invoking, viz.: 'For that most holy See has the sovereignty over the Churches which are in the whole world on many counts; and before all these, in that it has remained free from the stain of heresy, and none has ever sat in it with thoughts contrary [to the faith]; it has kept the Apostolic grace whole and uncorrupt.' He then expresses his readiness to acquiesce in its judgment, whatever it may be.

It is clear from this that it was not the judgment of the synod at Rome in itself that he sought, but the judgment of the Sovereign Pontiff, expressed, as it was wont to be, in synod. The synod was the apparatus, the machinery, the setting of the Papal judgment. The bishops of this synod could not be considered infallible as compared with other synods, except by reason of their relationship to the Holy See. It was the infallibility of this latter on which he distinctly placed reliance.

At the same time he wrote to Constantinople to Archbishop Anatolius, to induce him to persuade the emperor to allow him (since a bishop could not move without imperial leave and the assistance of the imperial purse)[4] 'to go to the

---

[1] *Ep.* xcii. c. 5.
[2] He was probably dead when Theodoret wrote to him. But Theodoret was insufficiently informed, according to Tillemont.
[3] *Ep.* cxvi.
[4] Through orders to the civil officials—as we should say, by free passes.

West and be judged by those bishops most beloved of God.' Theodoret was not simpleton enough to ask the emperor's leave for anything that contravened the laws of the Church as understood in the East; and yet he did ask the Bishop of Constantinople to get him leave to have his case tried at Rome. From which we may justly conclude that the transference of the case of a Greek bishop to Rome was not considered by either the Bishop of Constantinople or the emperor to be in contravention of the laws of the Church. It was not here the case of anything claimed by the Pope, but a glimpse of how Greek bishops understood the matter amongst themselves. These Western bishops, ' most beloved of God,' could possess no rights over an Eastern bishop, except as being the council of the sovereign ruler of the Church, as Theodoret had called the Roman Pontiff. But as the custom was ever to exercise the Pontifical authority by means of a council, it was all one to appeal to the Episcopal Council at Rome or to the Bishop of Rome himself. Theodoret's expressions concerning the latter necessitate this conclusion so far as his own judgment was concerned, and his letter to Anatolius gives his estimate of what the Bishop of Constantinople deemed a proper course for justice to take. It would, indeed, be difficult to express in clearer terms the teaching of the Vatican Council concerning the relationship of the Holy See to the rest of the Church than has been done by Theodoret. According to him that See is the Holy See, the Apostolic throne, the sovereign ruler of the Church throughout the world, and the one pure, true channel of the Church's faith.

It seems that the writings which Theodoret promised to send to Rome for inspection and judgment did not reach Leo until after the legates had left for Chalcedon; but on receiving them St. Leo at once passed sentence in Theodoret's favour. He was worthy to be restored to his see. Both St. Leo [1] and the commissioners [2] speak of the Papal 'judgment.' So that there can be no doubt that St. Leo passed actual sentence on Theodoret's individual case, and it follows that it was a regular appeal on the part of Theodoret. We may assume, indeed, that there was a careful examination of

[1] *Ep.* cxx. 5.   [2] Actio viii.

the case at Rome, considering the caution invariably exercised by this great Pontiff in admitting anyone to communion, who had been suspected of heresy. And Theodoret had been in active sympathy with Nestorius, but had detached himself from that heretic when the reconciliation took place between St. Cyril and John of Antioch. It is, therefore, in the highest degree improbable that St. Leo would pass judgment without careful and, presumably, conciliar examination of his present teaching. He had probably signed the dogmatic epistle to Flavian, or offered to sign it.

When, therefore, Theodoret came to Chalcedon, he was in the position of a man whose rights were secured by the Papal judgment, and who was entitled to act as bishop. The council, however, was called for the special purpose, amongst other things, of restoring the bishops who had been deposed in the Latrocinium (Robber Synod) ;[1] and St. Leo had commissioned it to act in the matter of such restoration.[2] Consequently it would seem that St. Leo wrote at once to the legates to say that he received Theodoret to communion and restored him to his see, so far as the right was concerned, although the complete execution of his sentence involving the actual restitution to this see would naturally remain in the hands of the synod, having been already devolved upon them by Leo himself.

When, therefore, the council opened its proceedings and Eusebius of Dorylæum had preferred the accusation against Diodorus, Theodoret was told by the imperial commissioners to enter ; but the Eutychian sympathisers amongst the bishops were indignant at his restoration. They were certain that Leo had been overreached ; and considering Theodoret's antecedents (his opposition to Cyril) it is not surprising that they should think this. For it was a matter in which, on the principles of the Vatican decrees, Leo might have been deceived. And the Eutychians, long years after this, maintained that Theodoret was insincere, and that St. Leo had been overreached. They ought, however, on any but the Papal theory of government, to have said that it made no difference whether he was deceived or not ; for what right had the

---

[1] *Ep.* lxxvii¹ [2] *Ep.* xciii. c. 3.

Bishop of Rome to restore a Greek bishop to his see at all? But this was not their contention; they neither blamed Theodoret for appealing to Rome, nor Rome for hearing his case. They simply objected that Theodoret had not placed his case honestly before the Bishop of Rome.[1] And in like manner, at Chalcedon, they demurred to the synodical acceptance of Theodoret as bishop, and clamoured for his extrusion.

The imperial commissioners, however, and the synod, decided that Theodoret's restoration by St. Leo must stand good so far as this, that he was to act as bishop, whilst any charge they had to prefer against him should be investigated later on. He was, I say, to act as bishop, for he was allowed to take his place as accuser, and was accepted as such by the whole council on the ground that he had been restored, or rather his deposition declared null and void, by the judgment of Leo. According to the arrangement of the Council of Constantinople (382), a degraded bishop could not act as accuser of another bishop; so that in admitting Theodoret as accuser of Dioscorus, the synod accepted the sentence of the Pope.

And, in point of fact, he subsequently acted as fully bishop in the course of the council. When the Illyrian bishops doubted about the meaning of some words in Leo's letter, Theodoret set them right, quoting from St. Cyril, on which the commissioners said: 'After this, who doubts?' and the bishops exclaimed, 'No one doubts!'[2]

In the fourth act Theodoret gave his judgment on the Tome of Leo; and in the sixth act he signed, saying, 'I, Theodoret, Bishop of Cyrus, defining have subscribed.'[3]

And now, in the seventh session (the eighth act), the bishops proceeded to satisfy the demands of the Illyrian and other bishops that Theodoret should anathematise Nestorius. They had consented to sit with him in synod on the ground that Leo had pronounced his deposition null and void; but they now—at least a certain portion of them—in deference to the clamours of the Egyptian bishops, desired that he should

---

[1] *E.g.* in the conference held before Justinian in 533.
[2] Mansi, t. vii. p. 19.   [3] *Ibid.* t. vii. p. 146.

assure the council that, whatever might have been his dispositions or avowals when Leo pronounced sentence in his favour, he was prepared to do what every bishop might be called upon to do, *i.e.* anathematise Nestorius. In this they were perfectly within their rights. The Egyptian bishops had been put off during the synod with the promise that they should have satisfaction later on. Theodoret, after a little fencing, anathematised Nestorius by name, and immediately the bishops burst into an exclamation of tremendous force, saying, 'Leo has judged after' (*i.e.* in accordance with the mind of) 'God!' It was Leo's judgment, as I have said above.

That the action of the bishops was in no way (on the principles of the Vatican decrees) an infringement of the authority of the Holy See, which Theodoret had invoked and described as presiding over the whole world, is certain from the following facts,[1] viz. that the legates took part in the matter and actually gave the decision—that the leader of the Illyrians was the Bishop of Thessaly, who entirely depended on Rome, being the Papal vicar in that region—and that Leo himself saw in the bishop's action no derogation of his authority,[2] and that in spite of the commissioners' attempt to soothe the Egyptians by saying Theodoret should not act as judge, he did, as a matter of fact, act as such though not in the case of Dioscorus which was the point of their objection.

So that the matter may be fairly summarised thus, St. Leo had given the bishops the fullest authority to deal with the cases of the bishops who had been 'deposed' at the Robber Synod. He had declared Theodoret, Bishop of Cyrus, to be deserving of his bishopric, having certified to his orthodoxy. Accordingly, in spite of the clamours of the Egyptian bishops, who had had to see their patriarch Dioscorus disgraced, and, *en revanche*, desired to make out that Theodoret had deceived St. Leo, he was allowed to act as judge in the matter of faith, though not in the deposition of their patriarch. When all was over, he was required to do what would satisfy the irritated Egyptian bishops, viz. anathematise Nestorius, and then, after saying, as it were, to these bishops, 'You see that Leo, as usual, was right,' they placed him in possession of his

---

[1] Cf. Natalis Alexander, *Diss. de Theodoreto*.   [2] *Ep.* xciii. *ad Theod.*

bishopric, their decision being expressed by the Papal legates. There was nothing in all this that placed the council above the Pope; on the contrary, the admission of Theodoret to the council as judge in doctrine, though not in the case of Dioscorus, of whom nevertheless he was allowed to be an accuser, which was forbidden to a degraded bishop, was a signal instance of the deference which was felt to be due to the sentence of the Bishop of Rome on the case of an Eastern bishop, who had expressly appealed to that judgment.

Another matter settled by the council concerned the See of Antioch, which had been occupied at the Robber Synod by a bishop named Domnus.

There was something pathetic about this man's career. He was nephew to the celebrated John of Antioch, and experienced a call to the solitary life. Fired, however, with the idea of recalling his uncle from his sympathies with Nestorius, he left his cell, contrary to the advice of the Abbot Euthymius, who predicted the misfortune that actually befel him. At Antioch he won his way to the episcopal throne, succeeding his uncle as successor of Peter in that third see of Christendom. But his weakness led him to show the white feather at the Robber Synod, and, cowed by Dioscorus, he consented to the restoration of Eutyches, and the condemnation of Flavian. But he reaped a rich reward of his cowardice in being deposed by Dioscorus, to whom he had truckled, on the ground of supposed sympathy in the past with Nestorius, and of having condemned Cyril. The indulgence shown to the other leaders of the Robber Synod on their repentance was not extended to Domnus by St. Leo, who forbade his restoration to the See of Antioch. He ended his days in penitent retirement.

Anatolius, in contravention of the Nicene Canons, ordained Maximus Bishop of Antioch in place of Domnus. And on the restoration at Chalcedon of the bishops who had lapsed at the Latrocinium, whilst other bishops were restored to their sees, Maximus was allowed to retain his intruded position on the sole ground that St. Leo had ordered that his ordination should hold good.[1]

A writer [2] who professes the greatest regard for the prero-

[1] Mansi, t. vii. p. 258.   [2] Quesnel.

gatives of the Sovereign Pontiff, but takes every opportunity of undermining their historical basis, remarks on this treatment of Domnus and Maximus, that if only the Act in which their case occurs were genuine, we should have in our hands an unequivocal testimony to 'the supreme authority of the Pontiff both over synods and over the Oriental bishops—the bishops of the greater sees.' His arguments against the genuineness of the record of this session were dealt with in a very satisfactory manner by Baluze, and in a still more trenchant way by Tillemont, who, in spite of his Gallican sympathies, pronounces Quesnel's array of arguments nothing less than imbecile. It was reserved, however, for the brothers Ballerini to set the matter at rest by means of a manuscript which Quesnel had not seen, and which is older even than Rusticus. Their refutation of Quesnel's objections is complete.[1]

The prerogative admitted, in this Act, as belonging to Leo, covers everything ever claimed by the Holy See in the way of jurisdiction. St. Leo dispensed with the irregularity of Maximus' ordination in contravention of the Nicene canons, doubtless because he had shown his fidelity to the true faith, whilst Domnus, after his cowardly conduct at the Latrocinium, did not ask for reinstatement, but eventually [2] elected to retire to his original seclusion.

Now the authoritative settlement on the part of the Bishop of Rome of the succession to that Oriental see, one of the three 'first' or 'greater' sees, was, if anything ever was, an exercise of Papal supremacy; and the acceptance of the settlement by these bishops assigning no other ground except that the settlement had been made by the Pope, amounts to a demonstration that, in the minds of the Eastern bishops of that time, the government of the Church was strictly and properly Papal.

But further, the acceptance of the Papal decision concerning the Antiochene succession occurred in the midst of a

[1] See an excellent summary of Baluze's proofs of the genuineness of the Act in Migne's *Leo the Great,* vol. ii. pp. 1269-75. The Ballerini afterwards clenched the matter by the Latin copy of an older Greek MS. alluded to in the text.

[2] For the sequence of events, see Migne's *Leonis Opp.* ed. Baller. t. ii. p. 726.

session which was dealing with the case of Ibas, Bishop of Edessa.[1] It was proposed that the minutes of the Robber Synod should be read. To this the Papal legates objected on the ground that the acts of that synod had been rendered null and void by 'the Apostolic Bishop of the city of Rome.' The Bishop of Constantinople (Anatolius) at once rose and said that he agreed that all that was done at that ill-fated synod was invalid, excepting only what was done in the matter of Maximus, Bishop of Antioch; and he gave as his reason for saying so, that the most holy Archbishop of Rome had received Maximus into communion, and had 'decided that he should preside over the Church of the Antiocheans.'[2] To this the rest of the bishops agreed.

So that the invalidity of the Robber Synod was assigned by these Eastern bishops simply and solely to the decision of the Bishop of Rome; and the single exception made to the general invalidity of its proceedings was one that the Pope had ordered, and its validity was attributed by these bishops to the Papal decision.

But whilst the Pope gave his sanction to Maximus' ordination to the See of Antioch, he refused it to the following compact now entered into by that bishop in regard to some provinces of his patriarchate.

Juvenal of Jerusalem had long set his heart upon the extension of his jurisdiction. He had succeeded in so completely gaining the ear of the emperor, Theodosius II., that he had been allowed to count in his rule the provinces of Phœnicia, and also of Arabia, and the three provinces of Palestine, which properly belonged to Antioch. St. Cyril had done his utmost to oppose this iniquitous proceeding, and appealed to the Pope, entreating him with earnest prayer ('sollicitâ prece')[3] to give no ground for such 'illicit attempts.' But Juvenal gained his case with the secular power by means of forged documents.

The quarrel over this lust of jurisdiction had gone on until

---

[1] The history of Ibas does not come within the scope of this book, but belongs rather to that of the fifth council.

[2] ἄρχειν τῆς Ἀντιοχέων ἐκκλησίας ἐδικαίωσεν (Mansi, t. vii. p. 258).

[3] *Leonis Ep.* cxix. *ad Maximum.*

the time of the council, when Maximus acquiesced in a compromise, by which Antioch was to be shorn of the three provinces of Palestine, and Juvenal was to give up all claim to the Phœnicians and Arabians. But Maximus consented to this arrangement only 'if it was approved by our venerable Father, the Archbishop of Greater Rome.'[1] Leo, however, withheld his sanction, and desired the Bishop of Antioch to keep him well informed as to what went on, reminding him that there must be some better reason for his allowing Antioch and Jerusalem to break the Nicene settlement than had been adduced.[2] He also informed him that the assent of his legates was necessarily provisional on matters on which they had no definite directions from himself. But the Pope did not, at least in that letter, absolutely and finally decide the matter. He only withdrew his sanction, and urged upon Maximus that he should 'share with the Apostolic See in this anxious matter,' and recognise the privileges of the 'third see' of Christendom.[3]

[1] Cf. MS. of Actio, edited by the Ballerini. The expression 'Greater Rome' is due to the account being from a Greek source.

[2] *Ep.* cxix. *ad Maximum.*

[3] The writer in the *Dict. of Chr. Biogr.* (vol. iii. p. 881) has completely misunderstood this phrase. He speaks of Leo exhorting Maximus, 'as a sharer in an Apostolical See,' to maintain the doctrine, &c. St. Leo says: 'Dignum est enim te Apostolicæ sedis in hac sollicitudine esse consortem et . . . privilegia tertiæ sedis agnoscere.'

CHAPTER XXVI.

THE BYZANTINE PLOT.

It had been well for the Church if the council had now dispersed. But it was not to be. The bishops who remained now engaged in a project which had long agitated the minds of a few leading spirits.

For more than eighty years Constantinople had nursed a thought which was destined to change the course of ecclesiastical history, and plunge her into a permanent schism. Photius, who consummated the schism between the East and West in the ninth century, claimed for the Bishop of Constantinople the title and position of 'Universal Bishop.' The Bishop of Rome had been such, according to his theory, until the capital of the empire passed from Rome to Byzantium. But the position of universal bishop was based, according to Photius, on the secular grandeur of the city; so that when Constantine left Rome it was only a matter of time for Byzantium to succeed to the honours of the original capital.

The difference between this theory and that which obtained in the fifth century involved the whole question of the property attributed to the Church in the Nicene Creed under the title 'Apostolic.' Under that title, in the mind of the early Church, was included the government of the Church by the Apostles and their successors; understanding by 'the Apostles,' as the primitive Church did, a body of men who were associated together by our Lord under a visible head. 'It has been known to all ages,' so it was said at Ephesus, 'and it is doubtful to none, that the blessed Apostle Peter, *the Prince and head of the Apostles*, the rock and foundation of the Catholic Church, received from our Saviour the keys of the Kingdom.' And the see of that Apostle, consecrated by the blood of the two Apostles, himself and St. Paul, became, in the words of St. Irenæus and St. Cyprian, the principal or ruling Church, that which, according to St. Ignatius of Antioch, writing in the second century, 'presided over the [covenant of] love,' and in which, according to St. Augustine, 'the principalship had ever been in force,' and was designated in the terminology of the whole Church, East and West, in the fifth century, 'the Apostolic See.'

The chasm between the teaching of the schismatic Bishop of Constantinople, Photius, in the ninth century, and his predecessor in the see in the fifth century at Chalcedon, is exactly expressed in the words of the latter when he said to Leo 'The see of Constantinople has for its parent your own Apostolic See, having specially joined itself thereunto.'[1]

But although Anatolius thus expressed the true relation between Rome and Constantinople, his action at Chalcedon prepared the way for the unhappy schism into which the East eventually plunged, under the guidance of the miserable Photius, with his claim to be 'universal bishop.' The term 'universal bishop' is one which might be properly used to express the relation of the Apostolic See to the rest of the Church, but even so it needed a certain care lest it should be thought to mean that other bishops were but legates or vice-bishops of the one universal bishop. In fear of this meaning being attached to the term, St. Gregory repudiated it. It was, however, freely used at the Council of Chalcedon. And there is no fear of any Catholic nowadays giving it such an unorthodox interpretation as St. Gregory detected in John's use of the term, and so there is no ground for refusing it to the occupant of the See of Rome. But on the lips of a bishop of Constantinople it necessarily implied a heresy, for it also implied the idea that the government of the Church was not apostolic but Erastian. The earthly emperor, according to this theory, by moving his capital, moved the centre of the Church's unity. So Photius argued. Neither he nor his predecessors were really prepared to carry out their theory to its logical issue, for, as a Sovereign Pontiff asked of his predecessors, were they prepared to call Ravenna, or Gangra, or

[1] 'Anatolius ad Leonem' (*Ep.* ci.).

Sirmium, the centre of the Church's government when the emperor made these, as he did, the centre of his rule?

The attack on the original constitution of the Church, which culminated, under favourable political circumstances, in the schismatic action of the East under Photius, was commenced in fact at the Council of Constantinople. There the bishops assembled under Nectarius had decreed a certain precedency of honour to the 'New Rome,' as Byzantine pride delighted to call the city of Constantine.

But they had not so much as ventured to send their canon to the West. It was a purely local arrangement, not sanctioned even by the rest of the East.[1] But it was continually being acted upon, and the titular precedency presently grew into a very real jurisdiction. Constantinople, being the centre of political and commercial interests, continually saw bishops from various parts staying in her midst, and convenience led to the custom of settling many an ecclesiastical dispute in meetings[2] composed of the Bishop of Constantinople and those bishops who happened to be in the imperial city. It came also to be sometimes a matter of convenience and sometimes a matter of secular advantage for bishops to be consecrated at Constantinople. And what began as an occasional practice attained in course of time to the rank of a regular custom, attended, as such customs usually are, with pecuniary advantages to the see that thus became an increasing centre.[3]

The lust of power, so infectious in an imperial centre, and sometimes a certain immediate disciplinary gain to the Church, had thus led to claims in the way of jurisdiction which found no countenance even in the third canon of the Council of Constantinople. Large provinces of the Church in the East had come under the practical jurisdiction of the Bishop of Constantinople, though not without struggles and alternations of submission and resistance.

Had Constantinople remained satisfied even with this, her

---

[1] Mr. Gore says (*Dict. of Chr. Biog.*, art. 'Leo,' p. 663) that 'Leo's statement that this canon had never taken effect is entirely untrue.' What St. Leo said was that the canon was null and void so far as the sanction of the West was concerned, and this was strictly true.

[2] Called the σύνοδος ἐνδημοῦσα.   [3] Cf. *Conc. Chalced.* Act xvi.

relations to the autonomous eparchies of Asia Minor and Pontus and Thrace might have been capable of adjustment. But she was continually being brought into contact with the 'greater sees,' as they were called, of Alexandria and Antioch. And their position of recognised superiority stood in the way of that programme of universal domination in the East which was now looming before her mind. She had made an enormous stride in the third canon of the Council of Constantinople. By the arrangement there proposed she took honorary precedence of Alexandria and Antioch. But this canon, having received no ecclesiastical sanction, had done no more than keep before the minds of the Eastern bishops her ideal of Church government.

It must not, however, be supposed that that ideal as at present conceived included any real equality of jurisdiction with Rome herself. Constantinople wished to be in the East what Rome was as patriarch of the West. Πατριαρχίας κληροῦσθε was St. Gregory of Nazianzus' condemnation of the East. The relation of Rome to the whole Church as the See of St. Peter—as in a peculiar and inalienable sense, the Apostolic See—was too firmly rooted in the mind of the Christian world for any idea of subverting that to enter as yet into even Byzantine schemes of exaltation; that was an after-thought. To be the Patriarch of the East over Alexandria and over Antioch was the summit of Constantinople's present ambition. And, as we shall see, Constantinople did not dream of the possibility of really securing this object of her ambition, *except with the permission of Rome, as representing the blessed Apostle Peter*.[1]

Now, Constantinople had met with more than one serious rebuff at the Council of Chalcedon. In discussing the complaint of Photius of Tyre a matter had come before the Fathers which touched the influence of Constantinople in her most sensitive part. The question had arisen whether the meetings of the Bishop of Constantinople and the other bishops resident or sojourning in the city could be called a synod, and the bishops at Chalcedon had refused to say that they could.

[1] Letter of the bishops to Leo.

This was throwing a serious slight on Constantinople's method of action at its very core.

Again, the bishops of Asia had desired that the bishops of Ephesus should not be ordained at Constantinople, and the council had refused to support Constantinople in this her growing custom.

Once more, the bishops had refused to give a definite sanction to Constantinople's custom of ordaining a bishop for Basilinopolis.

The time had therefore come for Constantinople to make one desperate effort to gain a quasi-synodical sanction for the position which she claimed as second only to Rome. Everything favoured her ambitious project. The bishops had left Chalcedon by the hundred, and amongst those that were left there was not one that might not be counted on for either assent or silence.

Of the two 'greater sees' Alexandria was vacant, and Antioch was occupied by a partisan of Anatolius, who owed to him his irregular elevation, which had been pardoned by Rome only (as Leo said) 'for the sake of peace.'[1]

Constantinople, therefore, had nothing to fear from these. She only needed a lack of scrupulous fairness on her own part to enable her to press the matter to a successful issue under these favourable circumstances. But further, she could count upon at least the silence of another leading prelate, viz. Juvenal of Jerusalem, who had himself just gained the object of his ambition for the last twenty years in the compromise by which he had wrested three provinces from Antioch. He at any rate was not in a position to complain of any illicit stretch of jurisdiction on the part of another. And Juvenal and Anatolius had a further bond in that both had come under the influence of Dioscorus and coquetted with Eutychianism. Then the Bishop of Heraclea, the Primate of Thrace, was absent, and he was very closely concerned in the project that Constantinople had before her of extending her actual jurisdiction as well as securing the semblance of synodical sanction for titular precedence. This primate was represented by Lucian, who was so friendly to Anatolius that

[1] 'Studio pacis.'

he was sent by him to Rome on this very matter. Ephesus, again, of supreme importance, as one of the exarchies to be robbed of its autonomy, was vacant, Bassian and Stephen having been deposed. Thalassius of Cæsarea was there, but did not subscribe. The Illyrians were not there, not even Thessalonia, neither was Ancyra, Corinth, Nicomedia, Cos, or Iconium, all of them important centres. In fact, the little knot of bishops whom Constantinople gathered round herself by various means could not by any stretch of language be called a representative ecclesiastical body. Moreover they had no leave from Rome to discuss the question now forced upon the bishops by Constantinople; it was no part of the council's programme. It was simply a plot against the Church's order, with hardly a name that would command the confidence of the Church except Eusebius of Dorylæum. The imperial commissioners were asked to assist at the session, but they refused. The legates also withdrew. There was not a single Western bishop present. But these 'astute' Orientals, as the African bishop Facundus called them, drew up a canon which flung the Nicene settlement as to precedence to the winds, and assigned, on the one hand, the first place in the East to Constantinople, and on the other hand gave her jurisdiction over Asia Minor, Thrace, and Pontus. Their metropolitans were to be deprived of their position as left to them by the Nicene Fathers, and Constantinople was to be not only New Rome in the civil order, but in the ecclesiastical hierarchy she was to stand second to Rome in point of titular precedence, and at the same time to receive an enormous extension of her jurisdiction in the East. She had hoped and tried to gain the confirmation and ordination of the provincial bishops as well as of the metropolitans, but owing to the opposition of some metropolitans she failed in this part of her project.

On the following day the Papal legates demanded an explanation of what had been done in their absence. They had absented themselves on the technical ground that after the definition of faith had been drawn up, and the matter of the lapsed bishops dealt with, their commission ended. But it turned out that they had also received orders from Rome to oppose any attempt at altering the relations of bishops on the ground of the civil *status* of their sees. Leo was already well aware of the ambitious projects of Constantinople.

Aetius, the archdeacon, now did his best to purge the action of the bishops of its irregularity. He said that it must be owned that the matters of faith had been decided in a fitting way, but pleaded that it was customary to take in hand other necessary matters; that they had asked the legates to be present, but without success, and that they had received the permission of the imperial commissioners to proceed with the business. The legates, however, maintained, and were probably justified in maintaining, that the bishops had signed in fear; that the proposed canon contravened the Nicene settlement; that it was professedly grounded on canons which had not been enrolled amongst those of the Church;[1] and, lastly, that if they had been benefiting by the said canon up till now, what need of anything further?—and if they had not, why do they now apply for sanction for that which is an infringement of the canons?—reasoning which was unanswerable.

In consequence of this mention of the canons, the commissioners requested that each side should read the canons on which they relied. The legates accordingly read the sixth canon of Nicæa, in which Alexandria and Antioch, and not Constantinople, come after Rome. Aetius is then supposed to have read first a slightly different version of the same canon, and then the third of Constantinople. But this is in the highest degree improbable, since his supposed reading of that version makes nothing for the point at issue. The rise of Constantinople took place after the Council of Nicæa; no one pretends, or pretended, that the Nicene canons in any way assisted Constantinople in its present aims. It was then an inferior see, and left so by the Nicene Fathers. It was on the third canon of Constantinople that these bishops took their stand, as their resolution in the previous session shows. The Nicene canon was their difficulty. Indeed, in one of the oldest versions of the Acts of Chalcedon that we possess, this

---

[1] 'Non conscripti.'

recitation of the sixth canon by Aetius does not appear.[1] There are also other indications that the text has been tampered with here; for between the supposed recitation of the sixth canon and that of the third of Constantinople occurs the statement that 'the same secretary read from the same codex the synodicon of the second synod,' which Mansi rightly transfers to the margin, as an impossible statement to have occurred in the original. The Council of Constantinople was not called 'the second synod' until after the Council of Chalcedon had placed it in that rank. The expression, therefore, belongs to a later period than the original of the Council of Chalcedon. Accordingly, Rusticus, who had before him very early manuscripts, omits this expression, although the sixth canon appears in his manuscript. The insertion, therefore, had been made before his time, doubtless, as has been suggested above, by a Greek scribe, who, seeing a Greek version of the sixth canon in the margin, put it into the text, and some after copyist inserted the remark about the second synod. Dr. Bright refers to the expression 'œcumenical,' used by the council of 382 of the council of 381;[2] but this could at that date only mean that it was a council of all the East, and it is certain that it had not yet been reckoned by the Church in general as the second synod. It would have been a simple impertinence to call it the second synod before it had received such a designation from the whole Church. Hefele seems to have misunderstood the Ballerini's argument, in urging that it was at Chalcedon that the Council of Constantinople took its place as second in the general councils. This is, of course, true; but the original of this Act could hardly have started the phrase.[3]

What, however, is of greater importance is the conclusion which the imperial commissioners now drew from the whole discussion. The legates had quoted the sixth Nicene canon,

[1] The *Codex Julianus*, now called *Parisiensis*. Baluze first noticed this, and has been followed by the Ballerini.

[2] *Notes on the Canons, &c.*, 1892, p. 228. The reader must not suppose that the reference to Theodoret which Dr. Bright gives contains any expression of that writer in favour of his opinion; it only contains the letter of the council of 382.

[3] Ballerini, *De Antiq. Collect. Canonum*, Part I. cap. vi. 8.

beginning 'Rome has always held the primacy,' and had read onwards about Alexandria and Antioch. The Archdeacon of Constantinople had read the third Canon of Constantinople. Several of the bishops had taken the side of Constantinople, and expressed their perfect willingness to subordinate their sees to that of the imperial city; Eusebius of Ancyra, however, whilst he proclaimed his willingness to do the same, protesting against the pecuniary exactions with which this subordination had been accompanied. The commissioners decided that two things were plain from the Acts and depositions—first, that the primacy ($\pi\rho\omega\tau\varepsilon\hat{\imath}\alpha$—the very word used in the sixth Nicene canon, as cited by the Papal legate) belonged to Old Rome. About this there had been no question, and it is obvious that the imperial commissioners could decide nothing about that. But, secondly, they decided that New Rome ought to have— not a primacy such as Rome had, which the whole history of the council proves to have involved jurisdiction in the minds of all the bishops—but the same honorary privileges, as Rome, besides her primacy, and as a consequence of it, also possessed. Rome, they had said, possessed two things—honorary precedence and primacy; Constantinople ought to possess in the East that honorary precedence which Rome possessed over the whole Church.[1]

Thus Constantinople laid the foundation of her desired patriarchate over the East, and supplied the premiss from which Photius was one day to draw the conclusion in claiming universal jurisdiction.

It is difficult to understand how Mr. Gore could manage to see 'Rome's self-assertion' at the bottom of all this. Canon Bright also reproduces with approval the sentence in which Mr. Gore makes the strange statement, that it is 'more than probable [sic] that the self-assertion of Rome excited the jealousy of the East, and thus Eastern bishops secretly

---

[1] πρὸ πάντων μὲν τὰ πρωτεῖα καὶ τὴν ἐξαίρετον τιμὴν κατὰ τοὺς κανόνας τῷ τῆς πρεσβύτιδος 'Ρώμης θεοφιλεστάτῳ ἀρχιεπισκόπῳ φυλάττεσθαι. I do not see how, in view of this undisputed original, it can be maintained, as it is by so many Anglican writers, that the legates' version was a forgery. I may mention Canon Bright, Canon Carter, Mr. Puller, and the Bishop of Lincoln, as amongst recent writers who lay great stress on this imaginary forgery. The Council clearly accepted the Papal legate's quotation as accurate.

felt that the cause of Constantinople was theirs.' It must have been *very* 'secretly' felt, for there is not a solitary allusion in their speeches to such an idea, whilst they are from end to end of the council brimful of acknowledgments of the service which Leo had rendered to the Church of God. So far as the records go, the bishops, whatever they 'secretly felt,' were open in their avowals that, to use their own words, 'God has given the synod a champion against every error in the person of the Roman bishop, who, like the ardent Peter, desires to lead everyone to God.' (Synod's letter to Marcian.) St. Nicolas said to Photius, of the crisis which arose in consequence of the Latrocinium, 'If the great Leo had not been divinely moved to open his mouth, the Christian religion would have perished outright.'

Mr. Gore's suggestion bears, indeed, no serious relation to the facts. It may be fairly said of it, as Canon Bright has said of a contention of the Ballerini, mentioned above, that 'nothing but an intelligible bias could account for a suggestion so futile.'[1] The 'self-assertion' was all on the part of Constantinople.

The legates entered their protest on the technical ground that the Apostolic See had not been consulted as to the discussion of this question,[2] and that the proposal was a violation of the Nicene canons. They ask that the proceedings of the previous day be cancelled, or else that their opposition be recorded, 'so that we may know what we ought to report to the Apostolic man, the Pope of the Universal Church, so that he himself may pass sentence on the injury done to his see or on the overthrow of the canons'—the injury done to the Holy See by debating the question without its consent, and the overthrow of the canons by displacing Alexandria in favour of Constantinople.

In spite, however, of the legates' protest the bishops voted the canon.

The matter could not, of course, stand there. Comparatively speaking, as we have seen, they were but a handful of

---

[1] Bright's *Notes on the Councils*, p. 148.
[2] This seems to be the meaning of the legates' words, which are obscure. It is most in accordance with what Leo says in his letters on the subject.

bishops,[1] most of them of sees grouped round Constantinople, and their leaders far from enjoying the esteem of the Catholic world. Their canon was the work 'rather of Greek sophists than of Fathers of the Church.'[2] They had adroitly tacked on their new claim over three large metropolitanates (which by the Nicene Council had been left autonomous) to the third canon of Constantinople, so that the new and old parts read like one, in which, as Canon Bright remarks, they were more 'astute than candid.' It was not true, as they asserted, that the Fathers (if the Nicene Fathers were meant) 'gave' her (patriarchal [3]) privileges to the See of Rome; they only recognised what was already ancient. It was not true that what the Nicene Fathers recognised as ancient custom was due to the secular position of the See of Rome. Her privileges were settled by herself as See of St. Peter. It was not true that the Fathers of Constantinople had bestowed anything in the way of jurisdiction, but merely the second rank in the way of honorary precedence. It was not true that Constantinople had any right over Pontus, Thrace, and Asia Minor. The bishops, moreover, enunciated a principle, which had its natural sequel in the present subservience of the Greek schism to the Czar on the one hand and to the Sultan on the other.[4] It so mixed up the movements of the Church and the State as to secularise the former and ensconce the latter in the position of the real determinant of the Church's jurisdiction. No wonder that only about 150 bishops out of the original 600 could be induced to sign, and that St. Leo could fearlessly call it an 'extorted subscription,' even after some few at the session had denied that they were compelled to subscribe. St. Leo knew that his legates were right in their estimate of the kind of influence that had been brought to bear upon these subservient bishops.

The matter, then, could not rest there. Indeed these bishops

---

[1] And yet Mr. Puller says that 'the Council, as a whole, passed it' (*Primitive Saints*, p. 20). Canon Bright more correctly speaks of the difference in number between these bishops and those who signed the Tome as 'significant.'

[2] Rohrbacher, *Hist.* vol. iv. p. 539.

[3] There is no indication that these bishops at Chalcedon were professing to deal with anything but the patriarchal rights of Rome: her primacy was left as it was.

[4] Cf. Rohrbacher, *Hist.* loc. cit.

themselves did not entertain the idea that their act was final; and accordingly they set to work to gain a favourable decision from Leo, in spite of his legates' protest. They had the emperor on their side, and the game was worth pursuing; for even if they lost in the present, they had taken a step forward for the future.

It is certainly astonishing that writers who are so full of Rome's supposed 'self-assertion' and 'exorbitant claims' should not only pardon but defend these arrogant pretensions of Constantinople. Yet it is the case that the most universally accepted writers amongst Anglicans have for the last three centuries taken their stand on this canon, and seen in it an acceptance, *by the Church,* of the principle that Rome owed *all* her privileges, not to her relationship to the Apostle Peter, and through him to our Lord's institution, but to her secular position as the capital of the Roman Empire. How, it may be asked, can the Church be identified with these Eastern adventurers, men whose antecedents were in almost every case sufficiently suspicious to deprive their judgment on such a matter of half its value? Anatolius, originally secretary to Dioscorus, and wavering in the Eutychian troubles; Juvenal, one of the leaders at the Robber Synod, and himself involved in an ambitious scheme for the stretch of his jurisdiction; Maximus, who had been irregularly ordained by Anatolius himself, his ordination only sanctioned by Leo for the sake of peace; Alexandria vacant; and the rest, most of them, in no position to withstand the pressure which the legates asserted had been put upon them by Constantinople—how can these be taken to represent the Church?

It may be asked, how did the Emperor Marcian come to second Constantinople's ambition? Perhaps the true answer is, that he saw in the proposed arrangement certain conveniences which commended it to his mind from a political point of view.[1] And it was undoubtedly the case that the proposed arrangement had something in its favour, and might have passed muster had it not conflicted with a higher principle of action. As things then stood, Constantinople having become the actual centre of life in the East, it was certainly a natural

[1] Cf. Hefele, *in loco.*

position for a politician to adopt, that the ecclesiastical apparatus should adapt itself to the new circumstances, and that the London of the East should become the root and womb of the Church in the future. But Marcian did not see that another principle was being introduced, which, if admitted, must have been subversive of the Church's spiritual and supernatural order, as, indeed, it proved to be under Peter the Czar. When Marcian saw this—indeed, as soon as he found that St. Leo was opposed to the arrangement—he dropped his patronage of the scheme.[1] But the bishops braced themselves to the work of persuading Leo that their canon was harmless and worthy of his necessary sanction.

[1] Cf. *infra*, p. 459.

CHAPTER XXVII.

THE EASTERNS' RECOGNITION OF PAPAL SUPREMACY.

No one will deny the incomparable importance of the letter which was now addressed to Leo by the remnant of the synod concerning their new proposal. The twenty-eighth Canon of Chalcedon is really the sheet-anchor of the Anglican position. Relying as that position does on the first four general councils, it is maintained that the judgment of the Council of Chalcedon, supposed to be expressed in this canon, is sufficient to establish the theory that the primacy of the Bishop of Rome was considered in the East to be due, not to his relation to St. Peter, but to the imperial position of the city of Rome. The belief in any real relationship to St. Peter postulates a divine origin for the primacy of the Bishop of Rome, for it involves the belief that our Lord included that primacy in His words to the Apostle.[1] And if the primacy be in any sense divine, it is indispensable. No amount of misconduct on the part of its representatives can justify us in altering the lines laid down by our Divine Lord Himself. But this twenty-eighth canon proves, so it is confidently asserted, that the Bishop of Rome only held a certain primacy by reason of his being Bishop of the Imperial City. He was, so it is said, only *primus inter pares.* Constantinople (it is urged) was placed by this canon in the second position on a principle which proves that Rome's primacy was one of mere presidency, of honour 'without definite powers '—in a word that the Bishop of Rome was only the 'First Patriarch.'

Now it is important to remember that the Bishop of Rome

---

[1] Cf. Lanfranc's argument at the Council of Windsor, which assumed that the commission to Peter included his successors—an assumption accepted on both sides, *i.e.* by the whole English Church.

was the first patriarch, and this canon recognises him as such. There is no dispute about this. Leo XIII. is to-day not only Bishop of Rome, but Patriarch of the West. The fault of the so-called twenty-eighth canon, therefore, did not lie in its recognition of Rome's patriarchal position; its mistake lay in attributing even that position purely to her connection with the imperial city, whereas the matter really stood thus:—St. Peter selected Rome, and Rome was the capital of the empire. His successors reaped the fruit of his wise choice, and utilised, as they were meant to do, the advantages of a natural centre. Ecclesiastical Rome was able to be what she was because she was the See of Peter; she was also able to do her work at first as she did because her influence radiated from the metropolis of the empire. Her patriarchal sway was subordinate to her apostolical jurisdiction; but it was a reality. It is difficult to draw the line between the apostolical and patriarchal elements of her position, for the latter is necessarily overshadowed, and coloured, and informed by the former; but her relationship to Peter, the prince and head of the Apostles, is clear, and occupied an unmistakable place in the thoughts of the bishops at Chalcedon. It was expressed emphatically and in the most precise terms by the comparatively few bishops who passed this canon in favour of Constantinople. The terms which they use in their letter to Leo cannot, without doing violence to the laws which govern men's minds, be attributed simply to flattery or general Eastern courtesy. This, which is the favourite Anglican explanation of these bishops' statements, is excluded by the circumstances which produced the letter.[1]

The bishops were, it is true, concerned to flatter St. Leo, if possible; they wanted to gain something from him. But what they wanted to gain was of that nature that the particular terms used by them were the last in the world that they would have dreamt of addressing to him at this juncture, merely with a view to flatter, even if they supposed that Leo was the man to be seduced by honeyed words in a matter of such supreme importance. Consider the circumstances under which they wrote. Leo had shown himself above all things

---

[1] *Leonis Ep.* xcviii.

zealous for the canons of the Church. It was this trait which the Emperor Marcian singled out for praise in his encomium of the Pontiff during this whole transaction. And the bishops at Chalcedon who passed the twenty-eighth canon were, as the African bishop Facundus described them in the next century, 'astute as serpents.' Is it to be supposed that these astute bishops would give away their case by telling St. Leo that he was in precisely that position which their canon, according to the Anglican interpretation, was concerned to deny or ignore? If they admitted that St. Leo was their 'head,' they were admitting that their position next after him was secondary in the sense of subordinate, and that their canon was valueless without his sanction. If they asserted that St. Leo was the instrument whereby the teaching of the Prince of the Apostles was made known *to them*, they were giving away the whole position which Anglicans consider essential to their own security. Complimentary terms which expressed, in plain Greek and Latin, a truth which Leo had all along maintained and acted upon, cease to be complimentary in the ordinary sense of the term; they denote the acceptance of the position.

Now the bishops did tell St. Leo that 'he was their head, and they but members.' What could be their idea in using, by way of compliment, such an expression as that? Did they suppose that Leo would not take them at their word and treat them as members and act as their head?

Then, again, they did tell St. Leo that he was their 'leader' in the council, through his legates. They used the very word which our Lord used to His Apostles when He told them that there should be a leader amongst them, and that their leader should be as He Himself was in their midst— 'Even as I am amongst you'—not lording it over them, but teaching, guiding, governing. Did they suppose that Leo would smile at the term and take no advantage of it?

Again, they did tell St. Leo that he had been to them 'the interpreter of the voice of Peter.' It was, on the Anglican supposition, exactly the wrong occasion to say that. They were not Eastern heathens addressing heathen rajahs, or Hindu suppliants before their conquerors. They were Christian bishops—not, it is true, the best specimens; but still, all

Eastern as they were, they had not lost all Christian sense of truth in spite of their Eastern cunning. On the other hand, they knew that it was the teaching of Leo that he was the successor of Peter, and as such the ruler of the Christian Church. And they were not so utterly devoid of all sense of truth, and of ordinary common sense, as to suppose that in putting such a weapon into Leo's hand as their own recognition of his position as successor of Peter, they would advance the cause of Constantinople. Whereas if the Christian world held that Leo was their head, their language was natural, for then they lost nothing by saying so.

Again they did tell St. Leo that 'the vineyard had been entrusted to him by the Saviour,' in a way which implied that he stood in a different relation to that vineyard from the rest of the bishops. And they did tell him that he was the 'father' of Constantinople, and trusted that he would 'extend his *wonted care* over that part of the vineyard.' In fact they as much as said there is no such thing as an independent national Church. Although we are the East, and under one emperor, and you are in the West and under another, still you have responsibilities towards the East, and a paternal relation to it, and you acted as our ruler in the council, and were the interpreter to us of the Prince of the Apostles, and we apply to you for that sanction without which our canon can never be the voice of the Catholic Church. This was what they said.

Indeed, they said more than this; for they told St. Leo that their own delivery of the truth to the children of the Church was but as the flowing forth of a stream from him as its apostolic source. 'Thou wast constituted the interpreter of the voice of blessed Peter to us all, and didst bring to all the blessing of his faith. *Whence we also* show the inheritance of truth to the children of the Church.'[1] And hence unity of teaching is secured through what they distinctly state as the mediatorial position of their head.

Of Eutyches, who, be it remembered, was deposed by the Synod of Constantinople, the Acts of which were sent to Leo,

[1] 'Unde et nos . . . ecclesiæ filiis hæreditatem sortemque veritatis ostendimus' (*Leon. Ep.* xcviii. c. 1).

these bishops say that 'his dignity was taken away by your Holiness'—which is the result arrived at above from a consideration of the facts. (Cap. 2.)

And of Dioscorus they say that he meditated an excommunication 'against thee, when thou wast all eager to unite the Church,' and 'he repudiated the letter of your Holiness.'

They speak also of being eager to 'confirm' the mercy of the Saviour towards him (which was what Leo had desired them to do)—not as if 'confirming' necessarily implies the action of a superior court, but in obedience to their Saviour's words. (Cap. 3.)

They speak of the actual help derived from St. Euphemia —'God was with us and Euphemia was with us'—on whose altar we know they placed their definition.

And then they ask that Leo will 'accept and confirm' their canon.

When they mention the legates' opposition to their canon, they profess to ascribe that opposition to the idea in the legates' minds that everything ought to originate with his Holiness, 'so that even as the right settlement of the faith is set down to your account, so also should that of good discipline.' They in fact acknowledge that the matter of faith was settled by Leo, but they thought that they might initiate a matter of discipline, which they had now brought before his Holiness for his acceptance and confirmation. 'Therefore, we entreat thee, honour the decision with your favourable judgment, and as we have introduced harmony with the head in the things that are excellent, so the head would supply to the children that which is becoming.'

They have (they say) sent the Acts to Leo, and they expressly state that 'the force of all' rests with his confirmation and ordering.

Now these are, many of them, positive statements of doctrine. Is sentence after sentence to be dismissed as mere compliment? Could anything but the exigencies of controversy have led Dr. Bright and Mr. Gore to disregard all these definite statements on the part of the bishops on the ground that they were mere compliments?

If they were 'compliments,' they were those of men who found themselves compelled to couch their compliments in terms which, if they wished to be independent of Rome, cut the ground from under their feet, sentence after sentence. They are not in the place in which compliments would come, nor are they of the nature of honorific expletives. They form the substance of the letter.

If insincerely used, they testify to the necessity under which these bishops found themselves, of crouching at the feet of a master in order to gain the object of their desires. If used in sincerity, they are the testimony of witnesses, naturally the most unwilling, to the position of headship which the East recognised in the occupant of the See of Peter. We cannot claim for them the authority of the council, for these men were not the council; but we are compelled to see in these terms the strongest possible evidence that the idea of the connection between Rome and St. Peter, and of such a consequent 'headship' of Rome over Constantinople that the latter could not arrange its own relations with other sees in the East without the acquiescence of Rome—we are compelled, I say, to acknowledge that this was so deeply rooted in the mind of the Eastern Church that it was simply useless to ignore it, and that the only thing to be done was to admit it plainly and to win the adhesion of Rome to their projected canon.

But side by side with this letter of the bishops is another written by Anatolius himself, not less emphatic in its witness to the Constantinopolitan conviction as to the Pope's supremacy. Anatolius speaks of the bishops at Chalcedon having confirmed 'the faith of the blessed and venerable Fathers' of Nicæa, 'and also your Holiness' letter agreeing with them'—showing that the attitude of the synod towards the Tome was the same as towards the Nicene faith, and that their confirmation of it was an acceptance of an authoritative statement. He then says that Bishop Lucentius is bringing the Acts of the synod, since 'it was a matter of necessity that all things should be brought to the cognisance of your Holiness.'[1] But beside these things, since some matters were trans-

---

[1] ἔδει ἅπαντα ἀναγκαίως. *Leon. Ep.* ci. cap. 1.

acted which specially concerned themselves,[1] and these *must also of necessity be brought to the knowledge of his Holiness*, Anatolius says that he sent these letters by the same messengers, to receive an answer concerning them. He then mentions the acts in order. First came Dioscorus' excommunication, which he feels sure will obtain his Holiness' assent. Next (Cap. 3) he speaks of the reception of the Tome in exact accordance with what we have seen above. He says that it was needful that 'the understanding of all should agree with the meaning of your orthodox faith,' and that this was the end for which the emperor convened the council—words which are completely corroborative of the view of the matter taken in chapter xv. Anatolius' words express the object of the session held after Dioscorus' excommunication, as that of obtaining an *intelligent adhesion* to the faith as propounded by Leo—*ut in rectæ vestræ fidei sensum omnium conveniret intelligentia*. Consequently, Anatolius says, that with prayers and tears, and with the help of Leo himself, assisting in spirit and co-operating by means of the well-beloved men whom his Holiness sent to the council, and under the protection of St. Euphemia, he and those with him had devoted themselves to the work—in allusion to the 'instruction' given in Anatolius' house to the Illyrian bishops. And when the time had come for all to issue an harmonious definition, they had done so, in spite of some contentious opposition from the first, and for the confirmation of their definition 'in accordance with that holy epistle of yours,' they placed it on the holy altar. This latter remark explains the statement of the bishops that their definition was offered by Euphemia to her divine Spouse.

So that Anatolius, writing thus publicly an account of the synod, emphasises (1) the *necessity* of agreement with the definition of faith issued by Leo, and (2) the *necessity* of reporting to the Pontiff whatever was done at the synod; and (3) describes the confirmation of their acts by Leo as at once necessary for them and free on his part.[2]

---

[1] διὰ τὸ ἰδικῶς ἡμῖν πέπραχθαί τινα—called 'negotia privata' in Pelagius II.'s letter to the Istrian bishops.

[2] Cf. *Leonis Ep.* ci., ed. Ballerini, note.

Having thus described the relation of a council to the Pope, in exact accordance with the present teaching of Leo XIII., Anatolius proceeds to introduce the subject of the canon. He describes it as having for its object the confirmation of the canon of the 150 Fathers, who decreed that the Bishop of Constantinople should have honour and precedence (not πρωτεῖα, primacy) next after the most holy throne of Rome, by reason of her being 'New Rome.' And, he says it decided (*i.e.* the canon drawn up at Chalcedon) that the ordination of the metropolitans of the diocese of Pontus, of Asia, and of Thrace, should rest with Constantinople; but that the bishops under them should not be ordained, as had been the case for sixty or seventy years, by the latter, but by their own metropolitans.

He then complains of the legates' opposition to all this, and speaks of the sanction of the emperor. He says that they paid all possible respect to the legates, but that they have now reported their decision to his Holiness, in hope of gaining his assent and confirmation, which they entreat him to give. ' For the throne of Constantinople has your Apostolic throne as its Father, having specially attached itself to you.' And so he asks for the ratification of the canon. Later on,[1] the archbishop tells the Pope that ' all the force and confirmation of what was thus done was reserved for the authority of your Blessedness.'

Now after these two letters—the one from the enacting bishops at Chalcedon, and the other from the Archbishop of Constantinople himself, it is idle to talk of the ' self-assertion ' of Rome as having anything to do with the twenty-eighth canon. St. Leo doubtless knew how to magnify his office. But, indeed, there was no need to do that here; it was already done for him. He was recognised publicly and unmistakably by these bishops of the Eastern part of the Church as the natural, and, indeed, the necessary guardian of the canons of the whole Church, and this, too, in virtue of his relationship, through his see, to the blessed Apostle Peter. To attribute all this plain dogmatic and public exposition of the

---

[1] *Ep.* cxxxii. c. 4 : ' Cum et sic gestorum vis omnis et confirmatio auctoritati vestræ beatitudinis fuerit reservata.'

relationship of the Holy See to the rest of the Church to mere courtesy can only be the shift of those who find themselves driven hard to explain untoward facts. The facts are that the bishops who drew up the twenty-eighth canon did avow their entire dependence on Rome as the See of St. Peter, and that the Archbishop of Constantinople himself counted the proposal canonically null and void without the subsequent confirmation of the Bishop of Rome. The explanation proposed and adopted by those writers who are out of communion with Rome, and have drawn up canons independently of her, is that all this plain speech was mere pretence. But something more than a mere conjecture is needed to set aside the plain facts of the case.

The letters of St. Leo in regard to all this are full of Christian royalty. Majestic, uncompromising, and tender, they would by themselves be sufficient to establish his claim to the title which Christendom has accorded to him—Leo the Great.

To Anatolius he wrote,[1] reminding him of the suspicion which had originally attached to his orthodoxy, praising the faith which he now exhibited, but regretting that he had allowed himself to be influenced by the lust of honour and power. He blames him for endeavouring to use a council, assembled for the matter of faith, for his ambitious projects, and for imagining that any number of bishops could override the Nicene settlement (cap. 2). He considers that Anatolius' blame of the Papal legates is their commendation, for they were bound to oppose any infringement of the Nicene canons (cap. 3). He says he is sure that Anatolius will please the royalties more by self-restraint than by ambition. The decision of 'some bishops,' sixty years ago, 'never transmitted to the Apostolic See,' is no support whatever. (In other words, the third canon of Constantinople is of no account.) Alexandria ought not to suffer because of Dioscorus, nor Antioch, where Peter first preached, be degraded (cap. 5). The Pontiff concludes with most earnestly and lovingly entreating Anatolius to cultivate humility and charity.

Already[2] Leo had written to the emperor, severely blam-

---

[1] *Ep.* cvi.   [2] *Ep.* civ.

ing Anatolius for not being content with being bishop of the royal city, but aiming at the rank of an apostolic see, which Constantinople can never become. And he tells the emperor that the Nicene arrangement cannot thus be set aside, and that in their defence, by the help of Christ, it is necessary for him to be a faithful servant unto the end, 'since a dispensation has been entrusted to me' ('dispensatio mihi credita est'), 'and the guilt will be mine if the rules sanctioned by the Fathers in the Synod of Nicæa, for the government of the whole Church, by the assistance of the Spirit of God, should be violated with my connivance, which God forbid.'

But as Leo's passing over the ordination of Maximus of Antioch by Anatolius might seem to be negligence, he adds that he has not rehandled that, out of love for the recovery of the faith and desire for peace.

To Pulcheria he writes [1] in the same strain, saying that he renders null and void ('in irritum mittimus') what the bishops agreed to contrary to the Nicene regulations, and that he does so by the authority of the blessed Apostle Peter.

In the following year the emperor wrote to St. Leo, telling him that he was unwilling to resort to extreme measures with the monks in Palestine until he could show them his (Leo's) confirmation of the Chalcedonian definition. He says that the Eutychianisers had thrown doubts on that confirmation.[2] The emperor, in this letter, yields the point of the twenty-eighth canon, and expresses his warm sympathy with the Pope for the stand he had made on behalf of historical veracity and the ancient ways. 'For assuredly,' wrote his Imperial Majesty,' 'your Holiness did excellently well, as became the Bishop of the Apostolic See, in so guarding the canons of the Church, as not to suffer any innovation on ancient custom or the order settled of old, and inviolably observed to this day.' Considering what Leo had written to Marcian, this public acknowledgment of the position of the Apostolic See as guardian of the canons, from an Eastern emperor who had his desires as to a rise in dignity for his

---

[1] *Ep.* cv.
[2] 'Whether your Blessedness has confirmed the things decreed (τυπωθέντα) in the synod,' *i.e.* on the matter of faith and excommunication of Dioscorus.

often mentioned in these pages. But he speaks of this French priest (Père Gratry) as 'noble and truth-loving.'[1] Now this 'noble and truth-loving' priest accepted the Vatican decree under peculiar circumstances. He had written against it in unmeasured terms, which he lived to regret. In the full exercise of his faculties, with the certainty that he must shortly stand before his Judge, owing to the rapid inroads of a fatal disease, he sent in to his archbishop his submission to that decree. He also wrote the following words to a friend: 'What I combated was *inspired* infallibility; the decree of the Council repudiates inspired infallibility. I combated *personal* infallibility; the decree lays down *official* infallibility. Writers of the school which I thought excessive would have no more infallibility *ex cathedrâ*, as being too narrow a limit; the decree lays down *ex cathedrâ* infallibility. I feared almost *scientific* infallibility, *political* and *governmental* infallibility, and the decree lays down only *doctrinal* infallibility in the matter of faith and morals. This does not mean that I have not committed error in my polemics. I have without doubt committed some on this and other subjects; but so soon as I perceive an error I efface it, and do not feel myself thereby humiliated.'[2]

It is with the prayer that some may perceive the error of opposing the dogma of Papal Supremacy and follow the example of this 'noble and truth-loving' priest, as Canon Bright calls him, that this work has been written. *Dominus illuminatio mea.*

---

[1] *Waymarks in Church History*, by W. Bright, D.D., Regius Professor of Ecclesiastical History, p. 241.

[2] *Souvenirs de ma Jeunesse*, par le P. Gratry. Œuvres Posthumes, p. 238.

APPENDICES.

APPENDIX I.

Rev. F. W. Puller's Interpretation of St. Cyprian.

Mr. Puller says, in reference to St. Cyprian's treatise on Unity, and especially the opening passage, 'Now, I put it to any candid Roman Catholic, Is this the way that he would write on the great subject of the Church's unity?' And again, 'You may read the whole treatise on Unity from beginning to end, and you will not find one single word about Rome, or about the Pope, or about any Papal jurisdiction derived from St. Peter.'[1] The argument from silence is very freely used by Mr. Puller throughout his book; but it requires an accurate knowledge of the circumstances under which a treatise is written to use such an argument with justice. The book of Esther does not contain the name of God; but it does not follow that the writer did not believe in God. St. John in his first epistle says nothing about the Church, but it does not follow that he did not believe in the Church. The question is, would it have been *ad rem* to write about the Papacy in St. Cyprian's case? The answer must be, that it would have been distinctly beside the purpose of his treatise, if the above estimate of that purpose is correct. It would have been nothing less than absurd to press the Papal jurisdiction on the Novatianists, with whom the question was, not as to the powers of the Papacy, but the legitimate occupant of the See of Rome. It would have been beside the purpose in the case of the lapsed, when the great point was to induce them to repair to their several diocesans for the requisite certificates. When Mr. Puller says further on,[2] 'The subject of the Church's unity required some treatment of the central jurisdiction. So St. Cyprian felt'—he is simply romancing.

[1] *Primitive Saints, &c.* p. 351.   [2] P. 353.

Where is there any evidence that St. Cyprian felt anything of the kind *at the time* when he wrote that short treatise?

Just before Mr. Puller says, 'Notice how twice over in this short passage St. Cyprian insists that St. Peter received no peculiar power,' that 'the other Apostles were what Peter was, endued with an equal fellowship both of honour and power. Can anything be more frigid and senseless than the Ultramontane reply that St. Cyprian is speaking of the power of order and not of the power of jurisdiction?' (p. 352).

Mr. Puller ought to have remembered that amongst these frigid and senseless Ultramontanes Bossuet himself must be numbered, to say nothing of his own master, Tillemont. But he ought, moreover, not to have forgotten that St. Cyprian qualifies the above statement when he says, in one of the passages to which Mr. Puller refers, that '*although* he gave the rest equal power, *nevertheless*, in order to manifest unity, he by his own authority instituted the *origin* of the same unity.' He is speaking, of course, of Peter. Why is it frigid and senseless to suppose that, since St. Cyprian plainly attributes a primacy of some kind to Peter (and Mr. Puller admits thus much), the equality is that of sacerdotal power and the difference that of supreme and subordinate jurisdiction?[1] Such an obvious explanation may seem 'frigid' to Mr. Puller, but to those who make it, it is full of inspiring teaching, since it shows that our Lord provided for the guardianship of unity by an institution whose history is the very history of the Church herself. On the other hand, what shall we say of the supposition that St. Cyprian knew so little of Holy Scripture as to imagine that our Lord consecrated St. Peter to the Apostleship first, apart from the others (which is Mr. Puller's curious interpretation of the Cyprianic teaching[2]), merely that the Apostles and

---

[1] *I.e.* whilst they all had jurisdiction, it was to be exercised in subordination to St. Peter.

[2] 'Some little time before the others' (p. 352). 'As we have already seen, St. Cyprian held that St. Peter was not only called first, but that he was also consecrated first. This notion is doubtless based on a mistake, but it ought to be kept in mind if we would understand St. Cyprian aright' (p. 354). Mr. Puller not merely corrects the frigid and senseless interpretations of Ultramontanes, but convicts St. Cyprian of a blunder of the first magnitude. If St. Cyprian blundered in such a vital manner as this concerning St. Peter, what is his witness worth? The fact is that the mistake is Mr. Puller's; but it was necessary that the mistake should have been Cyprian's, else his witness must be placed on the Papal side. What St. Cyprian held is what Bossuet expressed with his usual felicity when he said, in his sermon on the Unity of the Church, that our Lord first places all (Apostles included) under Peter by promising him

others might have an object lesson about unity? What shall we say of the theory that the place of honour assigned to Peter (and Mr. Puller says that the 'stream of Anglican Divines' assign the pre-eminence of leadership to Peter) did not even include presidency at a council? that his relationship to the other Apostles was only that of the Duke of Norfolk to the other peers of the realm?[1] I will not call such an explanation 'frigid' or 'senseless,' for that would not advance my argument, but I am bound to say it has no warrant in St. Cyprian's actual words.

Another of Mr. Puller's misinterpretations concerns the crucial expression which, as we shall see, St. Cyprian uses of the See of Peter, viz. 'the root' of the Church, but which Mr. Puller interprets of the Church herself. He rightly feels the importance of the expression, and informs us that if it could be 'solidly proved' that the Church of Rome is 'the centre and the root, the source and the matrix of Catholic unity' (as Father Bottalla correctly says it is, according to St. Cyprian), 'for the first time in my life I should begin to fear that the faith which God in His great mercy has ever given me in the Catholicity of my mother the Church of England has been the result of some illusion.' It is to be hoped that Mr. Puller may yet come to see that, so far as the Cyprianic literature is taken for evidence of the Church's teaching, it is certainly true that the Church of Rome is the 'root of Catholic unity.'

The word 'root' is connected by St. Cyprian with three other words. Speaking of the Church of Rome, he calls her 'the head and root of the Catholic Church,' 'the root and womb of the Catholic Church,' and 'the root and mother' of Catholic unity.

In using the first of these expressions, he is speaking of Pope St. Stephen. 'We, who hold the head and root of the one Church, know assuredly and are confident that to him' (*i.e.* Novatian, the anti-Pope at Rome), 'being outside the Church, nothing is lawful; and that baptism, which is one, is with us, where he also himself was formerly baptised.'[2] St. Cyprian's argument is that there is but one Church, and therefore but one baptism. He was mistaken the keys first and alone, and then he says 'the sequel does not reverse the beginning.' Golden words, which are the equivalent of St. Cyprian's teaching that our Lord 'provided (*disposuit*) by His own authority the origin of the same unity, beginning from one.' These words are absolutely subversive of Mr. Puller's fundamental contention that our Lord made Peter an object-lesson of unity ' as being the first-designated Apostle,' and so 'the symbol of unity' (p. 351). This would not be an exercise of 'authority,' nor the origination of unity, nor the beginning of a stream, such as St. Cyprian elsewhere describes the unity which started with Peter.

[1] P. 229, note 2.   [2] *Ep.* lxxiii. 2.

H H

in his application of this truth, but that does not affect the question as to the meaning of the expression 'head and root.' There were then at Rome two opposed heads. The Novatianists, he had already said, had set up an 'adulterous and opposed head without the Church.' St. Cyprian repudiated this 'adulterous and opposed head,' and says that he, together with Jubaianus, held to 'the head and root of the one Church,' *i.e.* St. Stephen, the legitimate Pope. Consequently (he argues) the baptism of Novatian is invalid. Mr. Puller appears to have missed the meaning of these words, from imagining that St. Cyprian is arguing with the Novatians. He thinks St. Cyprian is contrasting 'himself with Novatian' (p. 345, line 13); and he supposes that Novatian might answer, 'I am the Pope; I am the head and the root of the one Church.' But St. Cyprian is not arguing this question at all; he is engaged with a wholly different topic, viz. whether those whom he himself and Jubaianus both agreed were outside the Church, could validly baptise. It was not a 'controversy with Novatian'[1] in which he was engaged, but a controversy with certain bishops in Africa, destined soon, alas! to become a controversy with St. Stephen himself. Soon—but it had not as yet reached that stage. And consequently, Mr. Puller's argument[2] that 'it would have been absurd to base his argument in favour of baptising Novatians on his fellowship with Stephen, who *was treating him*' (the italics are mine) 'as a heretic because he baptised Novatians,' falls to the ground. He was doing no such thing.

Previously to this, St. Cyprian, writing to Cornelius, the Pope, speaks of the Novatians as having 'refused the bosom and embrace of the root and mother'[3]—not, as Mr. Puller translates it, 'of her who is their root and mother,' but simply 'the root and mother,' which is the same as the true 'head,' as he goes on to explain. Here we have the head, and root, and mother all in one, as in the treatise on the unity of the Church, he says 'there is one head, one origin, and one mother,' meaning the Church *and* Peter, whom Christ instituted as 'the origin of unity;' and as there he sees in the legitimate bishop the Peter for the time being, so here, in leaving Cornelius, they had left the true head and taken up (he says) with 'an adulterous and opposed head,' and so had 'refused the bosom and embrace of the root and mother,' the legitimate bishop. For the legitimate bishop is the root of the Church in each region, being himself rooted in that past which goes up to Peter and to his institution as the rock and key-bearer by Him

---

[1] *Loc. cit.* [2] P. 346.
[3] 'Radicis et matris sinum atque complexum' (*Ep.* xlv. 1).

Who is the Root of David, as He is the Rock, and the Father of the world to come, His own institution being the mother of us all.

But on another occasion St. Cyprian supplies an expression which is doubtless meant to be understood in the above passage. He calls the Church of Rome 'the root and womb *of the Catholic Church.*'¹ He is explaining to Cornelius that although he had not given those who sailed from Africa to Rome letters to himself, whilst there was a doubt, or strife, as to the validity of his election to the See of Rome, he had yet in no way opposed him. He had told them to 'recognise and hold to the root and womb of the Catholic Church,' whichever that might seem to be on proper inquiry.

Mr. Puller thinks that St. Cyprian meant simply by the above expression that the Catholic Church is 'the root and womb' to her children. And he thinks that 'St. Cyprian's advice was evidently meant to help them to discriminate.'² But this could hardly be the case if he merely told them to hold to the Catholic Church. How would that help them?

The fact is that Mr. Puller has misinterpreted the passage through omitting to notice (i.) one important word which he has omitted in his translation,³ and (ii.) from stopping short when he ought to have gone to the end of the paragraph.

St. Cyprian told his people during this period of difficulty (for it is obvious that he refers to that alone) that they were to be careful to '*acknowledge* and hold to the root and womb of the Catholic Church.' No one would talk of *acknowledging* the Catholic Church; but it is the natural word to use of the bishop, who is the root and womb of the Church.⁴ It is true that this would not help them to know which was the root and womb of the Catholic Church; but neither would his advice as interpreted by Mr. Puller. It was general advice. But St. Cyprian goes on to say that no sooner had he gained reliable information as to Cornelius' ordination than he had sent letters from all, everywhere throughout the province, so that 'all our colleagues might *approve and hold to*' (compare '*acknowledge and hold to* the root and womb') 'thee and thy communion, that is as well the unity as the charity of the Catholic Church.' I do not know why Mr. Puller has separated the two limbs of this paragraph and dealt with them,

---

¹ *Ep.* xlviii. 2.   ² P. 344.   ³ P. 343, line 3.

⁴ St. Pacian—whose works Dr. Pusey calls 'further fruits of the mind of St. Cyprian, whose writings St. Pacian quotes with reverence' (Pref. p. xxii), which he therefore bound up with St. Cyprian's Epistles in the *Lib. of the Fathers*—calls Cyprian the 'root' of his flock (*Ep.* ii. 3).

one on p. 344 and the other on p. 347; but it seems to me that through omitting to piece them together rightly, he has himself to accuse of 'forgetfulness,' and not Father Bottalla (p. 347, note 3). For had he taken the sentence as it stands in St. Cyprian he must, one would think, have seen that 'the root and womb of the Catholic Church,' which he (the Bishop of Carthage) told his subjects to acknowledge and hold to when at Rome, was, in that bishop's judgment, after all, Cornelius and his communion, which, on full examination, he bade all his colleagues 'approve and hold to,' being 'as well the unity as the charity of the Catholic Church.'

Thus the Church is our mother, *but the Church as represented and actualised by the See of Peter*, which is the root, and head, and origin of Catholic unity, on the principles which St. Cyprian's language, occasionally obscure and rhetorical, yet unmistakably enunciates.

Once more. Mr. Puller quotes Bossuet as on his side in this matter : ' He [Bossuet] understands the *radix et matrix*, as I do, of the Church's unity :—" Cette tige, cette racine de l'unité ! " [1] But Bossuet makes the 'root' something in the Church, not the Church herself—or, to speak more correctly, it is the Church putting herself forth in a long chain of teachers within the unity of the chair of Peter. 'There is in the Catholic Church a stem, a root, a force to reproduce ceaselessly new pastors to fill the same chairs with one and the same doctrine.' [2] And then he proceeds to explain this root of unity more fully. ' There is need of only a little good sense and good faith for one to acknowledge that the Christian Church has had from its origin for a mark of its unity its communion with the chair of St. Peter,' in which all the other " sees have preserved unity " ("in quâ sola unitas ab omnibus servaretur"—Opt. ' c. Parmen.' lib. 11), as the holy Fathers say ; so that by remaining therein as *we* [2] do, without anything being capable of withdrawing us from it, we are the body which has seen all those who separate themselves fall on the right and on the left. . . . When He [our Lord] said to His Apostles " I am with you," St. Peter was there with the rest, but he was there with his prerogative as the first of the stewards, *primus Petrus* (Matt. x. 2)—he was there with the mysterious name of Peter, which Jesus Christ had given to him (Mark iii. 17) to mark the solidity and force of his ministry ; he was there, in fine, as he who was to be the first to announce the faith in the name of his brethren, the Apostles, to confirm them in

---

[1] *Prim. SS.* p. 343, note 1.
[2] He is contrasting the Catholic (Roman) Church with schismatics.

it, and thereby to become the rock on which an "immortal edifice" should be built. Jesus Christ spoke to his successors as He spoke to the successors of the other Apostles, and the ministry of Peter became ordinary, principal, and fundamental in the whole Church.'[1]

This is the way in which Bossuet explains the root of unity. And in this last passage he gives the truth which corrects Mr. Puller's misunderstanding of St. Cyprian and of the general teaching of the Church. Peter was to have his successor, as the other Apostles had theirs; and if Peter were even merely a symbol and object-lesson of unity, we should expect that there would still be a successor of Peter distinct from the rest of the Episcopate, were it only to keep before our eyes the symbol of unity. As a matter of fact, our Lord made him the *origin*, not merely the symbol, of unity, and according to St. Cyprian, he was such, as having a chair, a succession—' the chair of Peter, whence episcopal unity took its rise.'

Mr. Puller's interpretation of St. Cyprian's doctrine comes to this:—Our Lord, according to that saint, ordained Peter first, and said, as it were, to His Apostles and others: 'Keep before your mind the unity of Peter, and how I ordained him by himself, that he might be a symbol of unity. He is one man, ordained by himself, and this will teach you unity. It is a picture for you to think about, and so keep together. It will always remind you that the Church ought to be one.'

APPENDIX II.

Are the Sardican Canons Nicene?

St. Julius, standing in the midst of Eastern bishops, who had been driven out by the Eusebians and had taken shelter in Rome, 'gave back,' says Sozomen, 'to each of them his own Church, inasmuch as the care of all belonged to him by reason of the dignity of his see,' or throne.[2] He also wrote the letter quoted above (p. 177), blaming the Eusebians for maintaining in the Council of Antioch that the Council of Tyre, which condemned Athanasius,

---

[1] *Instruction Pastorale sur les Promesses de l'Eglise* (Œuvres, ed. 1816, xxii. pp. 423, 424).

[2] οἶα δὲ τῆς πάντων κηδεμονίας αὐτῷ προσηκούσης διὰ τὴν ἀξίαν τοῦ θρόνου ἑκάστῳ τὴν ἰδίαν 'Εκκλησίαν ἀπέδωκε (Soz. iii. 8).

was subject to no revision on his (Julius') part. St. Athanasius was Bishop of Alexandria, and as such his case came necessarily under the cognisance of Rome.

In support of this assertion, St. Julius appealed to 'the directions of the Fathers,' which 'prescribed' the contrary course to that adopted by the Eusebians. He appealed to something 'written' by the Nicene Fathers—in other words, to a Nicene canon.[1] Where, then, is this canon containing 'the directions of the Fathers' to be found?

St. Athanasius, who produced this letter of Julius in his own behalf, must have known of it. St. Julius knows of no question as to its existence and genuineness. The exact contents as described by St. Julius are comprised in the 'Commonitorium' of St. Zosimus, sent to the African bishops when he commissioned his legate Faustinus to settle the affair of Apiarius in Africa. St. Zosimus called the canons, which embodied the principle for which St. Julius was contending, Nicene.

These canons have, since the seventh century, been called Sardican, and the question is, On what ground?

There are many reasons for believing that no canons were drawn up at Sardica. St. Athanasius, who was present at the Council of Sardica, and who professes to give an account of everything that happened there, says not a word about any canons, and his account leaves no room for any. Neither Socrates nor Sozomen, although professing to enumerate the acts of the council, make mention of any canons. No Pontiff, no one of the Fathers, of that century or the next, mentions any canons of Sardica; whilst St. Ambrose,[2] dealing with exactly the point settled in the so-called Sardican canons, appeals to the regulations of Nicæa, but not to Sardica.

But the most startling evidence against any canons having been drawn up at Sardica occurs in a letter of St. Innocent to the clergy of Constantinople.[3] The situation was exactly that which is contemplated in the so-called seventh (al. fifth) Sardican canon. St. Chrysostom had been deposed, and had appealed. On his return from exile, he had induced the emperor to summon a synod to put things right. Theophilus of Alexandria, who had done the mischief, and been told by the Pope to return to Constantinople and hold another synod in accordance with Nicene (or so-called Sardican) regulations,[4] had sent to Constantinople a copy of the very

---

[1] Athan. *Apol. c. Arianos*, n. 22.
[2] *Ep.* lvi. 'ad Theophilum.'
[3] *Ep.* vii.
[4] *Ep.* v. 'ad Theophilum.'

canon which the Eusebians had originally passed at Antioch, to prevent St. Athanasius from ministering again, because of his condemnation by the Council of Tyre. Thereupon,[1] St. Innocent joined issue on the subject of this said canon, and said that *no canons but the Nicene* were received by the Church, and these countenanced another synod being held. In the same paragraph he mentioned the Council of Sardica as having taken the same line, but not as having drawn up any canon. His language excludes the idea of there being any canons of Sardica. The evidence of this letter, if it stood alone, seems to me sufficient to warrant us in concluding against there having been any actually Sardican canons. But it does not, as a matter of fact, stand alone.

Further, St. Augustine and the African bishops had never heard of Sardican canons, though this may be otherwise explained.

St. Leo sketches the so-called Sardican canons, but calls them 'decrees of the canons drawn up at Nicæa,' when there was no reason for quoting them as Nicene, if they were Sardican, since as Sardican they would have been a sufficient authority for his purpose.[2] The same is true of St. Zosimus, St. Boniface, and St. Celestine, all of whom call these Sardican canons Nicene. They must have fallen back on the authority of Sardica, in meeting the difficulty of the African bishops, had any Sardican canons existed, for the Council of Sardica was only not numbered amongst the œcumenical councils because it did not deal with any new matter of faith but merely confirmed the Nicene.

Again, the formula used in these so-called Sardican canons is unique, except in Africa. They are introduced thus : 'Hosius said,' or 'Gratus said.'

And the introduction of the name of the reigning Pope in the third canon (viz. Julius, in some copies Sylvester) is altogether without precedent.

On these and other grounds it seems reasonable to conclude that these canons are possibly not Sardican.

And yet, whatever they were, they have been universally received in the Church, having been acted upon in the East, as well as in the West, and having been eventually incorporated even into the African code of canons, though for a while doubted there. John of Antioch incorporated them into the code of his Church in the reign of Justinian ; and the Constantinopolitan Council in Trullo, assembled to supply canons omitted in the fifth and sixth

---

[1] *Ep.* vii. 3.   [2] *Ep.* xliv. 'ad Theodosium.'

General Councils, inserted them in the Oriental code. But the most significant piece of evidence is their insertion into the 'Nomocanon' of Photius. It is true that Photius, in writing to Pope Nicolas, denied that these canons had ever been received at Constantinople. But it is as certainly true that Photius was telling a falsehood.[1] The Pope told Photius in reply that he was unable to believe his statement. He would have been able to convict him of a barefaced falsehood had he known that Photius had included these canons in every one of his successive editions of the canons considered to be binding on the whole Church. Theodore Balsamon, afterwards Patriarch of Antioch, wrote a commentary on the work of Photius and included the Sardican canons under those received in the East.[2]

Therefore, whatever these canons are, they express the mind of the Church as a whole. They can boast of œcumenical reception. What, then, is their real origin?

Some thirty years ago a theory was started by a professor at Rome, named Luigi Vincenzi, which satisfactorily accounts for most of the facts of the case.[3] This writer has endeavoured to show that in their present form the so-called Sardican canons are a commentary, or set of notes, on the Nicene canons by orthodox African bishops, the original Greek copies of those canons having been mutilated by the Arians. On the one hand we are led by the facts to doubt as to any canons having been drawn up at Sardica; on the other hand we are confronted with witness of unimpeachable character to the effect that the Nicene Fathers sanctioned certain canons for the guardianship of ecclesiastical discipline and with special reference to appeals to the Holy See, which correspond

---

[1] Photius also coined the Acts of a council, and tried to palm them off on the Catholic Church. He forged hundreds of signatures. His forgeries were committed to the flames by the eighth General Council. Nevertheless Mr. Puller (p. 153) uses his assertion to Pope Nicolas as conclusive evidence, prefacing that evidence with the recommendation that Photius 'was the most learned man who had ever sat on that throne.' Possibly he was, but he was also the most unscrupulous.

[2] Photius wrote first a collection of canons, then an arrangement in order of subject (*Syntagma*), and then a shorter form of the latter. The Sardican canons appear in all. The Pope had blamed Photius for reaching the episcopate *per saltum*, and had referred to the Sardican canons. Photius replied that these had not been received at Constantinople. As a matter of fact, he had quoted the tenth canon of Sardica by name under the heading 'concerning those who become bishops from lay condition,' both in his *Syntagma* and in his *Nomocanon*.

[3] *De Sacrâ Monarchiâ Hebr. et Christianorum.* Romæ, 1875.

to the provisions of the so-called Sardican canons. And again, in their present form these canons wear an African dress.

This seems to be the only adequate explanation of the passage in St. Julius' letter, which St. Athanasius considered so important that he incorporated it in his own defence. St. Julius there speaks of appeals to the Holy See, in case of difference arising amongst bishops, as a 'custom,' and he also calls this 'custom' something 'prescribed by the directions of the Fathers,' *i.e.* the Nicene Fathers, and also a custom sanctioned by 'the Great Synod,' thus appearing to indicate that he is referring to the sixth canon of Nicæa, which begins with speaking of 'ancient customs' prevailing. In its present condition that canon *suggests*, as has been shown above,[1] that Rome had jurisdiction over Alexandria; but it is only as expanded in the so-called Sardican canons that it fully justifies the argument derived from it by St. Julius and produced by St. Athanasius, himself the Bishop of Alexandria.

This theory also explains the otherwise inexplicable fact that when St. Julius told the Eusebians that they ought to come to Rome and have their cause tried there (in exact accordance with the provisions of the so-called Sardican canons); and this, on the ground that the Nicene Synod prescribed such a course, the Eusebians did not contradict St. Julius in their reply as to the canonical mode of procedure. They only made excuses which St. Athanasius calls unworthy of credit ($\dot{a}\pi\iota\theta\dot{a}\nu\text{ovs}$), such as the stress of circumstances and the length of the journey. They had, indeed, as St. Athanasius points out, themselves originally proposed to act on this very principle of having Julius for their judge (c. 20).

The explanation of the matter given by Canon Bright and others does not satisfy the facts of the case. St. Julius, says that writer (the italics are mine), 'when he wrote to the Eusebians that the Nicene Fathers decreed that one council's resolutions might be reviewed by another [Athan. 'Apol. c. Ari.' 22], means only that *they acted on this principle* by considering the Arian question *de novo* after it had been determined by the Synod of Alexandria.'[2] But St. Julius does not quote the example of the Nicene Fathers; he refers to their 'directions,' and he gives reasons, as does St. Athanasius, for the utility of the provision, showing that it was an actual *direction* for the future, and he emphasises in particular the special provision made in regard to the Bishop of Alexandria (the second Petrine See). His words, in fact, suggest the sixth Canon of 'the

---

[1] P. 166, *seq.*
[2] *Notes on the Canons of the first four General Councils*, 1882.

great Synod' (as he calls the Nicene), only in its fuller form, as quoted by his successors, and preserved, more or less, in the so-called Sardican canons. Indeed, this settlement at Nicæa, as I am supposing it to have been, runs through the action and letters of the Pontiffs and of the Fathers of the last half of the fourth century to an extent that requires some more reasonable explanation than that conscientious, high-minded, Christian rulers invented it or hailed the invention for their own ends.

But, further, St. Julius goes on to say that he is speaking of an 'ancient custom,' which was 'borne in mind and written down' in the Nicene Council.[1] It must then have been a definite regulation made in that council, not merely a principle of action to be deduced from their example.

Canon Bright says also : 'Just as the Roman series of canons in the fifth century confounded Sardican canons with Nicene, and led the Roman bishops, first in ignorance, as in the case of Zosimus and Boniface, and afterwards *in spite of authentic information* (as in the case of Leo, *Ep.* xliii.) to quote as Nicene what was really Sardican,' &c.

It has taken Canon Bright some years to arrive at a theory which thus impugns the honesty of the great champion of the Incarnation, the 'great' representative of the Christian religion at that era, whose holiness breathes through every line of his sermons and letters. In 1877 Canon Bright had only got as far as asking the question about St. Leo, 'Can he have known no better?'[2] In the former passage the question has become an assertion, and St. Leo the Great is presented to his readers as a deliberate liar.

The theory maintained in these pages makes no such demand on our moral sense. It requires us to believe, on the contrary, that when Pontiff after Pontiff quotes a canon as Nicene, and quotes it after it has been questioned as such, it is as good historical evidence as can well be obtained that the provision it contains was properly called Nicene.

It was, we may suppose, preserved after a while at Rome only, the home of accuracy, the metropolis of canonical lore. The various allusions in the letters of St. Julius and (by implication) St. Athanasius, of St. Ambrose, St. Innocent, St. Boniface, St. Celestine, and later on, in Gelasius' letter to Faustus, supply such strong evidence that there was some Nicene direction (for they all call it

---

[1] ἔθος παλαιὸν τυγχάνον, μνημονευθὲν δὲ καὶ γραφὲν ἐν τῇ μεγάλῃ συνόδῳ (*loc. cit.*).

[2] Cf. *Roman Claims tested by Antiquity*, p. 11.

Nicene) dealing with the question of appeals to Rome, corresponding to the provisions of the Sardican canons, that we may fairly suppose there has been some foul play in regard to some of the Nicene canons. It requires no stretch of imagination to suppose that the Arians, when in possession of the Eastern Sees, mutilated or burnt some of the canons. They were busy forgers—this we know from St. Athanasius. Their successor in heresy, the Emperor Anastasius, had the Acts of Chalcedon burnt outright; a more distant successor, Photius, forged a whole council, signatures and all. Rome alone was a safe refuge and guardian. Rome alone enjoyed an uninterrupted succession of high-minded orthodox prelates, and the maintenance of the canons of Nicæa was their special boast and glory. Their witness is a safer guide than the records of Alexandria and Constantinople, after these records had been in the perilous keeping of heretical bishops, who did worse things, as a matter of fact, even than mutilating records.

We may therefore safely reject the theory that saintly men like St. Innocent or St. Leo, with that uniform and tremendous sense of responsibility for the care of all the Churches which pervades their writings, were either ignorant of the laws they had to administer or deliberately changed their terms.

At the same time I am far from saying that this, which seems to me the most satisfactory, is the only tenable theory.

It is, I need hardly say, a perfectly tenable theory that these Sardican canons, having been passed at Sardica, were considered an appendix and explication of Nicene directions, and were, in such sense, Nicene. In that case they were launched upon the world with the authority of a council which reasserted the Nicene Faith, and whose acts received the confirmation of the Holy See. They were then part and parcel of the Nicene settlement, being a reassertion or explication of Nicene prescriptions, only not embodied in canons at Nicæa, because already considered part of 'ancient custom.'

At the Council of Florence, Mark, Bishop of Ephesus, when asked why the Constantinopolitan Creed was always called Nicene, replied, 'Because the latter virtually contains the former.' The Constantinopolitan was only a more lucid expression on a misunderstood portion of the Nicene Creed. In like manner the Nicene canons virtually contained the Sardican. The latter were only an authoritative explanation of the Nicene settlement, given to meet new emergencies and throw the cover of the Nicene rules over the champion of our Lord's Divinity. The Nicene Fathers had said, 'Let the Churches preserve their own privileges;' the Sardican

Fathers, many of them the same as at Nicæa, with the same president, explained what these privileges were: namely, that, for instance, the Bishop of Alexandria had an appeal to Rome from the Council of Tyre.

And if these canons were really Sardican, one can imagine a reason for speaking of them as Nicene to Africans.[1] For the Eusebians at Philippopolis called their meeting the Sardican Council, and sent their condemnation of St. Julius, St. Athanasius, and other orthodox bishops who had appealed to Rome, to Donatus at Carthage, and the Creed drawn up at this schismatic meeting was disseminated in Africa. This was what the Africans understood by Sardican, and therefore to call these canons Sardican would have been confusing. They were really (on the supposition which I am entertaining) Nicene, as confirmed at the true Council of Sardica. In point of authority and obligation to obedience they were Nicene. And possibly it was the discovery of this that led to the Church of North Africa dropping the matter and never returning to it, but eventually, when the fire of persecution had burnt out and they had been knit closer in bonds of amity to the See of Rome, incorporating them into their own African code.

On the whole, then, Canon Bright's theory may be said to be one that is not required by the facts of the case, and is somewhat revolting to Christian piety. Of the two counter-theories mentioned above, one is quite possible (namely, that these canons were Nicene in the same sense that the Constantinopolitan Creed is ever called the Nicene Creed), whilst the other (namely, that they were literally Nicene, and came, we know not how, to be called Sardican in the seventh century) explains all the facts.

One fact that specially makes for this theory is that St. Julius practically acted on a provision of the so-called Sardican canons, and that he wrote before the Council of Sardica met. And he called the provision one that had been 'written' in the 'great Synod.'

Note.—The discussion between Rome and Africa as to the Sardican canons throws no light on the question treated here, for we have no record as to its termination. Indeed, we have only two letters for the whole history of this discussion—one from African bishops to St. Boniface; the other to St. Celestine. The latter has every possible mark of forgery (cf. p. 303); and there are suspicious circumstances about the former. For the difference between Rome and Africa, as given in these letters, is mentioned nowhere else. Van Espen expresses himself as quite nonplussed

---

[1] Of course there are difficulties in this supposition, as is implied in what has been said above.

in regard to the council from which the letter to Boniface is supposed to have emanated.[1] The matter is not mentioned in Prosper's 'Chronicon,' nor in Possidius' 'Life of St. Augustine,' nor in Marius Mercator, nor in Paulinus' 'Libellus,' nor in Photius' 'Bibliotheca' (c. 52). Further, Balsamon gives the supposed letter from St. Cyril and from Atticus of Constantinople (accompanying their copies of the Nicene canons), which is obviously a translation from the Latin, suggesting that the original was a Latin forgery, and containing terminology found nowhere else in Cyril's writings. And how was it that Balsamon, himself of Antioch, could not produce the letter from Antioch? It must be admitted that grave suspicion rests on the whole of this supposed discussion.

APPENDIX III.

The Rev. F. W. Puller on St. Ambrose.

ST. AMBROSE was one of the primitive saints, and a very great saint. We have seen that he altogether differs from Mr. Puller on some points concerning the See of Rome, holding, as he did, that St. Peter was Bishop of Rome ('De Sacr.' i. 5), and that from that see 'the rights of venerable communion flow forth to all.' (Mansi, t. iii. p. 622.) But Mr. Puller has, nevertheless, claimed him as being to a certain extent on his side, on the ground that he says (Ep. xiii.), in reference (so Mr. Puller imagines) to the disputed succession at Antioch, and to a similar difficulty at Constantinople, in A.D. 381 or 382, that 'we do not assume to ourselves the prerogative of examining such things, but we ought to have a share in their examination.' This he considers moderate as compared with later claims; but Theodosius' answer 'to the Italians' (*i.e.* St. Ambrose and his council) decided that such matters should be 'settled in the East and by the East,' and this Mr. Puller considers to be the 'immemorial practice of the Church.' ('Primitive Saints,' &c. p. 274.) St. Ambrose says, No.

Theodosius had succeeded to the entire empire on Gratian's death. On his return to Constantinople from the West, he determined to make an effort to bring the schism at Antioch to an end. He accordingly summoned a synod to meet at Rome, and engaged that Flavian should attend. Flavian was accordingly summoned to Constantinople, to sail thence for Rome. He managed, however, to satisfy the emperor that he could not be expected to travel thus far in the winter season, in his eighty-second year, but promised to attend in

---

[1] *Jus Eccl.* vii. § 10, Art. 2. Lovanii, 1766.

the summer. The synod was held at Capua, and it was decided that both parties, whether they held to Flavian or Evagrius, should be considered to be in communion with Rome, so long as they held the true faith. The contest concerning the bishopric was remanded to the judgment of Theophilus of Alexandria, as having kept himself neutral, and the matter was to be confirmed by the Apostolic See.[1]

St. Ambrose, however, discovering that Flavian had 'had recourse again to the help of petitions and of imperial rescripts,' wrote a more stringent letter to Theodosius, and complained of the bishops having had all the trouble of going to Capua for nothing. He wrote at the same time to Theophilus, and spoke of Flavian as standing 'alone outside the law.' He neither came to Capua nor presented himself to the judges provided by the synod. The emperor wrote back somewhat sharply, and St. Ambrose replied. The letter of the emperor is not extant, and we can only guess at what he said from St. Ambrose's reply. The latter says (Ep. xiv.), that he must congratulate the emperor on seeming to have restored unity between the East and the West. He had summoned a council for the purpose. St. Ambrose and the bishops will not, they say, enter into the question of whose fault it has been that things were disturbed. He is glad that they made the endeavour, as it witnessed to their desire for peace. They deny that they could be accused of any partisanship, or too great readiness to believe either side, and they had met, not for the sake of defining, but of instruction. And since they have delegated the matter, they must be considered to have sought a just judgment rather than deferred to prejudice. The East had themselves wished for the council as well, and moreover had themselves set the example in reference to Paul, the Presbyter of Constantinople, when they asked for a synod within Achaia; but the West had thought Capua better, because they could travel more safely by sea than through Illyricum, which was in a state of disturbance ('movebatur'). They say that they are not innovating; they are not removing the landmarks of the Fathers, nor violating the rights of the Easterns; but on the contrary they are keeping the things defined by St. Athanasius, of holy memory, who was, as it were, a pillar of the faith, and by their holy Fathers of old in councils; neither are they violating the rights of hereditary communion, but whilst reserving the respect due to the Imperial Majesty, they are showing themselves eager for peace and quiet.'[2]

[1] Ambros. *Ep.* lvi. 7.

[2] *St. Ambrosii Epistol. Classis* i. *Ep.* xiv. Migne, vol. xv. The councils are obviously Nicæa and Sardica.

In an early part of the letter they remind the emperor that they had met together to consider also the case of those who tried to introduce the teaching of Apollinarius, who ought to be cut off in their presence, 'for he who has been convicted in the absence of the parties, as your clemency laid down in your august and magisterial (*principali*) reply, will always seize on a handle for questioning' the decision. And then they say that they asked for the council that 'no one might be able to compose a falsehood against the absent.'

These bishops, therefore, headed by St. Ambrose, do not admit to the emperor that this matter is one of those which must be concluded in the East, as neither does it appear that the emperor laid down the principle that *all* such matters should be concluded where they arose, seeing that he had originally contemplated the appearance of Flavian before Western bishops—namely, at Rome.

Tillemont, however, has made a conjecture concerning this letter of St. Ambrose which supports his Gallican views of the administration of the Church ; and his conjectures have recently been transformed into historical facts by Mr. Puller in his 'Primitive Saints and the See of Rome.'

Tillemont thought, as, indeed, others have, that the above letter of St. Ambrose was written *à propos* of the demand of the Council of Milan in 382 for a general council. But a close inspection of the letter will probably satisfy most readers that this is an untenable theory. For the council to which the letter refers is stated to have been summoned, not only to extinguish the Antiochian schism, but 'to take cognisance of those who are endeavouring to bring into the Church the dogma which Apollinarius is asserted to teach,' and this at a time when Illyricum was suspected of being in a state of disturbance, and therefore the sea journey (*i.e.* to Capua) was desired as being safer.[1] Now this was the state of things when Theodosius returned from Italy in 391. The Apollinarian heresy was then rising into greater prominence, and the barbarians were coming out of their hiding places and causing disturbance in Macedonia and Thessaly. Whereas there was no Gothic war nor known disturbances in Illyricum in 382. Things had been settled in 380. So that on these grounds the theory of Tillemont and others will not hold. Again, there was no idea of the West having in any way behaved reproachfully about the Convocation of the East in 381, as this letter of St. Ambrose states of the occasion of the council to which it alludes. The East answered the summons of the West

[1] 'Ideo maritima et tutiora quæsita sunt' (Ambr. *Ep.* iv. 3).

most courteously. So that the letter does not fit into the circumstances of 382. Further, on the occasion of St. Ambrose's letter, the West had been summoned by Theodosius, which could not be the case until Gratian's death. And since Theodosius could not, on Tillemont's theory, have written thus to St. Ambrose until towards the end of 382, it seems inconceivable that St. Ambrose should have answered in the name of the bishops whom he mentions, and not in that of the Roman Synod. Whereas everything fits in with the time immediately subsequent to the Synod of Capua, and it would seem that the very prominent paragraph about the Apollinarians applies to Vitalis, who had organised the Apollinarian party at Antioch, and took refuge under the pretext that he had not been condemned in person, which was true, and which was one main reason of St. Ambrose's wish for a general council, to which the said Apollinarist bishop, whom I am supposing to be Vitalis, should be summoned.

Mr. Puller, however, has improved on Tillemont. For Tillemont adds that what he says about the letter of Theodosius is only *conjectured* from this letter of St. Ambrose.[1] Mr. Puller professes to adduce Theodosius' letter itself, and compares it with that of St. Ambrose, and then compares the two with the action of Rome in 484 in deposing Acacius, and hence deduces 'a proof of the growth of the Papal and Italian claims.'[2] He first applies the letter to the circumstances of 382—which, as we have seen, is, to say the least, most improbable—and then quotes from another letter of St. Ambrose as follows: 'St. Ambrose and his council expressly say, "We do not assume to ourselves the prerogative of examining such things, but we ought to have a share in their examination."'

It must be noticed for the sake of English readers that the full force of the word 'prerogative' in the Latin is that of having the first vote in a matter, and that St. Ambrose and his council (in 382) do not repeat the word 'examination,' but use the word 'judgment' or 'decision.' They had just said (for we are now back in 382) that since Maximus was pleading his cause in the West they (the Easterns) 'ought to have waited for our judgment concerning him.' They in effect invoked the Niceno-Sardican canons. They then say that in thus claiming that the Easterns ought to have waited for the judgment of Rome—for that is what they certainly meant— 'we do not claim the prerogative of examination [*i.e.* the examina-

---

[1] 'Nous avons tiré ces choses par conjecture de la répo se que S. Ambroise et ses collègues firent à Théodose' (*Mémoires*, vol. x. p. 151).

[2] *The Primitive Saints and the See of Rome*, pp. 273, 274.

tion of the matter in the first instance), but there ought nevertheless to have been the participation of a common judgment.' It is to be noticed that there is no exact equivalent of Mr. Puller's words, 'such things,' which introduce the idea of a general rule instead of confining the sentiment to this particular matter. Mr. Puller then proceeds: 'The emperor wrote back to the Italians, &c., but he does not let his readers know that the emperor's letter is not extant, nor that Tillemont, from whom his words are taken, only gives them as conjectures. As has been seen above, 'the presence of the parties,' on which Mr. Puller lays stress, refers in all probability not to the affair of Nectarius at all, but to Flavian having absented himself on the ground that it was winter-time. But Mr. Puller proceeds more boldly still. He informs his readers that 'there can be no question that the emperor was stating the immemorial practice of the Church, not only in the East, but in Africa and elsewhere;' whereas St. Ambrose goes on to say that, on the contrary, there can be, or ought to be, no question that the immemorial practice of the Church has been precisely the other way. He instances St. Athanasius, and alludes to the Nicene Fathers as being against whatever it was that Theodosius said. It is but fair to retort on Mr. Puller what he says of some one else (*Prim. SS.* p. 327): 'If one may set aside evidence in such a way as that, history becomes an impossibility.'

APPENDIX IV.

The Apostolic See: Meaning of the Phrase.

THERE is one expression occurring again and again in the Acts of the Council of Ephesus, which gives what might be called the Christian name of the Bishop of Rome. He is the Archbishop of 'the Apostolic See, or Throne.' It is curious to notice how some writers fight shy of this title. Now Rome is, it is true, according to the Acts of the Councils, the Apostolic Throne of Greater or Old Rome; but it is also, what no other is, *simply* 'the Apostolic See.' It is a title accorded to her by emperors, empresses, patriarchs, individual bishops, and the entire synod of Ephesus.

The See of Rome, then, was, in 431, 'the Apostolic See;' hers was 'the' Apostolic throne; not, indeed to the exclusion of others, but in a super-eminent sense. During the Council of Ephesus, as a matter of fact, no other see is called apostolical at all, unless we except a doubtful passage in the speech of Juvenal of Jerusalem, *à propos* of the action of John of Antioch, in which he calls his see the Apostolic throne *of Jerusalem*—not simply 'the Apostolic See.'

Now, the natural inference from the use of the term 'the Apostolic See' as applied to Rome in the early councils is that the apostolicity of the Church in the matter of government was vested in the See of Rome, and flowed forth from thence to the rest of the sees of Christendom. This is the explanation which St. Leo gives in his sermon on St. Peter and St. Paul's Day. Canon Bright admits that 'on the whole, what Rome said in 431 amounts to this: All bishops succeed the Apostles, but Celestine, as heir of him who was the foremost Apostle, has a right to be foremost among bishops.'[1] The question is, of course, what constitutes the 'foremost place,' and by what sort of 'right' does Rome hold it? What did the Church at that date mean by so persistently attributing to Rome the title 'Apostolic'? Canon Bright says that in 431 'Rome did not say, as she now practically says, "The apostolic authority is concentrated in St. Peter's successor."' It is not quite plain what Dr. Bright means by 'concentrated.' But what is the explanation given by the history of the Council of Ephesus? It is as follows.

Celestine regarded himself, and was considered by others, as occupant of 'the Apostolic See.' As such he considered himself as, in a peculiar sense, clothed with apostolic authority, which he could exercise, as we have seen, in the way of deposing an Eastern bishop, the Bishop of Constantinople, the imperial city. No one in presence of the Acts of this council will deny thus much—viz. that he spoke of the authority of his see as in some sense pre-eminently apostolic, and that bishops (even Capreolus of Carthage[2]) speak of it as such, and that Celestine regarded his sentence on Nestorius as the judgment of God.

But he regards all the bishops as also true successors of the Apostles;[3] he rejoices in their gathering; he sees in their assembly a visible manifestation of the presence of the Holy Spirit, who is given to them all in common. He does not, indeed, say that all are *equally* partakers of the Holy Spirit, from an official point of view: that they all *equally* inherit the duties and graces of the apostolate. Dr. Pusey, in his endeavours to find contradictions between Popes on matters of faith, says that Celestine, according to the 'Roman' theory, must have been infallible when he said to the Council of Ephesus (the italics are his own) that—

'The charge of teaching has descended [from the Apostles] *equally* upon all bishops. We are all engaged in it *by an hereditary*

---

[1] *Church History*, p. 336, note *d*.   [2] Cf. *Ep. Capreoli ad Syn.* Act i.
[3] Cel. *Ep. ad Syn.* Act ii.

right; all we who have come in their stead preach in the name of the Lord to all countries in the world, according to what was said to them, "Go ye and teach all nations." You are to observe, my brethren, that the order (*mandatum*) we have received is a general order or command, and that He intended that we should all execute it when He charged them with it, as a duty devolving *equally* upon all. We ought all to enter into the labours of those *whom we have all succeeded in dignity*.'[1]

On this Dr. Pusey says, by way of comment, 'Not the Pope alone, but, according to Pope Celestine, the "assembly of priests," is the visible display of the presence of the Holy Ghost.'

Dr. Pusey here gives a turn to Celestine's words which neither the Greek nor Latin expresses. Celestine does not say that the assembly of priests is '*the* visible display,' but merely that it 'manifests (ἐμφανίζει, testatur) the presence of the Holy Ghost,' which is true on what Dr. Pusey calls the Ultramontane theory. Neither does Celestine use the word 'equally' at all; he says, 'in common,' and a gift received in common may be received in diversity of share.

As for its not being 'the Pope alone,' as Dr. Pusey puts it, no one ever supposed that the Pope enjoys a monopoly of the gifts of the Holy Spirit for the purpose of teaching or governing. The same remark applies to what Canon Bright says:

'It is certain that Celestine knew nothing of the theory which is now called "Ultramontane." He recognised apostolic authority in all bishops alike.'

It is curious that in the text[2] to which this is a note Canon Bright, in giving the applauses of the bishops at the council, omits precisely the exclamation which suggests the peculiarity of the Pope's position. The bishops called Celestine 'the guardian of the faith.' Canon Bright omits that. If by the word 'alike,' in the above note, he means 'equally,' then he is contradicted by the whole of Celestine's conduct at the council, and by the ending of this very letter. If Dr. Bright does not mean 'equally,' viz. that all bishops enjoyed, according to Celestine, equal apostolic authority, but uses the word 'alike' simply as redundant, he misinterprets the teaching to which he alludes. No Catholic theologian denies that the bishops 'all' enjoy apostolic authority. As Hettinger expresses it,[3] 'all received the same authority, but not all in the

---

[1] *Eirenicon*, p. 307.   [2] *Church History*, p. 336.
[3] Cf. *The Supremacy of the Apostolic See*, by Hettinger. Eng. trans. Edited by Archbishop Porter, S.J. (Burns & Oates), p. 15.

same degree or to the *same extent*.' And, as the same writer observes elsewhere, this does not the less make the bishops true bishops and true successors to the Apostles. For it will be admitted that Timothy and Titus were true bishops, and yet they were under apostolic authority. The Apostles had jurisdiction over the universal Church; and yet the bishops appointed by them, under their jurisdiction, were true bishops, placed by the Holy Ghost to rule the Church of God. The share of the episcopate in the apostolate of the Church is thus described by Hettinger:

'We know where to find the Catholic episcopate, the episcopate of the true Church of Christ, by the approbation its teaching receives from the Apostolic See; for where the members are in communion with their head, there is the unity appointed by God, the Catholic Church. . . . The primacy and the episcopacy are *both holders of the teaching office of the Church, but not ex æquo, on a par*. The head must teach the members and oblige them to accept his teaching; but the converse does not hold.'[1]

Bossuet, who insisted strongly on the apostolic authority of all bishops, nevertheless writes:

'When Christ chose St. Peter to be the foundation of His Church, He created for him a superiority in the Church and conferred on him the fullest plenitude of authority and majesty, that he might keep all bound together in unity.'[2] And he tells us that Celestine acted in the persuasion that he alone could judicially deal with Nestorius.

So that Dr. Pusey has no ground for translating Celestine's expression 'in common,' as though it were 'equally;' and Canon Bright is mistaken in supposing that our attribution of *special* authority to the Holy See annihilates the apostolic authority of the rest of the episcopate. And each of these writers is mistaken in supposing that St. Celestine held the equality of all bishops in their possession of the teaching office. They held it, according to St. Celestine, in common, but not in equal measure.[3]

---

[1] *Op. cit.* Part 2, ch. xviii.   [2] *Def. Decl. Cler. Gall.* xxi.

[3] Since writing the above I have noticed that Canon Bright translates Celestine's expression in the same way that Dr. Pusey does, as though he said that the teaching office 'had descended *equally* to all bishops' (*Roman Claims tested by Antiquity*, p. 11, note). St. Celestine says *in common*. 'Common Prayer' does not mean that Priest and people who pray are officially equal.

INDEX.

AETIUS, of Constantinople, reads the third Canon of Constantinople (not the sixth of Nicæa), 443

Africa, causes of bishops not to be terminated there, 142, 143; accepted Papal Infallibility, 289, 296; forbade inferior clergy to appeal to Rome, 297; deprecated legates *a latere*, 299; supposed letter to the Pope, probably spurious, 303

Alexandria, a see of Peter, 120; why above Antioch, 125; jurisdiction of, 167; subject to Rome, 177; Council of, 195; Acts sent to Rome, 197

Allies, T. W., 173

Ambrose, St., Bishop of Milan, on Damasus' election, 204; Gratian's adviser, 235, 237; teaching on the See of Peter, 242; at Aquileia, 264; at Rome, 273; contradicted by Mr. Puller, 479

Anatolius, Bishop of Constantinople, submits to Leo's demands, 393-396; signs the Tome and sends it round, 397; instructs bishops at council, 414; defends an inadequate formula, 419; grasps at supremacy in the East, 440; favouring circumstances, 441; his letter to Leo on the synod, 455

Anthony, Bishop, 301

Antioch, a see of Peter, 120; its relation to Rome, 123; to Alexandria, 126; Council of, 176, 179; dissensions under Meletius, 193

Apiarius, African priest, deceived the Pope, 297

Apollinarius, his heresy detected by Damasus, 212; condemned at Rome, 276

Aquileia, Council of, 264

Arles, Marcian, Bishop of, 70

Arles, Council of, 144; not superior to the Pope, 146; British bishops at, 146; regulation of Easter, 147; Archbishop Laud on the Council, 149, 152

Ascholius, St., baptises Theodosius, 243; Papal vicar, 246; meeting St. Ambrose, 273

Athanasius, St., and Julius' letter, 175, 178

Augustine, St., on Peter's primacy, 83; on Cyprian's speech, 93; opinion of St. Stephen, 113; on the Donatists, 140; on Melchiades' judgment, 141, 142; on the See of Peter, 143; on the Donatists' appeal, 144, 147; misinterpreted by Laud, 149; at Milevis, 287; letter to Pope Innocent, 288; his belief in Infallibility of the Holy See, 290; as Papal legate, 300

Auxentius, Bishop, 209

BARDESANES, 26

Basil, St., tender to Apollinarius, 211; looks to the West, 213; wishes for Papal legates, 214; letter of complaint as to Damasus, 220; on Western superciliousness, 222; recognises special grace in the Holy See, 224; admits Pope's power over Eastern bishops, 225; and to consecrate Bishop of Antioch by legate, 225

Basilides, Bishop, 73

Bigg, Dr., on the Clementine literature, 30

Bossuet, on *principalitas*, 36; on Victor and Irenæus, 43; on the Papal sentence against Nestorius, 335

Bottalla, Father, S.J., on relation of bishops to the Pope, 330

484 INDEX.

Bright, Dr. W., on *convenire ad*, 35; on Infallibility, 155; on 6th Nicene Canon, 171; quoted, 262; inadequate version of Celestine's judgment on Nestorius, 314; misunderstanding, 330; description of the sentence at Ephesus, 336; on John of Antioch's delay, 341; on the legate's speech at Ephesus, 349; on a supposed allusion to the Pope, 358 *seq.*; accusation of forgery, 445; translation of *communis*, 483

CÆCILIAN, Bishop of Carthage, 139 *seq.*
Canons, sixth of Nicæa, 166; of Sardica, 178, 183 *note*; why Popes quote, 183; third of Constantinople, 258 *seq.*; Nicene quoted as Sardican, 298, 302; third of Constantinople read at Chalcedon, 443; sixth Nicene only once, 444; twenty-eighth of Chalcedon, how carried, 441 *seq.*
Capreolus, Bishop of Carthage, letter on authority of Holy See, 317, 360
Carter, Canon, accusation of forgery, 445
Carthage, third Council about baptism, 89; letter to Pope Innocent, 286
Celestine, St. (Pope), 299; his character, 306, 311; letter condemning Nestorius, 309; real president at Ephesus, 321; his judgment on Nestorius accepted as authoritative, 334, 335; last letters, 354
Chalcedon, Nicene Canon at, 170. See Leo, Anatolius, Dioscorus, Theodoret, Maximus
Chrysologus, St. Peter, advises Eutyches to obey the Pope, 367
Church of Rome, authority same as that of the Bishop, 4
Church, the Catholic, its head and root, 85; her unity, 118, 119
Clement, St., of Rome, letter to Corinth, 1 *seq.*
Clementine literature, description, 12; used by Tübingen school, 13; by anti-papal writers, 13; not the parent of phrase 'See of Peter,' 16 *seq.*; subsequent to list of Hegesippus, 17-22; subsequent to Tertullian, 25; and Bardesanes, 26; reason of its acceptance at Rome, 31
Cœlestius, the Pelagian, 285; deceived the Pope, 292; was condemned, 295

Constantine, his wish for a council, 157
Corinth, Epistle of St. Clement to, 1; its effect, 32
Cyprian, St., treatise on Unity, reasons for writing, 50, 55; teaching as to Peter, 49, 54, 55; on the chair of Peter, 57; meaning of 'the head,' 61; on difference between orders and jurisdiction, 62; on Fortunatus going to Rome, 69; on Marcian of Arles, 70; deposition of Basilides, 73; on baptism by heretics, error, 77; on tradition, 82; expression 'bishop of bishops,' 92; his irritation, 99; summary by St. Vincent, 112
Cyprus, decision about, at Ephesus, wrong, 356
Cyril, St., of Alexandria, why intervened about Nestorius, 306; appeals to the Pope for judgment, 308; presided for the Pope, 321 *seq.*; presided after the legates' arrival, 350; sent by Celestine to preside, 348; his summary of the council, 351; defended by the synod, 353; praised by Celestine, 355; and by Sixtus, his successor, 356; his authorised letters accepted at Chalcedon, 411. See Ephesus.

DAMASUS, St. (Pope), his greatness, 203 *seq.*; election valid, 207; his rule, 208; estimate of Liberius' stand, 209; detection of Apollinarius, 211; and Macedonius, 212; his belief as to his see, 213; defined the Divinity of the Holy Ghost, 214; differed from Basil as to a legation, 215; annoyed Basil, 219; cool towards Meletius, 227; his religion as successor of Peter enforced in the East, 244, 247; on Maximus, 248; changes his opinion, 266; action in A.D. 382, 269; his glory, 278
Dionysius, St., of Rome, acts as supreme ruler, 122; on *Homoousios*, 156
Dionysius, St., of Alexandria, intercedes with the Pope, 81; letter for guidance, 114; defends himself to the Pope, 122
Dioscorus, Bishop of Alexandria, moves for a council, 368; presides at Ephesus, 379; acquitted Eutyches, 379; has to leave his seat at

INDEX. 485

Chalcedon, 400; sentenced by the Papal legates, 404

Döllinger, Dr., translation of St. Ignatius, 33; on *principalitas*, 36, 58; on communion with Rome, 38; on excommunication, 41; on Peter's primacy, 61; on Firmilian's letter, 100; on the sees of Peter, 125; on the peace at Antioch, 232; on the Pope as patriarch, 262; absurd notion of infallibility, 310; correct appreciation of Cyril's relation to Celestine, 313

Domnus, Bishop of Antioch, 433

Donatists, their origin, 139; ask for Gallic judges, 140; their appeal to the emperor, 144; their action misinterpreted by Laud, 149

EPHESUS, Council of (A.D. 431), due to Nestorius, 316; and to the emperor, 319; Celestine the president, 321; Cyril acted for him, 322; use of term 'Apostolic See' at Council of, App. IV. 479

Ephesus, Robber Council of (A.D. 449), not wished by Flavian, 369; Eutyches' plan, 368; why consented to by Leo, 375, 377; its constituents, 378; Flavian condemned, 379; appealed to Rome, 380; ill treated, 380

Epiphanius, St., on St. Clement's succession, 5, 21; at Rome, 273

Eusebians, their programme, 177, 179

Eusebius, on St. Clement's letter, 7; Papal lists, 19 *seq.*; on the Council of Nicæa, 157

Eusebius of Constantinople, 174

Eusebius of Vercellæ, Papal legate, 194; at Antioch, 199

Eustathius, St., Bishop of Antioch, 191

Eutyches, his teaching, 365; condemned by his bishop, 365; appeals to Rome, but not at the synod, 367; gains the emperor, 367; in concert with Dioscorus, moves for a council, 368; brings charges against his synod, 370; condemned by Leo, 373; acquitted at the Latrocinium, 379; his acquittal rendered null and void by the Pope, 385. *See* Flavian and Leo

Excommunication, different kinds, 41; of Asiatics by St. Victor, 42; of Marcian by the Pope, 71; of Firmilian, 81; lesser kind, 105; authorities against Cyprian's, 107; esp. St. Augustine, 109

FAUSTINUS, Papal legate, 299; not infallible, 300

Firmilian, 98; his letter, 101; probably altered his teaching, 111

Flavian, St., of Antioch, 253, 265

Flavian, Bishop of Constantinople, condemns Eutyches, 365; writes to the greater sees, but sends the Acts to Rome, 367; accepts censure from Leo, 369; prefers Papal brief to a general council, 369, 370; accepts legates from Rome, 373; murdered, 380; had appealed to Rome, 383

Francis of Sales, St., on Peter *quâ* foundation, 49

Freppel, Bishop, summary of Cyprianic dispute, 115

GELASIUS of Cyzicus, value of his lists, 163

Gore, Rev. C., refutation of Lightfoot, 7; interpretation of Irenæus, 36; his depreciation of Leo, 418; misinterpretation of Leo, 439; curious suggestion, 446

Gratian, Emperor, his attitude to the Church, 234; relationship to St. Ambrose, 235; gave civil effect to ecclesiastical judgments, 236; his rescripts conterminous with ecclesiastical arrangements, 237 *seq.*

Gregory, St., of Nazianzus, 245, 248; election confirmed, 249; opposes the election of Flavian, 252; resigns, 255

HEGESIPPUS, 17, 21, 30

Homoousios (Consubstantial), taught by St. Dionysius, 156

Hosius, Bishop, Papal legate at Nice, 163

IGNATIUS, St., on St. Clement's letter, 2, 19; the Church of Rome presiding, 33

Illyrian bishops at Chalcedon, their difficulty, 417

Infallibility, Papal, involves concurrence of the Church, 3; taught by Irenæus, 38; implied by Cyprian, 72; not inconsistent with Nicene

Council, 154; nor with Basil's words about Meletius, 220; accepted by the Church of North Africa, 290; assumed by Leo in writing to Theodosius, 387; Dr. Döllinger on infallibility, 417

Innocent I., St. (Pope), letters to Africa, 288; claim to infallibility received in Africa, 290

Irenæus, St., on St. Clement's letter, 2, 9; list of Popes, 22; on the sovereignty of the Church of Rome, 34-38

JEROME, ST., on St. Peter's episcopate, 21; on Liberius, 187; witness to Papal supremacy, 227; his age, 228; at Rome, 273, 277

John, Bishop of Antioch, counsels Nestorius to obey the Papal judgment, 315; his delay intentional, 320; holds a schismatic synod, 341; refuses to attend the council, 352; his deposition reserved to Rome, 353

Jubaianus, Cyprian's letter to, 85

Julian, Bishop, Pelagian, 317; wishes for a council, 318

Julius, St. (Pope), letter to the Eusebians, 175

Juvenal, Bishop of Jerusalem, on obedience to Rome, 352; wrests provinces from Antioch, 435

LATROCINIUM, i.e. Robber Synod. See Ephesus, Flavian, Dioscorus, Leo

Laud, Archbishop, mistranslation, 150

Leo the Great, St. (Pope), blames Flavian, 367; judges Eutyches in his Tome, 373; revises the Acts of the Eastern Synod, 373; consents to a council, 375; describes his Tome to the Archimandrites as *ex cathedrâ*, 376; and to the synod, *ibid.*; annulled the sentence on Eutyches, 385; acts on the Sardican Canon, 385; expounds Papal Infallibility to the emperor, 387; his demands on Anatolius, 393, 396; his Tome accepted as authoritative, 409; difficulty of some bishops about it, 413; instructed in committee, 414; free to examine, not to dissent, 416; Tome the rule of faith, 420; called by the synod 'the preaching of the See of Peter,' 422; Marcian's allocution on the Tome, 425; absolved Theodoret, 427; actual restoration left to the synod, 430; rejects the twenty-eighth Canon as contrary to Nicene Canons by virtue of his apostolic authority, 458-460

Liberius, St. (Pope), his support of Athanasius, 186; his lapse not proven, 187; his acts, 188; his second stand, 189; after Ariminum, 190

Lightfoot, Dr., on St. Clement's letter, 3, 8; on the Clementine literature, 14; on Hegesippus' list, 21; translation of St. Ignatius, 33

Lincoln, Bishop of, on the Clementine Romance, 14, 25; on Nicene Council, 168; unsubstantiated accusation of forgery, 445

Linus, successor of St. Peter, 19, 21, 22

Littledale, Dr., on Damasus, 205

Lucifer, St., of Cagliari, Papal legate, 194; consecrated Paulinus to Antioch, 199

Luciferians, 198, 206

MARCELLUS of Ancyra, 223

Marcian, Bishop of Arles, 70

Marcian, Emperor, why called a Council, 391-392; first supports, then gives up, the twenty-eighth Canon, 448, 459

Maximus of Constantinople, 246; ordination rejected, 249; appears in the West, 275

Maximus, Bishop of Antioch, his ordination validated by the Pope, 433; Eastern acceptance of Papal supremacy, 434; agrees to Juvenal's desire conditionally upon Leo's consent, 436

Melchiades, St., Bishop of Rome, his judgment on African bishops, 141; misrepresented by Laud, 149

Meletius, St., Bishop of Antioch, his election, 191; exile, 192; statement before Sapor, 194; dealt with at Alexandria, 195; Damasus cool towards, 227; compact with Paulinus, when made, 229; at peace with Rome (A.D. 379), 230; at Constantinople, 248; last acts and death, 250; proof that he died in communion with Rome, 267

Memnon, Bishop of Ephesus, held Nestorius condemned before the council, 319

INDEX. 487

Milan, Council of, 265
Milman, Dean, on the sentence of the Council of Ephesus, 337

NECTARIUS, Bishop, 255
Nestorius, his character and teaching, 306; idea of the council, 316; accused St. Cyril, 319
Nicæa, Council of, reasons for, 151; its president, 161; St. Boniface on, 165; sixth Canon, 166; supposed forgery, 171; directed from Rome, 210; are the Sardican Canons Nicene? 467 *seq.*
Norfolk, Duke of, not a type of the Pope, 224

OPTATUS, St., of Africa, on communion with Rome, 38, 274

PASCHAL Feast, dispute on, 39 *seq.*
Paschasinus, Papal legate, pronounces the deposition of Dioscorus, 405
Paul, St., relationship to See of Rome, 23
Paul of Samosata, his case referred to Rome, 123
Paulinus, Bishop of Antioch, 192; position sanctioned at Alexandria, 195 *seq.*; ordained by three bishops, 199; compact with Meletius, 229
Pelagius, his heresy, 284
Peter, St., ordained Clement, 19; relationship to the See of Rome, 23; Church built on, 47, 49, 60; place of, 55; chair of, 57, 67; primacy over Apostles, 83; three sees of, 120; mention of in the Sardican Canons, 180, 182
Philip, Papal legate at Ephesus, his exposition of Papal supremacy, 344; its acceptance by the synod, 347
Photius, of Constantinople, on Hosius, 163; his falsehood and forgeries, 470
Polycrates, 41
Popes, their witness, 129 *seq.*
Pulcheria, Empress, 389; beauty of character, 391; her joy at Anatolius' submission, 396
Puller, Rev. F. W., on the Clementine Romance, 14, 15, 25; on *principalitas*, 36; on St. Victor, 40, 42, 44; translations of Eusebius, 42, 46; on St. Cyprian, 47, 53; translation of *sacerdotalis unitas*, 58, 59; of *primatus*, 83; Old Testament teaching on unity compared with Cyprian's, 66; on going from Carthage to Rome, 69 *n.* 2; translation of *consulere rei*, 76; on the head and root of the Church, 85; on Stephen's excommunication of Cyprian, 106–111; mistake as to the sees of Peter, 126; repudiation of Popes as witnesses, 127; on the Nicene Council, 164; on sixth Canon, 167; on the Meletians at Antioch, 196 *n.*1, 197 *n.*3; note on his account of Meletius, 201; depreciation of Damasus, 205; on election of Damasus, 207; argument from titles unsound, 215 *n.* 2; on ἀκρίβεια, 217 *n.* 2; mistaken idea of papal teaching, 223; makes Gratian's Rescript wider than Rome's request—wrongly, 237 *seq.*; on the Council of Aquileia, 264 *n.* 2; mistranslation, 267; collapse of his argument about Meletius, 268; contradicts St. Ambrose, 271, 479; on North African Church, 283; assumption about African obedience, 302; on Philip's words at Ephesus, 350; on the Cyprian dispute, 357; accusation of forgery, 445; interpretations of Cyprian, App. I. 461–467; on St. Ambrose, App. III. 475
Pusey, Dr., argument about infallibility, 154; misunderstanding, 157; on Church of North Africa, 284; mistakes about St. Zosimus, 291 *seq.*; answered by St. Augustine, 293; account of the Council of Ephesus, 319; on John of Antioch's delay, 341; translation of *communis*, 483

RECOGNITIONS, the. Cf. Clementine literature
Rome, Church of. *See* Church
Rome, See of, relation to St. Peter and St. Paul, 23, 24; the Apostolic See, 118, App. IV

SALMON, Dr., tone of Clement's letter, 8, 11; his use of the Clementine literature, 13; undue depreciation of Council of Ephesus, 320; on the presidencies of councils, 321; ignoring Celestine's work, 327; depreciation of Nicene Council, 332; argument from resistance, 338
Sardica, Canons of, their meaning, 178 *seq.*, 183 *note*; quoted as Nicene,

298, 302; acted on by Leo towards the East, 385; are they Nicene? 467 *seq.*

Stephen, St. (Pope), asked to depose Marcian, 70; restores Basilides, 73; St. Vincent of Lerins on, 81; his letter to Cyprian, 89; his decree, 95; and the African legates, 97; his excommunication of Cyprian not proved, 107 *seq.*

Sylvester, St. (Pope), his action towards the Donatists, 146; sat in seat of the Apostles, 147; reason for accepting a Council, 158, 161

TERTULLIAN, not deceived by the Clementine Romance, 17; not contradicted by Irenæus, 23; definition of *principalitas*, 58

Theodoret, bishop and historian, account of compact at Antioch, 229; not allowed to judge Dioscorus, 401; acted as judge of the faith at Chalcedon, 431; synod did not review Papal judgment on, 432

Theodosius I., Emperor, enforces the faith of Rome, 244; decides on an Eastern Œcumenical Council, 246; second edict (A.D. 381), 247

Theodosius II., idea of the council at Ephesus, 319; takes Eutyches under his patronage, 367; appointed Dioscorus president at Ephesus, 379; ordered the presence of Barsumas, 378; refuses to convoke another council, 388

Timothy, of Alexandria, 254

Tyana, Synod of, admits Pope's power to restore Eastern bishops, 225

Tyre, Council of, 176, 179

URSINUS, schismatic, 207

VALENTINIAN, Emperor, letter to Theodosius on Papal jurisdiction, 389

Victor, St., 40 *scq.*

Vincent of Lerins, St., estimate of Stephen, 81; on the Donatists' use of Cyprian's name, 98; summary of Cyprian's case, 112; never mentioned by Mr. Puller, 112

Vitalis, Bishop, at Antioch, 218

WARD, Wilfrid, 224

Wordsworth, Bishop Christopher, 147; on the Ephesine sentence, 337

ZOSIMUS, St. (Pope), caution as to Cœlestius, 294; did not approve his heresy, 293; Marius Mercator, 294; his *ex cathedrâ* teaching, 296; received Apiarius, 298; quoted Nicene Canon, 298

Cardinal Newman's Works.

SERMONS.

PAROCHIAL and PLAIN SERMONS. Edited by the Rev. W. J. COPELAND, B.D. late Rector of Farnham, Essex. 8 vols. Cabinet Edition. Crown 8vo. 5s. each. Popular Edition. 8 vols. Crown 8vo. 3s. 6d. each.

SELECTION, adapted to the SEASONS of the ECCLE-SIASTICAL YEAR, from the 'Parochial and Plain Sermons.' Edited by the Rev. W. J. COPELAND, B.D. late Rector of Farnham, Essex. Cabinet Edition. Crown 8vo. 5s. Popular Edition. Crown 8vo. 3s. 6d.

FIFTEEN SERMONS PREACHED before the UNIVERSITY of OXFORD, between 1826 and 1843. Crown 8vo. 5s. Popular Edition. Crown 8vo. 3s. 6d.

SERMONS BEARING upon SUBJECTS of the DAY. Edited by the Rev. W. J. COPELAND, B.D. late Rector of Farnham, Essex. Crown 8vo. 5s. Popular Edition. Crown 8vo. 3s. 6d.

DISCOURSES ADDRESSED to MIXED CONGREGATIONS. Crown 8vo. 6s. Popular Edition. Crown 8vo. 3s. 6d.

SERMONS PREACHED on VARIOUS OCCASIONS. Crown 8vo. 6s. Popular Edition. Crown 8vo. 3s. 6d.

TREATISES.

LECTURES on the DOCTRINE of JUSTIFICATION. Crown 8vo. 5s. Popular Edition. Crown 8vo. 3s. 6d.

An ESSAY on the DEVELOPMENT of CHRISTIAN DOCTRINE. Cabinet Edition. Crown 8vo. 6s. Popular Edition. Crown 8vo. 3s. 6d.

The IDEA of a UNIVERSITY DEFINED and ILLUSTRATED. Cabinet Edition. Crown 8vo. 7s. Popular Edition. Crown 8vo. 3s. 6d.

An ESSAY in AID of a GRAMMAR of ASSENT. Cabinet Edition. Crown 8vo. 7s. 6d. Popular Edition. Crown 8vo. 3s. 6d.

POLEMICAL.

The VIA MEDIA of the ANGLICAN CHURCH. Illustrated in Lectures, Letters, and Tracts written between 1830 and 1841. With Notes. Vol. I. Prophetical Office of the Church. Vol. II. Occasional Letters and Tracts. Cabinet Edition. 2 vols. Crown 8vo. 6s. each. Popular Edition. 2 vols. Crown 8vo. 3s. 6d. each.

CERTAIN DIFFICULTIES FELT by ANGLICANS in CATHOLIC TEACHING CONSIDERED. Cabinet Edition. (2 vols.) Vol. I. Twelve Lectures. Crown 8vo. 7s. 6d. Vol. II. Letters to Dr. Pusey concerning the Blessed Virgin, and to the Duke of Norfolk in Defence of the Pope and Council. Crown 8vo. 5s. 6d. Popular Edition. (2 vols.) 3s. 6d. each.

The PRESENT POSITION of CATHOLICS in ENGLAND. Cabinet Edition. Crown 8vo. 7s. 6d. Popular Edition, 3s. 6d.

APOLOGIA PRO VITA SUA. Cabinet Edition. Crown 8vo. 6s. Popular Edition. Crown 8vo. 3s. 6d.

London : LONGMANS, GREEN, & CO.

CARDINAL NEWMAN'S WORKS (*continued*).

ESSAYS.

ESSAYS on BIBLICAL and on ECCLESIASTICAL MIRACLES.
Cabinet Edition. Crown 8vo. 6s. Popular Edition. Crown 8vo. 3s. 6d.

DISCUSSIONS and ARGUMENTS on VARIOUS SUBJECTS.
Cabinet Edition. Crown 8vo. 6s. Popular Edition. Crown 8vo. 3s. 6d.

CONTENTS.—1. How to accomplish it. 2. The Antichrist of the Fathers. 3. Scripture and the Creed. 4. Tamworth Reading Room. 5. Who's to Blame? 6. An Argument for Christianity.

ESSAYS CRITICAL and HISTORICAL. Cabinet Edition. 2 vols. Crown 8vo. 12s. Popular Edition. 2 vols. Crown 8vo. 7s.

CONTENTS.—1. Poetry. 2. Rationalism. 3. Apostolical Tradition. 4. De la Mennais. 5. Palmer on Faith and Unity. 6. St. Ignatius. 7. Prospects of the Anglican Church. 8. The Anglo-American Church. 9. Countess of Huntingdon. 10. Catholicity of the Anglican Church. 11. The Antichrist of Protestants. 12. Milman's Christianity. 13. Reformation of the Eleventh Century. 14. Private Judgment. 15. Davison. 16. Keble.

HISTORICAL.

HISTORICAL SKETCHES. 3 vols. Cabinet Edition. Crown 8vo. 6s. each. Popular Edition. Crown 8vo. 3s. 6d. each.

CONTENTS.—1. The Turks. 2. Cicero. 3. Apollonius. 4. Primitive Christianity. 5. Church of the Fathers. 6. St. Chrysostom. 7. Theodoret. 8. St. Benedict. 9. Benedictine Schools. 10. Universities. 11. Northmen and Normans. 12. Mediæval Oxford. 13. Convocation of Canterbury.

THEOLOGICAL.

The ARIANS of the FOURTH CENTURY. Cabinet Edition. Crown 8vo. 6s. Cheap Edition. Crown 8vo. 3s. 6d.

SELECT TREATISES of ST. ATHANASIUS in CONTROVERSY with the ARIANS. Freely Translated. 2 vols. Crown 8vo. 15s.

THEOLOGICAL TRACTS. Crown 8vo. 8s.

CONTENTS.—1. Dissertatiunculæ. 2. On the Text of the Seven Epistles of St. Ignatius. 3. Doctrinal Causes of Arianism. 4. Apollinarianism. 5. St. Cyril's Formula. 6. Ordo de Tempore. 7. Douay Version of Scripture.

LITERARY.

VERSES on VARIOUS OCCASIONS. Cabinet Edition. Crown 8vo. 6s. Popular Edition. Crown 8vo. 3s. 6d.

LOSS and GAIN: the Story of a Convert. Cabinet Edition. Crown 8vo. 6s. Popular Edition. Crown 8vo. 3s. 6d.

CALLISTA: a Tale of the Third Century. Cabinet Edition. Crown 8vo. 6s. Pupular Edition. Crown 8vo. 3s. 6d.

The DREAM of GERONTIUS. 16mo. 6d. sewed; 1s. cloth.

DEVOTIONAL.

MEDITATIONS and DEVOTIONS. Part I. Meditations for the Month of May. Novena of St. Philip. Part II. The Stations of the Cross. Meditations and Intercessions for Good Friday. Litanies, &c. Part III. Meditations on Christian Doctrine. Conclusion. Oblong Crown 8vo. 5s. net.

London: LONGMANS, GREEN, & CO.

www.ingramcontent.com/pod-product-compliance
Lightning Source LLC
Chambersburg PA
CBHW051156300426
44116CB00006B/325